BOOKS
of the
CENTURY

BOOKS

of the

CENTURY

A Hundred Years of
Authors, Ideas and Literature

From *The New York Times*

Edited by Charles McGrath
and the staff of the Book Review

ILLUSTRATIONS BY MARK SUMMERS

TIMES [T] BOOKS

RANDOM HOUSE

Library of Congress Cataloging-in-Publication Data

Books of the century: a hundred years of authors, ideas, and literature/ The New York Times Book Review; [editor, Charles McGrath]. — 1st ed.
p.   cm.
ISBN 0-8129-2965-9 (acid-free paper)
1. Books — United States — Reviews. I. McGrath, Charles. II. New York Times Book Review.
Z1003.2.C46 1998
028.1'0973 — dc21
98-5477

Random House website address: www.randomhouse.com
Printed in the United States of America on acid-free paper

9 8 7 6 5 4 3 2

First Edition

DESIGN BY BTD / SABRINA BOWERS

Acknowledgments

THANKS should be extended to all the members of the *Book Review* staff who worked on the original centennial issue: Michael Anderson, Alida Becker, Katharine Bouton, Don Bruckner, Margalit Fox, Tom Ferrell, Phyllis Gelfand, Caroline Rand Herron, David Kelly, Peter Keepnews, Michael Lichtenstein, Patricia T. O'Conner, and Arlene Youngman. Barry Gewen, Robert Harris, and Eden Ross Lipson deserve special mention for their contributions to the issue's time line of literary trivia, and so does Nancy Martinez-Ruiz for painstakingly retyping much of the material. The art director for that issue was Steve Heller, and the inspired literary caricatures, which are reprinted here, were done by Mark Summers, who has been an artist for the *Book Review* since 1985. Our original, intrepid freelance researchers were Elizabeth Hollow, David Jaffe, and Deborah Nelson. And, finally, thanks to Mitchel Levitas, himself a former editor of the *Book Review* and now Editorial Director of Book Development for the *Times*; he insisted that our Centennial efforts deserved to become a book and kept nudging us along the road to publication.

Contents

1920s

1930s

1940s

1950S

1960s

1970s

1980s

1990s

Introduction

TO READ THROUGH one hundred years of *The New York Times Book Review* is to be reminded, forcefully, that almost nothing lasts. The ninety-nine blue-bound volumes containing the *Book Review* so far are crammed together on metal shelving at the back of the *Times*'s editorial library, some of them unopened for years. They're a monument to continuity of a sort—to one hundred years of serious and careful attention to books, a record unequaled by any other publication—but they are also a chastening and depressing catalogue of once-famous books and authors now utterly forgotten. In those yellowing newsprint pages, mighty literary reputations rise and fall—Santayana, for example, and James Gould Cozzens—while redoubtable publishing flagships like Boni and Liveright sail bravely for a few decades and then sink, unnoticed, beneath the commercial waves. The haberdashery in authors' portraits changes, with frock coats giving way to the tweed jacket and Shetland sweater and then the T-shirt and the miniskirt, and so does the nature of the goods purveyed by the *Book Review*'s extra-literary advertisers. In the early days these pages used to sell bookcases and lessons in elocution, etiquette, and deportment; now there are ads for litter boxes, sex videos, and depilatory devices. For years, the *Book Review* is chastely black and white, and then, with a sudden splash, there's color. Meanwhile, books come and go—hundreds of thousands of them, giant forests' worth—some making an impression for a season or a year, even a generation, and many more slipping away unnoticed.

Book reviews are, by their very nature, even more transitory, more forgettable, than the books they purport to evaluate, and there's something slightly self-defeating about creating yet *another* book, eventually to be forgotten, by assembling within hard covers writing that was never intended (as most reviews are not) to be more than of the moment. If you look at enough reviews, though, and at reviews over a long enough period, amid the accidental changes you can spot some trends or alterations that seem instructive, if not reliably permanent. The dramatic emergence, for example, of that generation of writers—Hemingway, Dreiser, Fitzgerald, et al.—who in the years right after the First World War transformed the literary landscape and shifted its center to America. Or the flowering, in response to the baby boom, of children's literature in the '50s and '60s; the outpouring of extraordinary and original fiction in the '70s, and the great age of biography that seemed to sweep along afterward. Most evident of all, perhaps—if you look at *The New York Times Book Review*—is the gradual maturation of book reviewing itself. In the beginning the *Times* offered unsigned, often sniffy "notices" and "appreciations"; gradually, bylines and reviewer identifications began to appear and so, eventually, did true criticism, informed and readable and aimed at a discerning general audience. In a way, the *Book Review* grew up, and became more sophisticated, just as the American readership did.

In putting together this centennial volume, we've tried to demonstrate some of these changes, but the book, it should be emphasized, is not a comprehensive history of twentieth-century literature. It's not even a completely reliable index to changes in taste or to the ups and downs of critical reputations, or to the role of the literary marketplace. There are good and important books that get short shrift here, as they did in the *Times* originally, and there are others whose significance has perhaps been inflated. You will have to look very carefully here—or read between the lines—to discern some of the great changes that have surged through the publishing industry in the last hundred years; and you will look in vain for any consistent overview, any sense of where we and our literature might be headed.

What this book offers instead, we hope, is a vivid, entertaining, and at least occasionally enlightening sense of literary immediacy—of what it was like, of initial and immediate reaction, when some of the most important or most influential books of the century first came into view. The whole volume could easily be called, as we have called one of our features here, "First Impressions." It's a record, if you like, of some of our collective and instinctive responses—of how things first struck us—and, not surprisingly, it's often as interesting in its hesitations and uncertainties (what to make of W. E. B. Du Bois, for example, back in 1903) as it is in its outpourings and enthusiasms (as in the first, astonishingly prescient review of *Ulysses*).

This book is essentially an expansion of the centennial issue of the *Book Review*, which appeared in October 1996, on the occasion of the *Book Review*'s

100th anniversary. We've included a number of reviews that we didn't have room for back then, and also some nonreview material (the annual Editors' Choice selections for the twenty-five years 1972–1997, letters, essays, and commentary) intended to suggest a fuller sense not only of what the *Book Review* was actually like from week to week but also of some of the larger cultural issues that helped shape the literary climate at various points. But the editorial principle is the same in both the newspaper and book-length versions. In selecting material to reprint, we looked for two things: for books (or for controversies about books) that have in some way made a difference—by changing the way we think or by bringing us important news of ourselves and others—and for writing that is stylish and interesting enough to bear rereading. The latter is considerably harder to come by than the former, but, luckily, the two sometimes overlap. At least since the '20s, even in the *Book Review*'s dreariest issues, great books have often managed to elicit good (which is not necessarily to say favorable) reviews.

Often, but not always. Tastes alter, and as the material here abundantly testifies, critics are fallible. (If this book can be said to have a subtheme, in fact, it's that reviewing is not a science but, rather, an uneasy combination of description and opinion.) If a book that you deem an essential classic is not included here, it's possible that we overlooked it, but it's more likely that the original review failed to rise to the occasion, either by missing something essential or, more often, by being accurate but unmemorable. If there are fewer poetry reviews here than there ought to be, it's because for a long time the *Book Review* didn't pay a great deal of attention to poetry. If there's a noticeable scarcity of women reviewers, that's because in the *Book Review*'s early history women weren't invited to contribute very often. On the other hand, the present volume pays insufficient attention to translators, and for that those of us who put together the original centennial issue are to blame.

Though the years from 1896 until World War I saw no shortage of great books published, we had a hard time finding many reviews from that era that seemed fit to print again—though the fault here may not be so much the *Times*'s as the very nature of prewar critical prose. (Almost all the reviews, by the way, have been cut from their original lengths, some more drastically than others.) We had an equally hard time choosing among the many brilliant reviews that appeared in the late '60s and early '70s—a period that, from this distance, begins to look like a Golden Age of the Book Review, and perhaps of publishing in general. And when it came to the more current books—those from the late '80s and the '90s—we more or less threw up our hands and settled on ones that seem of particular relevance right now. When the enlightened and liberated editors come along to put together the second centennial volume of the *Book Review*, they will no doubt find many of our choices quaint, not to say incomprehensible. All those late-twentieth-century books on feminism and feminist issues, for example. What was *that* all about?

Nothing lasts—except, one hopes, the impulse that compels some people to write books and others to try to spread the word about them. The *Book Review* may not be the single most advantageous window from which to look back at the last one hundred years, but neither is it an entirely accidental one. It's a window inward as well as outward. Here, in one way or another, are our fears and anxieties and, more important, our longings and our dreams. This is really how we thought about what we thought, how we felt about what we felt.

The original, newspaper version of this centennial collection was put together by the editors of the *Book Review*, assisted by a SWAT team of freelance researchers who, equipped with magnifying glasses and ampules of injectable No-Doz, ventured back into the mustiest regions of the archives. The effort left many of us spent and blurry-eyed, and so for this book-length version we enlisted the services of Ken Emerson, who bravely took it upon himself to go back, one by one, through those same blue-bound volumes. Mr. Emerson is a former Articles Editor of *The New York Times Magazine*, an occasional contributor to the *Book Review* and the author of *Doo-dah!: Stephen Foster and the Rise of American Popular Culture*. Fortunately (and reassuringly), what he came back with mostly conformed to our original editorial judgments. He didn't find too many worthy reviews that we hadn't at least considered, that is. But he uncovered troves of valuable material—letters and essays, and some early glimpses of talent on the horizon—that we have gratefully included.

This may also be an appropriate moment to acknowledge the succession of talented editors who for the last half-century or so have overseen the *Book Review* and maintained its tradition of fairness and excellence. They are, in order, Francis Brown, John Leonard, Harvey Shapiro, Mitchel Levitas, and Rebecca Pepper Sinkler.

—CHARLES MCGRATH

BOOKS

of the

CENTURY

Henry James

Joseph Conrad • Émile Zola

W. E. B. Du Bois • Helen Keller

Jack London • Upton Sinclair • Kenneth

Grahame • Ernest Thompson Seton • Sir Robert

S. S. Baden-Powell • Fyodor Dostoyevsky

D. H. Lawrence • Anton Chekov • Edgar

Rice Burroughs • Robert Frost

Carl Jung • Henry Adams

John Reed

1897–1919

No Laughter, No Tears

The Spoils of Poynton by Henry James
February 20, 1897

MR. JAMES, in these later years, is spinning finer than ever. It is not only that his material in this novel is scant. Trollope and a dozen others have wrought skillfully with as little matter. But in the treatment of his subject Mr. James absolutely neglects all the opportunities any other novelist would seize upon. In the present case we have a mother, a son, and two young women, all of the "upper middle class," and in all the book not more than half a dozen other sketches of character for relief. Speaking broadly, the mother wants the son to marry one of the young women, and he intends to marry the other, and does. There, with another deserving hero, or even without one, would be material enough and to spare for the sentimental novelist.

But Mr. James makes nothing at all of the situation that he might be expected to make. He has few turns in the generally straight course of his narrative, and not one of them is obvious. He allows nothing for the romantic taste that is in us all. The study of character is his single aim, but it is invariably study pursued with no idea of giving the shallow entertainment; with no dwelling upon eccentric traits humorously, with no tenderness for the weak, with no appeal either for laughter or for tears, and it must be confessed, with a result which, if pleasing to one's finer senses, is yet scarcely tangible.

The most appreciative reader of this volume of exquisite English (always the only right word in the only proper place) will lay it down with no definite idea in his mind of the identity of Mrs. Gareth, Owen, Fleda Vetch, or Mona Brigstock. Once in a while, in his earlier novels, Mr. James so presented a personage that one felt, for a time, one knew him or her; as, for example, the protagonist of *The American*, the girl in *The Tragic Muse*, and that horrid brother and sister in *The Princess Casamassima*. But who remembers their names now? In his later books his aim has surely been far from making us care much for the creatures of his imagination.

It is sad to think that not one novel reader in ten thousand, probably, will be able to comprehend Mrs. Gareth's and Fleda Vetch's views of life, art, and conduct, leaving sympathy out of the question. But the appreciation of the one in ten thousand is worth working for, and the knowledge Mr. James must have that his delight in the book's subtlety and refinement, the grave, thoughtful piquancy which is its substitute for humor, will be keen while it lasts, is, perhaps, a sufficient reward. And counting all the tens of thousands of novel readers in the English speaking world, one from each of the tens of thousands will make up a company that is worth while. So that we need not grieve for Henry James.

1896

The first issue of the *Book Review,* called the *Saturday Book Review Supplement,* is published on October 10. Under the headline "Oscar Wilde's Forlorn State" runs a report on the playwright's plight in Reading Gaol.

1897

Samuel Butler proposes, in *The Authoress of the Odyssey,* that Homer was a woman. (See Harold Bloom, 1990)

1897

Publishers Weekly reports that 5,703 new books and new editions were published in 1896.

All at Sea

Lord Jim by Joseph Conrad
December 1, 1900

Oops!

December 25, 1897

The Invisible Man

BY H. G. WELLS

The scientific machinery
is not very delicately
constructed, and the
imagination of the reader
is decidedly overtaxed.

IT IS CONCEDED that Mr. Conrad, like Britannia, rules the waves. Other writers have told stirring tales of those "that do business in great waters," and have given vivid and picturesque descriptions of the ocean in its storms and in its calms. But when we open one of Mr. Conrad's books we are aware of none of this. At once there comes "so loud a calling of the sea" that we embark with the writer upon the great adventure of the deep. We know for ourselves "the magic monotony of existence between sky and water"; we feel all the prosaic exaction of the life, and, at the same time, we are fascinated and held by the mysterious, dominating spirit brooding always upon the sea.

Not less than in Mr. Conrad's surpassingly beautiful "Youth," peerless among short stories, do we feel all this in *Lord Jim*, but *Lord Jim* is much more than a romance of the sea. It is said that its author meant it to be a brief narrative, but that it took itself into its own hands, and swept its writer with it into a profound study of a psychic phenomenon. If this be true, we are grateful to the tale that thus assumed the mastership.

Lord Jim is the story of a boy born in a quiet English parsonage, but filled with a thirst for adventure that leads him early to a sailor's life. He has that sublime young egotism, that pathetic young faith in himself, that refusal to believe it possible that life can hold for him defeat or failure, in a word, that very spring and essence of youth. At last, when he is twenty-four years old, and mate of a vessel steaming through a calm Oriental sea, under the silent stars, with 800 peaceful pilgrims sleeping upon the deck, swiftly, appallingly rises beside him "the veiled opportunity"—the dream of his life. And, behold, he quails before it.

Here Mr. Conrad begins his study of a soul. He tells his tale not from within, but from without, putting it into the mouth of an interested observer that he himself may not assume the novelist's privilege of omniscience. He feels his way, step by step, along the obscure chambers of that clouded, crude young heart, which felt the full significance, the ineffaceable stain of its cowering moment, and yet which contrived, somehow, to piece together the shattered faith in its high potentialities.

In the psychology of the book Mr. Conrad's method reminds us not a little of that of Mr. Henry James. He pursues a situation to its last intrenchment; he subjects an emotion to its last analysis. He turns a problem over and over, until we see it in a hundred lights—but never, by any happy chance, does he solve it. Jim's case—that is the motif of the story. How does it look to Jim himself? How

1900

Sister Carrie, Theodore
Dreiser's first novel, is published. It is withdrawn after
the publisher's wife declares
it too sordid. Dreiser has a
nervous breakdown.

does it look to a man of honor? Where is the hope for Jim's future? What is his point of salvability? But there is, after all, no conclusion. We follow on, follow on, through one exquisitely put subtlety after another, until, in truth, we begin to feel, and we are ashamed of ourselves for feeling, just a little tired of so much analysis, of so many fine-drawn perplexities.

Why, we ask ourselves, can we not get hold of something definite? And what, after all, does all this theorizing amount to? We don't know that we are called to sit upon the judgment seat, weighing to the last scruple poor Jim's intention against his performance, and then why such a future? Would it not be the simple thing for his helpful friend to say: "You have fallen terribly, my boy, fallen, perhaps, through your own self-confident dreams. Get up and try again. No skulking, no evasion! Live this thing down, humbly and hopefully, in the light of day." This, or something like this, seems the plain and practical way out; and, for all their beauty, we cannot help becoming impatient of the labyrinthine mazes.

However one may weary of the slippery elusiveness of the psychic conclusions, or may rebel against the ultimate tragedy of the book, there are compensations of depth and beauty upon every page. Never were Mr. Conrad's felicity of phrase and charm of atmosphere more obvious than in *Lord Jim*. His danger is that, like Mr. James, he may become entangled in his own supreme literary art, and may sacrifice simplicity and directness of purpose to his very perfection of method.

As it stands, however, a book of the rare literary quality of *Lord Jim* is something to receive with gratitude and joy, and with a sense of a distinction conferred upon the readers of romance.

Interview

Émile Zola
April 27, 1901

BY WILLIAM WALLACE WHITELOCK

EMILE ZOLA is to-day the hardest literary man in France to get an interview with. "I have given up answering questions," he said to me in a courteous but decided tone that precluded protest. Indeed, to obtain the honor of a personal refusal of the "master" himself is beyond the good fortune of most applicants, who find their course blocked by the burly form of the porter at No. 21 bis, Rue de Bruxelles. "Monsieur Zola regrets infinitely his inability to receive Monsieur, but he is very busy at present; perhaps another time if Monsieur will kindly trouble himself to call again." So Monsieur kindly

Sigmund Freud publishes *Die Traumdeutung* (*The Interpretation of Dreams*) in German. Elsewhere, L. Frank Baum dreams up *The Wonderful Wizard of Oz*.

Andrew Carnegie donates $5.2 million to the New York Public Library.

troubles himself to call again and again, until in the end he reaches the conclusion that, like to-morrow, "another" time never comes. I do not in the least blame M. Zola for refusing to receive Tom, Dick, and Harry, since he saw fit to receive me, but doubtless Tom, Dick, and Harry are of different opinion; like anything else, it all depends upon the point of view, as the undertaker said in speaking of death.

He was sitting at his large table desk writing, and, immediately came out from behind it to receive me—a thick-set, rather short man of perhaps sixty years of age, with iron-gray hair retreating at the temples, short, stubby beard and mustache, deep-set brown eyes, and heavy features, indicative of force and perseverance rather than of perception and delicacy. He wore a shabby old working suit and had dispensed with the formality of a collar—"Émile Zola *en pantofles!*"

"Take a seat, Monsieur; now, what can I do for you?" The voice was round and full—that of an orator who delights in the power with which nature has endowed him.

1901

Thomas Mann's *Buddenbrooks* appears, despite the publisher's request that it be cut in half.

"I should appreciate it very much," I replied, "if you would favor me with a short interview; I shall detain you but a few minutes."

"But what do you want to know? What sort of interview?"

"Any sort; that is of no special importance. Perhaps you will tell me something about your start in literature?"

"No, I have stopped replying to questions of that sort. Besides, you can get all that out of a little book that appeared a year or so ago with my name for title. There, now you have seen me and you know what I look like, and you can tell the readers of *The New York Times* that I never answer personal questions. So you have got what you came for."

I had, however, not got what I came for, so I proceeded to sit down. Under the circumstances, M. Zola concluded that there was nothing to be gained by standing alone, so he seated himself in a comfortable chair facing me. The critical point had been safely but narrowly passed; once get a man seated, and the veriest tyro can manipulate him. On this occasion, however, no manipulation was required. The dam of reticence having been broken down, the words poured forth from his mouth in a torrent that swept away all attempts to turn the monologue into personal channels, and drowned all objections in a flood of rhetoric and universal assertion. It was evident that the speaker had made up his mind on every conceivable subject on earth, and that his convictions were endowed with the strength of fanaticism. The impression gained from hearing him talk is not so much that of a conceited man as of a man who is certain of being right and who takes himself and his mission on earth extremely seriously. He smiles frequently, but it is the smile of a kindly, rather than of a humorous, man.

Almost immediately our conversation turned upon the subject of war, and for half an hour I was treated to a disquisition on the unmitigated evils of this relic of barbarism.

"No, you are mistaken," he said, "there is no good side to war; it is all bad. You say that the Spanish-American war was a good thing for America. Perhaps. But what have I to do with America? *Je me moque d'Amérique,* just as I snap my fingers at Spain. You must look at the matter from a broader, more humanitarian standpoint. A war would put civilization in Europe back fifty years. There is, however, but little likelihood of such a thing occurring. None of the nations, except, perhaps, England, wants war. England, you see, has need of a big victory to regain the prestige she has lost in South Africa. There is also, of course, always a party in France that wants to plunge the country into war, but they are not the true patriots. The days of France's military glory have passed, and her mission now is to conquer the world by the power of her thought, not by the power of her arms. We are not in position to stand a war, even if we wanted one, which we do not. The trouble with Kipling, whom, I must confess, I know rather from articles about him than from those by him, seems to be that, despite undoubted genius, his influence is reactionary. I consider him an unfortunate element in literature."

It is evident that M. Zola, like the majority of his countrymen, wastes but little love or admiration on England or the English language. "To be sure," he remarked, "England has produced a number of great writers—and, after all, it is the writers that make a language—but I always feel that the English tongue is a mishmash, half German and half French, without the preciseness of the one or the strength of the other; it still has about it *beaucoup de petit nègre.* Yes, I admit what you say about its superiority to French in the matter of poetry; I was speaking of it as a medium of prose, and as such it is to be compared neither with French nor German."

"There," he cried, rising, "I have talked despite the fact that I said I would not. Can you make an article out of what I have said? Three? Well, you are welcome to do so if you can, but I don't believe it."

By this time we had reached the door, which the novelist held open for me to pass through. Then down the stairway, to the accompaniment of the "clip-clap" of his slippers, which were evidently loose at the heels.

As I heard the portal close behind me, I wondered whether it would ever be my fortune to pass through it again; I must confess, however, that I felt no special regret at the thought that I should probably never do so. M. Zola had displayed extreme courtesy in devoting so much of his time to me, yet the consequent sense of obligation was powerless to banish the feeling that I had passed the evening in the presence of a man of books, not letters, of knowledge, not of culture. It is a dangerous thing to meet an author.

Letter

Joseph Conrad
August 24, 1901

REFERRING TO *The New York Times Saturday Review* of July 13, it is impossible not to recognize in the review of one "extravagant story" the high impartiality exercised in estimating a work which, I fear, remains not wholly sympathetic to the critic.

A feeling of regret mingles with gratitude on that account. It is a great good fortune for a writer to be understood; and greater still to feel that he has made his aim perfectly clear. It might have been wished, too, that the fact of collaboration had been made more evident on the face of the notice. The book [*The Inheritors*, written with Ford Madox Hueffer (Ford)] is emphatically an experiment in collaboration; but only the first paragraph of the review mentions "the authors" in the plural—afterward it seems as if Mr. Conrad alone were credited with the qualities of style and conception detected by the friendly glance of the critic.

It is this feeling that gives him the courage to speak about the book—already written, printed, delivered, and cast to the four winds of publicity. Doubtless a novel that wants explaining is a bad novel; but this is only an extravagant story—and it is an experiment. An experiment may bear a certain amount of explanation without confessing itself a failure.

Therefore it may perhaps be permissible to point out that the story is not directed against "some of the most cherished traditions and achievements of Englishmen." It is rather directed at the self-seeking, at the falsehood that had been (to quote the book) "hiding under the words that for ages had spurred men to noble deeds, to self-sacrifice, and to heroism." It is not directed against tradition; still less does it attack personalities. The extravagance of its form is meant to point out forcibly the materialistic exaggeration of individualism, whose unscrupulous efficiency it is the temper of the time to worship.

It points it out simply—and no more; because the business of a work striving to be art is not to teach or to prophesy (as we have been charged, on this side, with attempting), nor yet to pronounce a definite conclusion.

This, the teaching, the conclusions, even to the prophesying, may be safely left to science, which, whatever authority it may claim, is not concerned with truth at all, but with the exact order of such phenomena as fall under the perception of the senses. Its conclusions are quite true enough if they can be made useful to the furtherance of our little schemes to make our earth a little more habitable. The laws it discovers remain certain and immovable for the time of several generations. But in the sphere of an art dealing with a subject-matter whose origin and end are alike unknown there is no possible conclusion. The only indisputable truth of life is our ignorance. Besides this there is nothing evident, nothing absolute, nothing uncontradicted; there is no principle, no instinct, no impulse that can stand alone at the beginning of things and look confidently to the end. Egoism, which is the moving force of the world, and altruism, which is its morality, these two contradictory instincts of which one is so plain and the other so mysterious cannot serve us unless in the incomprehensible alliance of their irreconcilable antagonism. Each alone would be fatal to our ambition. For, in the hour of undivided triumph one would make our inheritance too arid to be worth having and the other too sorrowful to own.

Fiction, at the point of development at which it has arrived, demands from the writer a spirit of scrupulous abnegation. The only legitimate basis of creative work lies in the courageous recognition of all the irreconcilable antagonisms that make our life so enigmatic, so burdensome, so fascinating, so dangerous— so full of hope. They exist! And this is the only fundamental truth of fiction. Its recognition must be critical in its nature, inasmuch that in its character it may be joyous. It may be sad; it may be angry with revolt, or submissive in resignation. The mood does not matter. It is only the writer's self-forgetful fidelity to his sensations that matters. But, whatever light he flashes on it, the fundamental truth remains, and it is only in its name that the barren struggle of contradictions assumes the dignity of moral strife going on ceaselessly to a mysterious end— with our consciousness powerless but concerned sitting enthroned like a melancholy parody of eternal wisdom above the dust of the contest.

The Tragedy of the Age

The Souls of Black Folk by W. E. B. Du Bois
April 25, 1903

IT IS GENERALLY CONCEDED that Booker T. Washington represents the best hope of the negro in America, and it is certain that of all the leaders of his people he has done the most for his fellows with the least friction with the whites who are most nearly concerned, those of the South. Here is another negro "educator," to use a current term, not brought up like Washington among the negroes of the South and to the manner of the Southern negro born, but one educated in New England—one who never saw a negro camp-meeting till he was grown to manhood and went among the people of his color as a teacher. Naturally he does not see everything as Booker Washington does; probably he does not understand his own people in their natural state as does the

1903

P. G. Wodehouse quits his bank job to write a column for *The London Globe*.

other; certainly he cannot understand the Southern white's point of view as the principal of Tuskegee does. Yet it is equally certain that *The Souls of Black Folk* throws much light upon the complexities of the negro problem, for it shows that the key note of at least some negro aspiration is still the abolition of the social color line. For it is the Jim Crow car, and the fact that he may not smoke a cigar and drink a cup of tea with the white man in the South, that most galls William E. Burghardt Du Bois of the Atlanta College for Negroes. That this social color line must in time vanish like the mists of the morning is the firm belief of the writer, as the opposite is the equally firm belief of the Southern white man; but in the meantime he admits the "hard fact" that the color line is, and for a long time must be.

The book is of curious warp and woof, and the poetical form of the title is the index to much of its content and phraseology. To a Southerner who knows the negro race as it exists in the South, it is plain that this negro of Northern education is, after all, as he says, "bone of the bone and flesh of the flesh" of the African race. Sentimental, poetical, picturesque, the acquired logic and the evident attempt to be critically fair-minded is strangely tangled with these racial characteristics and the racial rhetoric. After an eloquent appeal for a fair hearing in what he calls his "Forethought," he goes in some detail into the vexed history of the Freedman's Bureau and the work it did for good and ill; for he admits the ill as he insists upon the good. A review of such a work from the negro point of view, even the Northern negro's point of view, must have its value to any unprejudiced student—still more, perhaps, for the prejudiced who is yet willing to be a student. It is impossible here to give even a general idea of the impression that will be gained from reading the text, but the underlying idea seems to be that it was impossible for the negro to get justice in the Southern courts just after the war, and "almost equally" impossible for the white man to get justice in the extra judicial proceeding of the Freedman's Bureau officials which largely superseded the courts for a time. Much is remembered of these proceedings by older Southerners—much picturesque and sentimental fiction, with an ample basis of truth, has been written about them by Mr. Thomas Nelson Page and others. Here we have the other side.

While the whole book is interesting, especially to a Southerner, and while the self-restraint and temperateness of the manner of stating even things which the Southerner regards as impossibilities, deserve much praise and disarm harsh criticism, the part of the book which is more immediately concerned with an arraignment of the present plans of Booker T. Washington is for the present the most important.

In this matter the writer, speaking, as he says, for many educated negroes, makes two chief objections—first, that Washington is the leader of his race not by the suffrage of that race, but rather by virtue of the support of the whites, and, second, that, by yielding to the modern commercial spirit and confining the effort for uplifting the individual to practical education and the acquisition of property and decent ways, he is after all cutting off the negro from those higher aspirations which only, Du Bois says, make a people great. For instance, it is said that Booker Washington distinctly asks that black people give up, at least for the present, three things:

First, political power;

Second, insistence on civil rights;

Third, higher education for negro youth, and concentrate all their energies on industrial education, the accumulation of wealth, and the conciliation of the South. This policy has been courageously and insistently advocated for over fifteen years, and has been triumphant for perhaps ten years. As a result of this tender of the palm branch what has been the return? In these years there have occurred:

1. The disfranchisement of the negro.
2. The legal creation of a distinct status of civil inferiority for the negro.
3. The steady withdrawal of aid from institutions for the higher training of the negro.

These movements are not, to be sure, direct results of Washington's teachings, but his propaganda has, without a shadow of doubt, helped their speedier accomplishment.

The writer admits the great value of Booker Washington's work. However, he does not believe so much in the gospel of the lamb, and does think that a bolder attitude, one of standing firmly upon rights guaranteed by the war amendments, and alluded to in complimentary fashion in the Declaration of Independence,

1904

Opening of *Peter Pan*, a play by J. M. Barrie (text not published till 1928).

is both more becoming to a race such as he conceives the negro race to be, and more likely to advance that race. "We feel in conscience bound," he says, "to ask three things: 1, The right to vote; 2, Civic equality; 3, The education of youth according to ability" and he is especially insistent on the higher education of the negro—going into some statistics to show what the negro can do in that way. The value of these arguments and the force of the statistics can best be judged after the book is read.

Many passages of the book will be very interesting to the student of the negro character who regards the race ethnologically and not politically, not as a dark cloud threatening the future of the United States, but as a peculiar people, and one, after all, but little understood by the best of its friends or the worst of its enemies outside of what the author of *The Souls of Black Folk* is fond of calling the "Awful Veil." Throughout it should be recalled that it is the thought of a negro of Northern education who has lived long among his brethren of the South yet who cannot fully feel the meaning of some things which these brethren know by instinct—and which the Southern-bred white knows by a similar instinct; certain things which are by both accepted as facts—not theories—fundamental attitudes of race to race which are the product of conditions extending over centuries, as are the somewhat parallel attitudes of the gentry to the peasantry in other countries.

Awakening

The Story of My Life by Helen Keller
March 21, 1903

T HE TEDIOUS STEPS of the process of awakening the intelligence of a human being deprived of all the ordinary means of communication with her fellows at an age so early that practically no foundation has been laid by normal means—such is the material of this book on the life of Helen Keller, written partly by herself. The scientific interest of the process is great, both in itself and for the light it throws on the unconscious and unobserved processes by which children with all their senses learn the same things that have been laboriously acquired by this girl, stricken blind and deaf before she was two years old. The human interest of the story is hardly less great.

From recognizing the sign of one thing or of several things to the conception that everything had a sign was a long step, but here is the description of the dawning:

1904

James Joyce and Nora Barnacle have their first date, on June 16 (Bloomsday). When Joyce's father hears her last name, he says, "She'll never leave him."

Some one was drawing water, and my teacher placed my hand under the spout. As the cool stream gushed over one hand she spelled into the other the word "water," first slowly, then rapidly. I stood still, my whole attention fixed upon the motions of her fingers. Suddenly I felt a misty consciousness as of something forgotten—a thrill of returning thought; and somehow the mystery of language was revealed to me. I knew then that "w-a-t-e-r" meant the wonderful cool something that was flowing over my hand. That living word awakened my soul, gave it light, hope, joy; set it free!

So much has already been written about this remarkable young woman and her achievements in the face of fearful odds that most people do not need to be told that she has been attending Radcliffe College, and studying Greek, Latin, French, German, mathematics, literature, history—everything that other people study. She confesses, like Dr. Holmes, that she doesn't like mathematics. Where she cannot provide herself with a given textbook printed in the embossed letters used by the blind, she has Miss Sullivan read the lesson to her in finger language. In class her teacher sits beside her and repeats in the same finger language what the lecturer is saying, Miss Keller writes:

In this respect, I do not think I am much worse off than the girls who take notes. If the mind is occupied with the mechanical process of hearing and putting words on paper at pell-mell speed, I should not think one could pay much attention to the subject under consideration or the manner in which it is presented. I cannot make notes during lectures, because my hands are busy listening.

Letter

Jack London
September 2, 1905

AS ONE INTERESTED in the play of life and in the mental processes of his fellow-creatures, I have been somewhat amused by a certain feature of the criticisms of my prizefighting story, "The Game." This feature is the impeachment of my realism, the challenging of the facts of life as put down by me in that story. It is rather hard on a poor devil of a writer, when he has written what he has seen with his own eyes or experienced in his own body, to have it charged that said sights and experiences are unreal and impossible.

But this is no new experience, after all. I remember a review of *The Sea Wolf* by an Atlantic Coast critic who seemed very familiar with the sea. Said critic laughed hugely at me because I sent one of my characters aloft to shift over a gafftopsail. The critic said that no one ever went aloft to shift over a gafftopsail, and that he knew what he was talking about because he had seen many gafftopsails shifted over from the deck. Yet I, on a seven-months' cruise in a topmast schooner, had gone aloft, I suppose, a hundred times, and with my own hands shifted tacks and sheets of gafftopsails.

Now to come back to "The Game." As reviewed in *The New York Times Review of Books*, fault was found with my realism. I doubt if this reviewer has had as much experience in such matters as I have. I doubt if he knows what it is to be knocked out, or to knock out another man. I have had these experiences, and it was out of these experiences, plus a fairly intimate knowledge of prizefighting in general, that I wrote "The Game."

I quote from your critic: "Still more one gently doubts in this particular case that a blow delivered by Ponta on the point of Fleming's chin could throw the latter upon the padded canvas floor of the ring with enough force to smash in the whole back of his skull, as Mr. London describes."

All I can say in reply is, that a young fighter in the very club described in my book had his head smashed in this manner. Incidentally, this young fighter worked in a sail loft and took remarkably good care of his mother, brothers, and sisters.

And—oh! one word more. I have just received a letter from Jimmy Britt, lightweight champion of the world, in which he tells me that he particularly enjoyed "The Game" "on account of its trueness to life."

Up from the Stockyards

The Jungle by Upton Sinclair
March 3, 1906

INASMUCH as Mr. Upton Sinclair's co-workers in the field of Socialistic propaganda have acclaimed his book as "a great work," as a power that must make itself felt, "so simple, so true, so tragic, and so human," it becomes the plain duty of the reviewer to examine *The Jungle* with a candid and open mind, in order that its quality as literature and its efficiency as polemic may be fairly appraised. These young gentlemen who have so bravely come forward to assist in upsetting the established social order as a preparation for the Socialistic millennium on earth are all interesting. They burn with the zeal, the enthusiasm, and the full confidence of youth. Maturity has not moderated their buoyant trust in themselves; they are not plagued by the doubts that come with years nor by those habits of inquiry and prudent examination that experience inculcates. They have unbounded confidence in each other. They work in union and in harmony, without petty jealousies, unstintedly praising each other's productions, all for the advancement of the common cause.

Mr. Sinclair in *The Jungle* has given to the world a close, a striking, and, we may say, in many ways a brilliant study of the great industries of Chicago, beginning with the stockyards, using the characters of his story as subjects on which to demonstrate the effect upon human beings of the fierce struggle for work, for wages, and for life in those vast establishments. The "hero" or principal subject is Jurgis Rudkus, a Lithuanian immigrant, who with a group of neighbors and his kinsfolk has come across the seas to seek work and the living chance in the great Republic. He gets his first job in the "killing beds" of the great packing house of the Beef Trust. He is big, broad-shouldered, good-natured, full of energy, and with a tremendous capacity for work. He earns something more than a living wage, and he and his relatives lay by a little something every week until he feels able to marry the girl of his heart, who has come from Lithuania with her family. Their wedding feast cost them a hundred dollars—about one-third of his year's earnings. He and his Lithuanian friends are cheated right and left—by their own countrymen as well as by the natives. They buy a little house on the installment plan, paying over to the smooth-tongued agent nearly every cent of their savings. This all goes, of course, when Jurgis loses his job and they fall behind in the payments. Things go from bad to worse. Jurgis gets and loses one job after another, sometimes by the shutting down of work, sometimes through a disabling accident, until finally he is "blacklisted" for an assault upon a foreman who had misused his wife, Ona. Then things go very badly indeed with Jurgis. His wife dies. He begins to drink heavily, becomes sulky and sour-tempered, haunts the saloons, becomes engaged in frequent brawls, and finally, when his little boy dies, he loses hope and takes to the road as a tramp.

The progress of this victim of industrial oppression, as Mr. Sinclair depicts it, is rapidly and steadily downward. First the packing house, then the fertilizer works, then the harvester works, then the steel works; afterward he is a tramp, then a tunnel digger, then a thief, then a highwayman, later on a beggar, and after a brief and exciting experience as a "scab" workingman and an agent of the Beef Trust in oppressing organized labor, he enters Republican politics in the City of Chicago. This is evidently Mr. Upton Sinclair's idea of the progressive downward course. His pictures of the successive environments in which Jurgis is placed are vivid, full of local color, and often painted with much skill. They are without exception hideous. The language Mr. Sinclair employs is appropriate to the scene, the action, and the characters of his drama. For the gross words Dante occasionally employs in the *Inferno* the commentators make the excuse that as the action passes in Hell and the personages are many of them devils, uniform elegance and propriety of speech are not to be expected. The language of the stockyards, as employed by Mr. Sinclair, is often quite unquotable. The experienced reader will at once perceive that Mr. Sinclair has taken Zola for his model. The likeness is more than striking—it fairly forces itself upon the attention of the reader. The method is the same, and, although Mr. Sinclair writes no preface, it is evident that he expects his story to be taken as a scientific study of industrial conditions and his characters as "human documents." Zola with great solemnity and insistence forced upon his readers the scientific aspect of his work. Naturalism was the true method, the scientific spirit the only one in which to approach the study of social facts. He asked the world to accept him as a savant, as an investigator, a demonstrator. Now, between Mr. Upton Sinclair and Zola there is a wide interval. Zola was in his way a man of genius, while Mr. Sinclair, for the present at least, must be content to be set down as merely clever. But the shallowness of the scientific pretensions of both is equally evident. Zola forgot that his work was not done in the laboratory, but in the realm of the imagination; that his materials were not exhibited subject to the operation of natural law, but behaving as it occurred to his fertile invention to make them behave. As a presentation of industrial facts and social conditions Mr. Sinclair's work is open to that objection. Like Zola, he studies but one aspect, and that the meanest, the most hideous, and the most vicious and painful of the phases of human life and conduct that pass under his examination. Virtue, generosity, good impulses, morality, and honesty have their place and exert their influence in the stockyard population, no doubt. They do not attract the attention or engage the pen of Mr. Sinclair.

So the impression left upon the reader's mind by the descriptive part of his book is unsatisfactory. His pictures are not convincing. His work becomes mechanical in the carrying out, largely, no doubt, because of his attempt to make the naturalistic methods of Zola serve the purpose of demonstrating facts and conditions which he believed to exist and which he was determined that his public should believe to exist. The concluding chapters of *The Jungle*, in which the saving grace of Socialism is made to do its beneficent work upon Jurgis, are sufficient to put the reader quite out of the mood of belief and assent. If a biologist should exhibit to his class a robust and adult frog in his normal condition, and then, after having to some extent skinned and dissected the animal so as to lay bare his vital organs, exhibiting the ranuncular reflexes by applications of electricity, of divers chemicals, of heat, and of cold—if he should then apply to the frog some elixir of life of which he was the appointed "press agent," and present him to view once more sound and whole as an efficient and contented frog, the class would have to have a very unquestioning faith in the Professor if it did not at once suspect some hocus pocus that would altogether remove the experiment from the domain of science.

Jurgis is Mr. Upton Sinclair's frog. The frightful experiences through which he is made to pass as a workingman, ground down, oppressed, and brutally treated; as a drunkard, as a tramp, as a highway robber, and as a beggar, would not only have crushed his spirit, but would have put him beyond hope of regeneration. These cruelties would have beaten out and these poisons would have eaten out the whole soul of the man. Yet one day, as was his wont, having taken refuge from bitter cold and snow in a hall where a meeting was in progress for which no admission fee was charged, and having, as he had done upon previous occasions, fallen into an alcoholic drowse, he was aroused by the voice of a beautiful young woman, who implored him to sit up and listen. He listened. What he heard was a discourse by a Socialist, depicting the wretchedness of humanity as society is now organized, and setting forth the beauties and the beneficence of the Socialistic régime. Mr. Sinclair gives up several pages of his book to the Socialist's speech. Jurgis had hardly heard the word Socialism before, but that speech made him think. It was the dawn of hope in a bosom long occupied by black despair. The Socialists took him up. He learned to read and they supplied him with tracts. He attended many other meetings. The angel of the new faith guided his steps somehow to a Socialist who kept a hotel and who gladly employed Jurgis as a porter. Coming to a fuller knowledge of the doctrine and learning to talk, he became a Socialist speaker himself.

The greatest defect in the reasoning—or the dreaming—of all Socialists is that they put most of their carts before their horses. They assume that the unequal distribution of wealth is the cause of the inequality of condition, quite

Oops!

May 25, 1907

Sister Carrie

BY THEODORE DREISER

Theodore Dreiser's frankly realistic story called *Sister Carrie*, originally published seven years ago, is now republished and deserves to be received as a new book, for it did not get a chance for recognition when it first appeared. It may be added that the story even upon its first publication attracted much attention and won favorable recognition in England. We do not, however, recommend the book to the fastidious reader, or the one who clings to "old-fashioned ideas." It is a book one can very well get along without reading.

overlooking the fact that inequality of capacity is a somewhat important factor in bringing about the disparity in earthly possessions. They assume, too, that men and women need only to be emancipated from wage slavery and the barbarities of capitalism to become all at once high-minded, virtuous, generous, forbearing, honest, enamored of the Ten Commandments, and eager to do unto others as they would that others should do unto them. Jurgis is an example of this regeneration.

We lay aside *The Jungle* with a conviction that it is not, after all, a great and epoch-making work. We are afraid Mr. Sinclair has not been divinely appointed to be a deliverer of Labor lying prostrate. Somehow, in his tones the ear continuously catches the false note. There are spurious coins in every handful of his mintage. We cannot help being skeptical about his sincerity. His art is too obvious, his devices too trite, and he has too much joy in them. His delight is not so much in the thing he says as in the way he says it, which is often astonishingly clever. There is nothing spontaneous in the book save his imaginative descriptions of human disappointment and misery. In that he is at his best. He has been at pains to "get up" his facts thoroughly, and his realism is often striking. But he seems to write not from the heart but from the head, with that facile glitter of contrast and exaggeration that is characteristic of the school of young writers that have set out to deliver us from the evils of capitalism. Mr. Upton Sinclair does not remind the reader of John Knox or of Martin Luther, or of the leaders in the Abolition movement. He has not written a second *Uncle Tom's Cabin*.

First Impressions

The Wind in the Willows by Kenneth Grahame
October 24, 1908

THERE ARE CERTAIN BOOKS which are nearly always read furtively—at most, two congenial and properly grown-up souls may pore over their unexpurgated treasures in secret and behind locked doors, far away from a solemnly disapproving world. It would not do at all to give a list of these books, but any one who has ever met the Walrus and the Hatter in the land where jam is served every other day will quite understand just the class of literature indicated. It is necessary to be a bit cryptic, for if Mr. Kenneth Grahame's *The Wind in the Willows* should fall into the wrong hands it might suffer great indignities. Such, for instance, as being termed "an allegory," or, worse still, a "nature book." It might even be banished into the nursery, where it would simply be wasted, if it were not actively dangerous.

You must be quite grown up to appreciate the thrilling adventures of Mr. Toad, who would a-motoring go, even to the extent of stealing a car. For this rash act he was thrown into a deep dungeon, rescuing himself after sundry encounters with a fat barge woman, a gypsy, and a captured engine. The Toad is much more human than many people we read of in novels nowadays.

The Wind in the Willows is whimsical, fascinating by its apparent seriousness and that sense of underlying poetry which Mr. Grahame somehow manages to convey through all his nonsense. When the poor little Rat and Mole come to the enchanted isle, and, drawn by mysterious music, find themselves in the presence of the great God Pan himself, refuge and savior of weary, stricken wild creatures—well, you hope it is all true, and you know it is very beautiful.

Some may call it nature faking of the baldest sort, but such pedantry carries its own punishment. The book is not easily classified—it is simply destined to be one of those dog-eared volumes which one laughs over and loves. Which should be quite enough for any book to achieve.

1911

The *Book Review*, renamed the *Review of Books*, switches to Sunday on January 29.

First Impressions

The Boy Scouts of America by Ernest Thompson Seton and Sir Robert S. S. Baden-Powell
September 24, 1910

BRIMFUL of lore of woods and field, alluring with hints of the life out of doors, and containing the suggestive link between woodcraft and "life-craft," this handbook of woodcraft, scouting, and life-craft, by Ernest Thompson Seton and Lieut. Gen. Sir Robert S. S. Baden-Powell, K. C. B., appeared at an opportune moment. In the Summer season thousands of boys in large cities, and even in small towns and in the country, are thrown on their own resources for amusement and recreation. Keen observers have noticed the degenerating influence of undirected boyhood activities and particularly the rapidly growing numbers of spectators and lookers-on, rather than participators, in the sports and activities of our older boys and young men. We seem to be slowly evolving into a race of anaemics; the self-reliance, resourcefulness, and adaptability of our fathers are wanting. A remedy is sorely needed. "Something to do, something to think about, something to enjoy in the woods, with a view always to character building—for manhood, not scholarship—is the aim of education," best expresses the basis of the Boy Scout idea.

Under the direction of the Young Men's Christian Association and other influential societies and individuals, the Boy Scouts of America have been formed

Oops!

February 19, 1911

Howards End

BY E. M.
FORSTER

As a social philosopher, evidently, Mr. Edward M. Forster has not yet arrived at any very positive convictions. He evinces neither power nor inclination to come to grips with any vital human problem.

into a National organization, with Mr. Seton at its head, as "Chief Scout." Boys everywhere—in city and country—are collected into groups, competent volunteer instructors being appointed to guide their sports and recreations, and the secrets and rules of "life-craft" being taught through the interesting media of woodcraft, scouting, and real-boy games.

As a first step, *The Boy Scouts of America* has been issued in convenient and easily procurable form as the manual of organization of the movement. It contains all necessary information for instructors, as well as for the boy scouts themselves, and, in addition, a wealth of material on camping. Practical directions for the selection of camp outfits, instruction in wig-wag signaling, tracking, rope-knotting, first aid to the injured, and, in fact, everything one can imagine as necessary for the camper, we find in well-arranged, simple form, well adapted to the class of readers the book will reach. And even of greater value are the many pages of well-selected outdoor games, many of them new to the boys of America, that will go far toward holding the interest of those obliged to remain at home, as well as the more fortunate campers.

A Flood from the Soul

The Brothers Karamazov by Fyodor Dostoyevsky
June 30, 1912

W HEN, a few years ago, the dramatic essays of Bernard Shaw were occupying the attention of local playgoers, there was a story told of a young woman, after an evening spent at a theatre—face to face, it may be, with *Man and Superman*—who turned to another person present, and with a countenance transparently eloquent of what she felt, said: "Why, they talk about the things you think about at night when the light is out and you are all by yourself." The young woman must have been rather outspoken, as outspokenness went hereabouts at that remote period, or she would never have made such a speech.

We have advanced somewhat since that time. We have overcome reticences, cast down reserves. H. G. Wells's *Ann Veronica* has proved the advance agent of a deal of disturbing frankness. Mrs. Corra Harris, a purely domestic product, has learned to use a shocking freedom in telling things which in Mrs. Harris's set (and ours) used not to be mentioned even in a whisper. Novelists of ours and the English have gone to school to the Norwegians and the Russians, and done their best to imitate the frankness of those foreigners. Wells has tried it on. Galsworthy has tried it on. Bennett has domesticated the experiment in the Five Towns, and Robert Herrick has boldly undertaken to transplant it here.

Yet you have only to read any one of those Russians that they try to copy to realize that the trick of pouring out the contents of the human soul in talk is no more than views on art, "to be bought like trousers, ready made." Our English and American realists succeed in being piquantly and stupidly indiscreet by turns, but they no more tell the simple truth about themselves—or let their characters tell the simple truth about themselves—as the Russian does, than they would do if they practiced the old-fashioned method of reticence. What they tell is not less obviously told for false effect than what they used not to tell was withheld for false effect.

With these realistic writers of ours in mind, then, it is worth while even for a quite unliterary person to read such a book as Dostoyevsky's *The Brothers Karamazov* in an English version like that of Constance Garnett—a version which conceals nothing except, perhaps, certain idiomatic beauties of style, which the original Russian would reveal. It may not be necessary for such a person as has been suggested to read the whole book. That, though it is only a fragment of what the author intended to make it, extends to 840 pages of print. But it will prove very instructive to read some of it, and the reader—we are still taking here the case of the average American mildly interested in books, the American who has been no follower of the Russian literary school—will be astonished to find how much he does read. What makes him read it, too, is sheer breathless interest in the people and in the drama.

The reader we are speaking of, who, very likely, has a smattering of Tolstoy or Turgenev, or both, may already have got lodged in his head a sort of notion that Russian novels are inhabited chiefly by escaped lunatics and uncaught candidates for Bedlam. If he has, the history of the brothers Karamazov is admirably fitted to encourage that harmless presumption that Russia is little better than a vast mad-house in which the keepers share the affliction of the kept. And yet the reader in spite of this presumption will not be able to deny that everybody— every man, woman, and child introduced into these 840 pages is human—convincingly and horribly human. They are insane merely because they are so intensely self-conscious of every mood—because they live each mood as if it were the whole of life. Thus chronic hysteria pervades the whole lot from the point of view of the Western person who plays his game of life on a different system—an elaborate system of discounts, allowances, and compromises. For do we not balance our joy and our sorrow with a careful and calculating hand, measure our allowance of love, compound beforehand for our sins, pay to virtues we find it inconvenient to practice the homage of hypocrisy, and generally cultivate the tradesman's wisdom of common sense? By the way, let no man despise common sense because it is the tradesman's wisdom.

In other words, our approved plan for making life decently bearable to ourselves and outwardly acceptable in the sight of God and our fellowmen is never to admit the worst of the truth about it even to ourselves. It is not so with your Russians. They pour out the whole content of their souls in talk—talk that takes the place of what we esteem idle chatter. So Dostoyevsky pours out in a flood over these pages the souls of his Russians. Each pours his own soul out in talk to everybody. Old Karamazov, a Silenus, the three young Karamazovs, a hermit, a monk, a foolish widow, a crippled girlchild, an epileptic man cook; a haughty young woman with angry passions, another young woman with lovers, a broken Captain, a police commandant, a lawyer—each and all insist on making a clean breast of it till you are fairly overwhelmed with the indecency of so much truth telling.

You catch a glimmer, too, of a fact which you might never have guessed at otherwise—the fact that too insistent truth telling is almost as distorting to the just perspective of facts as plentiful lying. Here, for instance, is young Dmitri Karamazov, a quite lovable scoundrel who behaves, nevertheless, like a cur of low degree, chiefly—one may imagine—because he works off between times all his very considerable endowment of decent and even honorable and lofty feeling in rhetoric. On the other hand there is Ivan, his brother, who takes it all out in talk—vice and virtue alike. Russians recognize in him (we are told) the typical restless self-destructive intellectual type of the nation, the other young man being the "normal" Russian as nearly as Dostoyevsky's pathological twist allowed him to make anything normal. You might argue that this "normal" Dmitri was shown as the victim of conditions which might be considered normal for one of his age and class. He is a young officer reduced to dire shifts for money and driven upon his fate by these shifts and what comes of them. In any case he is a member of the human family whose kinship you dare not reject, and he is to the centre of a drama hardly less tremendous for being incomplete.

* * *

It was John Galsworthy who pointed out to the writer the exhaustion of the power to do that seemed to be incident to the Russian habit of trying it all out, and especially talking it all out. And very recently in his *Under Western Eyes* Joseph Conrad, who knows the Russian somewhat better than some of the rest

Oops!

September 14, 1913

O Pioneers!

BY WILLA SIBERT CATHER

Possibly some might call it a feminist novel, for the two heroines are stronger, cleverer and better balanced than their husbands and brothers— but we are sure Miss Cather had nothing so inartistic in mind.

of us, has undertaken to make a case in point concrete. Between the Russian as Conrad shows him in the person of his protagonist there and the Russian as Dostoyevsky shows him, however, lies all that difference that separates the Russian peasant and the European aristocrat. That difference—though Dostoyevsky died only in 1880—is roughly the span of twenty centuries—the span which separates civilized Europe from barbaric Russia. Those peasants with whom Dostoyevsky dealt as one of themselves belong to the age of Nero and earlier and the flowering of a hot-house literature which has followed the grafting of European culture—the intellectual part of it—upon a small minority on the top of this swarming ant heap of barbarians does not avail to wipe out those twenty centuries.

A Boy's Best Friend

Sons and Lovers by D. H. Lawrence
September 21, 1913

THERE IS PROBABLY no phrase much more hackneyed than that of "human document," yet it is the only one which at all describes this very unusual book. It is hardly a story; rather the first part of a man's life, from his birth until his 25th year, the conditions surrounding him, his strength and his numerous weaknesses, put before us in a manner which misses no subtlest effect either of emotion or environment. And the heroine of the book is not sweetheart, but mother; the mother with whose marriage the novel begins, with whose pathetic death it reaches its climax. The love for each other of the mother and her son, Paul Morel, is the mainspring of both their lives; it is portrayed tenderly, yet with a truthfulness which slurs nothing even of that friction which is unavoidable between the members of two different generations.

The scene is laid among the collieries of Derbyshire. Paul's father was a miner; his mother, Mrs. Morel, belonged a trifle higher up in the social scale, having made one of those "romantic" marriages with which the old-fashioned sentimental novel used to end, and with which the modern realistic one so frequently begins. The first chapter, which tells of their early married life before the coming of their second son, Paul, is an admirable account of a mismated couple. Walter Morel could never have amounted to very much, but had he possessed a less noble wife he might, by one of those strange contradictions of which life is full, have been a far better man than he actually was. His gradual degeneration is as pitiful as it is inevitable—the change from the joyous, lovable young man to the drunken, ill-tempered father, whose entrance hushed the children's laughter, the mere thought of whom could cast a shadow over all the house. Mrs. Morel was strong enough to remake for herself the life he had so nearly wrecked—he could only drift helplessly upon the rocks. It is wonderfully real, this daily life of the Morel family and the village wherein they lived as reflected in Mr. Lawrence's pages; the more real because he never flaunts his knowledge of the intimate details of the existence led by these households whose men folk toil underground. They slip from his pen so unobtrusively that it is only when we pause and consider that we recognize how full and complete is the background against which he projects his principal characters—Mr. and Mrs. Morel, Paul, Miriam, and Clara.

Paul himself is a person who awakens interest rather than sympathy; it is difficult not to despise him a little for his weakness, his constant need of that strengthening he sought from two other women, but which only his splendid, indomitable little mother could give him—a fact of which he was constantly aware, though he acknowledged it only at the very end. And it is not easy upon any grounds to excuse his treatment of Miriam, even though it was a spiritual self-defense which argued him to disloyalty. Mr. Lawrence has small regard for what we term conventional morality; nevertheless, though plain spoken to a degree, his book is not in the least offensive.

It is, in fact, fearless; never coarse, although the relations between Paul, Miriam, and Clara are portrayed with absolute frankness. And one must go far to find a better study of an intense woman, so over-spiritualized that she has almost lost touch with ordinary life and ordinary humanity, than he has given us in the person of Miriam. We pity her for her craving, the self-distrust that forbade her to take the thing she most wanted even when it was almost within her grasp; and yet Paul's final recoil is readily comprehensible, his feeling that she was making his very soul her own—would, as his mother said, leave nothing of him. The long, psychic battle between the two, a battle blindly fought, never really understood, is excellent in its revelation of those motives which lie at the very root of character—motives of which the persona they actuate are so often completely ignorant.

Clara is less remarkable than Miriam only because she is necessarily more obvious—a woman in whom the animal predominates, certain after a brief time to weary one like Paul. And better than either, strong of will, rich in love and sympathy, holding her place in her son's heart against even Miriam, who so nearly took him from her, reigning at last supreme over every rival stands the heroic little mother—the best-drawn character in a book which contains many admirable portrayals. From the moment when we first meet her taking her older children to the "wakes" and trying to nerve herself to endure a life which appears to be an endless waiting for something that can never come, until at the last she wages her valiant, losing fight against the cancer that is killing her by inches, she is always real, a fine, true woman, mother to the very core. Mr. Lawrence has mercifully spared us the terrible details of her illness; it is only her "tortured eyes" we see, and her children's grief and horror. Whether or not it was right for Paul to do the thing he did is an open question; only we are sure that in very truth he "loved her better than his own life." His impotent resentment of her growing weakness is an excellent bit of analysis, the effect upon him of her death, which he seemed to take so calmly—the blankness, the unreality and emptiness of all things—strikes home. Without her his life was meaningless; yet live he must, and for her sake. The book is full of short, vivid descriptions:

> The steep swoop of highroad lay, in its cool morning dust, splendid with patterns of sunshine and shadow, perfectly still. . . . Behind, the houses stood on the brim of the dip, black against the sky, like wild beasts glaring curiously with yellow eyes down into the darkness.

Each a picture drawn in a sentence. Although this is a novel of over 500 closely printed pages the style is terse—so terse that at times it produces an effect as of short, sharp hammer strokes. Yet it is flexible, too, as shown by its success in depicting varying shades of mood, in expressing those more intimate emotions which are so very nearly inexpressible. Yet, when all is said, it is the complex character of Miriam, she who was only Paul's "conscience, not his mate," and the beautiful bond between the restless son and the mother whom "his soul could not leave" even when she slept and "dreamed her young dream" which makes this book one of rare excellence.

Lightening the Gloom

Stories of Russian Life by Anton Chekov
June 7, 1914

ANTON CHEKOV has written in a letter to a friend:

> I fear those who look for hidden meanings between the lines, and those who look upon me as a liberator or as a guardian. I am neither a liberal nor a conservative, neither a monk nor an indifferent person . . . I only want to be an artist—that's all.

This demand that the artist shall be the leader has put an unfortunate bias to Russian literature, and Chekov realized it keenly. No sooner has a writer, surviving censorship, loomed up with the picture of his people, than all faces are turned to him. There is hope in every eye; hands are stretched out to him; because he understands misery it is taken for granted he knows how to end it. And overnight the artist is made into the man with a programme, overnight he is committed to the rôle of savior and leader. Anton Chekov had seen the big men before him, Tolstoy, Turgenev, even Gogol to some extent, succumbing to the pressure and mixing up of art and morals in a fashion that went out, as far as the rest of Europe is concerned, with Lessing and the eighteenth century. Chekov, as no one before him, realized that this was warping and narrowing, even while it deepened, Russian literature, and he fought against it. But the Russian mind—the mind of the Russian "intellectual," sees in literature only subject for debate or society reform. Chekov wrote a gloomy little tale—*The Peasants*—in which a working man who had longed all his life in the city to get back to his home, finally returned to the country and found it a wretched place indeed. Refusing to view the sketch as a sketch the Russian public snatched it up into the field of polemic and for months a controversy waged on the problem: Is living in the country worse than living in the city?

Chekov made an earnest effort to break with this tradition, built up by Tolstoy and Dostoyevsky and Turgenev, an effort to be non-Russian, or at best less Russian, and it is for this very reason, perhaps, that he is rated below his predecessors and his contemporaries. We are apt to make the skip from Tolstoy straight to Gorky and the newer company. Chekov tried to be different but he did not try hard enough. He tried to introduce into Russian literature not only an art for art's sake policy, but a delicate art for the sake of delicacy. He endeavored to relegate horrors to the background, to lighten the general gloom that has hung over Russian letters since the advent of the realist school under the influence of Dickens and Balzac. Nowhere is this shown better than in his swift sketches, the best of them collected in an English translation under the title *Stories of Russian Life*.

The story which opens the collection is wholly un-Russian in its deft funmaking, in its absence of any significance save that of an amusing picture. A surveyor finds himself driven along a lonely road at twilight by a murderous-looking peasant. The surveyor is a very little man and as the sunset burns itself out and the way becomes lonelier, he begins to talk about the three revolvers that he has concealed about him, about his almost superhuman strength where robbers are concerned, about three friends that are coming after him and will arrive in a few moments, and at length he has so thoroughly frightened the murderous-looking driver that he leaps from the seat and goes scuttling off into the darkness, leaving the surveyor with the prospect of spending the night in the cart alone, listening to the wolves. A mere trifle, for Chekov wrote like a flash, revising nothing—he finished one of his most successful plays in a single evening—but the touch is that of the artist, and the artist not burdened with the fact of being a Russian.

Chekov's endeavor has been largely negative. The best that he could do in the twenty years of his literary life was to refrain from writing his dramas and his sketches around some socialistic creed. There his vigor failed him. For the rest, the pressure of his time and of his environment was too strong, and he remains linked to the group from which he tried, however unconsciously, to break away. The delicacy and the sweetness which he brought as his contribution have been swamped by the salacious output of the "moderns." The whimsical humor which emerges from his pages has found no imitator. True it is that in his effort to break away from a preoccupation with ugliness and gloom, Chekov has slipped over to the sentimental. But sentimentalism and the Russian temperament are not long compatible, and Chekov's obvious admiration for the French school has also nipped the tendency in the bud. He has been called the de Maupassant of the Russians, but common points are few. He has perhaps taken over the swiftness of execution and the reserve of the French writer; his characters are never exhausted and never dominated by an abstract idea, but a genius of meditation which never crossed over into France, sits at his elbow, making his pen intimate that the greatest things have not yet been said, the large revelations not yet made. He is a pessimist to the core, a pessimist with only a vague glimmer of hope; he has all of the French cynicism but none of its *cynisme*. In short, to quote his own phrase, he is an artist—that's all.

First Impressions

Tarzan of the Apes by Edgar Rice Burroughs
July 5, 1914

A S THE RESULT of a mutiny aboardship, an English nobleman and his wife are marooned in a jungle inhabited by anthropoid apes. Here a child is born; a year later the mother dies. A great ape kills the father, but the baby boy is adopted by a female ape whose own child had just been killed by a fall. The subsequent adventures of Tarzan, as the boy is named by the tribe, make a story of many marvels. An ape in his agility and his prowess, heredity asserts itself; the boy tries to clothe himself, and, without ever having heard any save the ape language, without any conception of the sound of English, he teaches himself to read and write from books found in his father's cabin. With adventures and perils the book is replete, nor is a strange love story wanting. It closes with a great renunciation, but with the promise of another Tarzan book, which leads the reader to hope that the renunciation was not final. Crowded with impossibilities as the tale is, Mr. Burroughs has told it so well, and has so succeeded in carrying his readers with him, that there are few who will not look forward eagerly to the promised sequel.

Life Stripped of Externals

North of Boston by Robert Frost
May 16, 1915

BY JESSIE B. RITTENHOUSE

MR. ROBERT FROST has been fortunate in living down the fulsome and ill-considered praise with which he was introduced to the American public. When an American poet comes to us with an English reputation and prints upon his volume the English dictum that "his achievement is much finer, much more near the ground, and much more national than anything that Whitman gave to the world," one is likely to be prejudiced, not to say antagonized, at the outset. Just why a made-in-England reputation is so coveted by the poets of this country is difficult to fathom, particularly as English poets look so anxiously to America for acceptance of their own work.

Fortunately for Mr. Frost, his work is able to meet its own test. While it bears no more relation to the work of Whitman than a well-tilled field bears to the earth, this is to the credit of Mr. Frost. He is not a cosmic poet, not a great social seer, he is none of the things that Whitman was, and he refrains from assuming to be something that he is not. Mr. Frost is, indeed, too sincere a poet to look outside of his own experience for inspiration. The field that he has pre-empted is distinctly his own and one hitherto uncultivated in American poetry. It is the life of men and women on stony hill farms "north of Boston," life stripped of externals and lying sheer and bare to this analyst. There have been plenty to interpret rural New England in fiction, and Mr. Frost himself is a story teller plus the poet's spiritual focus upon the one essential motive of the story. He is able, as a writer of the short story (from the demands of the form) cannot do, to epitomize the many details of a narrative into some poignant episode which will illuminate the entire life he has chosen to reveal. For Mr. Frost is a psychologist, he is concerned entirely with the spiritual motives which actuate these folk on barren hill farms where life is largely reduced to its elemental expression. As faithfully as Sarah Orne Jewett has been able to interpret, through the much more flexible medium of the short story, the lives of these people, Mr. Frost in a few passages makes us free of their world.

It is a bleak world, infinitely sad. The spectre is always there, looking out of the eyes of men and women whom life has defrauded of joy. New England in literature is always stark and grim, but Mr. Frost is not an implacable realist; the grimness is there, but with it the tenderness of one who sees deeply into this phase of life because he has lived it. Mr. Frost was himself a farmer in New Hampshire and tilled his own acres before he converted them into the intangible estate of poetry.

Farm life, remote from centres, is much the same everywhere. The story of "The Hired Man" could be transferred without loss of color to any other section than New England. The pathetic old figure,

> *With nothing to look backward to with pride,*
> *And nothing to look forward to with hope,*
> *So now and never any different,*

is common to every community. What gives the poem its deep appeal is the insight of the woman who touches so tenderly the vagaries of the poor old derelict who has come back to die. Mr. Frost knows women and his truest studies are invariably of them. "Home Burial," perhaps the strongest of his poems, certainly the most dramatic, probes a woman's nature to the quick. One would have difficulty in finding, in such a compass, so powerful an illustration of the spiritual gulf between a man and a woman. The blunted sensibilities of the man who could dig his own child's grave, and the finer sensibilities of the woman upon whose soul every detail is stamped, could scarcely be rendered more effectively. A single passage from Mr. Frost's poem is hardly sufficient to suggest the play of character, but one may see in the following the truth of his psychology. To the remark,

> *"And so it's come to this,*
> *A man can't speak of his own child that's dead,"*

the wife replies,

> *"You can't because you don't know how.*
> *If you had any feelings, you that dug*
> *With your own hand—how could you?—his little grave;*

I saw you from that very window there,
Making the gravel leap and leap in air,
Leap up, like that, like that, and land so lightly
And roll back down the mound beside the hole.
I thought, Who is that man? I didn't know you.
And I crept down the stairs and up the stairs
To look again, and still your spade kept lifting.
Then you came in. I heard your rumbling voice
Out in the kitchen, and I don't know why,
But I went near to see with my own eyes.
You could sit there with the stains on your shoes
Of the fresh earth from your own baby's grave
And talk about your every-day concerns.
You had stood the spade up against the wall
Outside there in the entry, for I saw it."

In the last two lines Mr. Frost has one of his characteristic touches. To the man the spade was a spade, though he had dug his own child's grave with it; to the woman it was a thing of horror, and it was impossible to understand how he could calmly stand it up outside the door as upon any other occasion. It is in these little things that loom so large that one sees the subtlety of Mr. Frost's analysis. Psychology, however, does not make poetry, and one inevitably questions whether the short story would not fit this material quite as well as the form which Mr. Frost has chosen. There is little of poetry in the ordinary acceptance of the term, little of beauty, of magic, but there is the poetry of divination, the vision of souls, the poet's penetration into the one impulse which persists through all the deadening force of circumstance.

First Impressions

Psychology of the Unconscious by Carl Jung
May 21, 1916

FROM THE FIRST SUB-TITLE of this book there can be gained—by those more or less familiar with the new meanings which have been given to old words by Dr. Sigmund Freud, the Viennese psychologist—a general idea of its contents.

Jung is perhaps the most distinguished of Freud's European followers. He accepts with the gratitude of a faithful pupil the Freudian hypotheses as to the nature and processes of the unconscious or subconscious mind, but there his docility ends and for some of the Freudian conclusions Jung substitutes others of his own. He is, to that extent, in the eyes of the orthodox, a schismatic, starting, or endeavoring to start, a "school" of his own. Whether he will succeed in this remains for the disclosure of time. After all, it makes little practical difference as to the practical value of psychoanalysis whether, as Freud insists, the compulsive and obsessive neuroses come directly from psychic wounds suffered in early childhood, or whether Jung is right in viewing them as a return to one or another form of infantilism, caused by a later failure of adjustment to environment. The point is not unimportant, but it is not vital.

It is doubtful if many, or even any, readers of Jung's book who are not professional psychiatrists will fail to have, on closing it, a feeling that more than a few of its excursions into philosophy, etymology, and history are irrelevant, or too remotely and indirectly relevant, to his avowed subject. Americans will be apt to smile at the seriousness with which he treats the ethnology and mythology of *Hiawatha*, and to wonder if some other tales of eld, adduced in confirmation of his theory of transformations and symbolisms, are not as insecurely based. That, however, is decidedly amateur, and therefore futile, criticism. It is better to acknowledge frankly that Jung's book has deep interest, even when it does not convince, and that it has great value for all of the already large, and steadily increasing, number of people who have accepted the Freudian psychology as a long step, probably the longest ever taken, toward an understanding of mental mysteries hitherto insoluble.

1917

T. S. Eliot takes a job at Lloyds Bank, where he is employed for nine years, and in 1922 writes *The Waste Land*, which the *Book Review* never reviews.

The Adams Family

The Education of Henry Adams by Henry Adams
October 27, 1918

FOR THE AUTOBIOGRAPHY of Henry Adams we have waited for twelve years. It is a book of unique richness, of unforgettable comment and challenging thought, a book delightful, whimsical, deep-thinking, suggestive, a book greatly worth the waiting for. It has had a curious history. Written in 1905, *The Education of Henry Adams: A Study of Twentieth Century Multiplicity*, was a sequel to *Mont-Saint-Michel and Chartres: A Study of Thirteenth Century Unity*, which had been finished and privately printed the year before: 100 copies were privately printed, and sent to persons interested, in 1906; it is now published, by the Massachusetts Historical Society, for the first time. Yet in 1913, when the Institute of Architects published the *Mont-Saint-Michel*

1917

Modern Library is founded.

and Chartres, scholars already knew the *Education* well. Mr. Adams, however, to whose literary career a severe illness had put an end in 1912, had decided to have his autobiography, as Senator Lodge points out in his preface, "unpublished, avowedly incomplete, trusting that it might quietly fade from memory." It has not faded from memory. But it is unfortunate that the general public in his own country has given so little of its attention to the American historian who was Charles Francis Adams's son. It is to be hoped that the publication of *The Education of Henry Adams* will serve as introduction where that is needed. The book would be worth reading for no other purpose. It is worth reading for many purposes besides.

Its dry comment on things Bostonian and otherwise, its whimsical humor, its detached way of presenting the subject of the history—who is always referred to in the third person in this autobiography—its charming, tender, vivid portraits— all these are irresistible as matters of readability and as features of the author's literary style. His record of his childhood is unforgettable in its charm and vividness. Of the New England atmosphere in which he was brought up he writes:

> Resistance to something was the law of New England nature; the boy looked out on the world with the instinct of resistance; for numberless generations his predecessors had viewed the world chiefly as a thing to be reformed, filled with evil forces to be abolished, and they saw no reason to suppose that they had wholly succeeded in the abolition; the duty was unchanged. That duty implied not only resistance to evil, but hatred of it. Boys naturally look on all force as an enemy, and generally find it so, but the New Englander, whether boy or man, in his long struggle with a stingy or hostile universe had learned also to love the pleasure of hating; his joys were few.

Outstanding among the portraits of his boyhood are those of his grandfather, "the President," and his grandmother, "the Madame"—the latter "Louis Seize like the furniture" and not a Bostonian; his father, and his father's friend, who was the hero of his boyish worship, Charles Sumner. They are long pen-pictures—too long to quote—but once read they remain in the reader's own "portrait gallery."

School the boy disliked, and he always reckoned his school days as "time thrown away." From school he went, as all the Adamses and the Brookses had gone, to Harvard College, which, "so far as it educated at all, was a mild and liberal school, which sent men into the world with all they needed to make respectable citizens, and something of what they wanted to make useful ones."

1918

Ernest Poole's *His Family* wins the first Pulitzer Prize for fiction.

Henry Adams made friends in Harvard—as everywhere—but the most lasting academic impression came to him from James Russell Lowell, who had brought back from Germany the habit of private reading with his students, and who led Adams to go himself to Germany when he left college. As education, Germany was a failure. But the young American learned there that "the Germany he loved was the eighteenth century, which the Germans were ashamed of and were destroying as fast as they could. Of the Germany to come he knew nothing. Military Germany was his abhorrence." He liked "the blundering incapacity of the German for practical affairs"; German "system" was horrible to him.

He was twenty-three when his father was appointed Minister to Great Britain and took his son with him as private secretary. That was, as every one knows, in 1861, and the years to come were trying and perilous beyond words. "Of the year 1862 Henry Adams could never bear to think without a shudder." The history of those civil war years when English governmental feeling so strongly favored the Confederacy is told in a fashion arresting, personal, unique. There are sentences, paragraphs, whole pages that the reviewer is deeply tempted to quote. Suffice it again to recommend the public to read the book as a whole!

Dispatches from the Barricades

Ten Days That Shook the World by John Reed
April 27, 1919

BY CHARLES E. RUSSELL

ALL REVOLUTIONS are good; some revolutions are better than others; the Bolshevist revolution was of the best.

This is Mr. Reed's underlying thesis, and there is no doubt that he writes of it brilliantly and entertainingly. His familiar powers of graphic description and moving narrative are here at their best. In his own way he retells the story of the rise of the Provisional Government, of the gathering strength of the Bolshevist minority; the half-witted revolt of Korniloff, the blood-stained overthrow of the Kerensky administration, the dispersal of the Constituent Assembly, the fighting, the barricades, and the machine guns. It cannot be said that he adds anything to the essentials of the narrative already told by his talented wife or to that in the luminous pages of Miss Bessie Beattie. But he fills in some details (from his own point of view) and to those not familiar with the Bolshevist coup d'état his account will be virile and interesting, if not at all times clear.

Many of the incidents he relates afford new and convincing sidelights upon the Bolshevist spirit and methods. In the chapter called "Victory" (being the celebration of the final triumph of the armed Bolshevist minority over the unarmed or badly armed majority) he relates his ride to the front in a motor truck loaded at one and the same time with soldiers and with loose hand grenades and bombs filled with the most powerful of explosives. The bombs and grenades were allowed to roll and bounce around the bottom of the truck while Mr. Reed and his soldiers went on their joy ride, which might have ended any instant in the obliteration of them all.

> Occasionally a patrol tried to stop us. Soldiers ran out into the road before us, shouted "Shtoi!" and threw up their guns.
>
> We paid no attention. "The devil take you!" cried the Red Guards. "We don't stop for anybody! We're Red Guards!" And we thundered imperiously on.

Nothing could have been more typical. In a short time Mr. Reed was taken from the truck, which went on without him. Other soldiers now stood him against a wall and made rapid preparations to shoot him. What for? Apparently on blind impulse and because shooting people was the day's work. He had a pass from the central Bolshevist authority guaranteeing his safety. Of no avail was that; nobody could read it. By the merest chance he escaped the fate that befell thousands of others—befell them in the same way and for the same reason. Long live the revolution!

These flashlights come and go continually across his pages. It is hectic reading, but fascinating—to some minds. What is all the turmoil, shooting, and murder about? We are left at the close wholly uninformed. In this respect Mr. Reed differs in no way from the others of his faith that have essayed the apotheosis of the rifle as the arbiter of social progress. We are left with a clear sense of Mr. Reed's delight in these scenes, but not a suggestion as to why he should deem them delightful. No doubt the Bolsheviki slew with great energy and success; but what was the slaying for?

When less than one-sixth of a country's population undertakes with ruthless slaughter and horrible deeds to impose a program upon the unwilling remainder, persons not entranced with murder have some right to know what all this means. Assuredly their desires in this respect will not be supplied by anything in Mr. Reed's book. He himself propounds the question that is on so many million lips. "What is Bolshevism?" he asks, and the only hint of a response is that this is among the questions "that cannot be answered here." Nothing stranger has been known in human affairs. We have the adherents of a professed idea going forth with weapons to overthrow many Governments in Europe and threatening to overthrow government here, and yet none of them, apparently, able to tell what is the idea they serve or why there should be all this overthrowing. To revolt for the sake of revolting, to fight for the joy of fighting, to slay valiantly, to ride furiously, to shout vehemently, are activities glorious. This we can easily perceive from Mr. Reed's book, as from the others. But as to why we should revolt, fight, slay, ride, and shout we are left darkling.

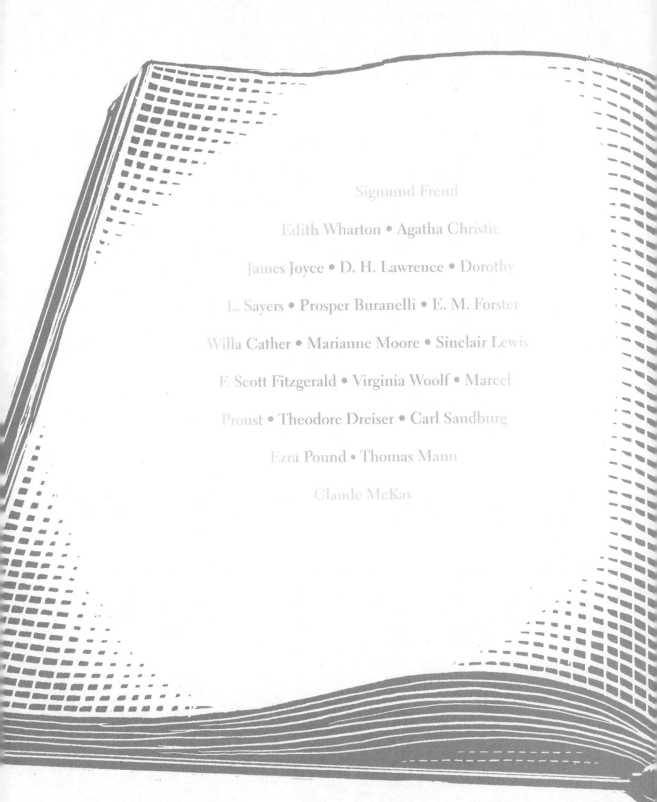

Sigmund Freud

Edith Wharton • Agatha Christie

James Joyce • D. H. Lawrence • Dorothy

L. Sayers • Prosper Buranelli • E. M. Forster

Willa Cather • Marianne Moore • Sinclair Lewis

F. Scott Fitzgerald • Virginia Woolf • Marcel

Proust • Theodore Dreiser • Carl Sandburg

Ezra Pound • Thomas Mann

Claude McKay

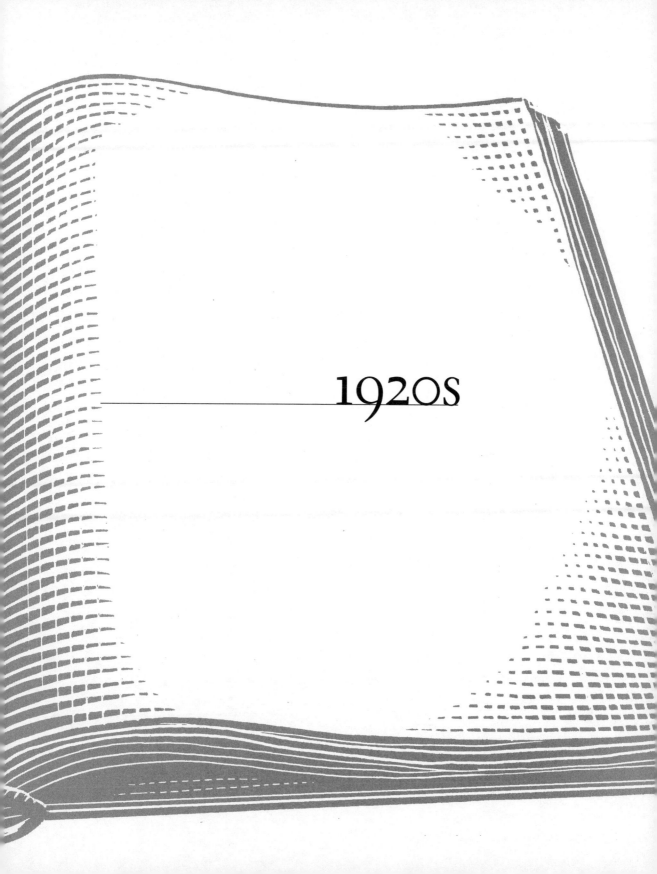

1920S

The Wizard of Dreams

A *General Introduction to Psychoanalysis* by Sigmund Freud
August 8, 1920

BY SMITH ELY JELLIFFE, M.D.

THERE IS A KINDLY MAN IN an old nursery song who, at the proper time, takes each child gently by the hand to lead him over into the marvels of an unknown land. This author, this kindly guide, is no other than Freud himself, who discovered the master key into the perplexities of human lives when he was working years ago with mental illnesses. Since then he has been using this key, turning it this way and that, penetrating with it doors at first unsuspected.

He has the assurance only of pragmatic truth. "Truth is truth when it works," and he has tested and proved. He has also the humble and genuine sympathy—for he has entered into his own analysis and that of others, as his lectures show—of one who has come face to face with the difficulties and perplexities of the hidden side of human nature and has had to clear a path through them. This means that among the facts which make up the unconscious mental life he has discovered the vital wishes that lie there unfulfilled and striving for fulfillment against an external demand largely hostile to them.

Freud begins with a universal manifestation of the psychic activity underneath the ordinary recognized conscious activity. This is that of errors, which in every life all day long ought to have reminded us of the fact that mental life does contain something, is subject to the action of mechanisms which are not explicable by the means at hand, those of ordinary rationalizing thinking.

In this way the reader finds himself in the looked-for field of the dream. This needs no apology for its existence, only for the importance and sense of it. All know the bewilderment, mingled with the satisfaction, of the prisoner, in the illustration used as a frontispiece to this volume, at the forms that flit across the surface of sleep. Not all can discern as can Freud, the now well-established wizard of dreams, the elements of wish fulfillment bringing themselves to realization through the reduplication and other mechanisms of the dream work which he has briefly applied to this illustration.

So far, naturally, the study of the dream leads directly into that field which has been the most important one in the practical application of psychoanalysis, that of the neuroses. Freud continually suggests other fields of human interest where psychoanalysis will penetrate in the future to prove itself as a method of understanding and guiding for all forms of human effort and endeavor. Freud realizes that psychoanalysis is a still undeveloped science and method and that whatever successes it has won, these are but the beginnings of that which may be done.

The Upholstered Life

The Age of Innocence by Edith Wharton
October 17, 1920

BY WILLIAM LYON PHELPS

IN THIS PRESENT YEAR of emancipation it is pleasant to record that in the front rank of American living novelists we find four women, who shall be named in alphabetical order—the only order that makes the world safe for democracy; much appreciated by opera impresarios, managers of stock companies and other great diplomats. The big four are Dorothy Canfield, Zona Gale, Anne Sedgwick, Edith Wharton.

Mrs. Wharton's admirable career is a progression from the external to the internal; she began as a decorator and is now an analyst. She has always been an expert in gardens and in furniture. Her first book was called *Decoration of Houses*, written in 1897 in collaboration with O. Codman, and in 1904 she produced a work on Italian villas and their gardens. These studies of interior decorating and landscape gardening are much in evidence in her novels; I do not remember when I have read a work of fiction that gives the reader so vivid an idea of the furnishing and illuminating of rooms in fashionable houses as one will find in *The Age of Innocence*.

Those who are interested in good dinners—and who is not?—will find much to admire in these brilliant pages. The formal and elaborate dinner parties in New York in the seventies are described here with a gusto that the steady undercurrent of irony quite fails to conceal; there were epicures in those days who sallied from their Fifth Avenue mausoleums not to talk, but to dine. They were professional diners-out, who noticed details—why does she allow her butler to cut the cucumbers with a steel knife?

It was *The House of Mirth* (1905), that gave Mrs. Wharton an international reputation; if one wishes to see how far her art has advanced since that popular book, one has merely to compare it with *The Age of Innocence*. By the side of the absolute mastery of plot, character and style displayed in her latest novel, *The House of Mirth* seems almost crude. That austere masterpiece, *Ethan Frome*,

---

Oops!

June 13, 1920

The Voyage Out

BY VIRGINIA
WOOLF

This English novel, by an English writer, gives promise in its opening chapters of much entertainment. Later, the reader is disappointed. That the author knows her London in its most interesting aspects there can be no doubt. But aside from a certain cleverness—which, being all in one key, palls on one after going through a hundred pages of it—there is little in this offering to make it stand out from the ruck of mediocre novels which make far less literary pretension.

1920

On June 27, the *Book Review* and the *Magazine* merge. The marriage lasts two years.

stands in a room all by itself; it is an illustration, however, of the fact that our novelist, who knows Paris and Continental urban scenes so well, was equally at home in a barren American village.

I think, with the exception of the novel now before us, *The Reef* is her finest full-length story. In one of the many intimate letters written to her by Henry James, and now published in the already famous two volumes, we find the following admirable remarks on *The Reef* and if one will read them immediately after finishing *The Age of Innocence*, one will see how perfectly they apply to Mrs. Wharton's style at its best:

> In the key of this, with all your reality, you have yet kept the whole thing, and, to deepen the harmony and accentuate the literary pitch, have never surpassed yourself for certain exquisite *moments*, certain images, analogies, metaphors, certain silver correspondences in your *façon de dire*, examples of which I could pluck out and numerically almost confound you with, were I not stammering in this in so handicapped a way.

The style of *The Age of Innocence* is filled with the "silver correspondences" spoken of by Henry James; and the book would be a solid satisfaction, as it is an exquisite delight, had the writer only possessed the homeliness, the rugged simplicity that is lost under the enamel of finished sophistication. The English critic, R. H. Hutton, said that Goethe was the wisest man of modern times that ever lacked the wisdom of a little child—this particular kind of wisdom is not to be found in the works of Mrs. Wharton, though we find everything but that.

Yet I am in no mood to complain. Edith Wharton is a writer who brings glory on the name America, and this is her best book. New York society and customs in the seventies are described with an accuracy that is almost uncanny; to read these pages is to live again. The absolute imprisonment in which her characters stagnate, their artificial and false standards, the desperate monotony of trivial routine, the slow petrification of generous ardours, the paralysis of emotion, the accumulation of ice around the heart, the total loss of life in upholstered existence—are depicted with a high excellence that never falters. And in the last few pages the younger generation comes in like fresh air. Mrs. Wharton is all for the new and against the old; here, at all events, her sympathies are warm.

The two young women of the story are contrasted in a manner that is of the essence of drama without being in the least artificial. The radiantly beautiful young wife might have had her way without a shadow on it, were it not for the appearance of the Countess Olenska, who is, what the other women are not, a personality. Newland Archer, between these two women, and loved by both, is not at all to be envied. The love scenes between him and Ellen are wonderful in their terrible, inarticulate passion; it is curious how much more real they are

1920

Edith Wharton's novel *The Age of Innocence* satirizes New York manners.

1920

Agatha Christie publishes her first book, *The Mysterious Affair at Styles*, and introduces the world to Hercule Poirot.

43

than the unrestrained detailed descriptions thought by so many writers to be "realism." Here is where Mrs. Wharton resembles Joseph Conrad and Henry James, for the love scenes in this book are fully worthy of those two men of genius. So little is said, so little is done, yet one feels the infinite passion in the finite hearts that burn.

I do not believe I shall ever forget three scenes between Archer and Ellen—the "outing" at Boston, the night carriage drive from the ferry in New York, and the interview in the corner of the Museum of Art, with its setting of relics. These are scenes of passion that Conrad, or Henry James, yes, that Turgenev might have written.

The appearance of such a book as *The Age of Innocence* by an American is a matter for public rejoicing. It is one of the best novels of the twentieth century and looks like a permanent addition to literature.

First Impressions

The Mysterious Affair at Styles by Agatha Christie
December 26, 1920

THOUGH THIS MAY be the first published book of Miss Agatha Christie, she betrays the cunning of an old hand. She first presents the mysterious affair of Styles as it became known to the world in July of a certain year of the war, and then proceeds to make it more and more mysterious by leading us gently to all sorts of wrong theories about the criminal. Mrs. Inglethorpe, a rich, elderly lady, is found early one morning writhing in pain from the effects, as is determined later, of poison. She dies with the name of her husband on her lips. This husband (her second) had been her secretary, and was twenty years younger than she. His intrusion had been highly resented by John and Lawrence Cavendish, sons of Mrs. Inglethorpe's first husband by a former marriage, by John's wife, half Russian by birth, by Miss Evie Howard, faithful companion and general factotum of Mrs. Inglethorpe, by Cynthia Murdoch, a young protégée of the old lady, and in general by all and every one composing the household at Styles Court in the English County of Essex. All these people were impecunious and some of them deeply in debt, so that all were deeply interested in the disposal of Mrs. Inglethorpe's estate. But the facts that there was "the most awful row" between Mr. and Mrs. Inglethorpe on the day preceding the crime, that on the same day Mr. Inglethorpe was declared by the village chemist to have bought a bottle of strychnine on the pretext of having to kill a dog, that the story was about that he had been conducting an intrigue with a cer-

1921

The first children's book column appears in the *Book Review.*

44

tain farmer's young and pretty wife, that he was absent from the house the night of the crime, that the remains of a burned will were found in the old lady's room, and that Mr. Inglethorpe, though denying all guilt, was quite unable to prove an alibi at the time that he was said to have visited the chemist's shop—all these things made the case very black for the young husband.

Mr. Inglethorpe would certainly have been arrested there and then had it not been for a certain delightful little old man, a refugee from Belgium and formerly a famous detective, who took a hand in the case. He prevented the arrest by producing an unimpeachable alibi for him, and secured that of John Cavendish. But if you think that that ends the story you are mistaken. You must wait for the last-but-one chapter in the book for the last link in the chain of evidence that enabled M. Poirot to unravel the whole complicated plot and lay the guilt where it really belonged. And you may safely make a wager with yourself that until you have heard M. Poirot's final word on the mysterious affair at Styles, you will be kept guessing at its solution and will certainly never lay down this most entertaining book.

A Fine Madness

Ulysses by James Joyce
May 28, 1922

BY DR. JOSEPH COLLINS

A FEW INTUITIVE, sensitive visionaries may understand and comprehend *Ulysses*, James Joyce's new and mammoth volume, without going through a course of training or instruction, but the average intelligent reader will glean little or nothing from it—even from careful perusal, one might properly say study, of it—save bewilderment and a sense of disgust. It should be companioned with a key and a glossary like the Berlitz books. Then the attentive and diligent reader would eventually get some comprehension of Mr. Joyce's message.

That he has a message there can be no doubt. He seeks to tell the world of the people that he has encountered in the forty years of sentient existence; to describe their conduct and speech and to analyze their motives, and to relate the effect the "world," sordid, turbulent, disorderly, with mephitic atmosphere engendered by alcohol and the dominant ecclesiasticism of his country, had upon him, an emotional Celt, an egocentric genius, whose chief diversion and keenest pleasure is self-analysis and whose lifelong important occupation has been keeping a notebook in which has been recorded incident encountered and

1922

Ulysses is published in Paris. It's banned in America until 1933 (a judge sets it free the same week Prohibition is repealed). The American edition of 1934 is its first legal printing in an English-speaking country.

speech heard with photographic accuracy and Boswellian fidelity. Moreover, he is determined to tell it in a new way. Not in straightforward, narrative fashion, with a certain sequentiality of idea, fact, occurrence, in sentence, phrase and paragraph that is comprehensible to a person of education and culture, but in parodies of classic prose and current slang, in perversions of sacred literature, in carefully metered prose with studied incoherence, in symbols so occult and mystic that only the initiated and profoundly versed can understand—in short, by means of every trick and illusion that a master artificer, or even magician, can play with the English language.

Before proceeding with a brief analysis of *Ulysses*, and comment on its construction and its content, I wish to characterize it. *Ulysses* is the most important contribution that has been made to fictional literature in the twentieth century. It will immortalize its author with the same certainty that *Gargantua and Pantagruel* immortalized Rabelais, and *The Brothers Karamazov* Dostoyevsky. It is likely that there is no one writing English today that could parallel Mr. Joyce's feat, and it is also likely that few would care to do it were they capable. That statement requires that it be said at once that Mr. Joyce has seen fit to use words and phrases that the entire world has covenanted and people in general, cultured and uncultured, civilized and savage, believer and heathen, have agreed shall not be used, and which are base, vulgar, vicious and depraved. Mr. Joyce's reply to this is: "This race and this country and this life produced me—I shall express myself as I am."

It is not unlikely that every thought that Mr. Joyce has had, every experience he has ever encountered, every person he has ever met, one might almost say everything he has ever read in sacred or profane literature, is to be encountered in the obscurities and in the franknesses of *Ulysses*. If personality is the sum total of all one's experiences, all one's thoughts and emotions, inhibitions and liberations, acquisitions and inheritances, then it may truthfully be said *Ulysses* comes nearer to being the perfect revelation of a personality than any book in existence. Rousseau's *Confessions*, Amiel's *Diary*, Bashkirtseff's vaporings and Casanova's *Memoirs* are first readers compared with it.

1922

Emily Post begins to teach America good manners with the first edition of *Etiquette in Society, in Business, in Politics and at Home*.

He is the only individual that the writer has encountered outside of a mad-house who has let flow from his pen random and purposeful thoughts just as they are produced. He does not seek to give them orderliness, sequence or interdependence. His literary output would seem to substantiate some of Freud's contentions. The majority of writers, practically all, transfer their conscious, deliberate thought to paper. Mr. Joyce transfers the product of his unconscious mind to paper without submitting it to the conscious mind, or, if he submits it, it is to receive approval and encouragement, perhaps even praise. He holds with Freud that the unconscious mind represents the real man, the man of nature, and the conscious mind the artificed man, the man of convention, of expediency, the slave of Mrs. Grundy, the sycophant of the Church, the plastic puppet of society and State. When a master technician of words and phrases sets himself the task of revealing the product of the unconscious mind of a moral monster, a pervert and an invert, an apostate to his race and his religion, the simulacrum of a man who has neither cultural background nor personal self-respect, who can neither be taught by experience nor lessoned by example, as Mr. Joyce has done in drawing the picture of Leopold Bloom, and giving a faithful reproduction of his thoughts, purposeful, vagrant and obsessive, he undoubtedly knew full well what he was undertaking, and how unacceptable the vile contents of that unconscious mind would be to ninety-nine men out of a hundred, and how incensed they would be at having the disgusting product thrown in their faces. But that has nothing to do with that with which I am here concerned, viz., has the job been done well and is it a work of art, to which there can be only an affirmative answer.

Mr. Joyce has no reverence for organized religion, for conventional morality, for literary style or form. He has no conception of the word obedience, and he bends the knee neither to God nor man. It is very interesting, and most important to have the revelations of such a personality, to have them first-hand and not dressed up. Heretofore our only avenues of information of such personalities led through the asylums for the insane, for it was there that such revelations as those of Mr. Joyce were made without reserve. Lest any one should construe this statement to be a subterfuge on my part to impugn the sanity of Mr. Joyce, let me say at once that he is one of the sanest geniuses that I have ever known.

Finally, I venture a prophecy: Not ten men or women out of a hundred can read *Ulysses* through, and of the ten who succeed in doing so, five of them will do it as a tour de force. I am probably the only person, aside from the author, that has ever read it twice from beginning to end. I have learned more psychology and psychiatry from it than I did in ten years at the Neurological Institute. There are other angles at which *Ulysses* can be viewed profitably, but they are not many.

1922

The Melcher family establishes the John Newbery Medal for children's literature. The first winner is *The Story of Mankind*, by Hendrik Willem van Loon.

Stephen Dedalus in his Parisian tranquility (if the modern Minos has been given the lethal warm bath) will pretend indifference to the publication of a laudatory study of *Ulysses* a hundred years hence, but he is as sure to get it as Dostoyevsky, and surer than Mallarmé.

Interview

D. H. Lawrence
August 27, 1922

BY HENRY JAMES FORMAN

IF MR. SUMNER, who is fond of "suppressing" D. H. Lawrence's books, could meet their author and have half an hour's conversation, he would probably never molest a Lawrence book again for the rest of his life.

For D. H. Lawrence is the mildest of men and one of the pleasantest of companions. With all that, he is perhaps the most serious artist I have ever met.

Last Winter Lawrence and the writer were neighbors hibernating on the rocks of Taormina. Lawrence occupied a small villa in the rugged hills back of the town, the Fontana Vecchia, approached like many other dwellings in the region only by a mule track. He was gravely ill during the Christmas holidays and the early part of January, with a virulent attack of influenza. Lawrence is frequently ill. He is tall and thin and delicate and his chest is not strong.

When during his convalescence, by the kindness of a common friend, I met Lawrence, I was surprised that he ever recovered. I walked up to his villa from the hotel, and the dripping foliage seemed every moment more dank and dripping as I drew nearer to his pink villa. It overhung a valley that with sunshine might have been radiant. But there was no sunshine then. Mrs. Lawrence opened the door and called out:

"Lawrence! Lawrence!" and turned promptly away to her household duties in the kitchen.

Lawrence came down in sandals and with his visitor sat down in the living room, of which the doors and window stood wide open. The mist of the valley floated in in damp, lazy drifts. I was wearing a Winter overcoat and felt comfortable enough. But Lawrence sat with his thin jacket and sandals, his lips blue with cold, and announced that he was quite over his influenza.

"It is a miracle," I told him, looking at the open doors and windows.

"Ah, I know," he said with a smile that his red beard makes sardonic, "you Americans want a lot of heat in your rooms. I couldn't stand stuffy rooms."

"Call this stuffy?" I murmured.

"No!" he laughed. "But think what it would be if I had steam heat here!"

It began to rain—a rain so wet and hopeless that it seemed almost to rain in the room. Lawrence grew visibly more cheerful as we looked out at the dismal picture.

An almost childlike, whimsical smile lighted his face.

"Sunny Sicily!" I murmured. He nodded, holding out his hands toward the miserable rain as though it were a crackling fire. That wretched weather was upsetting a generally popular notion that Sicily is always pleasant, forever romantically, idiotically sunny and bright. And to upset preconceived fixed notions of humanity with stark realism is Lawrence's delight. That weather, for the moment, was an ally of his, a prop to the tenets of his art. That is why he chuckled almost as if he were fondling that withering rain.

Ever since I had read *Sons and Lovers* I had been curious and interested in the personality of the writer who had produced it. Lawrence seldom speaks of his fictions unless he is asked direct questions about them. About *Sons and Lovers* he spoke freely and complained bitterly that he made not one penny out of the American edition.

"Why don't you write more books like that one?" I asked him one day as we were walking down the only street of Taormina, the Corso, on the way to the Post Office.

"That is what nearly everybody asks me." He smiled his peculiar half childlike, half sardonic smile. "But I don't want to write more books like that. I write every book three times," he went on. "By that I don't mean copying and revising as I go along, but literally. After I finish the first draft I put it aside and write another. Then I put the second aside and write a third. The first draft is generally somewhat like *Sons and Lovers*. And he laughed with a rising inflection that is like a little scream—a peculiarity of his.

"Very well," I told him firmly, "then in the next novel write one draft only and see how your sales will mount."

He laughed as though to say that that was the last thing that concerned him.

"I don't want to be rich," he murmured half to himself. "But I do want to be able to do absolutely as I please."

I tried, how unobtrusively soever, to discover why he injects into his novels not sex, but so much of the quality that evidently displeases Mr. Sumner and the soul of Anthony Comstock. To eliminate sex from a novel, the scheme of which requires the treatment of sex, would be as absurd as constantly using the phrase "dry grass" in place of the word hay, or forbidding the use of the word bread because some regions suffer famine. But some of his books undoubtedly seem, consciously or not, to stress the element of sex.

Well, I can only say that in his speech and conversation no priest could be

1923

Kahlil Gibran brings forth *The Prophet*; it is still Alfred A. Knopf's best-selling book.

purer or more austere. Always you get the impression of the simple, unaffected artist, with the childlike attachment to his art that one finds only in the great, out of reach of influences, either commercial or cliqueish.

I told him there were things in *Women in Love* that perhaps it might have been better to slur, particularly because the novel was, most of it, so fine, so excellent—or so it appeared to me.

"There were others who felt that way," he laughed.

"And when Hermione 'biffs' her irritating lover in the face," I told him, "even though it might have happened in real life, it is too preposterous for fiction. Don't you agree?"

He merely laughed again, but his wife spoke up bravely and declared:

"That outraged even me."

"Perhaps we are both old fogies," I told her.

Once, I remember, we took a long walk round the town and sat down upon a ledge of rock in the famous old Graeco-Roman Theatre of Taormina. The burden of our talk was the preponderance of the commercial spirit in the world today and the obstacles against which the artist today labored in those conditions.

1923

Ernest Hemingway sees his first bullfight.

"The only thing to do," he declared, "is to keep everlastingly combating it until at last some day things change."

The work of art is to him all important, for that work it is that must bring light into the world. He was looking forward to coming some day to America and living in the Arizona desert—a place of light and bracing vigorous air. I assured him that he could do nothing wiser or better for his health, physical and perhaps even mental. In the meanwhile he was going to India, to Ceylon. The life of the Buddhist monasteries there seemed to have a strange fascination for him.

We had a farewell party at his villa before we all dispersed. I have never seen a more delightful host. Mrs. Lawrence had loaded the tables with food, cakes and pastry of her own making. And Lawrence's chief concern was that we should consume all of it. The talk fluctuated vigorously between literature and food. I remember my wife asking him as he stood with a plate of cakes before her:

"Why do you leave Paul in *Sons and Lovers* so hopeless after his love affairs with Miriam and Clara—why so stripped of everything?"

"Ah, but he had his courage left," laughed Lawrence—"do have some of these cakes."

The impression of Lawrence that lingers in the memory is that of the vividly real personality, the austere artist living so frugally that many would call it poverty—devoted to the one supreme task, that of transcribing, interpreting life as he sees it.

First Impressions

Whose Body? by Dorothy L. Sayers
May 27, 1923

A NEW MEMBER of the extensive and entertaining fellowship of writers of detective stories, Miss Dorothy L. Sayers, presents as her initial and initiatory offering a very ingenious tale which she calls *Whose Body?* Its leading character is a certain genial and slightly eccentric Lord Peter Wimsey, younger brother of the Duke of Denver, who had taken up amateur detecting as a pastime. Closely associated with him was a professional from Scotland Yard, Mr. Parker, who did the, so to speak, routine work. Lord Peter himself is a likable and intelligent person, whose acquaintance we are glad to make, and to whom the ultra-cautious Parker, a veritable doubting Thomas, presents an admirable foil. Bunter, Lord Peter's very capable man, who tyrannized over him unmercifully in certain particulars, had a hobby of his own, and was useful in other ways than his avowed duties of valet and butler. The account he gives of his interview with the ingenuous Mr. Cummings is one of the most entertaining things in a book which contains a number of amusing bits.

The mystery which engaged the attention of these three very different persons—and of several others—during the course of the present narrative was a double one. In other words, there were two strange events, and in the beginning there was no apparent connection between them. The first was the discovery by a timorous and eminently respectable architect of the nude body of a murdered man, neatly disposed in his bathtub, and decorated with a pair of gold-rimmed pince-nez. The second was the strange disappearance of Sir Reuben Levy, the wealthy Jewish financier. Sir Reuben, his cook testified, had come home at midnight and gone to his room. Before morning he had vanished. But not one stitch of clothing had vanished with him; not even the spectacles, which his extreme nearsightedness made absolutely indispensable. What connection, if any, was there between these two events? And whose body was it which had been so deftly disposed in Mr. Thipps's bathtub, and which was very certainly not that of Sir Reuben Levy?

The tale is better written, and has a good deal more of characterization than one finds in the average detective story. It has been very cleverly worked out, and if the reader suspects the identity of the criminal before Lord Peter even dreams of it, this is entirely natural under the circumstances. The interest of the narrative is maintained up to the very end, and if Miss Sayers can maintain the standard she has set for herself in this tale, there seems to be no reason why the discerning, but by no means infallible, Lord Peter should not become one of the best-known and best-liked among the many amateur detectives of fiction.

First Impressions

The Cross Word Puzzle Book, edited by Prosper Buranelli, F. Gregory Hartswick, and Margaret Petherbridge
May 4, 1924

EVERY NOW AND THEN some game comes along that acts with a peculiar stimulus on the mass mind—perhaps something like catnip on cats—and sweeps across the country with a whirlwind rush that gathers in all but the strongest, or should one say the most obstinate, minds. For instance, there was the fifteen puzzle which elderly people recall as having produced in their youth a universal mild dementia which became in some cases so pronounced that its victims had to be sent to insane asylums. And along in the eighteen-nineties came the pigs-in-clover puzzle, which set everybody to tipping and manipulating the little pen with its tiny balls until it seemed as if the whole world had reached its second childhood. Now comes the cross word puzzle, which seems to be as catching as the "flu," and as certain in its conquering power.

This little book, said to be the first devoted to the subject, has fifty full-page puzzle designs, with the necessary directions on the opposite page, a prefatory chapter by each of the three editors and, all ready for use on the puzzles, a nicely sharpened pencil with an eraser tucked into a holder. The fifty puzzles have all been selected by the puzzle editors of *The New York World* from the thousands that have been submitted to that paper during recent months. The sudden growth of the fad is shown by the fact that that paper was until recently the only publication that indulged its readers in this form of amusement. Now, forty or more important newspapers in different parts of the country are featuring their cross word puzzle department.

Hopeless in Chandrapore

A Passage to India by E. M. Forster
August 17, 1924

BY HERBERT S. GORMAN

THERE ARE SOME NOVELISTS who creep into public esteem rather imperceptibly, and Mr. E. M. Forster is one of these. Already he has his rather small group of valiant disciples (at random one thinks of Mr. Leonard Woolf, Mr. Hamish Miles and Miss Rebecca West) who proclaim his merits with an insistence that would be provoking if there were not ample cause for the enthusiasm. A single reading of *A Passage to India* settles the question. Mr. E. M. Forster is indubitably one of the finest novelists living in England today, and *A Passage to India* is one of the saddest, keenest, most beautifully written ironic novels of the time. Saying so much one is forced to say much more, for Mr. Forster's quality is unique. In some respects it is like caviare, but not because one must cultivate a taste for it. It is difficult to conceive of any tastes being dissatisfied with *A Passage to India* unless it be fire-eating, gouty, retired Anglo-Indians now residing in Tunbridge Wells and kindred places.

A Passage to India is both a challenge and an indictment. It is also a revelation. But so intricately is this matter treated that the average reader is quite unaware of a smoldering subterranean passion in the depths of this carefully conceived study of two humanities—indeed, two worlds—in hopeless clash. A panorama of objective incidents and gestures is unfolded as one might unfold a carefully woven Indian carpet, and somehow the reader experiences an intense concern and despair before a situation that is both inevitable and impossible. Certain obvious words suggest themselves as descriptive of this book and among them are "subtle" and "acute." But they are not exact enough to describe that peculiar cool, clarified exposition that seems to miss nothing and that is so impregnated with unexplainable implications. Almost imperceptibly Mr. Forster develops a character until the reader has acquired the most meticulous comprehension of the deepest channels of being.

Such a proceeding was of the utmost difficulty in *A Passage to India*, for many of the characters who fit into the delicate structure of that book are Indians. It is easily understandable that mystery surrounds the East Indian, that his life is a conception peculiar to himself. Mr. Forster knows this and he conveys as much in his book. He also knows the Indian mind, and the clear shafts of his sentences pierce into it with a disturbing frequency until the reader is apt to wonder whether or not the Indian is as complicated a being as he seems to be. Yet in a last analysis he is. India remains India and no number of British civilians

1924

Billy Budd, completed just before Herman Melville's death in 1891, is published by one of his granddaughters.

or army corps can hope to divert that huge, semi-supine, dreaming giant from immemorial methods of existence. Broken and factious, throbbing with antagonistic religious sects and castes, it yet remains sullenly itself in spite of the long decades of English rule. Mr. Forster makes it quite clear that it is no dream of the Peacock Throne at Delhi that holds India apart, but the congenital differences of birth as well. Here again is Kipling's old dictum that "East is East and West is West." Yet if the idea be given that *A Passage to India* is the usual type of Indian novel in which patriotic impulses heroically manifest themselves, a genuine wrong is done the author. Mr. Forster is quite aware that right and wrong may not be so easily separated; that, in fact, both sides may be right and wrong at the same time. His objective is to show modern life in India, in Chandrapore, and to do this he draws with a superb finality a group of Indians and British civil officers and women. The utmost care is shown in interlocking the various urges in this book. The result is a bewilderingly vivid presentation of life.

A mere résumé of the novel gives no adequate idea of it, for the prime importance of Mr. Forster's work lies not so much in situation as in the development of a dozen apparently trivial incidents leading up to it. Odd words, single sentences, flashes of characterization, the general atmosphere which is so precisely built up—these are the touches that set Mr. Forster apart as a novelist. It conveys no more than his modus operandi to state that the book circles about a young Indian, Dr. Aziz, who is unjustly accused of attempted assault by a hysterical English girl and who therefore serves as a hinge from which both humanities—British and Indian—break. Certain things become apparent as the book progresses and not the least of them is the stupidity of the British. There is no other word for it. This system of the conqueror which prevents an Indian from being a member of a white man's club, which assumes a cocksure knowledge of the Indian mind when that knowledge is based on a dull misconception, which eternally suspects and belittles—this is the aspect of life in India which Mr. Forster brings out most clearly. A single episode may be noted as a fair exemplification of this. Dr. Aziz, calling on Fielding, the Englishman who stands by the Indians and commits the last sin by not blindfolding his judgment and sticking with the Britishers, gives the white man his collar button in a burst of generosity when that individual has broken his own. Later we find the City Magistrate, Heaslop, remarking: "Aziz was exquisitely dressed, from tie pin to spats, but he had forgotten his back collar stud, and there you have the Indian all over: inattention to detail; the fundamental slackness that reveals the race." Here, in a nutshell, Mr. Forster intimates, is the attitude of the Anglo-Indian toward the native; the slackness is instantly assumed; the Britisher sees the surface and no more.

The Indian portraits are superb. Dr. Aziz, of course, is more fully drawn than the others, for he serves as that aspect of India which Mr. Forster is anxious to bring to the fore—the educated Indian who understands British civilization, but who can never be really identified with it.

Indeed, one thing that *A Passage to India* seems to assert is the hopelessness of any agreement between India and her conquerors. Two peoples who will never mix are here, and when this is so there must always be two groups. The house will always be divided. The few points in this book which have been noted are but a tithe of the riches that may be found there. The crystal-clear portraiture, the delicate conveying of nuances of thought and life, and the astonishing command of his medium show that Mr. Forster is now at the height of his powers. It is not alone because the canvas is larger and the implications greater than in *Howards End* and *A Room with a View* that this is so. The real reason is implicit in the author's unmistakable growth, the deepening of his powers and the assurance of his technique. When Mr. Leonard Woolf states, "Mr. Forster seems now to have reached the point at which there is nothing too simple or too subtle for his pen," he is expressing an exact truth. Certainly *A Passage to India* should greatly widen that rather small audience that has relished his novels in the past. And that rather small audience should congratulate itself on its acumen.

Interview

Willa Cather
December 21, 1924

BY ROSE C. FELD

TEA WITH WILLA SIBERT CATHER is a rank failure. The fault is entirely hers. You get so highly interested in what she has to say and how she says it that you ask for cream when you prefer lemon and let the butter on your hot toast grow cold and smeary. It is vastly more important to you to watch her eyes and lips which betray her when she seems to be giving voice to a serious concept, but is really poking fun at the world—or at your own foolish question. For Willa Sibert Cather has rare good sense, homespun sense, if you will—and that is rare enough—which she drives home with a well-wrought mallet of humor.

It started with the question of books and the overwhelming quantities which the American public of today is buying. What exactly was the explanation of that? Did it mean that we were becoming a more cultured people, a more artistic people? Miss Cather was suffering from neuritis that day. It was difficult to understand, therefore, whether the twinge that crossed her face was caused by the pain we gave her or that of her temporary illness.

"Don't confuse reading with culture or art," she said, when her face cleared. There was laughter in her blue eyes. "Not in this country, at any rate. So many books are sold today because of the economic condition of this country, not the cultural. We have a great prosperous middle class, in cities, in suburbs, in small towns, on farms, to whom the expenditure of $2 for a book imposes no suffering. What's more, they have to read it. They want a book which will fill up commuting boredom every morning and evening, they want a book to read mornings after breakfast when the maid takes care of the apartment housework; they want a book to keep in the automobile while they're waiting for tardy friends or relatives; they want fillers-in, in a word, something to take off the edge of boredom and empty leisure. Publishers, who are, after all, business men, recognize the demand and pour forth their supply. It's good sense, it's good psychology. It's the same thing that is responsible for the success of the cinema. It is, as a matter of fact, the cinema public for whom this reading material is published. But it has no more to do with culture than with anarchy or philosophy. You might with equal reason ask whether we are becoming a more cultured people because so many more of us are buying chiffoniers and bureaus and mirrors and toilet sets. Forty or fifty years ago these things were not to be found in the average home. Forty or fifty years ago we couldn't afford them and today we can. As a result, every home has an increased modicum of comfort and luxury. But, carrying the thought a step further, every home has not increased in beauty.

"Not so long ago I was speaking to William Dean Howells about this subject of book reading and book publication. He said something which was of interest to me and which may be of interest to you. Forty years ago, he maintained, we were in the midst of a great literary period. Then, only good books were published, only cultivated people read. The others didn't read at all, or if they did it was the newspapers, the almanac, and the Bible on Sundays. This public doesn't exist today any more than the cinema public existed then. Fine books were written for fine people. Fine books are still written for fine people. Sometimes the others read them, too, and if they can stand it, it doesn't hurt them."

Her lips twitched in a smile she tried to suppress. She shook her head at a wayward thought.

"That discrimination is not a snobbish one," she went on. "Don't think that. By the fine reader I don't necessarily mean the man or woman with a cultivated background, an academic, or a wealthy background. I mean the person with quickness and richness of mentality, fineness of spirituality. You found it often in a carpenter or a blacksmith who went to his few books for recreation and inspiration. The son of a long line of college Presidents may be nothing but a dolt and idiot in spite of the fact that he knows how to enter a room properly or to take off a lady's wraps. It's the shape of the head that's of importance, it's the something that's in it that can bring an ardor and an honesty to a masterpiece and make it over until it becomes a personal possession.

"Because of this vast amount of writing and reading, there are many among us who make the mistake of thinking we are an artistic people. Talking about it won't make us that. We can build excellent bridges, we can put up beautiful office buildings, factories, in time, it may be, we shall be known for the architecture which our peculiar industrial progress has fostered here, but literary art, painting, sculpture, no. We haven't yet acquired the good sense of discrimination possessed by the French, for instance. They have a great purity of tradition; they all but murder originality, and yet they worship it. The taste of the nation is represented by the Academy; it is a corrective rod which the young artist ever dreads. He revolts against it but he cannot free himself from it. He cannot pull the wool over the eyes of the Academy by saying his is a new movement, an original movement, a breaking away from the old. His work is judged on its merits and if it isn't good, he gets spanked. Here in America, on the other hand, every little glimmer of color calls itself art, every youth that misuses a brush calls himself an artist and an adoring group of admirers flatter and gush over him. It's rather pathetic.

1925

Lorelei Lee makes her debut in *Gentlemen Prefer Blondes*, by Anita Loos.

"Read the life of Manet and Monet, both great artists, great masters. The French people had to be sure of their genius before it would acclaim them. Death almost took them before acknowledgment of their power was given them. It is good sense, deliberation and an eagerness for the beautiful that keeps up the fine front of French art. That is true of her literature as well as of her painting.

"Restlessness such as ours, success such as ours, striving such as ours, do not make for beauty. Other things must come first, good cookery, cottages that are homes, not playthings; gardens, repose. These are first-rate things and out of first-rate stuff is art made. It is possible that machinery has finished us as far as this is concerned. Nobody stays at home any more, nobody makes anything beautiful any more. Quick transportation is the death of art. We can't keep still because it is so easy to move about.

"Yet it isn't always a question of one country being artistic and another not. The world goes through periods or waves of art. Between these periods come great resting places. We may be resting right now. Older countries have their wealth of former years to fall back upon. We haven't. But, like older countries, we have a few individuals who have caught the flame of former years and are carrying the torch into the next period. Whistler was one of these, Whitman was another."

Miss Cather poured some tea into a cup and diluted it with the cream we asked for but didn't want. We let it stand on the arm of the chair and proceeded with a question that her words had awakened.

"If we have no tradition of years behind us, the people who come to live here have. Are they contributing anything to the artistic expression of the country?"

Again that twinge crossed her face. This time it was plain that the question had started it.

"Contribute? What shall they contribute? They are not peddlers with something to sell; they are not gypsies. They have come here to live in the sense that they lived in the Old World, and if they were let alone their lives might turn into the beautiful ways of their homeland. But they are not let alone. Social workers, missionaries—call them what you will—go after them, hound them, pursue them and devote their days and nights toward the great task of turning them into stupid replicas of smug American citizens. This passion for Americanizing everything and everybody is a deadly disease with us. We do it the way we build houses. Speed, uniformity, dispatch, nothing else matters."

We spoke about *My Ántonia*, Miss Cather's story about the immigrant family of Czechs.

"Is *My Ántonia* a good book because it is the story of the soil?" we asked. She shook her head.

"No, no, decidedly no. There is no formula, there is no reason. It was a story of people I knew. I expressed a mood, the core of which was like a folk-song, a thing Grieg could have written. That it was powerfully tied to the soil had nothing to do with it. Ántonia was tied to the soil. But I might have written the tale of a Czech baker in Chicago and it would have been the same. It was nice to have her in the country, it was more simple to handle, but Chicago could have told the same story. It would have been smearier, joltier, noisier, less sugar and more sand, but still a story that had as its purpose the desire to express the quality of these people. No, the country has nothing to do with it, the city has nothing to do with it, nothing contributes consciously. The thing worth while is always unplanned. Any art that is a result of preconcerted plans is a dead baby."

An Emotion of the Mind

Observations by Marianne Moore
February 1, 1925

BY HERBERT S. GORMAN

WHEN *THE DIAL* made its annual award of $2,000 to Miss Marianne Moore some weeks ago it gave inordinate pleasure to an audience of readers which had long since overgrown the limitations of a coterie. Almost simultaneously with *The Dial* award appeared *Observations*, Miss Moore's first book to be issued in the regular trade way and between cloth covers. It is interesting to note that Miss Moore is the first writer to be so honored who has such a small bulk of work behind her. Sherwood Anderson was the author of five or six volumes when he received the award. T. S. Eliot's output was more meagre, but besides his poetry he had to his credit *The Sacred Wood*, a volume of distinctly stimulating critical excursions. Miss Moore, therefore, is a lesser known personage in point of general circulation, and because this is so it is to be hoped that the award will quite definitely aid her in widening her audience. Certainly no one who possesses a quick interest in contemporary American poetry can afford to remain in ignorance of her sharp, intellectually compact, aristocratic work.

It is difficult to place Miss Moore. *Observations* inevitably becomes a starting point. From what ashes her Phoenix-like talent rises, with its sharp and glittering beak and, withal, gentle eye, becomes a matter of dubious speculation. Of one thing we may rest assured from the start—there is no pose, no dependence on unusual subterfuges, no willful attempts to astonish, here. *Observations* is the sort of a book it is because Miss Moore's mind is the sort of a mind it is. Her work—a sort of condensed intellectuality that sways between a matter-of-factness that is really about as matter-of-fact as a pearl and a symbolism that peers over these observations almost constantly—is compact with the lucidities of unusual mental attacks. What obscurity there may seem to be does not centre itself in her phraseology, broken lines or curious rhythmical effects. It is rather in her peculiar and somehow always pertinent approach toward the subject that is engrossing her for the moment. She observes visible phenomena with a rare and detached precision, and the acute speculations that result therefrom somehow seem to be just the right thing after one has pondered them. After all, the contemporary urge in art is split into two diverse directions. One of them is an attempted return to primitive values, high simplicities and starkness. The other proceeds along more formalized ways and is emphasized by those ritualistic adornments that become the elaborate adumbrations of difficult connotations. Miss Moore's art, possibly,

_1925_

Attilio Mussino's classic illustrations for _The Adventures of Pinocchio_ make Collodi's puppet fable a success in the United States.

emerges on this second way, although her complexities are no more than the cunning and subtle approximations of complicated and intellectual observation in itself. She is the direct opposite of sentimentality, blatancy, bathos, mere prettiness, fancy verbal adornment and melody for melody's sake. Because of this it is quite possible that her audience will continue to be a small gathering. Her art is not a democratic art in any sense of the word. But this is assuredly no belittlement of her essential value to contemporary American poetry, for she brings to it that fastidiousness and intellectualization that it sadly needs.

Her emotion is an emotion of the mind, an emotion that raised itself at moments in the work of Emily Dickinson, that is more ruddily circumscribed by Mrs. Elinor Wylie at times, that is emphatically lacking in the work of Miss Millay. In some of Miss Moore's shorter pieces she displays an epigrammatic savageness that is plainly the reflex of emotion. Even here, however, urbanity, a composure of the senses, cools what might in another poet have been an outcry. Miss Moore never escapes the intellectual observance; her mind instinctively deals with the subject. Her quick penetration and instant recognition of nuances is revealed in the last two lines of the short piece called "To Be Liked by You Would Be a Calamity."

> "Attack is more piquant than concord," but when
> You tell me frankly that you would like to feel
> My flesh beneath your feet,
>   I'm all abroad; I can but put
>   my weapon up, and
>   Bow you out.
> Gesticulation—it is half the language.
>   Let unsheathed gesticulation be the steel
>   Your courtesy must meet,
>   Since in your hearing words
>   are mute, which to my senses
>   Are a shout.

The question of color comes up. Nothing could do Miss Moore more wrong than the tacit espousal of the belittling assertion that her work is all compact of a dry cerebrality. It is true that her palette is primarily her own; not an untidy diffusion of primary hues, but a more selective equipment of subtler pigments. Yet reading through the various efforts in _Observations_ one will be halted constantly by pertinent pictures flung out with unquestioned vividness. They are not "set" for display, but are essential links in the progressing chain of thought or observation. One cannot get away from this word "observation," for it is peculiarly applicable to Miss Moore's work and she showed her usual rare judgment in so christening her book. These observations imply pictures as well as intellectual comment, and no one can read "A Talisman," "Black Earth," "Those Various Scalpels," "An Octopus," and "Sea Unicorns and Land Unicorns" without having pictures in the purest colors impinged on his mentality and that imaginary eye before which poetry passes like some sort of a burning pageant.

Here are pictures set forth with an undeniable clarity. Here also are those peculiar signatures upon a poem which show it to be Marianne Moore's craftsmanship, namely, the forced rhymes which are sometimes induced by splitting up a word. It is here, perhaps, that the professional cavilers will have their bumptious fun. This question of technique is a vexatious one, and the fairest approach to it seems to rest in the assertion that any technique is vindicated that becomes successful in best exploiting the personality and expression of the person who employs it. Miss Moore's technique is a dogmatic one, a conscious bit of mathematics, but it seems to suit her, and after one has read her poems a few times and gotten memories of Alfred, Lord Tennyson, out of one's mind the reader will discover a quaint pleasure in this new form. Rhythms will begin to hit his ear so dulled with the eternally even tomtoms of verse and he will perceive a reason for Miss Moore's particular form.

No particular attempt has been made here to go into the deeper significances of Miss Moore's thought. It is enough to assert that she exhibits a keen, restless yet urbane, scalpel-like intelligence that is quite undismayed in the face of difficulty. Where other poets would turn away or dismiss the mood in a gentle lyric, Miss Moore adjusts her perspicacity, investigates with a cool ardor, observes, comments and dissects. It is truth that she seeks essentially. In "In the Days of Prismatic Color" she ends the poem by exclaiming:

> Truth is no Apollo
> Belvedere, no formal thing. The
> wave may go over it if it likes.
> Know that it will be there when it says:
> "I shall be there when the wave
> has gone by."

It is that truth that will be there after all sorts of monstrous waves have gone by that Miss Moore is desirous to observe. She undoubtedly possesses an instinctive detestation of prettifications, adornments, veils and false gestures, and with the inspired keenness of the logician who knows that logic is not an end in itself she applies herself to the observation of phenomena, physical and spiritual, and draws her own conclusions.

House Call

Arrowsmith by Sinclair Lewis
March 8, 1925

BY HENRY LONGAN STUART

W HEN AN AUTHOR with the overwhelming popularity and intelligent following of Sinclair Lewis breaks a three years' silence, we approach the result with lively expectancy tinctured ever so little with apprehension. No one has ever made of the novel so potent an instrument for social satire or administered, through its medium, so many rough jolts to national complacency. In respect of sheer ground won his position is unprecedented. His first serious work (it is impossible to regard the early novels as anything save 'prentice-pieces—*brouillons*, in French phrase) showed the surprising direction his attack had taken and was to take. The next proved that it had simple resources of conviction at its back and was likely to be pressed far. Incidentally it furnished the language with a new word and hard pressed intellectuals with a weapon of great range and efficacy. To say "Babbitt"—"Babbittry" today is to utter a phrase that has all the force of an incantation.

A new book by Mr. Lewis now invites consideration, and even before opening its covers and plunging into its ample expanse, the general lines of the judgment it will invite define themselves. Will *Arrowsmith*, we ask, prove to be a logical sequence to *Main Street* and *Babbitt*, a true third in a trilogy of novels for which the word "great" is justified?

One closes the novel with a feeling that, if eternal verities be the ultimate objective, no great progress has been made. Mr. Lewis has attacked spiritedly, but he has not advanced. At the most he has turned roughly on a salient that enfiladed his theses and has straightened out his front. It was "high ground" from which a great deal of very telling criticism has been directed against his conclusions—criticism which would hardly have taken the form it did had he not chosen a doctor as contrast and protagonist in the novel that created his vogue and reputation. Rough, hearty Dr. Kennicot, speeding over dirt roads with his case of instruments under the back seat, had time and again been propounded as the best answer to the disgruntled esthetes of Gopher Prairie and Zenith. *Arrowsmith* in a sense, is a rejoinder to those who used him overconfidently. Mr. Lewis, reared, like Flaubert, in the atmosphere of antisepsis, son and grandson of physicians, has written a novel that is all about doctors, and that is an unsparing onslaught upon the healing art, as practiced in America.

Those to whom there is a *quid divinum* in the Hippocratic oath, and who demand vocational virtues from the Faculty, believing that the demand creates the supply, are hereby advised that severe trials are in store for their faith. Using for his theme the losing fight made by two men with whom scientific truth is religion, an unworldly old German bacteriologist and his young American disciple, Mr. Lewis draws a picture for us that is disquieting in its disillusionment. Here and there, in the long gallery through which we are sped at the breakneck pace of failure, are portraits of good doctors. But they are good men rather in spite of than because of their profession. For the rest, mean competition, with slander at times as its weapon, rule-of-thumb methods and impatience with the research that outdates them; eagerness to exploit real scientific discoveries commercially before they can be verified and safeguarded, social climbing and the inordinate chase for the dollar, quackery enthroned and genius seeking bread, these make the shadows in Mr. Lewis's acid-bitten picture. And, incidentally, out of this maelstrom of spite, injustice and blatancy, like a violet lifting its head shyly in a heap of shattered test tubes and retorts, is born for us one of the sweetest characters in all fiction—Leora the incomparable. If Mr. Lewis has done nothing else, he has come near giving us the great story of married love for which the world has been waiting. It was at the Zenith General Hospital, in Babbitt's home city, that Martin Arrowsmith first ran across Leora Tozer.

Martin came out of the common people. A shabby, rangy lad with a limited vocabulary, but with a thirst for knowledge quite Saharan. At 14, "by sheer brass and obstinacy," he was unpaid assistant to drunken old Doc Vickerson, who certified the population of Elk Mills into and out of life. At 18 he was one of 12,000 students at the State University of Winnemac. At Winnemac Mr. Lewis's long academy of doctors, in practice and to be, makes its inauspicious start. There is Dr. Robertshaw who "chirped about fussy little . . . maiden aunt experiments." Dr. Oliver Stout, who can "repeat more facts about the left little toe than you would have thought any one would care to learn"; Dr. Lloyd Davidson who "would have been a very successful shopkeeper. From him you could learn . . . the proper drugs to give a patient, particularly when you cannot discover what is the matter with him." There is Dr. Roscoe Geake, who "was a peddler. He would have done well with oil stock. As an otolaryngologist he believed that tonsils had been placed in the human organism for the purpose of providing specialists with closed motors." And Martin's fellow-students are not even made interesting by the possibilities of youth and enthusiasm. "No matter what they all thought, they all ground at learning the lists of names which enable a man to crawl through examinations and become an Educated Person with a market value of $5 an hour."

From now on Leora does more than dominate the story. She makes it. When she dies, tragically, and many will think needlessly, it is over. The brief remainder is a rather dreary anticlimax, while the men of research whose deterioration under the stress of social ambition and money has been shown to us turn to caricatures of themselves. She is a loving and fearless critic to her man.

"You're not a booster," she tells him, "you're a lie-hunter. . . . You belong in a laboratory, fishing things out, not advertising them. . . . Are you going on for the rest of your life, stumbling into respectability and having to be dug out again?"

If Leora lives and breathes throughout this splendid novel, Max Gottlieb, the old German chemist, haunts it like an avenging spectre, his voice uplifted from time to time with the cry of a prophet in Nineveh. He is the incarnation of the scientific conscience, to whose fanatical devotion the facile acceptors of nostrums, the commercial exploiters of laboratory formulae half worked out, are witch-doctors and spell-casters.

Intellectually, as has been said, *Arrowsmith* leaves Mr. Lewis about where he was. And that means it leaves him in a unique and unassailable position, with all his possibilities intact. Religious convictions, which are still the basis of so much human action, are not touched upon, or touched upon only in the person of one clownish hot-gospeller. It is a pagan novel for a pagan world.

Artistically, *Arrowsmith* is an authentic step forward. The novel is full of passages of a quite noble felicity and the old skill in presenting character through dialogue never fails. Babbitt is generic or he is nothing.

A Farewell to Flappers

The Great Gatsby by F. Scott Fitzgerald
April 19, 1925

BY EDWIN CLARK

O F THE MANY new writers that sprang into notice with the advent of the post-war period, Scott Fitzgerald has remained the steadiest performer and the most entertaining. Short stories, novels and a play have followed with consistent regularity since he became the philosopher of the flapper with *This Side of Paradise*. With shrewd observation and humor he reflected the Jazz Age. Now he has said farewell to his flappers—perhaps because they have grown up—and is writing of the other sisters that have married. But marriage has not changed their world, only the locale of their parties. To use a phrase of Burton Rascoe's—his hurt romantics are still seeking that other side of paradise. And it might almost be said that *The Great Gatsby* is the last stage of illusion in this absurd chase. For middle age is certainly creeping up on Mr. Fitzgerald's flappers.

In all great arid spots nature provides an oasis. So when the Atlantic seaboard was hermetically sealed by law, nature provided an outlet, or inlet rather, in Long Island. A place of innate natural charm, it became lush and luxurious under the stress of this excessive attention, a seat of festive activities. It expresses one phase of the great grotesque spectacle of our American scene. It is humor, irony, ribaldry, pathos and loveliness. Out of this grotesque fusion of incongruities has slowly become conscious a new humor—a strictly American product. It is not sensibility, as witness the writings of Don Marquis, Robert Benchley and Ring Lardner. It is the spirit of "Processional" and Donald Douglas's "The Grand Inquisitor"; a conflict of spirituality caught fast in the web of our commercial life. Both boisterous and tragic, it animates this new novel by Mr. Fitzgerald with whimsical magic and simple pathos that is realized with economy and restraint.

The story of Jay Gatsby of West Egg is told by Nick Carraway, who is one of the legion from the Middle West who have moved on to New York to win from its restless indifference—well, the aspiration that arises in the Middle West—and finds in Long Island a fascinating but dangerous playground. In the method of telling, *The Great Gatsby* is reminiscent of Henry James's *The Turn of the Screw*. You will recall that the evil of that mysterious tale which so endangered the two children was never exactly stated beyond a suggested generalization. Gatsby's fortune, business, even his connection with underworld figures, remain vague generalizations. He is wealthy, powerful, a man who knows how to get things done. He has no friends, only business associates, and the throngs who come to his Saturday night parties. Of his uncompromising love—his love for Daisy Buchanan—his effort to recapture the past romance—we are explicitly informed. This patient romantic hopefulness against existing conditions, symbolizes Gatsby. And like *The Turn of the Screw*, *The Great Gatsby* is more a long short story than a novel.

Nick Carraway had known Tom Buchanan at New Haven. Daisy, his wife, was a distant cousin. When he came East Nick was asked to call at their place at East Egg. The post-war reactions were at their height—every one was restless—every one was looking for a substitute for the excitement of the war years.

Buchanan had acquired another woman. Daisy was bored, broken in spirit and neglected. Gatsby, his parties and his mysterious wealth were the gossip of the hour. At the Buchanans' Nick met Jordan Baker; through them both Daisy again meets Gatsby, to whom she had been engaged before she married Buchanan. The inevitable consequence that follows, in which violence takes its toll, is almost incidental, for in the overtones—and this is a book of potent overtones—the decay of souls is more tragic. With sensitive insight and keen psychological observation, Fitzgerald discloses in these people a meanness of spirit, carelessness and absence of loyalties. He cannot hate them, for they are dumb in their insensate selfishness, and only to be pitied. The philosopher of the flapper has escaped the mordant, but he has turned grave. A curious book, a mystical, glamorous story of today. It takes a deeper cut at life than hitherto has been essayed by Mr. Fitzgerald. He writes well—he always has—for he writes naturally, and his sense of form is becoming perfected.

The Perfect Hostess

Mrs. Dalloway by Virginia Woolf
May 10, 1925

BY JOHN W. CRAWFORD

ONE DAY IN THE LIFE of Clarissa Dalloway, a June day in London, punctuated accurately, impersonally, unfeelingly, by the chimes of Big Ben and a fashionable party to end it, is the complete story of Mrs. Woolf's new novel, yet she contrives to enmesh all the inflections of Mrs. Dalloway's personality, and many of the implications of modern civilization, in the account of those twenty-four hours. Mrs. Dalloway in her own home is "the perfect hostess," even to her servants, to her daughter, her husband and her rejected suitor of long ago, who cannot free his mind of her. It is almost a perfect being that Mrs. Dalloway enjoys, but there is a resentfulness in her, some paucity of spiritual graces, or rather some positive hideousness.

Among Mrs. Woolf's contemporaries, there are not a few who have brought to the traditional forms of fiction, and the stated modes of writing, idioms which cannot but enlarge the resources of speech and the uses of narrative. Virginia Woolf is almost alone, however, in the intricate yet clear art of her composition. Clarissa's day, the impressions she gives and receives, the memories and recognitions which stir in her, the events which are initiated remotely and engineered almost to touching distance of the impervious Clarissa, capture in a definitive matrix the drift of thought and feeling in a period, the point of view of a class, and seem almost to indicate the strength and weakness of an entire civilization.

It is not only that Clarissa is giving, in fact does give, one of those parties at which the successful, the titled and the important pay a tacit homage to the political prestige of her husband, a member of Parliament, and an overt tribute to the fascinations of Clarissa herself. It is not alone that Clarissa's snobberies and exclusions, her hatred of ugliness and excess, her dainty wrapping of herself in cotton wool and her "tender superfluous probing into all that pollutes" are unerringly depicted. The whole progress of the circumstances of Clarissa's day, from the passing of a "somebody" in a closed motor car to the ignoring of a nobody at her party, make for a vivid interaction.

Clarissa might almost be one of those figures of high society which Mrs. Humphry Ward delighted in. She is as callous and vain as any of those earlier portraits. Clarissa is, however, conceived so brilliantly, dimensioned so thoroughly and documented so absolutely that her type, in the words of Constantin Stanislavsky, might be said to have been done "inviolably and for all time."

That Reminds Me. . . .

The Guermantes Way by Marcel Proust
July 5, 1925

BY ROSE LEE

A FRENCH CRITIC, Jacques Boulanger, has described Marcel Proust as a man shut up in his ego as in a railway carriage, indefatigably looking out of his window at the landscapes passing by. This description of *Remembrance of Things Past* as a series of psychological travel-pictures should be qualified by the fact that the train of M. Proust's ego moves backward, in pursuit of vanished scenes and sensations. It should also be added that M. Proust directs his own route and, however much he may seem to be deflected into the byways of associative memory, his side trips are never absolutely involuntary. On the contrary, he knew where he was going, and throughout this long, reminiscent journey his hand controlled the throttle.

Previous to the appearance of *Swann's Way* in 1913, he was known vaguely as a litterateur—the author of some slight sketches, some literary parodies in the styles of famous masters, and for fifteen years the translator of John Ruskin's writings. His unique talents had been recognized by the wise Anatole France, who, writing the preface to Proust's first book *(Pleasures and Days)*, hailed the 24-year-old author as an "ingenuous Petronius" and a "depraved Bernardin de Saint-Pierre." To most of the world, however, Marcel Proust appeared chiefly as a frail and fashionable dilettante—so sensitive that, lying in bed on the fifth floor of his house, he could feel a draught created by the opening of a door on the ground floor.

He was a full-fledged adult, stocked with the memories of many years, before he perceived what he calls "that invisible vocation, of which these volumes are the history." With the zeal almost of a visionary he set out upon his tremendous pilgrimage, to retrace his life in literature. Before his death in 1922—at the age of 51—he had, with incredible pains, completed fifteen volumes of *Remembrance of Things Past*. This novel, based for the most part on personal observation and experience, is the longest ever written within the memory of man; even so, it is incomplete, the later volumes being unrevised and faulty.

Through the deliberate recurrence of certain themes, persons, places, names and sensations, the successive volumes of Proust are subtly intertwined. The title of *The Guermantes Way*, for instance, refers back to the very first book, to Proust's childhood at Combray, when with his parents he walked on sunny afternoons along the hawthorn-hung paths of the Méséglise way or followed the Guermantes way beside the banks of the Vivonne. The loveliness of those walks filled his mind with images and indelible fantasies, which conditioned many of the tastes and reactions of his later life.

These perpetual returns to his own past impressions and childhood influences are certainly employed, to some extent, for literary effects; but they are actuated by motives of human sincerity as well. Among other things, they emphasize the particular bias of the author, they define the limits of that instrument of literary reproduction known as Marcel Proust. This is confirmed by the fact that Proust, in describing his own tendencies, is scientific, detached and singularly modest.

At the start, Proust abandons the devices of static description and characterization for a more tentative method. Making practical application of the psychological truism that all experience comes to us filtered through the lens of self, he seeks to tell his story solely through the medium of his own shifting perceptions. Persons and scenes unfold as in life, continually modified by the discovery of new facts or traits of behavior hitherto unseen. Sometimes the key to an important character is withheld and for hundreds of pages he will wander in an atmosphere of mystery and suspense, to be finally illumined in a perverse blaze of light, like M. de Charlus in the untranslated fragment of "Sodom and Gomorrah I." Often an apparently trivial discovery will give a novel turn to an almost forgotten situation as, for example, the discovery that Odette de Crecy was the mysterious Lady in Pink whom the little boy Marcel saw at his uncle's house five volumes earlier.

In spite of his independent manner Proust has managed to inspire his novel with the prudent technical virtues of suspense and unity. These signs of formal interest are what make *Remembrance of Things Past* a novel, rather than mere rambling reminiscence; but even in its technical aspects it seeks to follow the lines of life. It is held together by a method analogous to that which unifies actual human experience, repetition of events, physical and mental. That apparently accidental association of events in the external world which we call coincidence is to Proust an invaluable device. Even more he exploits the incorrigible tendency of the mind to associate present experience with suggested fragments of the past.

A name, a profile, a color will arouse a whole flock of allied mental pictures. A theme of music, heard in a strange house, recalls to Swann other scenes of its performance and all his happy, amorous hours with Odette. A bit of cake soaked in tea restores for Proust his Aunt Léonie and a train of childhood days at Combray. This trick of the mind, known to psychologists as mnemonic combination, permits a great many liberties when it is incorporated into a literary method. It annihilates space and time, allows the scene to shift at an instant's notice from Paris to Combray or Balbec in Brittany. It justifies M. Proust in dilating upon the most minute occurrences, so long as he maintains the air of spontaneous recollection. It injects dignity into otherwise trivial perceptions. It is a constant means of affirming Proust's belief in the essentially subjective nature of human experience.

When *The Guermantes Way* appeared in France, Ezra Pound said that the perfect criticism of it should be written in one paragraph, seven pages long and punctuated only by semicolons. That was hyperbole—Proust's sentences seldom run over a page and a half apiece—but it had the germs of accuracy. Those spiral sentences of Proust's, fastidious and tortured, have their physical counterpart in an incident of a revolving door in which Proust once found himself imprisoned. Just so (though on occasion he is capable of aphoristic brevity) he will involve himself in a sentence so full of similes and modifying clauses that one begins to wonder whether he can ever extricate himself. Certainly he was straining for sincerity rather than for effect. His elaborate style—a balance of broad vision and minute observation—reflects the man, delicate, abstruse, as fearful of overstating a mood as of allowing a shade of thought to escape him. To read him thoroughly constitutes a mental discipline, more humane, surely, but equal in rigor to Euclid. That is why, in spite of the piquant nature of much of his material, Proust will never be a widely popular writer.

Too Big to Write Smaller

An American Tragedy by Theodore Dreiser
January 10, 1926

BY ROBERT L. DUFFUS

IF ANY LESS WELL established writer than Mr. Dreiser had brought the manuscript of these two volumes into a publisher's office it is easy to guess what would have happened to him. He would have been told that his work was very promising indeed, and asked to take it away and cut it in half. The story is far too long, and there are scores of copy readers in newspaper and magazine offices who could shorten it and make it better. Mr. Dreiser not only reports his hero's love affairs in full, even in those details in which love affairs do not greatly differ, but he documents every other incident as carefully as a biographer endeavoring to establish a new conception of a famous character. He describes a murder trial as though he were a star reporter who had been told by his editor to take all the space he needed.

But whether Mr. Dreiser's 840 pages ought to be 420 is a vain question. Nothing that can be said to Mr. Dreiser or about him will in the least alter his artistic method. He has written *An American Tragedy* at this length and in this form because he cannot possibly write it in lesser length or other form. And this obstinacy, if it is that, is the defect of his strength. His name is well known today, and will continue to be known to all who are seriously interested in American literature, very largely because of the very fact that he would not listen to reason. Reason would have demanded in the '90s that he conform to the romantic requirements of the period. Reason might now demand that he consider the profits of serialization and motion-picture rights. But he has the unreasonableness of an author afflicted with a certain touch of genius.

The skeleton of the story is such as may be found, by a sufficiently astute reader, in almost any morning's newspaper. Clyde Griffiths is the son of a street preacher in Kansas City—a beaten, nondescript, shambling person. The mother is of stronger fibre, but her world is bounded by the Bethel Independent Mission. Youth will not be pinched within such narrow walls. Clyde's young sister meets a handsome actor and falls by the wayside. Clyde himself, at 16, breaks away and becomes a bellboy in "the very finest hotel in Kansas City." A few drinks, a visit to the tenderloin and a scrubby love affair, and the process of sophistication is complete. An escapade with a borrowed motor car, ending in tragedy, forces him, as he thinks, to leave the city. A chance meeting with his father's brother, Samuel Griffiths, a wealthy collar manufacturer of Lycurgus, N.Y., seems to promise a reversal of fortune. The uncle gives him a small place in the collar factory, and despite the opposition of his cousin Gilbert, Clyde sees the road to wealth and position opening before him. He even manages to make headway with Sondra Finchley, daughter of one of Lycurgus's upper-class families. And then what visions fill his somewhat ratlike brain!

Unfortunately he has been injudicious enough to enter into an affair with Roberta Alden, one of the operatives in the collar factory, and by the time he is tired of her it is clear that she is to become a mother. Clyde has no sense of responsibility, yet if he abandons Roberta she will expose him and he will lose Sondra. On the hook of this dilemma he is impaled. His mind has become fastened upon Sondra, and all that she represents, with the fatal tenacity of an obsession. He has the incurable selfishness and lack of imagination that sometimes do produce success. But he lacks the intellectual strength to extricate himself. He sinks in deeper and deeper. A chance newspaper clipping puts a gruesome idea in his head. Suppose a man and a girl go out in a canoe. Suppose the canoe tips over and only one returns. He finds himself led on, almost without willing it, into plotting murder.

From this point on, for some 120 pages, Mr. Dreiser gives us as fine and haunting a study of crime and punishment as he or any other novelist has written in America—a passage so penetrating, so poetic and of such weirdly dramatic power that the remaining 247 pages are something in the nature of an anti-climax. We see a vapid but not really evil little soul becoming, by easy steps, blood-guilty; it is almost as horrible as watching a vivisection:

And then once more on the water again—about 500 feet from shore, the while he fumbled aimlessly with the hard and heavy yet small camera that he now held, as the boat floated out nearer the centre. And then, at this point and time looking fearfully about. For now—now—in spite of himself, the long-evaded and yet commanding moment. And no voice or figure or sound on shore. No road or cabin or smoke! And the moment which he or something had planned for him, and which was now to decide his fate, at hand! The moment of action—of crisis! All that he needed to do now was to turn swiftly and savagely to one side or the other—leap up—upon the left wale or the right, and upset the boat; or, failing that, rock it swiftly, and if Roberta protested too much, strike her with the camera in his hand, or one of the oars free at his right. It could be done—it could be done—swiftly and simply, were he now of the mind and heart, or lack of it—with him swimming swiftly away thereafter to freedom—to success—of course—to Sondra and happiness—a new and greater and sweeter life than any he had ever known.

At the last there is a moment of hesitation. Did he mean to strike her with the camera? Did he commit murder?

H. L. Mencken has said of Dreiser, in a sentence quoted on the jacket of these volumes: "He stands isolated today, a figure weatherbeaten and lonely. Yet I know no American novelist who seems so secure or likely to endure." There is obviously at least this amount of accuracy in the statement: Mr. Dreiser is not imitative and belongs to no school. He is at heart a mysticist and a fatalist, though using the realistic method. He is a totally undisciplined, unorganized power—yet, on the evidence of this novel alone, nonetheless a power. *An American Tragedy* is not to be recommended as fireside reading for the tired business man: yet, as a portrayal of one of the darker phases of the American character, it demands attention.

Log Cabin Days

Abraham Lincoln: The Prairie Years by Carl Sandburg
February 14, 1926

A NEW EXPERIENCE awaits the reader of Carl Sandburg's book on Lincoln. There has never been biography quite like this before. But if Mr. Sandburg breaks new ground, it is not in the sense that Gamaliel Bradford and Lytton Strachey did. There is no question here of a new school of biographical writing. The thing Mr. Sandburg has done cannot well be repeated; his achievement is an intensely individual one, suffused by the qualities which are peculiarly his own as a poet. As those who have read him know, they are not the qualities of conventional poetry, nor is this new book of his a merely emotional rendering of the Lincoln story. It is as full of facts as Jack Horner's pie was full of plums. In the work of reporting, of assembling the vast stores of Lincoln material, Mr. Sandburg has been untiring. An extraordinary vitality pervades this story of Lincoln's life up to the time of his leaving Springfield for the White House. Part of that vitality comes from the poet's transforming touch, that power of suggestion which lies at the heart of poetry. Part of it comes from the quality of historic imagination, which is closely allied to poetry, for the surging, restless march of the westward movement streams through the book like the recurrent theme of a symphony. Part of it comes from a vivid sense of character, the play of which is not restricted to the central figure. And there are other elements which have gone into the fibre of *Abraham Lincoln: The Prairie Years.* Carl Sandburg grew up in that section of the country where the greater part of Lincoln's life was spent. He had in mind for more than thirty years the writing of such a book. It was not the President he would write about, but "the country lawyer and prairie politician."

Carl Sandburg prefers to see Lincoln as the product largely of those wilderness and prairie years. He emphasizes the loneliness in which the boy lived, "the wilderness loneliness," "not like that of people in cities who can look from a window on streets where faces pass and repass."

But if silence had a part in his making, so, too, did the early contact into which he came with the moving currents of American life. That is a fact worth remembering about Lincoln. While he was still a small boy, living on the Knob Creek farm in Kentucky, the Louisville and Nashville pike ran past the Lincoln cabin. Settlers in covered wagons, Congressmen, members of the Legislature on their way to Lexington, traveling preachers—all these passed and many stopped at the Lincoln door. And a few years later, when the boy was 10 years old and the family had moved on to Indiana, he ran a ferryboat across the Ohio River. It was a great highway of traffic and a fine vantage point for a boy with eager eyes and ears. One remembers, too, the voyage three years later, down the Mississippi and the new horizon unfolding at New Orleans.

When Lincoln, at 22, left his father and stepmother and went to New Salem to clerk in Denton Offut's store, he knew his way about among men. In the portrait of "the country lawyer and prairie politician" that he became, Carl Sandburg does not hesitate to leave in the crude, harsh lines. One meets with Lincoln the shrewd handler of men, the endless teller of stories, coarse often as not, the frankly office-seeking Lincoln, who never hesitated to write letters

1926

Winnie-the-Pooh, by A. A. Milne, a former assistant editor at *Punch*, is loosed upon the world.

urging the consideration of his claims. But there is marvelously little that can be said honestly today in disparagement of Lincoln. Carl Sandburg has written a book that merits the reading and meditation of every American. In the first place, for the extraordinary living warmth of the Lincoln he has drawn; and for such things as the beautiful tender handling of the story of Nancy Hanks and of Lincoln's unhappy love affair with Ann Rutledge.

Of that tragedy in Lincoln's life Mr. Sandburg has written with a splendid union of feeling and restraint. There is piercing sharpness in this brief paragraph in which he sets down the tragedy.

> Ann Rutledge lay fever-burned. Days passed; help arrived and was helpless. Moans came from her for the one man of her thoughts. They sent for him. He rode out from New Salem to the Sand Ridge farm. They let him in, they left the two together and alone a last hour in the log house, with slants of light on her face from an open clapboard door. It was two days later that death came.

Too little has been said here of the wider aspects of Carl Sandburg's book. Suffice it now to say that nobody can go through these two volumes without a more vivid sense of what the pioneer breed was really like, and a clearer perception of the forces that year after year were splitting the country until the ultimate gulf of disunion opened under it.

Making It New

Personae: The Collected Poems of Ezra Pound
January 23, 1927

BY HERBERT S. GORMAN

IN 1908 Ezra Pound published his first book, *A Lume Spento*, in Venice. It was a small book and possibly it made no impression on a public that was contented enough with the polite prettinesses of that interregnum period. Indeed, who was to know that the lank, red-bearded Ezra was to be the major prophet of an entire generation of poets who were, in 1908, still in primary school? Now that a score of years, less one, has passed and Ezra Pound has gathered his poetry into a single volume, *Personae*, it is possible to view the man and his work with some fair approximation of a perspective. Any summing up is a matter of perplexity and wonder, for Pound has never stood still. His career has fallen into two halves; one as the proselytizer, the preacher, the argumentative herald of a new order in literature; the other as the poet, and it is as the poet that he must be considered here.

Like some of the modern composers he is a heretic so far as the dogmas of composition are concerned, and he mingles freely a dozen traditions ranging from the manner of the ancient Chinese and the Provençal troubadours to the most modern vers libre in order to attain his effects. It is the effect, after all, that matters to him, the seizing upon the moment, and its emotional revelation in succinct form. And yet he can write the most delicate and poignant lines, lines filled with a twilight nostalgia and the shadow of wings. He is extraordinarily sensitive to the slightest moods, but he disciplines and lifts these moods to an intellectualized plane. It is not by any means a plane of dry celebration, but it is a terrain of sad gravity, an academe of the soul.

Except for his translations and his reconstructions from ancient literatures, his work is always the personal reflex of his furious opinions on life, love and art. There is therefore a vast vitality in his best work, a restlessness of the mind that consistently flings itself against saccharinity, stupidity, crumbled traditions and muddiness in thinking. This attitude naturally induces a satiric observance of certain phases of modern life. This satire may be either of the sledgehammer variety or a series of delicate rapier thrusts. In any case it is effective and serves its purpose admirably. He is concerned primarily with a liberated expression, with the fulfillment of one's self, with the recognition of a naked art unadorned with the rags of compromise. Above all things, beauty calls to him, beauty of emotion and beauty of intellect, and he follows it as the hound follows the doe. Nearly all of his work is threaded with passion and, though the passion may be restrained and disciplined, it loses none of its urgency.

Other writers reach a maturity, find themselves as individualities, and remain on the level so gained. But Pound is different. It is not that he has never found himself but that he continues to find himself constantly. There is no pause for him. He must go on, driven by his restless vitality to new experimentations and new utterances. Dredging constantly into the literatures and histories of the past he finds there a thousand and one nascent nuances that he must adapt to his peculiar personality.

It is impossible to judge his place as a poet today. Perhaps it is a much greater place than one may think, especially one somewhat blinded by his warfare as a propagandist for other writers and for a continuous series of new movements. The suspicion, however, rises that some of Pound's poetical strength has been dissipated by his activities as a prophet. If he had not leaped so gallantly to the defense of the poetic renascence in English he might have been a poetic renascence in himself. One must be thankful for what he is and realize that after years of ridicule from calf-brains he indubitably stands upon an eminence from which he may not be easily shaken. And besides this he offers to the public a harvesting of poetry in *Personae* that may well stand beside any collection of modern poetry of this era. There is strength, virility, beauty, sensitiveness, intellectual ardour, and experimentation in the book. Other books may suggest peaks reaching higher into Heaven, but few of them can suggest such a consistently high range. It is impossible to call Ezra Pound the finest American poet today, as some of his more enthusiastic friends insist, but it is not impossible to call him a fine American poet. And surely one may call him the finest American warrior for a liberalized expression in contemporary poetry.

Illness As Metaphor

The Magic Mountain by Thomas Mann
May 8, 1927

BY JOHN W. CRAWFORD

ARTIFICES WITHOUT END have appeared in fiction to crystallize out of complexities those stark clear values which have seemed to express man's dramatic relation to his world. It has remained for Thomas Mann to discover and to exploit the strangest device of all: a tuberculosis sanitarium. The character of Hans Castorp, one of the patients in the Berghof, in the Swiss Alps, provides the novelist with an additional degree of detachment, a further invitation to those more abstract concerns which have so little to do with the preoccupations of life in the flatlands. Hans Castorp passes the long, indistinguishable time intervals by taking stock of himself, his derivations, his significance in the world, and the meaning of the world to him. Castorp, further, comes in contact with other patients, representing every aspect of philosophy, whether reasoned and codified in thought or unthinkingly applied in living. Imperceptibly, yet overwhelmingly at the end, it becomes apparent that, through the supine, passive personality of Hans Castorp, situated in his removed, changeless sanitarium, Thomas Mann has wrought a synthesis out of the whole diversity of modern being.

As the novel opens, Hans Castorp is already on his way to the cure. He is "an unassuming young man," whose sole distinguishing characteristic is his faithfulness to a certain cigar. He is of an old burgher family of Hamburg, settled, sober people who have been the backbone of that tight oligarchy of trade for generations. Hans Castorp has just finished his engineering studies and has a position waiting for him with a firm of shipbuilders, conducted by traditional friends of his family's. He is going to spend three weeks in the company of his unhappy cousin, young Joachim Ziemssen. From the moment Joachim conducts his cousin from the narrow gauge railway compartment, it is apparent that a distinct mode of being exists upon that remote, bewitched mountain. "We up here," Joachim observes, "measure time on the grand scale, and consider three weeks nothing to speak of, a mere week-end."

Thomas Mann transforms Hans Castorp from a civilian with a part to play in the active business of Hamburg to a reflective, experimentative onlooker, by such gradual stages that the transitions are entirely organic. At one point, Castorp is nothing more than the visitor, making only those provisional adjustments to a new environment which spring from a natural wish to benefit by a vacation. Visibly he is inveigled and at length entirely absorbed by the conditions of these exotic surroundings. He develops a cold and a high fever. An examination and the revelations of the X-ray betray the little moist spot in his lungs which is destined to keep him at the Berghof for seven years instead of the original three weeks.

The sensible, physical universe of the Berghof is delimited by the Hofrat Behrens, the surgeon and head physician of the establishment; by the psychoanalyst, Dr. Krokowski; by five hearty meals each day; by the people at Castorp's table; by the strict regimen of rest, alcohol rubs, taking of temperature and so on, and by the imminence of death.

Hans Castorp soon has qualified these general conditions with the particular elements which appeal to him, and which serve to betray and accentuate his essential personality. Both his father and mother are dead, and his grandfather died when he was still a child. He himself is frail. He has not been a patient long before he discovers in himself an infinite, almost morbidly sensitive, tenderness toward suffering and dying. He sets himself the duty of visiting those who are about to end the fight for health, and be carried out, silently, and in the absence of the inmates, and put on bobsleds to be transported down the snow-covered mountainside to the railway.

Thomas Mann is infinitely, scrupulously fair. He is at pains to present Castorp in a dry light, free of prejudice. In addition, he gives unlimited license to all the speculators and theorists assembled at the Berghof, who inevitably cross the path of Castorp, and find his deference and his youth and his teachableness irresistible. The result is that Castorp listens to the Italian libertarian, son and grandson of classic humanitarians, and finds Ludovico Settembrini stimulating, provoking, sometimes aggravating. He also draws out the subtle Jesuit, Naphta. Hans is, too, the devoted friend and ally of the extraordinary Dutch Colonial, Pieter Peeperkorn.

It is impossible to read far into Thomas Mann without realizing that he is a tacit but inexorable advocate of the aristocratic principle. The democracy of Settembrini is allowed fullest expression, but there is always Naphta to riddle it, and to make the gallant Italian slightly ridiculous. In addition, there is the fascinating Russian woman, Clavdia Chauchat, bespeaking the life of the senses, and controverting with the spell of her greenish eyes and her red hair the austere humanity of Settembrini and its effect upon the impressionable Castorp. Further, there is Peeperkorn, reminding the Berghof inmates that sheer physical personality, deriving out of uncharted primitive forces, dominant in its own right, is an unanswerable challenge to reason and dialectic.

So soon as these tentative conclusions are reached, however, and the innate significance of the novel has appeared to have been deposited, crystalline-clear, once for all, the neatly arranged categories disappear at a breath, and it is all to do over again. Mynheer Peeperkorn, although he rules the oddly assorted little company, is yet diminished by the very power which has given him ascendency. He is aging, and that is the final answer, perhaps, to the form of the aristocratic principle which he represents.

The end of Peeperkorn is only one among many moments that would have tempted a lesser writer to rodomontade. Thomas Mann takes it all in his stride. He has established, early in the narration, an acceptance of this "eternal day that is ever the same" at the Berghof.

The reader looks in vain through *The Magic Mountain* for the docketed views and pat opinions of Thomas Mann. That in itself, considering the subject and the nature of the book, is a signal and grateful achievement. What he finds, instead, is the extraordinary spiritual, mental and physical adventures of Hans Castorp.

The recognition of Hans Castorp, on his isolated peak of arrested temporal experience, set free as he never could have been in the flatlands to explore and participate in many different ways of life and thought for himself, comes perilously, breath-takingly near to charting a discovery of the modern world. It is a fine, noble, inspiriting "Yes," which Thomas Mann returns to life. Yet *The Magic Mountain* falls just short of being that work upon which the thoughtful wanderer among contemporary perplexities may build a serene, untroubled, understanding acceptance of life. But it goes far on the way.

Jazz Days

Home to Harlem by Claude McKay
March 11, 1928

BY JOHN R. CHAMBERLAIN

HERE IS A BOOK that is beaten through with the rhythm of life that is a jazz rhythm. It is a story of a happy negro, of Jake Brown whose life in Harlem and elsewhere is a song of affirmation, of acceptance of the flesh as natural. Jake deserved Felice, and their happy departure from Harlem for Chicago at the close of the novel is no sentimental slop but the real thing in rightness.

Well, the story is Jake's story, but what of the man who wrote this jazz paean to nature? No doubt he included a little of himself in Jake, but there must be more of him in Ray, the educated Haitian, whose native tongue is French, and who quotes Wordsworth's sonnet on Toussaint L'Overture, that black Washington who is known to all school children with an eighth grade education in elocution. Ray, the outcast, the defeated, the man of mind, who has tasted philosophy, that dear delight, only to find out that good hors d'oeuvres make a bad dessert—there must be a lot of him in Claude McKay, pot-wrestler, dock-hand, fireman, artist, and friend of the social revolutionaries. For McKay comes from rebel stock and the tradition of rebellion is strong within him; and Ray, the exile, who cries out in the face of the white man's inhumanity to the black man, is obviously the birth in fiction of part of McKay's outlook. It is revealing that McKay dedicates his novel to Louise Bryant, who was the wife of Jack Reed, the Harvard boy who lies buried in Moscow as Tovarisch Jack, friend of the social revolutionists.

Mr. McKay's book assails the optical, the olfactory, the kinaesthetic antennae whereby the human being takes in the world about him. In less stilted phrases, you can see, smell and feel what he writes. He says of Spring in Harlem:

> The lovely trees of Seventh Avenue were a vivid flame-green. Children, lightly clad, skipped on the pavement. Light open coats prevailed and the smooth bare throats of brown girls were a token as charming as the first pussy-willows. Far and high above all, the sky was a grand blue benediction, and beneath it the wonderful air of New York tasted like fine dry champagne.

That paragraph captures a mood. When McKay says in the next paragraph "a colored couple dawdled by, their arms fondly caressing each other's hips. A white man forking a bit of ground stopped and stared expressively after them," he is shifting moods with an adroitness that is bardacious to behold.

Of course, *Home to Harlem* is not for the queasy of stomach. There are descriptions of parties, at Ginhead Susy's in Brooklyn and in Harlem, that might startle Anthony Comstock out of a year's growth in his heavenly expansion; and the scene in the Pittsburgh lodging house where the Pennsylvania Pullman porters, cooks and waiters stay and where Ray, Jake's new-found, sensitive pal, sniffs the happy dust in desperation, is realism in the peculiar modern overwrought sense of that word. There is talk of sex that is unrestrained; but for the most part it is joyous talk. And there is, in the book, "liquor-rich laughter, banana-ripe laughter"; as well as the smell of fried chicken, candied sweet potatoes, poke chops and beer. Not to mention the kaleidoscope of cabarets, saloons, joints, dives, dance halls, spohtin' houses, buffet flats and places of merriment, guzzling, gambling and scronching ad infinitum.

Much of the charm of *Home to Harlem* is in the easy, unforced conversation of the many characters. Whenever Jake and Zeddy and Felice and Billy talk the illusion is complete: one might be mixing again with the crowds in the Harlem streets on that cold Sunday when Florence Mills was buried. For here is talk that is a far cry from the stuff of the minstrel show and Octavus Roy Cohen.

It is when McKay begins talking about Gogol, Tolstoy, Chekhov, James Joyce and D. H. Lawrence that he is vague, that he seems to be glossing over. "During the war," he says of Ray, "he had been startled by James Joyce in The Little Review." Ray has aspirations to create art in words; but why, how and to what purpose Ray was startled by the aspect of Joyce's words is not explained by McKay. The talent of this negro writer is not for analysis or ideas, not for the essay; it is for dramatic depiction of rude, boisterous and Nietzschean lives. And it is not a strained halfhearted or skimpy talent, but one that is eminently worth more play than one novel.

First Impressions

Bambi by Felix Salten
July 8, 1928

BY JOHN R. CHAMBERLAIN

OUTSIDE, the heat radiates from the pavements. A forlorn sparrow cheeps in the dusty ailanthus. Trucks rumble by, taxis hoot, and gutter urchins play at one of the fifty variants of street baseball. But inside this book is the coolness of the woodland, and the Summer city is far away and almost forgotten.

For Felix Salten, in *Bambi*, takes you out of yourself. He has the gift of a tender, lucid style. His observation is next door to marvelous, and he invests the fruits of this observation with pure poetry. His comprehension makes his deer, his screech-owls, his butterflies, grasshoppers and hares, far more exciting to read about than hundreds of human beings who crowd the pages of our novels.

Bambi came into the world in the "middle of the thicket, in one of those little, hidden forest glades which seem to be entirely open, but are really screened in on all sides." "What a beautiful child," cried the magpie; but Bambi's mother pays no attention to this encomium for her first born. She continues to wash her child.

At first Bambi is as unorientated as a freshman in college. He can't understand what his elders mean when they utter the word "danger." He doesn't see why it isn't safe to play at any time on the meadow.

As the boy grows older he is initiated into the terrible idea of He, the hateful human who kills with a thundering "third hand" which He can throw from a great distance.

When the first Winter comes Bambi experiences the terror of being hunted by He. His mother is killed in a great massacre of forest folk, and he is forced thenceforward to rely upon himself.

It is from this point on that Salten shows increasing comprehension. Bambi's first shy advances to Faline, his early love, his maturity, his friendship with the old stag who teaches him the ways of the forest world and the necessity of being able to live alone if one is to become a philosopher and sage; and his own old age—all these stages in the life of a forest deer are set down in prose that is admirably translated by Whittaker Chambers.

Growing old, Bambi sees Faline, his old mate. "At that moment Bambi loved her with an overpowering, tender melancholy." But the days of his youthful impetuosity are gone forever. It is now time for him to learn his final lesson from his father confessor, the old Prince. The graybeard stag takes Bambi to where a poacher lies dead.

> "Do you see, Bambi," the old stag says, "do you see how He's lying dead, like one of us. Listen, Bambi. He isn't all-powerful, as they say. Everything that lives and grows doesn't come from Him. He isn't above us. He's just the same as we are. He has the same fears, the same needs and suffers in the same way. He can be killed like us, and then He lies helpless on the ground like all the rest of us, as you see Him now."

And Bambi replies that he understands. "There is Another who is over us all, over us and over Him," he answers with a sudden inspiration.

With such a salutary scene Salten puts man, the megalomaniac, in his place in the order of things and comes into his book's last pages.

This Is Progress?

Middletown: A Study in Contemporary American Culture
by Robert and Helen Lynd
January 20, 1929

BY R. L. DUFFUS

THE AMERICAN TOWN and small city have had to take some hard knocks in recent years, mostly from ungrateful natives who had escaped from them to Chicago, New York or the south of France. But these exposures have generally taken the form of fiction, and it was always possible to say that their authors had grievances. This particular charge cannot be brought against the authors of this book, who are scientific and sociological almost to a fault. They have looked at their sample American community with the cool eyes of anthropologists studying the habits of an alien species. They have collected case reports and their pages are larded with percentages and statistics. They had, consciously, at least, no axe to grind. According to Professor Clark Wissler, who writes a brief introduction, "no one had ever subjected an American community to such a scrutiny." Those who cling to their childhood illusions about their native land will wish that the Lynds had scrutinized the Patagonians instead. For the portrait of Middletown is not flattering. Not only does it make the reader wonder whether all that has happened since 1890 has been progress. It even arouses some doubt in his mind as to whether the present inhabitants of America have attained greater happiness per capita than did the Indians who preceded them. Of course this may be merely the result of viewing an objective piece of work in a subjective way. Even Athens under Pericles or Rome under the Antonines might have shown up badly under the statistical method. It may not be so much Middletown as the fundamental conditions of human life that are at fault. The American reader is shocked because, despite Sinclair Lewis, Theodore Dreiser, H. L. Mencken and others, he is invincibly optimistic.

Middletown comes into the picture as a town which has made great physical progress. In 1885 it was "an agricultural county seat of some 6,000 persons"; now it is an industrial city which in 1920 had a population of more than 35,000. Its wealth has greatly increased, its inhabitants have more things in their houses, better clothes on their backs and more means of amusement, and its health is decidedly better. But it gets less fun out of its job, its home life has pretty well gone to pot, it is inefficiently and often corruptly governed, and its ideas and habits are almost as regimented as those of a South Sea Islander under the taboo system. The individualism with which we endow the older generations is disappearing. A native returning to the familiar scenes notes a dismaying change.

"These people are all afraid of something," he writes. People are hemmed in by their social and economic affiliations. As the authors put it:

> Confronted by the difficulty of choosing among subtle group loyalties the Middletown citizen, particularly of the business class in this world of credit, tends to do with his ideas what he does with his breakfast food or his collars or his politics—he increasingly accepts a blanket pattern solution. He does not try to scratch the "good-fellow" ticket but votes it straight. To be "civic" and to "serve" is put over "Magic Middletown," the church, the party, a get-together dinner, a financial campaign, one's friends: it is to be a "booster, not a knocker"; to accept without question the symbols.

This group loyalty is more fatal to ideas than to action. The Chamber of Commerce naturally gets behind the "Buy in Middletown" campaign, but it does not hesitate to let contracts for its new building go to a builder using materials bought out of town. Competition is still the gospel of the city's business classes. A church which is raising a building fund refuses to lend its kitchen to another smaller church of the same denomination which is giving a benefit for its own building fund. In social and business life the man who conceals his thoughts, or possibly who has no thoughts, gets along best—assuming that we mean by thoughts a questioning of accepted beliefs. Of course, there are mavericks who indulge in private a fondness for speculative books, for the arts, even for producing literature. But they do not boast about these tastes unless—and this is a large exception in Middletown—they make money by them. Money making and money spending are current measures of quality in Middletown. A citizen explains that this is partly because they are such easy tests.

The impression with which the reader is left is that of a curiously contradictory community—united in supporting the meaningless gymnastics of the high school basketball team, clubbed together in numberless organizations for mutual advantage, yet rarely seeing or seeking true community good. Above all, Middletown seems to possess no sense of a community civilization. It is sophisticated in the mechanism of living and pitifully naïve in almost everything having to do with the purposes of living. Our authors do not tell us this in so many words. They are too unbiased and too scientific to do so. But the portrait of a community, representative of millions of our population, barely groping for a national culture still to be born, jumps out of their careful paragraphs. The only comfort is the possibility that Middletown is not altogether representative, after all.

Dashiell Hammett

Dorothy Parker • Frank Lloyd Wright

Margaret Sanger • Aldous Huxley • John Dos

Passos • Georges Simenon • William Faulkner

Nathanael West • James M. Cain • Roger Tory

Peterson • Zora Neale Hurston • Henry Roth

Margaret Mead • Margaret Mitchell • Dale Carnegie

M. F. K. Fisher • Franz Kafka • Dr. Seuss

Joseph Mitchell • Raymond Chandler

John Steinbeck

1930S

First Impressions

The Maltese Falcon by Dashiell Hammett
February 23, 1930

I F THE LOCUTION "hard-boiled" had not already been coined it would be necessary to coin it now to describe the characters of Dashiell Hammett's latest detective story. All of the persons of the book are of that description, and the hardest boiled one of the lot is Sam Spade, the private detective, who gives the impression that he is on the side of the law only when it suits his book. If Spade had a weakness it would be women, but appreciative as he is of their charms, never, even in his most intimate relations with them, does he forget to look out for the interests of Samuel Spade. And it is as well that he does, for the criminals, men and women, with whom he comes in contact in this story are almost as hard-boiled as he. Mr. Hammett, we understand, was once a Pinkerton operative, and he probably knows that there is very little romance about the detective business. There is none of it in his book, but there is plenty of excitement.

1930

Dashiell Hammett publishes *The Maltese Falcon* and introduces Sam Spade.

First Impressions

Laments for the Living by Dorothy Parker
June 15, 1930

T HE SEVERAL PIECES of short fiction, excoriating certain types of people, which Dorothy Parker has contributed over recent months to various magazines, are now brought together, the title being *Laments for the Living*. Miss Parker might with equal fitness have called her book a collection of laments for those who have never lived. But her people thought they were very much alive. Oh, yes indeed! And that is how the author gets in her good work with her well-known scalpel. For in the baker's dozen of short prose pieces of this not overlarge volume Dorothy Parker lives up to the reputation established by her verse, of being an exceedingly sharp-eyed observer. We should like it better if the gallery of subjects whose portraits she has done had been a little more various. But this is an initial venture into prose, and Miss Parker may yet move out of the speakeasy and extend her rambles more hither and yon. If she does, then it will behoove most of us to make a quick exit when she comes on the scene, for it is very probable that few, if any, would be pretty with the hide off and left to march around in our bones.

1930

Sinclair Lewis is the first American to win the Nobel Prize in Literature.

As the Depression deepens,
American readers become
enthralled with the plight of
Chinese peasants in
The Good Earth,
by Pearl S. Buck.

The opening story gives a useful key to the collection in a general sort of way. It is that story called "The Sexes," in which "the young man with the scenic cravat glanced nervously down the sofa at the girl in the fringed dress." The attempt at conversation is ludicrous, if conversation it can be called, for they are of the inarticulate class, and limited to:

"What's the matter?" he said.
  "Why, nothing," she said. "Why?"
  "You've been funny all the evening," he said.
  "I'm terribly sorry you haven't been having a good time," she said.

Until finally,

"I think you're just perfectly crazy," she said. "I was not sore! What on earth ever made you think I was? You're simply crazy. Ow, my hair-net! Wait a second till I take it off. There!"

It will be perceived that Miss Parker has here adumbrated a great deal, while saying nothing at all—which is precisely what her two young people achieved. But if we laugh at the thinness of the conversation, as the author intended us to do, we are well aware (as also she intended we should be) of the pathos of it all. And this is the saving grace of satire, without which it would be intolerable, that not only through it, but because of it, we see the sadness that brings, or should bring, tears.

O. Henry did not have all keys to the city—he had but one, the key of romance. And Dorothy Parker has but one key. As a guide, therefore, each has limitations. *Laments for the Living* is sharply keen in so far as it goes. But unless Miss Parker can go beyond it, not necessarily in method, but at least in range, the end of the course is already visible. One volume of *Laments* is admirable. Several would be insufferable.

The Tyranny of the Skyscraper

Modern Architecture by Frank Lloyd Wright
May 31, 1931

BY R. L. DUFFUS

AFTER A LONG PERIOD of obscurity Frank Lloyd Wright has come to be regarded in some quarters as America's most creative architect. These lectures, delivered at Princeton last year, help to explain both the obscurity and the present fame. For Wright is clearly a genius, as one would know by the mere reading of these 115 pages, and as such he is entirely uncompromising. Though he derived inspiration from Louis Sullivan, who may be called the father of the skyscraper, he now wishes us to be delivered from "The Tyranny of the Skyscraper"—as he calls one of his lectures. Though he is certainly "modern," he has little sympathy with "most of the cardboard houses of the 'modernistic' movement." He has broken with the old and he stands aloof from much that passes for new. Consequently he has had to follow a long trail and a lonely one.

And yet one may see in these lectures the signs that he is coming into his own. For he reflects an attitude which more and more the intelligent layman as well as the imaginative architect is likely to take—that is, that the old architectural forms are dead, that the time has come for absolutely new creations, that the machine will play its proper part in these creations, but that man himself ought not to be mechanized. The passing of classic forms was dramatized for Mr. Wright as it has been for few fledgling architects. Passing one day in his late teens around Capitol Square in Madison, Wis., he was just in time to witness the collapse of the new west wing of the Capitol, with death or serious injury to forty workmen. "A great 'classic' cornice," he remembers, "had been projecting boldly from the top of the building, against the sky. Its moorings partly torn away, this cornice now hung down in places, great hollow boxes of galvanized iron, hanging up there suspended on end. One great section of cornice I saw hanging from an upper window. A workman hung, head downward, his foot caught, crushed on the sill of this window by a falling beam." After this experience young Wright began "to examine cornices critically." He saw them as "images of a dead culture," and began to cast about for expressions of a new and living culture. He saw the "pilasters, architraves and rusticated walls" of late Victorian architecture as belonging to the same stuffy scheme of things as the "puffed sleeves, frizzes, furbelows and flounces" of the absurd feminine attire of the same period.

Looking further back, he came to believe that the Renaissance, whose work later architects had imitated, was an empty imitation of Greek and Roman forms, and that even the Greek forms had rested upon a false basis, so far as architecture was concerned, because the Greek builders had tried to imitate wood in stone. He concluded that all traditional forms must be swept away. "It is for us," he now says, "to bury Greek architecture deep. For us it is pagan poison. We have greater buildings to build upon a more substantial base—an ideal of organic architecture, complying with the ideal of true democracy." Imitations of dead styles are not, as Mr. Wright looks at them, "organic architecture," but neither are all attempts at a new style. In Mr. Wright's conception the style emerges out of the purposes of the building, though he necessarily differs from some of

August 9, 1931

Harmonium

BY WALLACE STEVENS

Unpleasant as it is to record such a conclusion, the very remarkable work of Wallace Stevens cannot endure. The verses which go to make up the volume *Harmonium* are as close to "pure poetry" as one could expect to come. And so far as rhythms and vowels and consonants may be substituted for musical notes, the volume is an achievement. But the achievement is not poetry, it is a tour de force, a "stunt" in the fantastic and the bizarre. From one end of the book to the other there is not an idea that can vitally affect the mind, there is not a word that can arouse emotion. The volume is a glittering edifice of icicles. Wallace Stevens is a martyr to a lost cause.

the mechanists in regarding the structure as a place where people are to live and work rather than as a ganglion of machinery. He never forgets that man is human and born of the earth. His first houses, built a generation ago, hugged the earth, let in sunlight, and centred about the ancient amenity of the hearth. He wiped out attics, bay windows, cellars, corner towers and scrollwork, and made his interiors at the same time airy and spacious and proportioned to the people who were to inhabit them. To his neighbors in the late '90s these ideas seemed so new "that what little prospect I had of ever earning a livelihood by making houses was nearly wrecked." There were some struggles between design and comfort. "I have been black and blue in some spot," he observes, "somewhere, almost all my life, from too intimate contacts with my own furniture."

Architecture is, for Mr. Wright, the expression of human life—the highest expression. If human beings working or living in hundred-story towers lead cramped and frustrated lives, then the towers have failed. And so, for Mr. Wright, "the skyscraper envelope is not ethical, beautiful or permanent. It is a commercial exploit or a mere expedient. It has no higher ideal of unity than commercial success."

Mr. Wright believes that "the city, as we know it today, is to die"; he does not believe that it can or should evolve into the "new machine-city of machine-prophecy as we see it outlined by Le Corbusier and his school." It is here that he diverges from a whole wing of the modernist movement. He does not see why men should continue to "go narrowly up, up, up, to come narrowly down, down, down—instead of freely going in and out and comfortably around about among the beautiful things to which their lives are related on this earth." He would "enable human life to be based squarely and fairly on the ground," and to follow that horizontal line, which "is the line of domesticity—the Earthline of human life." Cities there will be in his Utopia, but they will "be invaded at ten o'clock, abandoned at four, for three days of the week." People will get back to the land, to at least an acre of land apiece, carrying with them by means of modern invention—that is to say, the "Machine"—all and more than all they now find in the midst of urban congestion. The entire countryside will be "a well-developed park—buildings standing in it, tall or wide, with beauty and privacy for every one." In this environment "man will find the manlike freedom for himself and his that Democracy must mean."

This is, clearly, more than architecture—it is a way of life. If the way of life is not beautiful the architecture will not be—and vice versa. This philosophy he has stated lucidly and with a fine glow of enthusiasm. His message ought to stir the imaginations of youthful architects and of youthfulness, whether of years or of point of view, everywhere.

Memoirs of a Crusader

My Fight for Birth Control by Margaret Sanger
October 4, 1931

BY FLORENCE FINCH KELLY

ERILY, the way of the crusader is hard! Not even the proverbial discomforts of the path of the transgressor can exceed the pains and ills it visits upon those who tread the stones and suffer the revilings of its road. If any one doubts it let him read Mrs. Sanger's autobiographical account of the years, now almost a score, that she has spent upon her effort to legalize the dissemination of information on the subject of birth control. With her it has been, as every one knows who has had much knowledge of her or the movement, a real crusade that has called for the utmost she could give of courage, determination, energy, single-hearted devotion. From the start she has been inspired by sympathy with the overburdened wives and mothers of the submerged millions of poverty, and she has tried to convince that "other half" that knows nothing about their lives that here was a most necessary means of lessening the burdens imposed on society by pauperism, crime, and the demands of charity and social welfare work.

Before her marriage Mrs. Sanger was a trained nurse and her work in connection with hospitals and welfare agencies took her much into the poverty-stricken regions of the lower east side of New York City. After years of happy married life and motherhood it became necessary for her to take up again her vocation of nursing and again the work took her into the homes of the very poor. She found, she says, that life there offered "to mothers but one choice: either to abandon themselves to incessant child-bearing or to terminate their pregnancies through abortions. Is it any wonder they resigned themselves hopelessly, as the Jewish and Italian mothers, or fell into drunkenness, as the Irish and Scotch?"

Returning to her home from a case that had been particularly heart-breaking, she tells how the determination was born in her heart to try to help these helpless, hopeless women:

> As I stood at the window and looked out, the miseries and problems of that sleeping city arose before me in a clear vision like a panorama: crowded homes, too many children; babies dying in infancy; mothers overworked; baby nurseries; children neglected and hungry; mothers half sick most of their lives; women made into drudges; children working in cellars; children aged six and seven pushed into the labor market to earn a living; another baby on the way; still another; yet another; a baby born dead—great

1931

The Joy of Cooking, by Irma S. Rombauer, is (privately) published.

relief; an older child dies—sorrow, but nevertheless relief—insurance helps; a mother's death—children scattered into institutions, the father desperate, drunken. . . . Within five years four children are born. The mother, racked and worn, decides this can't go on, and attempts to interrupt the next pregnancy. The siren of the ambulance, death of the mother, orphan children, poverty, misery, slums, child labor, unhappiness, ignorance, destitution. . . . I watched the lights go out, I saw the darkness gradually give way to the first shimmer of dawn, and then a colorful sky heralded the rise of the sun. I knew a new day had come for me and a new world as well. I could now see clearly the various social strata of our life; all its mass problems seemed to be centered around uncontrolled breeding. There was only one thing to be done: call out, start the alarm, get the heather on fire! Awake the womanhood of America to free the motherhood of the world. . . . I would tell the world what was going on in the lives of these poor women. I *would* be heard. No matter what it should cost. *I would be heard.*

That decision gave to Mrs. Sanger the overmastering influence for all the rest of her life. She asked doctors what one could do and was told she'd better keep off that subject or Anthony Comstock would get her—as, indeed, he did in later years. She consulted progressive women, the "feminists," and they assured her that she couldn't do anything until women got the vote. She read and studied, she fell in with a group of social rebels, radical labor leaders, writers. But, she says, "I could not forget the mothers bringing to birth children in poverty and misery." A year or more of study, inquiry and consultation decided her that there was too little knowledge of the subject and too little interest in it anywhere in this country, even in the medical profession, for intelligent, effective work to be done here. She comments that "only the boys of the I.W.W. seemed to grasp the economic significance of this great social question." They gave her names of labor organizers and offered their help to get any knowledge she obtained on family limitation direct to workingmen and their wives. So she decided to go to France and study at first hand the results of generations of family limitation, and she spent there the year before the beginning of the war. She learned much in France, but was dissatisfied because she "wanted something more definite." "I longed," she says, "to see so powerful a force properly directed and controlled."

Back to the United States Mrs. Sanger came and started her magazine, *The Woman Rebel*, of which every now and then the New York Post Office suppressed an issue. It was the beginning of her crusade. Friends begged her to abandon her purpose and drop the paper, visioning for her trials in court and terms in prison. But to every argument she retorted, "Millions of mothers' lives against the comfort and security of one!" She kept the magazine going and wrote a practical pamphlet on "Family Limitation" "dedicated to the wives of workingmen" which she had great difficult in getting printed, because, as one liberal-minded printer told her, it was "a Sing Sing job." Twenty printers refused to touch it, but she would not give up until she found one willing to take the risk because he believed in her crusade. He did it in secret himself, when his shop was supposed to be closed and no one guessed that anything was going on in it.

From that time on there has rarely been an hour of Margaret Sanger's life that lacked excitement, suspense, the peril of arrest, the threat of prison. She tells it all in detail in this book. There is, indeed, so much detail that it blurs the clear-cut outlines of her story. Her account would have been more effective, though possibly it would have carried less of colorful personal interest, if she had omitted some of the less important particulars and had told some portions of her narrative in more summary fashion. But her share in the birth control movement is all here. And it is so large and so important a share that when the history of the whole movement comes to be written, impartially, as part of post-war social development, she will have to be accounted its initial inspiration and its dauntless and daring leader until it had got well on its feet as a worldwide, recognized factor of social evolution. Its high lights have been matters of big newspaper news during recent years. But she supplies the background for them by telling of the steady work of propaganda, of trying to reach and convert to her aid influential men and women, of trying to make the public realize the evil possibilities of the laws that sent her to prison and suppressed her literature, and especially of trying constantly to give the knowledge she had acquired to the wives and mothers of the poor. Now and then there is a brief and deeply touching glimpse of how much the phase of her work appealed to her and compelled her activities. There was the tragic face of a poor woman at her birth control clinic in Brownsville, who, when Mrs. Sanger was arrested and whisked away to trial and a thirty-day sentence in Queens County penitentiary, had run after the patrol wagon calling, "Come back and save me!" There are extended accounts and vivid description, from Mrs. Sanger's individual viewpoint, of the suppression by the police—although the author says that she telephoned Police Headquarters at once to ask why this action had been taken and was told that they had issued no such orders—of the Town Hall mass meeting in 1921 and of the police raid in 1929 on the offices in West Fifteenth Street of the Clinical Research Bureau she had organized and through several years had seen extend and increase its work. Mrs. Sanger makes known with emphasis and with frequent and apparently well-sustained charges the religious influence which she is very sure has instigated and pushed through these and other attempts to interfere with and nullify her crusade.

Not every crusader can see, after less than twenty years of work, such immediate, important and world-wide results as Mrs. Sanger counts up in the latter part of her book. In this country public opinion has swung around to her support, large church bodies and important organizations of men and women have declared in her favor and she begins to have hope that soon Federal legislation will bring ultimate victory. And at the end she affirms again, with undiminished faith, her conviction that the problem of birth control "concerns in its intimate aspects every one of us and in its remoter consequences the very life of the nation and the race."

The early chapters of the volume narrate interestingly some of the events and describe the environment of her childhood, thereby throwing much light on the author's temperament and endowments and making clear the force of the inner imperatives that have controlled her life.

Future Shock

Brave New World by Aldous Huxley
February 7, 1932

BY JOHN CHAMBERLAIN

DIGNITY, beyond all else, has attended the creation of the classic Utopias, from that of Plato on down to Edward Bellamy's perfectly geared industrial machine. Conceived in kindliness of spirit, dedicated to the high future of the race and offered with becoming humility as contributions to the questionable science of human happiness, these classic Utopias have only too often seemed mere parodies of the Napoleonic State, the Taylor system of the laboratory where guinea pigs are bred to predestined fates. It has remained for Aldous Huxley to build the Utopia to end Utopias—or such Utopias as go to mechanics for their inspiration, at any rate. He has satirized the imminent spiritual trustification of mankind, and has made rowdy and impertinent sport of the World State whose motto shall be Community, Identity, Stability.

This slogan, Mr. Huxley seems to be saying under the noise made by his knockabout farce, is thoroughly unbiological. Mankind moves forward by stumbling—we almost said progressing—from one unstable equilibrium to another unstable equilibrium; and if the human animal ever ceases to do this he will go to the ant (the sluggard!) and become a hived creature. Mr. Huxley doesn't like the prospect. So here we have him, as entertainingly atrabilious as ever he was in *Antic Hay* or *Point Counter Point*, mocking the Fords, the Hitlers, the Mussolinis, the Sir Alfred Monds, the Owen D. Youngs—all who would go back on laissez-faire and on toward the servile state. His Utopia has much in common with those of the nineteenth century—everything, in fact, but their informing and propulsive faith. It is as regimented as Etienne Cabet's Icaria, the communal Utopia seemingly made of breeding the bureaucracy of the first Napoleon with the ghostly positivism of Auguste Comte; and its ideas of dispensing *panem et circenses* to the populace are precisely those of Edward Bellamy's *Looking Backward* [2000–1887]—only Mr. Huxley, who has had the opportunity to visit moving-picture emporium and radio studio, knows the difference between possibility and actuality in popular entertainment. With the Highland Park and River Rouge plants, the Foster and Catchings ideology of consumption, the Five-Year Plan, the synthetic creation of vitamins, the spectacle of a chicken heart that lives on without benefit of surrounding chicken, the flight of Post and Gatty and the control of diabetics all behind him in point of time, Mr. Huxley has had an easy task to turn the nineteenth-century hope into a counsel of despair. And like an older utopian, Mr. Huxley finds no room for the poet in his Model T. world. His poets are all Emotional Engineers.

Behold, then, the gadget satirically enshrined. As Bellamy anticipated the radio in 1888, Mr. Huxley has foreseen the displacement of the talkie by the "feelie," a type of moving picture that will give tactile as well as visual and aural delight. Spearmint has given way to Sex Hormone gum—the favorite chew of one of Mr. Huxley's minor characters, Mr. Benito Hoover. Grammes of soma— a non-hangover-producing substitute for rum—are eaten daily by the populace; they drive away the blues. God had dissolved into Ford (sometimes called Freud), and the jingle goes "Ford's in his flivver, all's well with the world." Ford's book, *My Life and Work*, has become the new Bible. The Wurlitzer has been supplemented by the scent organ, which plays all the tunes from cinnamon to camphor, with occasional whiffs of kidney pudding for discord. Babies, of course, are born—or rather, decanted—in the laboratory; and by a process known as the Bodanovsky one egg can be made to proliferate into ninety-six children, all of them identical in feature, form and brain power. The Bodanovsky groups are used to man the factories, work the mines, and so on; there can be no jealousy in a Bodanovsky group, for its ideal is like-mindedness. But if there is little jealousy in Mr. Huxley's world, there is still shame; a girl blushes to think of having children in the good old viviparous way. To obviate the possibility of childbirth, the girls—or such of them as are not born sterile Freemartins—are put through daily Malthusian Drill in their impressionable 'teens. Buttons have disappeared and children play games of "Hunt the Zipper."

We are introduced at the outset to the Director of Hatcheries and Conditioning for Central London, who takes us through his plant and explains the creation of the various castes: Alphas, Betas, Gammas, Deltas and Epsilons, each caste ranging from minus to plus. Before a child is turned over to his station in life, he is thoroughly conditioned, by injection of hypnopaedic wisdom during sleep, to like precisely what he has to like. But slips there are, even in the most mechanical of all possible worlds, and owing to some oversight—possibly the spilling of alcohol into the blood surrogate upon which he was fed in his prenatal days—Bernard Marx, Mr. Huxley's hero, is dissatisfied.

Bernard loves Lenina Crowne in a sort of old-fashioned romantic way. He longs for *solitude à deux*. So with her he takes the rocket for a vacation in the New Mexican savage reservation. By sheer coincidence, the Director of Hatcheries and Conditioning for Central London had spent a vacation once upon a time in this reservation; and had lost his girl, a Betaminus, in a sudden and confusing desert thunderstorm. Bernard, of course, runs upon the girl—now an old woman—and her son, John, the Savage, born viviparously. Quickly he gets into touch with Mustapha Mond, his Fordship, the Resident Controller for Western Europe. Shall he bring them back by rocket to London? His Fordship thinks furiously and decides in the positive; and for the sake of educating the populace, the Savage and his mother are shot over to England.

It is Mr. Huxley's habit to be deadly in earnest. One feels that he is pointing a high moral lesson in satirizing Utopia. Yet it is a little difficult to take alarm, for, as the hell-diver sees not the mud, and the angle worm knows not the intricacies of the Einstein theory, so the inhabitants of Mr. Huxley's world could hardly be conscious of the satirical overtones of the Huxleyan prose. And the bogy of mass production seems a little overwrought, since the need for it as religion, in a world that could rigidly control its birth rate and in which no one could make any money out of advertising and selling, would be scarcely intelligible even to His Fordship. Finally, if Mr. Huxley is unduly bothered about the impending static world, let him go back to his biology and meditate on the possibility that even in laboratory-created children mutations might be inevitable. A highly mechanized world, yes; but it might breed one Rousseau to shake it to the foundations and send men back to the hills and the goatskins. Meanwhile, while we are waiting for *My Life and Work* to replace the Bible, *Brave New World* may divert us; it offers a stop-gap.

When Life Became Journalism

1919 by John Dos Passos
March 13, 1932

BY JOHN CHAMBERLAIN

IN 1919 John Dos Passos continues his explorations in the modern American and Americanized world which began with *The 42nd Parallel* and which will continue, one assumes, until the series is rounded off in either a trilogy or a tetralogy. The initial panel in the series commenced with an America that was growing up after the Spanish-American War; it ended, inconclusively, with Charlie Anderson, a kid from North Dakota, setting out for Paris at the outset of our own participation in the World War. *1919* goes on from where *The 42nd Parallel* leaves off. We meet old characters from the first book, and some new ones are introduced. Meanwhile, history spins on its crazy way; the war is fought; the peace is negotiated; A. Mitchell Palmer starts his Red-hunting campaign, which is resisted by Walter Lippmann and others; Wilson collapses; the Unknown Soldier is buried at Arlington, with President Harding making a speech. Some lives are explored by Mr. Dos Passos with finality; some are left poised on the edge of the unknown and waiting for the third panel of this *comédie humaine*. The trick of interspersing the separate stories of various characters with "newsreel" features (which recall to mind Mark Sullivan's books), with a "camera eye" department designed to give Dos Passos's own point of vantage in the time and space under consideration, and with driving, often splenetic Whitmanesque biographies of significant Americans, such as Randolph Bourne, John Reed, Woodrow Wilson and Theodore Roosevelt, is resorted to once more, as it was in *The 42nd Parallel*. The trick of evoking mood by interspersed data is, again, successful; it saves Mr. Dos Passos from being "discursive" in the middle of tense narrative, and yet it enables him to retain the values of discursiveness. Precedent for this sort of thing may be found in Hemingway's *In Our Time*.

Like *The 42nd Parallel*, 1919 is primarily a "news" novel. It is, of course, a satire on expansionist, "on the make," raffish and vulgar America. But it is more than a mere satire; it is also true characterization—more so than *The 42nd Parallel*. It is able to stick as close to the headlines of the newspapers as it does because its characters, after the manner of so many Americans, live in and by the news. Dick Savage, the Harvard man; Eveline Hutchins, the Chicago girl; Ben Compton, the radical; even Joe Williams, the sailor, all are "conditioned" by the daily papers to an extent that novelists of the past would be at a loss to understand. Even the personal problems of these people are shaped by the news and the men who make the news.

Because Mr. Dos Passos has realized that a shot fired in China, a kidnapped baby, a reconstruction finance corporation, a tennis tournament, a rumor that Baltimore and Ohio bonds are a good buy, and so on, can cause more perturbation or elation or depression in the minds of more people than traditional problems of virtue and vice, his novel is more true to life on a tightly meshed planet than most of us like to admit. The universal solvents of our grandfathers' world were, in settled areas, the community and the church, and the values engendered thereof; the solvents of our own urban life are the stock market quotation pages, the rumors of wars, the bulletins of the booms and the depressions. We have become, almost literally, all eyes and ears. Every one knows as much; but our novelists have been slow to realize it.

Mr. Dos Passos is, however, an exception; one may safely call him the most adventurous, the most widely experienced, the man with the broadest sympathies (we do not say the deepest), among our novelists since Sinclair Lewis bade goodbye to Martin Arrowsmith. Hemingway, who is Dos Passos's closest competitor in exploring the modern jungle, has been almost solely orientated in personal problems raised by the war; he is, as Malcolm Cowley has said, "not yet demobilized." Scott Fitzgerald, in *The Great Gatsby*, has utilized strictly contemporary material for a modern comedy of disenchantment; and a number of Southern writers have become fascinated by an agrarian decay that has been hastened by the onrush of industrialism. But no one has ranged as widely in post-Dreiserian and post-Howellsian America as Mr. Dos Passos.

Because of their living in and by the headlines, Mr. Dos Passos's characters are, sometimes, very flat and transparent. Mr. Moorehouse, for instance; this dollar-a-year man, who takes a government job in Paris and is seen moving about at the Peace Conference, is a four-flusher. Every newspaper reporter knows it, yet he has a mighty reputation. Daughter, the Texan, throws herself away because unharnessed energy, such as hers, must sputter out on thin air. And Joe Williams, who might have been content in a different society under his own vine and fig tree, is thrown about the world on tramp ships because that is the fate of willing souls without much brain-power in the contemporary world. We know of no better portrait in literature of the poor, dumb, driven devil than this Joe Williams.

Two of Mr. Dos Passos's characters are sounded out with much tenderness, sympathy and comprehension. They are Joe Williams and Eveline Hutchins; no characterizations in *The 42nd Parallel* can equal them. One character, Dick Savage, is less successful precisely because he has no character to get hold of. Daughter goes through the book like a rocket; she falls before we really can get a grip on her.

All of the characters, however, have a public reason for existing in Mr. Dos Passos's book. Through them we see, at one remove, how Clemenceau and Lloyd George turned the flank of Woodrow Wilson; we see the turmoil and the stridency of the nations at war and at peace. We go back to the newspapers of the war decade, not by visiting a library or a newspaper morgue, but by making the acquaintance of certain typical onlookers of the decade. These people's lives are a sort of ambulatory journalism; they reflect no deep meaning; even their tragedies pass away as a new crop of headlines calls the world to new news.

The prose instrument which Mr. Dos Passos has fashioned for himself in 1919 is vastly superior to that of *Three Soldiers*, his early war novel. Although it abounds in clichés, vulgarisms, curses, illiterate ellipses and shorthands of speech, the language of 1919 is really a literary language; Mr. Dos Passos has quintessentialized and distilled, compressed and foreshortened, until he is able to give the overtones of common chatter without resorting to a dreary literalism.

First Impressions

The Crime of Inspector Maigret and *The Death of Monsieur Gallet* by Georges Simenon
September 4, 1932

1932

BY ISAAC ANDERSON

Laura Ingalls Wilder's first book about her family, *Little House in the Big Woods*, appears.

THE YOUNG FRENCHMAN who writes under the name of Georges Simenon and who is introduced to the American public by the simultaneous publication of these two novels is only 28 years old and has already written 280 detective stories. He turns them out at the rate of four a month, and he has been known to write a book in four days. What is more to the point, they are, if one may judge from these two samples, well-constructed stories with unusual plots. In *The Crime of Inspector Maigret*, the inspector, having completed another case upon which he has been working, sees a man acting in a suspicious manner and decides to follow him. Technically, he becomes guilty of the crime of driving a man to suicide, but the net result of his investigations is the uncovering of a most bizarre crime committed many years earlier. In *The Death of Monsieur Gallet*, Inspector Maigret again finds that the death he has been assigned to investigate is the concluding episode of a drama of the past. Inspector Maigret's outstanding characteristics are infinite patience, dogged perseverance and a disinclination to be satisfied with anything less than a complete and logical solution of the problem upon which he happens to be engaged. Simenon's American publishers cannot expect to keep pace with the tremendous output of this extraordinarily prolific author, but they have promised to present more of his works from time to time. And that is good news for the detective story fans.

Mississippi Mud

Light in August
by William Faulkner
October 9, 1932

BY J. DONALD ADAMS

WITH THIS NEW NOVEL, Mr. Faulkner has taken a tremendous stride forward. To say that *Light in August* is an astonishing performance is not to use the word lightly. That somewhat crude and altogether brutal power which thrust itself through his previous work is in this book disciplined to a greater effectiveness than one would have believed possible in so short a time. There are still moments when Mr. Faulkner seems to write of what is horrible purely from a desire to shock his readers or else because it holds for him a fascination from which he cannot altogether escape. There are still moments when his furious contempt for the human species seems a little callow.

But no reader who has followed his work can fail to be enormously impressed by the transformation which has been worked upon it. Not only does Faulkner emerge from his book a stylist of striking strength and beauty; he permits some of his people, if not his chief protagonist, to act sometimes out of motives which are human in their decency; indeed, he permits the Rev. Gail Hightower to live his life by them. In a word, Faulkner has admitted justice and compassion to his scheme of things. There was a hint of this to come in the treatment of Benbow in *Sanctuary*. The gifts which he had to begin with are strengthened — the gifts for vivid narrative and the fresh-minted phrase. His eye for the ignoble in human nature is more keen than ever, but his vision is also less restricted.

There are two or three scenes in this book more searing than anything Faulkner has heretofore written, but they are also better integrated. Although the pattern of *Light in August* is streaked with red, there is a blending here with colors both more subdued and more luminous than were customary to his palette. The locale is again the "deep South"; and the characters include the white trash of which he has drawn such relentless portraits, plain folk of a better strain, whites of a higher order, Negroes, and for the subject of his most detailed attention a poor white with a probable mixture of Negro blood.

Light in August is a powerful novel, a book which secures Mr. Faulkner's place in the very front rank of American writers of fiction. He definitely has removed the objection made against him that he cannot lift his eyes above the dunghill. There are times when Mr. Faulkner is not unaware of the stars. One hesitates to make conjectures as to the inner lives of those who write about the lives of others, but Mr. Faulkner's work has seemed to be that of a man who has, at some time, been desperately hurt; a man whom life has at some point badly cheated. There are indications that he has regained his balance.

Sick of It All

Miss Lonelyhearts by Nathanael West
April 23, 1933

1933

Thomas Mann leaves Germany at the age of 57 for a brief lecture tour, and does not return for 16 years.

THIS IS HUMOR, if you like, or satire, if you see it that way. The orthodox communist critic would call its spirit "defeatism." Edmund Wilson speaks of the author as an original comic poet, a humorist with a philosophico-poetic point of view. Erskine Caldwell thinks the book will be hailed as clever and amusing by the general public, but to him it is a tragic story.

It is a difficult piece of work to put one's finger on, for it scarcely falls into any of the kinds of light reading with which we are familiar. Its wit and satire are as bitter as Swift's; and its despair, on its unambitious level, as profound. In short, the little volume is not to be classified with the *Gentlemen Prefer Blondes*, the Ring Lardner, the "Of Thee I Sing" or the "Once in a Lifetime" school of

American humorous satire. It is not directed at surface absurdities in a spirit of indignation, contempt, hatred or ironic amusement. It does have a philosophical undercurrent, and Mr. Wilson is right, too, in speaking of the poetic approach. That is borne out by the language. The philosophical undercurrent is similar to that in Dostoyevsky. Here is another record of "poor people" — but laid in hard twentieth-century America, not in mystical nineteenth-century Russia. Here the disturbing Christian pity for the rejected and despised turns against itself in revulsion and disgust. And wit, horseplay, liquor, excitement and hardboiledness overlie the pain of vicarious suffering with and for others. This, of course, is the gospel according to Tolstoy.

Miss Lonelyhearts, the young newspaper man detailed to conduct the advice column on a New York newspaper, scion of Puritans, finds a lump growing within him after a month spent in reading thirty or so letters a day from the sick, the discouraged, the broken-hearted, the bewildered. The letters begin to "get" him. He wonders if he has a "Christ complex." His hardboiled boss, Shrike, enjoys the joke and with his malicious and gleeful wit rubs salt into his wounds. When Miss Lonelyhearts gets sick from the strain, Shrike goes to his bedside and delivers himself of a very funny speech, pointing out to the sacrificial invalid what steps he might take to cleanse his soul from the slush and tosh he has been forced to write daily in answer to the sincere and pitiful appeals from his hundreds of pitiable readers. He might, says this Mephistopheles, go back to the farm. He might flee to the South Seas or turn hedonist or commit suicide or take to drugs. But, after pointing out the difficulties involved in pursuing any of these courses, the amiable Shrike advises him to turn to Christ, "the Miss Lonelyhearts of Miss Lonelyhearts," for his salvation. Shrike leaves, much pleased with himself. But the thing is no joke to Miss Lonelyhearts. On his spirit rests the burden of "Sick-of-it-all," "Desperate," "Harold S." and "Broad Shoulders" ("Don't think I am broad-shouldered, but that is the way I feel about life and me, I mean").

Miss Lonelyhearts's various adventures — with "the clean old man," the "dead pan," his girl, Mrs. Shrike, and finally with two of his correspondents in whose lives he becomes strangely involved — as he wavers between Christ and despair, between bouts of drinking and resolutions of humility, carry along the story.

The novel is ostensibly a piece of humorous fiction. But do not class it with the clever wisecracking little volumes that emerge seasonally from the presses to carry on the tradition of bald American exaggeration. It is ostensibly satiric. But its irony has roots to it. The wit is hard, brilliant and very funny. But the tragic letters seeking help and advice are human documents and well sustain the burden of the underlying meaning.

Miss Lonelyhearts stands to be one of the hits of the year, to win both popular and critical approval.

1933

The Nazis burn books, and Martin Heidegger joins the Nazi Party.

A Hymn of Hate

My Battle by Adolf Hitler
October 15, 1933

BY JAMES W. GERARD

THOSE WHO WOULD SOLVE the riddle of Hitlerism and the present extraordinary attitude of the German people must search the history of Germany. The Thirty Years' War, which ended in 1648, reduced the population of Germany from 24,000,000 to 4,000,000, polygamy was legalized and human flesh was on sale in the markets of Heidelberg. Only the strong and the ruthless survived.

Following the defeat of Prussia by Napoleon came quickly the battles of Leipzig and Waterloo, where with German aid Napoleon's power was destroyed, and then, later in the century, came the crushing of France in 1870, the establishment of the German Empire and the final hegemony of Prussia. And remember that feudalism existed nominally or psychologically until a late date. It was not until 1817 that serfdom was ended in Prussia and up to the World War the government service, as well as the army, was dominated by Prussian aristocrats. With the ending of the World War humiliation came to a nation which at that war's beginning was drunk with military power and commercial success.

The German people adore the tramp of massed men, the music of military bands, the waving of banners, the conquering songs of hundreds of thousands and all the "pomp and circumstance" of war. Hitler has catered to this feeling so that, today, Germany is a camp, unarmed, perhaps, but one great military camp, psychologically, if not materially, ready for a war of conquest and revenge. Hitler could not have attained such power unless he represented the thoughts and aspirations of a majority of the population.

With these historical facts in mind one is prepared for a better understanding of Hitler's *My Battle*. Now what manner of man, as disclosed by his book, is this Hitler, who has forced such a unification of Germany as Bismarck never dreamed of and who has arrayed a whole people from children to elders in a military formation which can only mean a war of revenge and who has revived the persecutions of the Middle Ages against an intellectual and harmless race? In the first place, do not think of this man Hitler as without brains and do not listen to the gossip which proclaims him morally unsound.

The first part of the book is an account of the author's life. In the first pages, in telling of his birth in a little town on the frontiers of Austria and Germany, he writes that at the outset of his career, when he was a poor workingman, he held to the hope, which at this moment he is endeavoring to realize, that Germany

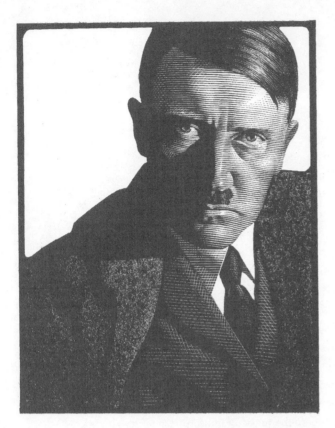

and Austria will become one. Vitally interesting as is his account of his early struggles, of the war, of his political life and revolutionary attempts, what we must look for in his book is an answer to the question, What are the policies, what are the aims of this extraordinary man who today rules Germany with a rod of steel?

In Hitler's ideal State the child is born, not a citizen, but someone who is a "subject of the State," and not until he has undergone the school education to be prescribed for every German and then the bodily exercises as laid down by the State and after that his training in the army under universal military service "the young man, if healthy and with a blameless record, will be solemnly invested with the rights of State citizenship." "The German girl is a subject of the State, but marriage makes her a citizen."

From this book we see what Hitler is in process of creating in Germany—an absolutely unified State, no longer Saxons, Bavarians or Prussians, only Germans—citizens of a Spartan State where all are educated alike, where all must undergo physical training and the discipline of the army, where wealth or birth will be of little account. Over this unified State is to preside one man.

For centuries the Jews have been persecuted and despised in the Central Empires of Europe. I believe that Hitler in his rise to power took advantage of this prejudice. And here it is necessary to compare the abridged book with the original work in German. Hitler's book in German in the current edition is of 781 pages. This translation is compressed into 297.

Even in the abridged translation there are pages and pages of attacks upon the Jews, but many more pages of such attacks are omitted and something of the spirit of the original is lost, much of the bitter prejudice and libel of the Jews. For instance, on page 63 of the German book occurs the sentence, "One could study in Vienna the connection of Jewry with prostitution and still more with white slavery," etc. I cannot find this in the book under review. Nor sentences like this, "Consequently this kind of Democracy [majority rule] has become the instrument of that race which must hide because of its inner aims from the sun, now and in all future times." And, "Only the Jew can praise an institution which is as dirty and untrue as he is himself."

Hitler is doing much for Germany, his unification of the Germans, his destruction of communism, his training of the young, his creation of a Spartan State animated by patriotism, his curbing of parliamentary government, so unsuited to the German character; his protection of the right of private property are all good; and, after all, what the Germans do in their own territory is their own business, except for one thing—the persecution and practical expulsion of the Jews.

These Jews have been German citizens for centuries. They fought for their country. No charge of spying, of treason, of cowardice in war has been brought against them. The civilized world took a strong stand against the Turks because of their massacres of the Bulgarians at one time, and of the Armenians at another, against the atrocities of the Belgian Congo, against the cruelties in the rubber forests of the Amazon. Now that the world is bound in smaller compass by radio, airplane, express steamers, by constant congresses of religions and commerce, we have all of us a right to criticize, to boycott a nation which reverts to the horrible persecutions of the Dark Ages.

It is with sadness, tinged with fear for the world's future, that we read Hitler's hymn of hate against that race which has added so many names to the roll of the great in science, in medicine, in surgery, in music and the arts, in literature and all uplifting human endeavor.

A Field Guide to the Birds, by Roger Tory Peterson, has never been out of print since its first edition.

First Impressions

The Post Man Always Rings Twice by James M. Cain
February 18, 1934

BY HAROLD STRAUSS

EVERY SO OFTEN a writer turns up who forces us to revalue our notions of the realistic manner, for, no less than reality itself, it is relative and inconstant, depending on the period, the fashion, the point of view. There is the feeling of realism, of intense realism, in James M. Cain's work, and yet he cannot be compared to such diverse types of realists as Zola, Ibsen, Sandburg, Dreiser, or Hemingway. It is the hard-boiled manner that has been heralded for some time, and is now upon us. It is the manner that James T. Farrell has been attempting in an inadequate way, that Dashiell Hammett has stumbled on. But Cain is to be compared to none of these, for where Farrell loses the strands of his story, Cain rushes forward like a hound on a hot scent; where Hammett's people act tough mostly out of boredom, Cain's are toughness itself. In short, Cain has developed the hard-boiled manner as a perfect instrument of narration.

He takes a young bum with a background of pool-rooms and rod-riding, a mug fresh from a binge in Tia Juana, and sets him down at a lonely roadside gas-station in California. Here is the first sentence: "They threw me off the hay truck about noon." The impact of that is tremendous. But more than that, it is a complete characterization of the hero, for there is just one kind of man who would ride a hay truck and be kicked off of it as an unwanted passenger, and then comment about it in just that manner.

Cain is an old newspaper man who learned his reporting well, so well that he makes Hemingway look like a lexicographer and Caldwell like a sob sister at her first eviction. He would be an asset to the tabloids, because he leaves lots of space for pictures. His story is a third as long as most novels, and its success is due entirely to one quality: Cain can get down to the primary impulses of greed and sex in fewer words than any writer we know of. He has exorcised all the inhibitions; there is a minimum of reason, of complexity, of what we commonly call civilization, between an impulse and its gratification. In the broadest sense he is no asset as yet to American literature, for he adds nothing in breadth, but only in intensity, to our consciousness of life. But we want to see more of his work. Meanwhile, we defy any one who has broached that remarkable first sentence to put his book down without finishing it.

First Impressions

A *Field Guide to the Birds* by Roger Tory Peterson
May 6, 1934

BY JOHN KIERAN

THIS HANDY VOLUME is offered as "a bird book on a new plan," possibly under the influence of the New Deal in wider but not always greener fields. The jacket warning includes the public notice that "This book will at once take its place as an indispensable pocket companion for Eastern bird students, both beginning and advanced." If the word "helpful" is substituted for the word "indispensable," this reviewer will accept the claim without further question.

This book was written for "popular" guidance. It is distinctly for amateurs, beginning or advanced. It tells, and shows by charts in color and black and white, how to distinguish the Royal from the Caspian tern, how to recognize the four little flycatchers, the Empidomax group, and just what to look for in trying to decide whether a shy sparrow in the underbrush is a Lincoln's or not. It is, in fact, a fine compendium of "field marks" and the "field mark" is as helpful to the wandering bird student as the highway signs are to a motoring tourist.

Even the scientists and field experts have their little debates over the best "field marks" or "diagnostic" points in difficult species, and possibly even the most advanced class in ornithology could pick up a few helpful hints for field work in this book. But definitely it is not for the scientist. The fact that, in the descriptions of the species, all measurements are omitted, is enough to settle that item at the outset.

But for the amateur, the eager bird student, the text and charts will be a real help in the big days afield or the quiet evenings at home when a satisfying expedition has been completed, or an even more ambitious one is being planned.

First Impressions

Jonah's Gourd Vine by Zora Neale Hurston
May 6, 1934

BY MARGARET WALLACE

JONAH'S GOURD VINE can be called without fear of exaggeration the most vital and original novel about the American Negro that has yet been written by a member of the Negro race. Miss Hurston, who is a graduate of Barnard College and a student of anthropology, has made the study of Negro folklore her special province. This may very well account for the brilliantly authentic flavor of her novel and for her excellent rendition of Negro dialect. Unlike the dialect in most novels about the American Negro, this does not seem to be merely the speech of white men with the spelling distorted. Its essence lies rather in the rhythm and balance of the sentences, in the warm artlessness of the phrasing.

No amount of special knowledge of her subject, however, could have made Jonah's Gourd Vine other than a mediocre novel if it were not for Miss Hurston's notable talents as a story-teller. In John, the big yellow Negro preacher, and in Lucy Potts, his tiny brown wife, she has created two characters who are intensely real and human and whose outlines will remain in the reader's memory long after the book has been laid aside. They are part and parcel of the tradition of their race, which is as different from ours as night from day; yet Miss Hurston has delineated them with such warmth and sympathy that they appeal to us first of all as human beings, confronting a complex of human problems with whatever grace and humor, intelligence and steadfastness they can muster.

John was a "yaller nigger," hated by his dusky foster-father because of the white blood in his veins. "His mamma named him Two-Eye John after a preacher she heered, but dey called him John-Buddy for short." When he was too big to be beaten or bullied the share-cropping Ned Crittenden turned him off the farm. John got a job on Mr. Alf Pearson's place, and created with his big young body and his rich voice a great stir among the brown maidens in Mr. Pearson's service, and fell in love with Lucy Potts, a bright-eyed little girl who could run faster and recite longer pieces than anybody else in school. In the interests of his ardent courtship, John learned to read, and when Lucy attained her fifteenth birthday they were married.

John really loved Lucy and intended to be true to her, but he was totally unable to resist the open and insistent blandishments of other women. Even after he felt a "call" to the ministry he was always mixed up with some woman or other, frequently to the point of an open breach with his horrified and interested congregation. John's long and futile struggle with his lusty appetites, Lucy's cleverness and devotion in protecting him from the consequences, his entanglement after Lucy's death with the magic-making Hattie, his public ruin and public regeneration all make an extraordinarily absorbing and credible tale.

Not the least charm of the book, however, is its language—rich, expressive and lacking in self-conscious artifice. From the rolling and dignified rhythms of John's last sermon to the humorous aptness of such a word as "shickalacked," to express the noise and motion of a locomotive, there will be much in it to delight the reader. It is to be hoped that Miss Hurston will give us other novels in the same colorful idiom.

The True Story If Not the Real One

Call It Sleep by Henry Roth
February 17, 1935

BY H. W. BOYNTON

ONE APPROACHES THIS NOVEL without much hope. Another story of the New York ghetto child, told by himself. How many of these documents have sprung already from that sultry soil! And how seldom they escape bathos, for all their insistence on the tragic dignity of their theme. Is the squalor of fact too much for them, so that they are unable to bring that enemy into necessary balance with the effort of its desperate challenger Man? Mere real life, of course, and any literal record of it, must be serenely indifferent to dramatic balance. But the autobiographical novel has no immunities beyond other kinds of novel. It must tell a story. And *Call It Sleep* does tell, dramatically for all its mass of detail, the true story if not the real one, of a new-born personality struggling desperately to salvage a place for itself and its dream out of the welter and squalor of "the melting pot."

The long narrative covers only the period that marks the passage of David Schearl from his eighth to his ninth year, and from a prolonged infancy to sudden initiation into some of the ruder mysteries of home and slum life. He is a sensitive and imaginative child, and up to this time his mother's coddling has kept him safe. Now he is terrified by the world that lies beyond sight and sound of her. And even within that zone he begins to feel unsafe. His father is a lean egotist with a persecution complex. He is unable to work with other men, fancies they are always sneering and laughing at him. Out of these imaginations brew sudden and furious rages that sometimes seek outlet in physical violence. Still, though he is always changing his jobs he is never without one. It is easier for him to make a living than a friend. But what is a life spent in making a living? He feels that he has been a stupid victim of betrayal: "I sell my days for a little silver—a little paper—sixteen smirched leaves a week—I'll never buy them back with gold." So he groans, but his wife, Mama Schearl, the patient, the abundant—hers is the deeper disillusion. Why does he want his days back? she asks—she wouldn't have any of hers.

Schearl is dimly conscious of something lacking in their relation, and jealousy of the boy leads to increasing harshness. From fear of him David at last dares leave the peril of home for his predestined playground, the street. There an inherited fastidiousness revolts from the filthy speech and habits of the gang with whom he is thrown. We are spared nothing of what he hears and sees. In this and other connections the book lays all possible stress on the nastiness of the human animal. It is the fashion, and we must make the best of the spectacle of a fine book deliberately and as it were doggedly smeared with verbal filthiness. Has the world arrived once more at the phase of decadence (Rome knew it, and France, and seventeenth-century England) which makes a cult of the excremental, and looks on queasiness under any provocation as a sign of mawkish reaction?

Young David, we say, does react, for a time, then the game gets him. But though he learns to speak filth it is always with a sense of sin, and this sense becomes in time an obsession. Therefore he thrills to the story of Isaiah and the angel-borne coal from the altar with which his lips were made pure. And in the end we find him venturing life itself in quest of a like purification. For the boy is a mystic, quivering in the presence of the unseen, often losing contact with reality.

Such is the thin outline of David's story, behind which, around which, moves the various pageantry of the East Side, its polyglot, polychrome crowds given to apparent promiscuity but governed by the sharp racial reservations of that strange world. Many figures detach themselves, with their special voices, from

1935

The WPA is created. Many writers make it through the Depression on the Federal Writers' Project.

the babel. And often the spotlight is diverted from the main scene to some by-vision, cellar or saloon or roof-top, in which a special aspect of the mad city comes to focus. Often, reading these pages, you recall the kaleidoscopic effect of *Manhattan Transfer* or *The 42nd Parallel*. Once, during that tremendous hour when David goes in search of death or his God, you come upon a tapestried pattern so strongly colored and firmly woven that you find yourself conceding, against all qualms, the rightness as well as the (you would have said) unspeakable grossness of its human ingredients.

Gender Bending

Sex and Temperament: In Three Primitive Societies
by Margaret Mead
May 26, 1935

BY FLORENCE FINCH KELLY

THIS MARGARET MEAD is a dangerous person. She goes down to New Guinea, studies primitive tribes for two years and comes back with a book like a bomb that she drops into the complacent, fundamental conviction of the Occidental world, both scientific and social, that the sexes are innately different in their psychological attributes and that the male is dominant by right of brain and brawn. Her bomb explodes and scatters fragments over all the surrounding area and the first thing she knows some indignant voice will be crying out that this is an outrage and there ought to be a law—.

Those who read her previous books, *Coming of Age in Samoa* and *Growing Up in New Guinea*, will know with what keen observation she studies her materials and with what vigorous thinking she correlates the results. But this new book delves even deeper into the roots of life and shows a more confident grasp of the significance of her findings. Whether or not one is disturbed by them, one must admire the fearlessness with which she challenges approved scientific principles and universally sanctioned social usage. For what Margaret Mead has brought back from the South Seas is a demonstration which she believes warrants her conclusion that there is no inherent psychologic difference between the sexes and that the differences that seem and are believed to be inherent are merely the result of social environment and training.

The major part of Miss Mead's book is devoted to describing the social roles which custom in each of three tribes in New Guinea demands shall be differentiated and played by the sexes separately. She takes up first the Arapesh, whose general portrait she draws as being, both men and women, gentle, amiable, cooperative, taking pleasure in subordinating self to the needs of those who are weaker and younger, feeling delight in "that part of parenthood which we consider to be specially maternal, the minute, loving care for the little child and the selfless delight in its progress toward maturity."

In astonishing contrast she found the culture of the Mundugumor, who were separated by only about a hundred miles from the Arapesh. The Mundugumor have gone to the opposite extreme and, again ignoring sex as a basis for the establishment of personality differences, "have standardized the behavior of both men and women as actively masculine, virile and without any of the softening and mellowing characteristics that we are accustomed to believe are inalienably womanly."

Next came study of the Tchambuli, a lake-dwelling people, possessing a lively artistic instinct which is manifest throughout "their pattern of social relations." Practice of art is largely confined to the men, for whom "it is the only important matter in life," while they depend upon the women for support. The women have the real position of power in their culture, they carry the family purse, and if a man wants to spend money he must wheedle it from his wife, "in return for languishing looks and soft words." The women make a solid group, "brisk, patronizing, jovial," while the men, although theoretically dominant, really play "a subservient rôle, depending upon the security given them by the women and even in sex-activity looking to women to give the leads."

In a smoothly flowing, vivid and interesting narrative that fills two-thirds of the book Miss Mead describes in detail the manners and customs, the social heritage and the culture pattern of each of these tribes. In each one she deals also with the social rebels, the deviants from the tribal culture, who flame out into violent behavior or shrink unhappily away into themselves, all of it interesting not only as primitive drama but also for the striking comparisons with similar rebellions in civilized society which she draws.

There was, for instance, Kavíwon, of the Tchambuli, a vigorous young man who rebelled against his subservient position as a man and gave vent to his anger by pushing his spear through his wife's cheek, because, he said, he could not stand her chatter any longer.

In the final chapters, keenly and clearly thought out and brilliantly written, Miss Mead reviews her findings, comes to her conclusions and casts her challenge to the theory and practice of the civilized world. She shows that "we are forced to conclude that human nature is almost unbelievably malleable, responding accurately and contrastingly to contrasting cultural conditions" and that "only to the impact of the whole of the integrated culture upon the growing child can we lay the formation of the contrasting types."

She comes to the conclusion that the distinctive male and female personalities

1936

Dale Carnegie's *How to Win Friends and Influence People* begins an avalanche of self-help books.

civilization believes to be inherent are "socially produced," that in America, "without conscious plan but none the less surely," social conditioning is doing away with the idea of male dominance, while in Europe, by the same means, fascism is forcing women back into an older and extreme type of subservience, while communism is endeavoring to make the two sexes as much alike as possible. Miss Mead would have civilization achieve a richer culture, with many contrasting values, by weaving "a less arbitrary social fabric, in which each diverse human gift will find a fitting place" and in which no individual will be forced by artificial distinctions, such as that of sex, "into an ill-fitting mold."

A Study in Scarlett

Gone With the Wind by Margaret Mitchell
July 5, 1936

THIS IS BEYOND a doubt one of the most remarkable first novels produced by an American writer. It is also one of the best. *Gone With the Wind* is by no means a great novel. But it is a long while since the American reading public has been offered such a bounteous feast of excellent story telling.

At least four of the people in this book achieve a quality of life as vivid as may be caught on the printed page. Many things happen in her book; it is full of movement, but the guns are offstage. So too are the great figures which the war produced; they are only spoken names, and the things which happened to Scarlett O'Hara and to Ashley Wilkes, to his wife Melanie and to Rhett Butler, are the things which happened to many other lives in that time and place.

The story opens in the plantation country of Northern Georgia, immediately before the war. Most of the action takes place in and about Atlanta, the sprawling new city of the South, a crossroads planted in the red mud and soon a hustling town, rising as the railroads come and cross it east and west and north and south. That choice of Atlanta (Miss Mitchell's native city) as the focal point of her novel was a happy one. Atlanta, once the war was begun, was much more the nerve center of the lower South than Charleston, where it was born, or the other older cities, like Savannah and Augusta, which looked pridefully askance at the blustering and arrogant newcomer.

But Miss Mitchell's real triumph is Scarlett O'Hara, a heroine lacking in many virtues—in nearly all, one might say, but courage. She is a vital creature, this Scarlett, alive in every inch of her, selfish, unprincipled, ruthless, greedy and dominating, but with a backbone of supple, springing steel. Daughter of an immigrant Irishman who by force of character and personal charm fought his way into the ranks of the plantation nabobs and married a belle of aristocratic family, she was earthily Irish, with but little trace of her mother's gentle strain, and a complete rebel against the standards and taboos of the society in which she was reared. She is a memorable figure in American fiction. But she lives in her own right, completely, and will, I suspect, for a long time to come.

An almost equally vital figure is Rhett Butler, scapegrace son of a Charleston family, cynical and hard-bitten realist (but no more realist than Scarlett herself), who saw the hopelessness of the South's position from the first, and who, as a daring blockade runner, lined his pockets during the war. The remarkable thing about Miss Mitchell's portrait of him is that she has taken a stock figure of melodrama and romance, even to the black mustache, the piercing eyes and the irresistible way with women, and made him credible and alive.

The battle of wills between these two, set against the cross-current of Scarlett's self-deceiving love for Ashley Wilkes, makes an uncommonly absorbing love story, and one that Miss Mitchell manages to tell with rarely a false note, and which she carries to a logical and unforced conclusion. Melanie, whom Ashley Wilkes married, and Ashley himself, are foils for these two. These are only Miss Mitchell's most fully drawn characters, the central figures of her story. She has a host of others, excellently if sketchily done. She draws on the whole social fabric of the ante-bellum, war time and Reconstruction South for her people.

He would be a rash critic who would make any prophecies as to Miss Mitchell's future. She has set herself a hard mark to match with a second book, and I hope only that she will not set too soon about it.

First Impressions

How to Win Friends and Influence People by Dale Carnegie
February 14, 1937

THE TRUTH WHICH this book lays down, and the precepts it offers, are as simple as the copy-book and as universal as humanity. In a brisk, cheerful, easy style, enlivened and emphasized by personal anecdote, this authority on "public speaking and human relations" tells us to smile and be friendly, not to argue or find fault, to get the other person's point of view, encourage and praise him, let him talk all he wants to, and persuade him that all the good ideas are his. He advises us also never to tell another person that he is wrong, but adds that if we are wrong ourselves we can turn a liability into an asset by admitting it "quickly and emphatically." If we do all that we are pretty sure to win friends. And if in addition we have the wit to dramatize our own ideas, our salesmanship will profit the more.

There is a subtle cynicism, to be sure, in directions which depend so largely upon flattering the other man's egotism. Mr. Carnegie's book offers very good advice, on bad assumptions. And it exemplifies thus the good and the bad of those "how to" philosophies which are sought by all the wishful millions who have never been able to influence other people much, who would like to begin life all over again even though they are past 40, who long to be told how they can think for themselves, who live alone and hate it, or who even are so far sunk in dullness and anxiety and unsuccess that they wake up every morning without any desire to live.

The good is in the simple, sound, practical common sense of Mr. Carnegie's counsel, and the lively and well-illustrated directness with which it is given. There is a great deal of that kind of good in this book. But there is bad, too: in the promise of what Lowell Thomas calls here a "short-cut to distinction"; in the suggestion that the superficial cultivation of "personality" may take the place of—or even be more important than—a sound foundation of knowledge, intelligence and ability; in the idea that one can—or should—whip up an effective "enthusiasm" without reference to the worth of the enthusiasm's object; and in the emphasis upon the supreme value of extraneous rewards.

First Impressions

Serve It Forth by M. F. K. Fisher
June 20, 1937

THIS IS A BOOK about food; but though food is universal, this book is unique. It is erudite and witty and experienced and young. The truth is that it is stamped on every page with a highly individualized personality. Sophisticated but not standardized, brilliant but never "swift-moving" or "streamlined," perfumed and a little mocking, direct and yet almost *précieuse,* the style of *Serve It Forth* is as unusual as its material is unfamiliar and odd.

And it really is a book about food. Mrs. Fisher even goes so far, in spite of preliminary assurances to the contrary, as to include two recipes—rare ones, both. But this is no book of practical counsel. These pages are filled with odd fact and obscure fantasy, illuminating comment, personal reflection and remembrance.

1937

Graham Greene provokes a libel suit with a film review in which he refers to the "dimpled depravity" of Shirley Temple.

The young author goes back to the simple and democratic food of the Egyptians and their simple lives; she dwells a bit on the Greeks. Then, with some horrible particularity of detail, she tells how "in their furious delicacy of palate and heavy-handed subtlety of selection the wealthy Romans left Greeks far behind." She explains how good cooking, like learning, was kept alive in the monasteries in the Dark Ages. She has surprising notes from Elizabethan England and Catherine de' Medici's France.

Of all the present nations France, says Mrs. Fisher, "has the simplest school of cooking." But when she explains the proper preparation of snails at their best (they ought to be starved to death, to be most appetizing), one realizes that there are different kinds of simplicity! Mrs. Fisher has lived in provincial France, and much of her oddest research and most pungent comment comes from that land of culinary supremacies; she brings some responsive human anecdotes from France, too. But most Americans, she declares, don't know how to eat: they are "taste blind."

Special K.

The Trial by Franz Kafka
October 24, 1937

BY LOUIS KRONENBERGER

WHEN THE LATE Franz Kafka's *The Castle* was published in this country some years ago, it created no general stir, but it was immediately seized upon by a few people as a very distinguished book. Time has passed, and other people—though still not many—have concurred in that conclusion. I must confess that I have not read *The Castle*, but I mean to, for I have read *The Trial*, and not in a long time have I come upon a novel which, without being in any vulgar sense spectacular, is more astonishing.

The Trial is not for everybody, and its peculiar air of excitement will seem flat enough to those who habitually feed on "exciting" books. It belongs not with the many novels that horrify, but with the many fewer novels which terrify. It does not trick out the world we know in grotesque and fantastic shapes; it is at once wholly of our world and wholly outside it. It keeps one foot so solidly on the ground that you can think of few books which stay there more firmly with both feet. But its other foot swings far out into space, conferring upon the literal action of the story a depth of meaning—or if meaning is often elusive, a power of suggestion—which can best be called visionary.

Something of the book's quality may be guessed from a brief mention of its plot. Joseph K., a young bank official, gets up one morning to find that he has been arrested. He knows he has committed no crime, and he is never then or later told what his crime is supposed to be. He is permitted his freedom, except that periodically he must go to court. Court is a weird place, full of other accused people and innumerable petty officials; there K. is allowed to assert his eloquence, but the business of his trial never makes any progress.

There is more to the story than an account of K.'s "trial"; we are told much about his life at the bank; about his relations with his landlady and with the young woman who has the room next to his. In all these things K. is made to feel just as uncertain and frustrated as in the matter of his trial; and this frustration contributes most of all to the dream character of the book. It is exactly the sensation we have during a lingering nightmare.

No summary can convey the atmosphere which Kafka cunningly distills— the atmosphere of some idiotic and hellish labyrinth where Joseph K. is forced to wander. The more he tries to control the situation, the more stranded he becomes. On psychological grounds alone the story has a peculiar force and distinction. But the impact of *The Trial* is much more moral than psychological. Kafka is at bottom a religious writer, with a powerful sense of right and wrong and an unquenchable yearning toward the unrevealed source of things. His story then is a great general parable. It is a proof of Kafka's other talents as a novelist, a humorist, a psychologist and a satirist that he does not leave his parable a bald one, but works into it every kind of human gesture and lifelike detail. The man who can, while writing symbolically, make a hilarious stuffed shirt out of K.'s advocate, and then—in a later scene—express his religious feeling in the richest organ tones, was a writer in whose death literature suffered a real loss.

First Impressions

And to Think That I Saw It on Mulberry Street by Dr. Seuss
November 14, 1937

ELLEN LEWIS BUELL

HIGHLY ORIGINAL and entertaining, Dr. Seuss's picture book partakes of the better qualities of those peculiarly American institutions, the funny papers and the tall tale. It is a masterly interpretation of the mind of a child in the act of creating one of those stories with which children often amuse themselves and bolster up their self-respect.

Little Marco has been chided by his father for his lack of observance in the ordinary routines of life, and, on his way home from school one day, he determines to have something of importance to tell. There is nothing very outstanding about a rattletrap cart and horse on Mulberry Street, yet Marco, once aroused, is not to be balked by mere realism. Tentatively he experiments, substituting in his rehearsed story a zebra for the horse. Fancy, unleashed, climbs to further heights. "Why not a chariot?" says Marco to himself. Logic, which has nothing to do with cold facts, intervenes, and with every step homeward the original report grows into a caravan of startling size and character, until a grand climax is reached, with its inevitable anticlimax in perfect keeping with Marco's character. The whole is told in rollicking verse, and in bright pictures, which though a bit crude in coloring are as spirited and comic as is the young hero's imagination. It is a book which will divert older readers as well as little children.

First Impressions

My Ears Are Bent by Joseph Mitchell
January 23, 1938

BY ROBERT VAN GELDER

MR. MITCHELL is a sort of Stephen Crane of this generation's newspaper city rooms, a somber athlete with an exceptional writing talent who finds Harlem and the lower East Side the most interesting localities in town. The book's title is his comment on the listening he has been obliged by his trade of daily newspaper interviewer to go through. He has become a connoisseur of talk and holds that the best talk is artless, made up of the wandering comments of people trying to reassure or comfort themselves. He particularly fancies the intimate confidences of those who might roughly be classified as "screwballs." For instance, there was a Mr. Samuel J. Burger who telephoned Mr. Mitchell's office to say that he was selling racing cockroaches to society people at 75 cents a pair. Mr. Mitchell went to interview him and found him in a Broadway delicatessen buying ham and cheese sandwiches for a couple of strip-tease women. Mr. Burger talked for a while about his cockroaches, and then mentioned a side line, the renting of monkeys. "I rent a lot of monkeys," he said. "People get lonesome and telephone me to send them a monkey to keep them company. After all, a monkey is a mammal, just like us."

Mr. Mitchell has decided that the most interesting human beings, so far as talk is concerned, are people whose occupations tend to restrain their own speech: anthropologists, farmers, prostitutes, psychiatrists, and an occasional bartender. The only people he does not care to listen to are society women, industrial leaders, distinguished authors, ministers, explorers, moving picture actors (except W. C. Fields and Stepin Fetchit), and any actress under the age of 35. His book is made

1938

The Melcher family establishes the Randolph Caldecott Medal for the most distinguished picture book for children, and the first winner is *Animals of the Bible*, illustrated by Dorothy P. Lathrop.

up of interviews with fan dancers, Negro evangelists, taxi drivers, politicians, persons engaged in the conjure business in one way or another, and people who own saloons. There are also some "atmosphere" sketches. The writing is always good and the book contains more of the strong, brash reds, yellows and blues that make New York the world's big town than any other book I ever have read.

First Impressions

The Big Sleep by Raymond Chandler
February 12, 1939

BY ISAAC ANDERSON

OST OF THE CHARACTERS in this story are tough, many of them are nasty and some of them are both. Phillip Marlowe, the private detective who is both the narrator and the chief character, is hard; he has to be hard to cope with the slimy racketeers who are preying on the Sternwood family. Nor do the Sternwoods themselves, particularly the two daughters, respond to gentle treatment. Spoiled is much too mild a term to describe these two young women. Marlowe is working for $25 a day and expenses and he earns every cent of it. Indeed, because of his loyalty to his employer, he passes up golden opportunities to make much more. Before the story is done Marlowe just misses being an eyewitness to two murders and by an even narrower margin misses being a victim. The language used in this book is often vile—at times so filthy that the publishers have been compelled to resort to the dash, a device seldom employed in these unsqueamish days. As a study in depravity, the story is excellent, with Marlowe standing out as almost the only fundamentally decent person in it.

1939

Pocket Books begins mass-producing paperbound books at 25 cents each, initiating a publishing revolution in America. The first 10 offerings include a volume of Shakespeare's tragedies, a self-help book, an Agatha Christie mystery, and *Bambi*.

Dust Bowl Blues

The Grapes of Wrath by John Steinbeck
April 16, 1939

BY PETER MONRO JACK

T IS A VERY LONG NOVEL, the longest that Steinbeck has written, and yet it reads as if it had been composed in a flash, ripped off the typewriter and delivered to the public as an ultimatum. It is a long and thoughtful novel as one thinks about it. It is a short and vivid scene as one feels it.

The journey across is done in superb style, one marvellous short story after another, and all melting into this long novel of the great trek.

Californians are not going to like this angry novel. The beauty and fertility of California conceal human fear, hatred and violence. "Scairt" is a Western farmer's word for the inhabitants, frightened of the influx of workers eager for jobs, and when they are frightened they become vicious and cruel. This part of the story reads like the news from Nazi Germany. Families from Oklahoma are known as "Okies." While they work they live in what might as well be called concentration camps. Only a few hundred are given jobs out of the thousands who traveled West. Their pay is cut from 30 cents an hour to 25, to 20. If any one objects he is a Red, an agitator, a trouble maker who had better get out of the country. Deputy sheriffs are around with guns, legally shooting or clubbing any one from the rest of the Union who questions the law of California. The Joad family find only one place of order and decency in this country of fear and violence, in a government camp, and it is a pleasure to follow the family as they take a shower bath and go to the Saturday night dances. But even here the deputy sheriffs, hired by the banks who run the Farmers Association, are poking in their guns, on the pretext of inciting to riot and the necessity of protective custody. The Joad family moves on through California, hunted by anonymous guns while they are picking peaches for 2½ cents a box, hoping only for a little land free of guns and dust on which they might settle and work as they were accustomed to. The promised grapes of California have turned into grapes of wrath that might come to fruition at any moment.

How true this may be no reviewer can say. It is easy to add that the novel comes to no conclusion, that the preacher is killed because he is a strikebreaker, that Tom disappears as a fugitive from California justice, that the novel ends on a minor and sentimental note; that the story stops after 600 pages merely because a story has to stop somewhere. All this is true enough but the real truth is that Steinbeck has written a novel from the depths of his heart with a sincerity seldom equaled. It may be an exaggeration, but it is the exaggeration of an honest and splendid writer.

Madeline, by Ludwig Bemelmans, fixes Paris forever in the minds and hearts of innumerable little American girls.

Richard Wright

Thomas Wolfe • Ernest Hemingway

Arthur Koestler • Rebecca West • Woody

Guthrie • T. S. Eliot • Stephen Spender

Malcolm Cowley • Evelyn Waugh • Christopher

Isherwood • Robert Lowell • John Hersey

James Michener • Alfred Kinsey • Winston S.

Churchill • Albert Camus • Sholom

Aleichem • George Orwell

1940s

Crime and Punishment and Explanation in Full

Native Son by Richard Wright
March 3, 1940

BY PETER MONRO JACK

A READY WAY to show the importance of this novel is to call it the Negro *American Tragedy* and to compare it roughly with Dreiser's masterpiece. Both deal seriously and powerfully with the problem of social maladjustment, with environment and individual behavior, and subsequently with crime and punishment. Both are tragedies and Dreiser's white boy and Wright's black boy are equally killed in the electric chair not for being criminals—since the crime in each case was unpremeditated—but for being social misfits. The pattern in both books is similar: the family, the adolescent, the lure of money and sex, fortuitous events, murder, trial and death. The conclusion in both is that society is to blame, that the environment into which each was born forced upon them their crimes, that they were the particular victims of a general injustice.

The startling difference in Mr. Wright's *Native Son* is that the injustice is a racial, not merely a social one. Dreiser's Clyde Griffiths represents a social "complex" that could be reasonably taken care of. Mr. Wright's Bigger Thomas is far beyond and outside of helpful social agencies. He represents an impasse rather than a complex, and his tragedy is to be born into a black and immutable minority race, literally, in his own words, "whipped before you born." Mr. Wright allows Bigger a brief moment of illumination into his hopeless condition before he is finally whipped out of the world.

The narrative of Bigger's life begins with a symbolic incident worth remarking on. He is 20 years old, living in a one-room tenement apartment in Chicago's South Side Black Belt, with his mother, his young sister, Vera, and younger brother, Buddy; they pay $8 rent a week; they are on relief. Bigger's first job when he wakes on the morning of his story is to kill a huge black rat that has got into the room. His intent destruction of the rat is a characteristic act.

It is later in the day when Bigger turns up to the job where the relief people have sent him, as chauffeur to one of Chicago's big executive types of the benevolent kind. This Mr. Dalton has given millions for social welfare, earmarked particularly for the Negro cause, for the National Association for the Advancement of Colored People, although most of it has dribbled into Ping-Pong tables in exemplary social clubs and the like. Bigger knows nothing about this, nor does he know that a good part of Mr. Dalton's money for charity comes from the exorbitant rents Dalton charges the Negroes to live in the overcrowded, rat-infested tenements that he owns in the Black Belt—in part, from the very room Bigger had left that morning.

On the night of the first day Bigger is to drive the daughter Mary to a university lecture. Mary has gone a little farther than her parents in practical sociology and directs Bigger to drive to Communist headquarters instead of the university. There she meets a practically perfect Communist, who shakes Bigger's hand and wants to be called by his first name, Jan. They drive together in the front seat to a Negro restaurant, drink a good deal, drive around the park while Jan and Mary make love, and finally Bigger brings a very drunk Mary home in the car about 2 in the morning, with a package of Communist pamphlets from Jan in his pocket.

How Bigger inadvertently murdered Mary that same night can be told only in the words that Mr. Wright uses. The necessary point is that he found he had killed her out of fear, out of his certain knowledge that he would be suspected (unjustly) of having raped the girl. When her mother, who is blind, comes to the bedroom to which Bigger has just carried her, Bigger puts a pillow over the girl's face to prevent her speaking of his presence there. Unconsciously he exerts more strength than he realizes. Mary is dead when Mrs. Dalton, believing that her daughter is merely drunk, leaves the bedroom without having discovered Bigger.

This is the beginning and end of Bigger's fatal history. The body he burns in the furnace, the head cut off with a hatchet because he cannot force it in, the exhaust fan switched on to clear the air of the basement of the smell of burning flesh. Bigger's mind reaches a rapid solution. As a Negro he will be the first suspect. But Jan, the Communist, he considers, is almost an equal object of job hatred. He has been told by the politicians that the Reds are the dirtiest kind of criminals; he can easily throw the blame on Jan by asserting that Jan went home with the girl, he can even collect kidnapping money on the pretense that Mary is still alive. This, one might say, is a typically criminal mind, but it is Mr. Wright's purpose to show it as a typical kind of social and racial conditioning. Bigger's crime is discovered. He commits another crime (this time merely the murder of his Negro mistress) to cover his tracks, but it is only now a matter of time between his flight and his fate. A Jewish Communist lawyer makes a brilliant speech in his defense, but there is nothing to be done save an attempt at explanation.

It will be argued, and I think with truth, that his character, Bigger, is made far too articulate, that he explains much too glibly in the latter part of the story how he came to meet his fate: "Seems sort of natural-like, me being here facing that death chair. Now I come to think of it, it seems like something like this just had to be." Later he has romanticized and rationalized himself into the declaration that "What I killed for must've been good! . . . It must have been good! When a man kills, it's for something . . . I didn't know I was really alive in this world until I felt things hard enough to kill for 'em." This, I believe, is so much romantic nonsense. Dreiser was wiser in allowing the reader to think out Clyde Griffiths in his own realistic terms: he did not interfere too much in the interpretation of his character. Mr. Wright does spoil his story at the end by insisting on Bigger's fate as representative of the whole Negro race and making Bigger himself say so. But this is a minor fault in a good cause. The story is a strong and powerful one and it alone will force the Negro issue into our attention. Certainly, *Native Son* declares Richard Wright's importance, not merely as the best Negro writer, but as an American author as distinctive as any of those now writing.

Look Forward, Angel

You Can't Go Home Again by Thomas Wolfe
September 22, 1940

BY J. DONALD ADAMS

T HIS NOVEL, the last work completed by Thomas Wolfe before his death two years ago at the age of 37, makes that event appear even more tragic now than then. When he died, and even last year, when *The Web and the Rock*, the first of the posthumous novels, was published, there seemed reason to doubt that this young man who was the most promising creative writer of his time in America would ever come to terms with his genius and realize its potentialities to the full. In reviewing *The Web and the Rock* I expressed such a doubt. It had no foundation in fact. The novel which is now published gives me, at least, every reason to believe that had Thomas Wolfe lived he would have become the greatest of all American novelists. There are things in his other books almost as fine as anything in this one, but *You Can't Go Home Again* will stand apart from everything else that he wrote, because this is the book of a man who had come to terms with himself, who was on the way to mastery of his art, who had something profoundly important to say. His death was the greatest loss to American letters in our time.

You Can't Go Home Again, like all Wolfe's other novels, is an intensely autobiographical book. Wolfe believed that enduring fiction must be written out of its author's personal experience of life. He would point to Tolstoy's *War and Peace* as supreme evidence of this truth. It is a truth which it seems to me futile to deny, but in Wolfe's case it did seem that he might never acquire the power to place himself outside the wide circle of his observation, to write with enough objectivity so that what he wrote would achieve that universality which is the distinguishing mark of the truly great novelists. Wolfe believed before he died that he had won through to that power, and this book confirms his belief.

The title derives from the last line of *The Web and the Rock*. It had, for Wolfe, many implications. "In a way," he writes of George Webber, who is Thomas Wolfe in this book as in its predecessor, "the phrase summed up everything he had ever learned." In the last analysis, it means, of course, that one must go forward in life, that there is no return to the things that were, however dear to us they may have been. And the application holds for Wolfe, in this book, beyond the individual; it holds for the world of man as a whole. We have come to the end of something, to the end of much, in our time, but we can't go home again; we must go forward. "I believe that we are lost here in America, but I believe we shall be found."

You Can't Go Home Again opens as George Webber's first novel is about to be published (*Look Homeward, Angel*, November, 1929). It closes with his visit to the Germany he had loved, and where he is now shocked into the realization that something abysmally evil and corrupt has entered the world, something that must be destroyed if men are to be once more proud and free. In between there is one of the most vital and wide-embracing pictures of American life that has ever been poured into the pages of a novel. The New York of the period just before the crash of 1929 and of the years immediately after is subjected here to a fierce illumination. What Scott Fitzgerald caught and gave a glimpse of in his best book, *The Great Gatsby*, is revealed here in its entirety, with all its implications defined, its meaning and its warning presented with passionate truth.

All of Wolfe's superb ability to transfix a scene, whether a casual incident or a momentous one such as that of the Jacks' party and the ensuing fire in the great Park Avenue apartment house (a succession of scenes which strip the whole society of a period to its naked essentials), is given full scope in this novel. There couldn't be a Wolfe novel without a description of a railroad journey, and there is that too. Or one without a host of sharply observed people, their outer and inner conformation indelibly drawn, whether they enter the book for a page or for its entirety. They are here in almost matchless profusion. Nor could there be a Wolfe novel without those soaring passages of poetry which were sometimes bombast but are here pure gold.

There are two portraits here, other than that of the author himself, of two other men who will be readily identified. They are both portraits which do their subjects honor, and there is no reason why they should not be named. One is of Sinclair Lewis; and it is, I think, at once the most vital and the most understanding one that has yet been made. The other is of the man who set Wolfe on the road to fame, the man whose belief in him never wavered, Maxwell Perkins of Scribner's. The letter to him with which Thomas Wolfe ends this book is one of the finest tributes that one human being ever laid at the feet of another. It is also one of the finest pieces of writing Wolfe ever accomplished. It is a fitting conclusion to a book which has the air of nobility about it. This is the story of a man who found himself, in relation to life, in relation to his time.

"Worth the Fighting For"

For Whom the Bell Tolls by Ernest Hemingway
October 20, 1940

BY J. DONALD ADAMS

THIS IS THE BEST book Ernest Hemingway has written, the fullest, the deepest, the truest. It will, I think, be one of the major novels in American literature.

There were those of us who felt, when *To Have and Have Not* was published, that Hemingway was through as a creative writer. That is always a dangerous assumption to make regarding any writer of much innate ability, but it did seem that Hemingway was blocked off from further development. We were badly mistaken. Technical skill he had long ago acquired; the doubt lay in where and how he could apply it, and that doubt he has now sweepingly erased. The skill is even further sharpened than it was, but with it has come an inner growth, a deeper and surer feeling for life, than he has previously displayed. Whatever brought about this growth—whether his experience of the Spanish war, out of which this novel was made, or something else, it is plainly to be seen in this book, from beginning to end. There are no traces of adolescence in the Hemingway of *For Whom the Bell Tolls*. This is the work of a mature artist, of a mature mind.

The title derives from John Donne. The passage from which it comes faces the book's first page:

> "No man is an *Iland*, intire of it selfe; every man is a peece of the *Continent*, a part of the *maine*; if a Clod bee washed away by the *Sea*, *Europe* is the lesse, as well as if a *Promontorie* were, as well as if a *Mannor* of thy *friends* or of *thine owne* were; any mans *death* diminishes *me*, because I am involved in *Mankinde*; And therefore never send to know for whom the *bell* tolls; it tolls for *thee*."

It is a fine title, and an apt one, for this is a book filled with the imminence of death, and the manner of man's meeting it. That is as it should be; this is a story of the Spanish war. But in it Hemingway has struck universal chords, and he has struck them vibrantly. Perhaps it conveys something of the measure of *For Whom the Bell Tolls* to say that with that theme, it is not a depressing but an uplifting book. It has the purging quality that lies in the presenting of tragic but profound truth. Hemingway has freed himself from the negation that held him in his other novels. As Robert Jordan lay facing death he looked down the hill slope and thought: "I have fought for what I believed in for a year now. If we win here we will win everywhere. The world is a fine place and worth the fighting for and I hate very much to leave it."

The frame of the story is a minor incident in the horror that was the war in Spain. Robert Jordan is a young American in the Loyalist ranks who has been detailed to the blowing up of a bridge which the General Staff wants destroyed to prevent the bringing up of enemy reinforcements. His mission carried him into hill country where he must seek the aid of guerrilla bands. Jordan destroys the bridge, but while he is escaping with his companions his horse is knocked from under him by an exploding shell, and we leave him lying on the hillside, his leg crushed by the animal's fall. He sends his companions on and waits, with a submachine gun beside him, for the enemy's approach.

Those who leave him are, with Jordan, the main figures in the story. Among them is the girl Maria, whom Jordan, in the four-day span of the story's action, has met and loved. And as *For Whom the Bell Tolls* is a better story of action than *A Farewell to Arms*, so too is this a finer love story than that of Lieutenant Henry and Catherine Barkley. That is saying a good deal, but it is true. I know of no love scenes in American fiction and few in any other to compare with those of *For Whom the Bell Tolls* in depth and sincerity of feeling. They are unerringly right, and as much beyond those of *A Farewell to Arms* as the latter were beyond the casual couplings of *The Sun Also Rises*.

The book holds, I think, the best character drawing that Hemingway has done. Robert Jordan is a fine portrait of a fighting idealist, and the Spanish figures are superbly done, in particular the woman Pilar, who should take her place among the memorable women of fiction—earthy and strong, tender, hard, wise, a woman who, as she said of herself, would have been a good man, and yet was a woman made for men. The brutal, unstable Pablo, in whom strength and evil were combined, the good and brave old man Anselmo—these and others are warmly living in this heroic story.

I wrote once that Ernest Hemingway can see and describe with a precision and a vividness unmatched since Kipling first displayed his great visual gift. There are scenes in this book finer than any he has done. The telling of how the Civil Guard was shot in Pablo's town and how the fascists were beaten to death between rows of men armed with flails and hurled over a cliff into the river 300 feet below, how the fascists walked out one by one from their prayers in the City Hall and severally met their deaths, has the thrust and power of one of the more terrible of Goya's pictures.

In all that goes to make a good novel *For Whom the Bell Tolls* is an advance beyond Hemingway's previous work. It is much more full-bodied in its drawing of character, visually more brilliant, and incomparably richer in content. Hemingway's style, too, has changed for the better. It was extraordinarily effective at times before, but it is shed now of the artificialities that clung to it. There is nothing obtrusive about the manner in which this book is written; the style is a part of the whole; there is no artifice to halt the eye. It has simplicity and power, delicacy and strength.

This is Hemingway's longest novel, and it could be, I think, as most books can, a little shorter, and with benefit. It seems to me that some of the long passages in which Robert Jordan's mind turns back to his days in Madrid retard the narrative unnecessarily and could well have been omitted. If there are other flaws in this fine performance, I have not yet found them. A very good novel it unquestionably is, and I am not at all sure that it may not prove to be a great one. That is not something to determine on a first reading. But this much more is certain: that Hemingway is now a writer of abundant talents whose work does not measure up to his equipment. *For Whom the Bell Tolls* is the book of a man who knows what life is about, and who can convey his knowledge. Hemingway has found bigger game than the kudu and the lion. The hunter is home from the hill.

Damnation by Faith

Darkness at Noon **by Arthur Koestler**
May 25, 1941

BY HAROLD STRAUSS

HERE, in a splendid novel, is an effective explanation of the riddle of the Moscow treason trials. It is the sort of novel that transcends ordinary limitations, and that may be read as a primary discourse in political philosophy. But this observation should frighten no one from the book, for it is written with such dramatic power, with such warmth of feeling, and with such persuasive simplicity that it is as absorbing as melodrama. It is a far cry from the bleak topical commentaries that sometimes pass as novels. It does not dwell on the merely circumstantial aspect of the trials; it bares no secrets; it seeks no escape in mystical generalizations about oriental psychology. The trials were peculiarly Russian in their garish externals. But at their core they were a clash between pragmatic absolutism and humanitarian democracy.

The central figure, Rubashov, is a composite of all the old Bolsheviks liquidated by Stalin. The novel opens in 1938 with his arrest, an arrest he has long been expecting. He has committed none of the crimes to which he will later confess. By our luxurious standards, he is innocent. But in his own mind he knows that he is guilty. Why? Because his are still the standards of a man who has dedicated himself unswervingly for forty years to the program of the revolution, to the struggle for its abstractly conceived ends by any necessary means, howsoever horrible. When such a man allows doubt to creep into his mind, when he questions whether the revolution might not after all cost too much in human suffering, he knows he is guilty. He understands that such humanitarian heresy must be punished by death. With great brilliance Koestler follows the course of Rubashov's thought down to the ultimate, immensely moving admission: "I no longer believe in my own infallibility. That is why I am lost."

Although this is a prison novel, it does not dwell unduly on oppressive details. Rubashov was not barbarously handled. The real, the truly moving dramatic emphasis, once his guilt has been established within the Soviet frame of reference, is on the great decision whether to confess at a public trial or die in silence.

The issue is in the hands of two investigating magistrates, Ivanov and Gletkin. They want Rubashov's agreement to a public confession because his is one of the great names of the Revolution, and his unexplained liquidation would have a demoralizing effect upon the people. Ivanov himself is an Old Bolshevik who can grasp Rubashov's thought processes.

Ivanov conducts the first two hearings. By inexorable logic he brings to light matters of which Rubashov himself is unaware. He shows Rubashov that the beginning of his disaffection was his return from Germany after two years of imprisonment by the Nazis. Rubashov had asked for a new mission abroad immediately, although he was entitled to an important job at home. "You did not feel at ease here, presumably? During your absence, certain changes had taken place which you evidently did not appreciate." Once Rubashov admits that he had not liked the liquidation of old comrades, the trap closes around him. For, in the Russian way of thinking, overt opposition must follow from inner disaffection.

Ivanov plays a magnificent game with Rubashov. He tries to recall him to his former acceptance of party discipline; he tries to persuade him to agree freely that he has erred. Actually he succeeds. But he is thought to have treated Rubashov too sympathetically, and he himself is shot. The last hearing, after Rubashov has already agreed to confess, is in Gletkin's hands. It is a prolonged agony of subtle torture. Its point is to implement the confession with specific crimes. It is difficult to suggest the protracted excitement of this intellectual duel; suffice to say that "an unspoken agreement had come into existence between them: if Gletkin could prove that the root of the charge was right—even when this root was only of a logical, abstract nature—he had a free hand to insert the missing details."

But while outwardly Gletkin wins the duel, inwardly great changes are occurring in Rubashov. He becomes once more a human being, a man of feeling, of subjective sensibilities. While with his mind he is assenting to Gletkin, in his heart he is acknowledging that perhaps man ought not to follow the logical consequences of his thought to the end—"perhaps reason alone was a defective compass, which led one on such a winding, twisting course that the goal finally disappeared in the mist."

The magic effect of *Darkness at Noon* is its magnificent tragic irony. For although in a deeply moving final sequence Rubashov makes a public confession and is shot, it is he who is the real victor over his oppressors.

1941

Céline writes of Hitler's anti-Semitism: "It is the side of Hitler that most people like the least . . . it is the side I like the most."

Travels Through History

Black Lamb and Grey Falcon by Rebecca West
October 26, 1941

BY KATHERINE WOODS

THE GREY FALCON is an enigmatic figure in a Slav folksong about a military defeat in the year 1389; and it offered the Serbian king a choice which expresses the sad dilemma of modern pacifism and points to its tragic results. The black lamb is the symbol, seen in a gypsy rite in Macedonia, of false—and thus of impious—sacrifice; and the terrible complexity of the choice between good and evil becomes not less but more tragic when man identifies himself with the false altar's helpless victim rather than with its cruel priest. For the king chose piety and immolation instead of the effective defense of Christian civilization against its oncoming enemy: "all was holy and honorable" within him, but like the celebrants of false sacrifice, he had set death before life. He and his soldiers died vainly on that consecrated but disastrous battlefield. And slavery closed down upon the Balkan peoples—no legend here, but history—for 500 years.

This may seem remote and recondite, but it is not. It is part—the distilled spiritual essence—of what may be accurately described as a most brilliantly objective travel book; although the travels are most significant for their observation of history.

In two almost incredibly full-packed volumes one of the most gifted and searching of modern English novelists and critics has produced not only the magnification and intensification of the travel book form, but, one may say, its apotheosis. Rebecca West's *Journey Through Yugoslavia* is carried out with tireless percipience, nourished from almost bewildering erudition, chronicled with a thoughtfulness itself fervent and poetic; and it explores the many-faceted being of Yugoslavia—its cities and villages, its history and ancient custom, its people and its soul, its meaning in our world.

The journey here specifically chronicled began with the arrival of Miss West and her husband at Zagreb at Eastertime in 1937. They were met by three friends of an earlier visit, and at once the "situation" began. For this was Croatia. Of the three Yugoslavs one, the Serbian poet Constantine, was an official in the Yugoslav Government; another, the middle-aged Croat Gregorievitch, had fought for his people's freedom and found it in union with "their free Slav brothers, the Serbs"; the third, the young Croat scientist Valetta, was a separatist. The meeting crystallizes the book's interest not only in its presentation of the Croatian problem, but in showing the reader with keen understanding what each of these patriots felt and why. And the character of the Yugoslav journey is caught in another way also: if there was much political argument in Zagreb, there was lively intellectual exercise in other talk, too. And Constantine, the poet, who had studied philosophy under Bergson, was the most fascinating talker, as he was also the most poetic and extravagantly individualized of them all. Throughout this book his talk runs like a clear stream, rippling or deep. But Constantine, who was to accompany his friends to Bosnia and Herzegovina and Macedonia and Serbia and Montenegro, was to show himself stricken by a division worse than the problem of Croatia: his blood was Jewish, his allegiance was Yugoslav, his culture was international; and he had a German wife.

Meanwhile, Rebecca West continued those travels in space and time, cause and effect, the Slav pattern of life, which give her book its three-dimensional wholeness. There was always a deep urgency of life among these peoples, which could keep their love of freedom rebellious in enslavement, their spirits proud and wise and dignified in poverty and ignorance, their minds speculative and individual. But there was dualism, too. Acceptance of tragedy, says Rebecca West, is the basis of Slav life. And it is not for nothing that the Manichaean glorification of suffering and death was strong among them long ago. Even so they did not lose sight of the value of independence; and if that very spirit, in its aspect of dissension, was played upon through centuries by the divide-and-rule policy of their various conquerors, still it gave them persistence, with fortitude: "The Slav is never subject, not even to himself."

With thousands of pieces, so, Rebecca West has made her mosaic. And her book is a true mosaic, each scene or event or character or re-creation of history a vivid whole, fitted with an art that seems almost casual into its place in the larger entity. From the point of view of continued reading a book of half-a-million words is, of course, far too long. The author never loses her freshness, but the reader may. Yet if it is not to be read at—so to speak!—a sitting, *Black Lamb and Grey Falcon* is to call the reader back, I think, in pertinent or haunting recollections, to many swift returns to read again. In the alchemy of Rebecca West's literary art those words are transmuted, to become elements of vital substance, enlightenment, and the stimulus of provocative and echoing thought; and this is the case whether they are concerned with Yugoslavia itself, with the terrible world we live in, or with the operation of the author's questing and decisive mind.

Reflection and the historical sense fuse in the epilogue which unites the picture of Yugoslavia with the vision of the world and gives the book its climax. "Violence was all I knew of the Balkans: all I knew of the South Slavs. . . . I had come to Yugoslavia because I knew that the past had made the present and I wanted to see how the process works," Rebecca West wrote in an early chapter.

1942

The best-seller list appears in the *Book Review* on August 9. During the previous 7 years, a monthly list based on sales figures from one book wholesaler was published intermittently.

_1942_

Twelve Little Golden Books
appear, each of 42 pages,
selling for 25 cents. One and
a half million copies are
sold within 5 months.

But long before the world's tragedy fills the horizon of her final pages the reader has grasped the inevitable sweep of her further purpose—to show "the past side by side with the present it created." For to do that is to look at the present, in sanity and valor, for what it is: the hairline of balance where the sad past of Yugoslavia may become the future of all the civilized world. The book that was begun in the thoughtful prescience of 1937 was finished in the dreadful empirical knowledge of 1941. It is so that the choice offered by the gray falcon, and the inner defeat of the black lamb's false sacrifice, hover in stark reality over all our present world.

First Impressions

Bound for Glory by Woody Guthrie
March 21, 1943

BY HORACE REYNOLDS

WOODY GUTHRIE is an American jongleur, a wandering minstrel, a guitar-busker who packs his guitar into saloons, 'burger joints, chili houses and plays for the nickels and dimes men throw into his hat. He has ridden in box cars and the jalopies of migratory workers singing:

> _This train don't carry no gamblers,_
> _Liars, thieves, and big-shot ramblers;_
> _This train is bound for glory,_
> _This train!_

He has slept under bridges and in four-bit flophouses and eaten out of cans in the jungle. A vagabond lover of life, he distills his joy into improvised song.

Out of that life he has made a book. Its action is the picaresque loafing, singing, starving, freezing, carousing life of the American road. Smoke boils out of the stacks of overworked locomotives, and Woody sweeps across the country from the green orchards of California to the sodden stones of New York's Ninth Avenue. Plenty happens. Sixty bums aboard a careening flat-wheeled boxcar coat themselves with blood and cement dust in a knockdown-drag-out brawl. Back in Oklahoma, where Woody was born and brung up, Charlie and Nora Guthrie's nice new place burns up. Their next house, not so nice, is destroyed in a cyclone which sets them a-runnin' like the folks in John Steuart Curry's picture, _Tornado Over Kansas_. An oil stove explodes and a little sister is burned to death. The mother goes crazy and dies in the crazy house. When the father went to West Texas, Woody took to combing the alleys and dump grounds with a junking sack. At 15 he hit the highway, and, I take it, has been hitting it ever since. He's done everything from shining shoes and telling fortunes to appearing on the radio and making Victor records.

He writes well. There's a glory hallelujah madness of imagery here which is exciting and compelling, a psychological counterpoint for the violence of the physical action. He writes much in the evangelical mood. As one reads him, one sees a Negro singing "On That Great Gittin'-Up Mornin'," his arms stretched up to heaven like a pair of crazy sticks. One catches echoes of *The Grapes of Wrath*.

The book is like pictures, both moving and still. The writing has that kind of vividness and that sort of limitation. It's exciting and it's a little flat and empty. But there's no mistaking Woody's talent for expression, his ability to sling the American slanguage. There's both the drawl of the South in it and the twang of the Middle West. His book is an eloquent piece of writing, wild as a train whistle in the mountains, a scrumptious picture of fighting, carousing, singing, laughing migratory America.

Some of this book is God gloomy, some of it's pathetic, some of it is a bit too strong for my stomach. Some of its violence has as little meaning as the action of a movie thriller. Some of it could have been pruned to advantage. But much of it is original, strong writing with the glint and sparkle of sunshine on it, gay as the ueklelaydillio to whose accompaniment Woody trolls his balladry.

Master Builder

The Fountainhead by Ayn Rand
May 16, 1943

BY LORINE PRUETTE

AYN RAND is a writer of great power. She has a subtle and ingenious mind and the capacity of writing brilliantly, beautifully, bitterly. *The Fountainhead*, her second novel, has been more than five years in preparation; it is a long but absorbing story of man's enduring battle with evil.

The background is architecture, a field relatively new to the fiction writer, and admirably adapted to the presentation of "the creator" and "the second-hander." Howard Roark is the creator, a tough guy who works

March 28, 1943

*The Way Some
People Live*

BY JOHN
CHEEVER

If the short story is merely a character in a crisis, Mr. Cheever's attempts fulfill the definition. This is not intended as a churlish comment; his talent is fine and incisive, he is definitely a writer to watch. But the crisis in any story, once it is stated, must be resolved in a way that touches off emotional responses in the reader, and this Mr. Cheever, for the most part, obstinately refuses to do. His people are seldom really angry, and almost never gay. When disaster impends, they usually run away from it, mix another Manhattan, or keep their reactions hidden from both the reader and themselves.

Unfortunately, this avoidance of anything resembling a climax, plus the author's misanthropic

(Continued)

cheerfully in the quarries if he is not allowed to build in his own way. Against his vision all the successful architects are combined: the ones who prattle of beauty and the sacredness of tradition, the ones who believe in mixing the best of all past periods. Against him is the charming lad who went to school with him and won all the prizes. Peter Keating continues to win all the prizes, to use his good looks, his personality and his lack of morals to make a rapid and fraudulent success. Against him, too, Dominique Francon, because she loves him and fears and hates the corrupting, engulfing world.

Above all, Mr. Ellsworth Toohey, who writes a famous newspaper column, is Roark's enemy. Ellsworth Toohey is a brilliant personification of a modern devil. Aiming at a society that shall be "an average drawn upon zeros," he knows exactly why he corrupts Peter Keating and explains his methods to the ruined and desolate young man in a passage that is a pyrotechnical display of the fascist mind at its best and its worst; the use of the ideal of altruism to destroy personal integrity, the use of humor and tolerance to destroy all standards, the use of sacrifice to enslave.

Miss Rand has taken her stand against collectivism, "the rule of the second-hander, the ancient monster" which has brought men "to a level of intellectual indecency never equaled on earth." She has written a hymn in praise of the individual.

All her characters are amazingly literate; they all speak with her voice, expressing in dynamic fashion the counterpoint of her argument. She uses mockery, irony, savagery, to portray her second-raters. Her characters are romanticized, larger than life as representations of good and evil. But nothing she has to say is said in a second-rate fashion. You have to think of *The Magic Mountain*, you have to think of *The Master Builder*, when you think of *The Fountainhead*.

Consumed by Fire

Four Quartets by T. S. Eliot
May 16, 1943

BY HORACE GREGORY

IT HAS BEEN SAID in certain quarters, thoughtlessly, I think, that the years of the present World War have failed to produce memorable poetry, and it has been implied that poetry in some mysterious way has failed to live up to great occasions. With Mr. T. S. Eliot's *Four Quartets* before me I wish to modify the gloomy accusation that the better poets of our time have been "irresponsible" or have failed to realize the seriousness of living through a difficult hour. For the past twenty years distinguished writers in England and in the United States have been aware of the potential existence of another world war, and they have warned their readers of its hidden forces long before its actual events took place, and in that sense most of the best poetry written in the present generation continues to be "war poetry."

It has been Mr. Eliot's destiny to anticipate, without seeming overtly prophetic, the mutations of feeling which have taken place within the past twenty years, and his perceptions have given him the right to speak with more than merely personal authority when he writes the following statement into his *Four Quartets:*

> *So here I am, in the middle way, having had twenty years—*
> *Twenty years largely wasted, the years of l'entre deux guerres.*

One recalls his "Difficulties of a Statesman," written long before the Munich pact; one remembers its notes of warning, its moments of satire, and its devotional spirit, for Mr. Eliot has held to the promises he gave his readers in "Ash Wednesday," and has continued his progress through the choruses of "The Rock," through the scenes of *Murder in the Cathedral,* and, most impressive of all, in his present collection of four poems, each bearing a place-name, "Burnt Norton," "East Coker," "The Dry Salvages" and "Little Gidding."

We may recognize East Coker as being on a guidebook route from London to Exeter, with beautiful churches near by and ancient factory yards, or The Dry Salvages as a small group of rocks off our North Atlantic Coast, or, perhaps more significantly, Little Gidding as an Anglican retreat, the scene of Nicholas Ferrar's "Protestant nunnery," which has been so memorably described in J. H. Shorthouse's finely tempered historical romance, *John Inglesant.* But these recognitions may be used as the content of footnotes merely to the four poems; one may photograph each place with anxious care, and yet not feel the emotion that the quartets with their melodic or lyrical interludes convey. The poems must be read for the quality of their emotion and its meaning—and I think I am not wrong when I say that the *Four Quartets* (without being in the least Wordsworthian) represent the best poetry of their kind since Wordsworth wrote *The Prelude.*

One remembers that *The Prelude* was somewhat portentously subtitled *Or Growth of a Poet's Mind: An Autobiographical Poem,* and though it is almost needless to say that Mr. Eliot's *Four Quartets* are not intended to sustain so weighty and so pretentious a claim upon the reader's interest in the philosophy of poetic composition, it is true that Mr. Eliot's new book contains a recapitulation

view of the human race, can only make for boredom, if you take your Cheever in large doses. Somewhere in this world (including the New York whose surface he scratches so brilliantly) Mr. Cheever could discover children who love their parents, people whose business doesn't fail, marriages that do not require twenty years of agony to build into a divorce, old folks whose minds are not as stuffy as New England attics, ladies who fall in love from uncomplicated motives, satyrs who are not suffering from vitamin deficiency.

Certainly such people must exist, but Mr. Cheever will have none of them. As a result, the characters in his own unhappy world have an astonishing and tortured similarity. *The Way Some People Live* is the perfect book for an up-and-coming dentist's anteroom. A few of those tense moments spent with Mr. Cheever's people and their off-center agonies will buck you up no end for the ordeal ahead.

The Swedish Academy, as a step toward peace, proposes to resume the Nobel Prize in Literature, withheld since 1939. But several members say German occupation in Europe has confused the situation; the prize is withheld again.

of very nearly everything he has written since _The Waste Land_ made its controversial appearance in _The Dial_ in 1922. In "Burnt Norton" (which, by the way, was the last of his poems in his _Collected Poems, 1909–1935_ and is reprinted here as the first of the four quartets), he greatly enriched the devotional premises of "Ash Wednesday"; and with the completion of "Little Gidding" we now know that the earlier poem was the first in a new vehicle of expression for Mr. Eliot's characteristic themes. And among them, not the least important is:

> _Seek only there_
> _Where the grey light meets the green air_
> _The hermit's chapel, the pilgrim's prayer._

However closely certain passages in the new poems may seem to echo the choruses of "The Rock" and of _Murder in the Cathedral_, or lines within the last scene of _The Family Reunion_, Mr. Eliot's quartets convey an impression of a newly awakened insight and of a control that seldom fails to delight the mind and eye and ear. Let us take the concluding passage of the third section of "The Dry Salvages," with its emotional temper reawakening the discourses between Krishna and Arjuna of the _Bhagavad-Gita_; and if one is so inclined, one may read a timely meaning into the cadences of what seems a timeless utterance:

> _O voyagers, O seamen,_
> _You who come to port, and you whose bodies_
> _Will suffer the trial and judgment of the sea,_
> _Or whatever event, this is your real destination._
> _So Krishna, as when he admonished Arjuna_
> _On the field of battle._
> > _Not fare well,_
> _But fare forward, voyagers._

And we might well say that this is Mr. Eliot's mature and deeply affirmative answer to his "Death by Water" passage in _The Waste Land_. More important than these considerations is the beauty of the new statement and its depth of feeling, for I happen to believe that the value of Mr. Eliot's sensibilities has been vastly underrated in favor of paying further tribute to his ingenuity and his acknowledged scholarship. His work is of a character that gives a pedant unholy delight in searching out its sources, and while such labors are not without their rewards, they tend to become irrelevant to the poetic gift which endows the following lyric from "Little Gidding" with such brilliantly inspired felicity:

The dove descending breaks the air
With flame of incandescent terror
Of which the tongues declare
The one discharge from sin and error.
The only hope, or the despair
  Lies in the choice of pyre or pyre—
  To be redeemed from fire by fire.

Who then devised the torment?
Love.
Love is the unfamiliar Name
Behind the hands that wave
The intolerable shirt of flame
Which human power cannot remove.
  We only live, only suspire
  Consumed by either fire or fire.

I submit this quotation as one of the finest lyrics written in our time; and for those who wish to take heart as against others who are convinced that poetry was among the early casualties of the present war, I strongly recommend a reading of Mr. T. S. Eliot's *Four Quartets.*

Essay

Stephen Spender on Henry James
March 12, 1944

A N AMERICAN SOLDIER said to me: "When I stand in the middle of Trafalgar Square I pinch myself to make sure I'm awake, and then I think: 'I'm here, in a certain time and at a certain place, a place which all my life I've heard and read about. I've never felt so much that I belong anywhere.' "

That is the authentic European spell, the situation of the American in Europe with his "point of view" which finds its supreme expression in Henry James's novels. Like all magic, it is alluring and at the same time dangerous. One has to pinch one's self to be sure one is not dreaming. There is evil, as well as charm and virtue, in the situation.

Henry James saw both the evil and the virtue, and in his earliest stories and

1944

Kurt Vonnegut is captured by German soldiers during the Battle of the Bulge.

139

novels—particularly in *Roderick Hudson, Daisy Miller* and *The American*—this evil can break out in surprising rashes of melodrama. Yet when the great explosion of a doom-ridden tradition of Europe took place in James's own time, he became an Englishman. He ceased to be "the American"; he identified himself passionately with the British point of view. His action was the counterpart of Aldous Huxley's in this war, who left Europe because it is involved in an inescapable self-destructive tradition.

Much of the European scene which is portrayed in James's novels is in course of being wiped off the map. The social class which he admired no longer enjoys the leisure, the wealth, the self-confidence, which enabled its members to cultivate the sensibility and fine shades of deep feeling of the characters in his novels. Yet although so much of his writing underlines the conditions which make the fine play of feeling possible, the world of his novels remains true even when the conditions are abolished. For this reason a revaluation of Henry James's world is necessary.

Re-reading him after the blitz (and our present counter-blitz) reveals, surely, a paradox which is a central obstruction to understanding him, unless it is fully explained. The paradox is this: that the greatest refinements in his novels often lead (by the most devious route) to crude situations in which characters cannot communicate with each other, so that, in fact, they behave with a kind of over-refined stupidity. James's characters often behave most stupidly when he is being his most clever, whereas, when he is being straightforward, or even creating an image which seems irrelevant, he often strikes his realest depths of perception. In Hollywood films, and in most contemporary novels, we are accustomed to the characters behaving with sub-human stupidity. What we do not expect is for them to behave with superhuman stupidity: to be too clever to understand one another. And yet the amount of unhappiness in the world of Henry James's novels and of lost opportunities, due to misunderstanding which could have been disposed of with a few straight words, is far greater than in real life. Unhappiness due not to passionate causes but to a "sense of style" in esthetic living is what really gives an air of artificiality to the Jamesian world—far more than his aristocrats and their golden hangings.

Misunderstandings in fiction are usually produced by different characters living according to different rules of moral conduct. The hero does not lie, does not give away secrets, plays the game according to rules not observed by the cad. Henry James also has his set of rules—which act as inhibiting forces to prevent his clever characters from understanding each other.

They are rules of a somewhat remarkable kind; the model Henry James characters, especially his women, are usually tremendous liars. They lie to conceal their feelings. A good example is Fleda Vetch in *The Spoils of Poynton*, who lies to her lover Owen Gereth; lies to his mother, of whom she is the confidante, and, by implication, lies to Mona, her rival, whom Owen marries. All these lies are of the heroic kind, but, clever as they are, they make the reader a little impatient.

The Spoils of Poynton, in fact, is an excellent example of James. It shows him at his very best: at the same time one sees a full application of all the extraordinary rules which do a kind of subtle violence to his human situations.

This short novel is a wonderful story of the havoc worked by a dominating personality (Mrs. Gereth), who cares more for exquisite objects than for the human beings who are closest to her. Mrs. Gereth's passion for her collection at Poynton—her house—is authentic, and her behavior is convincing from beginning to end. Her plans are clearly anchored to one central passion—for material things. Her mistakes are as real as her plots. Mrs. Gereth *is The Spoils of Poynton*. Because James understands her so fully, the story is a masterpiece.

Apart from Mrs. Gereth, there are Fleda Vetch, who shares Mrs. Gereth's appreciation of her works of art, but who, at the same time, cares for human beings. And there is Owen Gereth, Mrs. Gereth's son—stupid, handsome, remarkably English—and engaged to Mona, who has a coarse, hearty, back-slapping relationship with him.

The *objects* at Poynton, together with the house, have been left, in his father's will, unconditionally to Owen. It follows that when Owen marries, Mrs. Gereth will have to leave Poynton—unless, by chance, she finds a daughter-in-law who in some way accommodates her. Mrs. Gereth sees a chance to pair Fleda off with Owen—but, from the first, she bungles it. This kind of bungling is convincing because it is passionate, human bungling. But in the course of the highly involved action, Owen Gereth—having become engaged to Mona—falls in love with Fleda. In order to prevent Owen and Fleda falling into each other's arms—and Mrs. Gereth from coming to live with them—James makes use of all his inhibiting methods.

The first, familiar-inhibiting force in a James story is situation fortified by pattern. Fleda's situation is that she has thrown in her lot with Mrs. Gereth. They are both almost penniless, while Mona and Owen are, by right, the possessors. Loyal as she is to Mrs. Gereth, Fleda is obviously in an embarrassing position if she plots to oust Mona and get Poynton for herself, even if this is what Mrs. Gereth wants. Fleda is on the wrong side of the fence.

Also against the simple and straightforward fact that Owen and Fleda love each other, there are the principles of Fleda's character. Her sense of honor does not permit her to be a gold-digger—nor does it allow her to "plot" against Mona.

1944

William S. Burroughs becomes a junkie.

Therefore, she does not admit—until circumstances become too strong for her—that she loves Owen. Even then, she orders him to go back and marry Mona unless Mona freely releases him.

Unfortunately, just as Fleda does this, Mrs. Gereth, who has nabbed the spoils and taken them to another house, returns them, thinking that Mona has broken with Owen. Mona, getting the things she wants, accepts the man whom she will not take without the objects, and who does not love her. Thus, the principle that "love will find a way" is flouted; but, apart from Mrs. Gereth's destructive tactlessness and Owen's weakness, Fleda's behavior is too theoretical to be entirely convincing.

In his later novels, James introduces a curious moral value, which is the virtue of carrying off a crime with an air. In the *Wings of the Dove*, the adjective "beautiful" is frequently applied to Kate Croy at moments when she is really little better occupied than in mixing the poison which will kill the poor little rich girl, Milly. Charlotte, in *The Golden Bowl*, is another of James's characters who is "beautiful" as the tigress is beautiful. Here, again, James is only doing very circuitously what other writers do more straightforwardly. He is asking us to admire violence and wickedness because it is carried off with style, just as a writer like Hemingway will gild his thugs and bullfighters. He attempts to substitute a partly esthetic, partly snobbish, standard of behavior for a moral one.

At the same time, James is a moralist—and a great one. Two ideas exist side by side in his more highly organized books, and they are to some extent contradictory. One is the piercing moral vision which makes him see quite clearly the crimes perpetrated by the passion for *things* in social relationships; the crime of *The Spoils of Poynton*, for example. The other hare he pursues is the idea that social life has its own peculiar rules which have nothing to do with morality and nothing to do with happiness, the pursuit of which is "beautiful" and to be admired. Immorality may, to some extent, be atoned for by excellence at the social game.

There is good reason for this. James was aware that the life of cultured people sometimes depends on mountains of ill-gotten gain. But the virtuous rich people—the Millies and Maggies—who are already possessors of wealth, can afford to be good. The Kates and Charlottes are shabby immoralists going through the stage of initiation already passed by Milly and Maggie. James's tenderness toward them is that if they play the game when they get their wealth, the crime of initiation may be forgotten.

It is the life of the spirit which James cares about. And if he has surrounded that life with a barrier of wealth, who can contradict him? He has his own deep disturbances and uneasinesses. His true insight lies not so much in his ambiguous sense of values as in his piercing vision of the price people have to pay for everything in life. The amount his characters have to suffer, whether love or gain be their aim, is prodigious. Intelligence is all, and intelligence is the costliest of all.

His realization of this is what makes him, in spite of everything, one of the writers of life and love and death, and not just a snob writer caring for super-refined tastes and conversation. He cares for Poynton, he cares for human friendship, and he can throw Poynton into the flames at the end of the book, and the burning of the material symbols of James's world will seem a small thing beside the courage and desolation of poor Fleda's heart. Thus it is that the physical destruction of the beautiful objects in James's Europe does not make us feel that his novels were dependent on their gilt and stones. They can be thrown into the scale of our courage and our suffering, and the spirit of our civilization, which James loved, can still triumph.

Essay

Malcolm Cowley on "The Middle American Style"
July 15, 1945

MANY AMERICAN NOVELS TODAY, especially those by young men, are written in an exaggeratedly simple style, full of "ands," "all rights" and "anyways," full of accurate notes about the physical actions of the characters and flat statements about the way they felt. Book reviewers call it "the Hemingway style," using the phrase week after week. Literary historians explain that it began as a combination of what Hemingway learned from Sherwood Anderson and Gertrude Stein with his memories of people talking up in Michigan. The truth is that it goes back much farther into the American past, and it might be useful to trace its history in brief.

It began long ago as an attempt to reproduce the actual words and intonations of the American frontiersmen, and therefore it had little to do with the literary language used east of the Hudson. Its earliest appearance was in humorous sketches and notably in the great collection of tales that gathered round David Crockett, the Congressman from the Canebrakes. Robert Montgomery Bird of Philadelphia was possibly the first to use something like the real language of frontiersmen in the dialogue of a novel: *Nick of the Woods*, published in 1837. Mark Twain of Missouri was the first to write a whole book and a serious book in the new style: of course it was *Huckleberry Finn*.

It was published in 1884, with an introductory note explaining that several dialects were used in it: "the Missouri Negro dialect, the extremist form of the backwoods Southwestern dialect, the ordinary 'Pike County' dialect, and four modified versions of the last." All the dialects are exactly rendered, when the characters start talking, but that isn't the important feature of the book, even from the standpoint of style. Its importance there is that Huck tells the story in his own words and that, besides being a modified version of the Pike County dialect, those words are also a literary medium capable of being used for many different effects: not only backwoods humor but also pity and terror and the southward sweep of the River. Ernest Hemingway would say, many years later: "All modern American literature comes from one book by Mark Twain called *Huckleberry Finn*. There was nothing before. There has been nothing as good since."

There has been, however, a further development of this Middle American style as a literary instrument. In a sense, Mark Twain had apologized for using it, by putting it into the mouth of an illiterate hero; it was not at all his fashion of speaking for himself. The next step was for an educated author to use this style when writing ordinary third-person narrative. That was the step taken by Gertrude Stein in her first book, *Three Lives*, and it was a shocking step to her earliest readers. No publisher would accept the manuscript. A commercial printer hesitated to set it in type, even when payment of his charges was guaranteed. He sent an emissary to Miss Stein in Paris, to learn whether she was illiterate. "You see," her visitor said hesitantly, "the director of the Grafton Press is under the impression that perhaps your knowledge of English"—"But I am an American," said Miss Stein, as if that explained her whole manner of writing.

Unlike most of her later books, *Three Lives* told a recognizable story—three stories, in fact—and it had a clearly recognizable effect on Sherwood Anderson, who read it in his Chicago days and wrote in praise of the author. Hemingway read it, and in Paris after the war he adopted Miss Stein as his teacher and critic. He also felt an early, fervent and brief admiration for Sherwood Anderson. His style was not acquired from either of them—from the first it was largely his own invention—but Miss Stein in particular encouraged him to write a strictly Midwestern prose.

I have sketched this long development very briefly, mentioning only a few of the crucial books and authors. To illustrate the story, let me give a series of four quotations, extending over more than a century:

1. Old Tiger and Brutus were sitting upon the edge of the water, whining because they couldn't git over; and I had a mighty good dog named Carlow—he was standing in the water ready to swim; and I observed as the water passed by him it was right red—he was mighty badly cut. When I

come to notice my other dogs they were all right bloody, and it made me so mad that I harked 'em on, and determined to kill the bear.

I hardly spoke to 'em before there was a general plunge and each of my dogs just formed a streak going straight across. I watched 'em till they got out on the bank, when they all shook themselves, old Carlow opened, and off they all started. The water was right red where my dogs jumped in, and I loved 'em so much it made me mighty sorry.

—*Sketches and Eccentricities of Col. David Crockett of West Tennessee*, 1833.

2. I was powerful glad to get away from the feuds, and so was Jim to get away from the swamp. We said there warn't no home like a raft, after all. Other places do seem so cramped up and smothery, but a raft don't. You feel mighty free and easy and comfortable on a raft.

—*The Adventures of Huckleberry Finn*, by Mark Twain, 1884.

3. Jeff had never spoken to her at all about it. It just seemed as if it were well understood between them that nobody should know that they were so much together. It was as if it were agreed between them that they should be alone by themselves always, and so they would work out together what they meant by what they were always saying to each other.

—*Three Lives*, by Gertrude Stein, 1908.

4. As the shadow of the kingfisher moved up the stream, a big trout shot upstream in a long angle, then lost his shadow as he came through the surface of the water, caught the sun, and then, as he went back into the stream under the surface, his shadow seemed to float down the stream with the current, unresisting, to his post under the bridge where he tightened facing up into the current.

Nick's heart tightened as the trout moved. He felt all the old feeling.

—*In Our Time*, by Ernest Hemingway, 1925.

Even without dates or signatures, the casual reader of these four passages would assume that they were written by four different authors; yet he would also notice, I think, that they belong to the same prose tradition. Essentially it is a Midwestern style, but it is something more than a dialect, and it does not depend for its effect on misspellings or on violations of English grammar. If all the errors were edited out of the earlier passages; if Davy Crockett said "get" instead of "git" and Huck Finn said "wasn't any" instead of "warn't no"; if all the words listed as

1945

The first crime/mystery column appears in the *Book Review*.

Americanisms were changed to their English equivalents, these four quotations would still be American by virtue of the accents, the pauses, the fashion in which words are put together.

All four authors, beginning with the unknown journalist who listened to Davy Crockett's stories, reveal the same underlying attitude toward their material. They all have the same habit of making flat assertions about their emotional reactions ("It made me mighty sorry," "You feel mighty free and easy and comfortable on a raft," "He felt all the old feeling") that come after a series of violent physical images and therefore give the effect of understatement. Hemingway didn't invent that trick, any more than Crockett did; it was always part of the Midwestern tradition in story-telling.

Neither did Gertrude Stein invent the trick of repeating the same word in several sentences, so that it gives a keynote to the paragraph. Crockett found the trick instinctively: notice his repetition of "water" and "right red." Mark Twain used the word "raft" as keynote of the quoted sentences, which, by the way, have been echoed hundreds of times in contemporary writing. Hemingway used the words "stream" and "current" and "tightened." Most writers of standard English prose keep looking for synonyms, in order not to repeat the same words over and over. This Midwestern style, on the other hand, is based on a pattern of repetitions.

Here are a few of its other characteristics, as revealed in the quoted passages:

1. The words are simple in themselves, taken from common speech, and the authors make no effort to avoid a long succession of monosyllables. The "phrase"—that is, the group of words—tends to be rather longer than in standard English, and the accent or changed tone of voice falls on the last word in each group, almost as in French. Thus: "As the shadow of the *kingfisher* moved up the *stream,* a big trout shot upstream in a long *angle,* then lost his shadow as he came through the surface of the *water.*"

2. The sentence structure is generally looser than in standard English, with a number of simple statements connected by "and" or "but" or "when."

3. Most of these authors show a fondness for intensifying adverbs and adverbial expressions: "mighty," "right," "powerful," "just," "so," "at all." This, by the way, has always been a characteristic of American as a spoken language.

4. Some of the authors make an excessive use of present participles and participial tenses to give the effect of continued action: "they were always saying," "tightened facing up," etc.

5. All of them tend to avoid abstract nouns; instead, they use relative clauses to convey the same ideas. This tendency is especially clear in the passage from Gertrude Stein: she does not say "their meaning," but "what they meant"; she does not say "their conversation," but "what they were always saying to each other."

Some day I should like to see a more systematic analysis of this style that American novelists now seem to learn in the cradle. And some day I should like to see its development traced through the fiction of the last twenty years. It was certainly Hemingway who made it popular, but some of his contemporaries (including Fitzgerald and Dos Passos, but not Thomas Wolfe) seem to have approached it independently. It began to run riot among the novelists a little younger than Hemingway, like Steinbeck and Saroyan and Raymond Chandler. Curiously it has never gained a hold in contemporary poetry: Carl Sandburg's early experiments in the American language were widely read but had comparatively few imitators. The poets, most of them, write a tortured but late-classical English. The novelists try with more or less success to speak United States.

Remains of the Day

Brideshead Revisited by Evelyn Waugh
December 30, 1945

BY JOHN K. HUTCHENS

"**M**Y THEME**,**" says the narrator in Evelyn Waugh's latest, his most carefully written and deeply felt novel, "is memory, that winged host." And, with that, the brightly devastating satirist of England's Twenties and Thirties moves from one world to another and a larger one; from the lunacy of a burlesqued Mayfair, very glib and funny and masking the serious point in farce, to a world in which people credibly think and feel. Whether *Brideshead Revisited* is technically as expert, of its kind, as *Decline and Fall, Vile Bodies* or *A Handful of Dust* may be debatable. The important point just now is that it is bigger and richer, and that—to those of Mr. Waugh's admirers who might recently have suspected he was exhausting a rather limited field—it will almost certainly be his most interesting book in ten years; more interesting in story and in style, and not least in what it implies about its author and his growth as an analyst and an artist.

For Mr. Waugh is very definitely an artist, with something like a genius for precision and clarity not surpassed by any novelist writing in English in his time.

This has been apparent from the very beginning of his career—a career in which *Brideshead Revisited*, different in setting, tone and technique from all his earlier creative work, is yet a logical development.

Brideshead Revisited has the depth and weight that are found in a writer working in his prime, in the full powers of an eager, good mind and a skilled hand, retaining the best of what he has already learned. It tells an absorbing story in imaginative terms. By indirection it summarizes and comments upon a time and a society. It has an almost romantic sense of wonder, together with the provocative, personal point of view of a writer who sees life realistically. It is, in short, a large, inclusive novel with which the 1946 season begins, a novel more fully realized than any of the year now ending, whatever their other virtues.

Of the earlier Waugh, the moralist remains. For Mr. Waugh is, of course, a moralist after his fashion, and always was; when you look even slightly beneath the hilarity of those Mayfair studies, you see that he is performing the satirist's ancient function; he is excoriating the morals and standards of a society. Needless to say, he is too much the artist—and too astute as an entertainer—ever to be didactic; but inevitably it is there, the satirist's way with absurdity, including what is absurd in empty tradition; the moralist's hatred of injustice and his unspoken belief in the values of intelligence and simple decency.

Here, again, is the post–World War I England, but in very different focus; the story seen not through the eyes of a Paul Pennyfeather or a William Boot, comical character devices of earlier Waugh books, but told in the first person by a sensitive and intelligent observer, one Charles Ryder, architectural painter, captain in the British Army, looking back from middle-age at his youth. In the scheme of *Brideshead Revisited* that change in focus is all important, the frame in which the story is set between prologue and epilogue lending it perspective and narrative flexibility, the enchantment of experience recalled and sifted. The emotional tone and content of *Brideshead Revisited* are accordingly heightened beyond any Mr. Waugh has achieved before.

In the beginning it is gay enough—an affectionately ironic picture of Oxford in 1923, the sunflower estheticism, plovers' eggs and getting drunk at luncheon, the lively, small banter, the happy irresponsibility, *Antic Hay*. It is there that Ryder meets Lord Sebastian Flyte and forms a romantic friendship with him; Sebastian, the brilliant, charming, "half-heathen" second son of an old Catholic family that is verging on dissolution which, Mr. Waugh seems to suggest, parallels England's change from the old order to the new. Then, with the story's arrival at Brideshead and its baroque castle, the tone changes to a somber hue as the themes develop: the love story of Ryder and Sebastian's sister, Julia, of which Ryder's and Sebastian's friendship had been a spiritual forerunner; the Church giving haven to the soul-torn, drunken Sebastian and reclaiming Julia and even the Byronic father who comes home at last from Italy to die.

There is much of the earlier Waugh in this: the sharp phrasing, the keen and often deadly use of detail, the living speech, the scorn of vulgarity, the light summary touch with minor characters (Anthony Blanch, the Wildeean esthete; the narrator's crafty father, a mildly balmy old gentleman)—these traits and skills logically carry over, and you would expect them in any Waugh book, because they are part of him. What is quite new is a leisure, a spaciousness of style and structure. One sentence and one paragraph after another, of reflection and description, could have found no place in the staccato atmosphere of his other works. By comparison with them, this is as a full-bodied play to a deft vaudeville sketch. Nowhere, for example, even in *A Handful of Dust*, would you have found Mr. Waugh letting himself go to the extent of:

This was the creature, neither child nor woman, that drove me through the dusk that summer evening, untroubled by love, taken aback by the power of her own beauty, hesitating on the steps of life; one who had suddenly found herself armed, unawares; the heroine of a fairy story turning over in her hands the magic ring; she had only to stroke it with her fingertips, and whisper the charmed word, for the earth to open at her feet.

There will be, quite certainly, no little discussion and even controversy about the problem he poses, or rather the conclusion he offers. Mr. Waugh, a Catholic, is also, politically, a Tory. As a writer, as a story-teller and an artist, he insists on nothing. Of Catholicism as a factor in the lives of the Marchmains he writes so objectively, seeing it through the eyes of the non-Catholic narrator, that it could actually be construed as the slightly sardonic report of an unbeliever confronted with (and baffled by) "an entirely different outlook on life." What he is saying in effect is that faith is a saving answer to anyone who has it or has had it, which could scarcely be called propaganda, though he will surely be charged with propaganda. It will be said, too, that his political conservatism is patent in his reluctant acceptance of social change, and this will be true; the end of a Brideshead is to him a matter for regret and misgiving, for he believes in "order" and the continuity of tradition. Above all, he believes in responsibility, the absence of which in his own class he has castigated so fiercely.

But those who disagree with him on religious or political grounds, or both, will have a time for themselves in trying to prove that his beliefs have marred his literary artistry. *Brideshead Revisited* is Mr. Waugh's finest achievement.

The Courage of His Conventions

The Berlin Stories
(*The Last of Mr. Norris* and *Goodbye to Berlin*)
by Christopher Isherwood
February 12, 1946

BY ALFRED KAZIN

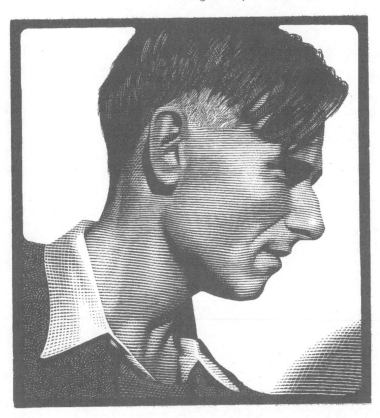

RECENTLY, while talking with a man just returned from Hollywood, I asked him what Isherwood was doing. "Oh, he's left the monastery and is writing movie scripts." The reply interested me, among other reasons, because it was said and received without mockery; it would have been funny enough of anyone else. For there is something about Christopher Isherwood's work that inspires respect and steady affection for the man, even when he chooses to cross the California bridge of sighs between a swami like Gerald Heard and the word factories of Culver City. Huxley, in his current Yogi period, has the look of a zealot; there is more than the suggestion in his latest that something pretty grim awaits you—the sterility of his own characters, in fact—if you do not follow his glacial prescriptions to sip the purgative of mysticism. But Huxley's religiosity repels me not because of its subject but because, like his fiction, it is outside people, society, politics. Isherwood's first concern, as a novelist, has always been with these. I have not followed his excursions into Vedanta, but I trust him to seek the truth in his own way, knowing that he seeks it for me, too. I believe in him, though I may never believe his gospel. He inspires the same good faith in his readers that is so much the secret, in himself, of his gift for creating character; of looking at the human problem with love and openness.

Isherwood is a real novelist, a real *minor* novelist. How minor he can be is seen in *Prater Violet*, which is a charming encore to his best work, notable for the loving portrait of Friedrich Bergmann, but slight and essentially retrospective — in its own way, I suspect, a way of postponing the integration of his creative gifts with his religious search. How good a novelist he has been can be seen in *The Berlin Stories*, which is the welcome reissue of his two most famous novels — *The Last of Mr. Norris* and that little diamond among modern narratives, *Goodbye to Berlin*.

It is a great distinction to be a minor novelist today; it is much more difficult than to imitate the great novelists. We have many excellent minor poets; we have almost no novelists — only great armies of people who have taken advantage of the deceptive looseness of the novel to write political tracts, memories of battle, romances, biographies and apocalyptic visions. To be a real minor novelist is to do the undisguisable work of fiction — which is to create a real human scene whose meanings follow from what has been freshly demonstrated — without the imperative world-meaning, the search for basic control, which has marked the crisis of modern thought. The great novelists of our day — the Kafkas, the Joyces, the Prousts, the Thomas Manns — have known how to transpose narrative into new keys for the understanding, but only by beating out whole new forms for the novel. The real minor novelist tends to stay in the well-pastured traditions of realism, finds his place rather than makes it, is easy in his ways and usually a clever innovator in style. He can survive as a novelist even if his total intellectual and religious life does not flow freely into his work. The Kafkas and Prousts could never begin with so much division in themselves. They cannot afford to be economical; they do not save themselves to write fiction; their only safety is in their creativity. The minor novelist is not a pioneer, but a well-bred artist. He stands for enjoyment, as the major novelists stand for a new conception of man and history. Isherwood is such a minor novelist, successful and delightful within his realm; but obviously only part of him gets into his fiction. He is interesting, among other reasons, because he is so fine-fibered an offshoot of the English genius. He writes his language — it is not always our language — with the tonal exactitude and humorous economy of a man who can be conventional, so distinct is his verbal inheritance. Isherwood's writing has the music of the old English fineness in it. It never presses or stammers; its correctness is implicit in its wit and it is always headed for the comic; he is a man who touches his language with affectionate brush strokes in exile.

He writes so well because he has been an exile for some time. England also has its refugees, its meditative wanderers standing outside the high world of nationalism and official political optimism. They are voluntary refugees, but involuntary defenders of a cause whose depths only all their lives and all their works will make clear to them. They are not less alienated from their country than the Thomas Manns or Friedrich Bergmanns are from theirs; and, though

1946

The French authorities prosecute Maurice Girodias for publishing Henry Miller; this is France's first obscenity case since *Madame Bovary* in 1857.

1946

Dr. Benjamin Spock's *Baby and Child Care* appears for the first time; its publishers will later call it the best seller of the century; others declare it the best seller in American publishing history (not counting the Bible).

their removal was less abrupt and less political, they are not less estranged. The real human background of *The Berlin Stories* is always Isherwood's own alienation from the England of the '20s and '30s, that slumbering pit in which Baldwin's pigs grunted in self-satisfaction and over which Chamberlain's umbrella rose like a forlorn tear. The hero of *Goodbye to Berlin* is in fact called Christopher Isherwood; he is and is not the man who wrote the story.

In a prefatory note Isherwood explains that the character called "Christopher Isherwood" is only a "ventriloquist's dummy," not to be identified as a matter of course with himself. His landlady, Fräulein Schroder, calls him "Herr Issyvoo." That suits him better. He is not really Christopher Isherwood; he is an impersonation of the author, tougher in some respects than the real Isherwood and more tender in others. Yet he is not someone else than Isherwood, or even his mask. He is the man who wrote the story as he lived it and is now teaching, replenishing the "real" Isherwood to put it down. He is the hero of the author's literary and moral imagination, as each of us has a hero, bearing our name and attired in our flesh, who is the negotiable self-portrait we have of ourselves. Our literary self-portraits are not necessarily better than we are; only easier to live with in our own minds; and for purposes of artistic production, more fertile. They are ourselves, as genial and exact observers.

First Impressions

Lord Weary's Castle by Robert Lowell
November 3, 1946

BY SELDEN RODMAN

O NE WOULD HAVE TO GO BACK as far as 1914, the year that saw the publication of Robert Frost's *North of Boston* or to T. S. Eliot's "The Love Song of J. Alfred Prufrock" to find a poet whose first public speech has had the invention and authority of Robert Lowell's. Lowell, like the two earlier poets, has the advantage of a complete break with currently fashionable tradition. Frost had gone back as far as Edward Rowland Sill and the still earlier New Englanders, and Eliot to the then unknown French symbolist Laforgue for his instruction. Lowell has as expertly adapted the angry mythologies of Herman Melville and John Milton to his strictly modern sensibility.

I saw the sky descending, black and white,
Not blue, on Boston where the winters wore
The skulls to jack-o'-lanterns on the slates,
And Hunger's skin-and-bone retrievers tore
The chickadee and shrike.

Like Melville, Lowell is filled with fury at the spectacle of mankind beating its brains out in a spurious race after the unattainable—call it the White Whale, World Conquest, the Perfect State, or what you will—and like Melville, he comes to endow the symbolism of this chase, inhuman and homicidal, with a greater reality than those who have seemed to lose their humanity in its madness. The great figures of history and religion are forced into line by Lowell as cavalierly and as inevitably—and sometimes, it must be admitted, as humorlessly—as by Milton.

At 29, Lowell's career already matches in stubborn heresy such of his forebears as "Rebel John," who grew orchids under glass in protest against Jefferson's plebeian politics, Imagist poet Amy with her long Manila cigars, and that Robert Traill Spence Lowell, his namesake, who took a slum parish in Newark, and then, "wearying of the high pulpit," became headmaster of St. Mark's and author of the narrative poem, "The Relief of Lucknow." Young Lowell, who began to write at St. Mark's and Harvard, is said to have refused Ferris Greenslet permission to include him in *The Lowells and Their Seven Worlds.* In 1943 he tried to enlist twice, but when drafted refused to serve on the grounds that the country was out of danger and that the bombing of civilians was unprincipled. He served six months in Federal prison, became a Catholic and in 1944 published 250 copies of *Land of Unlikeness,* which contained ten of the poems in the present volume and half a dozen others good enough to assure a lesser poet's reputation.

Lowell's command of the heroic line, his use of cacophony, alliteration and assonance is often awe-inspiring; but his rhetoric and violent imagery, especially in those religious poems which are not dramatized by the colloquial details of his own experience, sometimes becomes overpowering.

But at their best there is a great hope for poetry, and indeed for America, in these poems. Without Whitman's loose though buoyant optimism, they are directed just as surely at a people and a land of infinite, unfulfilled promise. The voice is vibrant enough to be heard, learned enough to speak with authority and savage enough to waken all but the dead.

1946

Ezra Pound is committed to St. Elizabeths Hospital for the criminally insane, where he spends the next 12 years.

It Was War, and We Had to Expect It

Hiroshima by John Hersey
November 10, 1946

BY CHARLES POORE

1946

Jack Kerouac meets Neal Cassady, who will become the model for Dean Moriarty in *On the Road*, and the two are soon making plans to travel across the country together.

IN THE WANING DAYS of last August people all over the United States who read *The New Yorker* suddenly began to discuss the harrowing experiences of a clerk in the personnel department of a tin works, a doctor in a private hospital, a tailor's widow, a priest, a young member of a surgical staff and the pastor of a church. The six were, of course, the principals in John Hersey's *Hiroshima*, which Alfred A. Knopf has just published in book form—the quietest, and the best, of all the stories that have been written about the most spectacular explosion in the time of man.

Hiroshima penetrated the tissue of complacency we had built up. It penetrated it all the more inexorably because it told its story not in terms of graphs and charts but in terms of ordinary human beings, Miss Sasaki, Dr. Fujii, Mrs. Nakamara, Father Kleinsorge, Dr. Sasaki, the Reverend Tanimoto, aliens and enemies though they were. Their stories had been taken down directly by Mr. Hersey, who brought to his interrogations and investigations the gifts he had already conspicuously shown as the Pulitzer Prize–winning author of *A Bell for Adano* and as an outstanding war correspondent.

Hiroshima seems destined to become about the most widely read article and book of our generation. What effect will it have on the thinking of our time, particularly the thinking of our own people?

The overwhelming response to Mr. Hersey's story would seem to provide one overwhelming answer. It is simply that millions of people have wanted to hear what he has to say and to have others hear it, too. Among the stacks of letters that have been written to *The New Yorker*, perhaps one in ten objected to the magazine's having printed *Hiroshima*, and the dissenters were generally people who thought the magazine had strayed grievously out of its field. Most thought the Japs had the bomb coming to them.

A very small minority believes that we should never have used the bomb at all; this is balanced by the lunatic fringe which has already picked targets on which it would like us to use it again. And among minorities there is considerable difference of opinion. When someone who thinks we should never have used the bomb at all encounters people whose brothers were in the Death March on Bataan or whose sons were among the immense forces poised for the final invasion of Japan's home islands that General Marshall outlined in his report, there must be a profound cleavage.

In the subtly contrapuntal text of *Hiroshima* opinion is divided. "It was war," Mrs. Nakamura says, "and we had to expect it," though Dr. Sasaki has a more violent view, while a priest writes in his report: "It seems logical that he who supports total war in principle cannot complain of a war against civilians."

As for those who, for various and somewhat disparate reasons, say that we did not need to use the bomb because the Japanese would have collapsed pretty soon anyway, various things are said in rebuttal. One is the example of the fanatic resistance at Okinawa and the knowledge that similar installations had been prepared in the home islands (at Hiroshima, for one place) but on a much vaster scale. Another is the very gruesomeness of arriving at the equation of American lives it would be proposed to offer in the gamble of saving a Japanese city.

There is abundant evidence that most Americans took the bomb as the epitome of all the instruments of war that maim and blast and burn and kill, and that *Hiroshima* has stirred thousands to a new awareness of the necessity for world action to stop using them all—not excepting the even more lethal instruments that may now be germinating in the strange mind of man.

First Impressions

Tales of the South Pacific by James Michener
February 2, 1947

BY DAVID DEMPSEY

TALES OF THE SOUTH PACIFIC is truly one of the most remarkable books to come out of the war in a long time. It was an unorthodox war that Mr. Michener fought, compounded of fiction and fact and cloaked in a romantic haze reminiscent of the novels of H. Rider Haggard. Certainly, the dirty, humdrum business of fighting (or waiting to fight) was never as much fun as Mr. Michener makes it seem throughout much of his book. Yet he has captured the phase of war that most GIs in the Pacific will want to remember—the flaming sunsets, the quiet, pellucid lagoons of some forgotten atoll, jungles that breathed mystery as well as malaria.

It was in this far-off land, where the native men wore bracelets of pigs' teeth and the women wore nothing, that a million Americans made their home for more than four years, superimposing a culture of jeeps and bulldozers over a

1947

Goodnight Moon, by Margaret Wise Brown, illustrated by Clement Hurd, settles the first baby boomers to sleep.

civilization as timeless as it is primitive. This juxtaposition of cultures forms the inspiration for most of Mr. Michener's tales. A visitor to dozens of islands himself, he came away from each with a story that will not be found in the official annals of the war. Bloody Mary and Colonel DeBecque and the Frenchman's Daughter and the descendants of the *Bounty* mutineers do not figure in our victory over the Japanese. Yet they are symbols of the casual asides that made the isolation and monotony of the Pacific endurable. They are also, Mr. Michener makes clear, the tempters and temptresses that lured many a good American into pursuing the will-o'-the-wisp of South Sea island romance.

Mr. Michener is a born story teller but, paradoxically, this ability results in the book's only real weakness—the interminable length of some of the tales. Mr. Michener saw so much, and his material is so rich, that he simply could not leave anything out. He re-enacts a love scene half a dozen times (including portal-to-portal by-play), when twice would do it. He ambushes the reader in the scenery. Some of his characters are altogether too windy. Fortunately, even when he is uneconomical, Mr. Michener is never dull. Nor is his lengthiness always a fault. He knows that some stories cannot be told in the conventional 5,000 words and, with the daring of an inspired amateur, he tells them in 10,000, and eloquently, too.

First Impressions

Sexual Behavior in the Human Male by Alfred Kinsey
January 4, 1948

BY HOWARD A. RUSK

JUST AS THIS was a difficult study to make, and a difficult book to write, so is it also a difficult book to review. Difficult, because of the magnitude of the subject—difficult, because it deals with man's basic drive to reproduce, a drive as strong as that for survival—difficult, because of our prejudices, taboos and preconceptions, preconceptions colored by personal experience which gives the individual the microscopic rather than the total concept. Now, after decades of hush-hush, comes a book that is sure to create an explosion and to be bitterly controversial.

The 12,000 subjects interviewed in the study by Professor Kinsey and his colleagues represented every level in our social strata—bootleggers and clergymen, professors and prostitutes, farmers and gamblers, ne'er-do-wells and social registerites. The final result—800 pages of text, with hundreds of charts and graphs

1947

Gentleman's Agreement, by Laura Z. Hobson, about a gentile who poses as a Jew, challenges anti-Semitism and group stereotyping.

analytically evaluated and statistically sound—is cold, dispassionate fact, starkly revealing our ignorance and prejudices.

We understand little of the range of human sex behavior. On the graph showing sexual frequency each individual differs only slightly from those next on the chart. This brings up the point of what is "normal" and "abnormal," and where such terms fit in a scientific study.

Dr. Kinsey points out that homosexual experience is much more common than previously thought. He indicates, however, that this is an extremely difficult problem to analyze "as very few individuals are all black or all white," and that one homosexual experience does not classify the individual as a homosexual. He decries the use of the noun, and finds that there is often a mixture of both homo- and heterosexual experience.

To have or not to have premarital intercourse is a more important issue for a larger number of males than any other aspect of sex. Individuals in our American society rarely adopt totally new patterns of sex behavior after their middle teens. The peak of sex drive and ability comes in the late teens rather than in the late 20's or 30's as heretofore believed.

Comparing the sexual activities of older and younger generations evidences the stability of our sexual mores and does not justify the opinion harbored by some that there are constant changes in such mores.

Because we are all human, every individual is bound to interpret this study in terms of personal experience. For some it will be clarifying. Others it will confuse. Some will be alarmed, others will be shocked; a few will interpret the general findings as grounds for personal license. After the initial impact, when time permits sober reflection and analysis—the end results should be healthy. They should bring about a better understanding of some of our emotional problems, and the bases for some of our psychiatric concepts.

1948

Alfred Kinsey's *Sexual Behavior in the Human Male* tries to bring science into the bedroom. The distaff side gets its turn in 1953.

The Supreme Test of His Mettle

The Gathering Storm by Winston S. Churchill
June 20, 1948

BY ANNE O'HARE MCCORMICK

WHAT GIVES WINSTON CHURCHILL his unique position among the figures of any age, indeed, is the extraordinary role he plays as the maker and the recorder of history. He is at once the hero of the drama and the dramatist. The dual character is immortalized in

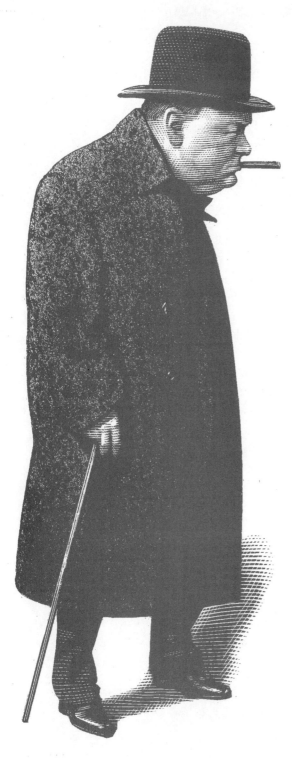

this book, the magnificent beginning of the crowning work of his life.

Here we see Churchill the historian looking at Churchill the statesman. The historian appreciates fully, often with relish, sometimes with a touch of awe, but never with surprise, the part the statesman plays. Nothing so small as vanity deforms his vision. Churchill is too well aware of the grand proportions of the drama of his time to overrate his own size. But he does not underrate it, either. Still less does he underrate his responsibility to history.

The Gathering Storm is the first volume of his memoirs of the Second World War, which are expected to fill five volumes. The first book in this volume, "From War to War," is a powerful indictment of the statesmanship that threw away every advantage won in the First World War in a policy of "easy-going placatory appeasement." The moral is that more resolute and far-sighted leadership could have averted disaster. Certainly if Churchill had been listened to in those years, Hitler would have been stopped cold before he had a chance to arm. But he was not listened to.

The second book is more revealing. Now Churchill is in action, in the government instead of out. In a series of heretofore unpublished letters and memoranda we get glimpses of the confused and inconclusive meetings of the War Cabinet and fresh insights into the state of physical and mental unpreparedness in which Britain and France entered the war. Churchill reached the height he had always aspired to in the lowest moment of British history. The volume ends on a note of excitement, the author's excitement in facing the supreme test of his mettle.

Churchill believes in man—and comprehends the uneven stuff of which he is made. His characterizations of the men he dealt with are probing but lenient. He manifests a curious sympathy for Chamberlain, "pack horse of our great affairs." Molotov, with his cannonball head, black moustache and comprehending eyes, his slab face, his verbal adroitness and imperturbable demeanor, "was above all men fitted to be the agent and instrument of the policy of an incalculable machine."

The temptation to keep on quoting is almost irresistible. Churchill is one of the most prolific writers of his generation, and some of the most glowing passages he has ever written illuminate this book. He cannot jot down a hasty memorandum except in the best literary style. He commands the English language as a skillful general commands armies, and it served him just as well, for Britain was saved in the first place because he was able to use the tongue of Shakespeare and Milton, Gibbon and the King James Bible, to evoke the great memories and loyalties that live and echo in his rolling rhythms. It is our immense good fortune that a man who presided over this crisis in history is able to turn the action he lived through into enduring literature.

Stricken

The Plague by Albert Camus
August 1, 1948

BY STEPHEN SPENDER

*T*HE PLAGUE is parable and sermon, and should be considered as such. To criticize it by standards which apply to most fiction would be to risk condemning it for moralizing, which is exactly where it is strongest. *The Plague* stands or falls by its message. The message is not the highest form of creative art, but it may be of such importance for our time that to dismiss it in the name of artistic criticism would be to blaspheme against the human spirit. What we have to judge is the urgency, for us, of M. Camus's morality. It seems to me to be of so much urgency that we would be wrong to ask how much significance people may attach to it tomorrow. There are certain things which need to be said now, without care for the future, and these are said, even with naïveté, in *The Plague*.

The pattern of the novel does permit M. Camus to exercise his considerable literary gifts of narrative and creating character. The city of Oran in Algiers is afflicted, in the year 194— with the plague. At first, the rats come out of the sewers and die in the streets. No one can understand this phenomenon. Then, a few weeks later, people start dying of a mysterious fever accompanied by horrible symptoms, all of them described with detached realism.

Zelda Sayre Fitzgerald, muse and author of the novel *Save Me the Waltz*, dies in a hospital fire.

M. Camus is a master of the Defoe-like narrative and of the African atmosphere. Against the background of events which he conveys with ease, he creates various attitudes of human beings toward the plague, heightened by touches of intimate observation. As far as possible he isolates his people from their private lives, and thrusts them into their public situation. It is a virtue of his artistic purpose that two of his main characters, the journalist Rambert and the doctor Rieux, should be separated by the plague from their women-folk throughout the whole narration. The other main characters are Father Paneloux, the priest; Tarrou, the idealistic celibate, and the shady character Cottard, of whose intimate life one hears nothing.

The plague becomes thus a kind of laboratory for studying attitudes toward itself. The attitude of the priest, who first regards it as a scourge of God against the wickedness of modern life, and later, with less complacency, as a test of Christian acceptance of terrible suffering; of the journalist Rambert, for whom it means separation from the woman he loves; of Tarrou, for whom it becomes the occasion of realizing his passion to correct an injustice at the center of society which he has always known; of Cottard, for whom it provides an opportunity of escaping justice and practicing black market activities.

In realizing these attitudes, M. Camus shows his rarest quality, which is charity. Its sympathy saves this novel from being mere noble pamphleteering and raises it to the level of art—and this sympathy establishes a relationship between his persons.

So much for the telling of the parable. What of the sermon and the morality? Here we encounter an inevitable naïveté, which will shock some critics. The plague is Social Catastrophe which is always with humanity—and which, in our own day, takes the form of modern war and the Occupation—too recognizable at moments in Camus's parable. But judging this book as parable, not as novel, one has to ask is the parable justified? One seeks the depth within the obvious: I think one finds this in the terrible and deeply moving passage which describes the death of the child of Othon, the judge. This death is the center of all the deaths in the book. Because it challenges the religious in being the death of a completely innocent victim, it raises the problem of social evil in the acutest form.

The two sermons of the Catholic priest Paneloux are, in a sense, false trails: the true message is contained in the confession of Tarrou toward the end of the period of plague. Tarrou tells how he grew up to regard himself as an enemy of established society because he realized that it was based on assassination. He joined the political forces which sought to overthrow society: "Needless to say, I knew that we too, on occasion, passed sentences of death. But I was told that these deaths were inevitable for the building up of a new world in which murder would cease to be. Until the day when I was present at an execution — it was in Hungary — and exactly the same dazed horror that I'd experienced as a youngster made everything reel before my eyes."

At this point Tarrou is obviously at the stage of the hero of Koestler's *Arrival and Departure*, disillusioned with communism and unhappily searching for a crusade without a cross. His conclusion is perhaps not satisfactory, but it takes us further than Koestler and than the existentialists. "All I maintain is that on this earth there are pestilences and there are victims, and it's up to us, as far as possible, not to join forces with the pestilences. I decided to take, in every predicament, the victim's side, so as to reduce the damage done. Among them I can at least try to understand how one attains to the third category; in other words, to peace."

In itself, this message does not perhaps take us much further than pacifist quakerism. But within the whole context of the parable of the plague it takes us a good deal further. For one thing, the problem of the victim is not that of one party member who kills a member of another party; it is the problem of the child, that is to say, the innocent life existing within every human being, destroyed by both parties. For another, the victims of the plague are the potential majority. They will continue to be the majority, until the healers fight the plague, until there are leaders to take the side of the innocent. Again, peace here is not pacifism; it is health and innocence and life itself. Lastly, Tarrou's confession turns the parable of the plague, which is a natural force, into a far more powerful parable of the evil which man wreaks on man.

M. Camus's method of parable is justified because it is impossible to state simply in political terms an attitude which seems outside political practicality. This attitude can only exist within an evocation of the human social situation so powerful that it overshadows the politics which are a part of that situation. What he has done is to state the anguish in the minds of those people who, because they were liberals, supported the anti-Fascist movement during the past decade, and who now see themselves poised between a powerful yet amorphous West and the police states of the East.

The question he poses is: Must people choose at all? Has not their position ceased now to be the famous "liberal dilemma" and become the overwhelming condition of all humanity? Sometimes to ask a question may be more effective than to support a cause. And if the world is divided into two warring sides — and if both these realistic-seeming sides are bankrupt — the realistic attitude may be to try to understand the meaning of peace.

First Impressions

Tevyeh's Daughters by Sholom Aleichem
January 23, 1949

BY THOMAS LASK

1949

**Margaret Mitchell is struck
and killed by a speeding
automobile in Atlanta.**

S o APPEALING, so warm and quick with life are the writings of Sholom Aleichem that he has stimulated translators all over the world. Sholom Aleichem could fashion an effective short story as well as the next one; but in his use of the common Yiddish speech he stands alone. It is both the substance and the medium, and he has wedded it to characters who raised dialect to the stature of art. These were the Jews of the Russian pale who flourished before the Holocaust and who were so poor that the spoken word was their only permanent possession. Their poverty was a function of their lives, and they raised it to "an art, a calling, a career." But through their speech they squared themselves with their condition, their assorted misfortunes, even with the Almighty Himself. As Maurice Samuel has remarked, life got the better of them, but they got the better of the argument.

But if Frances Butwin's translations are not the equal of the originals (and she would be the last to claim that they are), there is still a great deal that is amusing and delightful. Moreover, she has had the intelligence to concentrate on one of the most popular and effective of Sholom Aleichem's portraits, Tevyeh the Dairyman. Tevyeh had two major afflictions: his livelihood (or lack of one) and his seven marriageable daughters. No matter how he contrived or plotted to arrange suitable marriages, the girls had minds of their own and insisted on making their own destiny—with lamentable results. One spurns a rich man and marries a poor tailor who dies and bequeaths her a roomful of children. Another insists on marrying a revolutionary and sharing his exile. A third marries a Christian, and Tevyeh cuts the apostate from his life if not his heart. One, finally, does marry a rich magnate from Yehupetz, but this is the worst marriage of all—for money has been substituted for love and pride. In spite of his outward show, Tevyeh admires their independence. Throughout it all he struggles with his poverty, fences and argues with his wife, curses and communes with his nag and hides his sorrow.

All this may not seem the raw material for comedy, yet Tevyeh is one of the great humorous figures in literature. He has become so from his wit, from the play of his mind on the events, from his intellectual sprightliness. He is irrepressible. For every situation he has the quotation or twist of phrase that redeems it. His humor doesn't derive from the situation, but from the language that applies to it. It is a bittersweet optimism that is found so frequently in Sholom

Aleichem's writings. It can be seen in the note that Yosrolik writes to his friend after the Kishinev massacre: "Pogrom? Thank God we have nothing to fear. We have already had two of them and a third won't be worth while."

When Newspeak Was New

1984 by George Orwell
June 12, 1949

BY MARK SCHORER

J AMES JOYCE, in the person of Stephen Dedalus, made a now famous distinction between static and kinetic art. Great art is static in its effects; it exists in itself, it demands nothing beyond itself. Kinetic art exists in order to demand; not self-contained, it requires either loathing or desire to achieve its function. The quarrel about the fourth book of *Gulliver's Travels* that continues to bubble among scholars—was Swift's loathing of men so great, so hot, so far beyond the bounds of all propriety and objectivity that in this book he may make us loathe them and indubitably makes us loathe his imagination?—is really a quarrel founded on this distinction.

It has always seemed to the present writer that the fourth book of *Gulliver's Travels* is a great work of static art; no less, it would seem to him that George Orwell's new novel, *1984*, is a great work of kinetic art. This may mean that its greatness is only immediate, its power for us alone, now, in this generation, this decade, this year, that it is doomed to be the pawn of time. Nevertheless it is probable that no other work of this generation has made us desire freedom more earnestly or loathe tyranny with such fulness.

1984 appears at first glance to fall into that long-established tradition of satirical fiction, set either in future times or in imagined places or both, that contains works so diverse as *Gulliver's Travels* itself, Butler's *Erewhon*, and Huxley's *Brave New World*. Yet before one has finished reading the nearly bemused first page, it is evident that this is fiction of another order, and presently one makes the distinctly unpleasant discovery that it is not to be satire at all.

In the excesses of satire one may take a certain comfort. They provide a distance from the human condition as we meet it in our daily life that preserves our habitual refuge in sloth or blindness or self-righteousness. Mr. Orwell's earlier book, *Animal Farm*, is such a work. Its characters are animals, and its content is therefore fabulous, and its horror, shading into comedy, remains in the generalized realm of intellect, from which our feelings need fear no onslaught. But *1984* is a work of pure horror, and its horror is crushingly immediate.

1949

Reviewer identifications are added for all reviews in the *Book Review*.

The motives that seem to have caused the difference between these two novels provide an instructive lesson in the operations of the literary imagination. *Animal Farm* was, for all its ingenuity, a rather mechanical allegory; it was an expression of Mr. Orwell's moral and intellectual indignation before the concept of totalitarianism as localized in Russia. It was also bare and somewhat cold and, without being really very funny, undid its potential gravity and the very real gravity of its subject, through its comic devices. 1984 is likewise an expression of Mr. Orwell's moral and intellectual indignation before the concept of totalitarianism, but it is not only that.

It is also—and this is no doubt the hurdle over which many loyal liberals will stumble—it is also an expression of Mr. Orwell's irritation at many facets of British socialism, and most particularly, trivial as this may seem, at the drab gray pall that life in Britain today has drawn across the civilized amenities of life before the war.

In 1984, the world has been divided into three great super-states—Eastasia, Eurasia, and Oceania. Eurasia followed upon "the absorption of Europe by Russia," and Oceania, "of the British Empire by the United States." England is known as Airstrip One, and London is its capital. The English language is being transformed into something called Newspeak, a devastating bureaucratic jargon whose aim is to reduce the vocabulary to the minimum number of words so that ultimately there will be no tools for thinking outside the concepts provided by the state.

Oceania is controlled by the Inner Party. The Party itself comprises 25 percent of the population, and only the select members of the Inner Party do not live in total slavery. The bulk of the population is composed of the "proles," a depraved mass encouraged in a gross, inexpensive debauchery. For Party members, sexual love, like all love, is a crime, and female chastity has been institutionalized in the Anti-Sex League.

Party members cannot escape official opinion or official observation, for every room is equipped with a telescreen that cannot be shut off; it not only broadcasts at all hours, but it also registers precisely with the Thought Police every image and voice; it also controls all the activities that keep the private life public, such as morning calisthenics beside one's bed. It is the perpetually open eye and mouth. The dictator, who may or may not be alive but whose poster picture looks down from almost every open space, is known as B.B., or Big Brother, and the political form is called Ingsoc, the Newspeak equivalent of English socialism.

One cannot briefly outline the whole of Mr. Orwell's enormously careful and complete account of life in the super-state, nor do more than indicate its originality. He would seem to have thought of everything, and with vast skill he has woven everything into the life of one man, a minor Party member, one of perhaps hundreds of others who are in charge of the alteration of documents necessary to the preservation of the "truth" of the moment.

Through this life we are instructed in the intricate workings of what is called "thought-crime" (here Mr. Orwell would seem to have learned from Koestler's *Darkness at Noon*), but through this life we are likewise instructed in more public matters such as the devious economic structure of Oceania, and the nature and necessity of permanent war as two of the great super-states ally themselves against a third in an ever-shifting and ever-denied pattern of change. But most important, we are ourselves swept into the meaning and the means of a society which has as its single aim the total destruction of the individual identity.

To say more is to tell the personal history of Winston Smith in what is probably his thirty-ninth year, and one is not disposed to rob the reader of a fresh experience of the terrific, long crescendo and the quick decrescendo that George Orwell has made of this struggle for survival and the final extinction of a personality. It is in the intimate history, of course, that he reveals his stature as a novelist, for it is here that the moral and the psychological values with which he is concerned are brought out of the realm of political prophecy into that of personalized drama.

1984, the most contemporary novel of this year and who knows of how many past and to come, is a great examination into and dramatization of Lord Acton's famous apothegm, "Power tends to corrupt and absolute power corrupts absolutely."

L. Ron Hubbard

Alice B. Toklas • James Jones • Norman

Mailer • William F. Buckley • Ralph Ellison

Flannery O'Connor • Anne Frank • Bernard Malamud

E. B. White • Eudora Welty • Norman Vincent Peale

Dr. Seuss • Simone de Beauvoir • James Baldwin • Ian

Fleming • Randall Jarrell • J. R. R. Tolkien • W. H. Auden

Herman Wouk • Eugene O'Neill • Grace Metalious

Jack Kerouac • Alan Greenspan • Vladimir

Nabokov • William J. Lederer

Eugene Burdick

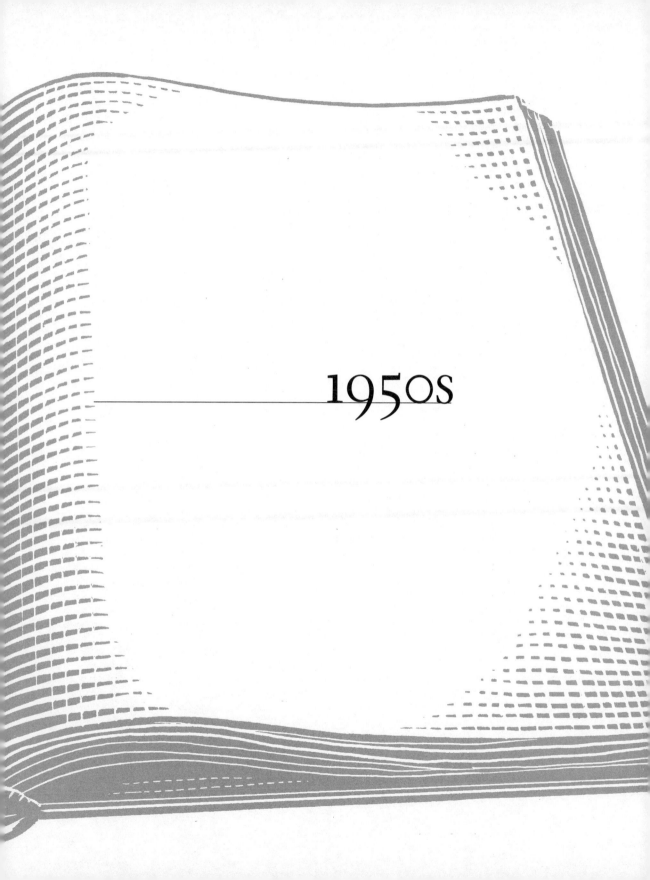

1950s

First Impressions

Dianetics: The Modern Science of Mental Health
by L. Ron Hubbard
July 2, 1950

BY ROLLO MAY

O N THE FIRST PAGE of *Dianetics* L. Ron Hubbard states that as a result of the theories presented in this book the "hidden source of all psychosomatic ills and human aberration has been discovered and skills have been developed for their invariable cure." A book which makes such claims needs to be scrutinized carefully.

Tremendous promises are made about what dianetics can do for one and the very simple way it can be used. It not only is supposed to eliminate any psychosomatic illness from which you suffer, and to help you "achieve at least one-third more than present capacity for work and happiness," but it also is held to raise your IQ substantially.

A few weeks of this therapy is held to equal several years of psychoanalysis, except that the person who has had dianetic therapy is certain not to relapse. One wonders at times in reading these fantastic claims whether the author is not writing with his tongue in his cheek, but there is no evidence that he does not mean his claims to be taken at face value.

The importance of *Dianetics*, in this reviewer's judgment, is that it so clearly illustrates the most common fallacy of our time in regard to psychological ills. This is the fallacy of trying to construct a simple science of human behavior based upon mathematics and using for its models the physical sciences and the machine.

In this book Hubbard often inveighs against shock therapy and psychosurgery—and one can sympathize with his intent at these points. But he does not see that the excessive use of shock therapy and surgical mutilation of the brain are based on the same assumptions as his own theory—namely, the oversimplification of complex human ailments and the endeavor to heal these ailments by mechanical methods.

It has required long and patient effort on the part of succeeding students of human behavior to arrive at the objective realization of the fact that man is a creature who lives in a social world, a creature who is responsible in ways a machine can never be. Hence the development of psychoanalysis has been away from the ideal of the "exact science" toward the inclusion of such disciplines as the social sciences, learning theory, and, latterly, ethics.

Books like this do harm by their grandiose promises to troubled persons and

1950

The Lion, the Witch and the Wardrobe, first of C. S. Lewis's *Chronicles of Narnia*, appears.

1950

Gwendolyn Brooks's book of poetry *Annie Allen* wins a Pulitzer Prize, the first Pulitzer award for literature given to a black author.

by their oversimplification of human psychological problems. This harm may be partially offset if such writings demonstrate to us again the absurdity of trying to view man as a machine, and encourage us to make of psychotherapy and psychoanalysis broad sciences of human relations.

Essay

Alice B. Toklas on Americans in Paris
August 6, 1950

BEFORE I CAME TO PARIS Henry James had already gone to live in England. When we went there in 1902 it had been arranged that we should spend a day with him at Rye, but to my bitter disappointment we received word that he was too indisposed to receive us on the appointed day, would we come some day on the following week? Alas, we had to return to Paris before then. It is my unique lost opportunity. The influence of the years Henry James spent in France is abundantly to be found in what he wrote in England. Could *The Spoils of Poynton,* though placed in England, have been so poignantly described without his having had intimate French experience? Did the foreign experience, first in Italy and then in France, finally in England, even his eventually becoming a British subject, did these make him less an American? Was his nationality not strengthened by his exterior conformity to the ways and habits of another country?

Fresh from the boat train the first person I met in Paris was the American writer Gertrude Stein. She so often wrote of her work, her friends and herself with intimacy and precision that one hesitates to add to the choice she considered appropriate to tell.

Americans were surprised, some of them shocked by her remaining so typically American, by her not having taken advantage of the foreign culture about her. Culture never did interest her.

Sherwood Anderson came to see G.S. on his first visit to Paris and frequently on his second. He had a winning brusquerie, a mordant wit and an all-inclusive heart—the combination was irresistible. He spoke no French but got on amazing well with the Parisians, particularly with the working people. He told us that when he had been for some time going about the country lecturing, one day he discovered that he held his audience in his hand the way an opera singer does, naturally he broke his contract at once and stopped lecturing. He was very handsome and incredibly charming and the story teller.

Scott Fitzgerald, the first of the lost generation as G.S. called them, was the only one at the time of their descent on Paris to have already given proof of a gift—and ample proof it was. He was distinguished, highly intelligent and completely attaching. He came to see G.S. on his thirtieth birthday and said that it was unbearable for him to have to face the fact that his youth was over. But you've been writing like a man of 30, she said with insistence. Have I, he said questioningly. He never believed what she told him about his work. It was too comforting to be true. He had a cynical wit. It's easy to flatter the old, he said apropos of the clumsiness of one of his contemporaries when they came to see us.

Then there was Dos Passos with his Latin charm and Glenway Wescott with his Canadian accent and Hemingway whose dark luminous eyes—they were that then—a flashing smile and the *guiches* he affected made him look like an Italian. He once told us he had Italian blood. The ambulance service into which he had volunteered had been attached to the Italian army and was at the front in time for Caporetto and the retreat which Hemingway described at length in *A Farewell to Arms*. Hemingway in speaking of a rich American and his wife who had come to Paris to become writers said that he had known them before they could read or write. And in a kind of way I feel that about Hemingway, that is that neither reading nor writing is a natural inevitable necessity for him.

Ezra Pound whom we met a few times in the Twenties had a great interest in Japanese prints, political economy and oriental music. He reminded me of Queen Victoria's remark after some one had most unfortunately selected to sing to the Queen "The Wearing of the Green," so sad and so very mistaken.

T. S. Eliot was brought to call upon G.S. once. He was a sober, almost solemn, not so young man who, refusing to give up his umbrella, sat clasping its handle while his eyes burned brightly in a non-committal face.

It wasn't until '34 that G.S. met Thornton Wilder. They immediately formed a warm friendship. Endless were their discussions, on walks in the country, in crowded city streets, in her home. Some of the solutions went into her work. Thornton's varied interests and activities fascinated her, they seemed to concentrate his qualities, not to disperse them.

Of the young American writers in Paris today there are the GIs with their Bill of Rights and their second novel on the way who are taking a course at the Sorbonne called French Civilization, for which at the end of the year they will be given a certificate of attendance. And there are the more serious Fulbright scholars who are writing tomes for their doctorate.

It would be well if one could end on an encouraging note but one can not completely ignore the highly colorful group in and about the cafés of Place Saint-Germain des Prés. They publish and contribute their writings to at least one little review. They may be gently dismissed with an "unpredictable future."

1950

V. S. Naipaul, 18 years old, arrives at Oxford from his home in Trinidad.

At War with Themselves

From Here to Eternity by James Jones
February 25, 1951

BY DAVID DEMPSEY

W HEN A BOOK IS as commanding in its narrative power and grasp of character as this one, it bears comparison with the very best that is being done in American fiction today. *From Here to Eternity* is the work of a major new American novelist. To anyone who reads this immensely long and deeply convincing story of life in the peacetime army, it will be apparent that in James Jones an original and utterly honest talent has restored American realism to a pre-eminent place in world literature.

Mr. Jones's novel, set at Schofield Barracks, Oahu, covers the years before and up through Pearl Harbor. It is about men who are at peace with the world and at war with themselves, about their rivalries, frustrations, hates and loneliness; about their women; about all the sutlers of virtue and camp-followers of vice that surround what is called, in peacetime, the Standing Army—an army, curiously enough, that always seems to be seated.

All this and hell too, for the moral azimuth of the novel is straight down. Since there are no great loves arising out of the priapic preoccupations of the soldiers, nor any heroic redemptions out of their sins, we would be wiser to turn to Margaret Mead rather than Dante as a guide. Mr. Jones is concerned with the almost biological relationship between the individual and the group, with the totems and taboos and orgiastic rites of a race of moral primitives, with the emotional pressures that fill the vacuum of life in the peacetime army. He has succeeded brilliantly in showing us the forces that destroy men when they live lives of rootless expediency.

The central theme is nonconformism. Using the Golden Boy idea, the author follows the career of a soldier who would rather bugle than box. There are no regulations in the army that decree that a man must box, but there are human improvisations which can make it tough for him if he doesn't. These are known as The Treatment and Pvt. Robert E. Lee Prewitt, the novel's principal character—a man who once played taps at Arlington—gets The Treatment.

His efforts to hold out against it form a study in the disintegration of a soldier and—in Thoreau's sense at least—the making of a man. Unfortunately, rebellion becomes an end in itself (all but one of Mr. Jones's recalcitrants fall into this fallacy) and the cause is lost.

This is not to suggest that the novel is involved with an elaborate symbolism; the book gives us the essence of a soldier's life rather than the symbols. It is the really eloquent virtue of *From Here to Eternity* that Mr. Jones makes us believe in his people, from the brass hats to the brass checks. They are human within the subhuman anonymity of the military machine—Prewitt, the bugler; Warden, the First Sergeant who manages his company with the dedication of a saint while seducing his commanding officer's wife; Bloom, who makes the one successful outward adjustment and then commits suicide; Malloy, the philosophical rebel.

They are talking about Bloom's suicide and Malloy expresses his approval:

"For every general in this world there have to be 6,000 privates. That's why I wouldn't stop any man from committing suicide. If he came up and asked to borrow my gun, I'd give it to him. Because he is either serious or else he's trying to maintain that illusion of freedom. If he was serious I'd want him to have it; if he was play-acting I'd want to call him _____. In our world, citizens, there's only one way a man can have freedom, and that is to die for it, and after he's died for it it don't do him any good. That's the whole problem, citizens. In a nutshell."

Yet their tragedy consists not alone in being among the 6,000 privates, but in the rootlessness of their lives, for which the army is no help.

From Here to Eternity is so uninhibited in its vocabulary, so outspoken in its descriptions, that it is bound to shock. It is a book for adults. Mr. Jones uses profanity skillfully, as do most soldiers for whom swearing is a way of making endurable the unendurable. Yet the book's extreme naturalism gives it a special importance at this time, when much of our serious fiction has turned introspective and somewhat effeminate in quest of psychological rather than social relationships.

In its statement of the ultimate values of a soldier's life, *From Here to Eternity* may not be as profound as Robert Henriques's *No Arms, No Armour*. Yet it will be read a long time for its minute and almost uncanny insight into army life, its pungent dialogue, its sheer narrative pull, its portrayal of the tenderness that sometimes is found beneath the crudest animal drives, its absence of mock heroics, its comic absurdities and irony and, above all else, its revelation of the perversity of human nature in the face of evil.

Mr. Jones has obviously written out of his own experiences. A native of Robinson, Ill., and a graduate of the Robinson High School, he served five years in the army, fought on Guadalcanal, where he was wounded, and witnessed the bombing of Pearl Harbor. At the time of his discharge he held the rank of private, having twice been reduced from (1) corporal and (2) sergeant.

Although his book ends shortly after the bombing of Pearl Harbor, it is a better "war" novel than those which have had war as a setting. Anyone who has ever worn the uniform of a soldier will recognize it as a definitive work, truer in its characterizations than *The Naked and the Dead*, less theme-ridden than *The Young Lions* and *Act of Love*, in every sense a work of heroic proportions.

In pushing forward the limits of naturalism while looking into the hearts of men, Mr. Jones does for our time what Stephen Crane did for his in *The Red Badge of Courage*. There have been more subtly written books about the American soldier, and books with more finished, conscious technique, but none that has been written with more integrity, or with a surer grasp of its material.

Make no mistake about it, *From Here to Eternity* is a major contribution to our literature, written with contempt for the forces that waste human life, and out of compassion for men who find love and honor and courage in the lower depths, where they are less apparent but sometimes more enduring. Its author speaks to us across an ocean of unshared experiences but from a world of common values. He makes us care about his soldiers and caring about them, we care about humanity.

Interview

Norman Mailer
June 3, 1951

BY HARVEY BREIT

O N JANUARY 31, Norman Mailer noted the fact that he had become 28 years old. "I was a young man in my prime," he said the other day with hardly any irony, "when I wrote *Naked and the Dead*. The army was the only milieu I ever had. It was like living in a society where rumor has the same validity as fact, like a tight community where you can weep about people you never saw. Like someone says, 'This guy got knocked off in a patrol.' And everyone feels bad."

If there is such an attribute as being restfully intense, Mr. Mailer has it. It is a quality of intensity that is without strain and makes no demands on a companion. Strangely, and comfortably let it be added, while Mr. Mailer's thought and speech have intensity, Mr. Mailer himself—beneath the mind and voice as it were—is perfectly relaxed. It is an attractive paradox that creates intellectual stimulation and physical relaxation simultaneously.

He said, "I wrote *Naked* in fifteen months. The new one, *Barbary Shore*, is half the size and took me three years. I don't think of myself as a realist," Mr. Mailer said after a pause, during which he obviously thought back to his first, and very impressive, novel. "That terrible word naturalism. It was my literary heritage—the things I learned from Dos Passos and Farrell. I took naturally to it, that's the way one wrote a book. But I really was off on a mystic kick. Actually—a funny thing—the biggest influence on *Naked* was *Moby-Dick*."

Had he known while writing it? Mr. Mailer nodded. "I was sure everyone would know. I had Ahab in it, and I suppose the mountain was Moby-Dick. Of course, I also think the book will stand or fall as a realistic novel.

"I may as well tell you what the title of the new book means," he said. "It has a double meaning. Barbary, for me, is a very rich word. One of the meanings is barbarism and the other, not in the Oxford dictionary, has romantic connotations. You think of the exotic, of pirates, of romantic things."

Were we coming back to romantic things? "I think the tendency as you come closer and closer to doom and disaster," Mr. Mailer said, and stopped and began again, "There is a tendency, given such a condition, to move closer and closer to amorous wish fulfillments."

How did Mr. Mailer feel about being an author in an age that was moving, as he put it, closer and closer to doom and disaster? "It is probably one of the worst periods in history for a writer," he said with hardly any hesitation. "To be a novelist today is absolutely a bone-cracker. The knowledge that you are embarking on a novel that may take ten years of your time is vitiated by what you read each day in the newspapers. I mean if you are trying to do work of the devotion of *Ulysses* or *Remembrance of Things Past* or *The Magic Mountain*. On top of that, the fundamental problem of knowledge is involved."

Mr. Mailer stared fixedly at his companion. "In the past," he said, "a novelist could create a world view, a whole thing in itself. It is different today because knowledge is broken down, departmentalized. Time and time again the novelist louses up his work with jargons and special knowledge. And yet you can't eschew it. It's better to fail that way than to ignore this condition and keep on in some little cubbyhole. If a writer really wants to be serious he has to become intellectual, and yet nothing is harder. Intellectuality delivers the writer to self-questioning and to despair at his own limitations; it vitiates the attempt at large, serious works because you are unable to suspend the critical faculties even at the times when you should."

Eliot once said perhaps the main difference between the good and bad poet was not so much one of talent as it was the inability of the bad poet to be *unconscious* at the right times. Mr. Mailer nodded at least in partial assent. "I'm beginning to have a pride in writers. They are radical, always disturbing. What they write has nothing to do with what they profess, which is usually silly.

"A great writer always goes to the root, he is always coming up with the contradictions, the impasses, the insoluble dilemmas of the particular time he lives in. The result is not to cement society but to question it and destroy it. Faulkner

Oops!

July 15, 1951

The Catcher in the Rye

BY J. D. SALINGER

This Salinger, he's a short-story guy. And he knows how to write about kids. This book though, it's too long. Gets kind of monotonous. And he should've cut out a lot about these jerks and all that crumby school. They depress me.

175

may profess all sorts of things, he may even be off on a white supremacy binge, but actually the total of his work has caught the horror at the same time that it has caught the fact that he loves it. A great writer has to be capable of knowing the rot, and he has to be able to strip it down to the stink, but he also has to love that rot. A writer has to have a tough mind, the toughest mind of his time. And he has to have a great heart."

First Impressions

God and Man at Yale by William F. Buckley
November 4, 1951

BY PETER VIERECK

WILLIAM BUCKLEY, Yale '50 and as a senior the able editor of *The Yale Daily News*, has written a book that challenges political, religious and educational liberalism. Nominally his book is about education at Yale. Actually it is about American politics.

How right he is to insist that man has a moral nature, that statism threatens it, that freedom depends on the traditional value-code of the West and that unmoral materialism results in a suicidal tolerance debunking all values as equally "relative." Specifically, Buckley attacks "statism and atheism" on the Yale campus. Yet what is his alternative? Nothing more inspiring than the most sterile Old Guard brand of Republicanism, far to the right of Taft.

Is there no "selfish materialism" at all among the National Association of Manufacturers as well as among the "New Deal collectivists" here denounced? Is it not humorless, or else blasphemous, for this eloquent advocate of Christianity, an unworldly and antieconomic religion, to enshrine jointly as equally sacrosanct: "Adam Smith and Ricardo, Jesus and Saint Paul?" And why is this veritable Eagle Scout of moral sternness silent on the moral implications of McCarthyism in his own camp?

In this urgent crisis, when our survival against Soviet aggression depends on cooperating with *both* conservatives *and* anti-Red heroes like the socialist Reuter in Europe, the author irresponsibly treats not only mild social democracy but even most social reform as almost crypto-communism. He damns communism, our main enemy, not half so violently as lesser enemies like the income tax and inheritance tax.

Has a young Saint Paul emerged from the Yale class of 1950 to bring us the long-awaited Good Tidings of a New Conservatism and Old Morality? The trumpets of advance publicity imply it. However, this Paul-in-a-hurry skips the prerequisite of first being a rebel Saul. The difference between a shallow and a profound conservatism is the difference between the easy, booster affirmation that precedes the dark night of the soul and the hard-won, tragic affirmation that follows it.

Great conservatives—immortals like Burke, Alexander Hamilton, Disraeli, Churchill, Pope and Swift—earned the right to be sunnily conservative by their long dark nights. You can earn it by being a tortured romantic Irishman like Burke. You can earn it by Churchill's bitter decade before his great hour in 1940. You do not earn a heart-felt and conviction-carrying conservatism by the short-cut of a popular campus clubman, without the inspiring agony of lonely, unrespectable soul-searching.

A Tale from Underground

Invisible Man by Ralph Ellison
April 13, 1952

BY WRIGHT MORRIS

THE GEOGRAPHY OF HELL is still in the process of being mapped. The borders shift, the shore lines erode, coral islands appear complete with new sirens, but all the men who have been there speak with a similar voice. These reports are seldom mistaken as coming from anywhere else. As varied as the life might be on the surface, the life underground has a good deal in common—the stamp of hell, the signature of pain, is on all of the inhabitants. Here, if anywhere, is the real brotherhood of man. Fleeing toward hell, Dante beheld a man whose voice seemed weak from a long silence, and he cried to him, saying, "Have pity on me, whoever thou art, shade or real man!"

Shade or real man? Visible or invisible? The Invisible Man would have smiled in recognition if hailed like that. He lives, he tells us, in an underground hole. To fill this dark hole with light, he burns 1,369 bulbs. He burns them free. A fine Dostoyevskyan touch. In his *Notes from the Underground* Dostoyevsky says: "We are discussing things seriously; but if you won't deign to give me your attention, I will drop your acquaintance. I can retreat into my underground hole."

The Invisible Man is also discussing things seriously. His report in this novel might be subtitled, "Notes From Underground America," or "The Invisible Black Man in the Visible White Man's World." That is part of his story, but the deeper layer, revealed, perhaps, in spite of himself, is the invisible man becoming visible. The word, against all of the odds, becoming the flesh. Neither black nor white flesh, however, for where the color line is drawn with profundity, as it is here, it also vanishes. There is not much to choose, under the skin, between being black and invisible, and being white, currently fashionable and opaque.

"Let us descend into the blind world here below," Virgil says, and the Invisible Man descends through the ivy-covered college doors. His report begins the day that rich men from the North, white philanthropists, appear on the campus of a Negro college in the South. They are there for the ceremony of Founders Day. The Invisible Man, a student at the college, is chosen to act as the chauffeur for one of them. He shows him, inadvertently, the underground black world that should not be seen. Before the day is over, both the millionaire and the student have been disillusioned, and the student, expelled from the college, leaves for New York.

In the city he becomes increasingly invisible. Hearing him rouse the crowd at the scene of a Harlem eviction, a key party bigwig sees a bright future for him in the brotherhood. The mysteries of the Order, revealed and unrevealed, as they fall to the lot of the Invisible Man, have the authentic air of unreality that must have bemused so many honest, tormented men. The climax of the book, and a model of vivid, memorable writing, is the night of the Harlem riots. Mr. Ellison handles this surrealist evening with so much authority and macabre humor, observing the forces with such detachment, that the reader is justified in feeling that in the process of mastering his rage, he has also mastered his art.

Perhaps it is the nature of the pilgrim in hell to see the visible world and its inhabitants in allegorical terms. They do not exist, so much as they represent. They appear to be forces, figures of good and evil, in a large symbolical frame, which makes for order, but diminishes our interest in their predicament as people. This may well be the price of living underground. We are deprived of uniqueness, no light illuminates our individuality.

The reader who is familiar with the traumatic phase of the black man's rage in America will find something more in Mr. Ellison's report. He will find the long anguished step toward its mastery. The author sells no phony forgiveness. He asks none himself. It is a resolutely honest, tormented, profoundly American book.

"Being invisible and without substance, a disembodied voice, as it were, what else could I do?" the Invisible Man asks us in closing. "What else but try to tell you what was really happening when your eyes were looking through! And it is this which frightens me: Who knows but that, on the lower frequencies, I speak for you?"

But this is not another journey to the end of the night. With this book the author maps a course from the underground world into the light. *Invisible Man* belongs on the shelf with the classical efforts man has made to chart the river Lethe from its mouth to its source.

The City of Fiendish Evangelists

Wise Blood by Flannery O'Connor
May 18, 1952

BY WILLIAM GOYEN

WRITTEN BY A SOUTHERNER from Georgia, this first novel, whose language is Tennessee-Georgia dialect expertly wrought into a clipped, elliptic and blunt style, introduces its author as a writer of power. There is in Flannery O'Connor a fierceness of literary gesture, an angriness of observation, a facility for catching, as an animal eye in a wilderness, cunningly and at one sharp glance, the shape and detail and animal intention of enemy and foe. The world of *Wise Blood* is one of clashing in a wilderness.

When Hazel Motes, from Eastrod, Tenn., is released from the army at the age of 22, he comes to a Southern city near his birthplace. He falls under the spell of Asa Hawks, a "blind" street preacher who shambles through the city with his degenerate daughter, Lily Sabbath Hawks, age 15. The encounter with Hawks turns Hazel Motes back into his childhood traumatic experience with his grandfather who was a preacher traveling about the South in an old Ford. The story of this novel, darting through rapid, brute, bare episodes told with power and keenness, develops the disintegration and final destruction of Hazel who physically and psychologically becomes Hawks and parrot-preaches (in vain) to the city crowds from the hood of his second-hand Essex.

In a series of grim picaresque incidents Hazel struggles to outfox and outpreach Hawks. He announces a new religion called "The Church Without Christ."

In Taulkinham, U.S.A., the city of Fiendish Evangelists, one is brought into a world not so much of accursed or victimized human beings as into the company of an ill-tempered and driven collection of one-dimensional creatures of sheer meanness and orneriness, scheming landladies, cursing waitresses, haunted-house people, prostitutes, fake blind men who take on, as they increase in number, the nature and small size of downright skulduggery and alum-mouthed contrariness. One is never convinced of any genuine evil in these people, only of a sourness; they seem not to belong to the human race at all, they are what the geneticist calls a race of "sports."

The stark dramatic power of the scenes is percussive and stabbing, but Miss O'Connor seems to tell her story through clenched teeth in a kind of Tomboy, Mean-Moll glee, and a few times she writes herself into episodes that have to contrive themselves to deliver her out of them, and then she is compelled to go on too far beyond or in the direction of sensationalism.

Miss O'Connor's style is tight to choking and as direct and uncompounded as the order to a firing squad to shoot a man against a wall. It perfectly communicates this devilish intent of the inhabitants of Taulkinham to be mean, or cadge or afflict each other. One cannot take this book lightly or lightly turn away from it, because it is inflicted upon one in the same way its people take their lives—like an indefensible blow delivered in the dark. Perhaps this sense of being physically struck and wounded is only the beginning of an arousal of one's questioning of the credibility of such a world of horror.

In such a world, all living things have vanished and what remains exists in a redemptionless clashing of unending vengeance, alienated from any source of understanding, the absence of which does not even define a world of darkness, not even that—for there has been no light to take away.

Life in the Secret Annex

The Diary of a Young Girl by Anne Frank
June 15, 1952

BY MEYER LEVIN

ANNE FRANK'S DIARY is too tenderly intimate a book to be frozen with the label "classic," and yet no lesser designation serves. For little Anne Frank, spirited, moody, witty, self-doubting, succeeded in communicating in virtually perfect, or classic, form the drama of puberty. But her book is not a classic to be left on the library shelf. It is a warm and stirring confession, to be read over and over for insight and enjoyment.

The diary is a classic on another level, too. It happened that during the two years that mark the most extraordinary changes in a girl's life, Anne Frank lived in astonishing circumstances: she was hidden with seven other people in a secret nest of rooms behind her father's place of business in Amsterdam. Thus, the diary tells the life of a group of Jews waiting in fear of being taken by the Nazis. It is, in reality, the kind of document that John Hersey invented for *The Wall*.

There is no lugubrious ghetto tale, no compilation of horrors. Reality can prove surprisingly different from invented reality, and Anne Frank's diary simply bubbles with amusement, love, discovery. It has its share of disgust, its moments of hatred, but it is so wondrously alive, so near, that one feels overwhelmingly the universalities of human nature. These people might be living next door; their within-the-family emotions, their tensions and satisfactions are those of human character and growth, anywhere.

Because the diary was not written in retrospect, it contains the trembling life of every moment—Anne Frank's voice becomes the voice of 6 million vanished Jewish souls. It is difficult to say in which respect the book is more "important," but one forgets the double significance of this document in experiencing it as an intimate whole, for one feels the presence of this child-becoming-woman as warmly as though she was snuggled on a near-by sofa.

Her father had already brought the family out of Germany in 1933. In June, 1942, a few weeks after the diary begins, the SS sends a call-up for Anne's sister, Margot, and the family goes into hiding. "I began to pack some of our most vital belongings into a school satchel . . . this diary, then hair curlers, handkerchiefs, schoolbooks, a comb, old letters." The Van Daans, with their 16-year-old son Peter, join the Franks. Later, because "Daddy says we must save another person if we can," an elderly dentist named Dussel is squeezed into the Secret Annex. He gets Anne's bed; she sleeps on a settee lengthened by chairs.

A born writer, Anne zestfully portrays the Annex inhabitants, with all their flaws and virtues. The common life effect which Mr. Hersey sought to suggest in *The Wall* here flowers with utter spontaneity. But Anne Frank's diary probes far deeper than *The Wall* into the core of human relations, and succeeds better than *The Wall* in bringing us an understanding of life under threat.

And this quality brings it home to any family in the world today. Just as the Franks lived in momentary fear of the Gestapo's knock on their hidden door, so every family today lives in fear of the knock of war. Anne's diary is a great affirmative answer to the life-question of today, for she shows how ordinary people, within this ordeal, consistently hold to the greater human values.

Two years passed in disciplined activities. The hidden ones kept busy with smuggled correspondence courses in speed shorthand, in Latin, in nursing; Dussel even attempted dental operations, hilariously described by Anne. She herself studied mythology, ballet, "family trees," while keeping up her schoolwork. She records the family disputes—Mrs. Van Daan violently resisting the sale of her fur coat, only to see it smoked up in black market tobacco! And the comic moments, as when her father lies on the floor trying to overhear an important business conference downstairs; Anne flattens herself beside him, lending a sharp ear. But business is so dull, she falls asleep.

Most wondrous of all is her love affair. Like a flower under a stone fulfilling itself, she came to her first love in her allotted time. "I give myself completely. But one thing, He may touch my face, but no more." All is told, from her potato-fetching devices for going up to Peter's attic lair, to the first misplaced kiss, on her ear. And the parents worrying about the youngsters trysting up there in the dusk, sitting by the window over the canal. And her fears that her older sister is lonely and jealous, leading to an amazing exchange of letters between the two girls, in those hidden rooms. Finally, there is even the tender disillusionment with Peter, as Anne reaches toward maturity, and a character understanding replaces the first tug of love. In all this there are perceptions in depth, striving toward mother, father, sister, containing love-anguish of the purest universality.

It is this unfolding psychological drama of a girl's growth, mingled with the physical danger of the group, that frees Anne's book from the horizontal effect of most diaries. Hers rises continuously, with the tension of a well-constructed novel.

The girl's last entries rather miraculously contain a climactic summation, a maturing self-analysis: "If I'm quite serious, everyone thinks it's a comedy, and then I have to get out of it by turning into a joke," she remarks with typical adolescent self-consciousness. "Finally, I twist my heart around again, so that the bad is on the outside and the good is on the inside. . . . I am guided by the pure Anne within, but outside I'm nothing but a frolicsome little goat who's broken loose."

This frolicsome little goat could write, "It's twice as hard for us young ones to hold our ground, and maintain our opinions, in a time when all ideals are being shattered and destroyed, when people are showing their worst side, and do not know whether to believe in truth and right and God.

"It's really a wonder that I haven't dropped all my ideals, because they seem so absurd and impossible to carry out. Yet I keep them, because in spite of everything I still believe that people are really good at heart. I simply can't build up my hopes on a foundation consisting of confusion, misery, and death. I see the world gradually being turned into a wilderness, I hear the ever-approaching thunder, which will destroy us too, I can feel the sufferings of millions and yet, if I look up into the heavens, I think that it will all come right, that this cruelty too will end, and that peace and tranquility will return again. . . .

"I want to go on living even after my death," Anne wrote. "I am grateful to God for giving me this gift, this possibility of developing myself and of writing, of expressing all that is in me." Hers was probably one of the bodies seen in the mass grave at Bergen-Belsen, for in August, 1944, the knock came on that hidden door in Amsterdam. After the people had been taken away, Dutch friends found Anne's diary in the debris, and saved it.

There is anguish in the thought of how much creative power, how much sheer beauty of living, was cut off through genocide. But through her diary Anne goes on living. From Holland to France, to Italy, Spain. The Germans too have published her book. And now she comes to America. Surely she will be widely loved, for this wise and wonderful young girl brings back a poignant delight in the infinite human spirit.

First Impressions

The Natural by Bernard Malamud
August 24, 1952

BY HARRY SYLVESTER

BACK IN THE THIRTIES the baseball writers making the swing through the West with the major league teams occasionally wondered whether one of their number would ever produce a serious novel about baseball. That novel has finally been written—and if the author does not come from the ranks of baseball reporters, at least he hails from Brooklyn and there are those who feel that qualifies him ex officio.

It's an unusually fine novel, too, although I don't know how the professionals are going to take it. For Bernard Malamud's interests go far beyond baseball. What he has done is to contrive a sustained and elaborate allegory in which the "natural" player—who operates with ease and the greatest skill, without having been taught—is equated with the natural man who, left alone by, say, politicians and advertising agencies, might achieve his real fulfillment.

The book's hero, Roy Hobbs, comes out of the West at the age of 19, brought to a major league training camp by a scout. He is shot by a girl in a hotel room

1952

The 16-year-old Allan Konigsberg has a joke published in Earl Wilson's newspaper column under the name Woody Allen.

and drops out of sight until, at the age of 34, he returns to the last place team in the National League and, with a trick bat—not unlike that used by Heinie Groh of the Cincinnati Reds back in the Twenties—almost single-handed leads the team into a tie for first place. Malamud has a mission and we grant him certain privileges, including the use of the super-realism he alternates with naturalism.

All the story is here of a natural man—hurt badly by his first love, recovering late for his profession, almost achieving greatness, then distracted or betrayed by people or objects or events all equated with elements in our environment. In his telling and always deliberate use of the vernacular alternated with passages evocative and almost lyrical, in his almost entirely successful relation of baseball in detail to the culture which elaborated it, Malamud has made a brilliant and unusual book.

Along Came a Spider

Charlotte's Web by E. B. White
October 19, 1952

BY EUDORA WELTY

E. B. WHITE has written a book for children, which is nice for us older ones as it calls for big type. The book has liveliness and felicity, tenderness and unexpectedness, grace and humor and praise of life, and the good backbone of succinctness that only the most highly imaginative stories seem to grow.

Wilbur is of sweet nature—he is a spring pig—affectionate, responsive to moods of the weather and the song of the crickets, has long eyelashes, is hopeful, partially willing to try anything, brave, subject to faints from bashfulness, is loyal to friends, enjoys a good appetite and a soft bed, and is a little likely to be overwhelmed by the sudden chance for complete freedom.

Charlotte A. Cavitica ("but just call me Charlotte") is the heroine, a large gray spider "about the size of a gumdrop." She has eight legs and can wave them in friendly greeting. When her friends wake up in the morning she says "Salutations!"—in spite of sometimes having been up all night herself, working. She tells Wilbur right away that she drinks blood, and Wilbur on first acquaintance begs her not to say that.

Another good character is Templeton, the rat. There is the goose, who can't be surprised by barnyard ways. "It's the old pail-trick, Wilbur. . . . He's trying to lure you into captivity-ivity. He's appealing to your stomach." The goose always repeats everything. "It is my idio-idio-idiosyncrasy."

What the book is about is friendship on earth, affection and protection, adventure and miracle, life and death, trust and treachery, pleasure and pain, and the passing of time. As a piece of work it is just about perfect, and just about magical in the way it is done. What it all proves—in the words of the minister in the story which he hands down to his congregation after Charlotte writes "Some Pig" in her web—is "that human beings must always be on the watch for the coming of wonders." Dr. Dorian says in another place, "Oh no, I don't understand it. But for that matter I don't understand how a spider learned to spin a web in the first place. When the words appeared, everyone said they were a miracle. But nobody pointed out that the web itself is a miracle." The author will only say, "Charlotte was in a class by herself."

"At-at-at, at the risk of repeating myself," as the goose says, *Charlotte's Web* is an adorable book.

First Impressions

The Power of Positive Thinking by Norman Vincent Peale
October 26, 1952

BY GEORGE R. STEPHENSON

A S MINISTER OF NEW YORK'S Marble Collegiate Church, Norman Vincent Peale has had wide experience with all sorts of people in all kinds of trouble.

There is no problem, difficulty, or defeat, the author claims, that cannot be solved or overcome by faith, positive thinking, and prayer to God. In citing proofs of his claim, he tells how people he knows have turned troubled minds into peaceful ones, improved their health, stopped worrying, increased their energy, and have become successful and popular.

Mr. Peale says that he does not ignore or minimize hardships and tragedies. In spite of this statement, these problems seem too easily solved, the success a bit too automatic and immediate, the answers a little too pat, and the underlying theology a shade too utilitarian.

Essay

Dr. Seuss on Writing for Children
November 16, 1952

THERE ARE MANY REASONS why an intelligent man should never ever write for children. Of all professions for a man, it is socially the most awkward. You go to a party, and how do they introduce you? The hostess says, "Dr. Seuss, meet Henry J. Bronkman. Mr. Bronkman manufactures automobiles, jet planes, battleships and bridges. Dr. Seuss . . . well, *he* writes the sweetest, dear, darlingest little whimsies for wee kiddies!"

Mr. Bronkman usually tries to be polite. He admits there *is* a place in the world for such activities. He admits he once was a kiddie himself. He even confesses to having read *Peter Rabbit*. Then abruptly he excuses himself and walks away in search of more vital and rugged companionship.

Wherever a juvenile writer goes, he is constantly subjected to humiliating indignities. When asked to take part in a panel discussion along with other members of the writing fraternity he is given the very end seat at the table . . . always one seat lower than the dusty anthologist who compiled *The Unpublished Letters of Dibble Sneth, Second Assistant Secretary of Something-or-Other under Polk.*

Besides that, since we don't make much money, our friends are always getting us aside and telling us, "Look, now. You can do better. After all, with all your education, there *must* be some way you could crack the Adult Field!"

The thing that's so hard to explain to our friends is that most of us who specialize in writing humor for children *have* cracked the adult field and, having cracked it, have decided definitely that we prefer to uncrack it. We are writing for the so-called Brat Field by choice. For, despite the fact this brands us as pariahs, despite the fact this turns us into literary untouchables, there is something we get when we write for the young that we never can hope to get in writing for you ancients. To be sure, in some ways you are superior to the young. You scream less. You burp less. You have fewer public tantrums. You ancients are, generally speaking, slightly more refined. But when it comes to trying to amuse you! . . . Have you ever stopped to consider what has happened to your sense of humor?

When you were a kid named Willy or Mary the one thing you did better than anything else was laugh. The one thing you got more fun out of than anything else was laughing. Why, I don't know. Maybe it has to do with juices. And when somebody knew how to stir those juices for you, you really rolled on the floor. Remember? Your sides almost really did split. Remember? You almost went crazy with the pain of having fun. You were a terrible blitz to your family. So what? Your juices were juicing. Your lava was seething. Your humor was spritzing. You really were living.

At that age you saw life through very clear windows. Small windows, of course. But very bright windows.

And, then, what happened?

You know what happened.

The grown-ups began to equip you with shutters. Your parents, your teachers, your everybody-around-you, your all-of-those-people who loved and adored you . . . they decided your humor was crude and too primitive. You were laughing too loud, too often and too happily. It was time you learned to laugh with a little more restraint.

They began pointing out to you that most of this wonderful giddy nonsense that you laughed at wasn't, after all, quite as funny as you thought.

"Now why," they asked, "are you laughing at *that*? It's completely pointless and utterly ridiculous."

"Nonsense," they told you, "is all right in its place. But it's time you learned how to *keep* it in its place. There's much more in this world than just nonsense."

Your imagination, they told you, was getting a little bit out of hand. Your young unfettered mind, they told you, was taking you on too many wild flights of fancy. It was time your imagination got its feet down on the ground. It was time your version of humor was given a practical, realistic base. They began to teach you *their* versions of humor. And the process of destroying your spontaneous laughter was under way.

A strange thing called conditioned laughter began to take its place. Now, conditioned laughter doesn't spring from the juices. It doesn't even spring. Conditioned laughter germinates, like toadstools on a stump.

And, unless you were a very lucky little Willy or Mary, you soon began to laugh at some very odd things. Your laughs, unfortunately, began to get mixed with sneers and smirks.

This conditioned laughter the grown-ups taught you depended entirely on *their* conditions. Financial conditions. Political conditions. Racial, religious and social conditions. You began to laugh at people your family feared or despised— people they felt inferior to, or people they felt better than.

If your father said a man named Herbert Hoover was an ass, and asses should be laughed at, you laughed at Herbert Hoover. Or, if you were born across the street, you laughed at Franklin Roosevelt. Who they were, you didn't know. But the local ground rules said you were to laugh at them. In the same way, you were supposed to guffaw when someone told a story which proved that Swedes are stupid, Scots are tight, Englishmen are stuffy and the Mexicans never wash.

1953

Casino Royale, the first James Bond book, is published—to little acclaim.

Your laughs were beginning to sound a little tinny. Then you learned it was socially advantageous to laugh at Protestants and/or Catholics. You readily learned, according to your conditions, that you could become the bright boy of the party by harpooning a hook into Jews (or Christians), labor (or capital), or the Turnverein or the Strawberry Festival.

You still laughed for fun, but the fun was getting hemmed in by a world of regulations. You were laughing at subjects according to their listing in the ledger. Every year, as you grew older, the laughs that used to split your sides diminished. The ledger furnished more sophisticated humor. You discovered a new form of humor based on sex. Sex, a taboo subject, called for very specialized laughter. It was a subject that was never considered funny in large gatherings. It was a form of humor you never indulged in at Sunday school. It was a form of humor that was subtle and smart and you learned to restrict it and reserve it for special friends.

And, by the time you had added that accomplishment to your repertoire, you know what had happened to you, Willy or Mary? Your capacity for healthy, silly, friendly laughter was smothered. You'd really grown up. You'd become adults, which is a word that means obsolete children.

As adults, before you laugh, you ask yourselves questions:

"Do I dare laugh at that in the presence of the boss? Sort of dangerous, when you consider how he feels about Taft-Hartley."

"How loud shall I laugh at *that* one? Mrs. Cuthbertson, my hostess, is laughing only fifteen decibels."

"Shall I come right out and say I thought the book was funny? The reviewer in *The Times* said the humor was downright silly."

These are the questions that children never ask. *The Times* reviewer and Mrs. Cuthbertson to the contrary notwithstanding, children never let their laughs out on a string. On their laughter there is no political or social pressure gauge.

That, I think, is why we maverick humorists prefer to write exclusively for children.

A World of One's Own

The Second Sex by Simone de Beauvoir
February 22, 1953

BY CLYDE KLUCKHOHN

O NE WONDERS if women still exist, if they will always exist, whether or not it is desirable that they should, what place they occupy in this world, what their place should be." The questions are radical enough, comprehensive enough, searching enough. And Simone de Beauvoir's answers are subtle and profound. This is no piece of flamboyant journalism and certainly not a petulant defense of her sex. Nor is it merely an extended essay, although it is indeed literature in the grand sense.

Essentially this is a treatise which integrates the most variegated strands of history, philosophy, economics, biology, belles-lettres, sociology and anthropology. I cannot think of a single American scholar, man or woman, who controls such a vast body of knowledge as this French writer.

The main themes are introduced at once. Women throughout history have been a disadvantaged group like the proletariat. Book One develops these themes with material from the facts of biology and history and from popular and literary myths.

There is a carefully constructed theoretical scheme for the analysis, coming largely from three sources: Existentialist philosophy (especially Sartre, of course, but with fairly numerous references to Kierkegaard and Heidegger), psychoanalysis and historical materialism.

The fact that Mlle. de Beauvoir approaches historical materialism with great discrimination—and also differentiates skeptically between Soviet propaganda and Soviet reality—is of topical interest in view of the current Camus-Sartre controversy.

If Book One is largely analytical and historical, Book Two is primarily clinical. And Simone de Beauvoir strikes me as a far better clinician than are most ointellectuals who have her analytic and verbal gifts. I suspect she understands herself very well indeed.

It is a truly magnificent book, even if sometimes irritating to a mere male. It

1953

The Olympia Press is founded in Paris. The following year, it publishes *Story of O* in French and English.

should be a required companion volume to all who read the forthcoming report of Kinsey and his associates. For Mlle. de Beauvoir says much about sexuality that is important which we are not likely to get from the Indiana group. Statistical tables of the incidence of various types of sexual acts need to be balanced by the historical depth, philosophical sophistication and exquisite psychological sensibilities of a Simone de Beauvoir.

My reservations are on a host of specific matters and two general issues. Of the former category I can mention only a few by way of example. If one presses some of the author's statements to their logical extremes, it would seem that she wanted and thought it possible that all women should become artists or intellectuals. We know that neither all men nor all women have such potentialities. Nor do they want to have them.

I think that perhaps there is too much about sexuality in *The Second Sex* and relatively little said (though well) about economic, political and social factors. In spite of her careful and precise attention to the facts of biology she seems at times to be saying, "Oh, but women can transcend all this." One is reminded occasionally of the one-line book review of another famous book by a woman: "Does she really know any culture in which the men have the babies?"

This reviewer was left with the conviction that Mlle. de Beauvoir was most reluctant to accept any genuine determination of woman's psyche by her biological nature.

Enough of this cavilling. *The Second Sex* has what Plutarch said of the buildings on the Acropolis: "There is such a certain flourishing freshness in it." It is a threadbare cliché to speak of not doing justice to a book, but in this case I must resort to the cliché, for I have never been so acutely conscious of incomplete justice.

First Impressions

Go Tell It on the Mountain by James Baldwin
May 17, 1953

BY DONALD BARR

THIS BOOK IS ABOUT PIETISM in Harlem—and, of the three sorts of novel (string, wind and percussion), it belongs to the first. It does not produce its story as an accumulation of shocks (as most novels of Negro life do), or by puffing into a rigid metaphysical system (as most novels about religion do); it makes its utterance by tension and friction.

The organizing event of the book is a 14-year-old boy's first religious experience. This experience is a fit, a brutal, unexpected seizure; for poor little John Grimes is the son, or thinks he is, of a deacon in one of the stomping, moaning, falling sects that ululate in converted stores around Harlem, the metropolis of grief. As a matter of fact, John and his real father had never known of each other's existence; Gabriel Grimes, a preaching widower up from the South, hard, without laughter, with a touch of the Messianic in his nature and a good deal of the trapped animal, had married John's mother and accepted John in expiation of his own carnal sins.

While John is in the holy spasm, Mr. Baldwin (who has really unusual substantive powers but conventional ingenuity in form) passes through three generations to find the antecedents of that hour. He has a curious attitude toward religion. He respects it. He does not find it comical, or anthropological, or pathetic. At its most grotesque, he will still have us know it in its own terms.

It is easy to explain. When the slaves, bred like animals and denied an equity in their own lives, were sent forth into monogamy, civil existence and the labor market, they received both freedom and the Law in the same instant. They then had the need of religion. In the religion that was most available (a vulgar export-model Puritanism) the notion of sin was central and fearfully inclusive. It included all but the most joyless releases of human needs. Guilt, guilt, guilt chimes through the book. Gabriel is guilty. His first wife Deborah is guilty, though she was the victim of rape. His second wife Elizabeth is guilty, though she loved much. Guilt is visited on his children. Hypocrisy will not sweeten the tragic dissonance. And guilt could not be removed, not by everyday contrition or penance—only by being born again altogether, as in baptism, but with huge pangs and convulsions. So it is writhing on the floor of "The Temple of the Fire Baptized" that John is saved.

Judicious men in their chairs may explain the sociology of guilt, and so explain Negro religion away. Mr. Baldwin will not have it away. In this beautiful, furious first novel, there are no such reductions.

1953

Ray Bradbury's *Fahrenheit 451* reminds us that books will still burn.

First Impressions

Casino Royale by Ian Fleming
April 25, 1954

BY ANTHONY BOUCHER

IAN FLEMING'S JAMES BOND is British Secret Service Operative 007, but his adventure in Casino Royale belongs pretty much to the private-eye school. The first part of the book is a brilliant novelette in itself, dealing with an unlikely but imaginative plot to ruin a Communist agent by gambling against him for high stakes. Mr. Fleming manages to make baccarat completely clear even to one who's never played it and produces as exciting a gambling sequence as I've ever read. But then he decides to pad out the book to novel length and leads the weary reader through a set of tough clichés to an ending which surprises no one save Operative 007. You should certainly begin this book; but you might as well stop when the baccarat game is over.

Making Mobiles at the Muse's Door

Poems, 1923–1954 by e. e. cummings
October 31, 1954

BY RANDALL JARRELL

E. E. CUMMINGS'S *Poems 1923–1954* contains "all the poems from all the collections of verse he has published to date." I've read these six hundred poems before, I think, and now I've read all six hundred again; and it seemed to me, as always, that Cummings is one of the most individual and American of poets, a man who has found his own one way and stuck to it with obstinate courage and integrity. There is a great deal of the world in the book, and a great deal more of one man. This formidable collection is going to get much praise and several prizes, and will be for many readers a veritable feast: all this year and next, people will be rising from the book stuffed, their ribs sore with laughter, their wits sharpened with typographical puzzles, their eyes shining with big lyric tears. "Good old Cummings!" they'll say. "There's nobody like him."

And I will nod: it's so. And then I will sit there dumbly, a stranger at a feast which, to me, is not a feast at all but a picnic—a picnic which goes on for yard after yard, mile after mile, of hot dogs, rat cheese, soda crackers, boiled ham curled into imitation rose petals. Valentines, jokes and favors from the Jokes and Magic Shop, warm chain-store beer. Here and there, I have to admit—I'm eager to admit—one comes on real wildflowers, the realest and brightest of chipmunks, a portable phonograph playing a wonderful popular song, a gold lock of a drunk girl's hair; and the sun sets behind the picnic, and the moon rises before it, like things from the *Iliad* or things from a nickel postcard.

It's a picnic which has its points—and what would life be without picnics? What I'm objecting to is calling it a Lucullan feast and Cummings the American Brillat-Savarin. "E. E. Cummings has achieved a permanent place among the great poets of this age," says his dust-jacket; has he, or has he a place off at the side, a special place all his own, among the good poets of the age? If Cummings is a great poet, what are you going to call Eliot and Frost? Rilke? Let's say together: "Great me no greats," and leave this grading to posterity.

So many critics have been more than just to Cummings's virtues—who could overlook so much life, individuality, charm, freshness, ingenuity?—that I should like to be unjust about his faults. Some of his sentimentality, his easy lyric sweetness I enjoy in the way one enjoys a rather commonplace composer's half-sweet, half-cloying melodies, but much of it is straight ham, straight corn. All too often Cummings splits man into a delicate unique Ariel, drifting through dew like moonlight, and into a Brooklyn Caliban who says, to prostitutes, dese, dem and dose. Some of all that Sex is there to shock, but more of it is there for its own sweet sake.

To Cummings words are things, exciting things excitingly manipulable: he sits at the Muse's door making mobiles. He is a magical but shallow rhetorician who specializes in turning inside out, fooling around with the rhetoric of popular songs, advertisements, bad romantic poetry. He invents a master-stroke, figures out the formula for it, and repeats it fifty times. The best rhetoric is less interested in itself, more interested in what it describes, than Cummings's.

Some of Cummings's humor is genuinely funny, some is crude and expected. He is, alas! a monotonous poet. Everything a poem does is, to old readers, expected. "Type Four," they murmur. "Well done!" Then they yawn. "Change in all things is sweet," said Aristotle; "They must often change who would be constant in happiness or wisdom," said Confucius; "Change the name of Arkansas? Never!" said Senator James Kimbrough Jones. Would that Cummings had listened to Aristotle and Confucius.

What I like least about Cummings's poems is their pride in Cummings and their contempt for most other people; the difference between the I and you of the poems, and other people, is the poems' favorite subject. All his work thanks God that he is not as other men are; none of it says, "Lord, be merciful to me, a sinner."

William Golding's *Lord of the Flies* changes forever our view of how boys will be boys.

Secular Hobbitism

The Fellowship of the Ring by J. R. R. Tolkien
October 31, 1954

BY W. H. AUDEN

SEVENTEEN YEARS AGO there appeared, without any fanfare, a book called *The Hobbit* which, in my opinion, is one of the best children's stories of this century. In *The Fellowship of the Ring*, which is the first volume of a trilogy, J. R. R. Tolkien continues the imaginative history of the imaginary world to which he introduced us in his earlier book but in a manner suited to adults, to those, that is, between the ages of 12 and 70. For anyone who likes the genre to which it belongs, the Heroic Quest, I cannot imagine a more wonderful Christmas present. All Quests are concerned with some numinous Object, the Waters of Life, the Grail, buried treasure etc.; normally this is a good Object which it is the Hero's task to find or to rescue from the Enemy, but the Ring of Mr. Tolkien's story was made by the Enemy and is so dangerous that even the good cannot use it without being corrupted.

The hero, Frodo Baggins, belongs to a race of beings called hobbits, who may be only three feet high, have hairy feet and prefer to live in underground

houses, but in their thinking and sensibility resemble very closely those arcadian rustics who inhabit so many British detective stories. For over a thousand years the hobbits have been living a peaceful existence in a fertile district called the Shire, incurious about the world outside. Actually, the latter is rather sinister; towns have fallen into ruins, roads into disrepair, fertile fields have returned to wilderness, wild beasts and evil beings are on the prowl, and travel is difficult and dangerous. In addition to the Hobbits, there are Elves who are wise and good, Dwarves who are skillful and good on the whole, and Men, some warriors, some wizards, who are good or bad. The present incarnation of the Enemy is Sauron, Lord of

Barad-Dûr, the Dark Tower in the Land of Mordor. Assisting him are Orcs, wolves and other horrid creatures and, of course, such men as his power attracts or overawes.

Of any imaginary world the reader demands that it seem real, and the standard of realism demanded today is much stricter than in the time, say, of Malory. Mr. Tolkien is fortunate in possessing an amazing gift for naming and a wonderfully exact eye for description; by the time one has finished his book one knows the histories of Hobbits, Elves, Dwarves and the landscape they inhabit as well as one knows one's own childhood.

If one is to take a tale of this kind seriously, one must feel that, however superficially unlike the world we live in its characters and events may be, it nevertheless holds up the mirror to the only nature we know, our own; in this, too, Mr. Tolkien has succeeded superbly, and what happened in the year of the Shire 1418 in the Third Age of Middle Earth is not only fascinating in A.D. 1954 but also a warning and an inspiration. No fiction I have read in the last five years has given me more joy than *The Fellowship of the Ring*.

1955

Publication of *The Poems of Emily Dickinson*, the first edition to contain all the poems and all the variant readings.

The Great Ruminator

The Shield of Achilles by W. H. Auden
February 20, 1955

BY KARL SHAPIRO

AUDEN IS THE GREAT RUMINATOR of modern poetry. In many ways he is also the typical poet of our age. In him are the rare words no one really wants to look up. In him are the negative convictions which are the trade-mark of modernism. Over most of the land of modern poetry he maintains his grumpy proprietorship. He is smugly unhappy. His whole work is a schoolroom, his universe a blackboard filled in with phyla, genera and species—all human types. His poems are playful games of Personification or the small Allegory, or colloquies of Ideas. His main theme is the quest for the Authentic City, a city neither in heaven nor earth, not the Unreal City and not the Accursed City of the self-damned poets, but the city in which human excellence is possible. Auden long ago gave up the conventional romantic visit to the New Jerusalem, but one still senses his nostalgia for it. Nowadays when Auden talks about the Good City or the Just City it is as if he were telling a story about a wonderful place where something terrible happened.

The shield of Achilles in Homer has emblazoned upon it the triumphs of the future. Auden, looking into the shield, sees the horrors of the modern state. But such a pattern, perfect though it is, seems to be too simple for the Auden of today.

Take, for example, the opening stanza of "Fleet Visit":

> *The sailors come ashore*
> *Out of their hollow ships,*
> *Mild-looking middle-class boys*
> *Who read the comic strips;*
> *One baseball game is more*
> *To them than fifty Troys.*

The romantic agonizing is almost gone from Auden's poetry. In its place we find a disarming first-person-singular Auden, almost as small as Cummings's little "i." This friendly, witty, serious, tutorial Auden chats comfortably of literary manners and the psychological phases of the mind. How he loves the dedicated man, the precise man, the productive man—those who have found their vocations! And how he splutters with impatience for the others—"all poor s-o-b's who never do anything properly." In this role of teacher Auden uses a strangely intimate vocabulary, as if he were always among old friends. And one is aware that his idiom has returned quietly to the most official English.

His new book contains two sequences of poems and one middle section made up of assorted pieces, several of which are superb examples of Auden at his most urbane. The opening sequence, called "Bucolics," is one of Auden's best works. The poems are named "Winds," "Woods," "Mountains," "Lakes," "Islands," "Plains" and "Streams." Auden's bucolics, naturally, are those of the city man. When he goes to the country he wonders how long he can stand it. The

poem "Plains" would make a good chapter for his autobiography: "If I were a plainsman I should hate us all." And "I should also like to own a cave with two exits." The poem "Streams" is one of the most beautiful pieces of writing in modern literature.

The other sequence, which ends the book, is "Horae Canonicae." Auden changes the canonical hours of prayer into seven periods of the day in which the poet examines his consciousness. He does this not in a clinical manner but with personal warmth, like an analyst who has fallen in love with the patient. In these poems we see Auden versus the crowd, Auden versus the world, Auden versus others. Like the "Bucolics," the seven poems of the canonical hours reveal the Auden Type. He is an Arcadian; his Anti-Type is a Utopian. Auden plays with these terms, creating himself phase by phase. We see the Arcadian, simple, peace-loving, good. And we see the Anti-Type, science-ridden, exacerbated, haughty. And everywhere in the poems we see a master of English poetry, whose stature increases with each new work.

Show Business Is Her Life

Marjorie Morningstar by Herman Wouk
September 4, 1955

BY MAXWELL GEISMAR

THE NOVELS OF HERMAN WOUK lie in a curious realm between art and entertainment. We have had a tradition of similar works from William Dean Howells to John P. Marquand, but few of these writers have been able to break through the formulas which have brought them popular success. It is more than a matter of money or prestige; it is a question of the writer's whole approach to experience, which wavers uneasily between his own convictions and the opinions which will soothe or delight his audience. These writers always seem to know more than they say, to feel more than they can express, and their typical literary form is irony.

Mr. Wouk takes pleasure in setting up a series of illusions that demonstrate his talent and perplex our minds. The central masculine figure in this new novel by the Pulitzer Prize–winning author of *The Caine Mutiny* is a frustrated artist who espouses a philosophy of "hits," or of extroverted egotism, as the driving force of life. Though Mr. Wouk is sardonic about his hero, there is a certain ambiguity of focus about the novel as a whole and we are never sure whether it is a romance or a satire.

The heroine is a young New York Jewish girl, Marjorie Morgenstern, who decides to be an actress, and picks an appropriate American name. Marjorie's talents are small, she never pursues her career very seriously, and the point of the novel is something else altogether.

What the story conveys, and often quite brilliantly, is the tragi-comic meeting of traditional Jewish culture and the American success myth. The children of the immigrants abandon the best part of their heritage in order to take on the worst aspects of their new environment, and Mr. Wouk has a sharp eye in describing their antics. There is a bar mitzvah scene very early in the novel, where Marjorie's poor Bronx relatives meet the prosperous West Side Jewish families whose ranks she aspires to join. "What's burning in that copper pot, I wonder," says one of these figures about the magnificent food. "Money," says another. The miracles of Lowenstein the caterer have replaced the presence of God.

The larger problem is of course the denigration of all immigrant culture by a society that marks its children only with the stamp of material success, and that, historically, gave up its own religious orientation somewhere around 1870. Marjorie is ashamed of her grasping, ambitious mother, her hardworking but uneducated father. To a certain degree she breaks away from the milieu of her youth where the size of the engagement ring determines the caliber of the bridegroom. She spends a period of her theatrical apprenticeship at a typical summer camp called South Wind and there she meets Noel Airman, another displaced Jewish conscience, who wants to be a Broadway playwright.

He is a shining apparition of the artistic life to a sheltered young girl, and he becomes Marjorie's great romance. (He is actually a volatile and disorganized bohemian who ends up quite correctly as a television writer.) Their anguished and tormented and rather adolescent love affair occupies a large part of this large novel, but during the course of this adventure Marjorie meets various other flamboyant and shady characters in the motion-picture and theatrical world.

Some of these minor portraits in the novel, like the disreputable Broadway producer, Guy Flamm, or the cynical Sam Rothmore of Paramount, or the witless and wolfish actor, Voen, are very well done, too. But the entertainment industry is both worse and better than this; and what Mr. Wouk is trying to establish, I think, is that his heroine's sentimental education is both typical of her culture and wrong. Marjorie finally marries a prosperous lawyer, settles down and has children in a little Westchester town and becomes a pillar of the community.

The young writer in the tale, Wally Wronken, who has always adored Marjorie from afar, finds her at last serene, matronly and dull. "You couldn't write a play about her that would run a week, or a novel that would sell a thousand copies. There's no angle." I would guess that Mr. Wouk's novel will sell much more than a thousand copies; and what it lacks is not an angle but a center.

In the juxtaposition of old and new forms of Jewish culture, one misses the real warmth, wisdom and humor of an ancient folk tradition whose transient resting place was the Bronx or Brooklyn. Mr. Wouk's Old World figures are stagey and contrived; he is more at home with their American descendants. And why should that narrow, complacent, comfort-loving petit-bourgeois world of commercial success, which Mr. Wouk satirizes so brilliantly at the start of the novel, become at the end the only possible horizon for his heroine?

If this is the story of a false emancipation, it is also that of a sterile compliance; and one has the impression that the author refuses to see the alternatives. The world of art or of intellect, for example—or even the profession of acting, which Marjorie abandons without a qualm—is not inhabited completely by the disorganized talents and esthetic frauds that the novel describes. And even in Westchester, is there no other course for Mr. Wouk's heroine except a total social conformity?

The problem of revolt and authority has preoccupied Mr. Wouk in the past. But here as in *The Caine Mutiny* it is settled by a final bow to the red-tape of a bureaucracy or to the proprieties of a social class, under the impression that these are among the eternal verities. *Marjorie Morningstar* is very good reading indeed. But to this reviewer at least, the values of true culture are as remote from its polished orbit as are, at base, the impulses of real life.

The Old Soaks at Home

Long Day's Journey into Night by Eugene O'Neill
February 19, 1956

BY BROOKS ATKINSON

A MONG THE PAPERS Eugene O'Neill left when he died in 1953 was the manuscript of an autobiography. Not an autobiography in the usual sense, however. For *Long Day's Journey into Night* is in the form of a play—a true O'Neill tragedy, set in 1912 in the summer home of a theatrical family that is isolated from the community by a kind of ingrown misery and a sense of doom.

As a piece for the stage *Long Day's Journey into Night*, finished in 1940, has certain faults that are inherent in the nature of the material. It is prolix and repetitious. It includes a number of long autobiographical speeches in which the characters go back into previous time to supply background facts. But the mass and weight of O'Neill tragedies often overwhelm things that look like faults in manuscript. As the portrait of the mind of a great dramatist, however, it is a thoroughly absorbing and characteristic work. It documents O'Neill's tragic point of view. In the play he gives the family the fictitious name of Tyrone. But it is

1956

Peyton Place starts giving off steam. Remember who wrote it? Grace Metalious.

obvious that the head of the family stands for O'Neill's father, James O'Neill, a fine actor trapped by his immense success in *The Count of Monte Cristo*. And the other characters represent the other members of the O'Neill family; the mother, a sweet woman lost in the oblivion of drug-taking; the dissolute older brother and the younger son, an unhappy, resentful youth, who devours pessimistic European literature and writes poetry.

The play is solely preoccupied with the private anguish of an overwrought family held together by incurable afflictions. In the affectionate inscription to his wife, O'Neill characterizes the work as a "play of old sorrow, written in tears and blood," but "with deep pity and understanding and forgiveness for all the haunted Tyrones." Originally, to spare the feelings of anyone associated with the family, the play was not to be published until twenty-five years after O'Neill's death. But O'Neill's father, mother and brother died in that order from 1920 to 1922. Since there seemed to be no further reason for keeping the play locked up, Mrs. O'Neill decided to add it to the O'Neill public record.

The immediate concern of *Long Day's Journey into Night* is the tuberculosis of the younger son. The malady is diagnosed by a local physician; the father and the physician select a sanatorium where the son can recover his health. This has more significance in the O'Neill saga than might appear. Historically, it was a crucial point in his career. After floundering around the world at loose ends, O'Neill did contract tuberculosis in 1912 and went for treatment to the Gaylord Farm in Wallingford, Conn. It was during this period of order and rest that he made up his mind to become a writer. Anyone who has read *The Straw* will understand how much he loathed the sanatorium to which his father had committed him.

Essentially, *Long Day's Journey into Night* is not so much a tale as O'Neill's remorseless attempt to tell the blunt truth about his family as a matter of artistic conscience. The truth is ugly. For the father has a peasant-like parsimony about his domestic affairs that embitters the family and alienates the sons. Ensnared in the meshes of the narcotic habit, the mother disintegrates as a human being while the family looks on in helpless horror. The older brother, drunken, crude, cynical, is pure evil. O'Neill does not forgive him for his malice.

But he analyzes the characters of the mother and father with a kind of austere understanding that ultimately spares them. Life has worn them down. The father has risen out of grinding poverty to a place in public life that he is incapable of mastering. Fear of returning to poverty poisons his instincts and judgment. And the mother's addiction to narcotics is a vice for which she is not responsible.

Both of these characters illustrate O'Neill's theory of tragedy. They are in the power of forces they cannot control. As the mother remarks in one of her few lucid moments: "None of us can help the things that life has done to us. They're done before you realize it, and once they're done they make you do other things until at last everything comes between you and what you'd like to be, and you've lost your true self forever."

Although the character of the younger son is the focal point of the drama, he is the one least developed or analyzed. Perhaps O'Neill felt inhibited here. Perhaps he was willing to let the long shelf of his published works stand as his own record. More likely, he felt shy about dramatizing himself or reluctant to take advantage of his authorship of an autobiographical drama to distinguish himself from his family.

Far from being idealized, however, the younger son emerges as the blood relative of a wretched family—petulant, overbearing, callow, cynical, dissipated. Here and there an illuminating remark appears. Worried about her responsibility, the mother declares: "He has never been happy. He never will be. Nor healthy. He was born nervous and too sensitive, and that's my fault."

Toward the end of the play, the younger son, who has drunk too much whisky, makes one wry remark that is the most subjective in the play. He says: "It was a great mistake, my being born a man. I would have been much more successful as a sea gull or a fish. As it is, I will always be a stranger who never feels at home, who does not really want and is not really wanted, who can never belong, who must always be a little in love with death."

That does sound like autobiography. It goes a long way toward accounting for O'Neill's detachment, his lonely brooding, his endless wandering from one home to another far away, his unsuccessful search for peace and health, his infatuation with death and oblivion. This bit of dialogue, romantic in tone, is as close to personal characterization as he gets.

It is interesting to compare the new play, completed in 1940, with *Ah, Wilderness!*, completed in 1933. In many respects the material is the same—New London in the summer, adolescent dissipation, the family car, the older brother, anarchistic ideas fresh from Europe. But *Ah, Wilderness!* is set in 1906 and the tone is like Booth Tarkington. When O'Neill was writing the play he was recollecting the past with humorous tranquillity and also writing one of the most beguiling comedies in American stage literature.

Six years later in the chronology of the O'Neill family, seven years later in the chronology of his writing career, O'Neill returned to New London wearing his tragic masque again. The story of *Long Day's Journey into Night* is no more devastating than others he told. But it seems more devastating because it is personal and as literal as a drama can be. This was the environment, respectably middle

1956

The characters in James Baldwin's new novel, *Giovanni's Room*, are white and gay.

class on the surface, obsessed and tortured inside, out of which our most gigantic writer of tragedy emerged.

First Impressions

Peyton Place by Grace Metalious
September 23, 1956

BY CARLOS BAKER

T HIS IS THE EARTHY novel of small-town life in New Hampshire which sprang into the news some weeks ago when the Gilmanton School Board dismissed young George Metalious from his position as principal of the local grammar school. "They told me it was because of my wife," said Mr. Metalious. "They don't like her book." Later, the school board said they had dismissed the young teacher for reasons of their own, which had no bearing on the novel. The author herself still insisted that word had got around Gilmanton that *Peyton Place* was a real shocker: "People suddenly decided that George is not the type to teach their sweet innocent children."

Whatever the merits of the Metalious case, the novel lives up very fully to its advance billing. We learn that life behind the scenes in New Hampshire is not widely different, fictionally speaking, from life in Winesburg, Ohio, Hecate County, Conn., or Gibbsville, Pa. It is only (if that is possible) a little "riper," a little more "hotly passionate," a little more frankly detailed—and, perhaps, a little more widely inclusive than the small-town chronicles of Messrs. Sherwood Anderson, Edmund Wilson and John O'Hara. The late Sinclair Lewis would no doubt have hailed Grace Metalious as a sister-in-arms against the false fronts and bourgeois pretensions of allegedly respectable communities, and certified her as a public accountant of what goes on in the basements, bedrooms and back porches of a "typical American town."

Mrs. Metalious, who is a pretty fair writer for a first novelist, is an emancipated modern authoress who knows the earthy words and rarely stints to use them. Samples of the adventures in store for readers of *Peyton Place* would include the following: Successive violations of a 14-year-old girl by her stepfather, leading to an abortion sadly performed by the town's admirable doctor. A murder in a "shacker's" hut with secret burial of the remains in a sheep pen. A suicide in a bedroom closet. A carnival accident which amputates a young girl's arm. A high-school seduction in which the girl is bought off by the boy's rich and corrupt father. The seduction of the local dress-shop proprietress by the vil-

1957

A *Death in the Family*, by James Agee, is published, two years after the author's death.

lage schoolmaster. The deflowering of her nubile novelist-daughter by an eroti-cally expert New York literary agent. A lengthy hard-cider binge in a locked cel-lar involving among others the town handyman who imbibes as a protest against his wife's multiple adulteries. The strangling of a pet tomcat at the feet of a dead spinster by a neurotic boy who has retchingly peered through a backyard hedge at the amorous activities of a neighbor couple.

If Mrs. Metalious can turn her emancipated talents to less lurid purposes, her future as novelist is a good bet. Another good bet is that the citizens of Gilman-ton, N.H., can look forward to a busy Indian summer of open or surreptitious reading.

The Long Joy-Ride

On the Road by Jack Kerouac
September 8, 1957

BY DAVID DEMPSEY

THIRTY YEARS AGO it was fashionable for the young and the weary—creatures of Hemingway and F. Scott Fitzgerald—simply to be "lost." Today, one depression and two wars later, in order to remain un-committed one must at least flirt with depravity. *On the Road* belongs to the new Bohemianism in American fiction in which an experimental style is combined with eccentric characters and a morally neutral point of view. It is not so much a novel as a long affectionate lark inspired by the so-called "beat" generation, and an example of the degree to which some of the most original work being done in this country has come to depend upon the bizarre and the offbeat for its creative stimulus. Jack Kerouac has written an enormously readable and enter-taining book but one reads it in the same mood that he might visit a sideshow— the freaks are fascinating although they are hardly part of our lives.

The story is told—with great relish—by Sal Paradise, a young college student who satisfies, through his association with a character named Dean Moriarty, his restlessness and search for "kicks." Moriarty, a good-natured and slap-happy reform-school alumnus, is pathologically given to aimless travel, women, car stealing, reefers, bop jazz, liquor and pseudo-intellectual talk, as though life were just one long joy-ride that can't be stopped. He is Mr. Kerouac's answer to the age of anxiety—and one of the author's real accomplishments is to make him both agreeable and sympathetic.

Through Moriarty we meet his three wives. We are also introduced to a dope

1957

While working as an actor, Harold Pinter is asked by a director friend to try writing a play.

1957

The Cat in the Hat, by Dr. Seuss, and *Little Bear*, by Else Holmelund Minarik, appear. Their child-friendliness and limited vo-cabularies, and the series they inspire, supplant Dick and Jane in the hearts and minds of boomers and their descendants.

1958

The Unnamable, the final
volume of Samuel Beckett's
trilogy (with *Molloy* and
Malone Dies) is published
in English.

addict, a poet—and an assortment of migratory decadents whose playground is
the vast American subcontinent of cheap lodgings, saloons, broken-down cars,
cross-country buses and all-night restaurants. Moriarty's continual roaming is interrupted only by a half-hearted attempt to find his alcoholic father. The incessant and frenetic moving around is the chief dynamic of *On the Road*, partly
because this is one of the symptoms of "beatness" but partly, too, because the hot
pursuit of pleasure enables Mr. Kerouac to serve up the great, raw slices of
America that give his book a descriptive excitement unmatched since the days
of Thomas Wolfe.

Unlike Wolfe, Nelson Algren or Saul Bellow (there are trace elements of all
three writers here), Mr. Kerouac throws his characters away, as it were. His
people are not developed but simply presented; they perform, take their bows
and do a handspring into the wings. It is the difference between a vaudeville act
and a play. The hedonism, the exquisite pointlessness of Moriarty's way of life is
not so much the subject of *On the Road* as a sightseeing device.

The non sequiturs of the beat generation become the author's own plotless
and themeless technique—having absolved his characters of all responsibility,
he can absolve himself of the writer's customary attention to motivation and
credibility. As a portrait of a disjointed segment of society acting out of its own
neurotic necessity, *On the Road* is a stunning achievement. But it is a road, as
far as the characters are concerned, that leads nowhere—and which the novelist himself cannot afford to travel more than once.

1958

Boris Pasternak, the author
of *Doctor Zhivago*, is forced
by the Soviet authorities to
turn down the Nobel Prize.

Letter

Alan Greenspan
November 3, 1957

A TLAS SHRUGGED by Ayn Rand is a celebration of life and happiness.
Justice is unrelenting. Creative individuals and undeviating purpose
and rationality achieve joy and fulfillment. Parasites who persistently
avoid either purpose or reason perish as they should. Mr. Granville Hicks suspi-
ciously wonders "about a person who sustains such a mood through the writing
of 1,168 pages and some fourteen years of work." This reader wonders about a
person who finds unrelenting justice personally disturbing.

Magnificent Obsession

Lolita by Vladimir Nabokov
August 17, 1958

BY ELIZABETH JANEWAY

T HE FIRST TIME I read *Lolita* I thought it was one of the funniest books I'd ever come on. (This was the abbreviated version published in the *Anchor Review* last year.) The second time I read it, uncut, I thought it was one of the saddest. I mention this personal reaction only because *Lolita* is one of those occasional books which arrive swishing behind them a long tail of opinion and reputation which can knock the unwary reader off his feet.

This is hard on any book. *Lolita* stands up to it wonderfully well, though even its author has felt it necessary to contribute an epilogue on his intentions. This, by the way, seems to me quite as misleading as the purposely absurd (and very funny) prologue by "John Ray Jr., Ph.D.," who is a beautifully constructed caricature of American Academic Bumbledom. But in providing a series of trompe-l'oeil frames for the action of his book, Vladimir Nabokov has undoubtedly been acting with intent; they are screens as well as frames.

He is fond of frames and their effects. A final one is provided within the book itself by the personality of the narrator, Humbert Humbert ("an assumed name"). Humbert is a close-to-40 European, a spoiled poet turned dilettante critic, the possessor of a small but adequate private income and an enormous and agonizing private problem: he is aroused to erotic desire only by girls on the edge of puberty, 9-to-14-year-old "nymphets."

Then, as in a fairy tale, his wish comes true, Lolita is its fulfillment. She is the quintessence of the nymphet, discovered by total accident in an Eastern American small town. To get her, Humbert puts himself through a pattern of erotic choreography that would shame a bower-bird. He is grotesque and horrible and unbearably funny, and he knows it.

1958

The Internal Revenue Service catches up with Edmund Wilson, who has failed to pay income taxes from 1946 to 1955.

1959

C. P. Snow warns in his lecture "The Two Cultures and the Scientific Revolution" that intellectual life in the West is becoming increasingly polarized into "literary" and "scientific" factions.

1959

D. H. Lawrence's *Lady Chatterley's Lover*, which was privately published in Italy in 1928 and banned in America, is reviewed on May 3.

In his epilogue, Mr. Nabokov informs us that *Lolita* has no moral. I can only say that Humbert's fate seems to me classically tragic, a most perfectly realized expression of the moral truth that Shakespeare summed up in the sonnet that begins, "The expense of spirit in a waste of shame / Is lust in action."

First Impressions

The Ugly American by William J. Lederer and Eugene Burdick
October 5, 1958

BY ROBERT TRUMBULL

IN THE UGLY AMERICAN, two experts on Southeast Asia spell out in illustrative anecdote why the free world is steadily losing ground in that part of the world to the Communists—often through the fault, the book says, of the Americans sent there to sell democracy.

This book should be a shocker to all Americans who believe that Asia is important. To make effective use of truth, unbelievable truth, without ruining careers and possibly inviting monumental libel actions, William J. Lederer and Eugene Burdick wrote this devastating indictment of American policy there as fiction. But any correspondent who has been any length of time in the locale of the story—the real, not the fictitious—will recognize its veracity.

The book—which began as a non-fiction project, was rewritten into short stories, and finally emerged as a novel—consists of the recital of a series of instances of American bungling and corresponding Russian successes among people like the Burmans, the Thais, the Vietnamese.

As the curtain rises, we find on stage a political hack named Louis Sears, lately rewarded with the Ambassadorship to Sarkhan—"a small country out toward Burma and Thailand"—who "wished to hell some American in the embassy could read Sarkhanese." He is succeeded as the United States envoy to this mythical, but typical, Southeast Asian country by Ambassador Gilbert MacWhite, a capable career officer who knows what to do about Asians and is forced to resign from the Foreign Service for precisely that reason.

Recognizable personalities among a parade of stuffed shirts, clowns and misfits and their helpless victims are the serious young agriculturist who is wined and dined into such euphoria that he forgets his ideals; the touring senator, essentially an astute and sincere man, who is cleverly misled into seeing things just as the embassy wants him to see them; the American missionary who really knows the country, but is considered a dangerous meddler by the Ambassador.

The attack on American policy in Asia this book makes is clothed in sharp characterizations, frequently humorous incident and perceptive descriptions of the countries and people where the action occurs. As a piece of literature, *The Ugly American* may fall into a permanent niche as a source of insight into the actual, day-by-day by-play of the present titanic political struggle for Asia that will engage future historians—unless, of course, the Communists win, and suppress all such books. After all, as the authors assure the reader in a foreword and in a closing chapter called "A Factual Epilogue," everything in this book actually happened.

William L. Shirer

Paul Goodman • J. D. Salinger • John

Updike • Rachel Carson • William S. Burroughs

Günter Grass • Aleksandr Solzhenitsyn • Thomas

Pynchon • George Plimpton • Hannah Arendt • Alfred

P. Sloan Jr. • Saul Bellow • Conrad Knickerbocker

Robert Lowell • Ingmar Bergman • Pauline Kael

Joseph Mitchell • Truman Capote • Masters and

Johnson • Malcolm X • Vladimir Nabokov

Philip Roth • Mario Puzo

1960s

World Power or Nothing

The Rise and Fall of the Third Reich by William L. Shirer
October 16, 1960

BY H. R. TREVOR-ROPER

I N 1923, in the years of inflation and economic crisis in Germany, Adolf Hitler, an Austrian subject who, like many other displaced or rootless ex-soldiers, had found a home in the nationalist asylum of Munich, attempted to carry out a *putsch.* It was a failure, and he was sentenced to a term in prison. When he emerged, he was bound over, and thereafter, as a learned professor wrote in 1929, "faded into oblivion."

The professor's verdict was premature, for in 1929 came another economic crisis, the Great Depression, and, as Hitler's chief ally Gregor Strasser wrote, "all that serves to precipitate the catastrophe is good, very good for us and our German revolution." In the new crisis, the Nazi party rose to new heights of power. Nevertheless, if the political structure of Germany had remained intact, Hitler might once again have faded, and this time finally, into oblivion. For by 1932 the economic crisis was on the way out, and recovery, of course, was bad, very bad, for nazism.

In August of that year Hitler, in a moment of gloom, thought of fleeing from Germany. In the November election his party lost 2 million votes. It was financially bankrupt, and its radical members were going over to communism. In December, Gregor Strasser sent in his resignation, and Hitler himself contemplated suicide. On January 15, 1933, General von Schleicher, the maker and unmaker of governments, declared that Hitler was no longer a problem, and his movement was "a thing of the past." On January 26, President Hindenburg said that he had "no intention whatsoever" of giving office to "that Austrian corporal." Only four days later he appointed the Austrian corporal Chancellor of Germany. The Thousand-Year Reich in Germany, the New Order in Europe had begun.

How can we even look objectively on the Third Reich? It was the greatest, most horrible phenomenon of the twentieth century. In ordinary circumstances it would be impossible, only half a generation after its end, in the twilight period between passion and documentation, to write its history. But with the Third Reich nothing was ordinary, not even its end. Hitler aimed at "world power or nothing," and after a brief period of world power ended up with nothing. In that total annihilation all the secrets of his rule were broken open, all the archives captured, their truth tested in court, their contents made public.

Now, as never before, the living witnesses can converge with the historical

1960

Growing Up Absurd, by Paul Goodman, ushers in the '60s.

Allen Drury's *Advise and Consent* wins the Pulitzer Prize for fiction; Saul Bellow's *Henderson the Rain King* doesn't.

truth. All they need is a historian. In William L. Shirer they have found him. He was himself in Germany from 1935 to 1941—need one refer to his *Berlin Diary*? Since the war he has studied the massive documents made available by Hitler's total defeat. And now he has brought together his experience and his study in a monumental work, a documented, 1,200-page history of the whole episode of Hitler's Third Reich.

The Nazis (like the Communists) represented their revolution as "inevitable," but in fact nothing is inevitable in history. A compromise peace in 1917 might have saved the world from communism; a strong President of Germany in 1932–33 might have saved it from nazism. But in fact, in that fatal year, the German President was a reactionary dotard, destitute of moral courage and ruled alternately by a few blind prejudices and those disreputable court schemers—Papen and, above all, Schleicher—who could exploit them. And so the political structure did not remain intact; it crumbled from within. Hitler, when his chances seemed already on the wane, was able to slip into power by a back door and carry out his greatest political triumph, the revolution that was in fact no revolution (there has never been a German revolution); the revolution from above, the revolution which followed, instead of preceding, the capture of power.

It is easy to describe Hitler's methods in retrospect: how, from his narrow basis, he gradually extended his power, enlarging his party in the Reichstag by controlled elections, converting it into a majority by expelling his rivals, and then into a dictatorship by the Enabling Act. We can go on to describe his consolidation of that dictatorship by wooing big business, until his finances were independent of it, the S.A. (storm troopers), until he could destroy it, and the army, until he had control over it. So, in the end, like the young cuckoo, he remained alone in his power, fed by those he had cheated and whose corpses lay scattered around the nest he had usurped. But even as we read of these now familiar episodes we find ourselves forced to ask questions. After all, the other Germans, the politicians, generals, business men and others, were human beings. They had minds of their own, wills of their own, power of their own. A nation of 65 million does not *need* to submit permanently to a foreign adventurer simply because an 86-year-old President appoints him to an office and he himself then exacts an illegal oath of personal allegiance. If they wish to repudiate him, the odds in their favor are great: 65 million to one.

Always, as we read the history of nazism, this is the problem. Mr. Shirer does not shirk it. First of all, he points out, Hitler was a man of political genius. He does not shrink, as so many historians do, from using that term. For a long time it has been fashionable to decry Hitler as a mere puppet of impersonal forces, froth thrown up by the waves of historic change. If one says or implies that he has genius, one is accused of admiring him, of being almost a Nazi one's self. I have endured a good deal of abuse from virtuous liberals and Socialists on this score. But it is really absurd to deny Hitler's genius, though it was the genius of a devil, a genius devoted to the destruction and degradation of humanity.

Hitler, says Mr. Shirer—and how I agree with him—was "possessed of a demonic personality, a granite will, uncanny instincts, a cold ruthlessness, a remarkable intellect, a soaring imagination and—until toward the end—an amazing capacity to size up people and situations." It is worth adding also, as evidence of this genius, that Hitler, alone of great revolutionaries, both launched his revolution and commanded all its stages. Nazism devoured its children but never its begetter. He was its prophet and tyrant alike. It began and ended with him, and the rise and fall of the Third Reich are synonymous with his career.

Nevertheless there is another side to the picture. Politicians, even politicians of genius, do not make revolutions alone. There are also their peoples. And the Nazi government was, as Mr. Shirer says, not only the most German but the only true German Government in history. The Habsburg Empire was cosmopolitan; Bismarck's Reich was created through war, the Weimar Republic imposed through defeat. On the other hand, "the Third Reich owed nothing to the fortunes of war or to foreign influence. It was inaugurated in peacetime, and peacefully, by the Germans themselves, out of both their weaknesses and their strengths. The Germans imposed the Nazi tyranny on themselves."

Moreover, they kept it on themselves. At every stage at which a protest might have been made, there was not merely inaction but silence. At best, the "good Germans" merely asked, as the generals asked in 1941, that the dirty work be done by other hands than theirs. At the worst, they not only did what they were told, but profited by it. In a nauseating story few things are more nauseating than the documents printed by Mr. Shirer which show German business men unctuously competing for contracts to supply poison gas, gas chambers and crematoria for Nazi extermination camps, and for desirable factory sites close to these constant supplies of cheap, exploitable, expendable labor. After the war all these, and such men with equal unction, protested their innocence. They had known nothing, they said. They had even been "anti-Nazis," members of "the Resistance." Well might a German author, recording the devastating forgotten past of some of these "resisters," write a book entitled *Das Verlorene Gewissen, The Forgotten Conscience.*

The forgotten conscience is one of the most dreadful lessons of the Nazi era. Mr. Shirer is keenly aware of it. He quotes Goethe's remark, "I have often felt a bitter sorrow at the thought of the German people, which is so estimable in the individual and so wretched in the generality. A comparison of the German people with other peoples arouses a painful feeling, which I try to overcome in

1960

Zora Neale Hurston, novelist, social critic, and once a star of the Harlem Renaissance, is buried in a pauper's grave in Florida.

every possible way." We should try to overcome it too; but not by overlooking the facts. The facts are in this book: massive, proved, indisputable. If anyone is tempted, by the evidence of Hitler's political and diplomatic achievements, to admire his indisputable genius, let him read Mr. Shirer's excellent chapter of the New Order and see, and remember, the hideous purpose to which 65 million Germans either actively helped or tacitly allowed it to lead them.

First Impressions

Growing Up Absurd by Paul Goodman
October 30, 1960

BY JOHN K. GALBRAITH

I HAVE A FEELING that a considerable part of the current spate of criticism of American life is coming to display the qualities being criticized. It is slick and superficial—designed for, and merchandised to, the mass market in criticism. If you are feeling a little at odds with your world, then there is nothing like a good, readable book on the sterility of suburbia, the sex mania of exurbia, the banality of Detroit design or the wastes of advertising to attest to your wholesome anger and show that you are right and the society wrong.

Criticism could not be put to a worse (or lesser) purpose. It imposes no responsibility upon the individual except the reading. Little is said of underlying causes and less of remedies. To put any blame on the President would be partisan. The networks must remain sovereign in their sadism; one doesn't want to raise the issue of government regulation. The automobile may have got out of hand but do its critics come up with studious proposals for solution? Much too controversial. I for one can see little merit in the man who finds much wrong but seeks neither an explanation nor a remedy.

All of this is by way of saying that Paul Goodman, a man deeply dissatisfied with things as they are, deserves more attention than other less conscientious objectors. His book is anything but slick. From the awkward title to the last appendix, reading is something of a struggle. And it is not strong on prescription, but it is a highly serious effort to understand the relation between society and the disaffected youngster.

In a common view, the disaffection which produces the delinquent—and also the angry and the beat—is the result of a failure in communication. Bring these young people into a proper relation to society, develop an understanding of social goals, and they will be all right. Mr. Goodman strongly disagrees. The

youngsters understand society all too well. They see it as it is—excessively organized for unimportant purposes. Once an apprentice mechanic could tackle a
recalcitrant Model T with the interesting and useful object of making it run.
Now the same automobile will have banged up some functionless protuberance or
it will have lost the use of some organ which was developed as a sales point in the
first place. The job no longer seems very important. If the youngster chivies the repair bill . . . well, wasn't the manufacturer also engaged in bamboozling the buyer
a bit?

Everywhere the diminishing marginal urgency of goods—the lessening importance of economic function—is robbing work of its purpose. Mere economic
achievement, being no longer sufficiently urgent, is no longer sufficient.

The Admirable Glasses

Franny and Zooey by J. D. Salinger
September 17, 1961

BY JOHN UPDIKE

QUITE SUDDENLY, as things go in the middle period of
J. D. Salinger, his later, longer stories are descending from the clouds
of old *New Yorkers* and assuming incarnations between hard covers.
Raise High the Roof Beam, Carpenters, became available last year in *Stories from
the New Yorker 1950–1960*, and now "Franny" and "Zooey" have a book to themselves. These two stories—the first medium-short, the second novella-length—
are contiguous in time, and have as their common subject Franny's spiritual
crisis.

In the first story, she arrives by train from a Smith-like college to spend the
week-end of the Yale game at what must be Princeton. She and her date, Lane
Coutell, go to a restaurant where it develops that she is not only unenthusiastic
but downright ill. She attempts to explain herself while her friend brags about a
superbly obnoxious term paper and eats frogs' legs. Finally, she faints, and is last
seen lying in the manager's office silently praying at the ceiling.

In the second story, Franny has returned to her home, a large apartment in
the East Seventies. It is the Monday following her unhappy Saturday. Only
Franny's mother, Bessie, and her youngest brother, Zooey, are home. While
Franny lies sleeplessly on the living-room sofa, her mother communicates, in an
interminably rendered conversation, her concern and affection to Zooey, who
then, after an even longer conversation with Franny, manages to gather from the

haunted atmosphere of the apartment the crucial word of consolation. Franny, "as if all of what little or much wisdom there is in the world were suddenly hers," smiles at the ceiling and falls asleep.

Few writers since Joyce would risk such a wealth of words upon events that are purely internal and deeds that are purely talk. We live in a world, however, where the decisive deed may invite the holocaust, and Salinger's conviction that our inner lives greatly matter peculiarly qualifies him to sing of an America where, for most of us, there seems little to do but to feel. Introversion, perhaps, has been forced upon history; an age of nuance, of ambiguous gestures and psychological jockeying on a national and private scale, is upon us, and Salinger's intense attention to gesture and intonation help make him, among his contemporaries, a uniquely relevant literary artist. His fiction, in its rather grim bravado, its humor, its morbidity, its wry but persistent hopefulness, matches the shape and tint of present American life. It pays the price, however, of becoming dangerously convoluted and static. A sense of composition is not among Salinger's strengths, and even these two stories, so apparently complementary, distinctly jangle as components of one book.

The Franny of "Franny" and the Franny of "Zooey" are not the same person. The heroine of "Franny" is a pretty college girl passing through a plausible moment of disgust. She has discovered—one feels rather recently—a certain ugliness in the hungry human ego and a certain fatuity in her college environment. She is attempting to find her way out with the help of a religious book, *The Way of a Pilgrim*, which was mentioned by a professor. She got the book out of the college library. Her family, glimpsed briefly in the P.S. of a letter she has written, appear to be standard upper-middle gentry. Their name is nowhere given as Glass; Franny never mentions any brothers.

The Franny of "Zooey," on the other hand, is Franny Glass, the youngest of the seven famous Glass children, all of whom have been in turn wondrously brilliant performers on a radio quiz program, *It's a Wise Child*. Their parents, a distinctly unstandard combination of Jewish and Irish, are an old vaudeville team. From infancy on, Franny has been saturated by her two oldest brothers, Seymour and Buddy, in the religious wisdom of the East. *The Way of a Pilgrim*,

1961

The Death and Life of Great American Cities, Jane Jacobs's polemic against modernist urban renewal, is published. It will become to city planning what *Silent Spring* became to the environmental movement.

far from being newly encountered at college, comes from Seymour's desk, where it has been for years.

One wonders how a girl raised in a home where Buddhism and crisis theology were table talk could have postponed her own crisis so long and, when it came, be so disarmed by it. At any rate, there is no question of her being pregnant; the very idea seems a violation of the awesome Glass ethereality.

The more Salinger writes about them, the more the seven Glass children melt indistinguishably together in an impossible radiance of personal beauty and intelligence. Franny is described thus: "Her skin was lovely, and her features were delicate and most distinctive. Her eyes were very nearly the same quite astonishing shade of blue as Zooey's but were set farther apart, as a sister's eyes no doubt should be." Of Zooey, we are assured he has a "somewhat preposterous ability to quote, instantaneously and, usually, verbatim, almost anything he had ever read, or even listened to, with genuine interest." The purpose of such sentences is surely not to particularize imaginary people but to instill in the reader a mood of blind worship, tinged with envy.

"Franny" takes place in what is recognizably our world; in "Zooey" we move into a dream world whose zealously animated details only emphasize an essential unreality. When Zooey says to Franny, "Yes, I have an ulcer, for Chrissake. This is Kaliyuga, buddy, the Iron Age," disbelief falls on the "buddy," as much as on "Kaliyuga," and the explanatory "the Iron Age" clinches our suspicion that a lecturer has usurped the writing stand. Not the least dismaying development of the Glass stories is the vehement editorializing on the obvious—television scripts are not generally good, not all section men are geniuses. Of course, the Glasses condemn the world only to condescend to it, to forgive it, in the end. Yet the pettishness of the condemnation diminishes the gallantry of the condescension.

Perhaps these are hard words; they are made hard to write by the extravagant self-consciousness of Salinger's later prose, wherein most of the objections one might raise are already raised. On the flap of this book jacket, he confesses, "There is a real-enough danger, I suppose, that sooner or later I'll bog down, perhaps disappear entirely, in my own methods, locutions, and mannerisms. On the whole, though, I'm very hopeful." Let me say, I am glad he is hopeful. I am one of those—to do some confessing of my own—for whom Salinger's work dawned as something of a revelation. I expect that further revelations are to come.

The Glass saga, as he has sketched it out, potentially contains great fiction. When all reservations have been entered, in the correctly unctuous and apprehensive tone, about the direction he has taken, it remains to acknowledge that it is a direction, and the refusal to rest content, the willingness to risk excess on behalf of one's obsessions, is what distinguishes artists from entertainers, and what makes some artists adventurers on behalf of us all.

Oops!

October 22, 1961

Catch-22

BY JOSEPH
HELLER

Catch-22 has much passion, comic and fervent, but it gasps for want of craft and sensibility. If *Catch*-22 were intended as a commentary novel, such sideswiping of character and action might be taken care of by thematic control. It fails here because half its incidents are farcical and fantastic.

The Poison Around Us

Silent Spring by Rachel Carson
September 23, 1962

BY LORUS AND MARGERY MILNER

P OISONING PEOPLE IS WRONG. Yet, for the sake of "controlling" all kinds of insects, fungi and weed plants, people today are being poisoned on a scale that the infamous Borgias never dreamed of. Cancer-inducing chemicals remain as residues in virtually everything we eat or drink. A continuation of present programs that use poisonous chemicals will soon exterminate much of our wild life and man as well. So claims Rachel Carson in her provocative new book, *Silent Spring.*

Silent Spring is similar in only one regard to Miss Carson's earlier books (*Under the Sea Wind, The Sea Around Us, The Edge of the Sea*); in it she deals once more, in an accurate, yet popularly written narrative, with the relation of life to environment. Her book is a cry to the reading public to help curb private and public programs which by use of poisons will end by destroying life on earth.

Know the facts and do something about the situation, she urges. To make sure that the facts are known, she recounts them and documents them with 55 pages of references. She intends to shock and hopes for action. She fears the insidious poisons, spread as sprays and dust or put in foods, far more than the radioactive debris from a nuclear war. Miss Carson, with the fervor of an Ezekiel, is trying to save nature and mankind from chemical biocides that John H. Baker (then President of the National Audubon Society) identified in 1958 as "The greatest threat to life on earth."

Her account of the present is dismal. It is not hopeless—at least not yet. But she demands a quick change in "our distorted sense of proportion." How can intelligent beings seek to control a few unwanted species by a method that contaminates the entire environment and brings the threat of disease and death even to our own kind? "For the first time in the history of the world," she writes, "every human being is now subjected to contact with dangerous chemicals from the moment of conception until death. . . . These chemicals are now stored in the bodies of the vast majority of human beings, regardless of age. They occur in the mother's milk, and probably in the tissues of the unborn child."

Albert Schweitzer has said, "Man can hardly recognize the devils of his own creation." Yet *Silent Spring* will remind some people that a few years ago they went without cranberry sauce at Thanksgiving rather than risk eating berries contaminated with a cancer-inducing chemical used improperly by some growers as a weed-killer in the cranberry bogs.

1962

The Other America, by Michael Harrington, plants some of the seeds of the War on Poverty.

"If the Bill of Rights contains no guarantee that a citizen shall be secure against lethal poisons distributed either by private individuals or by public officials, it is surely only because our forefathers, despite their considerable wisdom and foresights, could conceive of no such problem," she says.

The Big Fix

Naked Lunch by William S. Burroughs
November 25, 1962

BY HERBERT GOLD

ELDER STATESMAN of the beat fad, friend and adviser to Allen Ginsberg and Jack Kerouac, author of several novels as yet unavailable in this country, and pseudonymous author of a paperback novel about heroin addiction, William Burroughs has excellent credentials for producing the definitive hip book. He has followed the route of publication by the Olympia Press in Paris and by banned little magazines in the United States; extravagant international praise, with the usual admixture of gossip, has accumulated about his work and his person. Another convulsion of the true-believing bureaucrats of hipdom and the horrified censors, professors and policemen arrayed in mortal combat, now seems inevitable.

It happens that Burroughs possesses a special literary gift. *Naked Lunch* is less a novel than a series of essays, fantasies, prose poems, dramatic fragments, bitter arguments, jokes, puns, epigrams—all hovering about the explicit subject matter of making out on drugs while not making out in either work or love. The black humor of addiction—a religion as practiced by Burroughs—does not lend itself to that evolution of character and action within society which is traditional to the novel. No real people assist at the junkie's rituals: marks, suppliers, cops, but no friends or lovers.

In this book the single repetitive process of getting the fix replaces accumulating action or growth. There is a frozen dream of perfect isolation behind which Burroughs's intelligence retains its glitter. He sees the East River lined with gangsters in concrete blocks; he sees live monkeys sewn into the bodies of appendicitis victims by abstracted doctors. As in Swift's "A Modest Proposal," the satire proceeds from an apparent acceptance of the disposition of fate. Like Swift, Burroughs then drives through to an extreme of formal horror. He forms a college of American racial, commercial and social prejudices, placed upon a subject matter of perversion and nihilism. His businessman sells "adulterated shark repellent." We may start to smile but we stop.

1962

On December 8, a 114-day newspaper strike begins. Edmund Wilson observes, "The disappearance of the *Times* . . . book section at the time of the printers' strike only made us aware that it had never existed." The *New York Review of Books* is born in 1963.

Hero and villain of *Naked Lunch* are heroin. Burroughs makes it clear that addiction does not give pleasure—it is merely "something to do"—and he argues that the police collaborate with the addict, helping him find his something-to-do by making it hard for him, keeping him busy. Within the dry, husking rustle of Burroughs's prose lies a moral judgment. "I got the fear!" he writes, and runs from the dream of nothingness, no contact, toward his surreal fantasy. The world of men and women has let him down. The world of dream—no, of self-absorption—is the only alternative while he waits out his term on earth.

The literary technique will remind readers of Villon and Corbière, the gasping, torrid Céline and the furious Swift, Alfred Jarry and Jean Genet. But in a most American way, Burroughs rejects their yearnings for form in favor of a definition of the novel (read: Book) as receptacle. Repetitions of words, phrases, even episodes remain uncut. It is all there because it was *there* in his mind. He offers up a series of drug and sex transports, unseparated from the motion sickness of getting to the fantasy. He has the notion of suggesting heroin addiction as a treatment for schizophrenia. His logic: The schizophrenic loses contact with others; a heroin addict cannot ignore his need, therefore needs others, therefore needs efficient contact; therefore the addict will give up his madness in order to guarantee his supply.

Certainly a personal psychoanalysis is being wrought in this book. The climaxes are those of shock and the fix, and these are repeated obsessively, using a curious vocabulary which ranges from the pedantic to the childish. When the book flags, the attack is automatic and verbal, the mere play of an intelligent man diddling the language.

Many readers will turn from this book in disgust. Some literary snobs will use it as an occasion to cry masterpiece, forgiving its lack of shape and control; others will accuse it of being merely obscene, too stunned by the experience to admit its relevance to our time and to ride along with the driven, riven spirit that has gone into its making. The book is surely not pornographic. Sex is a target of immense disgust; the cruel language chills the reader, is as anaphrodisiac as heroin.

At its best, this book, which is not a novel but a booty brought back from nightmare, takes a coldly implacable look at the dark side of our nature. Civilization fails many; many fail civilization. William Burroughs has written the basic work for understanding that desperate symptom which is the beat style of life.

1963

Jean Cocteau dies, just hours after his longtime friend Edith Piaf.

He Won't Grow Up

The Tin Drum by Günter Grass
April 7, 1963

BY FREDERIC MORTON

AFTER WORLD WAR II there were two kinds of German writers. On the one hand was Thomas Mann: an enormous creative force, German in origin and experience, venerable and universal in his office as monarch in the world of letters. Mann's death left only the other kind: writers who have had an almost obligatory theme thrust upon them—the Third Reich and its legacies. Among them are men of genuine talent, yet none of them has contributed, like Alberto Moravia or Camus, to the international stock of characters or ideas. Now, suddenly, one of their countrymen has broken through.

Günter Grass turns the trick with *The Tin Drum*. When it was published in Germany three years ago, it immediately entered the mainstream of European literature. It won foreign praise and prizes, and created what no German since Thomas Mann has been able to create: international literary excitement. Grass works with a range of theatrical inventiveness that shades from Goethe at his most Mephisthophelean to Ionesco at his most perverse. *The Tin Drum* is a formidable, if formidably uneven, novel. It is also a prime example of The Novel of the Absurd.

Grass's hero, Oskar, begins as the misbegotten child of the Nazi era and ends—what could be more modern?—as a jazz musician in a mental hospital. In between, he enjoys a career made up of appalling and hilarious pranks. The arch-prank of all occurs when Oskar reaches his third year: he refuses to grow and thus exempts himself from all adult demands.

At the same time he receives a tin drum for a gift. Henceforth, he drums the way other people chain-smoke. To percussion, muffled or thunderous, he capers through life. He also develops a voice that cuts like a diamond: he can cut glass anywhere within range of his vocal cords, and among many other objects, he ruins his teacher's spectacles. He creeps under the rostrum at a Nazi rally and makes his drumsticks confuse the party faithful with "Jimmy the Tiger." He places his sticks in the hands of a stucco Jesus who then begins to drum. Reaching the age of romance, he seduces one of his loves with the help of fizz-powder he smuggles into her navel—among the unlikeliest aphrodisiac tricks in contemporary fiction.

All this, of course, can be read as one long macabre joke. But so can Thomas Mann's story of the confidence man, Felix Krull, with whom Grass's hero has been inevitably compared. Both Oskar and Felix are anti-bourgeois super-imps;

1963

Maurice Sendak's *Where the Wild Things Are* alters understanding of children's dreams. In 1964 it wins the Caldecott Medal.

both, relating their lives in the first person singular, parody the *Bildungsroman*, the German novel in which ideas are dramatized through the hero's character development. Felix Krull's tricks are governed by an artistic and aristocratic sensibility and by an Edwardian esthetic.

Oskar, by contrast, is a midcentury creation. Without manners or principles, he has only a capacity to be struck hard by the world's stupidity and viciousness. For him, pain is the engine of mockery. It spews out laughter at a universe made of wounds and voids.

1963

The poet John Hollander declares, "The defects of *The New York Times Book Review* are table talk even among those who write for it."

The details of this universe stud *The Tin Drum* with a persuasiveness which constitutes its primary source of power. Oskar, like his author, spent his childhood in Danzig. With masterful minutiae the petit-bourgeois background of an East Prussian port town is reconstructed. Everything is there: gossip, sausage picnics, money troubles. In the foreground is Oskar's family: his pretty mother, who when photographed likes to display an arch queen-of-hearts card to the lens; her husband Alfred, the industrious grocer who loves to cook; his friend Bronski, a well-manicured Polish post-office worker with whom Alfred's wife sleeps—but only at the respectable, circumspect afternoon hour appropriate to such affairs; and the evening card party uniting all three in sly but cozy peacefulness while Alfred cooks mushroom omelets in the kitchen.

Upon such a world Oskar, the demon dwarf, vents his derision. It is the sturdy hypocrisy, the homey corruption of his milieu that make Oskar's surrealist caricatures so inevitable. Through him the reader perceives the phosphorescent underbelly of the middle class. The Breughel landscape suddenly swarms with the consummate monsters of Hieronymus Bosch.

In its first pages *The Tin Drum* has no particular political coloration, but the book's weird double focus prepares the reader for Hitler's advent later on. Grass brings off what no German has managed or even dared to attempt—to show that the Nazis were not a black breed apart, imposing their exotic evil on the good little people. The Nazis were the good little people themselves. Alfred, the cuckolded, food-loving grocer, becomes a storm-trooper. He and his friends (not Bronski, who abrupty becomes an inferior Pole) go on posing for the family album, their pictures somehow enhanced by the brown uniforms.

Oskar's antics and experiences match in their savageness the general course of events. More than once the book insists on gratuitous shockers. For example, a tomb-cutter's boils are squeezed in rhythm to the prayer rite of a burial party. Such scenes scream out a blasphemy in high C as if—a frequent anxiety among avant-gardists—the only way to hold a reader were to offend him.

But the success or failure of this or that dithyramb matters little. What matters very much is Oskar's gradual and heartbreaking acquisition of a human face.

He drums himself into prosperity as a jazz musician during the postwar years. But who applauds, who surrounds him? Who if not more food-loving grocers cooking better omelets to feed even bigger phosphorescent underbellies? And is he, Oskar, any better than they?

Like the hump which abruptly, belatedly, curves out of Oskar's spine, so guilt and compassion afflict our dwarf. They deform him—into a man, a creature not merely fascinating but touching. At the end a human being crawls out from under the brilliant dramatic device. As a literary type Oskar's lineage goes back far beyond Krull, to King Lear's fool. As a human being he is real enough to make one wonder—despite all his excess—whether a little bit of him may not be lodged in many of us. At the end he flings his tiny self into a repentance an unrepentant world terms insane. And yet there must be a number of us worldlings who close the book and still hear the tin drum sounding.

First Impressions

One Day in the Life of Ivan Denisovich
by Aleksandr Solzhenitsyn
April 7, 1963

BY MARC SLONIM

THE DAY OF IVAN DENISOVICH, as the title reads in Russian, is the first work to break the taboo and to bring into the open the full truth about Russian concentration camps. Solzhenitsyn does not try to move the reader by haunting scenes and stories of dread. His writing is restrained and sober, with sparks of humor. He presents the most Kafkaesque situations, the most gruesome details in a matter-of-fact manner, without exaggeration or indignation. His is a calm, stylized narrative by an extremely observant and intelligent man.

The hero of the novelette, Shukhov, is a humble, hard-working peasant, and everything is seen through his eyes. During the war his unit had been encircled, and he had been taken prisoner by the Germans. He escaped, came back to the Russian lines where he was arrested, accused of spying for the enemy and sentenced to 10 years of hard labor. He has accepted his fate with resignation and is only trying to stay alive. The struggle for survival is the main theme of *One Day*.

Solzhenitsyn follows with minute details the daily routine of Shukhov's life: reveille at 5 A.M., with the risk of three days in solitary confinement if one is late in jumping out of a bug-ridden bunk; breakfast in the crowded mess hall—mush

Oops!

April 7, 1963

The Feminine Mystique

BY BETTY FRIEDAN

Sweeping generalities, in which this book necessarily abounds, may hold a certain amount of truth but often obscure the deeper issues. It is superficial to blame the "culture" and its handmaidens, the women's magazines, as she does. What is to stop a woman who is interested in national and international affairs from reading magazines that deal with those subjects?

and boiled gruel with fish skeletons floating next to rotten cabbage leaves; roll call in the polar frost, the prisoners lined up with their numbers sewn on their caps, breasts, knees and backs, and frisked by the guards. Then departure for work, in slow procession, under the escort of police dogs and wardens who shoot at anyone who makes a step to right or left of the ranks; the desolation of the Northern steppe where prisoners mix cement and build walls and roofs; short intervals for lunch and supper, and again roll call, the search of each inmate, and heavy slumber in cold barracks, 240 men in each of them piling up everything they find to warm their frozen limbs.

Shukhov "defends" himself well: he chews slowly each crumb of his bread ration, he succeeds in hiding from the guards a piece of wire and a string that may come handy some day, he saves a pinch of tobacco, and enjoys a whiff of warm air while running errands in the infirmary and in the Staff Headquarters. At the end of a day of hard labor and minor incidents, he feels that he has been lucky: he has not fallen ill, he has escaped the cell, managed to eat an extra bowl of soup, got some tobacco. The story ends: "Almost a happy day. There were 3,053 days like that in his sentence, from reveille to lights out. The three extra ones were because of the leap years."

The great literary merit of *One Day in the Life of Ivan Denisovich* is its unity of tone and its stylistic originality. Shukhov's thoughts and impressions are rendered in a language that mingles popular speech with prisoners' slang.

Alexander Tvardovsky, a prominent poet and editor-in-chief of *Novy Mir*, who went to Khrushchev to obtain the authorization to publish Solzhenitsyn, insists that the novelette is a literary as well as a political event. He finds particularly attractive the ring of sincerity and authenticity in every line of Solzhenitsyn's work—a relief after the false pathos of most Soviet fiction. The maturity of Solzhenitsyn's art is surprising in a newcomer to literature.

The Whole Sick Crew

V by Thomas Pynchon
April 21, 1963

BY GEORGE PLIMPTON

SINCE THE WAR a category of the American novel has been developed by a number of writers: American picaresque one might call the archetype, and its more notable practitioners would include Saul Bellow with *The Adventures of Augie March*, Jack Kerouac, *On the Road*, Joseph Heller, *Catch-22*, Clancy Sigal, *Going Away*, and Harry Matthews, who last fall produced a generally overlooked though brilliant novel entitled *Conversions*. The genus is distinguished by what the word "picaresque" implies—the doings of a character or characters completely removed from socio-political attachments, thus on the loose, and, above all, uncommitted.

Such novels are invariably lengthy, heavily populated with eccentrics, deviates, grotesques with funny names (so they can be remembered), and are usually composed of a series of bizarre adventures or episodes in which the central character is involved, then removed and flung abruptly into another. Very often a Quest is incorporated, which keeps the central character on the move.

For the author, the form of the picaresque is convenient: he can string together the short stories he has at hand (publishers are reluctant to publish short-story collections, which would suggest the genre is perhaps a type of compensation). Moreover—the well-made, the realistic not being his concern—the author can afford to take chances, to be excessive, even prolix, knowing that in a work of great length stretches of doubtful value can be excused. The author can tell his favorite jokes, throw in a song, indulge in a fantasy or so, include his own verse, display an intimate knowledge of such disparate subjects as physics, astronomy, art, jazz, how a nose-job is done, the wildlife in the New York sewage system. These indeed are some of the topics which constitute a recent and remarkable example of the genre: a brilliant and turbulent first novel published this month by a young Cornell graduate, Thomas Pynchon. He calls his book *V*.

V has two main characters. One of them is Benny Profane—on the loose in New York City following a Navy hitch and a spell as a road-laborer. Born in 1932, Profane is Depression-formed, and his function in the novel is to perfect his state of "schlemihlhood"—that is to say being the *victim*, buffeted by circumstance and not caring to do much about it—resigned to being behind the 8-ball. Indeed, in one poolroom fracas the 8-ball rolls up to Profane, prostrate on the floor, and stares him in the eye. His friends are called the Whole Sick Crew, a fine collection of disaffected about whom one observer says "there is not one you can point to and say is well." Typical of them is the itinerant artist Slab, who calls himself a catatonic expressionist. Beset by a curious block he can only paint cheese danishes—Cheese Danish No. 56 is his subject at one stage of the book.

Set in contrast to Profane is a young adventurer named Stencil. He is active as opposed to passive, obsessed by a self-imposed duty which he follows, somewhat joylessly—a Quest to discover the identity of V, a woman's initial which occurs in the journals of his father, a British Foreign Office man, drowned in a waterspout off Malta. The search for V, a puzzle slowly fitted together by a series of brilliant episodic flashbacks, provides the unifying device of the novel—a framework encompassing a considerable panorama of history and character. V, turning up first as a young girl in Cairo at the start of the century, reappears

Oops!

April 7, 1963

A Clockwork Orange

BY ANTHONY BURGESS

A satirical horror novel by one of Britain's most talented observers of the social scene. In Mr. Burgess's Slav-oriented state of the future, the Lower Orders are in ascendence and happy hooligans roam the London streets, bashing senior citizens in the eyes with bicycle chains. The protagonist is a 15-year-old psychopath named Alex who undergoes a corrective brainwashing that makes him allergic to violence. With his tongue popping in and out of his cheek, Mr. Burgess satirizes both the sociological and the penal approach to juvenile crime, literary proletarianism, and anything else in his path. Written in a pseudo-criminal cant, *A Clockwork Orange* is an interesting tour-de-force, though not up to the level of the author's two previous novels.

under various names and guises, invariably at times of strife and riot, in Florence, Paris, Malta, South Africa. Finally one finds her disguised as a Manichaean priest, trapped under a beam in a World War II bombing raid on Malta and being literally disassembled by a crowd of children.

The identity of V, what her many guises are meant to suggest, will cause much speculation. What will be remembered, whether or not V remains elusive, is Pynchon's remarkable ability—which includes a vigorous and imaginative style, a robust humor, a tremendous reservoir of information (one suspects that he could churn out a passable almanac in a fortnight's time) and, above all, a sense of how to use and balance these talents. True, in a plan as complicated and varied as a Hieronymus Bosch triptych, sections turn up which are dull—the author backing and filling, shuffling the pieces of his enormous puzzle to no effect—but these stretches are far fewer than one might expect.

Pynchon is in his early twenties; he writes in Mexico City—a recluse. It is hard to find out anything more about him. At least there is at hand a testament—this first novel V—which suggests that no matter what his circumstances, or where he's doing it, there is at work a young writer of staggering promise.

No Ordinary Criminal

Eichmann in Jerusalem: A Report on the Banality of Evil
by Hannah Arendt
May 19, 1963

BY MICHAEL A. MUSMANNO

ADOLF EICHMANN, one of Hitler's principal instruments in the Nazi program to exterminate the Jews of Europe, was hanged on May 31, 1962, but in this book he is very much alive. We see him energetically striding from page to page, we observe him in shining, black-leather boots stamping into governmental, military and diplomatic offices in all parts of Europe. We follow him, his ornamented cap at a sharp angle, storming into hotels, concentration camps, railroad trains, human abattoirs and emerging with neither a dirty spot on his immaculate uniform, nor—according to Eichmann, with Hannah Arendt apparently supporting his boast—a dirty spot on his conscience.

That is what this book is principally about: Adolf Eichmann's conscience.

The author covered the trial of Eichmann in Jerusalem for *The New Yorker*, and the series of articles in that magazine, which form the bulk of this book, stirred controversy as a strong wind agitates the waters of a lake. The book, which follows the articles as a gale succeeds a rising wind, will probably evoke a great deal of pensive reflection; Eichmann was no ordinary criminal, and his deeds were not the subject of the ordinary court of assizes.

There will be those who will wonder how Miss Arendt, after attending the Eichmann trial and studying the record and pertinent material, could announce, as she solemnly does in this book, that Eichmann was not really a Nazi at heart, that he did not know Hitler's program when he joined the Nazi party, that the Gestapo were helpful to the Jews in Palestinian immigration, that Himmler (Himmler!) had a sense of pity, that the Jewish gas-killing program grew out of Hitler's euthanasia program and that, all in all, Eichmann was really a modest man.

Miss Arendt devotes considerable space to Eichmann's conscience and informs us that one of Eichmann's points in his own defense was "that there were no voices from the outside to arouse his conscience." How abysmally asleep is a conscience when it must be aroused to be told there is something morally wrong about pressing candy upon a little boy to induce him to enter a gas chamber of death?

The author believes that Eichmann was misjudged in Jerusalem and quotes, with astounding credulity, his statement: "I myself had no hatred for the Jews." Sympathizing with Eichmann, she laments, "Alas, nobody believed him." Should anyone be blamed for lifting an eyebrow to the suggestion that Eichmann loved the Jews? At the end of the war he exclaimed: "I shall laugh when I jump into the grave, because of the feeling that I killed five million Jews. This gives me a lot of satisfaction and pleasure."

Miss Arendt defends Eichmann against his own words here arguing that it would be "preposterous" to believe he personally slew five million people. But his guilt did not depend on personal physical annihilation. The District Court of Jerusalem specified: "The legal and moral responsibility of him who delivers the victim to his death is, in our opinion, no smaller, and may even be greater, than the liability of him who does the victim to death." Eichmann headed the incredibly monstrous project to exterminate coldbloodedly a segment of the human race. He rounded up his victims in cities, villages and the remotest corners of a continent; he had them jammed, herring fashion, into box cars; he had a hand in supplying the gas which eventually killed them.

If, in recalling the period, one could shut one's eyes to the scenes of brutal massacre and stop one's ears to the screams of horror-stricken women and terrorized children as they saw the tornado of death sweeping toward them, one

1963

The Group, by Mary McCarthy, shows that an intellectual can write a sexy commercial novel.

could almost assume that in some parts of the book the author is being whimsical. For instance, she says that Eichmann was a Zionist and helped Jews to get to Palestine. The facts, as set forth in the judgment handed down by the District Court of Jerusalem, are entirely to the contrary. As far back as November, 1937, after an espionage trip into the Middle East he reported that the plan for emigration of Jews to Palestine "was out of the question," it being "the policy of the Reich to avoid the creation of an independent Jewish State in Palestine."

Miss Arendt says that the only time Eichmann gave an "order to kill" was in the autumn of 1941 when he "proposed killing by shooting" of 8,000 Serbian Jews. This is quibbling. While heading the "Eichmann Special Operation Unit" in Hungary, he shipped, in less than two months, 434,351 Jews in 147 trains of sealed freight cars to Auschwitz where the gas chambers had to work at full capacity to kill the human cargoes. These 434,351 Jews died as the result of Eichmann's orders as much as if he had personally directed the gassing and the cremating crews.

The disparity between what Miss Arendt states, and what the ascertained facts are, occurs with such disturbing frequency in her book that it can hardly be accepted as an authoritative historical work. She says Eichmann never "actually attended a mass execution by shooting" or watched a "gassing process." Eichmann himself spoke of attending a mass shooting and described seeing "marksmen . . . shooting into the pit." The pit was "full of corpses." The Court, in its final judgment, described Eichmann at Treblinka, one of the death camps in the East, watching "the naked Jews being led to the gas chambers along paths surrounded by barbed wire."

According to Miss Arendt, Eichmann never saw "the killing installations" at Auschwitz, although she admits he went to this charnel house "repeatedly." Her observation is like saying that one repeatedly sojourned at Niagara Falls but never noticed the falling water. Eichmann dispatched over two million Jews into the Auschwitz "destruction machinery" of which, Miss Arendt admits, he saw "enough to be fully informed."

The author supports Eichmann's incredible claim that he was ignorant of the *Kristallnacht* or Night of Broken Glass, even though the whole world knew of the conflagration of hatred which burned down synagogues, smashed 7,500 Jewish shop windows and drove 20,000 Jews into concentration camps.

Another unfortunate feature of this book is that the author, an eminent scholar, should reveal so frequently evidences of purely private prejudice. She attacks the State of Israel, its laws and institutions, wholly unrelated to the Eichmann case; she pours scorn on Prime Minister Ben-Gurion.

Miss Arendt says that Eichmann, "to a truly extraordinary degree," received the "cooperation" of the Jews in their own destruction. This astonishing conclusion is predicated on statements of others that some Jewish leaders dealt with Eichmann, and that, in certain instances, Jews took part in police work. The fact that Eichmann with threats of death coerced occasional Quislings and Lavals into "cooperation" only adds to the horror of his crimes.

Driving Ambition

My Years with General Motors by Alfred P. Sloan Jr.
January 19, 1964

BY LOUIS M. HACKER

THE MAJOR FORCE BEHIND the industrial growth of modern nations is not the classical triad of land, labor and capital. It is entrepreneurship. Those who exercise it are the restless, imaginative and resourceful men and families who are willing to break through the hard crust of custom, inertia and bureaucratic indifference.

The United States has been more fortunate than most countries in making possible the emergence of entrepreneurs; and yet, it had to be so, for we have been a people without a past in the sense that the absence of tradition and inherited privilege has given opportunity for the quick recognition of talent. The road to entrepreneurial success, usually, has not been an easy one; but those who have traveled it saw it almost at once as an open way, yet straight and narrow. It was McCormick's move from Virginia to Chicago—the center of the then wheat country—and his devotion to the manufacture and distribution of reapers exclusively that revolutionized America's agriculture. Edison concentrated on incandescent lighting. Andrew Carnegie worked only in heavy steel: his perspicacity caught at once iron's first opportunity in modernizing the country's railroads and, when these were largely finished, in the late 1880s, its second in the manufacture of the structural steel that made possible our great cities. It was when the elder Rockefeller turned to transportation—the control of his own pipelines and tank cars—that the Standard Oil Company of Ohio began to outstrip its many rivals in the highly competitive business of oil refining. It was the du Pont shift over from powder to chemicals that helped give such great vitality to the 1920s. And as for Henry Ford and the automobile: he had been working on cars for more than a decade—on the same obscure and unrewarding basis as had been hundreds of other tinkerers like himself all over the Western World— when in 1908 he announced his Model T: a single, spare, utility model, at a low price, made on the assembly line for a mass market (of farmers). This was his vision; and the world has never been the same since.

Alfred P. Sloan Jr. was cut from the same cloth; his chance as entrepreneur came in 1920 when that imaginative and volatile genius William C. Durant, who in the same 1908 had founded the General Motors Company, saw his personal speculations overextended and his company on the verge of bankruptcy. Durant stepped out; Pierre S. du Pont stepped in (the family owned almost 30 percent of General Motors stock). The company weathered the lean years 1921–22, thanks in part to financing from the du Ponts and Morgan, but thanks as much to a conception of organization and broad manufacturing policy for which Sloan was responsible.

Sloan was born in 1875, the son of a wholesale tea and coffee merchant who was able to send him to the Massachusetts Institute of Technology and to stake him in a partnership (the investment was $5,000) in the Hyatt Roller Bearing Company. General Motors absorbed the United Motors Corporation (of which Hyatt had become a part) in 1918 and Sloan went with it—becoming president of General Motors in 1923 and remaining active in its affairs as chief executive and board member for almost forty years. This book covers those years when General Motors became the largest industrial concern in the world and a showpiece and showcase of American entrepreneurial versatility.

Every step that Sloan took, in shaping General Motors in his own image, was preceded by a position paper from his own hand (here reprinted) that was mulled over, discussed and in the great majority of cases adopted entire by his associates. We have here, in effect, the full record of a campaign laid out in general in the 1920s and carried out and won, from objective to objective, in the following three decades.

By 1927, the Chevrolet was closing in on the Ford; after that, Ford had leadership over General Motors in only the three years 1929, 1930 and 1935. Ford did not understand the ever-shifting (but not capricious) market; that "middle-income people, assisted by trade-in and installment financing, thus created the demand not for basic transportation but for progress in new cars, for comfort, convenience, power, and style."

The decision to offer new models every year was first taken in 1925 and fully installed as policy in the 1930s. About this highly controversial matter Sloan has much to say. Is it one of the examples of the weaknesses and wastefulness of J. K. Galbraith's "affluent society"? Or is it evidence of the vitality—what Joseph Schumpeter called the "creative destruction"—of capitalism? Sloan definitely adheres to the latter position and he says it with an eloquence that even Schumpeter could not match. The annual model—which takes two years in the planning and involves thousands of General Motors' best minds and hands—is "the

_1964_

It's legal to publish *Tropic of Cancer* (Henry Miller) in the United States. American fans began smuggling it in from France in 1934.

spur to which the organization must respond or die. The urge to satisfy this requirement is the dynamism of General Motors, its will, its drive, its pride and its defense."

It is something else: here is the proving ground, the annual baptism of fire to which the younger men are exposed. Here talents emerge—or early promise fails to mature. The routineers are sorted out and retained as "middle executives"—for there are innumerable day-by-day tasks that have to be done. Those with flair, imagination, and boldness rapidly ascend.

What does the future hold for General Motors? Will it sooner or later diversify? Will it recognize the new opportunities in transportation—and changing tastes—that the manufacture of pleasure watercraft, hydrofoil boats, cheap and standardized helicopters, possibly even monorail trains, presents? After all, General Motors, by its very successes, has helped to create problems: our congested highways and our urban communities threatened with blight at their centers exactly because so many cars and trucks choke off mobility. These challenges are for other innovators to face up to; for Sloan has done his share in demonstrating the vitality, imagination, and broad and general social gains of American capitalist enterprise.

Chain Letter

Herzog by Saul Bellow
September 20, 1964

BY JULIAN MOYNAHAN

THE POSITION of the 43-year-old hero and title character of Saul Bellow's latest and best novel is absurd. Moses E. Herzog believes in reason, but is suffering from a protracted nervous crisis, following the collapse of his second marriage, that leads him to the brink of suicide. He deplores the current vogue for crisis ethics, dionysiac revivals and thrilling apocalypses, yet is professionally an intellectual historian of the Romantic Movement who travels about with a paperback volume of Blake's poems in his valise.

He is an urbanite from Montreal who has spent most of his life in Chicago and New York, yet the only thing he owns is a decaying farmhouse in a depopulated area of the Berkshires. He believes that "brotherhood is what makes a man human," yet he has been cuckolded by his best friend and has come to manhood in a period when 6 million of his fellow Jews were exterminated by the Nazis and their allies.

He sees his mission as "this great bone-breaking burden of selfhood and self-development," but he has apparently failed as a father, a lover, a husband, a writer, an academic, and he faces each day and each night the real possibility that his psyche is being invaded by the self-disintegrative processes of an actual psychosis.

And he sees in a last absurd paradox that his balance, if it is to come, must come "from instability." The novel, in its almost perfect narrative art, makes us see the truth and wisdom of that paradox, not only for Herzog himself but for all of us at this point—at this "post-Christian" point, as the book hesitantly but finally puts it—of modern history.

Over the past 10 or 15 years, Jewish writers—Bernard Malamud, J. D. Salinger, Norman Mailer, Philip Roth, inter alia—have emerged as a dominant movement in our literature. *Herzog*, in several senses, is the great pay-off book of that movement. It is a masterpiece, the first the movement has produced (unless Henry Roth's magnificent try at a masterpiece, *Call it Sleep*, written in the 1930s, can somehow be brought into the picture), and it is Bellow's most Jewish book. There are no gentiles in it. It is full of Jewish wit, humor, pathos, intellectual and moral passion, hipness about European social thought and foreign literatures. Like the prophets, Herzog cries out for "a change of heart," and like all Jews in this generation, he feels himself to be a survivor with the responsibility of testifying to the continued existence of values which the Eichmanns had tried to send up in the smoke of burning flesh.

Herzog is a great book because it has great characters. First, Herzog himself. He wanders about, distracted, charming and nervy, a kind of intellectual Oblomov on the run, a Pierre Bezhukhov of the thermonuclear century. His mood shifts in great swoops and glides; he revisits in imagination the scenes of his broken marriages, his broken career, his childhood. He disappears from New York, turns up in Vineyard Haven, flies to Chicago, where, gun in hand, he spies through a window his ex-wife's lover bathing Herzog's own small daughter and realizes he can never seize the swift logic of the assassin.

At last he comes back to the Massachusetts farmhouse where owls roost on the posts of his former marriage bed and the toilet bowl contains the tiny skeletons of birds. Throughout his mental and physical journeying, he has been composing letters—to friends and enemies, professional rivals and colleagues, to General Eisenhower and Friedrich Nietzsche, to his second wife, Madeleine, to a woman named Wanda with whom he had a brief affair during a foundation-sponsored lecture tour in the Iron Curtain countries.

Some of Herzog's letters are playful, some are pixilated; but all of them are, in the last analysis, responsible. Taken together they compose a credo for the times. Through his nervous and distracted hero Bellow appears to me to be saying this:

The age is full of fearful abysses. If people are to go ahead they must move into and through these abysses. The old definitions of balance and sanity do not help on this journey, but the ideals these terms gesture at remain, even though they require fresh definition. Love still counts, justice still counts, and particularly intellectual and emotional courage still count. The book reserves its sharpest criticism for those people—and no doubt they are to be found among public men as well as among theologians and artists—who try to cope homeopathically with the threat of violence under which we all live by cultivating an analogous, imaginative violence or intemperate despair. As Moses E. Herzog says in his manner of "strange diatribe":

We love apocalypses too much. . . . and florid extremism with its thrilling language. Excuse me, no, I've had all the monstrosity I want.

Essay

Conrad Knickerbocker on Black Humor
September 27, 1964

SOMETHING TERRIBLE (to many people) and marvelous (to others) has happened to the national sense of humor since World War II. Not only is more serious American fiction funnier, but our comic writers, like medieval magicians, have divided into two camps, white and black. "White" humorists such as Max Shulman and William Brinkley are as harmless as Lucille Ball or the Flintstones. They chuckle at our foibles, but when the chips are down, they support the familiar comforts of the status quo. Their adherents are many, for everyone agrees that a good laugh—moderate of course—is a wonderful tonic in this careworn world of ours.

Everyone, that is, except an immoderate new breed of American writers, who have wrenched the status quo until it begins to emit tormented laughter. Bitter, perverse, sadistic and *sick*—as the righteous defenders of a sick society aver—the new humor is black in its pessimism, its refusal of compromise and its mortal sting. Its adherents are few as yet but increasing. Bored beyond tears by solemnity and pap, an increasing audience finds in black humor no tonic, but the gall of truth. There are no more happy endings. A cheery wave and a fast shuffle no longer leave them laughing. New for us, black humor has been part of the response of wiser peoples in other times. Its appearance in American fiction may signal the end of certain innocences.

The list of American talents who have opted for a Bronx cheer instead of a handshake has been growing for 10 years. Terry Southern unmasks fraud in its slickest guises. J. P. Donleavy demolishes matrimony. William Burroughs hoots at our ideas of criminal behavior. Warren Miller conjures new saviors and the free state of Harlem. Bruce Jay Friedman aborts motherhood. Charles Simmons unsmuts smut. Thomas Pynchon, Hughes Rudd, William Gaddis, John Barth, Joseph Heller, Donald Barthelme, Elliott Baker, Ivan Gold and Richard G. Stern, all in their various ways are stampeding the vast herd of American sacred cows.

These writers belong to no round table. The mass book audience has not heard of most of them. They work independently in Mexico City, Chicago or Connecticut. Their views, which have in common the savagery of their conclusions, signal a major new, and perhaps the only new, development in American fiction since the war.

Incapable of a détente, the black humorists torment the American mind by taking nothing at face value. They hate preconceptions, stereotypes and spiritual fat. They laugh in tune with the man on the gallows who asked, "Are you sure this thing is safe?" because their social realities seem just as precarious. They are afraid not so much of the cliché of the Bomb as the more awful prospect that we will survive after all only to win the space race and eliminate washday blues.

We have always had satirists, but *A Connecticut Yankee* and *Main Street* are gentle nudges in the ribs compared to the neo-Swiftian assaults of Mr. Southern's *The Magic Christian* or Mr. Burroughs's *Naked Lunch*. Petronius Arbiter, his barbs incurring the wrath of Nero, opened his veins and recited frivolous verses to his friends as he died. Certain modern humorists may instead shoot heroin into their veins, but the message is the same. As societies convulse, art turns emetic. Whether the new humor ominously resembles the Latin satire that flourished while the totalitarian power of the Empire grew, or the glittering harpoons of Dr. Johnson's age that drew their aim on stupendous social arrogance, indifference and misery, depends on who has the last laugh. One thing is certain: the new humorists bear witness to convulsions.

"I am in the position of liking the roots, somehow, of America and loathing everything it stands for today," James Purdy, one of the grimmest of the grim humorists, wrote a friend recently. "We live in the stupidest cultural era of American history. It is so stupid it inspires me."

Only disappointment—an irremediable sense of expectations betrayed—can account for the violent and amusing shapes that fill his novel *Malcolm* and stories like "Daddy Wolf." "The theme of my work is the estrangement of the human being in America," he has said, an America "based on money and competition, inhuman, terrified of love, sexual and other, obsessed with homosexuality (Hemingway, O'Hara, etc.) and brutality . . . opposing anything that opposes money."

With a kind of glossolalia of imagery, the new humorists testify to a world filled with discontinuities too huge for normal expression. Benny Profane, the "human yo-yo" who is the hero of Mr. Pynchon's novel V, finds solace in New York sewers shooting the gift alligators children have flushed down toilets. Starting from scratch and with an evangelical momentum, these shaggy anchorites in a desert avoid the amenities, the little courtesies to reader and reviewer that have enervated many of our more "normal" writers. Their freedom gives them the elbow room for onslaught, the vigor to deal directly, as the traditional novel seems less and less able to do.

"Normal" novelists prefer to seduce the reader with clever mixtures of the probable and the derived; this kind of fiction waits coyly to be consumed and explained in the normal fashion. The black humorists prefer rape. They ambush the reader and savage his convictions that war, success, big cars, families and fancy restaurants are worth living for.

It was more than 15 years after V-J Day before any American author raised the point that a war of noble purpose could also be a boondoggle not dissimilar to some gigantic used-car auction. Mr. Heller did it in *Catch-22*. Thousands of ex-GIs winced but also winked. Stanley Elkin's *Boswell* concerns a wrestler who worships the ideal of strength, but muscles grown too large bind into immobility. Mr. Gaddis's *The Recognitions*, one of the most serious, most memorable novels of the 1950s, has long stretches of black humor that amplify its themes of spiritual and artistic forgery. These novels bear one message, forceful, repetitive, almost repetitious: in the midst of progress, as we photograph moon craters, as wars continue, and as power structures proliferate, we regress.

It began to show in the 1930s, even as various new orders seemed to promise solutions. Nathanael West in America and Louis-Ferdinand Céline in France used black humor to warn against dream merchants. The French bought Céline's *Death on the Installment Plan* by the thousands. Later the panzers of the greatest dream merchant of them all rolled into Paris. Nobody here paid a great deal of attention to West. We were busy with a new order of our own, rebuilding prosperity, bolstering our souls with DeMille.

The enemy, according to the black humorists, is made up of men of gesture, manipulators of acceptable ideas, wise in the incantation of popular brainstorms. The new humor is anti-intellectual in the conventional sense. The idea, the concept logically advanced by critics, professors, senators and psychiatrists, has been tried and found wanting. John Barth's *The Sot-Weed Factor*, a novel of

1964

Jean-Paul Sartre chooses to decline the Nobel Prize in Literature.

great learning, has as its target the edifice of the intellect, particularly as guarded by its chief articulator, the university. Purportedly a ribald account of colonial American life, the book squares off at the Ph.D. candidate, with his view that history is somehow redemptive and that progress is the natural order of things. Our early national aspirations were just as squalid as those of the next nation's. The only difference is that we prefer delusions to illusions, Mr. Barth tells us, and he uses the techniques of a doctoral dissertation to give the coup-de-grace.

Most national styles of humor contain elements of social criticism, but the target usually lies without, unless there are worms within. Englishmen used to prefer jokes about the French and Irish; now the English physic themselves continually. In earlier days on the American stage, Uncle Sam and the Yankee trader told jokes about the English; now Mort Sahl tells jokes about the liberal intellectual; the liberal intellectual explains why, and Mr. Barth calls a plague on both houses. The new humor is self-directed. Underneath lie spasms of self-loathing.

Why has satire appealed to so many exceptional talents in the last dozen years, when a generation ago, the more "normal" forms of social commentary — the essay, the social novel — were the accepted channels of protest? One reason is reaction: traditional forms cannot accommodate a reality which now includes Jack Ruby. More, we have begun to lose our accustomed responses to the event. The excesses of civilization have stupefied us. Brutalized, we scream "Jump!" to the man on the ledge.

A number of writers no longer use ideas to explain events, for events have become too mysterious. The black humorists recount events in their natural — which is to say nonlogical — sequence. Events can, after all, be found in similar sequence on the front page of any newspaper, equally incomprehensible. *Naked Lunch* consists of a series of dispatches from America and abroad interlaced with a treatise on narcotics addiction. Never mind that the geography is hallucinated. Our laughter is the sad delight of recognition, not to be found in pamphlets on the national purpose.

A collection of short-stories by Donald Barthelme, *Come Back, Dr. Caligari,* is a testament to the non-sequiturs of the contemporary event. The stories become prose pop art, spilling past the hitherto agreed-on limits of fiction into realms as mysterious as daily life. Ideally, one should read them while drinking beer, reading *Time,* watching television, and listening to Dizzy Gillespie. More than stories, they are literary "happenings." In "A Shower of Gold," the hero is selected as a contestant on a television program called *Who Am I?* The master of ceremonies asks the hero if he loves his mother. "Yes," he replies, but a bell rings, the tote board flashes, and the announcer screams, "He's lying!" Shortly before this, he has been visited by the player of a cat-piano, a sinister device encasing eight live cats. His mother, furthermore, had always paid for his karate lessons. He is confused.

"Turn off your television sets," he finally rages in the pandemonium of the studio. "Cash in your life insurance, indulge in a mindless optimism. Visit girls at dusk. Play the guitar . . . Think back and remember how it was." The audience shrieks and howls.

Certain critics may tell us the spirit of alienation—a vitalizing force in much of our best literature—is dying, and that American fiction is moving into a period of accommodation with things-as-they-are. This idea may have been suggested by the present self-satisfaction of our traditional novelists. As always, trying to hear what has already sounded, critics tend to ignore new thunder on the horizon.

Traditional art forms, in which the surfaces of life fit neatly together, cope less and less. Black humor more and more expertly points out the inconstancies of modern experience, the fragmented zaniness of a day at any office. Laughter itself may be a form of accommodation, as the critic Webster Schott has suggested, but if so, it is the only point of juncture between the black humorists and the times in which they live. They are irreconcilable.

So, indeed, are more of us than the image-packagers would care to admit. Black humor has infiltrated middle culture in movies such as *Dr. Strangelove*, in theater with *Who's Afraid of Virginia Woolf?* and *Oh What a Lovely War*, in the nightclub dementia of Lenny Bruce and Jonathan Winters, in the pop-art put-ons of Roy Lichtenstein and Andy Warhol. The Ginger Man might not speak for all of us, but his mockery prophesies a time when life will be lived exactly as blueprinted in the beer commercials, unless we hoot loud enough.

By default, the black humorists have become keepers of conscience. Strident, apt, they challenge the hypnotists and the hysterics. They urge choices on us. Amid the banality, the emptiness and excess, they offer the terrors and possibilities of self-knowledge. "There ought to be no barriers," Terry Southern recently told a *Life* magazine interviewer in an enigmatic put-on. Stop kidding yourself and recover joy, he may have meant. Has the age of hollow laughter dawned? Soon, perhaps, we will move forward to the sound of exploding windbags all around.

Interview

Robert Lowell
October 4, 1964

BY STANLEY KUNITZ

R OBERT LOWELL SPEAKS with an air of gentle authority. Surprisingly, for a New Englander, his voice has a soft Southern tincture, which may be traced back to his formative years when he modeled himself on the Southerners Allen Tate and John Crowe Ransom. His wife, who supplies another auditory influence, is the Kentucky-born novelist and critic, Elizabeth Hardwick, one of the founding editors of *The New York Review of Books*.

Since 1960, when the Lowells braved the shock of transplanting themselves from Boston, they have figured prominently in the literary and intellectual life of New York. With their daughter Harriet, an ebullient 7-year-old, from whose flights of fancy and rhetoric her father has been known to borrow, they occupy a cooperative duplex apartment in mid-Manhattan, off Central Park. The Victorian décor, dominated by "an unauthenticated Burne-Jones" hanging above the fireplace, and the majestic proportions of the book-lined living room, with its 20-foot ceiling, recall the turn of the century, when the building was designed as a luxurious nest of studio apartments for nonstruggling artists.

"Our move from Boston to New York gave me a tremendous push," says Lowell. "Boston is all history and recollection; New York is ahead of one. Sympathetic spirits are a rarity elsewhere. Here there is a whole community of the arts, an endlessly stimulating fellowship . . . at times too stimulating. No one is too great for New York, and yet I grant there is something frightening about it."

He is asked to comment on a passage from his remarks at the Boston Arts Festival in 1960, when he was the honored poet: "Writing is neither transport nor a technique. My own owes everything to a few of our poets who have tried to write directly about what mattered to them, and yet to keep faith with their calling's tricky, specialized, unpopular possibilities for good workmanship. When I finished *Life Studies*, I was left hanging on a question mark. I am still hanging there. I don't know whether it is a death rope or a lifeline."

"Thankfully," he responds with the hint of a smile, "the lifeline seems to me both longer and stronger than I thought at that time."

He notes that he is feeling unusually fit, as his bronzed look confirms, after a summer in Castine, Me., where the Lowells have an old house on the Commons, a gift from his cousin Harriet Winslow. His weight—he has a tendency to gain—is down to 170 pounds, ideal for his 6-foot frame.

"In *Life Studies*," he continues, "I wanted to see how much of my personal story and memories I could get into poetry. To a large extent, it was a technical problem, as most problems in poetry are. But it was also something of a cause: to extend the poem to include, without compromise, what I felt and knew. Afterwards, having done it, I did not have the same necessity. My new book, *For the Union Dead*, is more mixed, and the poems in it are separate entities. I'm after invention rather than memory, and I'd like to achieve some music and elegance and splendor, but not in any programmatic sense. Some of the poems may be close to symbolism. After all, it's a bore to keep putting down just the things you know."

As Lowell talks, slumped in his chair until he is practically sitting on his spine, he knits his brow and stirs an invisible broth with his right index finger. The troubled blue eyes, intense and roving behind the thick glasses, rarely come to rest.

"The kind of poet I am was largely determined by the fact that I grew up in the heyday of The New Criticism, with Eliot's magical scrutiny of the text as a critical example. From the beginning I was preoccupied with technique, fascinated by the past, and tempted by other languages. It is hard for me to imagine a poet not interested in the classics. The task is to get something new into old forms, even at the risk of breaking them.

"So much of the effort of the poem is to arrive at something essentially human, to find the right voice for what we have to say. In life we speak with many false voices; occasionally, if we are lucky, we find a true one in our poems. A poem needs to include a man's contradictions. One side of me, for example, is a conventional liberal, concerned with causes, agitated about peace and justice and equality, as so many people are. My other side is deeply conservative, wanting to get at the roots of things, wanting to slow down the whole modern process of mechanization and dehumanization, knowing that liberalism can be a form of death too. In the writing of a poem all our compulsions and biases should get in, so that finally we don't know what we mean."

The contradictions of which Lowell speaks are present in his face and manner. The sensitive curved mouth contrasts with the jutting, fleshy chin; the nose is small, with wide circular nostrils; he is articulate, informed and positive, but his gestures are vague and rather endearingly awkward. With his friends he has an air of affectionate dependency, which makes him seem perpetually boyish, despite the 47 years, the grizzled hair, the deep parentheses etched at the corners of his mouth. He is knowing about fame and power, but no less knowing about his weaknesses. His ambition and pride are real, but so is his modesty.

He has a great gift for friendship. No one is more generous than Robert Lowell in acknowledging his indebtedness to anybody who has ever helped him with a problem or with a poem.

"The poets who most directly influenced me," he says, "were Allen Tate, Elizabeth Bishop and William Carlos Williams. An unlikely combination! . . . but you can see that Bishop is a sort of bridge between Tate's formalism and Williams's informal art. For sheer language, Williams beats anybody. And who compares with him for aliveness and keenness of observation? I admire Pound but find it impossible to imitate him. Nor do I know how to use Eliot or Auden—their voice is so personal. Williams can be used, partly because he is somewhat anonymous. His poems are as perfect as anybody's, but they lead one to think of the possibility of writing them in different ways—for example, putting them into rhyme."

Lowell has no secondary skills or hobbies to distract him from his absorption in literature. At 9:30 every morning, when he is in the city, he retires to his separate and private apartment on an upper floor of the building in which he lives. There he spends at least five or six hours reading and writing. He reads only three or four novels a year now, but is quite omnivorous in his capacity for literary periodicals and for books of poetry, criticism and history. He makes a point of returning regularly to the classics "with the aid of some sort of trot." Recently he has been reading Juvenal and Dante. Some of his scholarship is specifically designed to prepare him for his courses at Harvard, where he teaches two days a week. "I have had the advantage," he reflects, "of an independent income, which made it unnecessary for me to work for a living. I came to teaching voluntarily and quite late, having been unfit for it in my youth."

Lowell occupies himself tirelessly with literary evaluations, comparisons and ratings. "The modern poem of length that interests me most," he remarks sweepingly, "is Pound's *Cantos*, the only long poem of the century that really comes off, even with all its flaws. One reason for my sustained interest in it is that it continues to puzzle me. In so many respects Pound remains a pre-Raphaelite figure, filled with nostalgia for the pure song of the troubadours and a lost pre-Renaissance innocence. What saved him as a poet was his bad politics, which got him involved in the contemporary world. The *Cantos* are not so good as Faulkner, but they are better than Hemingway and better than the work of any other novelist we've had since James. Dreiser's *American Tragedy*, which is comparable in scale, is humanly superior to the *Cantos*, but technically and stylistically inferior."

His taste for fine prose is as keen as his taste for verse. "As Pound said, poetry ought to be at least as well-written as prose. Furthermore, if you have sufficient control of the measure, you ought to be able to say anything in poetry that you can say in prose. The main difference between prose and poetry is a matter of technique: prose is written in paragraphs, poetry in lines. I am fascinated by the prose grip on things that somehow lets the music in and invites the noble splendor of a formal art. Swinburne's voice is dead because it's all music and no experience. Hardy owed a great deal to Swinburne, as we know from his elegy, but his grasp on reality put him out of Swinburne's class.

"Some of the intricate musical stanzas in Hardy have the solidity of a stone-mason's job. In an anthology that I was reading the other day I came across 'The Frigate Pelican' of Marianne Moore's with a sense of relief and liberation, not because it wasn't well-made but because it was made differently, outside the groove of conventional poetics. It caused the other poems to wither. I am still tempted by metrical forms and continue to write them on occasion, but I am aware that meter can develop into a kind of paralysis. Sometimes I start regular and end irregular; sometimes the other way around."

With an accelerated stir of his finger, Lowell tries to sum up his argument on the relationship between prose and poetry. "In general, the poets of the last generation have lasted much better than the novelists. By way of illustration, contrast Williams with Thomas Wolfe. Yet the poets need the prose-writers and have a lot to learn from them. The style of a Flaubert or of a Faulkner affects the tradition of poetry as much as it affects the tradition of fiction. An ideal poetic language is more likely to resemble the art of Chekhov than that of Dylan Thomas. Maybe Thomas's language is too sonorous to be at the center of poetry. The best poets have an enormous respect for prose. After all, the great novelists of the nineteenth century make *Idylls of the King* seem frivolous. The supreme epic of the last 150 years is *War and Peace*, of the last 50 years, *Ulysses*."

The conversation veers to the subject of poetic reputation. Lowell is without doubt the most celebrated poet in English of his generation. Almost from the beginning it seemed that he could do no wrong. Why? After several false starts and a deepening of the furrows in his brow, Lowell proposes a tentative reply:

"I can't really explain why that much attention has been paid to me. Looking back at *Lord Weary's Castle*, for example, my first full-length collection, I see it as out of the mainstream, a rather repellent, odd, symbolic Catholic piece of work. It may be that some people have turned to my poems because of the very things that are wrong with me, I mean the difficulty I have with ordinary living, the impracticability, the myopia. Seeing less than others can be a great strain. One has to learn how to live with one's limitations. I don't like to admit that my gift is for short pieces, but I'm better off knowing it."

The British critic, A. Alvarez, has recently paired Lowell with John Berryman as writers of "poetry of immense skill and intelligence which coped openly with the quick of their experience, experience sometimes on the edge of disintegration and breakdown. . . . Where once Lowell tried to externalize his disturbances theologically in Catholicism and rhetorically in certain mannerisms of language and rhythm, he is now . . . trying to cope with them nakedly, and without evasion."

Lowell does not try to skirt the issue, though it is difficult for him to discuss. "We are more conscious of our wounds," he ruminates, "than the poets before us, but we are not necessarily more wounded. Is Stevens or Eliot or Pound really any sadder at the heart or more vulnerable than Keats or Coleridge? The difference may be that modern art tries more deliberately to save the unsavable by giving it form. I am inclined to argue that it is better to be happy and kind than to be a poet. The truth is that no sort of life seems to preclude poetry. Poetry can come out of utterly miserable or disorderly lives, as in the case of a Rimbaud or a Hart Crane. But to make the poems possible a huge amount of health has to go into the misery."

Exhausted as he is, at 2 in the morning, after more than five vehement hours of conversation, he is loth to let you go until the final resolving word has been spoken.

"You wouldn't write poetry unless you felt it had some chance of lasting. But if you get too concerned about posterity, you're in danger of becoming pompous and fraudulent. The poet needs to keep turning to something immediate and alive . . . something impertinent, engaging, un-Olympian. It's a waste of time to dream about immortality, but it's important to try for a poem that continues to be good, even though you realize that it's somehow a mockery for a poem to last longer than you do.

"You write poetry without hoping to attract too much attention, and it would be foolish to aim for a great audience that doesn't exist. Most people have a contempt for poetry—it's so ineffectual—but there may be some envy mixed up in that reaction. Today 'poet' is a slightly laughable and glamorous word."

The Magician

Four Screenplays of Ingmar Bergman by Ingmar Bergman
February 21, 1965

BY PAULINE KAEL

WHAT ARE THESE "SCREENPLAYS" and for whom are they intended? This double question is not so simple-minded as it may appear; nor are the answers obvious.

A reader who has seen the movies of the Swedish director Ingmar Bergman and wants the screenplays so that he can check out his responses to the four films here—*Smiles of a Summer Night, The Seventh Seal, Wild Strawberries* and

The Magician—is likely to be confused, because the screenplays don't exactly correspond to the completed films. He may begin to think his memory is playing tricks; he may become uncertain about just what he did see and hear. A reader who hasn't seen the films has almost no way of discovering how these screenplays were used, how they became part of the style and texture of the films, or what the finished films were like.

What we have here is the dialogue of the film set in a descriptive narration—sort of a cross between a play and a novel—and each can be read as dramatic literature. They resemble plays that have discarded the classic unities (which is not really such a bad description of a dramatic movie). The translators have not given the dialogue the care and polish that would (hopefully) be given to plays they were preparing for performance; still, Bergman's considerable dramatic gifts and accomplishments can be detected even in the inelegant English. Taken simply and loosely as dramatic literature, as story outlines plus dialogue, these screenplays are surprisingly rich reading.

Would the screenplays of other writer-directors attract anything like the attention this collection has drawn since it was first published in 1960? I think not. The reasons for the interest in these screenplays are integral to the modern history of movies, and to the special appeal of Bergman's work.

By the late fifties movies had reached an all-time low: Educated people who still attended American movies did so furtively. The country that had pioneered the only great modern new art had mechanized and commercialized the art—and the interest—out of it; American movies had become a bad joke. And art or foreign movies had come to mean Brigitte Bardot in and out of towel and sheet and Italian Amazons in and out of slips and beds. Several early Ingmar Bergman pictures were imported and exploited as sex films; gradually a few of them reached a more discerning audience. It was not until 1959 that *Wild Strawberries*, capturing a large audience, caused a revolution in American moviegoing, a new adult interest in motion picture art. It was Bergman's 18th film.

In newspapers and magazines Bergman was discussed as a bona fide creative spirit, and his films as "personal statements." When it came to analyzing these personal statements, demonic prose began to haunt movie reviews—such terms as anguish, conjuror, tormented, humiliation, bleak (not as a pejorative but as indicating truthfulness, honesty), harsh, despair, symbolic, the meaninglessness of existence, the reality beyond reality, uncompromising and, of course, brooding—as in "the brooding surf," "a brooding story of reason and faith," "two incestuously brooding sisters." In classic Bergman-reviewer prose, those same two girls were described as "a tormented rationalist" and "a brooding sensualist."

Movie audiences that had grown up on and grown beyond the anonymous Hollywood products discovered a "new" art—the "personal" cinema of Berg-

1965

Robert Lowell makes front-page news with a letter to President Lyndon B. Johnson. Saying that he can follow American foreign policy only with "the greatest dismay and distrust," Lowell refuses to participate in the White House Festival of the Arts.

man, and soon the work of Fellini, Truffaut, Godard, Resnais and Antonioni. But of all the new directors, it was Bergman who developed the most loyal following. He is the only director who has had retrospective showings—"Bergman festivals"—playing throughout the country. Perhaps after years of standardized, pretested, mindless entertainment, the movie audience was well prepared to accept nineteenth-century metaphysical speculation as profound. It was reminded that art was said to have its origins—or was it its significance?—in religious mystery.

In his introduction to the screenplays, Bergman writes that "art lost its basic creative drive the moment it was separated from worship. It severed an umbilical cord and now lives its own sterile life, generating and degenerating itself." One may be puzzled by his imagery (should grown men dangle from an umbilical cord?) and even more perplexed by the appeal of these views; but the gloom of pronouncements like "nobody can live with Death before his eyes, and knowledge of the nothingness of all things" was positively refreshing to people who felt it gave them something to think about.

Much of Bergman's power to affect audiences derives from the peculiar circumstance that the nineteenth-century dichotomies of religion vs. science, faith vs. reason, and so forth, have a new pulling power in the postbomb world. The Bergman films (and some of Fellini's) provide a scapegoat (the rationalist-critic-materialist) and a panacea (love). The filmmaker himself assumes the traditional mystic role of artist-poet-magician. And reviewers, anxious to prove that they are not cold and unfeeling, that they are not those dreadful rational enemies of art who presumably made the world what it is today, come up with moth-eaten blanket remarks like "His characters are tragic victims of a black age."

This "victimization" of his characters—or alienation, as it is generally described—is the most fashionable ailment in modern movies, a kind of super-disease that film directors no longer think it necessary to explain. But it is a mistake to assume that alienation in Bergman's movies is the modern dislocation of sensibility produced by city life, routine work, mass culture, etc.

His famous "ambiguities" are just plain contradictions: God is both dead and diabolic in his films, but there is no ambiguity about it—alienation is the result of skepticism. The only cure he sees is the sweetest, the most fashionable of wonder drugs: "What matters most of all in life is being able to make contact with another human. If you can take that first step toward communication, toward understanding, toward love, then you are saved."

The simple solution of his movie sermons—his exhortation to love on penalty of death—is a kind of universal all-purpose "artistic" solution—an incontrovertible blessing, which, of course, seems more profound than practical attempts to solve actual, complex problems like how can we make a living and still do something worth doing or how can we find or make an environment that has the vitality of a big city without the depersonalization of a big city?

Some of the "magic" of art may be nothing more mysterious than that certain artists have an instinctive grasp of what their audiences want to feel, and the eloquence or audacity to give it expression. Bergman is not the artist-magician that some of his followers believe him to be. He is an extremely uneven artist who, at worst (as in the introduction to this volume), presents himself as a false magician.

When Bergman said of *The Seventh Seal* that "man's dignity lies in his ability to question again and again the seemingly incoherent logic of our destiny," it sounded rather grand. Yet many pictures later he's still asking the same questions—like a compulsive child who doesn't want to learn from the answers. Bergman is suffering from what so few film artists have ever had the glorious opportunity to suffer from: freedom.

There is reason to fear that Bergman is returning the art film to the situation from which he rescued it. Ironically, he can go farther in explicit sexuality than almost anyone else because he is an internationally acclaimed artist, and—a more sinister reason—because he moralistically and puritanically makes sex so disgusting—as a life-denying escape from communication and love!—that in legal terms it isn't pornographic. As a matter of depressing fact, when you come out of some of his movies, you don't want to do *anything*.

The Man Who Was Greenwich Village

Joe Gould's Secret by Joseph Mitchell
September 19, 1965

BY HARRY ROSKOLENKO

BASED ON TWO PROFILES written for *The New Yorker* between 1942 and 1964, Joseph Mitchell's enchanting account of the frenetic Bohemian, Joe Gould, is also an equally touching and sensitive portrait of a man who became a puckish, ribald myth during his life—and, one can almost add, before he was born.

Joseph Ferdinand Gould was an extraordinary intellectual savage; a poet who was not a poet and a historian who was not a historian. He was, as one recalls from this vivid rendering of his frantic antics, as much Greenwich Village, when it counted, as Washington Square Park—now the last port of call for beatniks, ugly girls, cultural expatriates from Harlem, dope pushers, and the folk-singing fraternity.

Joe Gould came to the Village in 1916 after graduating from Harvard with a "magna cum difficultate, class of 1911." He tried, with some amateurish enthusiasm, to take up cultural anthropology, and he measured Indian heads for a season in North Dakota. His father, Dr. Clarke Storer Gould, tried to take Joe into medicine; but Joe, instead, took a job with *The New York Evening Mail*—and it was to be his first and last job. By 1917, he had thought up that poetic, historical, folksy, cum-Gould conceit, "An Oral History of Our Times"—a massive project that took him through the next 40 years, and reached, so he told every paying listener, over 9 million great words.

Between the twenties and the fifties one saw Gould all over the Village, hugging old notebooks containing his "history" of the times. He was the patron of every café, bar and cafeteria in the Village, and the main organizer of the "Joe Gould Fund"—which meant friends with money who kept the burgeoning historian in cigarettes, beer, hangovers, flophouses, cigarette holders (for butts) and all the essentials to keep Gould's "Oral History" on an uneven keel, until publication date. He was to become a night wanderer with a portfolio containing odds and ends, including his indecipherable notebooks of interviews with bums, poets, barflies, taxi drivers and landladies—the outcome of his fabulous sallies into the folkway of our times. Despite his flophouse-and-hangover life, Gould kept his monumental history going—or so he told the tourists in the Village before bumming them for the "Joe Gould Fund." He was fascinating to watch at work. Pixyish, short, wildeyed, wearing hand-me-downs, chasing girls, kidding savagely with a real poet like Maxwell Bodenheim, he also went among the Communist proletarian poets and recited to these cultists from Moscow:

> *The Comrades die!*
> *The Comrades die!*
> *The Comrades die!*
> *And behind these barricades,*
> *The comrades die—*
> *Of overeating.*

He knew the literary élite, including Malcolm Cowley, Burton Rascoe, E. E. Cummings, Ezra Pound, William Saroyan, Horace Gregory and Marianne Moore. He wrote occasional reviews for newspapers. And select passages of his "Oral History" were published in *The Dial*, which he lampooned:

> " *'Who killed The Dial?'*
> *'Who killed The Dial?'*
> *'I,' said Joe Gould,*

'With my inimitable style,
I killed The Dial.'"

Mitchell's book, which is nobly written, flares and drums with Gould's personal history as Mitchell attempts to discover the final whereabouts of the real "Oral History," the hundreds of notebooks about everything, that Gould was supposed to have left with friends in New York, Long Island and Connecticut. For, through the many years of their friendship, and Gould's incessant monologues in bars and bistros, Mitchell kept seeing these notebooks. Oddly, they always had the same headings: "Death of Dr. Clarke Storer Gould—A Chapter of Joe Gould's 'Oral History' "; "The Dread Tomato Habit—A Chapter of Joe Gould's 'Oral History' "; "Drunk as a Skunk, or How I Measured the Heads of Fifteen Hundred Indians in Zero Weather—A Chapter of Joe Gould's 'Oral History' "; "An Infinitude of Bushwa," etc.

Gould was a comedian who did, so he insisted, the sacred Indian dances. For collection purposes, Gould turned himself into a dancing translator of purist Sea Gull, claiming that Longfellow's *Hiawatha* was a much better poem in bird-shrieking Sea Gull. Gould, who had an endless audience through his Bohemian and burlesque years in the Village, was waspish and elfin, satirical and lovable, witty and whimsical—and he was always hungry.

Having read some of the *found* notebooks that Gould left behind with the artist, Harold Anton, I've seen the secret that Mitchell finally extracted from Joe Gould. There was no "Oral History." It was in Gould's head and conversations, to stimulate his listeners to buy him bed, board and booze. The notebooks are one and the same, repeating the chapters on the "Death of Dr. Clarke Storer Gould," "An Infinitude of Bushwa," and "The Dread Tomato Habit."

Joe Gould, who attended Harvard with some great people, was another sort of a Harvard graduate. He was to become the kibitzer of the passing scene, incapable of writing a history but capable of living it. In 1952, he was picked up on the Bowery and hospitalized. He died of arteriosclerotic senility in 1957 at Pilgrim State Hospital—while imitating a sea gull.

1965

Allen Ginsberg is elected
King of the May
by Czechoslovak students
in Prague, anticipating the
spring of 1968.

Kansas Death Trip

In Cold Blood by Truman Capote
January 16, 1966

THE PLAINS OF WESTERN KANSAS are even lonelier than the sea. Men, farm houses and windmills becoming specks against the vast sky. At night, the wind seems to have come from hundreds of miles distant. Diesel-engine horns echo immensity. During the day, one drives flat out through shimmering mirages. Highways all roll straight to the point of infinity on a far horizon. Tires click; tumbleweed rustles; Coca-Cola signs endlessly creak.

On the Indian summer night of November 14, 1959, two criminals visited this haunting geography. With a knife and a 12-gauge shotgun, they robbed and murdered a man and his wife and their son and daughter. The deed filled the scene. It echoed through the lives of all who lived nearby, rushing toward some appalling, mysterious point of psychic infinity. It made haggard men out of the guardians of order. Eventually, through a fluke almost as gratuitous as the killing itself, they captured the murderers. On an April night last year, as rain beat on the roof, the two were hanged in a chilly warehouse in the corner of the yard of the Kansas State Penitentiary at Lansing.

To the Midwestern newspaper reader, the crime and its aftermath, while awful enough, were not especially astonishing. Spectacular violence seems appropriate to the empty stage of the plains, as though by such cosmic acts mankind must occasionally signal its presence. Charlie Starkweather, accompanied by his teen-age lover, killed 10 people. George Ronald York and James Douglas Latham murdered seven. Lowell Lee Andrews, the mild, fat student with dreams of becoming a Chicago gunman, dispatched his father, mother, and older sister with 21 bullets. Last May, Duane Pope, a clean-cut young football player, shot four people (three of them fatally) who were lying face down on the floor of a rural bank in Nebraska. Multiple murder is one of the traditional expressions of youthful hostility.

To Truman Capote, the killings in western Kansas seemed less commonplace. Already he had explored beyond the lush settings and moonlit characters that had made him famous. The very forms of novel and short story seemed to him increasingly inadequate to the weird dynamics of the age. *Breakfast at Tiffany's* was a bon-bon, but in *The Muses Are Heard*, with its improbable cast of Negro performers and Russian and American culturati, he demonstrated that reality, if heard out patiently, could orchestrate its own full range. He did not intend to be merely the novelist-as-journalist, writing diversionary occasional pieces. He had already done all that in *Local Color*. In the completer role of novelist-as-journalist-as-artist, he was after a new kind of statement. He wanted the facts to declare a reality that transcended reality.

He went west, to Kansas City, to Garden City and Holcomb, Kan., the hamlet where the murders took place. With the obsessiveness of a man demonstrating a profound new hypothesis, he spent more than five years unraveling and following to its end every thread in the killing of Herbert W. Clutter and his family. *In Cold Blood*, the resulting chronicle, is a masterpiece — agonizing, terrible, possessed, proof that the times, so surfeited with disasters, are still capable of tragedy.

The tragedy was existential. The murder was seemingly without motive. The killers, Perry Smith and Richard Hickock, almost parodied the literary anti-hero. Social dropouts filled with nausea, disillusioned romantics, they were the perfect loners. Their relationship, if not physical, was spiritually homosexual, similar to the exalted Freundschaft, bound in blood, of SS brothers. Smith, the archetypal underground exile, had the usual existential loathing of the body; he hated his crushed legs. Chewing aspirin and drinking root beer, he daydreamed in his crushed heart of a Mexican beach paradise with treasure under the sea. At night, sometimes, afflicted with enuresis, he dreamed of a giant yellow bird that would lift him to salvation. Sometimes his captors saw in him the violence and power of a maimed jungle animal. Hickock, on the other hand, was nothing, merely the kid next door gone totally wrong. He was only charming while unloading hot checks on clothing salesmen. One of his weaknesses was little girls, and to the end he loudly asserted he was "a normal."

The Clutters made especially poignant victims. It was not that they wanted killing, but their lives, like so many of their countrymen's rigid, solidly reliant on the grace of affluence, denied the possibility of evil and thus were crucially diminished. Mr. Clutter tolerated no drinkers among those who worked on his farm. He ate apples in the morning and bought everything by check. The wax on the floors of his $40,000 house exuded a lemon scent. His daughter, Nancy, lovely and virginal, baked pies and attended 4-H Club meetings. Once, her father caught her kissing a boy, but she could never marry him because he was a Catholic. His son Kenyon made good things with his hands in the basement workshop. Mrs. Clutter, the pious Bonnie, afflicted with deathly cold shivers and fits of anxiety amid the sunny bounties of a Kansas farm, was the only discordant element in this American dream. Finally they knew terror, and the knowledge in Mr. Capote's words becomes heartbreaking.

There are two Truman Capotes. One is the artful charmer, prone to the gossamer and the exquisite, of *The Grass Harp* and Holly Golightly. The other,

1966

Legal publication in the United States of *Memoirs of a Woman of Pleasure*, better known as *Fanny Hill*, 216 years after it first appeared in England.

darker and stronger, is the discoverer of death. He began the latter exploration as a very young man in his first novel *Other Voices, Other Rooms* and in such stories as "Master Misery," "The Headless Hawk" and "A Tree of Night." He has traveled far from the misty, moss-hung Southern-Gothic landscapes of his youth. He now broods with the austerity of a Greek or an Elizabethan.

As he says in his interview with George Plimpton, he wrote *In Cold Blood* without mechanical aids—tape recorder or shorthand book. He memorized the event and its dialogues so thoroughly, and so totally committed a large piece of his life to it, that he was able to write it as a novel. Yet it is difficult to imagine such a work appearing at a time other than the electronic age. The sound of the book creates the illusion of tape. Its taut cross-cutting is cinematic. Tape and film, documentaries, instant news, have sensitized us to the glare of surfaces and close-ups. He gratifies our electronically induced appetite for massive quantities of detail, but at the same time, like an ironic magician, he shows that appearances are nothing.

In Cold Blood also mocks many of the advances (on paper) of anti-realism. It presents the metaphysics of anti-realism through a total evocation of reality. Not the least of the book's merits is that it manages a major moral judgment without the author's appearance once on stage. At a time when the external happening has become largely meaningless and our reaction to it brutalized, when we shout "Jump!" to the man on the ledge, Mr. Capote has restored dignity to the event. His book is also a grieving testament of faith in what used to be called the soul.

First Impressions

Human Sexual Response by William H. Masters and Virginia E. Johnson
May 29, 1966

BY ALAN F. GUTTMACHER

NEARLY HALF A CENTURY AGO, when I was an undergraduate student at the Johns Hopkins University, Dr. William Welch addressed the senior class on "Medicine as a Career." I remember his words, "Some of you are hesitant to take up medicine because you cringe from the sight of a dead body. Well so do I. I cannot make myself look at a friend laid out in a casket, but the same friend on the marble slab of the autopsy table presents an entirely comfortable image."

I recalled these words on reading *Human Sexual Response* by my good friends William H. Masters and Virginia E. Johnson. I first encountered their fascinating studies in the chaste pages of the *Western Journal of Surgery*, where they seemed in place. To be sure, the subject, the physiology of human mating, was unique, a topic previously shunned by scientists. I read with interest, and also profit, much that they wrote. However, this same material put together in a hardcover book with a four-toned, dignified jacket, under the imprint of a general publisher reads differently.

Most of the vast public that will read this book are not disciplined to keep constantly in mind the fact that the study population represents an extraordinarily skewed sample. In the first place, the original research group consisted of 118 female and 27 male prostitutes. They were the guinea pigs who taught the facts of sex to the authors. Though the authors take precise pains to exclude from the book both historical and laboratory data obtained from these prostitutes, undoubtedly their contributions must have made some impression on the study team.

Despite the authors' efforts, I doubt that a lay public is capable of maintaining in clear perspective the bizarre and strange nature of such a study population. I venture the opinion that they will falsely conclude that the data present the sexual response profile of Mrs. (or Miss) and Mr. America. And when they compare their own sexual capacity and performance to such a troupe of sexual athletes (one male subject was observed to ejaculate three times within ten minutes), most will feel abjectly inferior.

Human Sexual Response is a good book written by competent scientists in a scientific manner with tables and graphs. Alfred C. Kinsey and his associates some years ago pioneered the study of human sexual response through the case-history method, that is, what their sample did. Masters and Johnson pioneer the technique of observing, recording and measuring what the sample does, and how it does it. Both contributions are subject to the same question: How applicable are findings and conclusions based on a restricted, atypical study universe to a large, unselected universe? The Masters-Johnson study interposes an additional question, the weight of the modifying factors of nonspontaneity and laboratory environment. Nevertheless, a scientific study of human sexuality needs to be begun, and we owe a debt to both groups for having cracked the armored barrier of scientific reticence, taboo and prudery.

Essay

Saul Bellow on Intellectuals
July 10, 1966

W E CAN'T MASTER CHANGE. It is too vast, too swift. We'd kill ourselves trying. It is essential, however, to try to understand transformations directly affecting us. That may not be possible either, but we have no choice.

The changes on which I would like to comment are those in the relations between the writer and the public in the English-speaking countries. I shall begin with the sort of description of these relations an avant-garde writer might have given 30 years ago.

He would certainly have referred to himself as a highbrow. Not without irony, but seriously nevertheless, he would have distinguished himself from the middle-brow, the ape of culture, and from the low-brow or no-brow, that philistine hater of all that was good and beautiful in the modern tradition. This is not to say that the highbrow writer invariably loved his isolation and that he rejected the great public out of pride or decadent class-feeling. On the contrary, the division of cultures into high and low caused much bitterness and was considered by many highbrows to be dangerous to society and to civilization as a whole.

Perhaps overlooking the humiliations of the poet under patronage, the vanguardist of the thirties was often nostalgic for the eighteenth century and the small, refined and aristocratic public of that age of masterpieces. In his view the nineteenth-century public was already fully vulgarized—enthusiastic, perhaps, but coarse-grained, an audience of shopkeepers. The weaknesses of this public were aggravated by commercial exploitation, by promoters who made great fortunes in cheap novels, bringing mass culture into the world. The vanguard minority, by this vanguard account, grew smaller and smaller. The specialist now appeared, the technician, a new sort of intellectual with little or no understanding of art and small sympathy for the life of the mind.

Finally, in the twentieth century, to state the case as it was stated by a brilliant critic and observer, the late Wyndham Lewis, an authentic highbrow, civilization cut itself in two, driving into pens and reservations all that was most creative and intelligent. The vanguard artist, like the American Indian, was shut up in barren places, sequestered in the ivory tower, deprived of human contact and influence. Probably all this would end in the total liquidation of intellectuals. Only a few twilight masterpieces by men like Joyce or Paul Klee would remain, and we would reach the stage of final degradation, the era of brutal unrelieved stupidity.

This in some ways resembles the description of the bourgeois situation given by the nineteenth-century romantic, not wholly unjustified but containing certain exaggerations. The romantic saw himself cut off from society, held in contempt by its rulers, separated from the people and longing to be reunited with them.

Wyndham Lewis was a thoughtful and original observer, but it is apparent that he made any number of wrong guesses. Intellectuals have not been liquidated. On the contrary they have increased in number and in influence. They are now spoken of with respect, even with awe, as indispensable to the government, as makers of educated opinion, as sources of symbolic legitimacy—replacing the clergy. Old Walt Whitman, announcing, "The priest departs, the divine literatus arrives," does not sound as unhinged as he did 30 years ago.

I do not speak of the *quality* of these literati (that is another matter; they are still a little remote from divinity) but of the growth of their power.

On the eve of World War II the highbrow public was indeed very small. This is no longer the case. We now have a growing class of intellectuals or near-intellectuals. There are millions of college graduates. A college degree may not mean much. It does, however, indicate exposure to high culture. And the literary culture to which these students are exposed was the creation of highbrow geniuses—disaffected, subversive, radical. The millions who go to art museums today admire there the strangely beautiful, powerful paintings of artists who worked in what Lewis called the thickening twilight of modernism. The millions who take courses in literature become acquainted with the poems and novels of men who rejected the average preferences of their contemporaries.

The minority public is no longer that handful of connoisseurs that read *Transition* in the twenties or discussed "significant form." We have at present a large literary community and something we can call, *faute de mieux*, a literary culture, in my opinion a very bad one.

For one thing, the universities have now embraced modern literature. Stony old pedants two generations ago refused to discuss anyone newer than Browning, but their power was broken in the thirties, and all universities permit the study of contemporary writers. Thousands of teachers turn out millions of graduates in literature. Some of these teachers, a very small minority, are quite useful; others are harmless enough, textual editors, antiquarians and fuddyduddies. Others are influential interpreters. Or misinterpreters.

It is in the universities that literary intellectuals are made, not on Grub Street, not in Bohemia. The mass media and the university-sponsored quarterlies have between them swallowed up literary journalism. The salaried professor will supply literary articles cheaply and has all but wiped out his professional competitors. Bohemia, too, has been relocated in new quarters, near to university campuses.

The university therefore is producing quantities of literary intellectuals who teach, write or go into publishing houses. So far as I can see this new group, greatly influenced by the modern classics, by Joyce, Proust, Eliot, Lawrence, Gide, Valéry, etc., have done little more than convert these classics into other forms of discourse, translating imagination into opinion, or art into cognitions. What they do is to put it all differently. They redescribe everything, usually making it less accessible. For feeling or response they substitute acts of comprehension.

Sometimes they seem to be manufacturing "intellectual history," creating a sort of subculture more congenial to them and to their students than art itself. Sometimes I think they are trying to form a new model of the civilized intelligence for the twentieth century, an intelligence to which a more worthy art will one day be offered—the zeitgeist permitting. Perhaps the "dehumanization of art" of which Ortega speaks reflects the demands made upon art by literary intellectuals. It may in part be a result of the pressure they put upon it for meanings.

Redescription can be intriguing and useful, and succeeding generations must, like Adam and Eve in the Garden of Eden, rename their beasts. Molière revealed the comic possibilities of this when M. Jourdain discovered that all his life he had been speaking prose. We Americans take great satisfaction in this comedy of terms. We pay psychologists to penetrate our characters and redescribe them to us scientifically, rationalizing consciousness on the verbal level at least. We are delighted to hear that we are introverted, fixated, have a repression here, a cathexis there, are attached to our mothers thus and so. Such new accounts seem valuable in themselves, worth the money we pay for them.

Yet what our literary intelligentsia does is to redescribe everything downward, blackening the present age and denying creative scope to their contemporaries. They assume themselves to be the only heirs of the modern classical writers. Our most respected men of letters identify themselves with Joyce, Proust, et cetera, and present themselves as the distinguished representatives, indeed the only representatives of these masters. The agents, managers or impresarios (popularizers) of James or the French symbolists consider themselves the only successors of these writers. Thus they enjoy a certain genteel prestige. They are the happy few.

There are clear signs that intellectuals in what American universities call the humanities are trying to appropriate literature for themselves, taking it away from writers. These intellectuals are like the British princess who said to her husband during the honeymoon, "Do the servants do this too? Much too good for them." Literature is too good for contemporary novelists, those poor untutored drudges.

And what do these intellectuals do with literature? Why, they talk about it; they treasure it; they make careers of it; they become an élite through it; they adorn themselves with it; they make discourse of it. It is their material, their capital. They take from it what they need for their own work in culture history, journalism or criticism of manners producing hybrid works, partly literary, sometimes interesting in themselves, but postulating almost always the decadence or obsolescence of contemporary literature. They want to use the literature of the modern tradition to make something far better; they project a higher, more valuable mental realm, a realm of dazzling intellectuality.

In his latest book, *Beyond Culture*, Professor Lionel Trilling tells us that we now have a sizable group of people in the United States educated in the modern classics. He thinks they have not turned out very well. One sees his point.

They seem to have it both ways. On the one hand these teachers, editors or culture-bureaucrats have absorbed the dislike of the modern classic writers for modern civilization. They are repelled by the effrontery of power and the degradation of the urban crowd. They have made the *Waste Land* outlook their own. On the other hand they are very well off. They have money, position, privileges, power; they send their children to private schools; they can afford elegant dental care, jet holidays in Europe. They have stocks, bonds, houses, even yachts, and with all this, owing to their education, they enjoy a particular and intimate sympathy with the heroic artistic life. Their tastes and judgments were formed by Rimbaud and D. H. Lawrence. Could anything be neater?

Yet this may be the way things are in the modern world, a consequence perhaps of the decline in belief, or of certain doubts about the value of human actions. Thus in a short life one feels free to combine all things of value. People pursue luxury but try to keep by some means values conceived in austerity. They combine private security with rebellious attitudes, monogamy with sexual experiment, conventional family life with bohemian attitudes, the dolce vita with the great books. Vice presidents during the working day, they may be anarchists or utopians at cocktail time. In the higher income brackets, insulated from the dirt and danger of New York, they retain as a matter of course all the sentiments of alienation, honor-bound to be sullen, ungrateful, dissatisfied, suspicious and theoretically defiant of authority.

There is nothing very new in this. Dostoyevsky observed that people who recited Schiller's odes with tears in their eyes were also very good at managing their bureaucratic careers. No wonder Professor Trilling is upset. He sees that a literary education may be a mixed blessing, and that the critics, writers and executives sent into the world by English departments have not turned out very well.

This then is the situation. Critics and professors have declared themselves the true heirs and successors of the modern classic writers. They have obscured the connection between the contemporary writer and his predecessors. They have not shaped the opinions of the educated classes. They have done nothing to create a new public. They have miseducated the young. They are responsible for a great increase in what Veblen called "trained incapacity."

Furthermore, they have projected the kind of art and literature that suits them and have the power to recruit painters and novelists who will meet their requirements. Novels are written which contain attitudes, positions or fantasies pleasing to the literary intelligentsia. These are of course given serious consideration, though they may be little more than the footnotes of fashionable doctrines.

Literature is becoming important for what one can do with it. It is becoming a source of orientations, postures, lifestyles, positions. These positions are made up of odds and ends of Marxism, Freudianism, existentialism, mythology, surrealism, absurdism, *undsoweiter*—the debris of modernism, with apocalyptic leftovers added.

I am speaking of educated and indeed supercivilized people who believe that a correct position makes one illusionless, that to be illusionless is more important than anything else, and that it is enlightened to expose, to disenchant, to hate and to experience disgust. Wyndham Lewis had an excellent term for this last phenomenon—he spoke of the vulgarization of once aristocratic disgust by the modern romantics. One might add that the skepticism of the Enlightenment has also been vulgarized, and that it is at present thought blessed to see through to the class origins of one's affection for one's grandfather, or to reveal the hypocritical weakness and baseness at the heart of friendships.

Nevertheless there are friendships, affinities, natural feelings, rooted norms. People do on the whole agree, for instance, that it is wrong to murder. And even if they are unable to offer rational arguments for this, they are not necessarily driven to commit gratuitous acts of violence. It seems to me that writers might really do well to start thinking about such questions again. Evidently they will have to do this without the aid of the critics. The critics are too romantic to deal with these problems.

A final word about the avant-garde. To labor to create vanguard conditions is historicism. It means that people have been reading books of culture-history and have concluded retrospectively that originality is impossible without such conditions. But genius is always, without strain, avant-garde. Its departure from tradition is not the result of caprice or of policy but of an inner necessity.

As for the highbrow public of an earlier time, it has now been assimilated by our literary culture and transformed into something else. For the time being the writer will have to do without it. He will have to believe that what he writes will evoke a public, that the new forms he creates will create a new public, summoned up by the force of his truth.

Up from Thuggery

The Autobiography of Malcolm X
September 11, 1966

BY ROBERT BONE

IN THE MONTH OF JUNE, 1966, the Negro protest movement entered a new phase. For the first time, during the so-called "Meredith march" to Jackson, Miss., the younger activists raised the slogan of "Black Power!" In the same month, less than a year after its initial publication, Grove Press brought out a paperback edition of *The Autobiography of Malcolm X*. The two events are linked by more than a coincidence. For Malcolm's book, without a doubt, has had a major impact on the younger generation.

White liberals and Negro leaders alike have joined in condemnation of the new slogan. But before we fill the air with charges of "nihilism" and "black nationalism," it behooves us to read, and even to reread Malcolm's book, and especially the last five chapters, which describe the transformation that took place in his mind and heart after his break with Elijah Muhammad and the Black Muslims.

The main events of Malcolm's life are by now familiar. His childhood in Michigan was a nightmare, replete with images of violence and misery. He became a pusher, a procurer, a gunman, and eventually was sentenced to 10 years in prison for armed robbery. There he was converted to the Nation of Islam, and for 12 years he devoted to the Muslim cause his impressive forensic and administrative talents. Not much more than a year before his death, he was "isolated indefinitely" by the Black Muslims.

Malcolm's inner history is less widely understood. His life has been from start to finish a challenge and rebuke to historic Christianity. The son of a Baptist minister, he encountered only violence and humiliation from "the good Christian white people" of his native state. He retaliated through a life of crime, which proclaimed louder than words his denial of Christian community and negation of Christian values. It was the Nation of Islam, with its anti-Christian demonology, that rescued Malcolm from criminality and elevated his rebellion to a metaphysical plane.

In the end, it is Malcolm's metaphysical revolt that matters. For around his quarrel with the Christian God clusters a series of explosive issues that are of paramount concern to Negroes of the coming generation. These include the historic relationship of Christianity to white power, the freeing of the black man's mind from the tyranny of white culture and the formation by the American

Negro of an adequate self-image—or putting it another way, his conquest of shame. To all of these issues Malcolm addressed himself with eloquence and passion from the time of his conversion to the Nation of Islam. It is to that curious sect that we must therefore turn in order to discover the sources of his personal power.

The Muslim indictment of historic Christianity might be summarized as follows. The Christian religion is the tribal religion of white Europe. Since the time of the Crusades, the Christian church has instigated, championed, and proclaimed as holy the white man's depredations into Africa. Throughout the centuries, and in every corner of the globe, the church has been the willing instrument of white power.

In the consolidation of white power, the church has played a crucial part. The whip and gun, although in ample evidence, remained a last resort. Far handier was the apathy, resignation, or even willing cooperation of the victim in his own enslavement. To secure this acquiescence, the blessings of the white slavemaster's religion were bestowed upon the blacks. They were taught to endure humbly and without complaint the cruelties of the slavemaster.

The permanent effects of this indoctrination are apparent in "the brainwashed black Christian" of the present day. He has been convinced of his inferiority; his manhood has been crushed by an overwhelming sense of shame. And here again, the Muslims claim, it is the church that taught the Negro to hold his blackness in contempt, and to revere the color white.

All of this, as Malcolm never ceases to affirm, rings true to the potential Muslim convert. It corresponds to his experience, his knowledge of the white world. It comes in a package, to be sure, which also contains a good deal of magic, Puritan fanaticism, ignorance and hate. These extraneous features of the sect, Malcolm came to realize, had limited its growth and obscured its central insight. What if they were cut away? A movement might emerge shorn of racism, separatism, and blind hate, which yet preserved the explosive force and liberating energy of the Muslim myth. This is the direction in which Malcolm X was moving for a year or more before his death.

When he returned from his pilgrimage to Mecca, he announced to the reporters, "In the past, yes, I have made sweeping indictments of *all* white people. I never will be guilty of that again—as I know now that some white people *are* truly sincere, that some truly are capable of being brotherly toward a black man."

Malcolm's explanation of his new attitude toward whites ought not to be accepted at face value. The casual encounters, however gratifying, of a visit to a foreign land, do not constitute an adequate basis for a profound personality change. What took place in Malcolm's heart was perhaps confirmed in Mecca, but initiated in Chicago: namely, his betrayal by Elijah Muhammad and expulsion from the Muslim sect.

What is at issue is Malcolm's education in the nature of evil. For 12 years he endorsed a demonology which proclaims that the white man is a devil. When betrayal came, however, it was by a black man and in Malcolm's world, *the* black man par excellence. Under the impact of this trauma, the simple equation of white with evil had to fall. If a man's moral nature cannot be reliably inferred from the color of his skin, then we must confront what James Baldwin has called the mysteries and conundrums of the human heart.

It was this confrontation, this inner growth, that made possible the next stage in Malcolm's political development. For want of a better term, it might be described as a *tactical* black nationalism. Toward the end of his life, Malcolm wrote that he now wanted "an all-black organization whose ultimate objective was to help create a society in which there could exist an honest white-black brotherhood."

Perhaps, in the light of Malcolm's book, we can better understand the rivalry between the youthful militants of SNCC and their erstwhile parent organization, the Southern Christian Leadership Conference. For these young men are finished with appeals to Christian conscience; that is the meaning of their new slogan. "Freedom Now!" is addressed to whites; it is a shorthand version of "Give us our freedom now!" But "Black Power!" is addressed to Negroes; it is a call to mobilize their full social weight for the achievement of specific goals. The essence of the shift is psychological. It has nothing to do with black supremacy, but much to do with manhood and self-reliance.

First Impressions

Down These Mean Streets by Piri Thomas
May 21, 1967

BY DANIEL STERN

THIS IS THE AUTOBIOGRAPHY of Piri Thomas, son of a light-skinned Puerto Rican mother and a dark-skinned Puerto Rican father. The book's literary qualities are primitive. Yet it has an undeniable power that I think comes from the fact that it is a report from the guts and heart of a submerged population group, itself submerged in the guts and hearts of our cities. It claims our attention and emotional response because of the honesty and pain of a life led in outlaw, fringe status, where the dream is always to escape.

The American Negro has, of course, developed his own argot, partly to put the white man off, partly to put him down. The Puerto Rican living in New York faces an even more complex fate and linguistic adjustment. He shares with the Negro the neologisms of the street, but the Puerto Rican's are mixed with a heavy complement of Spanish. One does not need to be reminded that the Puerto Ricans are Spanish-speaking United States citizens. What I, for one, did not know until I read Piri Thomas's tough, lyrical autobiography was the pervasiveness of the Hispanic cultural and social legacy, particularly that phenomenon known as *machismo*, which can be roughly translated as a kind of insistent maleness.

The uniqueness of this story begins when Piri—finally bugged beyond endurance by the question of whether he should accept himself as a Negro because he is black, as a Puerto Rican because of his national origin, or some confused mixture of the two—takes off for the South. Why the South? Where better could a Puerto Rican cat who was also a black cat find out who he was?

One of the funniest—and most bitter—is the scene in Galveston where Piri convinces the proprietor of a local whorehouse that he is not a "real nigger" by speaking only Spanish, and manages to sleep with a white prostitute. As he leaves, he triumphantly tells the astonished girl that she has slept with a "nigger . . . *a black man*." (The nightmare fantasy of color runs throughout the book. The girl could see he was a "black man." But he wasn't black until she thought he wasn't a Puerto Rican. The mind boggles.)

From the inferno of the sidewalks Thomas has written another stanza in the passionate poem of color and color-hatred being written today all over the world. James Baldwin tells us he was brought up to believe white was good and black was bad. Piri Thomas had to prove for himself that this was not true. In speaking for the black as well as for the poor and alien, he speaks for all who are buried alive in a society that troubles itself only minimally with its inarticulate miserable, its humiliated, its defeated and self-defeating.

1967

William Styron unintentionally raises a storm of controversy over race in history and literature with *The Confessions of Nat Turner*.

Interview

Vladimir Nabokov
May 12, 1968

OR A NUMBER OF YEARS Vladimir Nabokov and his wife Vera have been living in the resort town of Montreux at the eastern end of Lake Geneva. They occupy all the rooms overlooking the lake from the sixth floor, with one additional room on the far side of the corridor, recently rented for overflow books. When he is interviewed, Mr. Nabokov prefers to receive the questions in writing and respond in kind, a practice he followed here.

How do you work and relax?

After waking up between six and seven in the morning, I write till ten-thirty, generally at a lectern which faces a bright corner of the room instead of the bright audiences of my professorial days. The first half-hour of relaxation is breakfast with my wife around eight-thirty, and the creaming of our mail. One kind of letter that goes into the wastepaper basket at once, with its enclosed stamped envelope and my picture, is the one from the person who tells me he has a large collection of autographs (Somerset Maugham, Abu Abdul, Karen Korona, Charles Dodgson Jr., etc.) and would like to add my name, which he misspells. Around eleven, I soak for 20 minutes in a hot bath, with a sponge on my head and a wordsman's worry in it, encroaching, alas, upon the nirvana. A stroll with my wife along the lake is followed by a frugal lunch and a two-hour nap, after which I resume my work until dinner at seven. An American friend gave us a Scrabble set in Cyrillic alphabet, manufactured in Newtown, Conn.; so we play *skrebl* for an hour or two after dinner. Then I read in bed—periodicals or one of the novels that proud publishers optimistically send us. Between eleven and midnight begins my usual fight with insomnia. Such are my habits in the cold season. Summers I spend in the stumbling pursuit of lepidoptera on flowery slopes and mountain screes; and, of course, after my daily hike of fifteen miles or more, I sleep even worse than in winter. My last resort in this business of relaxation is the composing of chess problems. The recent publication of two of them (in *The Sunday Times* and *The Evening News of London*) gave me more pleasure, I think, than the printing of my first poems half a century ago in St. Petersburg.

What about your social circle?

The tufted ducks and crested grebes of Geneva Lake. The characters in my new novel. My sister Elena in Geneva. A few friends in Lausanne and Vevey. A steady stream of brilliant American intellectuals visiting me in the riparian solitude of a beautifully reflected sunset. A Mr. Van Veen who travels down from his mountain chalet every other day to meet a dark lady whose name I cannot divulge, on a street that I glimpse from my mammoth-tusk tower. Who else? A Mr. Vivian Badlook.

Why did you recently drop your publisher?

Nabokov produced an index card with the following answer, which he reads to long-distance phone inquiries of a similar kind: "Putnam's position was that Mr. Nabokov was much too good a writer to fuss about such sordid trifles as more money for more books and Mr. Nabokov's position was that no matter how good he was he should get enough money to buy pencil sharpeners and support his family. It was the clash of two philosophies, one—Putnam's—idealistic, the other—Nabokov's—practical."

How do you feel about your work?

My feelings about my work are, on the whole, not unfriendly. Boundless modesty and what people call "humility" (the same people who use such journalistic metaphors as the atrocious "dialogue") are virtues scarcely conducive to one's complacently dwelling upon one's own work—particularly when one lacks them. I see it segmented into four stages. First comes meditation (including the accumulation of seemingly haphazard notes, the secret arrowheads of research); then the actual writing, and rewriting, on special index cards that my stationer orders for me: "special" because those you buy here come lined on both sides, and if, in the process of writing, a blast of inspiration sweeps a card onto the floor, and you pick it up without looking and go on writing, it may happen—it has happened—that you fill in its underside, numbering it, say, 107, and then cannot find your 103 which lurks on the side used before. When the fair copy on cards is ready, my wife reads it, checking it for legibility and spelling, and has it transferred onto pages by a typist who knows English; the reading of galleys is a further part of that third stage. After the book is out, foreign rights come into play. I am trilingual, in the proper sense of writing, and not only speaking, three languages (in that sense practically all the writers I personally know or knew in America, including a babel of paraphrasts, are strictly monolinguists). *Lolita* I have translated myself into Russian (recently published in New York by Phaedra, Inc.); but otherwise I am able to control only the French translations of my novels. That process entails a good deal of wrestling with boo-boos and boners, but on the other hand allows me to reach my fourth, and final, stage—that of re-reading my book a few months after the original printing. What

1968

Russian tanks roll into Prague, and within two years Milan Kundera will lose his teaching job, while his books are removed from libraries in Czechoslovakia.

judgment do I then pronounce? Am I still satisfied with my work? Does the afterglow of achievement correspond to the foreglow of conception? It should and it does.

What is your attitude to the modern world?

I doubt if we can postulate the objective existence of a "modern world" on which an artist should have any definite and important opinion. It has been tried, of course, and even carried to extravagant lengths. A hundred years ago, in Russia, the most eloquent and influential reviewers were left-wing, radical, utilitarian political critics, who demanded that Russian novelists and poets portray and sift the modern scene. In those distant times, in that remote country, a typical critic would insist that a literary artist be a "reporter on the topics of the day," a social commentator, a class-war correspondent. That was half-a-century before the Bolshevist police not only revived the dismal so-called progressive (really regressive) trend characteristic of the eighteen-sixties and -seventies, but, as we all know, enforced it. In the old days, to be sure, great lyrical poets or the incomparable prose artist who composed *Anna Karenin* (which should be transliterated without the closing "a"—she was not a ballerina) could cheerfully ignore the left-wing progressive philistines who requested Tyutchev or Tolstoy to mirror politico-social soap-box gesticulations instead of dwelling on an aristocratic love affair or the beauties of nature. The dreary principles, once voiced in the reign of Alexander II, and their subsequent sinister transmutation into the decrees of gloomy police states (Kosygin's dour face expresses that gloom far better than Stalin's dashing moustache) come to my mind whenever I hear today retro-progressive book reviewers in America and England plead for a little more social comment, a little less artistic whimsy. The accepted notion of a "modern world" continuously flowing around us belongs to the same type of abstraction as, say, the "quaternary period" of paleontology. What I feel to be the real modern world is the world the artist creates, his own *mirage*, which becomes a new *mir* ("world" in Russian) by the very act of his shedding, as it were, the age he lives in. My mirage is produced in my private desert, an arid but ardent place, with the sign No Caravans Allowed on the trunk of a lone palm. No doubt, good minds exist whose caravans of general ideas lead somewhere—to curious bazaars, to photogenetic temples; but an independent novelist cannot derive much true benefit from tagging along.

What then would be your politics?

Here again I would want to establish first a specific definition of the term politics, and that might mean dipping again in the remote past. Let me simplify matters by saying that in my parlor politics as well as in open-air statements

(when subduing, for instance, a glib foreigner who is always glad to join our domestic demonstrators in attacking America), I content myself with remarking
that what is bad for the Reds is good for me. I will abstain from details (they
might lead to a veritable slalom of qualificatory parentheses), adding merely that
I do not have any neatly limited political views or rather that such views as I have
shade off into a vague old-fashioned liberalism. Much less vaguely—quite
adamantically, or even adamantinely—I am aware of a central core of spirit in
me that flashes and jeers at the brutal farce of totalitarian states, such as Russia,
and her embarrassing tumors, such as China. A feature of my inner prospect is
the absolute abyss yawning between the barbed-wire tangle of police states and
the spacious freedom of thought we enjoy in America and Western Europe.

How does this attitude reflect itself in your views about contemporary literature?

I am bored by writers who join the social-comment racket. I despise the corny
philistine fad of flaunting four-letter words. I also refuse to find merit in a novel
just because it is by a brave black in Africa or a brave white in Russia—or by any
representative of any single group in America. Frankly, a national, folklore,
class, Masonic, religious, or any other communal aura involuntarily prejudices
me against a novel, making it harder for me to peel the offered fruit so as to get
at the nectar of possible talent. I could name, but will not, a number of modern
artists whom I read purely for pleasure, and not for edification. I find comic the
amalgamation of certain writers under a common label of, say, "Cape Codpiece
Resistance" or "Welsh Working-Upperclass Rehabilitation" or "New Hairwave
School." Incidentally I frequently hear the distant whining of people who complain in print that I dislike the writers whom *they* venerate such as Faulkner,
Mann, Camus, Dreiser, and of course Dostoyevski. But I can assure them that
because I detest certain writers I am not impairing the well-being of the plain-
tiffs in whom the images of my victims happen to form organic galaxies of esteem. I can prove, indeed, that the works of those authors really exist
independently and separately from the organs of affection throbbing in the systems of irate strangers.

Wouldn't Lolita *be considered square by today's youth, who turn on with drugs instead of chewing bubble gum?*

Drug addicts, especially young ones, are conformists flocking together in
sticky groups, and I do not write for groups, nor approve of group therapy (the big
scene in the Freudian farce); as I have said often enough, I write for myself in
multiplicate, a not unfamiliar phenomenon on the horizon of shimmering
deserts. Young dunces who turn to drugs cannot read *Lolita*, or any of my books,
some in fact cannot read at all. Let me also observe that the term "square" already

dates as a slang word, for nothing dates quicker than conservative youth, nor is there anything more philistine, more bourgeois, more ovine than this business of drug duncery. Half a century ago, a similar fashion among the smart set of St. Petersburg was cocaine sniffing combined with phony orientalities. The better and brighter minds of my young American readers are far removed from those juvenile fads and faddists. I also used to know in the past a Communist agent who got so involved in trying to wreck anti-Bolshevist groups by distributing drugs among them that he became an addict himself and lapsed into a dreamy state of commendable metempsychic sloth. He must be grazing today on some grassy slope in Tibet if he has not yet lined the coat of his fortunate shepherd.

Guilty Pleasures

Portnoy's Complaint by **Philip Roth**
February 23, 1969

BY JOSH GREENFELD

G UILT-EDGED INSECURITY is far more important when it comes to the making—and unmaking—of an American Jew than, say, chicken soup or chopped liver. For guilt is as traditionally American as Thanksgiving Day pumpkin pie and, at the same time, on native grounds as far as Jews are concerned: it was the Jews who originated that mother lode of guilt,

the theological concept of original sin; it was a Jew who developed psychoanalysis, that clinical faith based on a belief in the transferability and negotiability of long-term debts and credits in guilt.

So, not surprisingly, a special blend of guilt-power usually fuels the American-Jewish character in fiction, sends him soaring to his manic highs and plummeting to his abject lows.

But while the American-Jewish novelist has thus had a subject, though he has been

searching diligently, questing imaginatively, he has lacked an ideal form. Now, with *Portnoy's Complaint*, Philip Roth (*Goodbye, Columbus, Letting Go, When She Was Good*) has finally come up with the existentially quintessential form for any American-Jewish tale bearing—or baring—guilt. He has done so by simply but brilliantly casting his American Jewish hero—so obviously long in need of therapy—upon a psychoanalyst's couch (the current American-Jewish equivalent of the confessional box) and allowed him to rant and rave and rend himself there. The result is not only one of those bullseye hits in the ever-darkening field of humor, a novel that is playfully and painfully moving, but also a work that is certainly catholic in appeal, potentially monumental in effect—and, perhaps more important, a deliciously funny book, absurd and exuberant, wild and uproarious.

The novel ends at a beginning, with the straight-man analyst speaking his only line: "So. Now vee may perhaps to begin. Yes?"

I feel very much the same way about the ultimate significance of this much ballyhooed, eagerly awaited novel. If viewed as the apotheosis of a genre, the culmination of a fictional quest—and it is, I think, as I've tried to say, the very novel that every American-Jewish writer has been trying to write in one guise or another since the end of World War II—then it may very well be what is called a masterpiece—but so what? It could still also be nothing more than a cul-de-sac.

However, if by this definitive outpouring into a definitive vessel of a recurring theme, thus guilt (screaming, strident, hysterical, hyperbolic, hyperthyroid) has been successfully expatiated, and future American-Jewish novels will be all the quieter, subtler, more reflective and reasoned because of it, then this novel can truly be judged a milestone.

First Impressions

The Godfather by Mario Puzo
April 27, 1969

BY DICK SCHAAP

THERE ARE STRONG SIMILARITIES between Michael Corleone and Alexander Portnoy. Neither of them, for instance, wishes to enter his father's line of work. Each of them falls for a White Anglo-Saxon Protestant girl. Of course, there are some differences, too. When Alexander Portnoy's father is frustrated, he gets constipated; when Michael Corleone's father is frustrated, he gets someone killed.

1969

Isaac Asimov publishes his 100th book, and will publish almost 400 more before his death in 1992.

The Godfather is the coming of age of Michael Corleone in a world that Philip Roth never knew. It is the world of the Mafia in America, and the dialogue and the logic of *The Godfather* ring true enough to raise the suspicion that, at least by hearsay, Mario Puzo knows his subject well.

If Philip Roth has created a Jewish mother who can actually give you heartburn, Mario Puzo has created a Sicilian father who will make you shiver every time you stroll on Mulberry Street. And, with loving care and detail, what Roth has done for masturbation, Puzo has done for murder.

Yet it is unfair to carry the analogy too far. *The Godfather* is not written nearly so artfully as *Portnoy's Complaint*. Nor does it approach the humor of Roth's work. Yet *The Godfather* is such a compelling story, a better-written Sicilian entry into the Irving sweepstakes, the truth-disguised-and-distorted-as-fiction genre, that any day now, I am certain, the Portnoy family and the Corleone family will end up sharing the heady heights of best-sellerdom as comfortably as the Jews and the Italians have long shared the pleasures of salami.

Kate Millett

Gabriel García Márquez • Charles A.

Reich • Germaine Greer • Hunter S. Thompson

John Leonard • Doris Lessing • Erica Jong • Timothy

Leary • Erma Bombeck • Leslie A. Fiedler • E. L.

Doctorow • Edward O. Wilson • John Ashbery • Alice

Walker • Irving Howe • Anne Rice • E. B. White • John

Cheever • Joan Didion • Toni Morrison • Allen Ginsberg

Michael Herr • I. B. Singer • Christopher Lasch

V. S. Naipaul • Norman Mailer

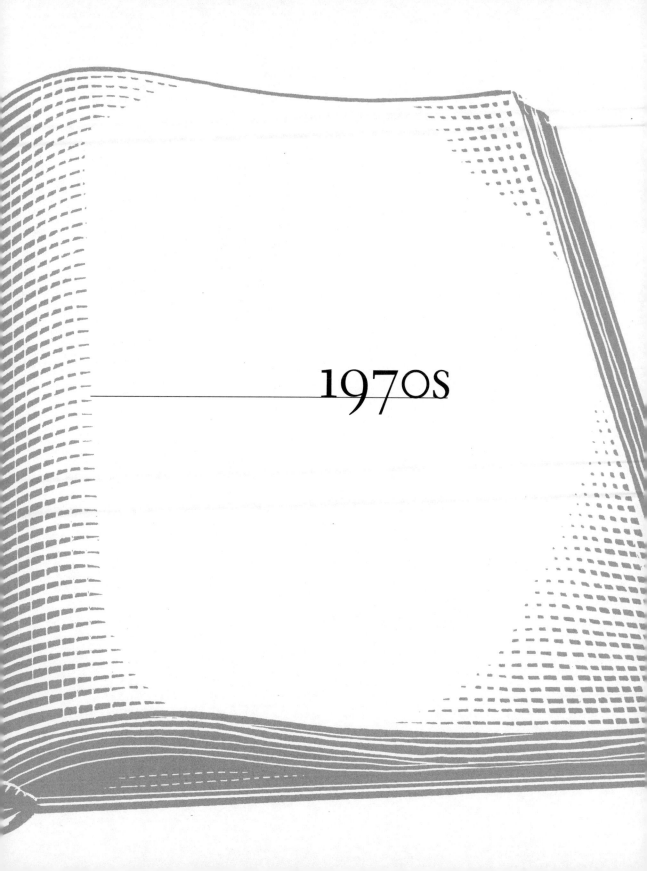

1970S

Real Magic

One Hundred Years of Solitude
by Gabriel García Márquez
March 8, 1970

BY ROBERT KIELY

T O SPEAK OF A LAND of enchantment, even in reference to a contemporary novel, is to conjure up images of elves, moonbeams and slippery mountains. Along with the midgets and fairies, one can expect
marvelous feats and moral portents, but not much humor and almost certainly
no sex. The idea, it would seem, is to forget the earth. At least that is one idea of
enchantment.

It is obviously not shared
by the Colombian novelist
Gabriel García Márquez, who
has created in *One Hundred
Years of Solitude* an enchanted
place that does everything but
cloy. Macondo oozes, reeks
and burns even when it is
most tantalizing and entertaining. It is a place flooded
with lies and liars and yet it
spills over with reality. Lovers
in this novel can idealize each
other into bodiless spirits,
howl with pleasure in their
hammocks or, as in one case, smear themselves with peach jam and roll naked
on the front porch. The hero can lead a quixotic expedition across the jungle,
but although his goal is never reached, the language describing his quest is pungent with life:

> The men on the expedition felt overwhelmed by their most ancient mem-
> ories in that paradise of dampness and silence, going back to before origi-
> nal sin, as their boots sank into pools of steaming oil and their machetes
> destroyed bloody lilies and golden salamanders. For a week, almost with-
> out speaking, they went ahead like sleepwalkers through a universe of
> grief, lighted only by the tenuous reflection of luminous insects, and their
> lungs were overwhelmed by a suffocating smell of blood.

This is the language of a poet who knows the earth and does not fear it as the enemy of the dreamer.

Near the end of *One Hundred Years of Solitude* a character finds a parchment manuscript in which the history of his family had been recorded "one hundred years ahead of time" by an old gypsy. The writer "had not put events in the order of man's conventional time, but had concentrated a century of daily episodes in such a way that they coexisted in one instant." The narrative is a magician's trick in which memory and prophecy, illusion and reality are mixed and often made to look the same. It is, in short, very much like García Márquez's astonishing novel.

It is not easy to describe the techniques and themes of the book without making it sound absurdly complicated, labored and almost impossible to read. In fact, it is none of these things. Though concocted of quirks, ancient mysteries, family secrets and peculiar contradictions, it makes sense and gives pleasure in dozens of immediate ways.

García Márquez creates a continuum, a web of connections and relationships. However bizarre or grotesque some particulars may be, the larger effect is one of great gusto and good humor and, even more, of sanity and compassion.

1970

Jim Bouton's *Ball Four* rocks baseball and starts a tradition of tell-all memoirs.

Consciousness Raising

Sexual Politics by Kate Millett
September 6, 1970

BY BARBARA HARDY

ON THE DELICATE SKIN of the Rokeby Venus in London's National Gallery are the slashmarks made by the suffragettes. The aggressive women, the odalisque represented, the model, the painter celebrating such form and flesh, and the consumers of such high pornography are all victims of corrupted sex. Like race and class, sex is a subject we cannot simply write "about," for it is our sex that writes. Aloofness is no merit, being inappropriately tolerant. Corrupted lovers all, we find it hard to keep heart and head in the right place.

Kate Millett's book on "sexual politics" is thus a rare achievement. Its measure of detachment is earned by learning, reason and love, its measure of involvement is frankly set out. It is a piece of passionate thinking on a life-and-death aspect of our public and private lives.

We are plunged in at the deep end, in a not unappreciative commentary on a scene of sex in and just out of the bath, from Henry Miller's *Sexus*, rapidly followed by a more complexly brutal passage from Mailer's *An American Dream*. Permissive fiction proffers rich materials. The pornographic element now so assimilated by imaginative literature as to confound the legal distinctions of censorship has exposed far more than beds and bodies. Its freedom shows truths and fantasies about sex hitherto disguised. Moreover, the act of sexual description is itself aggressive, indulgent, attractive, repulsive. These scenes are crucial. The power-politics of a patriarchal society creates the complacent zest of Miller's hero as he subdues his women, and creates too the desperate arrogance of Mailer's Rojack.

The texts Kate Millett has chosen have to transcend pornography, too. They are rich in the revelation of complexities of corrupt reason, ethic, language and sensuality. The third extract is from *The Thief's Journal*. In a wide-ranging and self-effacing commentary, Kate Millett brings out the nature of Genet's homosexual parody of the heterosexual "parent world" where "most of us imagine we are at home." Genet makes his plea and his satire from the most honorable place to be, the very bottom of the pecking-order, secure, kept alive by pain, given a good view and a right to criticize. From this experience Genet moves on, especially in his play *The Balcony*, to demonstrate, both in "content" and "form," that social change without a change in sex only keeps you in the vicious circle.

Beginning with these texts from Miller, Mailer and Genet gives a taste, a method and a theme, leading persuasively into a historical and intellectual history of sexual politics, taking in art, anthropology, physiology, psychology, politics and economics. Genet's novels and plays are at the center of the plea for change. It is unlike the Victorian plea for a change of heart in being much more firmly and optimistically related to current signs of a change of consciousness.

But this close and original analysis of individuals serves a larger cause. This is a book that analyzes revolution in order to serve revolution. It has to look at individual cases both because it is concerned with culture and because its subject is human consciousness. Yet it cannot be solely concerned with individual expression in art and language. It needs to demonstrate more broadly the nature of the patriarchal society and the nature of that revolution which started to overthrow patriarchal laws, values and relations. This sexual revolution partly succeeded, was arrested and temporarily defeated, but is once more active. Kate Millett shows why and how.

It is in order to expose the inadequacy of the revolution and the strength of the counterrevolution that she makes her analysis of literature. The writers and thinkers give the evidence of the slow and complex erosion of patterns of feeling. You need sympathy and toughness to analyze such complexities, and Kate Millett manages brilliantly, whether she is looking at Tennyson's better-than-nothing struggles in "The Princess" or Mill's excellent analysis, slightly underplaying

1970

Are You There, God? It's Me, Margaret, by Judy Blume, articulates authentic anxiety about adolescence previously hidden from print.

1970

Yukio Mishima leads an
attack on an army
headquarters in Tokyo, ties
up the commander, lectures
the troops on Japan's
military decline, and then
commits suicide.

economics, but superior to Engels in a courageous appraisal of the future of the family.

If Genet is the Wise Fool in this drama, Ruskin and Freud are simpler clowns. Ruskin provides a comic modern image of chivalric compensation and swindling. Freud is admired for his work on the unconscious and on infantile sexuality, but seen as ironically basing observations about female character on pathological cases, social victims. The ghost of penis-envy is finally laid, beautifully and good-temperedly, and the author generally refrains from too many laughs at penis-pride; when she occasionally succumbs, she is not strident or complacent. The book's humor is part of its warmth and tenderness, and in striking contrast, I thought, to the chill humorlessness of those other two great feminists, Simone de Beauvoir and Doris Lessing.

"Oh Wow!"

The Greening of America by Charles A. Reich
November 8, 1970

BY PETER MARIN

WE ARE WELL INTO strange and crucial times in America, turbulent and anguished days, but it is difficult, in the midst of everything, to break through the haze of image and rhetoric to any real vision of what is happening. *The Greening of America* is an attempt to do that: an analysis of what is happening to consciousness in this country. In many of its parts it is both intelligent and moving, and it will probably be widely accepted as an important book; for these reasons I want to treat it as seriously, as severely, as I can.

Charles Reich's strongest points are those he makes in his often brilliant description of the growth and nature of the corporate state, but the heart of his work is a schematic arrangement of American consciousness into three categories.

"Consciousness I" is the consciousness behind the original American dream: a mixture of individual dignity and rapacity—at best that of the settler and builder, at worst that of the robber barons. "Consciousness II" is the dominant consciousness of the corporate state: the traditionally liberal, the New Deal, the systematic solution, what Reich calls the machine. "Consciousness III" is what has begun to emerge from all this in the young: "the energy of enthusiasm, of hope." Its basic stance, writes Reich, "is one of openness to any and all experience, is always in a state of becoming." His version of that new consciousness is a romantic one, lovely and almost pietistic.

He begins with a long and somewhat empty celebration of young people's clothes—bellbottoms and skins—but moves beyond that to their music and their sense of celebration, their seeming release from cultural limits, their slant toward sensuality and cosmic consciousness. What lies behind it all, he writes, is "a childlike, breathless sense of wonder . . . to which [they] give [their] ultimate sign of reverence, vulnerability and innocence, 'Oh wow!' "

Oh wow! Well, what can one make of that? The entire scheme is a delusive reduction of things to an unreal but orderly form, and its forced imposition upon what is actually happening does some violence to both the harsh political realities of our time and the quality of individual lives. The consciousness Reich celebrates so carelessly is far more complex and anguished than he realizes: a lived philosophic and existential maze that too often reduces the young to psychosis. Reich fails to explore the critical contradictions within this consciousness—without much effort one can list so many problems he ignores:

(1) The extreme terror and isolation inherent in it. (2) The repressive reaction to it and the increasing repression or destruction of "new" persons. (3) The fact that "liberated" persons are part of a monied class still living off stolen land, labor and time. (4) The inability of those with new consciousness to find any viable way to express it in politics. (5) The existence of a growing, revolutionary and almost "traditional" violence among those with Consciousness III. (6) The simultaneously unliberated condition of every minority group. (7) The fact that no new consciousness is ever as pure as Reich makes it, but a tangle of present and past, and all too often a disguise for older kinds of transcendence, withdrawal, passivity or alienation.

The flower children I know have been driven to exile or heroin, or else now arm themselves with guns instead of flowers. The first wave of exhilaration is over, and the young have moved on to something lonelier and far more real, a kind of mythic struggle in a darkness more profound than any Reich recognizes or has chosen to enter.

He writes:

> There is a great discovery awaiting those who choose a new set of values . . . there is nobody whatever on the other side. Nobody wants inadequate housing and medical care—only the machine. Nobody wants war except the machine. And even businessmen, once liberated, would like to roll in the grass and lie in the sun. There is no need then to fight any group of people in America. . . . There is no reason to fight the machine.

I am almost embarrassed to quote that passage. Who would dare say those words to the Soledad brothers or Huey Newton or Timothy Leary or Kent State's students? Who is it that runs New York's prisons? Murders Panthers? Who,

1971

Abbie Hoffman causes some disruption in bookstores with *Steal This Book.*

indeed, is Nixon, and Agnew, and Mitchell, and Daley, and Rizzo? God knows the businessmen and police I know don't roll in the grass. And I have seen enough "liberated" adults to know that there is nothing new in most of them to move them toward life or genuine tolerance.

All men are, at bottom, redeemable, but there is still an enemy, the "other side," and whoever it is, whatever it is, every day it slides closer in America to fascism. We ought to know by now that death appears in many guises; it can wear modish costumes; and wigs and flowered ties are not necessarily signs of changed or life-giving consciousness.

The willingness to create and defend life means more than a new style or rhetoric or even intention: it is a tough, sustained kind of daring and commitment still very rare among us, and it really thrives only in healthy communities and through living connection. It is precisely these things that we increasingly ache for in America and do not have.

Reich's thesis is perhaps half-right: there *is* an opening up, a new sense of space. But that space is also a void, a terrifying sense in the young of disconnection, impotence, sorrow and rage that exceeds anything one finds elsewhere in the world. The problem is that the dissolution of culture both releases and betrays us. It gives us the space to create new styles, new gods and connections, but it denies us the strengths and talents to do it; for these are learned in relationships and community, and the dissolution of culture deprives us of them.

Everything whispers to me that it is too soon, too easy, to believe we are as "safe" as Reich implies. If too many of us mistake his cheerful conclusions for the whole truth, we will forget what is actually missing here, and what *is* happening, and how men really live and thrive, and what we still owe one another and the young.

1971

Neil Sheehan, a correspondent in *The Times*'s Washington bureau, writes a controversial front-page review of 33 books about the Vietnam War by authors like Seymour M. Hersh, Jonathan Schell, Telford Taylor, Noam Chomsky, and David Dellinger.

Germaine Matters

The Female Eunuch by Germaine Greer
April 25, 1971

BY SALLY KEMPTON

I MUST ADMIT I approached *The Female Eunuch* with suspicion. I first heard about it last fall from a male magazine editor who had read the British edition and said it was the most brilliant piece of feminist writing he had ever read, and it has since been recommended to me by four different men, not to mention Norman Mailer, who plugged it in the course of his anti-feminist tirade in the February *Harper's*.

It seemed to me that there must be something odd about a feminist book which gave pleasure to Norman Mailer, and when the prepublication publicity started—the photographs of Germaine Greer buttressed with quotations and pieces of biography (born in Australia, educated at Cambridge), headed off by some hopeful interviewer with the line, "At last, a feminist who doesn't hate men"—I began to be afraid that they were foisting upon us a ringer, appointing for us a spokesman whose only qualification for the post was her ability to traffic with the enemy.

In fact, *The Female Eunuch* is a great pleasure to read. It is brilliantly written, quirky and sensible, full of bile and insight; if many of its insights are available to us in the work of other feminist writers that does not make the book less interesting.

Her book is a conglomeration of fact and speculation and polemic, arranged under chapter headings that follow each other with almost poetic logic, and if *The Female Eunuch* is not in the least confessional, it is highly personal in the sense that the essays of Lamb and Hazlitt and Virginia Woolf were personal. An essayist may give the reader new information or merely rearrange other people's ideas, but more than anything else a good essay reveals the qualities of its author's mind. The things Germaine Greer tells us about women and men are true and often brilliant, and often, as I have said, they are things we knew before. Her art consists in the looseness and ease with which she puts it all together and, telling us about women, tells us also about herself.

It is Greer's fundamental insight that women have been systematically robbed of productive energy by society's insistence on confining them to a passive sexual role. When all activism is assumed to be male, and femininity is defined as merely receptive (and hence irresponsible), then women must repress their normally human drive toward active sexuality in order to conform with the male supremacist idea of what is feminine. Woman's energy, Greer maintains, is then channeled by the denial of her sexuality into a system of repression which extends into every area of her life.

She may even be right when she criticizes the woman's movement on the grounds that to demand liberty from men is to perpetuate the estrangement of the sexes; liberty is in any case something one takes without asking, as the woman's movement has come very well to understand. I would like to believe, as she does, that love between men and women is possible even in the course of a feminist revolution.

Horatio Alger on Drugs

Fear and Loathing in Las Vegas by Hunter S. Thompson
July 23, 1972

BY CRAWFORD WOODS

WE WERE SOMEWHERE around Barstow on the edge of the desert when the drugs began to take hold." The hold deepens for two days, and the language keeps pace for 200 pages, in what is by far the best book yet written on the decade of dope gone by.

Fear and Loathing in Las Vegas is a number of things, most of them elusive on first reading and illusory thereafter. A solid second act by the author of *Hell's Angels*, it is an apposite gloss on the more history-laden rock lyrics ("to live outside the law you must be honest") and—Don Quixote in a Chevy—a trendy English teacher's dream, a text for the type who teaches Emily Dickenson and Paul Simon from the same mimeograph sheet. It is, as well, a custom-crafted study of paranoia, a spew from the 1960s and—in all its hysteria, insolence, insult, and rot—a desperate and important book, a wired nightmare, the funniest piece of American prose since *Naked Lunch*.

What a lot of madness! These are the tracks of a man who might be dismissed as just another savage-sixties kook, were it not for the fact that he has already written himself into the history of American literature, in what I suspect will be a permanent way. Because, regardless of individual reader-reactions, his new book is a highballing heavyweight, whose ripples spread from Huckleberry Finn to F. Scott's Rockville grave.

The bones of the story are no more than spareribs. Thompson ("Raoul Duke" in the book), under contract to *Sports Illustrated*, travels with his attorney, Dr. Gonzo, to Las Vegas. They have been summoned to cover a dirt-track motorcycle race, the Mint 400, by a mysterious phone call. "But what *was* the story? Nobody had bothered to say. So we would have to drum it up on our own. Free Enterprise. The American Dream. Horatio Alger gone mad on drugs in Las Vegas. Do it *now*: pure Gonzo journalism."

Down the desert. The trunk of their car looks like a "mobile police narcotics lab"; a towel soaked in ether washes vapors over them from the floorboards. But their reception in the city is none too friendly, even when they represent themselves as the factory crew of the Vincent Black Shadow, the world's most frightening motorcycle—perhaps because they are stoned into a state of sustained paranoia that turns everyone they deal with into some sort of reptilian foe.

A flurry of picaresque disasters alters their plans as the dope alters their minds. Drug and dream, event and recollection become inseparable. (Thompson now says that when he rereads his book he can't remember what he made up and what really happened. Pure Gonzo journalism. Pure Gonzo fiction.)

But the sporting life collapses in any case when a wire comes from *Rolling Stone*, keeping the crew in Vegas to report on a national district attorneys' conference on dangerous drugs. Coverage of the conference is the book's centerpiece. It includes an imbecilic meeting of narcotics agents, where the officers are solemnly assured that a marijuana butt is called a roach "because it resembles a cockroach"; and a macabre, incredibly funny conversation with a Georgia cop, who is warned of a smackhead migration to his state because they like warm weather. Vegas, Duke decides, "is not a good town for psychedelic drugs. Reality itself is too twisted."

The book is about that twisting. Like Mailer's, Thompson's American dream is a fanfare of baroque fantasy. It should not, despite its preemptive title, be mistaken for a synopsis of the American experience (even though the narrator comes to think of himself as a "monster reincarnation of Horatio Alger"). But its limits are no narrower than the limits of lunacy, and its method is as adventurous as any to be found in all the free-fire-zone writing of the past dozen years.

"Writing" is as exact a label as the book will carry. Neither novel nor nonfiction, it arrives with fashion's special sanction. Its roots are in the particular sense of the nineteen-sixties that a new voice was demanded—by the way people's public and private lives were coming together in a sensual panic stew, with murder its meat and potatoes, grass and acid its spice. How to tell the story of a time when all fiction was science fiction, all facts lies? The New Journalism was born.

But who taps fashion for wisdom gets poison in the sap, and *Fear and Loathing* is the quick assassin of the form it follows. Not the least of Thompson's accomplishments is to suggest that, by now, the New Journalism is to the world what the New Criticism was to the word: seductive, commanding—and, finally, inadequate. The form that reached apotheosis in *Armies of the Night* reaches the end of its rope in *Fear and Loathing*, a chronicle of addiction and dismemberment so vicious that it requires a lot of resilience to sense that the author's purpose is more moralizing than sadistic. He is moving in a country where only a few cranky saviors—Jonathan Swift for one—have gone before. And he moves with the cool integrity of an artist indifferent to his reception.

For the things the book mocks—hippies, Leary, Lennon, journalism, drugs themselves—are calculated to throw Thompson to the wolves of his own subculture. And the language in which it mocks them is designed to look celebratory to the stolid reader, and debased to established critics. This book is such a mind storm that we may need a little time to know that it is also, *ting!* literature.

Much the same thing happened with Henry Miller—with whom Thompson has perhaps even more kinship than with Burroughs. Hero of all his books,

drowning in sex and drink, Miller makes holy what Thompson makes fundamental: appetite. In both writers, the world is celebrated/excoriated through the
senses. But the taste of the one is for rebellion, of the other for apocalypse writ
small.

Apart from the artistry, it is a modestly eschatological vision that lifts *Fear and
Loathing* from the category of mere funky reminiscence. It unfolds a parable of
the nineteen-sixties palatable to those of us who lived them in a mood—perhaps
more melodramatic than astute—of social strife, surreal politics and the chemical feast. And it does so in language that retires neither into the watery sociology
of the news weeklies nor the zoo-Zen of the more verbally hip. Far out. Thompson trusts the authority of his senses, and the clarity of a brain poised between
brilliance and burnout.

The book's highest art is to be the drug it is about, whether chemical or political. To read it is to swim through the highs and lows of the smokes and fluids
that shatter the mind, to survive again the terror of the politics of unreason.
Since plot has been scrapped, the whole thing must be done in the details, in
cameo sketches and weird encounters that flare and fade into the backdrop of
the reader's imagination. These details are technically accurate, which is a contemporary form of literary precision, with all ambiguity intact.

The same accuracy is preserved in the use of drugs as metaphor. The suggestion is that to drop acid in 1966 was to seek the flower at the heart of the cosmos, but to shoot heroin in 1972 is to hide from the pain of the President's face.
("It is worth noting, historically, that downers came in with Nixon . . .") Dope—
once mystic, private and ecstatic—has become just another way to kiss goodbye.

Essay

John Leonard on Doris Lessing
May 13, 1973

I THINK *The Summer Before the Dark* is not only Doris Lessing's best novel,
but the best novel to have appeared here since García Márquez's *One Hundred Years of Solitude*.

It is not as though Lessing hasn't dealt with this material before. She has consistently gone underground into a woman's being, into the being of our species,
tunneling through memory and myth, through Marxism and madness. She has
investigated our role-playing, our racism, our sexual oppression, our radical political activity, our psychoses. Indeed, she has tried every nostrum that arrives in

an aluminum can from the vending machine of twentieth-century thought: what we buy with coins of hope and schism. Dissatisfied, even angry, she has proceeded to mine Sufi mysticism, to traffic in R. D. Laing (most egregiously in "Briefing for a Descent into Hell") and to rendezvous with archetypes.

However: the two most important products of this exhaustive inquiry, *The Golden Notebook* and *The Four-Gated City*, have been less novels than they have been pythons. We saw the lumps of thought in the process of being digested. The voracity and the devouring resulted in esthetic distortions. Even as distortions, they were infinitely more compelling than most of the pretty stylistic lollipops that masquerade as fiction these days, but emotion and intellect were not brought into a satisfying proximity. Both novels stopped because they ran into a brick wall: not a resolution, but a giving up to despair. The artfulness that makes the difference between information and wisdom was missing.

What, technically, distinguishes *The Summer Before the Dark* from Lessing's previous fiction is its artfulness. It is a novel of selection, exclusion and concentration. From the beginning, when we are introduced to 45-year-old Kate Brown at home with her family (there have been electrical power failures all day long: she is preparing tea outside over an open fire) to the end, when she returns to that family (after power failures of her own, after a testing of herself on an open fire of the mind), the book has an almost biological development and the closure of an organic system. Her adventures in between—a summer job with the international civil service, an affair, illness, madness, renewal, too many dreams about bringing a wounded seal to safety—are genuine discoveries. There is little that is unnecessary in this novel, little that is not indispensable. Its power is in its containment.

What, thematically, distinguishes *The Summer Before the Dark* is that it is as much about middle age, the autumn of the body and the mind, the coming of death, as it is about being a woman. Lessing is not *reminding* us that we are going to die (information); she is *persuading* us (the beginning of wisdom is the capacity to imagine this first fact). The intersecting arcs of discovery are thrown from the still point of a single memory: the young girl Kate once was, during a year in Portugal by the Indian Ocean, "precious and despised," the sex object. That was spring; now it is autumn; the emotional weather in between has been that of "caring"—caring for her husband, caring for the civil servants, caring for the young man wasted by fever in Spain, caring finally for herself.

How astonishing, then, to discover during the summer before the dark, when her husband has gone to America for scientific conferences and her children have scattered throughout Europe for vacations, that the "caring" which they held in such low regard, her mother-habit which they so take for granted, is worth a great deal of money in the international civil service. There she is paid

1973

Erica Jong's *Fear of Flying* is published, and if you didn't understand it, you could look at the illustrations in *The Joy of Sex*, by Alex Comfort, published a year earlier.

to care, and when she is done caring for one group of experts, there is another group in another hotel for another round of seminars. Her caring is a marketable skill; she is not doing anything different from what she was doing at home, but value is ascribed to it in the only way we seem to be able to ascribe value: by paying dearly for it, cash on delivery.

This is obviously not enough for Kate Brown, who has developed the habit of slipping in and out of herself, as though to surprise and trap an essence in conflicting attitudes. She will take up with the young man, and borrow from him his sickness. (Lessing has never been terribly good at getting into the minds of men; one of the strengths of this novel is that men have so little to do with the action and she has thereby finessed a weakness.) She will descend into frumpdom, changing personalities along with clothes. She will find a surrogate-daughter, Maureen, who is the 1960s equivalent of what Kate was long ago in Portugal. The arcs form a sphere; the circle is complete; while Maureen is deciding on a husband, Kate is deciding to go home again.

But changed. I must emphasize that *The Summer Before the Dark* is about Kate's rehabilitation, not her destruction. She has been broken and has mended herself, become an adept in ambiguities.

Her experiences of the last months, her discoveries, her self-definition; what she hoped were now strengths, were concentrated here—that she would walk into her home with her hair undressed, with her hair tied straight back for utility; rough and streaky, and the widening gray band showing like a statement of intent. . . . She had lived among words, and people bred to use and be used by words. But now that it was important to her, a matter of self-preservation, that she should be able to make a statement, that she should be understood, then she would, and would not, do certain things to her hair . . . the only part of her that felt nothing if it was stroked, pinched or handled.

Her hair! I leave it to the ideologues of sexism—our newest critical category—to comb out the ironies from this resolution. But it *is* a resolution, achieved with fine economy, bespeaking a subterranean independence, a capacity to choose after a precise imagining of the consequences of choice: wisdom, not despair.

1973

Eudora Welty, the Mississippi writer who worked on the *Book Review* staff during World War II before returning to Jackson, where she still lives, wins a Pulitzer Prize for her most autobiographical novel, *The Optimist's Daughter*.

First Impressions

Fear of Flying by Erica Jong
November 11, 1973

BY TERRY STOKES

ISADORA ZELDA WHITE STOLLERMAN WING, J.A.P. (Jewish American Poet), the narrator of Erica Jong's first novel, finds herself on a plane with her second husband, Bennett, a Chinese-American Freudian analyst, and 116 other psychoanalysts, as well as their families. Where are they going? To Vienna. Why? To attend a psychoanalytic convention right in Freud's old backyard. This convention is not called a convention, it's a "Congress." You know what that means: "An ideal beginning for the nightmare the trip was going to become."

On to the thrust of the book, whoops. Isadora is not allowed to register for the Congress, she doesn't have the right credentials; she's writing an article for *Voyeur* magazine. Enter Adrian Goodlove, a Laingian analyst. He grabs her behind and says he will try to get her into the Congress. Any congress, I suppose.

They get a cup of coffee and check their libidos. Adrian spills his coffee on her lap. She likes it. Pretty hot stuff. "Adrian kept on grinning. Both of us knew I had finally met the real zipless f. . . ." The essential ingredients of Isadora's Z.F. fantasy are "anonymity" and "brevity." Adrian will fill the bill.

The complications continue. If there is a *Kama Sutra* of the spirit, Isadora is entangled in one of those positions that look good on paper but prove untenable in the execution. Although there is a lot of conjecture about mutability in the novel, nothing changes. Isadora is as passive in the end as she was in the beginning. Oddly, the narrator denigrates all women by casting them in her mold; people who don't know what they want. The male figures are portrayed as either lifeless or fall guys for Isadora's proclamations. There is some great humor in the book, but often Isadora's condescension and self-consciousness reduce the experience for the reader. Adrian says insightfully, "You and Bennett do seem to *whine* an awful lot." It is the whining that gets in the way of this otherwise energetic, bawdy, well-conceived first novel.

1973

Anne Rice turns her short story "Interview with the Vampire" into a novel in 5 weeks.

Letter

Timothy Leary
November 11, 1973

FOR 30 YEARS, I have read critiques in your pages dealing with the great scoundrels of history: Hitler, Stalin, Mao, Nixon, et al. I cannot recall any of your reviewers being so angry at a public figure as to confess homicidal wishes. Now comes Midge Decter, whose review of Myra Friedman's book, *Buried Alive: The Biography of Janis Joplin*, has just reached me. It finds the behavior of a contemporary artist (the subject of the Friedman biography) "so profoundly infuriating" that "one [i.e., Decter] would have been driven to throttle her on the spot."

Your middle-aged, middle-class readership will love Midge Decter's comments. She tells them what they wish to hear: the bad girl takes dope and comes to a bad end. Her review is important because it states clearly the causes of the genocidal hatred of a generation for its young.

Decter knows nothing of Janis—or of the culture of which Janis was a part. Perhaps your reviewer claims Sinatra for *her* philosophical guru . . . but the rock fan did, and still does, dig Joplin as one especially brilliant young person trying to find her way in a confusing, rapidly changing period. Joplin was one of several million such searchers, all tuned to the same circuit, all sharing certain hopes, and the same revulsion for the ethic Decter tries, so incoherently, to defend. Did she never hear of Bob Dylan, of the fabulously diverse Beatles? Did she never listen to the kid next door?

I have probably talked to more of the children of famous Americans than any man my age. A consistent concern of these extraordinary young people is the loss of communication with their parents. They know, only too well, what previous generations espoused. They feel sad that their parents (whom they love) can't tune in to their new experiences, listen to some new perspectives. And they *are* new and different.

Midge Decter, the truth of the sexual liberation of the 1960s is worse, much worse than the wildest fantasies of the aging. You can read about the Mogul courts, gossip about the King of Saudi Arabia, leaf through erotic art books, watch porn at your neighborhood theater. If you were born before 1940, there is little chance that you can share the erotic experiences of the new neurological generation. I regret this as much as you should regret it.

Janis sang "Take another little piece of my heart now, baby / You know you got it if it makes you feel good." Do you really think she would have wanted to "work" for a "lasting career"? Like Bob Hope? She preferred to die young, rather than to live old. Full-Tilt Boogie was the name of her last band.

She died, of course, as all "stars" die—after "no more than a moment's enthusiasm." And millions of us still live a little warmer because of her generous radiation.

I'd rather shoot heroin with Janis than shoot heroines with Midge. It's easier for me to kick a habit than kick a star.

First Impressions

Free to Be . . . You and Me edited by Marlo Thomas
April 21, 1974

BY ERMA BOMBECK

U P UNTIL NOW the Women's Liberation movement has done for humor what Woody Allen has done for the centerfold. All that housewives have had to combat boredom, depression, neurosis, exploitation and submission with has been a clenched fist and a nocturnal headache.

It would appear some help is on the way for the woman who wants to make things better without sacrificing the family structure or discarding something worth saving to do it. It's a positive, refreshing book for children and adults that tells you not who you should be or ought to be, but who you can be. It's like a streaker running through *As the World Turns*.

Marlo Thomas has gathered together some of the most noted disciples of human dignity preaching today . . . Gloria Steinem, Letty Cottin Pogrebin, Shel Silverstein, Carl Reiner and Kurt Vonnegut Jr., to name a few. They have filled the book with songs to be played on your piano or guitar, poems to be read aloud or to yourself and stories often illustrated by the crayon crowd . . . all with the underlying theme . . . you are free to be yourself.

As a Mother I couldn't resist the temptation to grade myself on how many sexist sins I had committed in the name of tradition.

Do I object to men crying? Hardly. Mine not only cries over the checkbook, he has been known to bite right through 400 cancelled scenic checks.

Do I object to role changing? Get serious. I live for the day when my husband becomes known at the redemption center as old Glue Breath, and the high spot in his week is when it rains on his Tupperware party.

Am I raising my children to regard one another as individuals and not stereotypes?

1974

All the President's Men, by Bob Woodward and Carl Bernstein, appears just before the Watergate scandals conclude with the resignation of President Richard Nixon.

The other night when my son punched his sister in the face I said to him, "Why did you do that? Is it because she is a girl and you felt a superior, masculine dominance in putting her in her place?"

"No," he said, "I punched her because she is a rotten human being."

I'm doing something right.

Essay

Leslie A. Fiedler on Tarzan
June 9, 1974

I T IS HARD TO THINK OF Tarzan without thinking of one's own childhood. Yet that immortal myth of the abandoned child of civilization who survives to become Lord of the Jungle was not written for children at all—as I keep explaining to my 9-year-old son whenever he snatches from my desk the volume I am currently reading. "Look," I tell him, "the only two books Burroughs ever deliberately wrote for kids are lousy. Stupid. And besides," I add, "your teen-age brother and your mother are next in line after me. *Then* you." But in some sense he has the prior claim. Certainly I was his age when I began the series, and I am his age still when I return to it now. Or rather, I realize returning to it that, at my deepest level of response, I have remained faithful to the dream which moved me then.

It has been a long time, however, since I last dreamed the dream all the way through—near tears as I finished the last volume, though I knew I could always begin again. And again. And again. Not that the Lord of the Jungle has ever completely disappeared from my life; but for many years I have encountered him chiefly in comics and movies, on radio—and especially in those old films endlessly replayed on Sunday morning television. Tarzan between commercials. Tarzan as Johnny Weissmuller and Buster Crabbe. And however such versions may falsify details of the original text, they cannot betray the myth, which like all authentic myths has passed into the public domain, and must be re-embodied in whatever vulgar commercial form has preempted the popular imagination.

How could Burroughs, who died reading the Sunday comics, have objected? True, in *Tarzan and the Lion Man*, which appeared in 1934, he satirized what Hollywood had made of his creation, showing in a final scene his hero being rejected as "not the type" to play himself. But in *Tarzan and the Foreign Legion*, published 13 years later, he puts into the mouth of a sympathetic character, confronted with the actual Ape Man, the words, "Is dat Johnny Weissmuller?" It is

Burroughs's own last word on the subject, his final irony, directed this time not at the moviemakers but his own belief that the myth he created belonged solely to him.

From the start, I believed it belonged to me, a small Jewish boy in Newark, N.J., appalled at the grayness of the urban world between the two Great Wars. It was a Green World I needed to dream of but not a pastoral or Arcadian one, which is to say, a world unremittingly green. No, it was a Darwinian world, one green in leaf, but red in fang and claw that the times and I demanded. And this Burroughs provided, aware somehow that though, in his own heyday, the jurors at the Scopes Trial may have voted against evolution, the mass audience had decided otherwise. In the cities at least, Burroughs's Chicago, my Newark, no one could doubt the Struggle for Existence, the Survival of the Fittest, the bloody triumph of homo sapiens over the lesser beasts.

It is this triumph which Burroughs celebrates in the tale of Tarzan, making him the first Wild Man Saviour to have been suckled by a she-ape rather than a she-wolf. The latter had fostered mythic heroes from the Romulus and Remus to the Mowgli of Kipling's *The Jungle Books*; but *On the Origin of Species* had persuaded Burroughs that apes are our closest kin. And the popular imagination had transformed them into our actual progenitors, twisting classical evolutionary theory just enough to suggest that our remotest ancestors have survived, and can be seen in the nearest zoo. Or better still, in their native habitat, the living past of "Africa." Taking his myth for a fact, literal-minded readers are appalled by the mistakes Burroughs makes about the Dark Continent—especially about its fauna, or the languages spoken by its natives. But it is merely a convenient name for the absolute Elsewhere, where the pop Darwinian Jungle shelters Indian Tigers and African Lions side by side. And Burroughs relocated it, when he was so moved, in Sumatra, for instance, or the *Island of Uxmal*, or the Center of the Earth: the imaginary womb of the Great Mother civilization has in fact sullied and raped.

Darwin alone, however, could not teach Burroughs to convert science to myth. This he learned from other tellers of tales, like Jack London and Kipling, for whom he has registered his admiration and gratitude. But a third great popular myth-maker, H. Rider Haggard, whom he does not mention, seems to me equally important for him. It was Haggard who first suggested the notion that in the preserved past of "Africa," a castaway from the present could reenact not only the victory of man over the beasts, but also the encounter of the male with the mystery of woman, the invention of eros.

Again and again, in the midst of human sacrifice, torture and the eating of raw flesh, Tarzan confronts erotically potent, unredeemably exotic and invariably naked females. As divine and mythic as he, they offer to yield up their

1974 —————

Aleksandr Solzhenitsyn
is expelled from the
Soviet Union.

divinity for his love, striving to win him with caresses and the threat of death. But always, of course, in vain. And the prototype of them all is La of Opar, whom Tarzan rejects like the rest, but returns to over and over—in quest not only of the treasure she guards, but also the renewal of their endless flirtation. But La is clearly blood sister to the title character of H. Rider Haggard's *She*, a pop masterpiece as universally appealing (among its admirers are Carl Jung, Henry Miller, D. H. Lawrence and Andrew Lang) as *Tarzan of the Apes*. The infamous schoolteacher of Downey, Calif., was, therefore, right when, in 1961, she removed two volumes of Tarzan from her library shelves as "pornographic"—wrong in particular (she thought Tarzan had never married Jane), but right in general. And Philip Jose Farmer, greatest living authority on Burroughs, was even more right when, in a pornotravesty called *A Feast Unknown*, he revealed the sadomasochistic and homosexual aspects of Tarzan's eros.

As a boy, however, I scarcely noticed the erotic episodes, skipping ahead impatiently, as my 9-year-old does now, whenever some languorous charmer appeared. Yet Burroughs, I have learned since, thought of himself as a "dirty writer," refusing, for instance, to dictate aloud to his secretary, as was his custom, passages he felt to be too titillating. To be sure, he uses only the chastest language, and never describes the sex act at all. Even the consummation of Tarzan's marriage occurs off-scene, though he does render in detail the two occasions on which Jane *almost* yields to the Ape Man before they are duly wed.

Resisted seduction and failed rape: these are for Burroughs the paradigms of passion. And rape is more central than seduction. Few rapes are ever consummated in his books but the unconsummated variety occurs with an astonishing frequency. One industrious critic has counted 76 rapes in the books Burroughs wrote in the first four years of his career and time did not slow down his pace. Indeed, "good women" exist in his fiction almost entirely to be threatened with violation and rescued. Jane is, of course, the target-in-chief, desired on sight by all males of the "lesser breeds": great apes, gorillas, black cannibals, Russians, Germans, Lascars, Japanese. And worst among them are the Kings and High Priests, those Bad Fathers, whose frustrated passion and eventual destruction Burroughs especially delights in imagining.

After a while, Burroughs seems to grow weary of Jane, whom, it would appear, he had never really wanted Tarzan to marry. His first volume ends in fact with Tarzan's rejection of her. And though his editors persuaded Burroughs to give her another chance, he keeps the pair separated for ever longer periods; perhaps because he senses dimly that his Forest God should have remained forever virgin. For a while, he relishes portraying her in the arms of some frustrated bestial attacker, but even this runs out eventually.

The theme of rape, however, does not disappear with Jane, since every young woman who wanders into Burroughs's "Africa" is threatened with that fate. And in tyrannical gynocracies, like that portrayed in *Tarzan and the Ant Men*, males, too, are sexually assaulted—including Tarzan himself. But more customarily, he watches from concealment, like a child at the bedroom door, convinced that the groans of his beloved mother mean she is being forced by his hairy father. In Burroughs's Primeval Forest, Freud's Primal Scene is eternally reenacted. And interpreted as rape and miscegenation.

How else could sex possibly be interpreted in that world of eternal war: the war of man against beast and man, and of beast against man and beast, which is to say, the world of Darwin's nature; though it is the world of "civilization," too, in which nation wars against nation, class against class, race against race, sex against sex and generation against generation? Burroughs imagined a score of civilizations lost in the interior of "Africa," in each of which two tribes are locked in warfare. And why not? His father had served in the Civil War, and he himself lived through the three major conflicts which followed, without, however, seeing combat duty in any. Not until World War II, during which he was in his late sixties, did he even see battle action from a safe distance; but he imagined Tarzan a combatant in both World Wars, and even a participant in the Cold War which outlasted both. The single historical character I can remember in the Tarzan books is, in fact, "Stalin, the dictator of Red Russia," who personally dispatches an OGPU agent to liquidate the Ape Man.

Combat existed for Burroughs, as it did for most of his readers, in the press, the mass media which reinforced in him attitudes already inculcated by pointless drill in a military school, and dull army duty in a West from which the Indian enemy had long since been driven. A lifetime of unconsummated macho dreams created in him a reverence for rank and order, and a hatred for those who threatened them from within or without: the "inferior races" against whom his country had fought or might some day fight, along with rebellious blacks and discontented women. By force homo sapiens had established and maintained the hierarchy which sets him above beasts; and by force the Anglo-Saxon male would prove, within the species, his right to rule over not just Krauts, Japs and, of course, blacks, but women of his own kind as well. Was there not even among the lower animals a rank order, at the top of which stood Numa the Lion and Tantor the Elephant; while at the bottom skulked Hista the Snake, Ungo the Jackal and Ska the Vulture?

What popular anthropology taught and the army enforced, the nose confirmed; for the lower orders *stank*, whether man or beast, as only the highest of creatures, Tarzan the White-Skinned, could fully perceive. Above that demigod there was nothing for Burroughs, who seemed as certain as Nietzsche that the traditional God was dead and the Superman had already been born. Between the highest of creatures and the lower there could, however, be communication and a kind of love, so long as both knew their places. Tarzan found that communion easier with animals, perhaps, than with humans; with Nkima the Monkey, Sheeta the Leopard, Jad-bal-Ja the Golden Lion, and especially Tantor the Elephant. There is something deeply sensuous and wholly committed in the caresses of Tarzan and the half-blind Tantor: a tenderness he never quite manages with women, who in any case communicate not in the Old Language common to the whole animal kingdom, but in the divided tongues of the modern world.

Black males, however, who have learned to call him master, can join in communion with the Jungle Lord and his beasts, though always there is a note of reservation. His faithful Waziri, in particular, saves him time and again, as Tantor and Nkima also do, though never a woman. And with them he almost forgets that it was one of their kind, a bestial black, who killed his ape-mother, Kala. That aboriginal crime taught him terror, converting him into a one-man Ku Klux Klan, burning, killing and hanging (though he had first to invent the noose) hundreds of black victims. And here perhaps is a clue not only to Tarzan's deepest emotion but his continuing appeal.

However totally amnesia overcomes him, he never forgets his natural mother, his animal inheritance, his suckling in the woods. It is everything else he forgets: his "real" white parents and the imperialism they serve, his aristocratic descent, his having been switched in the cradle. Not until the very end of the first volume, in which the total myth is already present, does Tarzan learn of his European heritage and the fortune it entails. And when he "lyingly" denies his "true" origin, it is not for the sentimental reasons Burroughs describes. It is to the exigencies of the myth, the deeper truth his author did not have to know he was telling, that Tarzan responds, saying, "My mother was an ape . . . I never knew who my father was."

Who can hate the hero who loves his mother and kills—over and over and over—his father? Not I or my wife or either of my sons; and certainly not the young, re-enacting the myth of agricultural communes or dreaming it in universities. In *Morgan*, the first film to protect a hero appropriate to their dreams, that protagonist is, therefore, quite properly portrayed as haunted by images out of old Tarzan movies. The "anti-psychiatrist," R. D. Laing, may have presided over the conception of that film, but Edgar Rice Burroughs played a role in it, too. And his role may indeed be the critical one; since unlike Laing and the later blander apologists for the "counter-culture" he does not deny that to keep faith with our sweet ravaged Mother, we must be willing to enter a world of brutality, fraternal and filial strife, even murder and cannibalism. Latter-day refugees from civilization may pretend that they can take with them into the wilderness effete ideologies like Vegetarianism, Pacifism and Universal Love. Not so Burroughs.

How could he, being more like Archie Bunker, an embattled spokesman for the Veterans of Foreign Wars, or the Sigmund Freud of *Totem and Taboo* than Theodore Roszak or Gary Snyder or the Laing of *The Politics of Experience*. Aware of this, we can understand why the fathers of the anti-urban young, and their fathers as well, also relished Tarzan. Making it in the gray cities, they, too, at whatever buried level, dreamed the Green World Restored; dreamed prophetically what would drive their children and grandchildren out of their comfortable homes. If they tend now to deny this, so also do their children and grandchildren deny that they dream still, at levels even more deeply buried, perhaps, what moved their progenitors: the fear of rape by the Other, the resolve to survive at all costs, the lust for murder and the eating of bloody flesh. What else cues their nightmares and "bad trips" on drugs? Such nightmares they cannot exorcise in their daytime lives, only disguise and invert them; even as their fathers inverted and disguised the rejected side of their ambivalence. But for both sides, it is necessary to live out their ambivalence, even if this means giving aid and comfort to what they have come to consider "the Enemy." But this, for most men and women, is possible only through the mediation of pop texts like *Tarzan of the Apes*, archetypal and unpretentious.

The Heavy Breath of History

Ragtime by E. L. Doctorow
July 6, 1975

BY GEORGE STADE

THE PROBLEM IS NOT so much *what* as *how*. Since the time of Henry James, at least, serious novelists have had more trouble deciding how to write than what to write about. Most have felt that the traditional methods of narration had exhausted their possibilities, that they were bound up with conceptions of exterior and interior reality we no longer share, that they were the product of vicious or extinct social conditions; and many novelists also felt that a work of art should be an object in its own right, rather than a report or illustration, that a work of art should explore, not represent, that esthetic like scientific truths can be proved only by experimentation, that, in short, new realities call for new fictions or that new fictions remake reality.

The greatest and most experimental of experimental novelists is still James Joyce. Writing to a friend about *Ulysses* Joyce explained that "each adventure (that is, every hour, every organ, every art being interconnected and interrelated in the structural scheme of the whole) should not only condition but even create its own technique." Joyce chose to let his subjects dictate his methods rather than to impose a method upon his subjects. And that is in part why his experiments remain significant, unlike most of those conducted less out of solicitude toward a subject than out of an aptitude for self-absorption. The special significance of E. L. Doctorow's new novel is that the *what* for which he has found a *how* is a historical moment, as opposed, say, to a single adventure or a theory about the self.

A method for giving us the *feel* of a historical moment—as distinct from information about it—is something that more and more of our novelists may soon be after, now that Thomas Pynchon and Doctorow have shown us how it is done, now that the millennial sixties are over and we are looking back to see what happened rather than forward to see what next. The method of his new novel is dictated by the lives and times of Americans during that moment between the turn of the century and World War I, the moment of arrival for the Model T, the assembly line, the moving picture, and Scott Joplin's rags. *Ragtime* succeeds entirely—as his three earlier books did not—in absorbing rather than annotating the images and rhythms of its subject, in measuring the shadows of myth cast by naturalistic detail, in rousing our senses and in treating us to some serious fun.

Mameh, Tateh and the Little Girl in the pinafore live in one room and everybody works. Mameh and the Little Girl sew knee pants and get 70 cents a dozen. Tateh is a peddler, but has the wrong temperament for his work. One day when two weeks' rent is due, Mameh lets her employer have his way with her on a cutting table. Tateh drives her from the house and mourns her as though she were dead. Tateh is a socialist.

He is also an artist, president, in fact, of the Socialist Artists' Alliance of the Lower East Side. On a hot June just this side of 1900, he stands on the sidewalk before a display cart of framed silhouette portraits. One end of a clothesline is tied around his waist, the other around the wrist of his beautiful Little Girl. White slavers lurk everywhere. For 15 cents, he will cut your image on a piece of white paper and mount it on a black background. "With his scissors he suggested not merely outlines, but textures, moods, character, despair."

To amuse his daughter he puts 120 silhouettes on pages no bigger than your hand. He binds them with a piece of string. She flips the pages with her thumb and watches herself skating away and skating back, gliding into a figure eight, returning, pirouetting and making a lovely bow to her audience. Now catch the movement of images in this bit of prose describing the sidewalk artist's world:

> . . . by the end of the month a serious heat wave had begun to kill infants all over the slums. The tenements glowed like furnaces and the tenants had no water to drink. The sink at the bottom of the stairs was dry. Fathers raced through the streets looking for ice. Tammany Hall had been destroyed by reformers but the hustlers on the ward still cornered the ice supply and sold little chips of it at exorbitant prices. Pillows were placed on the sidewalks. Families slept on stoops and in doorways. Horses collapsed and died in the streets. The Department of Sanitation sent drays around the city to drag away horses that had died. But it was not an efficient service. Horses exploded in the heat. Their exposed intestines heaved with rats. And up through the slum alleys, through the grey clothes hanging listlessly on lines strung across air shafts, rose the smell of fried fish.

Such sentences are the verbal equivalents of riffling silhouettes. They are all plane and outline, nothing filled in. They do not caricature; even less do they travesty; nor do they simplify, exactly; their effect is to clarify what would otherwise be lost in featureless detail. Yet they suggest every depth and quality of texture, mood, character and despair. But wait.

Living in New Rochelle, rather than New York, is another anonymous family, another family in silhouette. There is Father, manufacturer of flags, buntings, fireworks and other accouterments of patriotism, president of the New York Explorers Club, companion of Peary during his third expedition to the Pole. There is Mother, blonde, beautiful, full-bodied, whose golden gestures are outlined as by the rays of the late-afternoon sun. There is Grandfather, retired professor of classics. There is the Little Boy, who learns from Grandfather's stories out of Ovid that the forms of life are volatile and that everything in the world has been and will be something else. There is Mother's Younger Brother, who is thought to be having difficulty finding himself and who is in love with the notorious Evelyn Nesbit, over whom the infamous Harry K. Thaw shot the famous architect Stanford White. The murder occurs during the opening night of *Mamzelle Champagne* on the roof garden at Madison Square at the beginning of the June heat wave that kills infants all over the slums.

One day Mother nearly steps on an infant buried, but not very deep, in her flower garden. The baby is still alive and has a brown skin. Mother takes in not only the child, but also its mother, Sarah, whose last name no one ever discovers. Father is dubious. He becomes more dubious still when Coalhouse Walker

1975

With *A Division of Spoils*, Paul Scott completes his series of novels about India, *The Raj Quartet*. The earlier volumes are *The Jewel in the Crown*, *The Day of the Scorpion*, and *The Towers of Silence*.

Jr. appears one Sunday to court Sarah. Correct, fastidious and resolute, Walker arrives in his gleaming Model T Ford every Sunday for over a year until the equally proud Sarah relents and agrees to marry him.

Formerly a traveling man, Coalhouse Walker is now permanently located in Harlem, where he works as pianist for the Jim Europe Clef Club Orchestra. "The clusters of syncopating chords and the thumping octaves" of Scott Joplin's "Maple Leaf Rag" are like a revelation to the family.

Plink-a-plink, a-plink-plink, a-plink-plink. The rhythm of the sentences and events in this novel is the verbal equivalent of ragtime. The left hand pounds out the beat of historical change. It modulates from the WASP to the immigrant to the black families as through the tonic, dominant and subdominant chords upon which the right hand builds its syncopating improvisations. These are variations on themes provided by representative figures and events of the time.

By the end of the novel Grandfather is dead, having slipped while doing a jig to welcome in spring. Father is dead, blown up with his own munitions and the *Lusitania*. Mameh is dead, swallowed up by the slum. J. P. Morgan is dead, after having spent a night in the Great Pyramid of Giza awaiting a vision. Sarah is dead, mistaken for a terrorist. Coalhouse Walker Jr. is dead, after a career of terrorism that begins when fire-house rowdies vandalize his car and ends with his hand on a detonator inside the J. P. Morgan Library. Mother's Younger Brother is dead, fallen by the side of Emiliano Zapata.

But Mother has been rejuvenated by her marriage to Tateh, now the Baron Ashkenazy, a film-maker. The Baron, looking at his beautiful olive-skinned Little Girl, at his handsome blond stepson, and at Coalhouse Walker III, his ward, gets an idea for a movie. He has a vision of a gang of kids of different colors, classes, kinds, like all of us, getting into scrapes and getting out of them. "And by that time the era of Ragtime had run out, with the heavy breath of the machine, as if history were no more than a tune on a player piano."

And so it is in this excellent novel, whose silhouettes and rags not only make fiction out of history but also reveal the fictions out of which history is made. It incorporates the fictions and realities of the era of ragtime while it rags our fictions about it. It is an anti-nostalgic novel that incorporates our nostalgia about its subject. It is cool, hard, controlled, utterly unsentimental, an art of sharp outlines and clipped phrases. Yet it implies all we could ask for in the way of texture, mood, character and despair.

The Slime Molds and Us

Sociobiology by Edward O. Wilson
July 17, 1975

BY JOHN PFEIFFER

A T SUNSET IN THE KALAHARI it is still possible to catch a glimpse
of how all men once lived. Some 30 bushmen sit in the midst of a
desert, inside a circle of low grass huts, gathered around their hearth
fires. A child cries, and a woman is there within arm's reach to pick it up and
console it. Individuals several hearths apart converse, and their soft voices carry
easily across the circle. When they laugh, the sound spreads like a ripple from
fireside to fireside. They are huddled together, bodies actually touching much
of the time, in what one observer has called "the human press."

Most of us live in a human press rather less intimate than that found among
the world's last hunter-gatherers. But it is no less basic. We also come together
because we must, moving always in response to the play of many forces, including the same forces which determine the behavior of other social creatures from
apes and lions to whales, dolphins and wallabies. And there are societies all the
way down the ladder of life, almost to the very bottom rung, among the simplest
singled-celled animals whose ancestors appeared on earth some 3,500,000,000
years ago, give or take half an eon or so.

These are exciting times in the search for universals, laws shaping societies at
all evolutionary levels. That the discovery of such laws may be imminent is a
central message of *Sociobiology: The New Synthesis* by Edward O. Wilson, a
Harvard zoologist, author of *Insect Societies*, who specializes in studying social
insects, mainly ants—and who, unlike most specialists, has the desire, knowledge and courage to discuss matters outside his chosen field.

Wilson turns a connoisseur's eye on contemporary societies, judging them on
the basis of how completely individuals work together, how effectively individuality or ego has been modified for the good of the whole. Going by that criterion,
he concludes that "four groups occupy pinnacles above the others: the colonial
invertebrates, the social insects, the nonhuman mammals, and man." The first
group, which includes certain molds, corals, sponges and jellyfish-like creatures, wins top rating by a wide margin, as nature's closest approach to social perfection.

For example, some so-called slime molds start life as free-ranging cells, preda-
tory amebas engulfing bacteria and multiplying by fission at a great rate—that is,
until their food supply starts dwindling. Then, faced with the threat of famine,

these rugged individualists lose their identities and merge into a tight-knit organization. Streaming together by the thousands, they form a sausage-shaped body which swims off in search of richer hunting grounds. Individuality is almost entirely submerged among advanced floating colonies with stinging tentacles like the oceanic Portuguese man-of-war, whose cells or "zooids" never enjoy amebic freedom and are joined together in a permanent union of specialists.

Such harmony is not found among more complex species. As evolution proceeds from colonies of single cells to colonies of multi-celled organisms (colonies of colonies), individuals tend to become less and less manageable. That even holds for those paragons of industriousness, social insects, in Wilson's book the next highest evolutionary pinnacle to colonial invertebrates.

The insects' world is no Eden. Female workers in some of the simpler bee societies may challenge the queen's egg-laying monopoly, attempt to lay eggs of their own, and are attacked for their troubles. They may also fight among themselves for the right to take the queen's place when she dies or is removed from the hive by an inquisitive investigator.

Tension increases by several orders of magnitude in mammals. Something about cerebral complexity, brains made up of millions rather than hundreds of thousands of nerve cells or neurons, seems to encourage individuality at the expense of group solidarity. The wolf pack, with its food-sharing and cooperative hunting and baby sitters left behind to protect the young, may represent a high point of cooperative living for nonhuman mammals. By insect standards, however, it is practically anarchy. A "lone wolf" would be unthinkable in a colony of ants, which arose more than 100,000,000 years ago from nonsocial solitary wasps.

Still, there are some interesting new developments among mammals. Evolution is probably making a virtue out of the antisocial behavior of the loner who, too young or weak or nonconforming to make it in the central hierarchy, the Establishment, is forced to explore new territories and living styles. Social misfits may have helped lead our remote ancestors out of the forests into wide-open savanna lands. Another, subtler development is a sharp increase in play. Insects with nothing better to do simply rest; the same goes for fish, amphibians and reptiles. A few birds, notably the more intelligent species such as crows and jackdaws, engage in odd stunts for the sheer pleasure of it. But mammals are the animal kingdom's supreme players—and of all mammals man, the fourth and latest evolutionary pinnacle, is the most playful.

Wilson falters somewhat in presenting the human story. For one thing, he subscribes rather uncritically to the notion that big-game hunting was primarily responsible for the sort of evolution which marks the emergence of man—a process apparently dominated by culture rather than genes, by learning and tradition rather than heredity. Man never lived by big game alone. It was only one item in his diet, and rarely the major item.

Wilson can also be faulted for his vision of the future. He is fairly confident on this point. Mankind will arrive at "an ecological steady state," a balanced position with respect to other species, involving stability without conflict, or at least with only a subdued undercurrent of conflict analogous to that observed among advanced insect societies. It will be the end of our kind of evolution. We will achieve "total knowledge, right down to the levels of the neuron and gene," utter insight with hardly any illusions and hardly any art or neurosis. All this, he says, will probably happen by the end of the twenty-first century.

We could indeed wind up in some such steady-state world. But there are alternatives that depend less on the weak assumption that somehow things will work out in the future as they always have in times past. There is always the prospect of an all-out nuclear war, which is rapidly replacing death as a subject to be avoided in social gatherings, of returning with a big bang to a near-ape existence. Or culture, representing the driving force of a new level of evolution, could continue to operate in and through us. We could develop indefinitely, creating fresh syntheses and continually replenishing surprise on our way to other plants and solar systems.

In any case, *Sociobiology: The New Synthesis* has much to say about what is happening to us here and now. It is devoted largely to discussions of factors favoring cooperation—defense against predators, outcompeting competitors, more effective feeding and breeding, and so on. It also goes into more abstract matters such as the new arithmetic of altruism which helps explain how evolution can favor the survival of individuals genetically predisposed to die for others. Actually the book may be regarded as an evolutionary event in itself, announcing for all who can hear that we are on the verge of breakthroughs in the effort to understand our place in the scheme of things.

Giving Chance a Chance

Self-Portrait in a Convex Mirror by John Ashbery
August 10, 1975

BY JOHN MALCOLM BRINNIN

IN THE PAGES OF AN ART JOURNAL some years ago, John Ashbery wrote: "Most reckless things are beautiful in some way, and recklessness is what makes experimental art beautiful, just as religions are beautiful because of the strong possibility that they are founded on nothing." Ashbery's own kind of recklessness takes the form of an austere refusal to honor any of the claims of sentiment, beauty and good conscience that poetry is supposed to make. Worse than that, he has brought into American poetry the practice of randomness—a method of composition-by-chance familiar to readers of French poets (Mallarmé, Valéry, Michaux) in whose works the last vestiges of moral instruction and spiritual uplift are crowded out by uncertified sensations and unsanctioned feelings. The factor of chance has already modified certain conceptions in the realm of physics and, to music and painting, has achieved almost the status of a mode. Yet in poetry it is still suspect and open to charges of frivolity. The publication of this remarkable book should make one thing obvious: if chance is going to have a chance in the pious annals of American poetry, Ashbery is the man to provide it.

In contrast with the long meditative excursions that have recently become his hallmark, Ashbery used to work with comparative deliberateness. The titles of his early poems usually indicated some connection with the stanzas beneath them. His conventional skills could be observed in his handling of forms as rigorous as the sestina. Most of his poems satisfied the normal expectation that anything introduced would eventually be resolved. But when the vast possibilities implicit in randomness became apparent to him, Ashbery soon left convention behind. Instead of willfully "seeking" a poem or even pursuing a subject, his way was to sit still, to relax into a sort of magnetic sense of being in which all the materials of poems would come to him in indiscriminate clusters.

Consequently, a typical Ashbery poem was not a composition but a continuum. Meanings gave way to cognitions, structure gave way to process. When this happened, he lost an audience and gained a reputation. Except for those readers already initiated into the "reckless" excesses of English literature from *Euphues* to *Tender Buttons*, reading Ashbery was hard going. The span of attention any page of his work demanded was simply too wide and of too little programmatic interest for most people to tolerate. In this new book there are signs that, after many years apart, the deliberate and the random are moving toward rapprochement. The result is a collection of poems of breathtaking freshness and adventure in which dazzling orchestrations of language open up whole areas of consciousness no other American poet has even begun to explore.

"For where a mirage has been," says Ashbery, "life must be." This notion supplies a clue to the difficulties of certain of his poems and an index of his general method. The method is one of constant investigation of the vision and its source; a meshing of the real and the unreal so absolute as, finally, to remove the distinction. The consequence is a poetry of discovery—an endless, endlessly repeated, journey into the interior. Yet the nature of Ashbery's quest is crucially different from nearly all others in the history of allegory; it does not occur in time but, instantaneously, in space. Instead of setting out on a path that will take him from here to the enchanted castle by way of the duck pond, the carrousel, the two-headed prophet and the cave of the winds, Ashbery lets the castle and all the adventitious stuff of the journey come to him. When he begins a poem, all the characters and all the scenery are immanently there. Everything that might happen *has* happened before the journey is begun. The substance of a poem becomes a collocation of possibilities. The message of the poem is that there is no message—yet the castle still sits in the mist and the two-headed prophet still spells out his riddles.

Ashbery can be discussed most congenially in the company of French poets, yet very often he reminds one of Wallace Stevens—Stevens carried one logical step further, Stevens dispossessed of his subjects. For readers who can accept Stevens's arabesques of verbal delight but continue to find Ashbery's impenetrable, the affinity may be instructive. When, for instance, Stevens speaks of "a little island full of geese and stars," he is not referring to an island off the coast of Maine or Scotland or Japan. He is dealing with the idea of an island in which flocks of geese and nights clear enough to reveal stars are wholly contingent. So it is with Ashbery: what can be imagined, *is*.

As with Stevens, poetry for Ashbery is not a discrimination among units of intellectual or emotive attention but an ongoing process—"The poem of the act of the mind." In this view, poetry becomes synonymous with imagination and a book of poems becomes a sequence of demonstrations: the workings of the mind are offered to the observer much like those machines which, encased in glass for exhibition purposes, show how they function without any obvious reference to what they produce.

A somewhat surprising aspect of Ashbery is his broad easy usage of the colloquial. Phrases that would seem to belong only in some lexicon of the vulgar tongue run through his works like a gritty seam: "a blah morning" . . . "Bombed out of our minds" . . . "they stuck to their guns" . . . "betting on a sure thing" . . . "Aw nerts . . . this guy's too much for me." Metaphysical poets aren't supposed to talk this way. Yet Ashbery continually reminds his readers that he is no stranger to the bargain basements of language without for a moment suggesting that what he finds there isn't in its way as expressive as what might be available on higher levels.

His use of "homely" materials for lofty purposes brings to mind that brief phase of Cubism designated "synthetic"—the interregnum of the *papier collé* and the *tableau-objet*. This was the period between 1912 and 1914 when first Braque and then Picasso found that the new territory they had opened up could be charted by their noses: cigarette packets, bottle labels, bus tickets, fragments of café menus, snatches of newsprint and wallpaper. These little emblems of everyday life helped them to enlarge the scope of Cubism and to produce works as naïvely pure in fact and as expressive in effect as anything in modern art. Ashbery's use of slang and street lingo serves the same purpose—it anchors his metaphysics in common speech, keeps his feet "on the ground" and shows that a well-worn cliché nicely placed can be as resonant as a newly minted metaphor.

On the kinds of technique Ashbery has borrowed from movie makers I can only speculate, yet I have a feeling that they contribute importantly to the several ways by which he presents his materials. As early as 1962, in *The Tennis Court Oath*, there were poems that moved with the blinking speed of movies, others that seemed to have been "written" by a camera that had zoomed off its tripod, still others that looked as though they had been spliced together out of sweepings from a cutting-room floor. Buried in the unassorted contents of these movie-like poems there were indications of Ashbery's affection for the world of movies before movies became art and of his nostalgia for the trashy icons of art deco which gave that world its character. "Forties Flick" in the current volume gives a hint of a matinee at Loew's Paradise and the magic moment that will reveal Ida Lupino in her spunky wedgies, but in general the influence of films now shows in Ashbery's deft control of just those cinematic devices a poet can most usefully appropriate. Crosscut, flashback, montage, close-up, fade-out—he employs them all to generate the kinetic excitement that starts on the first page of his book and continues to the last.

This excitement comes mostly from finding yourself in places where you've never been and have never even dreamed of. It also comes from finding yourself caught off guard between an observation of sobering profundity and one smack next to it that makes you laugh out loud. No one quite likes to think of himself or herself as an extra in a divine comedy, yet Ashbery extends no option. His humor charges the air he breathes like static electricity; you can't go three pages into his book without hearing its crackle. Once aware of this, you are on your way to reading him on his own terms—"A little puttering around. / Some relaxing, a lot of plans and ideas" and toward taking him at his own word—"Hope to have more time to tell you about / The latter in the foreseeable future."

Letter

Alice Walker
November 30, 1975

RE: MARY ELLEN GALE'S review of Susan Brownmiller's *Against Our Will:*

As an 11-year-old growing up in a small town in the South 20 years ago, I was haunted by a photograph in *Jet* magazine showing the badly decomposed body of Emmett Till immediately after it was dragged from the river. Even more gruesome than the photograph, in which Till was hardly recognizable as a human being, not to mention a specific person, was the story of how his murder had occurred. Till, aged 13 (by some accounts as old as 14) was visiting relatives in Mississippi during the summer of 1955, whistled at a white woman in a grocery store and that night disappeared. He was kidnapped by two white men, unmercifully beaten, mutilated and shot, his hands tied behind his back, his body weighted down with chains and dumped in the river. The lesson for black men, as it had been for generations in the South, was stay away from white women. I do not believe any black men of that period misread the message.

It comes as something of a shock to read in Mary Ellen Gale's review that Brownmiller "came to realize 'Till's action was more than a kid's brash prank,' that among the things at stake was the age-old male claim to free access to all women, and that Till's insult, though no justification for murder, formed another link in a long chain of verbal and physical abuse."

Black men have never, until quite recently, made any claim to "free access to all women"; even a cursory reading of racial history in this country proves this. Perhaps that is why Eldridge Cleaver—a singular personality unfairly generalized—was "inspired" to rape white women. If the excuse of Till's lynching had not existed, he would have invented it.

Till, practically a child at the time of his death, is a poor example of black on white rape. He cannot be blamed for Cleaver's appropriation of his martyrdom. Emmett Till was not a rapist. He was not even a man. He was a child who did not understand that whistling at a white woman could cost him his life.

Black rapists of white women do exist, however, and I trust Brownmiller's book to offer more convincing examples of masculine aggression than the case of Emmett Till.

Bedraggled and Inspired

World of Our Fathers by Irving Howe
February 1, 1976

T HE FIRST GENERATION tries to retain as much as possible, the second to forget, the third to remember. Little wonder that the out-cropping of American-Jewish writing in the past 30 years is so often a literature of memory, an attempt to recover the world of childhood and adolescence as the last place the trail of Jewish identity was seen before it faded into the lawns of suburbia and the bright corridors of the professions. Why this interest, though? "Why not stick to the present," as my father would say. "The farther back you go, the more miserable it gets."

The main reason, I think, is that the third-generation Jew like myself intermittently experiences himself as walking around in America with a case of cultural amnesia, full of ancestral promptings and demurrers pulsing away. That's why *Portnoy's Complaint* rang bells like mad. But Roth's novel was a two-generational psychological farce—Freud played by the Marx Brothers—which can only explore its point by simplifying and tickling it. The secret communications between the generations are more long-term and broad and vague, and run through other switchboards besides the Oedipal one. So one also reads Bellow and Leonard Michaels, Grace Paley and Malamud, Cynthia Ozick and I. B. Singer, among many others, looking for kinship and instruction. Or one can study Judaism, even learn Hebrew, hoping to find the way back to its shaping significance on one's spirit that must have preceded the tense, perfunctory bar mitzvah lessons and seders of one's childhood. However, contemporary fiction tends to be too immediate and too stylized to carry one back far enough, while the covenants, principles and movements of Judaism, like its warming but remote observances, are difficult to carry forward (except perhaps for Hasidism).

So the context of these intuitions of Jewish being, or these moral slants and emotional tilts in the way you do your work, relate to your children, vote, justify your life, chase your desires remains elusive, full of blank spaces and darkness. A temporal link seems to be missing.

Jewishness, then, is like a language in which one knows only a few words and yet is thoroughly responsive to its intonations and rhythms, its lights and darks of feeling. Like Russian, as I found out on a recent visit. And, more to the point, like Yiddish. Yes! The dark language in which our parents mainly kept their secrets from us. What remains are a few expressions, a coarseness to the ear which once had a stigma attached, like slurping soup; also a certain long breathing frenzy underneath that makes it seem a little dizzying; also a vibrant tone, a mingling of laughter, heartfulness, irony. So one puts these bits and drops into one's English, now and then, like salt and pepper and a touch of horseradish. But one also does so because they feel right, confirm something basic.

Of course, one says, hitting his head at finding what was before the eyes, or rather, on the tongue. The missing link is Yiddish, and the evasive context, as one recognizes and recognizes in reading *World of Our Fathers*, is *Yiddishkeit*, the culture of our grandfathers.

Irving Howe has written a great book. Those who are not Jewish can still read a marvelous narrative about two generations of "bedraggled and inspired" Jewish immigrants on the Lower East Side and beyond in virtually all of their social and cultural bearings and in most of their political and economic ones.

But if you are Jewish you will also realize that Howe has written a necessary book, particularly for those of you who need its blow on the head to deliver you from your amnesia or, better, to help you begin to rescue yourself. Not that Howe's pages are ever particularly startling. Their effect is cumulative—the slow, dawning realization that this world is as familiar to you as it is fresh. Howe's just, remarkably just, descriptions and explanations, along with the voices of his sources, will minister to your residues of Jewish intuition and memory and cause them to unfold and blossom like those Japanese pellets which when put into water turn into flowers. As you read along, it is often difficult to distinguish between what you are discovering and what you are recollecting of this all-but-vanished life. For this life, as you will see, still lives—right behind your sense of your own distinctive mind and heart and face. And slowly you will begin to understand.

A few examples—some almonds and raisins and a bite of honeycake for remembrance sake. Savor for a moment Howe's detail that the Yiddish word for excommunication, *herem*, is also the word for a boycott. Or Howe's image of Jacob Adler, the matinee idol of the Yiddish theater, lying in state, as he instructed, in English morning coat, Windsor cravat and *talit*. Or a sketch by Z. Libin—a writer from the terrible first years, the era of the "*farloyrene menschen*," "the lost souls"—about a worker who fears that because a wall blocking his window has been torn down he will have to pay more rent.

In order to perceive the force of the attitudes and values that *Yiddishkeit* pumped through the generational conduits, one often has to recover the conditions that charged and shaped them. It is a platitude, for example, that Jews are mercenary because our forefathers were desperately poor, that Jewish mothers dote on and stuff, worry about their children because of the immigrants' experience of hunger, illness, self-sacrifice and hope. How banal, one says, until he reads Howe's harrowing account of the poverty of the Lower East Side during the 1880s and '90s. "Have you ever seen a hungry child cry?" asks the social worker Lillian Wald, explaining the dedication of her life. By 1885, the crying was everywhere. Wages in the garment industry—the main source of jobs— were cut in half. The population density of the Lower East Side was soon greater than in the worst sections of Bombay, the mortality rate was double that of the rest of the city. Project these figures into conditions and you get men working 70 hours a week in the unspeakable sweatshops and taking piecework home to scrape by, of people sleeping five or six to a room with their boarders, of near epidemics of dysentery, typhoid fever, and of course tuberculosis, the "tailors' disease." For 20 years or so, it was as though the fabled wretchedness of the steerage passage never ended, that those dark packed ships simply came upon land and turned into factory lofts and tenements.

What was most traumatic was the inner darkness. Totally uprooted and alien, driven by a tempo they had never known before, their austere, decorous spirits assaulted and derided by the brutal dog-eat-dog conditions of their existence, their religious institutions in disarray, the immigrants seemed to lose their main possession, the culture that had preserved so many generations of the Pale despite poverty and other oppressions. The collapse of its center, rabbinical authority, is brought home by the anecdote Howe tells of the attempt to establish a chief rabbi to restore order: soon there were three—a Lithuanian and a Galician (traditional antagonists) and a newcomer from Moscow. When asked who had made *him* the chief rabbi, he replied "the sign painter."

In a radical newspaper of the day, Howe tells us, "the word *finsternish*, darkness, recurs again and again. . . . their lives are overcome by *finsternish* and it is to escape from *finsternish* that men must learn to act." So they listened meekly to their flamboyant agitators, went on bitter and usually doomed strikes, saved their pennies for the Yiddish theater, but mainly lived on their last hope that "here they might yet see their sons and daughters move on to something better."

Finsternish didn't begin in the New York ghetto. It came in the immigrants' luggage and dreams, the darkness of being cooped up for centuries in their decaying villages and prayer-houses and in their sustaining but hapless messianism. But in the Russian Pale it was already lifting, thanks in good part to the Bund, the nascent Jewish socialists from the cities.

In America, it was the distinctively Jewish socialism developed by the Bund that largely rebuilt the community and morale the immigrants had lost. Indeed socialism, mostly through the organizing of the garment trades, provided a collective enterprise, not only as a consequence of despair but also as a movement

1976

Irving Howe's *World of Our Fathers* helps make a generation nostalgic for the Lower East Side.

toward the vision of a "normal life" at last, not merely as a response to privation but also as a recycled moral yearning. Jewish socialism derived, as Howe shows, from Jewish messianism, in which the worldly and other-worldly were aspects of the same destiny, a tradition that was quick to produce political and social movements that had a strong utopian, universalist cast and fervor.

Reading Howe's pages on Jewish socialism and the labor movements, one can see the powerful strains of Jewish idealism and skepticism working away like yeast in bread. Also in Howe's descriptions of the intricate, shifting, but always bitter struggle between the left and right, of the slow giving way of radical aspirations to practical ambitions in the rank-and-file, one can find an evolving paradigm of the political behavior of Jews in America as well, perhaps, of the ideological tensions that mark one's own politics.

The other powerful force that brought the immigrant community together and enabled it even to flourish was *Yiddishkeit*, also originally an East European movement of the late nineteenth century. Its marrow was the vernacular of the Jews, "a language crackling with cleverness and turmoil, ironic to its bones." Its substance was the Jewish way of life, through thick and thin, the "shared experience, which goes beyond opinion and ideology." Its function was to hold a people together who were undergoing one challenge after another, including, after 1881, dispersion and acculturation in a totally strange secular society. Its spirit was an ironic acceptance of its role of straddling two world views—the religious and secular—which were slowly moving apart and one of which was withering.

Even so, it performed wonders while it lasted. It carried the fragmented, rivalrous East European Jews into the modern world. It provided an essential network of communications between the Pale and New York that reached into their respective theaters, union halls, newspaper offices, poetry movements, political cells, lifestyles, schools of fiction. It also negotiated the uneven and fateful transactions between tradition and modernity, between communal and individual expression, between its own survival and its people's acculturation. In its very premises that the Jews could remain Jews and yet regain their worldly bearings and lead a "normal life" in Russia and America, lay the sources of its enormous energies and contradictions, its startling full life and its inexorable destruction.

The sense of this rich and terrible brevity provides the tone of *World of Our Fathers*—the note of up-and-doing, striving, even frenzy mingling with the note of frustration, sacrifice, incompleteness. This tone, now brisk, now elegiac, also arises from Howe's feeling for the tragic dialectic of his story—that the "normal life" that these self-educated workers and their tribunes strove to create proved to be but a staging area for their children's escape from the family, community and culture. Perhaps the last word fittingly belongs to David Goldenbloom, a self-educated worker whom Howe, like the world he lived in, has rescued from near-oblivion:

> What else can I tell you. My children went their own way. I am proud of them, but there are things we can't talk about. Still, I have no complaints. My circumstances were what they were. My family has been a whole world to me. I still take pleasure in Sholom Aleichem, and to me Bazarov and Raskolnikov are like friends of my youth. But to think of them is to be reminded that there was a door which, for me, never opened.

First Impressions

Interview with the Vampire *by Anne Rice*
May 2, 1976

BY LEO BRAUDY

THE MONSTERS WHO BEGAN to roam through English and European literature in the Age of Enlightenment attracted and allured readers because—like the earlier figures of the highwayman and whore—they embodied urges that were ignored or actively repressed by a society fervently dedicated to industrialization, social order and scientific progress. Through Gothic fiction, readers could for a while escape from the cold demanding daylight into the almost unthinkable thrill of the night.

The power of those early images of the unacknowledged self lasted well into the twentieth century, extended and elaborated by the technological magic of film. But at least until recently it seemed that we were no longer getting the same solace and sense of expansion from the old myths. Many horror films and Gothic novels of recent years have been arch and archaic. They were largely nostalgic exercises, feeble attempts to summon up the old power by allusion and gesture, like the superheroes of Marvel comics, who muse aloud over the psychic pressures of being different (and of course better) than anyone else.

But vampires have had a resurgence in popularity, and the appearance of Anne Rice's first novel, *Interview with the Vampire*, its film sale to Paramount, and its huge paperback sale argue that at least someone in a large office somewhere thinks the myths retain their power, that Freud has not yet supplanted Bram Stoker.

Vampires are the aristocrats of the monster world. Unlike the man-made monsters such as Frankenstein's, forever trying to make their creators pay attention to them, or the Wolfmen, the Mr. Hydes and other eruptive lower beings whose more social selves wish only to be relieved of their tendency to change into something uncontrollable, the vampire is a creature of will, comfortable in his monsterhood, his specialness, and even egalitarian enough to want to help selected others join him. Vampire stories explore the lure of being totally different, without guilt. If the choice had to be made, who would rather be Mr. Hyde than Dracula?

Anne Rice's publishers mention *The Collector* and *The Other*, but it is really *The Exorcist* to which *Interview with the Vampire* should be compared, and both novelist William Peter Blatty and filmmaker William Friedkin, whatever their faults, did it there much better. The desire to be an individual, different from anyone else, and simultaneously to be part of a loving, nurturing community is a basic theme in American culture. But *Interview with the Vampire* states this more than feels this. The publicity tells us Rice is "a dazzling storyteller." But there is no story here, only a series of sometimes effective but always essentially static tableaus out of Roger Corman films, and some self-conscious soliloquizing out of Spider-Man comics, all wrapped in a ballooning, pompous language. Maybe the movie will be better, but the book is too superficial, too impersonal and too obviously made, to touch the sources of real terror and feeling.

The Elements of His Style

Letters of E. B. White
November 21, 1976

BY WILFRID SHEED

NEW YORKER WRITERS have always denied that there is such a thing as a *New Yorker* style, and by now they are probably right. (All rumors about that magazine are automatically denied, but some are false nevertheless.) But in the heyday of Gibbs, Thurber and White, readers knew better. There was such a style, and its name was E. B. White.

Not that all the writers used the style (in fact, most of the best avoided it). But White's notes and comments established, as they say in Rock, The Sound. "Harold Ross and Katharine Angell, his literary editor [and later White's wife], were not slow to perceive that here were the perfect eye and ear, the authentic voice and accent for their struggling magazine," wrote Thurber in 1938 before his blindness had stiffened everything into private myth; and no one knew sounds better than Thurber. In fact, he was a bit of a mimic on the side and presumably without trying, he himself took White's style and ran with it. But from comparing their juvenilia, there's no question that White got there first, by about 20 years.

Enough. White doggedly downplays this kind of talk because down-playing is his very essence. A nimbus of modesty surrounds him, as it does the magazine itself, because boasting is so second-rate. But if you read these letters with half an ear, the jig is up. White's notes to the milkman achieve effects that the others sat up all night for. If the present editor has allowed the style to semi-retire, it is not just because of his own raised consciousness, but because too many people were sitting up all night to too little purpose. They don't make writers like White anymore, and rather than plug on with inferior imitations, William Shawn has wisely let in new subject matter with the new voices to match.

Still, it was, and is, an intriguing style, and any American writer, from pastoral to Spillane, who hasn't learned from it has missed a trick or two. Essentially it combines the English sensible (as crystallized in Fowler's *English Usage*) with the rustic colloquial. Look for phrases like "horn in on," "going some" and "mighty" followed by adjective: look, in short, for an imitation of a New England farmer, and a darn good one (or jimdandy). This inspired concoction removed at a blow much of the lace and stuffing from American belles lettres and even commanded the respect of the British, who have yielded their language rather more grudgingly than their empire. On the evidence, White began writing this way around the age of 11.

Not exactly of course. One of the grim pleasures of reading collected letters comes in watching a style being built year by year until it resembles a model prison, with the writer on the inside. Only in this case, White had a magazine in there with him. Because, since you could only say certain things in White's style, light dry quick things, the magazine tended only to say those things too.

Which was fine so long as humor was the main order of business: but humor is a young man's game, after that it is just a chore, and by World War II we find White declaring himself heartily sick of Eustace Tilley, the dandy with the monocle who personified *The New Yorker*. Yet it proved hard to convert Eustace to serious purposes. This fretful fellow was accustomed to feeling "jumpy," "edgy" and plain "scared" over things like the disappearance of ferry boats and double-decker buses; now suddenly he was asked to feel jumpy about the erosion of freedom and such, and it didn't sound right.

So one turns to White's letters first off to find how much of this was manner and how much White; and the first thing you discover is that he is indeed jumpy, edgy and nervous about just about everything. Where Thurber had used edginess as a purely comic device (the edge of a tantrum as often as not) with White it was a simple statement of fact. He is, it seems, so finely strung that keeping his sanity has been a struggle at times and writing brightly for *The New Yorker* a potential torture. No wonder his stuff seemed almost preternaturally sane and well-balanced. It had to.

All this puts into new perspective White's retreat to Maine in the thirties, which had seemed the ultimate in fastidiousness. In fact he was closer to running for his life. Near breakdowns in his thirties and forties left his head feeling funny, as if something bad was running around in the attic (a painful image: he had been scared of the attic in his childhood home in White Plains). In such a state he took, like Hemingway's shell-shocked Nick Adams, to fishing and doing simple country tasks well.

Much of this he describes here to his friends in such painstaking detail that it could be a boy writing home from camp. The act of description seems itself a country task, a necessary branch of farming. Just as you could barely tell by the end whether Hemingway was writing or fishing, White hammering a nail and fashioning a sentence looks more and more like the same fellow.

The effect was obviously good for his prose and his nerves, and a treat for his friends (he is clearly a charming man). Yet, as nature writing goes, White's still gives off a slight sense of a city boy writing about the country: not precisely a Eustace Tilley, but someone just a little too delighted with everything, whether the birth of a lamb or the ways of the titmouse. This is an urban mind in exile, trying to find the same quaint excitements among animals that it used to find on the sidewalks.

This country is merciless to good small talents. A writer who doesn't take chances and swing for the fences (whether or not he has a prayer of reaching them) is less than a man. White must surely have been aware of this. In the mid-thirties he took a year off to write something "major" and found that he just couldn't. Maybe it rattled his nerves too much; maybe the creature in the attic would have got loose; most likely, it simply went against the grain of his style. So instead he made the common mistake of enlarging the subject matter while playing the same basic notes: like a minuet in honor of Napoleon.

One reads the book for the words, which should be good enough for anyone. The studied informality of his *New Yorker* style turns out not to be studied at all but bred in the bone. And it loosens just the right bit more for his friends. Hemingway's writing "reminded me of the farting of an old horse." (Too bad he couldn't have said things like that out loud.) A famous trick of his, of doubling back on a word or phrase and playing with it like a cat shows up early. To wit: "The only Earp I ever knew was neither Wyatt nor Henry—he was Fred Earp, a copy-reader on the *Seattle Times*. All this is getting us nowhere, all this Earp business. It earps me. I suspect it earps you, too." This is the secret of *The New*

Yorker's famous one-line newsbreaks and, formula or no, no one else has been able to do it. In fact, being inimitable within a formula is the very definition of White's genius.

Letters by a living man are a bit like a stately home with the owner around—one isn't sure how much one can touch. Keeping psycho-history to a minimum, we are confronted with a passion for independence that seems alternately fearful and almost truculent. In the twenties he breaks off from a girl with a curiously icy letter and in the thirties he appears to send his wife packing for a year, with a similar *demand* for loneliness.

In that same ambitious decade (his thirties and ours), he even tried to distance himself from *The New Yorker*, once again for breathing room. Being identified with a great magazine was no substitute for being a great writer, and he made a brief break for *Harper's* and freedom. In the same prickly vein, he has always refused to be exploited, to make money on the cheap or to have his children's books butchered by the media.

That is the plus side of his gift for saying no: but on the other hand is a sorry stream of negation, a refusal to do virtually anything at all, from lecturing to joining the American Academy of Arts and Sciences. He had his good reasons: the few times he ventured out he erupted in a wild array of disorders issuing from head and stomach. But the malaise seemed to spread to the magazine itself, whose psycho-history *is* fair game. One had a picture of *New Yorker* writers (whom one seldom saw) vying with each other in feats of hypochondria and shyness: also of flinching and shrinking, jumping at small sounds, and holing up in the country. American writers will compete at just about anything.

Not White's fault, of course: he never tried to influence anybody. But his retreat from life sounded so tasteful and amusing that it cried out for imitation. When the Whites phased up to Maine in the thirties and forties, they became gray eminences with a vengeance. It was rumored that they disapproved of Thurber's book on Harold Ross, a harmless enough ragbag of too-often-told anecdotes; but then one fancied that they didn't approve of much that was written about *The New Yorker*. When Tom Wolfe did a feckless spoof of the magazine for *New York*, a slew of contributors, including White, dashed off indignant letters which, while more than justified, unwittingly bore out Wolfe's image of *The New Yorker* as an old person with bad nerves. The young magazine would have handled it better.

But White's era at *The New Yorker* was a great one, unique in magazine history. Surely never before has a house-style influenced the prose of a generation for the better—even if White isn't strictly speaking a house. And his personal era continues of course as chirpy as ever, as he rides out sickness and the loss of friends with good humor, kindness and courage. A valuable man, but beware of imitations. His letters are equivalent to a weekend in the country and should be read as such. The shorter, sharper ones he wrote in the City give hints of another kind of writer, but we may never know for sure. Meanwhile, the one we got is fine with me.

Afflicted with Nostalgia

Falconer by John Cheever
March 6, 1977

BY JOAN DIDION

SOME OF US ARE NOT JEWS. Neither are some of us Southerners, nor children of the Iroquois, nor the inheritors of any other notably dark and bloodied ground. Some of us are even Episcopalians. In the popular mind this absence of any particular claim on the conscience of the world is generally construed as a historical advantage, but in the small society of those who read and write it renders us "different," and a little suspect. We are not quite accredited for suffering, nor do we have tickets for the human comedy. We are believed to have known no poverty except that of our own life-force. We are seen by the tolerant as carriers merely of an exhausted culture, and by the less tolerant as carriers of some potentially demonic social virus. We are seen as dealers in obscure manners and unwarranted pessimism. We are always "looking back." We are always lamenting the loss of our psychic home, a loss which is easy to dismiss—given our particular history in this particular country—as deficient in generality and even in credibility. Yet in a very real way the white middle-class Protestant writer in America is in fact homeless—as absent from the world of his fathers as he is "different" within the world of letters—and it is precisely this note of "homelessness" that John Cheever strikes with an almost liturgical intensity in his extraordinary new novel, *Falconer.*

Of course this note of exile and estrangement has always been present in Cheever's fiction, from the early stories on. But in the beginning Cheever characters appeared to be exiled merely by their own errors or passions or foolishness: lost wives and quixotic husbands, apparently golden individuals who conceived their children at the St. Regis Hotel and tumbled their card houses down for love of the grocery boy, love of the plumber, love of the neighbor who came to collect for Muscular Dystrophy and had six drinks and let her hair fall down. They tried to behave well and they drank too much. Their best light was that which dapples lawns on late summer afternoons, and their favorite note was "plaintive": everything they heard was "plaintive," and served to remind them that life and love were but fleeting shadows, to teach them to number their days and to call them home across those summer lawns. They yearned always after some abstraction symbolized by the word "home," after "tenderness," after "gentleness," after remembered houses where the fires were laid and the silver was polished and everything could be "decent" and "radiant" and "clear."

Such houses were hard to find in prime condition. To approach one was to hear the quarreling inside. To reach another was to find it boarded up, obscene with graffiti, lost for taxes. There was some gap between what these Cheever people searching for home had been led to expect and what they got, some error in expectations, and it became increasingly clear that Cheever did not locate the error entirely in the hearts of the searchers.

"Nostalgia" is in our time a pejorative word, and the emotion it represents is widely perceived as retrograde, sentimental and even "false." Yet Cheever has persisted throughout his career in telling us a story in which nostalgia is "real," and every time he tells this story he refines it more, gets closer to the bone, elides another summer lawn and pulls the rug from under another of his own successful performances. He is like a magician who insists on revealing how every trick was done. Every time he goes on stage he sets for himself more severe limits, as if finally he might want to engrave the act on the head of a pin. "The time for banal irony, the voice-over, is long gone," reflects Ezekiel Farragut, the entirely sentient protagonist of Cheever's new novel, *Falconer*. "Give me the unchanging profundity of nostalgia, love and death." In this sense of obsessive compression and abandoned artifice *Falconer* is a better book than the *Wapshot* novels, a better book even than *Bullet Park*, for in *Falconer* those summer lawns are gone altogether, and the main narrative line is only a memory.

Falconer is the name of a prison (actually the name of the prison is *Daybreak House*, but this "had never caught on"), and it is at Falconer that Farragut is serving time for the murder of his brother. "I thought that my life was one hundred per cent frustration," Farragut is advised by his wife, Marcia, when she visits Falconer for the first time. "But when you killed your brother I saw that I had underestimated my problems." Marcia would have visited sooner had she not been in Jamaica. "I," Marcia informs the guard who tells her the visitors' rules, "am a taxpayer. It costs me more to keep my husband in here than it costs me to send my son to a good school."

Cheever has a famous ear, but he is up to something more in *Falconer* than a comedy of prison manners. On its surface *Falconer* seems at first to be a conventional novel of crime and punishment and redemption—a story about a man who kills his brother, goes to prison for it and escapes, changed for the better—

and yet the "crime" in this novel bears no more relation to the "punishment" than the punishment bears to the redemption. The surface here glitters and deceives. Causes and effects run deeper.

Of course Farragut has been, all his life, afflicted with nostalgia. Of course "home" has been hard to locate. Of course he has resorted to anodynes—in this case heroin—to dull his affliction. "There is a Degas painting of a woman with a bowl of chrysanthemums that had come to represent to Farragut the great serenity of 'mother.' The world kept urging him to match his own mother, a famous arsonist, snob, gas pumper and wing shot, against this image . . . why had the universe encouraged this gap?"

At Falconer there is no heroin to blur this question and Farragut must manage with methadone. "When do you think you'll be clean," Marcia asks. "I find it hard to imagine cleanliness," Farragut answers. "I can claim to imagine this, but it would be false. It would be as though I had claimed to reinstall myself in some afternoon of my youth." "That's why you're a lightweight," Marcia says. "Yes," Farragut says.

Yes and no. Of all those Cheever characters who have suffered nostalgia, Farragut is perhaps the first to apprehend that the home from which he has been gone too long is not necessarily on the map. He seems to be undergoing a Dark Night of the Soul, a purification, a period of suffering in order to re-enter the ceremonies of innocence, and in this context the question of when he will be "clean" has considerable poignance. As a matter of fact it is this question that Cheever has been asking all along—*when will I be clean?* was the question on every summer lawn—but he has never before asked it outright, and with such transcendent arrogance of style. Farragut is not the first Cheever character to survive despite his father's attempt to abort him, but in the past it took more words. Farragut is not the first Cheever character to see freedom as the option to book a seat on the Tokyo plane, but in the past the option was open. Addiction has been common, but not before to heroin. The spirit of fratricide has been general, but not until now the act. In this way *Falconer* is a kind of contemplation in shorthand, a meditation on the abstraction Cheever has always called "home" but has never before located so explicitly in the life of the spirit.

The Adventures of Macon Dead

Song of Solomon by Toni Morrison
September 11, 1977

BY REYNOLDS PRICE

TONI MORRISON'S first two books—*The Bluest Eye* with the purity of its terrors and *Sula* with its dense poetry and the depth of its probing into a small circle of lives—were strong novels. Yet, firm as they both were in achievement and promise, they didn't fully forecast her new book, *Song of Solomon*. Here the depths of the younger work are still evident, but now they thrust outward, into wider fields, for longer intervals, encompassing many more lives. The result is a long prose tale that surveys nearly a century of American history as it impinges upon a single family. In short, this is a full novel—rich, slow enough to impress itself upon us like a love affair or a sickness—not the two-hour penny dreadful which is again in vogue nor one of the airless cat's cradles custom-woven for the delight and job-assistance of graduate students of all ages.

Song of Solomon isn't, however, cast in the basically realistic mode of most family novels. In fact, its negotiations with fantasy, fable, song and allegory are so organic, continuous and unpredictable as to make any summary of its plot sound absurd; but absurdity is neither Morrison's strategy nor purpose. The purpose seems to be communication of painfully discovered and powerfully held convictions about the possibility of transcendence within human life, on the time-scale of a single life. The strategies are multiple and depend upon the actions of a large cast of black Americans, most of them related by blood. But after the loving, comical and demanding polyphony of the early chapters (set in Michigan in the early 1930s), the theme begins to settle on one character and to develop around and out of him.

His name is Macon Dead, called "Milkman" because his mother nursed him well past infancy. He is the son of an upper-middle-class Northern black mother and a father with obscure working-class Southern origins. These origins, which Milkman's father is intent on concealing, fuel him in a merciless drive toward money and safety—over and past the happiness of wife and daughters and son. So the son grows up into chaos and genuine danger—the homicidal intentions of a woman he spurned after years of love, and an accidental involvement with a secret ring of lifelong acquaintances who are sworn to avenge white violence, eye for eye.

Near midpoint in the book—when we may begin to wonder if the spectacle of Milkman's apparently thwarted life is sufficient to hold our attention much longer—there is an abrupt shift. Through his involvement with his father's sister, the bizarre and anarchic Pilate (whose dedication to life and feeling is directly opposed to her brother's methodical acquisition of things), and with Guitar, one of the black avengers, Milkman is flung out of his private maelstrom. He is forced to discover, explore, comprehend and accept a world more dangerous than the Blood Bank (the ghetto neighborhood of idle eccentrics, whores, bullies and lunatics, which he visited as a boy). But this world is also rewarding, as it opens into the larger, freer sphere of time and human contingency and reveals the possibility of knowing one's origins and of realizing the potential found in the lives, failures and victories of one's ancestors.

Although it begins as a hungry hunt for a cache of gold that his father and Pilate left in a cave in Virginia, Milkman's search is finally a search for family history. As he travels through Pennsylvania and Virginia, acquiring the jagged pieces of a story that he slowly assembles into a long pattern of courage and literal transcendence of tragedy, he is strengthened to face the mortal threat that rises from his own careless past to meet him at the end.

The end is unresolved. Does Milkman survive to use his new knowledge, or does he die at the hands of a hateful friend? The hint is that he lives—in which case Toni Morrison has her next novel ready and waiting: Milkman's real manhood, the means he invents for transmitting or squandering the legacy he has discovered.

But that very uncertainty is one more sign of the book's larger truthfulness (no big, good novel has ever really ended; and none can, until it authoritatively describes the extinction from the universe of all human life); and while there are problems (occasional abortive pursuits of a character who vanishes, occasional luxuriant pauses on detail and the understandable but weakening omission of active white characters), *Song of Solomon* easily lifts above them on the wide slow wings of human sympathy, well-informed wit and the rare plain power to speak wisdom to other human beings. A long story, then, and better than good. Toni Morrison has earned attention and praise. Few Americans know, and can say, more than she has in this wise and spacious novel.

Interview

Allen Ginsberg
October 23, 1977

BY KENNETH KOCH

What do you like best about your own poetry?

Cranky music.

Meaning?

Vowelic melodiousness, adjusted towards speech syncopation.

Vowelic?

Assonance, long mellow mouthings of assonance. Classic example: Moloch Moloch. In "Howl," Moloch whose skyscrapers stand in the long streets and so on.

You like the music in your poetry more than you like the content?

My ambition for my content was to be totally personal. So it could rest on fact. I mean the world I knew. But the sound in my throat, that mellow music's part of the world I know. So if I get "hot" poetically, the vowels heat up.

Would you explain getting "hot" in poetry?

I mean inspiration in a literal way, as deep breath flowing out unobstructedly as long vowels, musical.

What brings on this state, if you can say anything about that? I believe some people have the idea about your work that you get poetic inspiration from, or have gotten it from, certain drugs, from certain political experiences, and so on. What's the truth about this?

The vowelic heat comes from single-minded devotional awareness of death. And the preciousness of the human body alive. Drugs have been a side experiment, just to cover those classical possibilities—Baudelaire, Gautier, old Bohemia. Buddhist Vajrayana studies reinforce natural inspiration. Because it's practice of breath awareness.

What helps you most to be in a single-minded devotional state?

Not trying to. It's accident, from resting in ordinary mind.

What things do you think keep you from having that experience, if any? Do your travels, your political activity, your literary ambitions, etc.?

All those, including the telephone and excessive masturbatory activity as a man of letters—publishing journals, teaching, trying to keep up with punk rock.

What would you consider an ideal existence for yourself as a poet?

Retiring from the world, living in a mountain hut, practicing certain special meditation exercises half the day, and composing epics as the sun sets. I did that actually, for 10 days early September in a mountain hut in Southern Colorado.

How long would you have had to stay to feel good about writing?

About a thousand days. There is in Tantric study a specific three-year, three-month solitary retreat doing non-conceptual practices.

What does that do for you as a poet?

It clears the mind of false poetry, let's say. That is to say, self-centered poetry.

You said earlier your ideal in poetry was to be completely personal. Can one be that and not be self-centered?

That's a problem I have, and I'm working on it. I think there is, though. One would still be looking out of one's ego eyes, without attachment. If you sat for three years not doing anything you'd sure wind up that way, if you had a good teacher.

About non-attachment—your poetry seems so admirably attached to the world.

I'd rather use the word "involved."

Could you explain the difference?

Involved means present in the middle of, with complete awareness, and active. *Attached* means neurotically self-centered in the activity. That's the way I'm using those words.

Do you think your poetry may have gotten some of its energy from a conflict between being attached and wishing not to be?

No, I think the biggest energy is probably in the Moloch section of "Howl" and the "Hymns to Death" in "Kaddish" and the dramatic rants in my new "Contest of Bards" poem. That energy, in the first two cases, comes from total belief in the subject—annihilation of civilization, inevitability of death. In the "Contest of Bards" I found a dramatic form to go all-out into total self-belief through the mouths of characters. They can say anything I want. I don't have to take responsibility.

Could you say something more about "Contest of Bards"?

That poem came in a burst of all-night writing. Thirty pages—later to be touched up, unscrambled a little. A few times my attention lapsed and the page got cross-hatched with corrections. But mostly a continuous stream of improvisation. Symmetric and perfect. Like "Howl," "Kaddish" and another poem I love, "September on Jessore Road." Poe said a long poem was impossible because he couldn't conceive of a long poem being written in one sitting. He thought you'd lose the lyric impulse if you worked on it over a period of years—months, years. But I think most poets have found that every few years they're liberated into a composition. That they can accomplish a vast epic in one night. Vast 30, 40 pages. I think most poets have that experience—most big poets. How long did it take Shelley to write "Ode to the West Wind"? Teatime? Before breakfast?

I think he wrote it in a park in Florence in one afternoon or one day.

On the other hand, I write a little bit every other day. I just write when I have a thought. Sometimes I have big thoughts, sometimes little thoughts. The deal is to accept whatever comes. Or work with whatever comes. Leave yourself open.

What do you have to have, or to be, to start with, in order to leave yourself open to produce good poetry?

A little glimpse of death, and the looseness and tolerance that brings.

I think I understand about the glimpse of death, but haven't ambition and passion and the wish for fame and power been at least as important in making you a good poet?

No, I think a glimpse of the death of power, fame and ambition liberated me from rigid interpretation of those stereotypes. Not that they don't exist in my head, but they exist side by side with taxicab noises and the gaps in between sounds.

You have a way of speaking easily and openly about things (including what you like in your work)—I wonder if Whitman influenced you at all to be able to do that.

In the "Journals" I put myself down a lot too. There's a lot of depreciation. I'm just registering what comes in my head. I wouldn't be studying Buddhism if I thought I were ego-less. I wouldn't be such a religious fanatic. As for registering what's going on in one's feelings, it's too much work to do anything else but reproduce as exactly as possible the fluctuations.

Do you feel this makes you a disconcerting person?

I try to be less and less disconcerting as I grow older.

Could you tell me another line in your work that has the witty quality you like?

Taxi September along Jessore Road

Oxcart skeletons drag charcoal load.

There's a certain nostalgia in the first line, as of some old supper-club lyric ("September in the Rain") followed by a Daumier-like, objectively-observed fact—condensed into cartoon, literally, charcoal loads dragged by oxen whose ribs are showing—minute particulars, yet in the first line there's this funny Jerome Kern sentimentality, but the statement I'm making is all newspaper-true.

Did you feel the Jerome Kern sentimentality at the time of the taxi ride or when you wrote the poem?

Both. That's what I meant by awareness of mortality.

Please explain.

Part of the sentimental nostalgia of show tunes like "September Song" is a little glimmer of actual feeling of the transitoriness and dream-illusory nature of our presence here on the scene. At the same time as the gruesome bones of suffering show in the oxcart skeletons. Same time, there's an odd humor in noticing they're dragging a load of charcoal through the mud. I don't know if that answers the question. In some respects the lines are humorous because they reflect ordinary mind. What actually passes through your head. Which you recollect and accept if you're a poet.

What do you mean by what passes through your "head"?

I mean that literally: the pictures that occur in an area about two inches before the forehead and the couple of inches into the skull where you see mental images. What Pound called Phanopoeia. Which I'm locating physiologically. There are pictures, and then there are the words. And the words—or soundtrack connected with the pictures—seem to occur physiologically along the surface of the tongue and down into the larynx. And the activity of poetry can include bare attention to those two areas which provide sharply defined detailed photos and a running commentary—spontaneous and so to speak, unborn (you can't trace their origin)—on the picture show. I'm suggesting if the reader takes a quiet moment to pay attention to his mental activities located in those areas he'll discover that process is going on all the time.

Do you feel these pictures and sounds are worth reproducing in poetry, and, if so, why?

Well, where else in your head are you going to find matter for writing?

Some have thought to find it in the experience of passionate love, others in singing of the history of their people, others in writing about flowers, streets, etc.

Well, I'm simply pointing out that exact pictures of flower-power street riots can be observed in detail for such purposes in the mind's eye, which I've tried to locate physiologically, as an *aide-memoire.* No contradiction. Does that make any sense?

Everything you say makes sense, but I want to be sure I'm getting the same sense you do.

Really. If somebody wants to write about a love affair they once had, they'll have to remember it in pictures and words.

Couldn't what the love made the poet feel be used to create a poem about something not the love affair? Or might not made-up pictures give a better sense of the love affair than the "real" ones?

Certainly your statement is right. I was just pointing out the easiest place to look for an objective correlative. But then if you substitute a roller-coaster ride for the flash of belly you kissed, the roller-coaster picture will occur somewhere around your forehead.

Do you think all words are accompanied by pictures?

No. But for that combination of visual particularity that Pound praises so highly in Catullus, with accurate verbal captions, look to the forehead and tongue. If you go to a restaurant and want to order eggs over easy, bacon and hash browns, you'll find yourself formulating it subvocally till the waitress arrives at your table. So when you're trying to describe your grandmother's amethyst necklace, that pretty detail arrives at your tongue involuntarily the same time as the picture in the mind's eye. I mean, how do you think I got "amethyst necklace"?

How would you distinguish "mind's-eye" lines like those in "Jessore Road" from those in, say, the Moloch section of "Howl"?

The Moloch section really has accurate pictures. "Moloch whose smoke-stacks and antennae crown the cities." That you can see entering or leaving

Chicago by train or bus—swift sketch panoramic vista. I would say those are directly mind's-eye lines. Not as particular as Williams's, because we're dealing with panoramic megalopolis. Not saxifrage cracking a Rutherford sidewalk on Ridge Road.

How do you change "mind's-eye" material so as to make it into lines like that?

By paying attention to the soundtrack along the surface of the tongue. You're riding along on the bus. You see these weird wires, gas flares, industrial smokestacks, antennae, covering the outskirts, surrounding the city. They have names. Listen to what you're thinking in the base of the throat. "Smokestacks and antennae crowning the city." How else do you think of the words? Listen to your foot? Yes. Rhythmically. But the words march in rhythm through the throat. That's pretty good. What I'm saying is taking off from Kerouac's motto: "Don't stop to think of the words. Stop to see the picture better." Sure, anybody can write all the subconscious verbal gossip, but if it's connected with a picture, there's likely to be some substance there. If you can focus on details of the picture, the descriptive words rise naturally.

Could you tell me briefly which twentieth-century poets have influenced your work?

Most recently, enormously, Charles Reznikoff, for his particular focus on sidewalks, parks and subways of New York. Williams, originally, for a large body of haiku-like concrete particulars in which "things are symbols of themselves." Particularly one poem of Williams lately—"Thursday"—which for me is the intersecting point between Buddhist "mind-fullness" and American poetics. Then, further, Kerouac's spontaneous melodiousness (his long-sentence, Melville-like prose paeans to American disillusionment). Hart Crane's Shelley-like apostrophes. Their musical structure. Eliot's nostalgic silent movies—"A crowd flowed over London Bridge, so many." Marsden Hartley's plainness and localism. Robert Creeley's and Charles Olson's mystique of syllables and physiology—that is, the line as an extension of the breath has affected me. In the New York schools, glamorization of the informal.

I thought I noticed in some recent short poems something closer to Gary Snyder than I'd seen before in your poetry.

Gary's always an influence. Toward muscular Chinese. That is to say, sharp specific images rising from actual physical work and familiarity—with woodchopping, Ponderosa pine, Sierra trails, and carpentry. Other influences, particularly toward music, have been the Blues of Richard "Rabbit" Brown (a '20s New Orleans guitar singer) and Dylan's marvelous use of rhyme.

Allen, you're a remarkable man. And I've known you for 25 years, and this is our first long conversation. It's been good to get around to it.

It's about time.

Gimme Shelter

Dispatches by Michael Herr
November 20, 1977

BY C. D. B. BRYAN

DURING THE PAST FEW YEARS I have tried to read most of the Vietnam books that have been published. I read them hoping to understand the war, to know what it was like to fight there, how it differed from all our other wars. Some, like Bernard J. Fall's devastating Dienbienphu book, *Hell in a Very Small Place*, already seem distant and dated. Others, like Daniel Lang's *Casualties of War* and Jonathan Schell's *Village of Ben Suc*, were chilling in their reflection of some of our servicemen's murderous detachment. I tried to finish Frances FitzGerald's *Fire in the Lake*, but although I was dazzled by the brilliance with which she illuminated Vietnam's political landscape, her book never quite penetrated my tangled emotions. Gloria Emerson's *Winners and Losers: Battles, Retreats, Gains, Losses and Ruins from a Long War* intrigued me, but for the wrong reasons: I was far more moved by the obvious impact the war had had on her than I was by its impact on those she wrote about.

Certain books seemed to me to capture exactly the mood and madness of specific aspects of the war; I am thinking here of Mailer's *Armies of the Night*, Mary McCarthy's *Medina*, Seymour Hersh's book on My Lai, Tom Wolfe's Navy carrier-pilot piece, "The Truest Sport: Jousting with Sam and Charlie," from his collection *Mauve Gloves & Madmen, Clutter & Vine*, and Robert Jay Lifton's heartbreaking study of returning veterans in *Home from the War*. Ron Kovic's mortification in *Born on the Fourth of July* and Ronald J. Glasser's burn ward memories in *365 Days* haunt and hurt. But now there is a book that seems to be making all the right sort of incoming noises that indicate a direct hit: Michael Herr's *Dispatches*.

Quite simply, *Dispatches* is the best book to have been written about the Vietnam War.

Dispatches must be read because, even if there already exists a surprisingly rich selection of writings on Vietnam, nothing else so far has even come close to conveying how different this war was from any we fought—or how utterly different were the methods and the men who fought for us.

Vietnam required not only new techniques of warfare, but new techniques in writing as well. News cameramen and photographers could show us sometimes what the war looked like, but an entirely new language, imagery and style were needed so that we could understand and feel. Until Michael Herr, no reporter or writer seemed to capture it. The previous books seem to have been trapped in styles left over from previous wars, and I read them feeling as dissatisfied with their attempts to explain the Vietnam experience as I have been with the astronauts' tedious responses to questions on what it was really like to orbit in space or walk on the moon. (Only Yuri Gagarin's thrilling "I am Eagle!" tells me anything at all.)

Herr's literary style derives from the era of acid rock, the Beatles' films, of that druggy, Hunter Thompson once-removed-from-reality appreciation of The Great Cosmic Joke. He was covering Vietnam for *Esquire*—"*Esquire*, wow, they got a guy over here?" a Marine asks him. "What . . . for? You tell 'em what we're wearin'?" (General Westmoreland asked Herr if he planned on doing "humoristical" pieces.) Secondly, as Herr notes, he wasn't there to fight, he "was there to watch. . . . Talk about impersonating an identity, about locking into a role, about irony: I went to cover the war and the war covered me; an old story, unless of course you've never heard it." While the newspaper and news magazine correspondents were writing against daily or weekly deadlines, Herr's stories wouldn't appear in *Esquire* until five months after they'd been written. This lag gave him the opportunity to write thoughtful, polished, tough, compassionate pieces in which he could be careful to capture the image exactly: "Sitting in Saigon," he tells us, "was like sitting inside the petals of a poisoned flower."

To Michael Herr's everlasting credit he never ceased to feel deeply for the men with whom he served; he never became callous, always worried for them, agonized over them, on occasion even took up arms to defend them. His greatest service, I'm convinced, is this book. What more need one really say about our young who fought in Vietnam than this: "Along the road," Herr writes, "there is a two-dollar piece of issue. A poncho which has just been used to cover a dead Marine, a blood-puddled, mud-wet poncho going stiff in the wind. It has reared up there by the road in a horrible streaked ball. I'm walking along this road with two black grunts, and one of them gives the poncho a vicious, helpless kick. 'Go easy, man,' the other one says. 'That's the American flag you gettin' your foot into.' "

Interview

I. B. Singer
July 23, 1978

BY LAURIE COLWIN

Readers of all ages, nations, backgrounds and creeds read and love your books. Can you explain why you are so popular? What do you think are the elements that make it possible for everyone to appreciate what you write?

First of all, I don't think I'm so popular. All I would say is that, in the languages into which I am translated, there are people who are interested. A writer, like a woman, never knows why people like him or why people dislike him. We never know.

Why don't you take a guess?

The guess is that there is always a kinship between souls. Souls are either close to one another or far from one another. There are people who, when they read me, they like what I say. And there's nothing else I can tell you. I wouldn't say Jewish people, because I'm translated into Japanese. The Japanese translate everything I write, immediately. And how could I explain why some Japanese in Yokohama will like to read what I write? Just as I would enjoy a Japanese writer, a Japanese man may enjoy a Yiddish writer.

What sort of things would draw you to a Japanese writer?

I will tell you. I know nothing about the Japanese—really nothing. And, let's say, I read two Japanese books. I will say one is a good book and one is a bad book. How do I know, since I haven't lived in Japan? It seems that to enjoy a book you don't really have to go there and to know the land and the people, because human beings, although they are different, also have many things in common. And through this you get a notion which writer says the truth and which writer is fabricating.

How does it come that we read the Bible, which was written, parts of it, 3,000 years ago, and we understand the story of Joseph and the other stories? It seems that we are very much today basically as we were 3,000 years ago, and we are able to understand what another human being does.

I even suspect that if books are written on another planet somewhere in the universe, and if someone would make a translation, a reader would understand what is good and what is bad. But this is already too far-fetched. Unless, one day, you would bring me a translation from the planet Mars, then we will see.

You must have some notion of what you're doing that is this attractive. There must be some quality. You have been mentioned for a Nobel Prize.

Are you trying to convince me that I'm a big shot?

You are a big shot. Now, tell me why you are.

I will tell you, Laurie: When I sit down to write a story, I'm not saying to myself I'm going to write a Jewish story. Just like when a Frenchman builds a house in France. He doesn't say he's going to build a French house. He's going to build a house for his wife and children, a convenient house. Since it's built in France, it comes out French.

When I sit down to write a story, I will write the kind of stories which I write. It's true that since I know the Jewish people best and since I know the Yiddish language best, so my heroes, the people of my stories, are always Jewish and speak Yiddish. I am at home with these people. But just the same, I'm not just writing about them because they speak Yiddish and are Jewish. I'm interested in the same things you are interested in and the Japanese are interested in: in love, and in treachery and in hopes and in disappointments.

Do you ever feel that, like a photographer, you're preserving the last part of a vanished culture?

People tell me this, and while they tell me this I have a moment of feeling, yes, it is so. But I never sit down to write with this idea. I wouldn't be a writer if I would sit down to preserve the Yiddish language, or life in Poland, or make a better world or bring peace. I don't have all these illusions.

I know that my story will not do anything else but entertain a reader for half an hour. And this is enough for me. The word entertainment has become, lately, a very bad word. I call it the 13-letter word which writers are afraid to use, because the word entertainer means for them a cheap grade of writing. But it isn't so.

The great writers of the nineteenth century—Tolstoy and Dostoyevsky and Gogol and Dickens—were great entertainers. And Balzac. They wrote a novel or a story so that there was some suspense in it. When you began to read it, you wanted to know what would happen next. And they also published, some of them, their stories in magazines and in newspapers, where it was written, "It continues next week." And the reader had to be interested to read the continuation.

A serial.

A serial, yes.

You still do that in The Forward, *don't you?*

I still do it in *The Forward,* and I know whatever I write is immediately read, I would say, at least by 15,000 or 20,000 people, because we still have about 40,000 readers. And, since *The Forward* is a small newspaper, those who read it read everything in it, even the advertisements.

So I'm still connected with the reader. And these readers also don't read my story because they are Jewish, because Jewishness is not something new for them. They have been Jews all their life. They judge a writer from the point of view: Is he interesting or not interesting? Also, although some of them are ignorant people and primitive people, they know that a writer's not going to redeem the world, as some of the young writers think.

So, in other words, I'm before everything else a writer, not just Jewish, and I'm not doing it with some illusion that I'm going to do great things. I just feel that I have to tell a story.

I have said this a few times before, and I can repeat it: I need three conditions to write a story. One condition is I have to have a plot. I don't believe that you can write a story without a story—in other words, just sit down and write a slice of life hoping against hope that it will come out right. It happens once in a while, but most of the time if you don't have a plan there won't be a story.

The second condition is: I must have a desire to write the story—or a passion to write it. I must get up with an appetite to do this story.

And the third condition: I must have the illusion that I am the only one who can write such a story. Since I know the Yiddish writers, more or less, so I know what they could do and what I can do.

If I have these three conditions, I will sit down and do the work without worrying too much whether it is good for the Jews or bad for the Jews; whether it will redeem humanity immediately or whether it may take a few weeks until humanity is redeemed. I do the story, and I leave the rest to the reader, or to the critic—let them draw their own conclusions. Sometimes they find in it something.

Once I wrote a book called *The Magician of Lublin.* The hero repents at the end and hardens himself against the temptation of running after women. So once a psychoanalyst called me up, and he said: "I was delighted to see how you made your hero go back to his mother's womb." This had never occurred to me. But then I said to myself: He is just as good a reader as anybody else, and if he sees this it's just as good.

In other words, once you have written a story, it's not your private property anymore. And if someone wants to find in it sociological truths or psychological truths, he's entitled to do it. In my case, all I want is to write a story.

How do you go about making up a plot? Do you know the steps your mind takes?

No, I'm not making up a plot. The plot comes to me.

Does it just come like a flash?

I would say: if something happens to me. And things happen—I'm alive, I am with people, I also have memory. I've had affairs in my life and women and all kinds of things. And I think about these things. Suddenly, I say, here is a story. In other words, I don't wake up in the morning and go out into the street to make a plot. This never happens.

What kind of things do you like to read?

I love to read a story with real suspense. I mean, not that there should be only suspense—I don't read detective stories—but if it has a literary value and it has suspense. I often go back to the writers of the nineteenth century. I'm ashamed to tell you.

Everybody does that. What interests you? Love? Treachery? Sex?

Yes. Love and sex more than anything else.

Treachery is second?

If there's love, there is treachery. And then, also, crime interests me. When I was a boy of 12 years old *Crime and Punishment* came out in Yiddish, and I began to read it. A large book—in Yiddish it's twice as large as in English—and I was fascinated. I couldn't put it away. And I must tell you, a boy of 12 years there in Warsaw, I knew nothing of the world except what I studied in school, but I suddenly felt: Here is a great work.

So, if a boy of 12 years, in Warsaw, who had no experience in life could understand, more or less, *Crime and Punishment,* there is really no reason why the Japanese and the Turks should not understand what you write or what I write. So, actually, the writer should never be afraid that he is not going to be understood. Those writers who are afraid of that really underestimate the reader. The reader is—I assume so—an intelligent person; he knows about life and love and crime and everything, just as much as I and in some cases much more than I. So, I really don't worry that if I'm going to be translated one day into Chinese that no one will understand what a Hasid is and what a rabbi is. They will understand it very well. If they have learned in the last few years how to build machine guns and airplanes, they will also understand what I have to say. What I worry about is if what I do is good enough to be translated or to be read, and I work accordingly.

You once said that an army of Kafkas was killing literature. What do you mean by that?

Yes, yes, I will tell you. Avant-garde writers like Kafka and Joyce say to themselves: I don't care for the reader or for the critic or for anybody. I am going to say what I want. I have to please myself and nobody else.

I assume this is what they say. I wasn't there to listen to them, but this is more or less how they think. To me, Kafka was made of the material of genius. But just the same, he did things which a writer who writes for people, who has the audience before his eyes, would not do.

Let's say, if a writer imitates Tolstoy—and I think that Solzhenitsyn tries to write like Tolstoy—there is no misfortune, because, if he has talent and if he tries to write like Tolstoy and even if it doesn't come out 100 percent, it's still good. But if you try to imitate Kafka, Joyce, and you don't have their talent, it will come out completely bad. Because only a great talent can afford to say: I'm speaking only to myself.

If you were a Ph.D. candidate and you had to do your thesis on Isaac Singer, what would your topic be?

I would do what all the students do. I would read the author's books and I would try to find what they call the central idea.

What would the central idea be in the work of I. B. Singer?

I would say that the idea behind everything is that one should not belittle any emotion. The philosophers all belittle the emotions—especially a man like Spinoza, who considered all emotions as evil. I have convinced myself that everything that goes through our minds, no matter how trivial, no matter how silly, and no matter how terrible sometimes, is of some value. In other words, take away the emotions from a human being, and no matter how much logic he will have, he will be a vegetable. The emotions and man are the same. And I'm interested, especially, in the emotions that become passions.

Spinoza says in his *Ethics* that everything can become a passion, and I know that this is true. There is nothing that cannot become a passion. Especially if they are connected either with sex or with the supernatural—and I would say for me sex and the supernatural go very much together. I feel that the desire of one human being for another is not only a desire of the body but also of the soul. The two—a man and woman, or two men, or two women—when they embrace and they say they cannot live one without the other, and they fall one upon the other with a madness, that this is not just an act of the flesh, it's more than the flesh.

So, in other words, your topic would be emotion and excess in the works of Isaac Bashevis Singer?

Yes, and if I would be the dean I would give you the Ph.D. right this minute.

Sparing the Rod, Spoiling Ourselves

The Culture of Narcissism: American Life in an Age of Diminishing Expectations **by Christopher Lasch**
January 14, 1979

BY FRANK KERMODE

AT ALL GREAT CRISES of human affairs (and to be in the midst of such a crisis is what we all want, for it makes us more interesting, is indeed an aspect of our narcissism) a pattern of thought and feeling forms that has decadence as its motif. But almost invariably it coexists with an antithetical pattern devoted to renovation. The two patterns run into each other when we say that the old order is falling apart to make room for the new.

Christopher Lasch is a professor of history at the University of Rochester. His first well-known book was *The New Radicalism in America*, published in 1965. In it he examined, sympathetically but not without skepticism, the role and the delusions of intellectuals in modern American society. His tone was cool, but nobody could have supposed him to be committed to a wholly pessimistic view of the future. If anything, he was a renovationist. But in this new book he speaks only rarely of a possible better world; his concern is with decadence. Ranging with much virtuosity over the whole of modern American life, he finds evidence only of change and decay.

So here we have a civilized hellfire sermon, with little promise of salvation. From the tumult of ideas we have lived through Professor Lasch thinks there are only bitter lessons to be learned—that nobody ever learns anything; that we are all tainted with the same modern diseases; that hope itself is an illusion fostered by the very powers that are destroying our lives. Having lost our sense of communion with the past, we feel no responsibility for the future. Our schools, our attitudes toward sex, the family and old age, our acquiescence in the rule of bureaucracy, our muddled liberal attitudes toward punishment, even our acceptance of the corruption of sport into showbiz, all provide Professor Lasch with evidence that what we have given up—an older style of capitalism, more candidly exploitative, the disciplines of marriage and family—was better than what we have got instead. Better the unjust patriarchal rigor of a Hobbesian world than our unconstrained pursuit of pleasure as the highest good. Ours is a world in which Moll Flanders succeeds rather than Crusoe, the whore rather than the industrious self-made man.

"The political crisis of capitalism reflects a general crisis of Western culture, which reveals itself in a pervasive despair of understanding the course of modern history or of subjecting it to rational direction." If history is bankrupt, so are sociology and psychoanalysis. As for cultural radicalism, it merely seems to attack the status quo; in fact it unwittingly supports it. The final product of bourgeois individualism is psychological man, who lives entirely for the present, demands instant gratification, and yet exists in a state of restless, unsatisfied desire.

Professor Lasch believes that changes in psychoanalytic practice mirror changes in society; we need a more modern doctrine of narcissism than Freud's. He dealt with patients who had to come to terms with a rigid censorship; the modern therapist deals not with repression but with excessive "acting out," with shallowness in personal relations, with inability to mourn, with a pathological narcissism made all the worse by the ubiquity of the camera, and by the fact that the narcissistic personality is often fashionable and successful, at any rate when young and seductive. But age brings only worries, especially about health; and the doctors are not slow to profit from the senescence of Narcissus.

The entire society collaborates, says Professor Lasch, in intensifying the narcissistic syndrome. Its chief agent is probably advertising, but the substitution of credibility for truth in politics helps along the process of returning us to a form of society in which there is a war of all against all. The extravagances of art and technology have given us a substitute for Hobbes's nature, a very plush one, of course; if we're lucky our lives will be solitary, rich, nasty, brutish and long. We allow the language of sex to be contaminated by the violence of the slum. Our secondary schools are playpens, our colleges cafeterias "from which the students select so many credits." How should we care for our schools, since we have no care for posterity? And the arts dismally echo the society; they mock and destroy the old beneficent illusions of order, and they exalt narcissistic performance above all other values.

Performance invades other spheres. Parents unduly concerned with their performances as parents exercise no authority. Those archaic images make the modern superego extremely ferocious; and the standards it sets are such that the ego must fail. Here is a source of rage and guilt; and however permissive we may be about libido, we cannot be permissive about aggression. Lack of discipline thus breeds failure and death; the new freedom turns out to be a worse servitude. So the arrival of the sexually liberated woman eases no problems. Sex becomes a performance, and men who not so long ago complained of women's frigidity now complain of their demand for limitless orgasm. Professor Lasch even thinks things were better when people thought sex was dirty; the modern insistence that it isn't "expresses a desire to sanitize it by washing away its unconscious associations."

How shall we redeem the time? A return to "the moral discipline formerly associated with the work ethic" might help, says Professor Lasch not very hopefully. Women might come to see that their subordination, far from being an effect of economic causes, is rooted in nature. We could, as citizens, rebel against bureaucracy and capitalism in its modern form, and create "communities of competence."

All this sounds pretty hopeless, and however much one agrees with some of the diagnosis, the cure is both unpromising and unappealing. Professor Lasch believes that many of our ills are related to the removal from our society of visible sanctions; by sparing the rod we spoil not only the child but ourselves. The danger here, I think, is precisely that the introjected archaic parent also favors terror. In early modernism we had several instances of the way in which a desire for order and discipline may be transformed into support for political terror.

And what is to be offered to ordinary people when their dismal pleasures have been taken from them? The right to be poor, to be beaten in childhood, constrained by a savage penal system, compelled to suffer through an unhappy marriage, to be openly instead of covertly exploited, and to die young? For those conditions are as much a part of the relevant past as sobriety, ambition and discipline. And most of us, given a choice, would stick to what we've got. Because women may be exigent about orgasm, do we want a world in which most of them hardly know what the word means? For all that one agrees with Professor Lasch about the debasement of sports, do we want the great performers to return to wage slavery? And is their experience really so unusual? The painters made it in the sixteenth century, the actors in the eighteenth; no longer artisans or vagabonds, they were valued performers. And so with ballplayers now; their success is concededly accompanied by many less agreeable signs of corruption, but you could find people ready to argue that the same is true of the success of the painters and actors.

Perhaps the world has changed less than Professor Lasch believes. He condemns the modern painters for their insistence on formal qualities, their flaunting of illusion; yet they are only doing what Velázquez did before them, though they may be more interested than he was in the theory of what they are doing. For ours is an age of theory, and much of the situation Professor Lasch deplores may arise from an unduly heavy feedback of theory into practice. Historians lose confidence in history partly because the theory of history turns out to be so complex, and history so hard to distinguish from lying. It might even be argued that

we have a more honest understanding of our intellectual plight than our predecessors, and that this accounts for our mistrust of simple rules and remedies. We
are bound to be skeptical, of renovation as well as of decadence. But one thing
we do know: there is no going back. We cannot destroy television, prohibit con-
traceptives, restore the work ethic, and if we did we should hardly be better off.
What Professor Lasch has done—with somber force and occasionally with
gloomy wit—is to provide us with a black survey of the way we live now, and leave
us to use all our resources of theory and skepticism to make the best we can of it.

In the Shadow of the Big Man

A *Bend in the River* by V. S. Naipaul
May 13, 1979

BY IRVING HOWE

FOR SHEER ABUNDANCE OF TALENT there can hardly be a
writer alive who surpasses V. S. Naipaul. Whatever we may want in a
novelist is to be found in his books: an almost Conradian gift for tensing
a story, a serious involvement with human issues, a supple English prose, a hard-
edged wit, a personal vision of things. Best of all, he is a novelist unafraid of
using his brains—he would surely jeer at the common American notion that the
exercise of mind saps a writer's vital juices. His novels are packed with thought,
not as lumps of abstraction but as one fictional element among others, fluid in
the stream of narrative.

Born to Hindu parents in Trinidad in 1932, Naipaul has lived as an outsider,
first by virtue of fate and then, apparently, by clear-minded decision. His knowledge of the India from which his family stems is not large, nor his feeling for it
secure. He resides in England, but no one could take him for an Englishman.
What, then, is he? I would say: the world's writer, a master of language and perception, our sardonic blessing.

"Every writer," Naipaul has remarked, "is, in the long run, on his own; but it
helps, in the most practical way, to have a tradition. The English language was
mine; the [English] tradition was not." Yet precisely from this deracination he
has drawn novelistic strength. It enables a steely perspective, the scraped honesty
of the margin. It spurs him to a cool precision, trusting his own eyes. In novels
such as *In a Free State* (a dazzling tour de force), *Guerrillas* and now, perhaps
best of all, *A Bend in the River,* Naipaul struggles with the ordeals and absurdities of living in new "third world" countries. He is free of any romantic moon-
shine about the moral charms of primitives or the glories of blood-stained

dictators. Nor does he show a trace of Western condescension or nostalgia for colonialism. He is a tough-spirited writer, undeluded about the sleaziness of much contemporary history and not especially hopeful about its consequences.

There was a time when Naipaul did come rather close to being the "lovable" performer that Westerners have often looked for in colonial writers. His long Dickensian novel, *A House for Mr. Biswas*, chronicling the decay of traditional Indian life in the exile of Port of Spain, has its touches of humor and affection. But since publishing that book in 1961, Naipaul has grown more astringent. In recent fictions set in the Caribbean and Africa, he is hardly even a "likable" writer, for he no longer performs and barely troubles to please. He is now in the grip of a complex, entangling vision of what happens in those unfortunate countries that have just toppled out of a tribal past, or freed themselves from colonial rule, but cannot reach the uncertain blessings of modernity. He is obsessed with the shallowness of proclaimed liberations and the low cost of spilling blood. Reading his novels, one finds oneself driven to discomfiting reflections on how precarious is the very idea of civilization—reflections that jolt intellectual biases and political preconceptions. But that is one of the things literature should do.

A Bend in the River is set in an unnamed East African country, a bit perhaps like Uganda, but finally Naipaul's own turf. Independence has been won, civil war concluded. "The Big Man," president for life, rules by rhetoric, guile, sorcery and a strong helping of terror. There is a new dispensation: "black men assuming the lies of white men."

At the novel's center is Salim, a Muslim of Indian family, whose people have lived for several generations in a coastal town, trading quietly, rutted in traditionalism. Both the narrative voice and dominant consciousness, Salim is a decent fellow, impressionable, thoughtful, not at all an intellectual. (This creates problems, since Naipaul has to force some decidedly complex observations through Salim's limited awareness.) "Our way of life," Salim tells himself about the Indian settlement in Africa, "was antiquated and almost at an end." He is an outsider, watching with the outsider's nervousness.

The country, presumably Salim's too, has now entered modern history, or at least a coarse parody of it. Impressive buildings go up, for no clear purpose; local toughs are bundled into the army; young people are sent off to schools and universities; the population listens to three-hour radio orations by the Big Man. For the blacks in the bush, for the Indians on the coast, even for the quavering elite supposed to run the country, everything is unsettled, dependent on the whim of the Big Man. It's a country perhaps, but hardly a coherent society. The fading of the tribes, the feebleness of all social classes in the towns, the absence of a self-assured intelligentsia: all lead to making the army the single source of power, and within and over the army, the Big Man.

The Big Man has a genius for destructive manipulation, cutting down his army (through a brilliantly evoked gang of white mercenaries, crew-cut killers) in order to quash potential rivals. The country's new elite—raw, fearful, greedy, but specked with idealism—is kept constantly on edge: it is a tool in the hands of the Big Man, but a tool he has reason to fear. To the disenchanted Indian, Mahesh, "It isn't that there's no right and wrong here. There's no right." To the more patient Salim, the moral obligation of "outsiders" is to wait, be patient, try to avoid passing judgment.

Inexorably he is pushed into a kind of despair, saddened by a growing persuasion that, at least in the Big Man's country, human effort must burn itself out into waste, while ideas and ideals shrink to mere covers for power. Civilized norms are all we have to defend ourselves against ourselves, and they form, at best, a thin shield.

Beyond this, Naipaul offers no intimations of hope or signals of perspective. It may be that the reality he grapples with allows him nothing but grimness of voice. There is a complicated literary-moral problem here that cannot be solved in a few sentences, if solved at all. A novelist has to be faithful to what he sees, and few see as well as Naipaul; yet one may wonder whether, in some final reckoning, a serious writer can simply allow the wretchedness of his depicted scene to become the limit of his vision. Such novelists as Dostoyevsky, Conrad and Turgenev, also dealing with painful aspects of political life, struggled in some ways to "surmount" or "transcend" them. Naipaul seems right now to be a writer beleaguered by his own truths, unable to get past them. That is surely an honorable difficulty, far better than indulging in sentimental or ideological uplift; but it exacts a price.

I raise this question with much uneasiness, since the last thing I want to do is to badger Naipaul (a writer not easily badgered) with requests for facile tokens of "positive" belief or value. Perhaps, given the subject that grips him and the moment in which he lives, there is no choice. Perhaps we ought simply to be content that, in his austere and brilliant way, he holds fast to the bitterness before his eyes.

"Let's Do It"

The Executioner's Song by Norman Mailer
October 7, 1979

BY JOAN DIDION

I T I S O N E O F T H O S E testimonies to the tenacity of self-regard in the lit-erary life that large numbers of people remain persuaded that Norman Mailer is no better than their reading of him. They condescend to him, they dismiss his most original work in favor of the more literal and predictable rhythms of *The Armies of the Night*; they regard *The Naked and the Dead* as a promise later broken and every book since as a quick turn for his creditors, a stalling action, a spangled substitute, tarted up to deceive, for the "big book" he

cannot write. In fact he has written this "big book" at least three times now. He wrote it the first time in 1955 with *The Deer Park* and he wrote it a second time in 1965 with *An American Dream* and he wrote it a third time in 1967 with *Why Are We in Vietnam?* and now, with *The Executioner's Song,* he has probably written it a fourth.

The Executioner's Song did not suggest, in its inception, the book it became. It began as a project put together by Lawrence Schiller, the photographer and producer who several years before had contracted with Mailer to write *Marilyn,* and it was widely referred to as "the Gary Gilmore book." This "Gary Gilmore book" of Mailer's was understood in a general way to be an account of or a con-templation on the death or the life or the last nine months in the life of Gary Mark Gilmore, those nine months representing the period between the day in April of 1976 when he was released from the United States Penitentiary at Marion, Illinois, and the morning in January of 1977 on which he was executed by having four shots fired into his heart at the Utah State Prison at Point of the Mountain, Utah.

It seemed one of those lives in which the narrative would yield no further meaning. Gary Gilmore had been in and out of prison, mostly in, for 22 of his 36 years. Gary Gilmore had a highly developed kind of con style that caught the national imagination. "Unless it's a joke or something, I want to go ahead and do it," Gary Gilmore said when he refused legal efforts to reverse the jury's verdict of death on felony murder. "Let's do it," Gary Gilmore said in the moments before the hood was lowered and the muzzles of the rifles emerged from the executioner's blind.

What Mailer could make of this apparently intractable material was unclear. It might well have been only another test hole in a field he had drilled before, a few further reflections on murder as an existential act, an appropriation for himself of the book he invented for *An American Dream*, Stephen Rojack's *The Psychology of the Hangman*. Instead Mailer wrote a novel, a thousand-page novel in a meticulously limited vocabulary and a voice as flat as the horizon, a novel which takes for its incident and characters real events in the lives of real people.

I think no one but Mailer could have dared this book. The authentic Western voice, the voice heard in *The Executioner's Song*, is one heard often in life but only rarely in literature, the reason being that to truly know the West is to lack all will to write it down. The very subject of *The Executioner's Song* is that vast emptiness at the center of the Western experience, a nihilism antithetical not only to literature but to most other forms of human endeavor, a dread so close to zero that human voices fade out, trail off, like skywriting.

In a world in which every road runs into the desert or the Interstate or the Rocky Mountains, people develop a pretty precarious sense of their place in the larger scheme. People get sick for love, think they want to die for love, shoot up the town for love, and then they move away, move on, forget the face. People commit their daughters, and move to Midway Island. People get in their cars at night and drive across two states to get a beer, see about a loan on a pickup, keep from going crazy because crazy people get committed again, and can no longer get in their cars and drive across two states to get a beer.

The Executioner's Song is structured in two long symphonic movements: "Western Voices," or Book One, voices which are most strongly voices of women, and "Eastern Voices," Book Two, voices which are not literally those of Easterners but are largely those of men—the voices of the lawyers, the prosecutors, the reporters, the people who move in the larger world and believe that they can influence events. The "Western" book is a fatalistic drift, a tension, an overwhelming and passive rush toward the inevitable events that will end in Gary Gilmore's death. The "Eastern" book is the release of that tension, the resolution, the playing out of the execution, the active sequence that effectively ends on the January morning when Lawrence Schiller goes up in a six-seat plane and watches as Gary Gilmore's ashes are let loose from a plastic bag to blow over

Provo. The bag surprises Schiller. The bag is a bread bag, "with the printing from the bread company clearly on it . . . a 59-cent loaf of bread."

The women in the "Western" book are surprised by very little. They do not on the whole believe that events can be influenced. A kind of desolate wind seems to blow through the lives of these women in *The Executioner's Song*, all these women who have dealings with Gary Gilmore from the April night when he lands in town with his black plastic penitentiary shoes until the day in January when he is just ash blowing over Provo. The wind seems to blow away memory, balance. The sensation of falling is constant. Nicole Baker, still trying at 19 to "digest her life, her three marriages, her two kids, and more guys than you wanted to count," plus Gary Gilmore, plus Gary Gilmore's insistence that she meet him beyond the grave, reads a letter from Gary in prison and the words go "in and out of her head like a wind blowing off the top of the world."

These women move in and out of paying attention to events, of noticing their own fate. They seem distracted by bad dreams, by some dim apprehension of this well of dread, this "unhappiness at the bottom of things." Inside Bessie Gilmore's trailer south of the Portland city line, down a four-lane avenue of bars and eateries and discount stores and a gas station with a World War II surplus Boeing bomber fixed above the pumps, there is a sense that Bessie can describe only as "a suction-type feeling." She fears disintegration. She wonders where the houses in which she once lived have gone, she wonders about her husband being gone, her children gone, the 78 cousins she knew in Provo scattered and gone and maybe in the ground. She wonders if, when Gary goes, they would "all descend another step into that pit where they gave up searching for one another." She has no sense of "how much was her fault, and how much was the fault of the ongoing world that ground along like iron-banded wagon wheels in the prairie grass." When I read this, I remembered that the tracks made by the wagon wheels are still visible from the air over Utah, like the footprints made on the moon. This is an absolutely astonishing book.

Eudora Welty • Milan

Kundera • Philip Roth • Max Apple

Nadine Gordimer • Gabriel García Márquez • John

Updike • Garrison Keillor • Roy Blount Jr. • Cynthia Ozick

I. B. Singer • Sue Grafton • Elizabeth Bishop • Raymond

Carver • E. L. Doctorow • Edna O'Brien • Jay McInerney • Charles

Murray • Oliver Sacks • Winston Groom • John le Carré • Frank

Conroy • Bernard Malamud • Ben Yagoda • Art Spiegelman • John

Barth • Tom Wolfe • Randy Shilts • James Baldwin • Primo

Levi • Anne Tyler • Salman Rushdie • Henry Louis

Gates Jr. • Raymond Carver • Michael

Lewis • Ray Bradbury

1980s

Interview

Eudora Welty
November 2, 1980

BY ANNE TYLER

S HE LIVES IN ONE OF THOSE TOWNS that seem to have outgrown themselves overnight, sprouting—on reclaimed swampland—a profusion of modern hospitals and real estate offices, travel agencies and a Drive-Thru Beer Barn. (She can remember, she says, when Jackson, Miss., was so small that you could go on foot anywhere you wanted. On summer evenings you'd pass the neighbors' lawns scented with petunias, hear their pianos through the open windows. Everybody's life was more accessible.) And when her father, a country boy from Ohio, built his family a house back in 1925, he chose a spot near Belhaven College so he'd be sure to keep a bit of green around them, but that college has added so many parking lots, and there are so many cars whizzing by nowadays.

Still, Eudora Welty's street is shaded by tall trees. Her driveway is a sheet of pine needles, and her house is dark and cool, with high ceilings, polished floors, comfortable furniture and a wonderfully stark old kitchen. She has lived here since she was in high school (and lived in Jackson all her life). Now she is alone, the last of a family of five. She loves the house, she says, but worries that she isn't able to keep it up properly: A porch she screened with $44 from the *Southern Review*, during the Depression, needs screening once again for a price so high that she has simply closed it off. One corner of the foundation has had to be rescued from sinking into the clay, which she describes as "shifting about like an elephant's hide."

But the house seems solid and well tended, and it's clear that she has the vitality to fill its spare rooms. Every flat surface is covered with tidy stacks of books and papers. A collection of widely varied paintings—each with its own special reason for being there—hangs on wires from the picture rails. One of them is a portrait of Eudora Welty as a young woman—blond-haired, with large and luminous eyes.

Her hair is white now, and she walks with some care and wears an Ace bandage around her wrist to ease a touch of arthritis. But the eyes are still as luminous as ever, radiating kindness and . . . attention, you would have to call it; but attention of a special quality, with some gentle amusement accompanying it. When she laughs, you can see how she must have looked as a girl—shy and delighted. She will often pause in the middle of a sentence to say, "Oh, I'm just enjoying this so much!" and she does seem to be that rare kind of person who takes an active joy in small, present moments. In particular, she is pleased by *words*, by ways of saying things, snatches of dialogue overheard, objects' names discovered and properly applied. (She likes to read technical manuals and diagrams with the parts labeled. Her whole face lights up when she describes how she heard a country woman confess to a "gnawing and a craving" for something. "Wasn't that a wonderful way of putting it?" she asks. "A gnawing and a craving.")

Even in conversation, the proper word matters deeply to her and is worth a brief pause while she hunts for it. She searches for a way to describe a recent heat wave: The heat, she says, was like something waiting for you, something out to *get* you; when you climbed the stairs at night, even the stair railing felt like, oh, like warm toast. She shares my fear of merging into freeway traffic because, she says, it's like entering a round of hot-pepper in a jump-rope game: " 'Oh, well,' you think, 'maybe the next time it comes by. . . .' " (I always did know freeways reminded me of something; I just couldn't decide what it was.) And when she re-read her collected stories, some of which date back to the 1930s: "It was the strangest experience. It was like watching a negative develop, slowly coming clear before your eyes. It was like recovering a memory."

A couple of her stories, she says, she really had wished to drop from the collection, but was persuaded not to. Others, the very earliest, were written in the days before she learned to rewrite ("I didn't know you *could* rewrite"), and although she left them as they were, she has privately revised her own printed copies by hand. Still others continue to satisfy her—especially those in *The Golden Apples*—and she laughs at herself for saying how much she loves "June Recital" and "The Wanderers." But her pleasure in these stories is, I think, part and parcel of her whole attitude toward writing: She sees it as truly joyful work, as something she can hardly wait to get down to in the mornings.

Unlike most writers she imposes no schedule on herself. Instead she waits for things to "brood"—usually situations from her own life which, in time, are alchemized into something entirely different, with different characters and plots. From then on, it goes very quickly. She wakes early, has coffee and sets to work. She writes as long as she can keep at it, maybe pausing for a brief tomato sandwich at noon. (And she can tell you exactly who used to make the best tomato sandwiches in Jackson, back during her grade-school days when everybody swapped lunches. It was Frances MacWillie's grandmother, Mrs. Nannie MacWillie.)

What's written she types soon afterward; she feels that her handwriting is too intimate to re-read objectively. Then she scribbles revisions all over the manuscript, and cuts up parts of pages and pins them into different locations with dressmakers' pins—sometimes moving whole scenes, sometimes a single word.

Her favorite working time is summer, when everything is quiet and it's "too hot to go forth" and she can sit next to an open window. (The danger is that any passing friend can interrupt her: "I saw you just sitting at your typewriter. . . .")

Describing the process of writing, she is matter-of-fact. It's simply her life's work, which has occupied her for more than 40 years. She speaks with calm faith of her own instincts, and is pleased to have been blessed with a visual mind—"the best shorthand a writer can have." When she's asked who first set her on her path (this woman who has, whether she knows it or not, set so many later writers on *their* paths), she says that she doesn't believe she ever did get anything from other writers. "It's the experience of living," she says—leaving unanswered, as I suppose she must, the question of just how she, and not some next-door neighbor, mined the stuff of books from the ordinary experiences of growing up in Jackson, Miss., daughter of an insurance man and a schoolteacher; of begging her brothers to teach her golf; bicycling to the library in two petticoats so the librarian wouldn't say, "I can see straight through you," and send her home; and spending her honor roll prize—a free pass—to watch her favorite third baseman play ball.

And where (she wonders aloud) did she get the idea she was bound to succeed as a writer, sending off stories on her own as she did and promptly receiving them back? How long would she have gone on doing that?

Fortunately, she didn't have to find out. Diarmuid Russell—then just starting as a literary agent—offered to represent her. He was downright *fierce* about representing her, at one time remarking that if a certain story were rejected, the editor "ought to be horsewhipped." (It wasn't rejected.) And there were others who took a special interest in her—notably the editor John Woodburn, and Katherine Anne Porter. (Katherine Anne Porter invited her to visit. Eudora Welty was so overwhelmed that she only got there after a false start, turning back at Natchez when her courage failed.) A photo she keeps from around this period shows a party honoring the publication of her first book: a tableful of admiring editors, a heartbreakingly young Diarmuid Russell, and in their midst Eudora Welty, all dressed up and wearing a corsage and looking like a bashful, charming schoolgirl. She does not admit to belonging to a literary community, but what she means is that she was never part of a formal circle of writers. You sense, in fact, that she would be uncomfortable in a self-consciously literary environment. (Once she went to the writers' colony at Yaddo but didn't get a thing done, and spent her time attending the races and "running around with a bunch of Spaniards." She'd suspected all along, she says, that a place like that wouldn't work out for her.)

In a profession where one's resources seem likely to shrink with time (or so most writers fear), Eudora Welty is supremely indifferent to her age. She says,

1980

Lillian Hellman sues Mary McCarthy for $2.25 million after McCarthy says of Hellman, "Every word she writes is a lie, including 'and' and 'the.' "

when asked, that it does bother her a little that there's a certain depletion of physical energy—that she can't make unlimited appearances at colleges nowadays, much as she enjoys doing that, and still have anything left for writing. (Colleges keep inviting her because, she claims, "I'm so well behaved, I'm always on time and I don't get drunk or hole up in a motel with my lover.") But it's plain that her *internal* energy is as powerful as ever. In fact, she says, the trouble with publishing her collected stories is the implication that there won't be any more—and there certainly will be, she says. She takes it as a challenge.

She does not, as it turns out, go to those ladies' luncheons with the tinted cream cheese flowers that she describes so well in her stories. (I'd always wondered.) Her life in Jackson revolves around a few long-time friends, with a quiet social evening now and then—somebody's birthday party, say. Her phone rings frequently just around noon, when it's assumed that she's finished her morning's work. And one friend, an excellent cook, might drop off a dish she's prepared.

Nor is she entirely bound to Jackson. She loves to travel, and she positively glows when describing her trips. "Oh, I would hate to be confined," she says. Her only regret is that now you have to take the plane. She remembers what it was like to approach the coast of Spain by ship—to see a narrow pink band on the horizon and then hear the tinkling of bells across the water.

When she talks like this, it's difficult to remember that I'm supposed to be taking notes.

Is there anything she especially wants known about herself—anything she'd like a chance to say? Yes, she says, and she doesn't even have to think about it: She wants to express her thankfulness for all those people who helped and encouraged her so long ago. "Reading my stories over," she says, "brings back their presence. I feel that I've been very lucky."

Interview

Milan Kundera
November 30, 1980

BY PHILIP ROTH

THIS INTERVIEW IS CONDENSED from two conversations I had with Milan Kundera after reading a translated manuscript of his *Book of Laughter and Forgetting*—one conversation while he was visiting London for the first time, the other when he was on his first visit to the United States. He took these trips from France; since 1975 he and his wife have been living there as émigrés, in Rennes where he taught at the University, and now in

Paris. During our conversations, Kundera spoke sporadically in French, but mostly in Czech, and his wife Vera served as his translator and mine. A final Czech text was translated into English by Peter Kussi.

Do you think the destruction of the world is coming soon?

That depends on what you mean by the word "soon."

Tomorrow or the day after.

The feeling that the world is rushing to ruin is an ancient one.

So then we have nothing to worry about.

On the contrary. If a fear has been present in the human mind for ages, there must be something to it.

In any event, it seems to me that this concern is the background against which all the stories in your latest book take place, even those that are of a decidedly humorous nature.

If someone had told me as a boy: One day you will see your nation vanish from the world, I would have considered it nonsense, something I couldn't possibly imagine. A man knows he is mortal, but he takes it for granted that his nation possesses a kind of eternal life. But after the Russian invasion of 1968, every Czech was confronted with the thought that his nation could be quietly erased from Europe, just as over the past five decades 40 million Ukrainians have been quietly vanishing from the world without the world paying any heed. Or Lithuanians. Do you know that in the seventeenth century Lithuania was a powerful European nation? Today the Russians keep Lithuanians on their reservation like a half-extinct tribe; they are sealed off from visitors to prevent knowledge about their existence from reaching the outside. I don't know what the future holds for my own nation. It is certain that the Russians will do everything they can to dissolve it gradually into their own civilization. Nobody knows whether they will succeed. But the *possibility* is here. And the sudden realization that such a possibility exists is enough to change one's whole sense of life. Nowadays I even see Europe as fragile, mortal.

And yet, are not the fates of Eastern Europe and Western Europe radically different matters?

As a concept of cultural history, Eastern Europe is Russia, with its quite specific history anchored in the Byzantine world. Bohemia, Poland, Hungary, just like Austria have never been part of Eastern Europe. From the very beginning they have taken part in the great adventure of Western civilization, with its Gothic, its

Renaissance, its Reformation—a movement which has its cradle precisely in this region. It was here, in Central Europe, that modern culture found its greatest impulses: psychoanalysis, structuralism, dodecaphony, Bartók's music, Kafka's and Musil's new esthetics of the novel. The postwar annexation of Central Europe (or at least its major part) by Russian civilization caused Western culture to lose its vital center of gravity. It is the most significant event in the history of the West in our century, and we cannot dismiss the possibility that the end of Central Europe marked the beginning of the end for Europe as a whole.

During the Prague Spring, your novel The Joke *and your stories* Laughable Loves *were published in editions of 150,000. After the Russian invasion you were dismissed from your teaching post at the film academy and all your books were removed from the shelves of public libraries. Seven years later you and your wife tossed a few books and some clothes in the back of your car and drove off to France, where you've become one of the most widely read of foreign authors. How do you feel as an émigré?*

For a writer, the experience of living in a number of countries is an enormous boon. You can only understand the world if you see it from several sides. My latest book, which came into being in France, unfolds in a special geographic space: Those events which take place in Prague are seen through West European eyes, while what happens in France is seen through the eyes of Prague. It is an encounter of two worlds. On one side, my native country: In the course of a mere half-century, it experienced democracy, fascism, revolution, Stalinist terror as well as the disintegration of Stalinism, German and Russian occupation, mass deportations, the death of the West in its own land. It is thus sinking under the weight of history, and looks at the world with immense skepticism. On the other side, France: For centuries it was the center of the world and nowadays it is suffering from the lack of great historic events. This is why it revels in radical ideologic postures. It is the lyrical, neurotic expectation of some great deed of its own which however is not coming, and will never come.

Are you living in France as a stranger or do you feel culturally at home?

I am enormously fond of French culture and I am greatly indebted to it. Especially to the older literature. Rabelais is dearest to me of all writers. And Diderot. I love his *Jacques le fataliste* as much as I do Laurence Sterne. Those were the greatest experimenters of all time in the form of the novel. And their experiments were, so to say, amusing, full of happiness and joy, which have by now vanished from French literature and without which everything in art loses its significance. Sterne and Diderot understood the novel as a *great game*. They discovered the *humor* of the novelistic form. When I hear learned arguments that the novel has exhausted its possibilities, I have precisely the opposite feeling: In the course of its history the novel *missed* many of its possibilities. For example, impulses for the development of the novel hidden in Sterne and Diderot have not been picked up by any successors.

Your latest book is not called a novel, and yet in the text you declare: This book is a novel in the form of variations. So then—is it a novel or not?

As far as my own quite personal esthetic judgment goes, it really is a novel, but I have no wish to force this opinion on anyone. There is enormous freedom latent within the novelistic form. It is a mistake to regard a certain stereotyped structure as the inviolable essence of the novel.

Yet surely there is something which makes a novel a novel, and which limits this freedom.

A novel is a long piece of synthetic prose based on play with invented characters. These are the only limits. By the term synthetic I have in mind the novelist's desire to grasp his subject from all sides and in the fullest possible completeness. Ironic essay, novelistic narrative, autobiographical fragment, historic fact, flight of fantasy: The synthetic power of the novel is capable of combining everything into a unified whole like the voices of polyphonic music. The unity of a book need not stem from the plot, but can be provided by the theme. In my latest book, there are two such themes: laughter and forgetting.

Laughter has always been close to you. Your books provoke laughter through humor or irony. When your characters come to grief it is because they bump against a world that has lost its sense of humor.

I learned the value of humor during the time of Stalinist terror. I was 20 then. I could always recognize a person who was not a Stalinist, a person whom I needn't fear, by the way he smiled. A sense of humor was a trustworthy sign of recognition. Ever since, I have been terrified by a world that is losing its sense of humor.

In your last book, though, something else is involved. In a little parable you compare the laughter of angels with the laughter of the devil. The devil laughs because God's world seems senseless to him; the angel laughs with joy because everything in God's world has its meaning.

Yes, man uses the same physiologic manifestation—laughter—to express two different metaphysical attitudes. Someone's hat drops on the coffin in a freshly dug grave, the funeral loses its meaning and laughter is born. Two lovers race through the meadow, holding hands, laughing. Their laughter has nothing to do with jokes or humor, it is the *serious* laughter of angels expressing their joy of being. Both kinds of laughter belong among life's pleasures, but when it is carried to extremes it also denotes a dual apocalypse: the enthusiastic laughter of angel-fanatics, who are so convinced of their world's significance that they are ready to hang anyone not sharing their joy. And the other laughter, sounding from the opposite side, which proclaims that everything has become meaningless, that even funerals are ridiculous and group sex a mere comical pantomime. Human life is bounded by two chasms: fanaticism on one side, absolute skepticism on the other.

What you now call the laughter of angels is a new term for the "lyrical attitude to life" of your previous novels. In one of your books you characterize the era of Stalinist terror as the reign of the hangman and the poet.

Totalitarianism is not only hell, but also the dream of paradise—the age-old dream of a world where everybody would live in harmony, united by a single common will and faith, without secrets from one another. André Breton, too, dreamed of this paradise when he talked about the glass house in which he longed to live. If totalitarianism did not exploit these archetypes, which are deep inside us all and rooted deep in all religions, it could never attract so many people, especially during the early phases of its existence. Once the dream of paradise starts to turn into reality, however, here and there people begin to crop up who stand in its way, and so the rulers of paradise must build a little gulag on the side of Eden. In the course of time this gulag grows ever bigger and more perfect, while the adjoining paradise gets ever smaller and poorer.

In your book, the great French poet Eluard soars over paradise and gulag, singing. Is this bit of history which you mention in the book authentic?

After the war, Paul Eluard abandoned surrealism and became the greatest exponent of what I might call the "poesy of totalitarianism." He sang for brotherhood, peace, justice, better tomorrows, he sang for comradeship and against isolation, for joy and against gloom, for innocence and against cynicism. When in 1950 the rulers of paradise sentenced Eluard's Prague friend, the surrealist Závis Kalandra, to death by hanging, Eluard suppressed his personal feelings of friendship for the sake of supra-personal ideals, and publicly declared his approval of his comrade's execution. The hangman killed while the poet sang.

And not just the poet. The whole period of Stalinist terror was a period of collective lyrical delirium. This has by now been completely forgotten but it is the crux of the matter. People like to say: Revolution is beautiful, it is only the terror arising from it which is evil. But this is not true. The evil is already present in the beautiful, hell is already contained in the dream of paradise and if we wish to understand the essence of hell we must examine the essence of the paradise from which it originated. It is extremely easy to condemn gulags, but to reject the totalitarian poesy which leads to the gulag by way of paradise is as difficult as ever. Nowadays, people all over the world unequivocally reject the idea of gulags, yet they are still willing to let themselves be hypnotized by totalitarian poesy and to march to new gulags to the tune of the same lyrical song piped by Eluard when he soared over Prague like the great archangel of the lyre, while the smoke of Kalandra's body rose to the sky from the crematory chimney.

What is so characteristic of your prose is the constant confrontation of the private and the public. But not in the sense that private stories take place against a political backdrop, nor that political events encroach on private lives. Rather, you continually show that political events are governed by the same laws as private happenings, so that your prose is a kind of psychoanalysis of politics.

The metaphysics of man is the same in the private sphere as in the public one. Take the other theme of the book, forgetting. This is the great private problem of man: death as the loss of the self. But what is this self? It is the sum of everything we remember. Thus, what terrifies us about death is not the loss of the future but the loss of the past. Forgetting is a form of death ever present within life. This is the problem of my heroine, in desperately trying to preserve the vanishing memories of her beloved dead husband. But forgetting is also the great problem of politics. When a big power wants to deprive a small country of its national consciousness it uses the method of *organized forgetting*. This is what is currently happening in Bohemia. Contemporary Czech literature, insofar as it has any value at all, has not been printed for 12 years; 200 Czech writers have been proscribed, including the dead Franz Kafka; 145 Czech historians have been dismissed from their posts, history has been rewritten, monuments demolished. A nation which loses awareness of its past gradually loses its self. And so the political situation has brutally illuminated the ordinary metaphysical problem of forgetting that we face all the time, every day, without paying any attention. Politics unmasks the metaphysics of private life, private life unmasks the metaphysics of politics.

In the sixth part of your book of variations the main heroine, Tamina, reaches an island where there are only children. In the end they hound her to death. Is this a dream, a fairy tale, an allegory?

Nothing is more foreign to me than allegory, a story invented by the author in order to illustrate some thesis. Events, whether realistic or imaginary, must be significant in themselves, and the reader is meant to be naïvely seduced by their power and poetry. I have always been haunted by this image, and during one period of my life it kept recurring in my dreams: A person finds himself in a world of children, from which he cannot escape. And suddenly childhood, which we all lyricize and adore, reveals itself as pure horror. As a trap. This story is not allegory. But my book is a polyphony in which various stories mutually explain, illumine, complement each other. The basic event of the book is the story of totalitarianism, which deprives people of memory and thus retools them into a nation of children. All totalitarianisms do this. And perhaps our entire technical age does this, with its cult of the future, its cult of youth and childhood, its indifference to the past and mistrust of thought. In the midst of a relentlessly juvenile society, an adult equipped with memory and irony feels like Tamina on the isle of children.

Almost all your novels, in fact all the individual parts of your latest book, find their denouement in great scenes of coitus. Even that part which goes by the innocent name of "Mother" is but one long scene of three-way sex, with a prologue and epilogue. What does sex mean to you as a novelist?

These days, when sexuality is no longer taboo, mere description, mere sexual confession, has become noticeably boring. How dated Lawrence seems, or even Henry Miller with his lyricism of obscenity! And yet certain erotic passages of George Bataille have made a lasting impression on me. Perhaps it is because they are not lyrical but philosophic. You are right that with me everything ends in great erotic scenes. I have the feeling that a scene of physical love generates an extremely sharp light which suddenly reveals the essence of characters and sums up their life situation. The erotic scene is the focus where all the themes of the story converge and where its deepest secrets are located.

There is a certain imaginary dividing line beyond which things appear senseless and ridiculous. A person asks himself: Isn't it nonsensical for me to get up in the morning? to go to work? to strive for anything? to belong to a nation just because I was born that way? Man lives in close proximity to this boundary, and can easily find himself on the other side. That boundary exists everywhere, in all areas of human life and even in the deepest, most biological of all: sexuality. And precisely because it is the deepest region of life the question posed to sexuality is the deepest question.

A novel does not assert anything; a novel searches and poses questions. I don't know whether my nation will perish and I don't know which of my characters is right. I invent stories, confront one with another, and by this means I ask questions. The stupidity of people comes from having an answer for everything. The wisdom of the novel comes from having a question for everything. When Don Quixote went out into the world, that world turned into a mystery before his eyes. That is the legacy of the first European novel to the entire subsequent history of the novel. The novelist teaches the reader to comprehend the world as a question. There is wisdom and tolerance in that attitude. In a world built on sacrosanct certainties the novel is dead. The totalitarian world, whether founded on Marx, Islam or anything else, is a world of answers rather than questions. There, the novel has no place. In any case, it seems to me that all over the world people nowadays prefer to judge rather than to understand, to answer rather than ask, so that the voice of the novel can hardly be heard over the noisy foolishness of human certainties.

Essay

Max Apple on Learning and Loving English
March 22, 1981

I GREW UP IN THE HEYDAY of ventriloquism, when the dummy Jerry Mahoney was everyone's sweetheart. You could hardly go a day without hearing a joke about buttoning your lip or having a wooden head. On the playground of my elementary school I practiced with all my might. I kept my lips close to the chain-link fence so that if they moved I would know it by the touch of cold steel against them. My friends were doing the same.

Finally I got my dummy. An elderly cousin, moved by the seriousness of my tight-lipped practicing, sent me an expensive one, a three-foot-high Jerry Mahoney in a cowboy outfit with an embossed half-smile on his face. By the time my Jerry arrived he was too late; ventriloquism had already faded. The contestants on *The Original Amateur Hour* went back to thigh-slapping and whistling through combs. My schoolmates, too, abandoned the fence for kickball and pulling girls' hair. My dummy languished then as my wok and my food processor do now.

It took another 20 years for me to cast my voice again, this time into stories rather than dummies. It's a weak analogy, I know, and yet fiction seems sometimes like my dummy, like that part of myself that should get all the best lines. I want to be the "straight man" so that the very difference between us will be a part of the tension that I crave in each sentence, in every utterance of those wooden lips redeemed from silence because I practiced.

Yet the voice from the silence, the otherness that fiction is, doesn't need any metaphoric explanations. It's true that I tried ventriloquism, but it was my fascination with the English language itself that made me a writer. Its endless suggestiveness has carried me through many a plot, entertained me when nothing else could. If not for love of words I couldn't have managed sitting next to Wayne Bruining during lunch in eighth grade, listening to the details of his escapades as a hunter. These were not adventure stories of life in the wild, they were the drab minutiae of taxidermy. While I held an oily tuna sandwich, Wayne lectured on how to skin a squirrel. He brought pelts to school and supplied the entire class with rabbits' feet. As Wayne droned on, I wondered in all the words that were new to me if he hunted in fens, glades, moors, vales and dales. Though his subject was gory, Wayne was a good teacher. I could probably skin a squirrel based on my memory of his conversations. I imagine that Wayne is still at it somewhere deep in the Michigan woods, showing his own son how to position a dressed buck over the hood of the car and then wipe the knife clean on the outside of his trousers.

My grandmother had a word for Wayne and most of my other friends: "goyim." It explained everything: the hunting, hubcap stealing, smoking, fighting—all were universal gentile attributes. "Goy" was a flat, almost unemotional word that defined everything I was not. There was some difficulty. Grand Rapids, Mich., in the 1950s was not an East European ghetto, although my grandma did her best to blur the distinctions. The First World War and poverty had moved her from her Lithuanian village, but even 40 years in the wilderness of America did not make her learn English. She chose, above all, to avoid the language of the goyim. I told her about Wayne and everything else in Yiddish, which was the natural language of talking. I remember in kindergarten being surprised that everything happened in English. To us English was the official language, useful perhaps for legal documents and high school graduation speeches but not for everyday life.

My grandmother and I were quite a pair in the supermarket. Proud that I could read, I read all pertinent labels to her in loud Yiddish. The two of us could spend a long time in aisle four at the A & P, sorting over the differences between tomato paste and tomato sauce while all around us gentiles roamed, loading their carts with what we knew were slabs of pork and shotgun shells.

While my grandmother daydreamed in Yiddish, my grandfather worked in the American Bakery among ovens that could bake 200 loaves at once. He wore a white shirt, white trousers, a white apron and a white cap. His hair was white and fine-textured. Puffs of flour emanated from him as he walked toward me. The high baking tables, the smell of the bread, the flour floating like mist gave the bakery a kind of angelic feeling. In the front, two clerks sold the bread and customers talked in plain English. In the back, where the dough was rising, my grandpa yelled Yiddish and Polish, urging his fellow bakers to hurry. He went to the bakery long before dawn, and would sometimes work 24 hours nonstop. He was already in his 70s. Twenty-four hours he considered part-time.

He did not bake what you might think: The American Bakery was true to its name. My grandpa toiled over white bread, sticky air-filled white bread, and cookies shaped like Christmas trees, green at the edges, blood-red in the middle. He baked cakes for Polish weddings and doughnuts by the millions. My grandmother preferred store-bought baked goods. Their ghetto curses and Old World superstitions interrupted *I Love Lucy* and *The $64,000 Question*. He wished upon her a great cholera, a boil in her entrails, a solipsism deeper than despair.

My mother spent her energy running the household. My father earned our living as a scrap dealer. His work meant driving long distances in order to buy and then load upon his short-wheelbase Dodge tons of steel shavings, aluminum borings, defective machinery—anything that could eventually be melted down to a more pristine condition. I rode with him when he didn't have very far to go. I had a pair of leather mittens, my work gloves, which I wore as I strutted among the barrels of refuse at the back of factories. I touched the dirtied metals; I wanted to work the way my father did, using his strength to roll the barrels from the loading dock to the truck.

When he came home, he washed his hands with Boraxo, then drank a double shot of Seagram's Seven from a long-stemmed shot glass. I imitated him with Coke or ginger ale. He alone knew what I wanted and loved. My grandfather wanted me to be a rabbinic scholar, my grandmother thought I should own at least two stores, my sisters and my mother groomed me for a career as a lawyer or "public speaker." My father knew that I wanted to play second base for the Tigers and have a level swing like Al Kaline. I probably love and write about sports so much as a way of remembering him. I carry a baseball with me the way he carried my mittens in the glove compartment of a half-dozen trucks to remind him of his little boy who grew up to study the secrets of literature but still does not forget to check the Tigers' box score every morning of the season.

When I was not listening to the Tigers or playing baseball or basketball myself, I was reading. A tunnel under Bridge Street connected the Catholic school next to the American Bakery to the west side branch of the public library. I don't know what use the Catholic school made of the tunnel, but it was my lifeline. I would have a snack at the bakery, then move through the tunnel to reappear seconds later in that palatial library. In the high-ceilinged reading room I sat at a mahogany table. Across the street my grampa in the heat of the ovens was yelling at Joe Post in Polish and at Philip Allen in Yiddish; here the librarians whispered in English and decorated me with ribbons like a war hero just because I loved to read.

The books all in order, the smiling ladies to approve me, the smooth tables, even the maps on the wall seemed perfect to me. The marble floors of that library were the stones of heaven, my Harvard and my Yale, my refuge in the English language. What I learned from those books was indeed American Literature. Wayne Bruining skinning squirrels was too close, too ugly, too goyish. But in the reading room Huckleberry Finn and the Kid from Tomkinsville were my true buddies. I wanted to bedeck them with ribbons the way the librarians decorated me, or better yet take them through the tunnel for a quick doughnut at the bakery.

When I read *Les Misérables*, my taste changed. I checked out the book to impress the librarian with its thickness. I also liked the odd title, which I did not recognize as French. But in that sentimental overwritten novel, I recognized for the first time the deep pleasure of reading about a whole life even when that life is filled with misfortune and awful coincidence. I suffered with Jean Valjean as I had not suffered with ballplayers or space travelers. His life affected me then; it still does. As I read about Jean Valjean moving through the sewers of Paris, I too moved, four bookcases to the left—adult fiction.

When I came home from the library, I sometimes told my grandmother in Yiddish about the books. We wondered together about space travel and the speed of light and life on other planets. If there was life on other worlds she thought it was only the souls of the dead. She urged me to read less and think about someday owning my own store.

I think it was in that library that I finally came to distinguish the separateness of the Yiddish and English languages. I could speak and think in both, but reading and writing was all English. I specialized in reading and writing as if to solidify once and for all the fact that the written language was mine.

My sisters found the language through speaking. They won "I Speak for Democracy" contests; they were the Yankees and Dodgers of debate tournaments. I could barely hit my weight in Little League, but their speech trophies lined the windowsills. They stood in front of our gilded dining room mirror, speaking earnestly and judging their looks at the same time. They used their arms to gesture, they quoted *Time* magazine, their bosoms heaved. My mother stopped her chores to swoon at her lovely daughters. My grandma thought their padded bras were a clever way to keep warm. Patrick Henry himself could not have outdone the rhetoric in our dining room.

My sisters wanted it for me too, that state championship in debate that seemed automatic just because we spoke English. I resisted the temptation, just as a few years later I resisted law school. I admired my sisters before the mirror, and I too longed to understand *Time* magazine, but I didn't want to win anything with my words; I just wanted to play with them. I was already in love. Instead of debate I took printing.

I too made words, but laboriously; words composed on a "stick," with "leads" and "slugs"; words spelled out letter by letter with precise spacing; words that had to be read, not heard.

My hero was Ben Franklin. On his tombstone it said only, "Ben Franklin, Printer."

"Did he make a living?" my grandmother wanted to know.

"He made the country. He and George Washington and Alexander Hamilton, they made the whole country."

"Go on," she said, "you believe everything they tell you in school."

I did believe everything I learned, but I listened to her too. Her stories were sometimes about the very things I was studying. She had lived through the Russian Revolution. A shoemaker's daughter, she waited out the war in a house in Odessa until she could join her baker husband, already sporting two-tone shoes and a gold watch on the shores of Lake Michigan.

She had no political ideology: The Czar and the Communists were equally barbarous in her eyes. Once, though, she did hide a young Jew pursued by the Czar's police. It was my favorite story. To me that young Russian became Trotsky himself, hiding for half an hour among my grandmother's wedding aprons, featherbeds, long-sleeved dresses and thick combs—the very objects I hid among in our Michigan attic.

My grandmother didn't care about Trotsky or Ben Franklin, only about her grandson, who she thought was making a mistake by becoming a scribe rather than a merchant. Only shortly before she died did I convince her that being a scribe was not my intention: "I make things up. I don't just copy them."

"I've been doing that all my life," she told me. "Everyone can do that."

In a way she was right; making things up is not very difficult. The difficulty is getting the sentences to sound exactly right. I have been working at that for as long as I've known what a sentence is. Those early years of rapturous reading were training, the best training, I think, though I also admit to eavesdropping, listening to gossip, and the interpretation of insignificant looks and gestures. I do all of this because memory alone is not enough to feed sentences always hungry for detail. I have to fill in gaps, make things up, sometimes even change the memories. I was in my late 20s before I got all the sentences right in a single story.

I would still prefer to be the ventriloquist—to let the words come from a smiling dummy—but I'm not good enough at buttoning my lip. An awkward, hesitant, clumsy sentence emerges. I nurse it, love it in all its distress. I see in it the hope of an entire narrative, the suggestion of the fullness of time. I write a second sentence, and then I cross that first one out as if it never existed. This infidelity is rhythm, voice, finally style itself. It is a truth more profound to me than meaning, which is always elusive and perhaps belongs more to the reader.

Jacob wrestled with angels and I with sentences. There's a big difference, I know. Still, to me they are angels, this crowd of syllables. My great-uncle, who came from the Russian army in 1909 straight to the American West, told me he never had to really learn English. "I knew Russian," he said. "English was just like it." He bought horses, cattle, land. He lived 90 years, and when he died he left me his floor safe, which sits now, all 980 pounds, alongside me in the room where I write. My 8-year-old daughter knows the combination, but there is nothing inside.

I don't know if that's a trope too, that safe that comforts me almost as if there was a way to be safe. There is no safety: not for my uncle, not for my sentences so quickly guillotined, not for me either. Yet I wish for the security of exact words, the security I knew as a 4-year-old reciting the Gettysburg Address at patriotic assemblies in the Turner School Auditorium.

I learned the Gettysburg Address from a book of great American documents that my father turned up in the scrap. It was a true found poem; Lincoln's cadences thrilled me long before I knew what they meant. Abe Lincoln was as anonymous as that Russian hiding in my grandmother's boudoir, but I could say his words, say them in English, in American. My parents coached me in Yiddish. I know that they wanted me to be an American, to recite "Fourscore and seven years ago" in order to prove beyond a doubt that I was an insider to this new lingo—to prove that our whole family understood, through my words, that somehow we had arrived, featherbeds and all, to live next door to squirrel skinners.

Perhaps my grandmother was right: A store or two or even a law office makes a lot more sense than a love affair with words. At least in a business your goods and services are all there, all out in the open, and most of the time you even see your customers. To confront them and know what you're selling—those are pleasures the writer rarely knows. Believe me, reader, I would like to know you; most of the time I am just like you, curled up on the sofa hoping not to be distracted, ready to enter someone else's fabric of words just as you are now in mine.

Across the room from me my great-uncle's safe is stuck half-open. My son's tiny socks lie beside it, my daughter's lovely drawing of a horse, the sky, a cloud and a flower. I wish I could tell you more, and I will perhaps in stories and novels. There I'll tell you more than I know. There I'll conjure lives far richer than mine, which is so pedestrian that it would make you seem heroic were you here beside me. Take comfort, though, in these sentences. They came all the way from Odessa at the very least, and have been waiting a long time. To you they're entertainment, to me breath.

White Flight

July's People by Nadine Gordimer
June 7, 1981

BY ANNE TYLER

BAM AND MAUREEN SMALES, middle-class white liberals from Johannesburg, South Africa, begin their day with a tea tray carried in by their black manservant, July. However, there's something wrong here. The tea is served in two cheap glass cups, along with a jaggedly opened tin of milk. The door at which July knocks is only an aperture in the thick mud wall of an African hut.

The Smaleses are people who have overstayed. Extensions of Nadine Gordimer's earlier characters—those uneasy, conscience-stricken whites at-

tempting to come to terms with the ambiguities of South African life—they find themselves face to face with the ultimate: total revolution. The time is the very near future, when rioting blacks have taken over the country. Airports are being bombed, and whites cannot leave. Bam and Maureen, with their three young children, have no choice but to flee to July's isolated village.

On a superficial level, this is a wonderful adventure story. It has the ingenuity and suspense of *Robinson Crusoe*, the wry twists of

The Admirable Crichton. The Smaleses, whose hastily packed baggage includes a gadget for removing dry cleaners' tags without damaging the fingernails, are forced to adapt to a life of weed gathering and mealie cooking, of shivering in a rainstorm while the hut walls grow sodden and flying cockroaches zip through the dark. The clay vessels of the sort that Maureen used to collect as ornaments are now her kitchen utensils.

On a deeper level, of course, *July's People* is much more than another survival story; and this level succeeds so extraordinarily because of the Smaleses' liberalism. It would have been too easy to make them racists, who finally see the light while roughing it with the natives. Instead, they are from the outset sensitive, politically aware, genuinely concerned with the welfare of black South Africans. How ironic, then, is their discovery that even in the underbrush, reactionaries exist! And how much subtler and more complicated is the hostility that develops between Maureen and July! In a scene with July that's especially affecting because it takes place in another language—a language she doesn't speak—Maureen perceives the truth: For July "to be intelligent, honest, dignified for *her* was nothing; his measure as a man was taken elsewhere and by others. She was not his mother, his wife, his sister, his friend, his people."

Nadine Gordimer has always been an admirable writer, combining skill with social conscience; but here she has outdone herself. *July's People* demonstrates with breathtaking clarity the tensions and complex interdependencies between whites and blacks in South Africa. It is so flawlessly written that every one of its events seems chillingly, ominously possible.

Essay

Gabriel García Márquez on Hemingway
July 26, 1981

I RECOGNIZED HIM IMMEDIATELY, passing with his wife Mary Welsh on the Boulevard St. Michel in Paris one rainy spring day in 1957. He walked on the other side of the street, in the direction of the Luxembourg Gardens, wearing a very worn pair of cowboy pants, a plaid shirt and a ballplayer's cap. The only thing that didn't look as if it belonged to him was a pair of metal-rimmed glasses, tiny and round, which gave him a premature grandfatherly air. He had turned 59, and he was large and almost too visible, but he didn't give the impression of brutal strength that he undoubtedly wished to, because his hips were narrow and his legs looked a little emaciated above his coarse lumberjack shoes. He looked so alive amid the secondhand bookstalls and the youthful torrent from the Sorbonne that it was impossible to imagine he had but four years left to live.

For a fraction of a second, as always seemed to be the case, I found myself divided between my two competing roles. I didn't know whether to ask him for an interview or cross the avenue to express my unqualified admiration for him. But with either proposition, I faced the same great inconvenience. At the time, I spoke the same rudimentary English that I still speak now, and I wasn't very sure about his bullfighter's Spanish. And so I didn't do either of the things that could have spoiled that moment, but instead cupped both hands over my mouth and, like Tarzan in the jungle, yelled from one sidewalk to the other: "Maaaeeestro!"

Ernest Hemingway understood that there could be no other master amid the multitude of students, and he turned, raised his hand and shouted to me in Castillian in a very childish voice, "Adióoos, amigo!" It was the only time I saw him.

At the time, I was a 28-year-old newspaperman with a published novel and a literary prize in Colombia, but I was adrift and without direction in Paris. My great masters were the two North American novelists who seemed to have the least in common. I had read everything they had published until then, but not as complementary reading—rather, just the opposite, as two distinct and almost mutually exclusive forms of conceiving of literature. One of them was William Faulkner, whom I had never laid eyes on and whom I could only imagine as the farmer in shirtsleeves scratching his arm beside two little white dogs in the celebrated portrait of him taken by Cartier-Bresson. The other was the ephemeral man who had just said goodbye to me from across the street, leaving me with the impression that something had happened in my life, and had happened for all time.

I don't know who said that novelists read the novels of others only to figure out how they are written. I believe it's true. We aren't satisfied with the secrets exposed on the surface of the page: we turn the book around to find the seams. In a way that's impossible to explain, we break the book down to its essential parts and then put it back together after we understand the mysteries of its personal clockwork. The effort is disheartening in Faulkner's books, because he doesn't seem to have an organic system of writing, but instead walks blindly through his biblical universe, like a herd of goats loosed in a shop full of crystal. Managing to dismantle a page of his, one has the impression of springs and screws left over, that it's impossible to put back together in its original state. Hemingway, by contrast, with less inspiration, with less passion and less craziness but with a splendid severity, left the screws fully exposed, as they are on freight cars. Maybe for that reason Faulkner is a writer who has had much to do with my soul, but Hemingway is the one who had the most to do with my craft—not simply for his books, but for his astounding knowledge of the aspect of craftsmanship in the science of writing. In his historic interview with George Plimpton in *The Paris Review*, he showed for all time—contrary to the Romantic notion of creativity—that economic comfort and good health are conducive to writing; that one of the chief difficulties is arranging the words well; that when writing becomes hard it is good to reread one's own books, in order to remember that it always was hard; that one can write anywhere so long as there are no visitors and no telephone; and that it is not true that journalism finishes off a writer, as has so often been said—rather, just the opposite, so long as one leaves it behind soon enough. "Once writing has become the principal vice and the greatest pleasure," he said, "only death can put an end to it." Finally, his lesson was the discovery that each day's work should only be interrupted when one knows where to begin again the next day. I don't think that any more useful advice has ever been given about writing. It is, no more and no less, the absolute remedy for the most terrible specter of writers: the morning agony of facing the blank page.

All of Hemingway's work shows that his spirit was brilliant but short-lived. And it is understandable. An internal tension like his, subjected to such a severe dominance of technique, can't be sustained within the vast and hazardous reaches of a novel. It was his nature, and his error was to try to exceed his own splendid limits. And that is why everything superfluous is more noticeable in him than in other writers. His novels are like short stories that are out of proportion, that include too much. In contrast, the best thing about his stories is that they give the impression something is missing, and this is precisely what confers their mystery and their beauty. Jorge Luis Borges, who is one of the great writers of our time, has the same limits, but has had the sense not to try to surpass them.

Francis Macomber's single shot at the lion demonstrates a great deal as a lesson in hunting, but also as a summation of the science of writing. In one of his stories, Hemingway wrote that a bull from Liria, after brushing past the chest of the matador, returned like "a cat turning a corner." I believe, in all humility, that that observation is one of those inspired bits of foolishness which come only from the most magnificent writers. Hemingway's work is full of such simple and dazzling discoveries, which reveal the point at which he adjusted his definition of literary writing: that, like an iceberg, it is only well grounded if it is supported below by seven-eighths of its volume.

That consciousness of technique is unquestionably the reason Hemingway won't achieve glory with his novels, but will with his more disciplined short stories. Talking of *For Whom the Bell Tolls*, he said that he had no preconceived plan for constructing the book, but rather invented it each day as he went along. He didn't have to say it: it's obvious. In contrast, his instantaneously inspired short stories are unassailable. Like the three he wrote one May afternoon in a Madrid pension, when a snowstorm forced the cancellation of a bullfight at the feast of San Isidro. Those stories, as he himself told George Plimpton, were "The Killers," "Ten Indians" and "Today Is Friday," and all three are magisterial. Along those lines, for my taste, the story in which his powers are most compressed is one of his shortest ones, "Cat in the Rain."

Nevertheless, even if it appears to be a mockery of his own fate, it seems to me that his most charming and human work is his least successful one: *Across the River and into the Trees*. It is, as he himself revealed, something that began as a story and went astray into the mangrove jungle of a novel. It is hard to understand so many structural cracks and so many errors of literary mechanics in such a wise technician—and dialogue so artificial, even contrived, in one of the most brilliant goldsmiths in the history of letters. When the book was published in 1950, the criticism was fierce but misguided. Hemingway felt wounded where he hurt most, and he defended himself from Havana, sending a passionate telegram that seemed undignified for an author of his stature. Not only was it his best novel, it was also his most personal, for he had written it at the dawn of an uncertain autumn, with nostalgia for the irretrievable years already lived and a poignant premonition of the few years he had left to live. In none of his books did he leave much of himself, nor did he find—with all the beauty and all the tenderness—a way to give form to the essential sentiment of his work and his life: the uselessness of victory. The death of his protagonist, ostensibly so peaceful and natural, was the disguised prefiguration of his own suicide.

When one lives for so long with a writer's work, and with such intensity and affection, one is left without a way of separating fiction from reality. I have spent many hours of many days reading in that café in the Place St. Michel that he considered good for writing because it seemed pleasant, warm, clean and friendly, and I have always hoped to find once again the girl he saw enter one wild, cold, blowing day, a girl who was very pretty and fresh-looking, with her hair cut diagonally across her face like a crow's wing. "You belong to me and Paris belongs to me," he wrote for her, with that relentless power of appropriation that his writing had. Everything he described, every instant that was his, belongs to him forever. I can't pass by No. 12 Rue de l'Odéon in Paris without seeing him in conversation with Sylvia Beach, in a bookstore that is now no longer the same, killing time until six in the evening, when James Joyce might happen to drop by. On the Kenya prairie, seeing them only once, he became the owner of his buffaloes and his lions, and of the most intimate secrets of hunting. He became the owner of bullfighters and prizefighters, of artists and gunmen who existed only for an instant while they became his. Italy, Spain, Cuba—half the world is filled with the places that he appropriated simply by mentioning them. In Cojimar, a little village near Havana where the solitary fisherman of *The Old Man and the Sea* lived, there is a plaque commemorating his heroic exploits, with a gilded bust of Hemingway. In Finca de la Vigía, his Cuban refuge, where he lived until shortly before his death, the house remains intact amid the shady trees, with his diverse collection of books, his hunting trophies, his writing lectern, his enormous dead man's shoes, the countless trinkets of life from all over the world that were his until his death, and that go on living without him, with the soul he gave them by the mere magic of his owning them.

Some years ago, I got into the car of Fidel Castro—who is a tenacious reader of literature—and on the seat I saw a small book bound in red leather. "It's my master Hemingway," Fidel Castro told me. Really, Hemingway continues to be where one least expects to find him—20 years after his death—as enduring yet ephemeral as on that morning, perhaps in May, when he said "Goodbye, amigo" from across the Boulevard St. Michel.

Interview

John Updike
September 27, 1981

S OME YEARS AGO, on the occasion of the publication of *Rabbit Redux*, John Updike was interviewed for *The Book Review* by Henry Bech—critic, aspiring author and hero of Mr. Updike's novel, *Bech: A Book*. Mr. Updike has consented to sit for another talk with his creation on the subject of his new novel.

In the 10 years since your hypothetical interviewer bearded the beardless Updike in his Ipswich (Mass.) den, the skittish author has moved some miles inland, to a town without qualities called Georgetown—a nexus of route numbers on the edge of that New England hinterland best known for its bygone Indian massacres. As if to announce his willingness to assume the mothballed mantle of Sinclair Lewis, Updike lives on Main Street. He works, if that is the word, in a former antique shop now crammed with editions of his 20-odd books in 20-odd languages, including Finnish, Serbo-Croatian, Hebrew and Korean. The years have not been terrifically unkind to him; trembling on the verge of 50, he has retained his figure, which is that of a pot-bellied ectomorph, and his hair, which if not quite silvery is certainly pewter. His complexion has not improved during the Me Decade, and his stammer has grown worse. He gives the impression, reciting his responses into the tape recorder with many a fidget and static pause, of a word processor with some slipped bits; the effort, one feels, of visualizing every utterance in print has somewhat dimpled the flow of language within him, and cast him like a gasping crab onto one dry bank of the onrushing human orality alongside of which literature is just so many irrigation ditches.

However, he is most at home among his own characters, and therefore appeared relatively relaxed with me. I confessed that I had not, due to press of other business, made much headway into his new novel, concerning the adventures of another old friend, Harold C. Angstrom, of Brewer, Pa. I reminded him, though, that at our last interview he had promised that the sequel to *Rabbit Redux* would be, in 10 years, a volume entitled "Rural Rabbit," to be then followed, in 1991, with *Rabbit Is Rich*. Updike squirmed and, making sure that the tape recorder was running, stiffly dictated:

Well, this novel really has "Rural Rabbit" in it, since he keeps going out into the country to spy on this girl he thinks might be his daughter. Ever since his girl baby drowned in *Rabbit, Run*, Harry has been looking for a daughter. It's the theme that has been pressing forward, without my willing it or understanding it exactly, through these novels.

(primly) Please, let's not give the plot away. Or do the work of that third, who is among us.
(spooked) Who? Who's that? (He darts his scum-green eyes all around the memorabilia-choked shelves of his atelier, genuinely alarmed.)

The author of the review with which this interview must appear in tandem, and with whose silent voice we are singing a curious duet, perhaps in grotesque disharmony.
(whispering) Can he hear us?

He or she. I doubt it. Reviewers don't read more than they have to. Anyway, what matters surely is the book itself, in its final thumb-worn library state, stripped of its jacket of publicity and passing financial trauma, a mysterious cloth and paper casket waiting to be broken open by the trumpet call of an unknown reader's mind. All else is dross.
You've taken the words right out of my mouth.

I know you pretty well. Your theme, in this latest artifact in your habitual 10-point Janson, is inflation, am I correct?
Yes, and the trouble with inflation as a theme is that inflation overtakes it. The book was inspired by my sense of outrage at paying 99 cents a gallon for gasoline, and now that would be a bargain. Harry is meant to feel rich, but the income I assigned him as of 1979 will within a few years drop him below the poverty line. I fear my sense of the dollar is hopelessly retrograde; I live in a world where you can still buy two sparrows for a farthing. The very price of this novel—who can afford it? My first novel not 22 years ago sold for $3.50, and that seemed a lot to ask. There is a terror to all this.

(in Bech's best psychoanalytical manner) Let's talk about that.
Oh, Lordy. The terror of launching yourself into the blank paper. A writer hang-glides all the time, out over that terrible whiteness. The abyss is you, your own life, your mind. It's a terrifying thing to exist at all, and an author with every

creation tries to exist twice over; it is as when in poker you try to bluff a nothing hand through, and the dark face opposite raises, so you raise him back. And the bookstores—there's terror there, especially this time of year, all those bright books of life fighting it out in their armor of embossed lettering, stacks of them being carted out to make room for the fresh contenders, all these sensibilities the educational system is churning out, dying to describe their parents, their seductions, they keep coming, wave upon wave, and the old sensibilities won't even die off, modern medicine is too good. Who can even spot a trend anymore? Whatever happened to Black Humor, to the Imperial Novel? We live in a coral reef, smothered in a glut of self-regard. And the reviews? There's terror for you, all those muddy paws, even the ones trying to give you a pat.

Yet you yourself are a reviewer.

(holding up his muddy paws) Mea culpa. Print is guilt. Life is guilt. I believe it.

(smoothly) And take considerable satisfaction in it, it would appear.

I've been lucky. My heroes tend to be lucky. But as long as there is one unlucky person in the world, life is grim.

And writing?

Makes it less so. I cannot do justice to the bliss that attends getting even a single string of dialogue or the name of a weed right. Naming our weeds, in fact, seems to be exactly where it's at. I've been going out into my acre here (gestures toward a scruffy meadow visible from his windows) and trying to identify the wildflowers along the fringes with the aid of a book, and it's remarkably difficult to match reality and diagram. Reality keeps a pace or two ahead, scribble though we will. If you were to ask me what the aim of my fiction is—

I will. I do.

It's bringing the corners forward. Or throwing light into them, if you'd rather. Singing the hitherto unsung. That's applied democracy, in my book. And applied Christianity, for that matter. I distrust books involving spectacular people, or spectacular events. Let *People* and *The National Enquirer* pander to our taste for the extraordinary; let literature concern itself, as the Gospels do, with the inner lives of hidden men. The collective consciousness that once found itself in the noble must now rest content with the typical.

You've taken the words right out of my mouth.

I've been through a lot of interviews.

Yet you say you dislike them.

I don't dislike the spouting off, the conjuring up of opinions. That's show biz, and you don't go into this business without a touch of ham. But as a practitioner trying to keep practicing in an age of publicity, I can only decry the drain on the brain, the assumption that a writer is a mass of opinions to be trucked in and carted off for his annual six minutes on the pan-American talk show. He is not; he is a secreter of images, some of which he prays will have the immortal resonance of Don Quixote's windmills, of Proust's madeleine, of Huck Finn's raft. As a secreter he must be at heart secret, patient, wicked even. His duty is, in a sense, to turn his back. This is not easy to understand in an era when everybody says "Have a nice day" and even two o'clock in the morning is lit by the phosphorescent glow of money going rotten.

Has the writer's condition changed, do you think, in the 20-odd years since you took up a pen with a professional purpose?

When I began to write, publishers were gentlemen in tweed jackets puffing pipes. Now the only one who looks like that is Hugh Hefner. Publishing houses are owned by oil companies or their cat's-paws, and their interest is naturally in the big strike, the gusher. I don't want to write gushers. I want to write books that are hard and curvy, like keys, and that unlock the traffic jam in everybody's head. Something like $E = mc^2$, only in words, one after the other.

And speaking of after the other, what can you tell us about the "Rabbit" book to follow this in 10 years?

Nothing, except that I hope it exists. I hope, that is, that both Harry and I survive the decade. I have ominous feelings about the '80s, and it's not just Orwell's book. North America has been by and large an unmolested continent for over a century, and there is a possible perspective from which the postwar decades, decry them though we have, will look as halcyon as the summer of 1914. However, I will hope for the best, and hope to rendezvous with my ex-basketball player and fellow pilgrim one more time, proving that two plus two equals four.

And in the meantime?

I have dreams, I have corners picked out for a web or two. I always am trying to relearn my job, taking into sober account the reproaches of friend and enemy alike and seeking out the great exemplars. I've been reading the late Melville lately, to see what went wrong, if anything. A wonderful man he was, refusing all his life to call the puzzle solved. Let me quote: "Yea and Nay— / Each hath his say; / But God He keeps the middle way."

(getting down to business) Now I have here a number of more specific and personal questions which

Tape Recorder: Click.

First Impressions

Happy to Be Here by Garrison Keillor
February 28, 1982

BY ROY BLOUNT JR.

IT MAY WELL BE, as a recent reviewer asserted, that "Donald Barthelme's manner represents a kind of culmination of national humor." Barthelme may have refined American cheek to the point that no known tongue can turn another corner in it. But there is one humor writer who, although lighter (I guess the word is) than Barthelme, also attains the sublime. At this point I recommend that the reader throw away this review and pick up Garrison Keillor's first collection of pieces, *Happy to Be Here*.

In 1933, wrote James Thurber, a humorist tended to be plagued by "the suspicion that a piece he was working on for two long days was done much better and probably more quickly by Robert Benchley in 1924." Today, a humorist may feel that way about Keillor. Like Benchley's, Keillor's best stuff is clean (in the sense that lines are clean), down to earth, exquisitely good-hearted, highly ludicrous and as labored as nitrous oxide. His stuff is more cerebral than Benchley's, though, and spiritually more interesting, and . . . even harder to describe.

Keillor's stuff is calmly, acrobatically droll, yet makes no bones about its fondness for decency and its distaste for bullies. Keillor's sympathy goes out readily, but his feet are on the ground. In one of his several baseball pieces the new manager of a losing team observes: "It seemed pointless to berate players for mistakes that stemmed from deep-seated attitudes, to tell them to respond to grounders logically and not emotionally." Another one, "Attitude," speaks of how exactly to "spit the expert spit of a veteran ballplayer" after being forgiven a dumb play, and reaches this conclusion: "This is ball, ladies and gentlemen. This is what it's all about."

The way Keillor plays is ball. But not just sportive. "The Drunkard's Sunday" is downright grave, but redemptive in the way of high comedy. And the book's last sentence, given all that has come before, is brave and moving in the spirit of Dickens.

Letter

Cynthia Ozick
February 28, 1982

L ESLIE EPSTEIN, arguing for "the kind of resolution we rightly demand from imaginative fiction" in his review of *Levitation* complains that in my stories "the game is no longer being played by the rules of fiction. Probability, necessity, recognizable human feelings are replaced by the laws of what can only be called mystical vision."

Who keeps the tablets whereon this "right demand" is graven? Where abides the omniscience charging us with these "rules of fiction"? One longs to cry out: Leslie Epstein! Why do you willfully seek to bind imagination and dictate where it may or may not turn?

One of the oldest and profoundest tales is precisely about the unraveling of a resolution rightly demanded. Abraham has just bound Isaac for an offering, and we are set up for recognizable human feelings: a father's tragic bereavement. Instead, something quirky happens, breaking all the rules of probability and necessity. An angel—a mystical vision?—puts a ram in a thicket. Isaac lives; in a flash the resolution rightly demanded is thwarted. Plausibility, foreseeable emotions, reasonable presumptions, above all the sanity and focus of the narrative—everything has been shattered, scattered, stunned and shunned by an act of the liberating imagination. The story has taken a jarring turn, and the world is reborn free of human sacrifice and—as a model for all stories ever afterward—freed from the bondage of pious expectation.

Leslie Epstein! Undo your blasphemy! Revoke your impertinence! If God Himself allowed the First Plot to walk away from its script for the sake of an original thought, who are you to insist on the binding, hand and foot, of narrative freedom?

Nice Jewish Demons

Collected Stories of I. B. Singer
March 21, 1982

BY CYNTHIA OZICK

S OME TIME AGO, when Isaac Bashevis Singer first mounted the public platform to speak in English, he was asked whether he really believed in *sheydim*—in imps and demons, ghosts and spirits. The response, partly a skip and partly a glint, followed considerable playful pondering and ended in a long shrug: "Yes and no." The rebuke of an imp guarding secrets, one might judge—but surely a lesser imp, capable mainly of smaller mischiefs: the knotting of elflocks in the audience's hair, perhaps.

Years pass; the astonishing stories accumulate; the great Nobel is almost upon Singer, and the question reliably recurs. Now the answer is direct and speedy: "Yes, I believe there are unknown forces." This is no longer the voice of a teasing imp. Never mind that its tone clearly belongs to a seasoned celebrity who can negotiate a Question Period with a certain shameless readiness; it is also a deliberate leaning into the wind of some powerful dark wing, fearsomely descried.

Whether the majesty of the Nobel Prize in Literature has since altered Singer's manipulation of this essential question, I do not know. Nevertheless the question remains central, though not quite so guileless as it appears. Should we believe that Singer believes in the uncanny and the preternatural? Is there ever a trustworthy moment when a storymonger is not making things up, especially about his own substance and sources? Doesn't an antic fancy devoted to cataloguing folly always trifle with earnest expectation? And what are we to think of the goblin cunning of a man who has taken his mother's name—Bashevis (i.e., Bathsheba)—to mark out the middle of his own? Singer's readers in Yiddish call him, simply, "Bashevis." A sentimental nom de plume? His is anything but a nostalgic imagination. Does the taking on of "Bashevis" imply a man wishing to be a woman? Or does it mean that a woman is hiding inside a man? Or does Singer hope somehow to entangle his own passions in one of literature's lewdest and nastiest plots: King David's crafty devisings concerning the original Bathsheba? Or does he dream of attracting to himself the engendering powers of his mother's soul through the assumption of her name? Given the witness of the tales themselves, we are obliged to suspect any or all of these notions, as well as others we have not the wit or fantasy to conjure up.

On one flank Singer is a trickster, a prankster, a Loki, a Puck. His themes are lust, greed, pride, obsession, misfortune, unreason, the oceanic surprises of the mind's underside, the fiery cauldron of the self, the assaults of time and place. His stories offer no "epiphanies" and no pious resolutions; no linguistic circumscriptions or Hemingwayesque self-deprivations. Their plenitudes chiefly serve undefended curiosity, the gossip's lure of what comes next. Singer's stories have plots that unravel not because they are "old-fashioned"—they are mostly originals and have few recognizable modes other than their own—but because they contain the whole human world of affliction, error, quagmire, pain, calamity, catastrophe, woe. Things happen; life is an ambush, a snare; one's fate can never be predicted. His driven mercurial processions of predicaments and transmogrifications are limitless, often stupendous. There are whole fistfuls of masterpieces in this one volume: a cornucopia of invention.

Because he cracks open decorum to find lust, because he peers through convention into the pit of fear, Singer has in the past been condemned by other Yiddish writers outraged by his seemingly pagan matter, his superstitious villagers, his daring leaps into gnostic furies. The moral grain of Jewish feeling that irradiates the mainstream aspirations of Yiddish literature has always been a kind of organic extension of Talmudic ethical ideals: family devotion, community probity, *derekh erets*—self-respect and respect for others—the stringent expectations of high public civility and indefatigable integrity, the dream of messianic betterment. In Singer, much of this seems absent or overlooked or simply mocked; it is as if he has willed the crashing down of traditional Jewish sanity and sensibility. As a result, in Yiddish literary circles he is sometimes viewed as—it is the title of one of these stories—"The Betrayer of Israel."

In fact, he betrays nothing and no one, least of all Jewish idealism. That is the meaning of his imps and demons: that human character, left to itself, is drawn to cleanliness of heart; that human motivation, on its own, is attracted to clarity and valor. Here is Singer's other flank, and it is the broader one. The goblin cunning leads straight to this; Singer is a moralist. He tells us that it is natural to be good, and unholy to go astray. It is the inhuman, the antihuman, forces that are to blame for harms and sorrows. Surely these imps must be believed in; they may have the telltale feet of geese, like Satan their sire, but their difficult, shaming, lubricious urges are terrestrially familiar. Yet however lamentably known they are, Singer's demons are intruders, invaders, no true or welcome part of ourselves. They are "psychology"; and history; and terror; above all, obsessive will. If he believes in them, so, unwillingly but genuinely, do we.

And to understand Singer's imps is to correct another misapprehension: that he is the recorder of a lost world, the preserver of a vanished sociology. Singer is an artist and transcendent inventor, not a curator. His tales—though dense with the dailiness of a God-covenanted culture, its folkways, its rounded sufficiency, especially the rich intensities of the yeshiva and its bottomless studies—are in no way documents. The Jewish townlets that truly were are only seeds for his febrile conflagrations: Where, outside of peevish imagination, can one come on the protagonist of "Henne Fire," a living firebrand, a spitfire burning up with spite, who ultimately, through the spontaneous combustion of pure fury, collapses into "one piece of coal"? Though every doorstep might be described, and every feature of a head catalogued (and Singer's portraits are brilliantly particularized), parables and fables are no more tied to real places and faces than Aesop's beasts are beasts.

This is not to say that Singer's stories do not mourn those murdered Jewish townlets of Poland, every single one of which, with nearly every inhabitant, was destroyed by the lords and drones of the Nazi Gehenna. This volume includes a masterly memorial to that destruction, the brokenhearted testimony of "The Last Demon," which begins emphatically with a judgment on Europe: "I, a demon, bear witness that there are no more demons left. Why demons, when man himself is a demon?"

In Singer the demons are rarely stilled. In "The Unseen," a prosperous and decent husband runs off with a lusty maidservant at the urging of a demon; he ends in destitution, a hidden beggar tended by his remarried wife. "The Gentleman from Cracow" corrupts a whole town with gold; he turns out to be Ketev Mriri, Satan himself. In "The Destruction of Kreshev," a scholar who is a secret Sabbatean and devil worshiper induces his wife to commit adultery with a Pan-like coachman. Elsewhere, excessive intellectual passion destroys genius. Character and motive are turned inside out at the bidding of imps who shove, snarl, seduce, bribe, cajole. Allure ends in rot; lure becomes punishment.

This phantasmagorical universe of ordeal and mutation and shock is, finally, as intimately persuasive as logic itself. There is no fantasy in it. It is the true world we know, where we have come to expect anguish as the consequence of our own inspirations, where we crash up against the very circumstance from which we had always imagined we were exempt. In this true world, suffering is endemic and few are forgiven. Yet it may be that for Singer the concrete presence of the unholy attests the hovering redemptive holy, whose incandescence can scatter demons. "Yes, I believe in unknown forces."

First Impressions

"A" Is for Alibi by Sue Grafton
May 23, 1982

BY NEWGATE CALLENDAR

MEET A NEW PRIVATE EYE—Kinsey Millhone. Locale, California, near Los Angeles. Sex, female. Integrity, high. Previous marriages, two; currently single. She appears in "A" Is for Alibi by Sue Grafton. She's already scheduled to appear again in "B" Is for Burglar.

Will the series take hold? This first book is competent enough, but not particularly original. Miss Grafton uses deliberately flat prose in an effort at realism. Kinsey Millhone, not a very interesting woman, is a cliché-ridden character representing the loneliness and alienation of her male counterparts.

In Alibi, Millhone is hired to clear a woman who is serving time for murder. The trail is eight years old, but it will take a very dull reader not to figure out who the villain is, though Miss Grafton does introduce a surprise en route. What is basically wrong with the book is that the writing lacks real flair. It is no better or no worse than the majority of related books, and that is about all.

Morality and Invention

The Complete Poems: 1927–1979 by Elizabeth Bishop
February 27, 1983

BY DAVID BROMWICH

ELIZABETH BISHOP'S steadily widening audience and her endurance among the readers she has once claimed are the reward of constancy to an ideal object. Her reputation is founded on perhaps 25 poems, among them "Love Lies Sleeping," "The Unbeliever," "The Shampoo," "Over 2,000 Illustrations and a Complete Concordance," "Arrival at Santos" and "First Death in Nova Scotia." Altogether that looks like a modest achievement until one considers that most of the larger poetic reputations of the past century have been founded on similar evidence. The difference is that Bishop's masterpieces stand in a higher ratio to her work as a whole.

Throughout her career Bishop aimed to bring morality and invention together in a single thought. One can feel this especially in "The Weed," with its Herbert-like meditation on the birth of a new feeling; in "The Armadillo," which shows the complicity of esthetic pleasures in any grand spectacle, even a scene of suffering; in "Roosters" and "The Fish," those guilty and strangely conciliatory professions of human strength.

In four poems above all—"The Map," "The Monument," "At the Fishhouses" and "The End of March"—Bishop announced her task as a poet and confirmed her dedication to it. Varied as they are, these poems have the authority of self-portraits, and they depict her, poignantly at times but always masterfully, as a creator of more than secondary imaginings. Her errors, or wanderings from fact, have for her the finality of fact, and her wish is to make a reader see them that way.

From her very first poems, Bishop's fascination for travel was an interest in seeing the place the map told of, the "lion sun" that you meet after turning away from a dream house "littered with correspondences." She speaks too of the dangers of travel for those nourished on art: The title of "Brazil, January 1, 1502" alludes to the landing of the conquistadors, who brought to the New World what she calls elsewhere "an active displacement in perspective." A "tapestried landscape" was all European eyes were prepared to see in the jungle. The actual landscape, with its terrors, somehow evaded them, "retreating, always retreating" behind "the hanging fabric" of the continent until the invaders settled in what they had known before they came—"an old dream of wealth and luxury / already out of style when they left home."

It seems almost an impertinence to add that of the poets of her generation, with temperaments often more conspicuously adaptable than hers, Elizabeth Bishop alone now seems secure beyond the disputation of schools or the sway of period loyalties. Like all great poets, she was less a maker of poems than a maker of feelings.

First Impressions

In Pursuit of Excellence by Thomas J. Peters and Robert H. Waterman Jr.
March 6, 1983

BY FRAN R. SCHUMER

BACK IN THE 1950S, when workers were only too happy to be turning out "tailfins for a tailfin-hungry world," as Thomas J. Peters and Robert H. Waterman Jr. put it, American business favored the rationalist mode. Theory and analysis had replaced seat-of-the-pants techniques, and success became something you could study at school.

This highly readable and sensible book, however, finds the secret of business success not in the head but in the heart. Mr. Peters and Mr. Waterman, management consultants, find that "excellent" companies are distinguished by good old-fashioned values—respect for the individual, devotion to service and attention to the customer. That Ray Kroc, the former chairman of McDonald's, waxes poetic about hamburger buns says more about the chain's success than any company earnings report can.

"Label a man a loser and he'll start acting like one," Mr. Peters and Mr. Waterman caution, which is why the excellent companies set lower, not higher, quotas, with the surprising result of greater productivity. They tolerate mistakes.

What didn't work for 3M as a brassiere cup eventually became a standard worker safety mask. (Not even excellent companies adhere to all their rules. The worker who perfected the safety mask was told by the company to "knock it off." He completed the project at home.)

Injecting a little Nietzsche, a little Zen and a lot of the Protestant work ethic, the authors strike a tone that is remarkably sane, although they occasionally succumb to corporate boosterism. To illustrate the excellent companies' ample use of hoopla, they cite admiringly the I.B.M. manager who rented New Jersey's Meadowlands Stadium for a company rally. As each worker ran out to the field, his name beamed from the electronic scoreboard to the cheers of relatives and friends. One wonders whether such tactics really work, and if they do, whether they should.

Ordinary People

Cathedral by Raymond Carver
September 11, 1983

BY IRVING HOWE

T HERE ARE ARTISTS who reach the strange by staying with the ordinary. Maurice Utrillo paints European streets that narrow into enigmatic space and Edward Hopper American houses that seem laden with disquiet. How they do this only a very good art critic can explain, but that it happens everyone who looks at pictures must know.

Raymond Carver, an American writer now in his mid-40s, has been writing stories for some years that, on a smaller emotional scale, create similar effects. His settings are American towns, semi-industrial and often depressed. His characters, plebeian loners struggling for speech, now and then find work as factory hands and waitresses. His actions skid across the troubles of daily life and then, through some eerie turn of chance or perhaps a darker cause, collapse into failed marriages and broken lives. Familiar enough on the surface, these stories leave one with tremors that resemble the start of a breakdown. The familiar controls guiding daily life fall apart; panic takes over.

Mr. Carver has been mostly a writer of strong but limited effects—the sort of writer who shapes and twists his material to a high point of stylization. In his newest collection of stories, *Cathedral*, there are a few that suggest he is moving toward a greater ease of manner and generosity of feeling; but in most of his work it's his own presence, the hard grip of his will, that is the strongest force. It's not that he imposes moral or political judgments; in that respect, he's quite self-effacing. It's that his abrupt rhythms and compressions come to be utterly decisive.

In a brilliant story from an earlier collection, "They're Not Your Husband," a man distraught over losing his job goes to the restaurant where his wife works as a waitress and, out of some unprobed need for self-humiliation, repeats the vulgarities several customers have been making about his wife's exposed flesh. The story strikes at the nerves, creating ripples of anxiety. In a perhaps richer story, "What We Talk About When We Talk About Love," two couples chat somewhat aimlessly about the vagaries of love until their talk leads to an atmosphere of brooding reflectiveness. They cannot leave their chairs but must sit silently, fixed into anxiety.

Cathedral contains a number of similar stories, very skillful within their narrow limits, written with a dry intensity, and moving, at their climaxes, from the commonplace to the unnerving.

These stories yield neither the familiar recognitions of realistic narrative nor the ambiguous motifs of symbolic fiction. They cast us adrift, into a void on the far side of the ordinary. Ordinary life is threatening; ordinary life is the enemy of ordinary people.

Behind Mr. Carver's stories there are strong American literary traditions. Formally, they summon remembrances of Hemingway and perhaps Stephen Crane, masters of tightly packed fiction. In subject matter they draw upon the American voice of loneliness and stoicism, the native soul locked in this continent's space. Mr. Carver's characters, like those of many earlier American writers, lack a vocabulary that can release their feelings, so they must express themselves mainly through obscure gesture and berserk display.

It's a meager life that Mr. Carver portrays, without religion or politics or culture, without the shelter of class or ethnicity, without the support of strong folkways or conscious rebellion. It's the life of people who cluster in the folds of our society. They are not bad or stupid; they merely lack the capacity to understand the nature of their deprivation—the one thing, as it happens, that might ease or redeem it. When they get the breaks, they can manage; but once there's a sign of trouble, they turn out to be terribly brittle. Lacking an imagination for strangeness, they succumb to the strangeness of their trouble.

A few of Mr. Carver's stories—"They're Not Your Husband," "Where I'm Calling From" and "A Serious Talk"—can already be counted among the masterpieces of American fiction; a number of others are very strong. But something of the emotional meagerness that he portrays seeps into the narrative. His art is an art of exclusion—many of life's shadings and surprises, pleasures and possibilities, are cut away by the stringency of his form.

In his earlier years Raymond Carver led the kind of shapeless life he depicts in his fiction, drifting from job to job, town to town. Slowly and, one gathers, at

1983

The Road Less Traveled, by M. Scott Peck, hits the bestseller list on October 16. It stays there most weeks until April 6, 1997, its 694th week on the paperback list—far more than any other book.

some expense to himself and his family, he worked out his strategy of composition: taut plot, detached voice, austere setting, brilliant shock effect.

But the hazard of this artfulness is that he succumbs at times to bravura, with stylization declining into mannerism. Having learned to control the devices that make him so notable a writer, he began, in his second book of stories, to slip into self-imitation. What makes *Cathedral* so interesting—apart from the intrinsic merit of the stories—is that it shows he has become aware of his temptations and perils.

A literary friend whose judgment I respect dislikes Mr. Carver's work because he finds it "cold." If he means that Mr. Carver employs devices of distancing which keep us from the inner life of his figures, I see no reason to be troubled. Greater writers have used such devices. But if my friend means that there creeps into Mr. Carver's stories a note of disdain toward the people he creates, then the charge is sometimes—by no means always—accurate. I suspect this happens because Mr. Carver grows impatient with, even grieved by, the resignation of his characters. It's as if he wished they would rebel against the constrictions of their lives, rebel even against the stylized constraints he puts upon them. But they don't.

I think Mr. Carver is showing us at least part of the truth about a segment of American experience few of our writers trouble to notice. Neoconservative critics, intent upon pasting a smile onto the country's face, may charge him with programmatic gloom and other heresies, but at his best he is probing, as many American writers have done before, the waste and destructiveness that prevail beneath the affluence of American life.

In *Cathedral* a few stories move past Mr. Carver's expert tautness and venture on a less secure but finer rendering of experience. The title story is a lovely piece about a blind man who asks an acquaintance to guide his hand in sketching a cathedral he has never seen. At the end, the two hands moving together—one guided by sight and the other not—come to seem a gesture of fraternity.

Cathedral shows a gifted writer struggling for a larger scope of reference, a finer touch of nuance. What he has already done makes one eager to read his future work.

Choiceless in Czechoslovakia

The Unbearable Lightness of Being by Milan Kundera
April 29, 1984

BY E. L. DOCTOROW

I AM BORED BY NARRATIVE," Virginia Woolf wrote in her diary in 1929, thus suggesting how the novel has been kept alive in our century by novelists' assaults on its conventions. Writers have chosen to write novels without plots or characters or the illusion of time passing. They have disdained to represent real life, as the painters did a half century before them. They have compacted their given languages, or invented their own, or revised the idea of composition entirely by assembling their books as collages.

Appearing noticeably in the United States 15 or 20 years ago was the disclaimed fiction in which the author deliberately broke the mimetic spell of his text and insisted that the reader should not take his story to heart or believe in the existence of his characters. Disclaiming had the theoretical advantage of breaking through to some approximation of the chaos and loss of structure in life. The subject of these fictions became the impossibility of maintaining them, and the author by his candor became the only character the reader could believe in. John Barth is one writer who comes to mind as having explored the possibilities of this strategy, and the distinguished Czech novelist Milan Kundera in his new book, *The Unbearable Lightness of Being,* continues to find it useful.

"And once more I see him the way he appeared to me at the very beginning of the novel," Mr. Kundera says of one of his characters. "This is the image from which he was born. . . . Characters are not born, like people, of woman; they are born of a situation, a sentence, a metaphor, containing in a nutshell a basic human possibility . . . the characters in my novels are my own unrealized possibilities. That is why I am equally fond of them and equally horrified by them. . . . But enough. Let us return to Tomas."

The question may reasonably be asked if this convention too isn't ready for assault. May it not be too late to return to Tomas? Do we have to be told where he comes from any more than we have to be told where babies come from? There is a particular hazard to the author who intrudes on his text: He had better be as interesting as the characters he competes with and the story he subverts or we may find him self-indulgent or, worse, coy, like those animated cartoons where a hand draws a little animal and colors it in and pushes it along to its adventure down the road.

Even now, in our age, there is a sanctity to the story. Because it is supremely valuable to us—as valuable as science or religion—we feel all violence done to it must finally be in its service. Virginia Woolf's experiment in avoiding narrative, *Mrs. Dalloway*, discovered another way to construct it or, perhaps, another place in which it could occur. The idea has always been to make it beat with life's beating heart.

Let us return to Tomas. Mr. Kundera has made him a successful surgeon. In Prague, in the spring of 1968, when Alexander Dubček is trying to make the Czech Communist Government more human, Tomas writes a letter to a newspaper to add his voice to a public debate. Thereafter, the Russians invade Prague, Dubček is replaced, public debate ceases, and Tomas is asked by the authorities to sign a statement retracting the sentiments of his letter. But he knows that once he does, if he ever again speaks out the Government will publish his retraction and his name among his fellow Czechs will be ruined. So he refuses and for his intransigence is then asked to sign a letter avowing his love for the Soviet Union, a possibility so unthinkable that he quits medicine and becomes a window washer. He hopes that now that he is down at the bottom he will no longer matter to the authorities and they will let him alone. What he discovers is that he no longer matters to anyone. When he was supposed by his hospital colleagues to be thinking of signing the retraction in order to keep his job they turned up their noses at him. Now that he's been declassed for maintaining his integrity, he's become an untouchable.

The first thing to note about this character's fate is that it is a gloss on Orwell: To destroy Tomas, Mr. Kundera is saying, the powerfully inertial police apparatus doesn't have to expend the energy required to torture him. It need only send around an affable plainclothesman with a letter to be signed. Once the policeman appears, no matter how Tomas responds his life is ruined.

The second thing to note is the idea of the exhaustion of meaningful choice. Tomas is one of four main characters born frankly of images in Mr. Kundera's mind. All of them to one extent or another enact the paradox of choices that are not choices, of courses of action that are indistinguishable in consequence from their opposite.

There is a pattern in the subservience of his characters to Mr. Kundera's will. They all exemplify the central act of his imagination, which is to conceive of a paradox and express it elegantly. The paradox he is most fond of is the essential identity of opposites, and he plays with it over and over again, with minor characters as well as major ones and with little essays and one-line observations. For instance, he shows us a dissident Czech émigré in Paris in the act of reproaching his fellow émigrés for their lack of anti-Communist fervor, and he finds in him the same bullying quality of mind as in the former head of state, Antonin Novotny, who ruled Czechoslovakia for 14 years. The elegance lies in the image Mr. Kundera uses to make the observation that both the émigré and the former ruler point their index fingers at whomever they address. In fact, people of this sort, Mr. Kundera tells us, have index fingers longer than their middle fingers.

Whether personal or political, all attitudes, stands, positions in the Kunderian vision come up short. He will kill off three of his quartet and allow the fourth to disappear from the book, presumably from a lightness of being; but his true story, the one to which he gives honest service, is the operation of his own mind as it formulates and finds images for the disastrous history of his country in his lifetime. The paradox of the essential identity of opposites describes an intractable world in which human beings are deprived of a proper context for their humanity. The author who ostentatiously intrudes in his characters' lives and tells them how to behave mimics, of course, the government that interferes deeply in its citizens' lives and tells them how to behave.

Readers of the author's celebrated novel *The Book of Laughter and Forgetting* will recognize here his structural use of leitmotif, the repertoire of phrases and fancies among which he circulates and recirculates. They will find the same ironic tone and brilliance of annotation of the fearful emptiness of Eastern European life under Communist management. Here too is the author's familiarity with music, his preoccupation with Don Juanism, his almost voyeuristic attention to the female body and its clothes. And the pointed, surreal image: Park benches from the city of Prague, colored red, yellow and blue, floating inexplicably on the Vltava River. Like Gabriel García Márquez, Mr. Kundera knows how to get ahead of his story and circle back to it and run it through again with a different emphasis. But the prose is sparer here, and the García Márquez levitations are not events now, but ideas. There is less clutter in the prose, less of the stuff of life, as if the author had decided to send the myriad furnishings of novels, its particulars, down the Vltava, after the benches. This is a kind of conceptualist fiction, a generic-brand, no-frills fiction, at least in Michael Henry Heim's translation. Mr. Kundera is not inclined to dwell on the feel of human experience except as it prepares us for his thought.

It is a not unattractive philosophical bent that sends Mr. Kundera into his speculative exercises. He has a first-rate mind and, like Bernard Shaw, the capacity to argue both sides of a question and make each side seem reasonable in its turn. But every now and then a wryly argued proposition seems flawed, a weakness for literary idea rather than a strength of thought—that a concentration camp, for instance, is defined first and foremost by the complete absence of privacy; it might be argued that slave labor and starvation and mass graves are its primary characteristics.

One recurrent theme in the book is that the ideal of social perfection is what inevitably causes the troubles of mankind, that the desire for utopia is the basis of the world's ills, there being no revolution and therefore no totalitarianism without it. This idea has currency among expatriate Eastern European intellectuals, and perhaps their bitter experience entitles them to it. But the history of revolutions begins, more likely, in the desire to eat or to breathe than in the thought that man must be perfected. And a revolutionary document like the American Constitution is filled with instructions and standards for civilized life under equitable law; and it is truly utopian, but its ideals are our saving grace and drive us to our best selves, not our worst.

It is not exactly self-indulgence or coyness that threatens *The Unbearable Lightness of Being*. The mind Mr. Kundera puts on display is truly formidable, and the subject of its concern is substantively alarming. But, given this subject, why are we forced to wonder, as we read, where his crisis of faith locates itself, in the world or in his art? The depiction of a universe in which all human choice wallows in irresolution, in which, as Yeats wrote, "The best lack all conviction, while the worst / Are full of passionate intensity," sometimes sets off the technique of this novel as an act of ego in excess of the sincere demands of despair. Mr. Kundera's master, the prophet Kafka, we can't help remembering, wrote a conceptualist no-frills fiction in which, however, he never appeared.

All this said, the work of reconceiving and redesigning the novel continues through the individual struggles of novelists all over the world, like an instinct of our breed. What is fine and valiant in Mr. Kundera is the enormous struggle not to be characterized as a writer by his exile and by his nation's disenfranchisement, even though they are the conditions his nose is rubbed in by Czechoslovak history. He works with cunning and wit and elegiac sadness to express "the trap the world has become," and this means he wants to reconceive not only narrative but the language and history of politicized life if he is to accord his experience the dimensions of its tragedy. This is in direct contrast to the problem of the American writer who must remember not to write of life as if it had no political content whatsoever. We can hope, with Milan Kundera, not to enact one of his elegant paradoxes in our separate choices and discover that either one leads to the same exhausted end.

Interview

Edna O'Brien
November 18, 1984

BY PHILIP ROTH

THE IRISH WRITER EDNA O'BRIEN, who has lived in London now for many years, moved recently to a wide boulevard of imposing nineteenth-century facades, a street that in the 1870s, when it was built, was renowned, she tells me, for its mistresses and kept women.

Because everything she's wearing for the interview is black, you cannot, of course, miss the white skin, the green eyes and the auburn hair; the coloring is dramatically Irish—as is the mellifluous fluency.

In Malone Dies, *your compatriot Samuel Beckett writes: "Let us say before I go any further, that I forgive nobody. I wish them all an atrocious life in the fires of icy hell and in the execrable generations to come." This quotation stands as the epigraph of* Mother Ireland, *a memoir you published in 1976. Frankly, I don't feel such harshness in your work.*

I picked the epigraph because I am, or was, especially at that time, unforgiving about lots of things in my life and I picked somebody who said it more eloquently and more ferociously than I could say it.

The fact is that your fiction argues against your unforgivingness.

To some extent it does but that is because I am a creature of conflicts. When I vituperate, I subsequently feel I should appease. That happens throughout my life. I am not a natural out-and-out hater any more than I am a natural, or thorough, out-and-out lover, which means I am often rather at odds with myself and others!

Who is the most unforgiven creature in your imagination?

Up to the time he died—which was a year ago—it was my father. But through death a metamorphosis happens: within. Since he died I have written a play about him embodying all his traits—his anger, his sexuality, his rapaciousness, etc.—and now I feel differently toward him. I do not want to relive my life with him or be reincarnated as the same daughter but I do forgive him. My mother is a different matter. I loved her, over-loved her, yet she visited a different legacy on me, an all-embracing guilt. I still have a sense of her over my shoulder, judging.

Here you are, a woman of experience, talking about forgiving your mother and father. Do you think that still worrying those problems has largely to do with your being a writer? If you weren't a writer, if you were a lawyer, if you were a doctor, perhaps you wouldn't be thinking about these people so much.

Absolutely. It's the price of being a writer. One is dogged by the past—pain, sensations, rejections, all of it. I do believe that this clinging to the past is a zealous, albeit hopeless desire to reinvent it so that one could change it. Doctors, lawyers and many other stable citizens are not afflicted by a persistent memory. In their way, they might be just as disturbed as you or I, except that they don't know it. They don't delve.

But not all writers feast on their childhood as much as you have.

I am obsessive, also I am industrious. Besides, the time when you are most alive and most aware is in childhood and one is trying to recapture that heightened awareness.

As a writer, how much or how little do you owe to the primitive rural world you often describe in stories about the Ireland of your childhood?

There's no telling, really. If I had grown up on the steppes of Russia, or in Brooklyn—my parents lived there when they were first married—my material would have been different but my apprehension might be just the same. I happened to grow up in a country that was and is breathlessly beautiful so the feeling for nature, for verdure and for the soil was instilled into me. Secondly, there was no truck with culture or literature so that my longing to write, sprung up of its own accord, was spontaneous. The only books in our house were prayer books, cookery books and blood-stock reports. I was privy to the world around me, was aware of everyone's little history, the stuff from which stories and novels are made. On the personal level, it was pretty drastic. So all these things combined to make me what I am.

But are you surprised that you survived the isolated farm and the violent father and the provincial convent without having lost the freedom of mind to be able to write?

I am surprised by my own sturdiness—yes; but I do not think that I am unscarred. Such things as driving a car or swimming are quite beyond me. In a lot of ways I feel a cripple. The body was as sacred as a tabernacle and everything a potential occasion of sin. It is funny now, but not that funny—the body contains the life story just as much as the brain. I console myself by thinking that if one part is destroyed another flourishes.

How do you account for your ability to reconstruct with such passionate exactness an Irish world you haven't fully lived in for decades? How does your memory keep it alive, and why won't this vanished world leave you alone?

At certain times I am sucked back there and the ordinary world and the present time recede. This recollection, or whatever it is, invades me. It is not something that I can summon up, it simply comes and I am the servant of it. My hand does the work and I don't have to think; in fact, were I to think it would stop the flow. It's like a dam in the brain that bursts.

Do you visit Ireland to help this recall along?

When I visit Ireland, I always secretly hope that something will spark off the hidden world and the hidden stories waiting to be released, but it doesn't happen like that! It happens, as you well know, much more convolutedly, through one's dreams, through chance and, in my case, through the welter of emotion stimulated by a love affair and its aftermath.

I wonder if you haven't chosen the way you live—living by yourself—to prevent anything emotionally too powerful from separating you from that past.

I'm sure I have. I rail against my loneliness but it is as dear to me as the thought of unity with a man. I have often said that I would like to divide my life into alternating periods of penance, cavorting and work, but as you can see that would not strictly fit in with a conventional married life.

Most American writers I know would be greatly unnerved by the prospect of living away from the country that's their subject and the source of their language and obsessions.

To establish oneself in a particular place and to use it as the locale for fiction is both a strength to the writer and a signpost to the reader. But you have to go if you find your roots too threatening, too impinging. Joyce said that Ireland is the sow that eats its farrow—he was referring to their attitude to their writers, they savage them. It is no accident that our two greatest illustrati—himself and Mr. Beckett—left and stayed away, though they never lost their particular Irish consciousness. In my own case, I do not think that I would have written anything if I had stayed. I feel I would have been watched, would have been judged (even more!) and would have lost that priceless commodity called freedom. Writers are always on the run and I was on the run from many things. Yes, I dispossessed myself and I am sure that I lost something, lost the continuity, lost the day-to-day contact with reality. However, compared with Eastern European writers, I have the advantage that I can always go back. For them it must be terrible, the finality of it, the utter banishment, like a soul shut out of heaven.

What has Joyce meant to you, and how intimidating is it for an Irish writer to have as precursor this great verbal behemoth who has chewed up everything Irish in sight?

In the constellation of geniuses, he is a blinding light and father of us all. (I exclude Shakespeare because for Shakespeare no human epithet is enough.) When I first read Joyce, it was a little book edited by T. S. Eliot which I bought on the quays in Dublin, second-hand, for fourpence. Before that, I had read very few books and they were mostly gushing and outlandish. I was a pharmaceutical apprentice who dreamed of writing. Now here was "The Dead" and a section of *A Portrait of the Artist as a Young Man* which stunned me not only by the bewitchment of style but because they were so true to life, they *were* life. Then, or rather later, I came to read *Ulysses*, but as a young girl I balked, because it was really too much for me, it was too inaccessible and too masculine, apart from the famous Molly Bloom section. I now think *Ulysses* is the most diverting, brilliant, intricate and unboring book that I have ever read. I can pick it up at any time, read a few pages and feel that I have just had a brain transfusion. As for his being intimidating, it doesn't arise—he is simply out of bounds, beyond us all, "the far Azores," as he might call it.

You write about women without a taint of ideology, or, as far as I can see, any concern with taking a correct position.

The correct position is to write the truth, to write what one feels regardless of any public consideration or any clique. I think an artist never takes a position either through expediency or umbrage. Artists detest and suspect positions because they know that the minute you take a fixed position you are something else, you are a journalist or you are a politician. What I am after is a bit of magic and I do not want to write tracts or to read them. I have depicted women in lonely, desperate and often humiliated situations, very often the butt of men and almost always searching for an emotional catharsis that does not come. This is my territory and one that I know from hard-earned experience. If you want to know what I regard as the principal crux of female despair, it is this: in the Greek myth of Oedipus and in Freud's exploration of it, the son's desire for his mother is admitted; the infant daughter also desires its mother but it is unthinkable, either in myth, in fantasy or in fact, that that desire can be consummated.

Yet you can't be oblivious to the changes in consciousness that have been occasioned by the women's movement.

Yes, certain things have been changed for the better, women are not chattels, they express their right to earn as much as men, to be respected, not to be *The Second Sex*, but in the mating area things have not changed. Attraction and sexual love are spurred not by consciousness but by instinct and passion, and in this men and women are radically different. The man still has the greater authority and the greater autonomy. It's biological. The woman's fate is to receive the sperm and to retain it, but the man's is to give it and in the giving he spends himself and then subsequently withdraws. While she is in a sense being fed, he is in the opposite sense being drained, and to resuscitate himself he takes temporary flight. As a result, you get the woman's resentment at being abandoned, however briefly, his guilt at going and, above all, his innate sense of self-protection in order to re-find himself so as to reaffirm himself. Closeness is therefore always only relative. A man may help with the dishes and so forth but his commitment is more ambiguous and he has a roving eye.

Are there no women as promiscuous?

They sometimes are but it doesn't give them the same sense of achievement. A woman, I dare to say, is capable of a deeper and more lasting love. I would also add that a woman is more afraid of being left. That still stands. Go into any woman's canteen, dress department, hairdresser's, gymnasium and you will see plenty of desperation and plenty of competition. People utter a lot of slogans but they are only slogans and what we feel and do is what determines us. Women are no more secure in their emotions than they ever were. They simply are better at coming to terms with them. The only real security would be to turn away from men, to detach, but that would be a little death—at least, for me it would.

Why do you write so many love stories?

First of all, I think love replaced religion for me in my sense of fervor. When I began to look for earthly love (i.e., sex), I felt that I was cutting myself off from God. By taking on the mantle of religion, sex assumed proportions that are rather far-fetched. It became the central thing in my life, the goal. I was very prone to the Heathcliff, Mr. Rochester syndrome and still am. The sexual excitement was to a great extent linked with pain and separation. My sexual life is pivotal to me as I believe it is for everyone else. It takes up a lot of time both in the thinking and the doing, the former often taking pride of place. For me, primarily, it is secretive and contains elements of mystery and plunder. My daily life and my sexual life are not of a whole—they are separated. Part of my Irish heritage!

Do you think there are difficulties you have writing as a woman that I don't have as a man—and do you imagine that there might be difficulties I have that you don't?

I think it is different being a man and a woman, it is very different. I think you as a man have waiting for you in the wings of the world a whole cortege of women—potential wives, mistresses, muses, nurses. Women writers do not have that bonus. The examples are numerous, the Brontë sisters, Jane Austen, Carson McCullers, Flannery O'Connor, Emily Dickinson, Marina Tsvetayeva. I think it was Dashiell Hammett who said he wouldn't want to live with a woman who had more problems than himself. I think the signals men get from me alarm them.

You will have to find a Leonard Woolf.

I do not want a Leonard Woolf. I want Lord Byron and Leonard Woolf mixed in together.

But does the job fundamentally come down to the same difficulties then, regardless of gender?

Absolutely. There is no difference at all, you, like me, are trying to make something out of nothing and the anxiety is extreme. Flaubert's description of his room echoing with curses and cries of distress could be any writer's room. Yet I doubt that we would welcome an alternative life, there is something stoical about soldiering on all alone.

First Impressions

Bright Lights, Big City by Jay McInerney
November 25, 1984

BY WILLIAM KOTZWINKLE

A YOUNG MAN works for a New York magazine in the Department of Factual Verification, where facts are tracked "through dusty volumes, along skeins of microfilm, across transcontinental telephone cables, till they prove good or are exposed as error." Factual error cannot appear in this magazine, and it sure sounds like *The New Yorker*, though it is never named in Jay McInerney's first novel, *Brights Lights, Big City*. In any event, our hero does not fit in. "Should you call up the president of the Polar Explorers and ask if it's true that someone was wearing a headdress made out of walrus skin?" asks the narrator, who uses present-tense verbs and second-person pronouns, presumably apostrophizing himself. "Does it matter?"

It matters a great deal to the magazine, but our young man has had many long nights at New York clubs, utilizing a substance he refers to as "Bolivian Marching Powder." He is an amusing fellow, and he meets strange people—a baldheaded girl, for instance, with a scar tattooed on her scalp. "Her voice . . . is like the New Jersey State Anthem played through an electric shaver."

An employee whose head is filled with "crusted snow" and who on his lunch hour contemplates buying a leashed ferret from a street hustler is bound to clash with the Ivy League tradition of the magazine. He is, in fact, fired after allowing a mistake-riddled article on French politics to go to press.

His wife, Amanda, is a high-fashion model who has left him. He appears at a fashion show in the Waldorf-Astoria. Drunk, he tries to accost her on the runway. He is thrown out. A friend asks him why he married her at all.

> "Weren't you suspicious when you saw the sign on her forehead?"
> "Which sign was that?"
> "The one that said, *Space to Let. Long and Short Term Leasing.*"
> "We met in a bar. It was too dark to read."

Mr. McInerney has wandered Manhattan with its shadows taking shape in his soul. He and his narrator know the lounges and the lizards who wait there, gazing into dreams and hallucinations. There is also a fine assortment of street purveyors, not only of ferrets but of watches and other objects, most of which the narrator is ready to purchase, none of which work:

> "My man, check it out here. Genuine Cartier watches. Wear the watch that'll make 'em watch you."
> "How do I know it's real?"
> "How do you know anything's real?"

This is the echo of New York, all right, and if you have a love affair with it, you'll recognize the truth in Mr. McInerney's landscapes. Oh, yes, the new Cartier watch "dies at three-fifteen. You shake it, then wind it. The winding knob falls off in your hand."

Welfare As We Knew It

Losing Ground: American Social Policy, 1950–1980
by Charles Murray
December 16, 1984

BY LAWRENCE M. MEAD

D URING THE GREAT SOCIETY PERIOD, from the early 1960s to the late 1970s, many poor people escaped poverty, but a substantial number became mired even more deeply in welfarism, crime and other social problems. Conservatives now assert that Federal programs for the poor have failed, and their animus has helped justify the Reagan Administration's cuts in these programs.

How could programs to help the poor make many of them *worse* off? After all, Charles Murray, a senior research fellow at the Manhattan Institute for Policy Research, finds that social welfare spending was 20 times higher in 1980 than in 1950, even allowing for inflation. In *Losing Ground*, his answer is that the programs "changed the rules" that govern the poor. By the late '60s, he argues, welfare and other programs that use means tests gave so much to recipients relative to what they could earn that they no longer felt much reason to get ahead on their own. At the same time, with the decline of standards in urban schools, which took away incentives to learn, and lenient law enforcement, which reduced the penalties for crime, the semiskilled or unmotivated could now tell themselves that a life of welfare and/or hustling paid as well as or better than getting a job or going straight. Thus an underclass appeared in American cities. Its members may appear deviant, but they are really responding "rationally" to "changes in the rules of the game."

The argument is not new, but it is well made. Mr. Murray's case is distinguished by its accessibility. He writes with clarity and style. To support his argument, however, he is not above reading the statistics his way. In showing how welfare tempts recipients not to work, for example, he compares the meager benefits of 1960 with the much more generous payments of 1970—ignoring the decline of benefits since 1970 due to inflation.

The author's difficulties come in explaining trends and suggesting remedies. He blames the buildup of welfare and other programs on an "elite wisdom" that shifted the responsibility for poverty entirely from the poor to "the system." But the crusade against poverty was endorsed by Congress and the public. In reality, the welfare state is deeply rooted in American politics. Its origins stretch back at least to the New Deal, of which the Great Society was an extension. Political support for welfare, if not for its abuses, is strong.

While Mr. Murray says social programs do too much for the poor, liberals would say too little. Their dispute is over the size of government, the primordial battle in American politics. My own view is that the nature of government may be more important. The problem with the welfare state is not its size but its permissiveness. As yet, few serious work or other requirements are attached to Federal benefit programs. Recipients seldom have to work or otherwise function in return for support. If they did, there is some evidence they would function better. Work requirements, however, are hardly mentioned in *Losing Ground*.

Mr. Murray would reform social policy mainly by abolishing it. He would revamp education through stiffer standards and a voucher system to make schools compete for students. But he would eliminate all preferential treatment for minorities and virtually all welfare for adults, leaving "the working-aged person with no recourse whatsoever except the job market, family members, friends,

_1985_

Angelica Garnett's memoir,
Deceived with Kindness,
gives the Bloomsbury rage
a new twist.

and public or private locally funded services. It is the Alexandrian solution: cut the knot, for there is no way to untie it." This program reflects the hard-line, meritocratic tone of the book. The author indicts current policy for refusing to recognize "more inequality" and to admit that those who succeed "are in some practical way _better_" than those who do not. His own motto is "Billions for equal opportunity, not one cent for equal outcome."

Such proposals are completely impolitic, and this tells us much about the conservative mind. Conservatives believe that adult recipients could really take care of themselves if forced. This pays the poor a greater compliment than many of them can stand. Some adults really do need Government's support and guidance. Mr. Murray suffers from the besetting problem of the right—an inability to define any meaning for equality beyond equal opportunity. He does not reckon with the insistence of most Americans that social policy define some kind of community in which everyone has a place, regardless of his or her fortunes in the marketplace.

Conservatives needlessly let liberals monopolize the value of equality, the trump card of modern politics. Why do they assume that equality must mean a leveling of income and status distinctions, the bugaboo of the right? For most Americans, it simply means equal participation in the rights _and_ obligations of citizenship. In social policy, that would mean support for the poor plus insistence that they function in integrating ways. The answer to poverty may be not fewer programs but more authoritative programs that seriously require work, learning and obedience to the law from those they support. But to do this, conservatives will have to give up their suspicions of government and instead use it for conservative ends.

The Scientist Who Talks of the Soul

The Man Who Mistook His Wife for a Hat by Oliver Sacks
March 2, 1986

BY JOHN C. MARSHALL

WHEN THE PSALMIST lamented the Jewish exile by the waters of Babylon he wrote: "If I forget thee, O Jerusalem, let my right hand lose its cunning and my tongue cleave to the roof of my mouth if I remember thee not." The Psalmist's style differs somewhat from that of current medical journals, yet the writer is describing a neurological condition well known to the modern physician. Now, as then, many people who are unfortunate enough to suffer a cerebrovascular accident—a stroke—become paralyzed on the right side of the body and lose their command of speech. Many other examples of severe but relatively isolated disorders of perception, knowledge or skilled action consequent upon injury to the brain were described by scholars of the ancient world.

We now have fancy, classical-sounding names for these conditions and some knowledge of the underlying pathologies that are their proximate cause: disorders in the expression and comprehension of language (the aphasias) are typically associated with damage to the left cerebral hemisphere; failure to recognize familiar faces (prosopagnosia) is usually provoked by bilateral injury to more posterior regions of the brain; an inability to remember the happenings of the day, or even the last minute (amnesia) is found with bilateral damage to more central areas of the brain. So far, so clear. But do we really understand such phenomena, either scientifically (whatever that means!) or in terms of how a fellow human feels about and copes with such drastic changes in his or her capacities?

Oliver Sacks has a decidedly original approach to these problems. In addition to possessing the technical skills of a twentieth-century doctor, the London-born Dr. Sacks, a professor of clinical neurology at the Albert Einstein College of Medicine in the Bronx, sees the human condition like a philosopher-poet. The resultant mixture is insightful, compassionate, moving and, on occasion, simply infuriating. One could call these essays neurological case histories, and correctly so, although Dr. Sacks's own expression — "clinical tales" — is far more apt. Dr. Sacks tells some two dozen stories about people who are also patients, and who manifest strange and striking peculiarities of perception, emotion, language, thought, memory or action. And he recounts these histories with the lucidity and power of a gifted short-story writer.

In the title story, Dr. P., a distinguished musician and teacher of music, lost the ability to recognize people and common objects at a glance. Although his visual acuity was perfectly normal, he would mistake his wife's head for his hat and act accordingly, attempting to lift it off and put it on. It is important to realize that Dr. P. was in no sense demented. There was no primary disorder of memory; he could carry on an intelligent and entertaining conversation and could play the piano with all his old skill (although he could no longer read music). The ability to recognize objects and scenes was not totally lost, for Dr. P. could still slowly and laboriously work out what an object must be by analyzing out loud what it looked like. He could then, as it were, construct by logic and reasoning the identity of objects in his world.

Such reports illustrate that there are often two (or more) ways of reaching the same goal but that for biologically essential functions nature has endowed our brains with special-purpose organs that achieve the goal (in this case, the recognition of objects) "unconsciously," rapidly and efficiently. Dr. Sacks's description succeeds admirably in making us feel what it might be like to "see" our nearest and dearest by strategies more akin to those we normally employ in solving a crossword puzzle or designing an apartment block.

Many of Dr. Sacks's other tales of loss display the same imaginative facility to convey life in a partial world. His description of Jimmie G., a patient with severe amnesia, is a little masterpiece of clinical writing. We begin to share the experience of living in a specious present, divorced from a coherent autobiographical understanding, where only spasmodic, disconnected memories occasionally surface to remind one of who one is. We might expect such an experimental world to be drained of emotion, as indeed it seems to be for many amnesia patients. And one might in an unguarded moment toy with the notion of such a person as a "lost soul." It is entirely to Dr. Sacks's credit that he does not dismiss such locutions as unprofessional reverie.

Even in these liberal times, the scientist who talks of the soul is usually regarded as being on vacation. This taboo does not inhibit Dr. Sacks from asking in all seriousness whether Jimmie G., with his profound loss of autobiographical self, has also lost his soul. The nuns in the home where Jimmie lives respond to Dr. Sacks's question with the suggestion: "Watch Jimmie in chapel and judge for yourself." His concentration held and absorbed by the rite, Jimmie at Holy Communion "found himself, found continuity and reality, in the absoluteness of spiritual attention and act." However one describes what remains to the amnesia patient, one would be a fool to dismiss those realms of experience that are opaque to the scientific method and understanding.

Dr. Sacks's admirable presentation of seemingly bizarre phenomena and difficult concepts is marred by only one weakness. It is stylistic, but nonetheless extremely annoying. He constantly plays naïve about the neurological literature. He would have us believe that an experienced neurologist could fail to have read anything about many of the standard syndromes of behavioral neurology until he had himself seen a particularly pure case of the condition in question. Dr. Sacks is too sophisticated to convince the reader of such ignorance. For the rest, I can think of no better neurological introduction to the psyche, often in pain and distress but always struggling to remain human.

1986

Stranger in Two Worlds is on the best-seller list for three weeks. It is the autobiography of Jean Harris, who in 1980 murdered Dr. Herman Tarnower, author of *The Complete Scarsdale Medical Diet*, a much bigger best seller.

First Impressions

Forrest Gump by Winston Groom
March 9, 1986

T HIS NOVEL IS A TALE told by an idiot (with an IQ, he tells us,
"near 70") who, in the course of his travels through three decades of
American landscape, becomes a football star, a war hero, a Ping-Pong
ace, a one-man band, a chess champion, a movie actor, an astronaut, a professional wrestler and a business tycoon. Forrest Gump also gets to visit China—he
in fact saves Mao Zedong from drowning—and he spends four years in the jungles of New Guinea among cannibals. Winston Groom's picaresque novel is a
kind of defanged *Candide*, an unabrasive satire of the idiocy of life in our time
as manifested in various touchstone events and institutions.

"Let me say this," Forrest begins, "bein a idiot is no box of chocolates. People
laugh, lose patience, treat you shabby. Now they says folks sposed to be kind to
the afflicted, but let me tell you—it ain't always that way. Even so, I got no complaints, cause I reckon I done live a pretty interestin life, so to speak."

The narrative voice is an impressively sustained impersonation, but finally
not a human voice. As long as *Forrest Gump* remains a satiric cartoon, it doesn't
matter that Forrest exists for us essentially as a device, an overabundant collection of unassimilated attributes. The sweetness and humor of the voice suffice.
When the novel tries to move us with human tragedies, it goes off pitch, vitiates
its most interesting aspirations, turns sentimental. One can be amused by Forrest and like him, but one can't accept this comic-strip figure as someone capable of real human pain.

If charm were everything, *Forrest Gump* might be some kind of masterpiece.
This light satiric novel has many pleasures to offer. As a serious work, which is
its sometime ambition, it is too ingratiating, too lacking in genuine surprise, too
undemanding of itself. The novel tends to fade from memory with surprising
dispatch. It leaves no aftertaste. *Forrest Gump* succeeds at the expense of muting
its outrage, of repressing an original and possibly dangerous vision. This seemingly audacious work sells short its best and deepest impulses.

Magnus Pym Is Missing

A *Perfect Spy* by John le Carré
April 13, 1986

BY FRANK CONROY

IRST, A SMALL TECHNICAL MATTER. Pains will be taken in this review to reveal nothing from the plot of *A Perfect Spy* that might take away from the pleasure of reading the book. Were I reading *Great Expectations* for the first time I would not, for instance, want some loudmouth to reveal the identity of the mysterious benefactor, thank you very much. Despite a few leaks about *A Perfect Spy* printed elsewhere, adherence to a literary equivalent of the Official Secrets Act seems appropriate because, whatever else it is, John le Carré's new book is a first-rate espionage novel, perhaps the best of his already impressive oeuvre. The author has gone to great lengths to create a tense balance between the narrative drive of the plot and the intelligent, artful richness of the style. I say tense because the book is a page-turner as well as a very satisfying read—you want to move fast so you can find out what will happen and you want to go slow so as to relish the writing. Out of respect for this remarkable achievement, discretion will prevail.

We have Magnus Pym, a middle-aged senior official in British Intelligence, holed up in his own personal safe house on the Devon coast. His father, Rick, has just died, and Magnus is in extremis, whether as a result of his father's death, his job, or some combination of these and other factors, we do not know. Pym has isolated himself in order to write, "to tell it straight . . . word for word the truth." He writes specifically to his son Tom, and to his espionage colleague Jack, and perhaps for posterity. Magnus's writings, about the past, are interspersed by Mr. le Carré with actions in the present involving Tom, Jack, Magnus's wife, Mary, and others animated by Magnus's disappearance. (The disappearance of a high-ranking intelligence officer of course constitutes a serious emergency that automatically sets off various procedures, flaps and political infighting of satisfying complexity.) The structure of *A Perfect Spy* is straightforward, and those readers who have complained that Mr. le Carré has on occasion been overly Byzantine—to the point of self-indulgence—will have no trouble on that account. After some fluttering of tenses and slightly nervous hopping through time and space in the first chapter (which serves to make the reader read carefully), the narrative settles down nicely for the rest of the book.

A rich novel emerges, full of interweaving stories, a wide variety of believable characters and any number of quietly resonating central images (the old copy of *Simplicissimus*, a pun on the word Poppy, the green filing cabinet, etc.). It is the life of Magnus Pym—first as a boy, and then as a man who remains a boy. Pym has many secrets, but the most fundamental is the fact that he never grew up. He must play the adult and hide the childlike (and by now grotesque) narcissism and self-absorption that have dominated his emotions all along.

Magnus Pym's father is Rick Pym, a flamboyant, powerful confidence man who lives entirely on the surface of experience. He lies, cheats and steals without emotional involvement. There is, as it were, nobody home inside the body of Rick Pym. He is no more than a bundle of sophisticated reflexes, every one of them self-serving. Magnus's mother goes mad while the boy emerges from infancy. Magnus is in a far worse position than an orphan. He has before him the body of a father, a tantalizing presence, but not the substance. To the father, the boy is just another mark, a fact that Magnus, as long as he lives, will never be able to fully accept. The agenda of Magnus's life is to find something in the world to fill the void in himself created by the harrowing relationship with his father. Espionage is quite precisely it—a cabal of powerful men, working secretly, following highly ritualized procedures, espousing clear codes of behavior, offering protection, security and even love to the deserving young man who can prove himself. For Magnus the church was too dull, the military too full of nitwits and the academy too vague. He needed the pressurized, one-on-one world of spying, of devoted service to a loving master. "I wish I could adequately describe to you," Magnus writes at one point, "the pleasure of being really well run."

As simple as this idea may sound in synopsis, it is anything but simple in the book. Mr. le Carré mines this vein very deeply, creating parallelisms, symbols, psychological motivations and complex metaphors that echo and expand. He works with a thoroughness that inevitably brings to mind the nineteenth century.

Mr. le Carré's model is Charles Dickens. He has skipped over John Buchan, W. Somerset Maugham, Wilkie Collins et al. and gone to the master, who died writing *The Mystery of Edwin Drood*. (A sad piece of work that would doubtless have been even sadder had it been finished.) Mr. le Carré is exceptionally good at creating vivid minor characters, laying false trails, spiraling the narrative instead of setting it out in a sort of linear step one, step two fashion, and at playing with the tension of withheld information, techniques we associate with Dickens. He knows how to drop an ambiguous word or phrase into the narrative as a sort of code word, or key, with which to illuminate subsequent action—"Poppy" in *A Perfect Spy*, "Recalled to life" in *A Tale of Two Cities*. It's a credit to both writers that these technical devices can travel so far and still work so well, particularly since, at bottom, the writers have such different preoccupations.

Dickens paid a lot of attention to money, because it allows for survival and

1986

The first four volumes of *The Baby-Sitters Club*, a wholesome paperback series for school-age girls by Ann M. Martin, appear. There are now 311 titles in the series and its spin-offs, plus the author's biography.

security. He celebrated romantic love, and what might be called family love (Mr. and Mrs. Micawber!), cared about social justice and, above all, he loved his characters, even the villains. Dickens loved the world and believed that things could be done (in his novels as in his life) to make it a better place. His childhood—father in debtor's prison, factory work as a boy—both haunted and energized him, and he wrote on a grand scale and worked his way free.

Mr. le Carré writes in a philosophically darker age. As a theme, money and economic survival are not relevant, indeed dealing with them might obscure his main preoccupation, which is individual psychological survival under conditions of extreme stress. The world, in the novels of Mr. le Carré, is bleak, to say the least. Romantic love, if it ever existed, does not last, does not nourish anybody (the Smiley books). Sex is a weapon (*The Little Drummer Girl*). Family love degenerates to a kind of world-weary nostalgia, since marriage and generational connections have been hopelessly corrupted by deceit, withdrawal or allegiance to self.

Social justice is not really a concern. It doesn't matter what side you're on, East or West, or somewhere in between, what matters is how you behave, what sort of personal existential ethic you live by. Mr. le Carré gives us the image of the mother country, for instance, to make the point that re-defectors, from wherever they may have originated, are weak men, psychologically infantile. It is their lack of a personal code that is reprehensible. In Mr. le Carré's books people do not spend time discussing concepts of social justice, except in scathing or perfunctory asides. What matters is personal loyalty among men, and loyalty to country, whatever the country. The world is in such bad shape—so full of lies, hypocrisy and betrayal—that no one can possibly make it better. Security is a meaningless concept. There is only survival, and everyone fights for it more or less alone.

A Perfect Spy contains autobiographical elements. Mr. le Carré's mother vanished when he was quite young, his father was a confidence man who once spent some time in jail, and at another time ran for Parliament. (An exact parallel with Rick Pym in the book.) Magnus Pym's experiences, traveling as a student, being recruited into British intelligence, etc., seem to fit what we know, or can guess, about young le Carré.

The most important element here is the father-son relationship. The author was consistently lied to and manipulated by his father for as long as the old man was alive—so says Mr. le Carré—and love was absent. The old man used false love in the attempt to make his son feel guilty, to con him and get money or whatever else he needed out of him. The father was pathological, but he was strong, apparently very strong, and Mr. le Carré has not thus far worked his way free. Mr. le Carré says somewhere (not in this book) that the monsters of one's childhood were not in fact as monstrous as one remembers them having been. But he also says we never reach a plane of detachment regarding our parents, however wise and old we may become, and to pretend otherwise is to cheat.

I cannot agree with that statement. We may perhaps never be fully detached, but we can expand our understanding of the world to the point where our parents, or other figures powerful in our childhood, can be seen in perspective. Without getting too psychoanalytical about it, they are reduced from mythological proportions when we finally give up the ghost and stop projecting our needs and emotions onto them. There are plenty of people who have done it (I would include Dickens) without pretense, and without cheating. But if Mr. le Carré remains obsessed with the memory of his father, it is our good luck, because we get a splendid book out of it.

Essay

Philip Roth on Bernard Malamud
April 20, 1986

> "Mourning is a hard business," Cesare said. "If people knew there'd be less death."
>
> —from *Life Is Better Than Death* by Bernard Malamud

IN FEBRUARY 1961 I traveled west from Iowa City, where I was teaching in the Writers' Workshop of the university and finishing a second book, to give a lecture called "Writing American Fiction" at a small community college in Monmouth, Ore. A close buddy from my graduate school days at the University of Chicago was teaching there and had arranged the invitation, promising that if I came out he'd also arrange for me to meet Bernard Malamud.

Bern taught nearby at the state university in Eugene, Ore. He'd been in Eugene (pop. 50,000) since leaving New York (pop. 8,000,000) and a night school teaching job there in 1949—12 years in the Far West instructing freshman Oregonians in the fundamentals of English composition, and writing his unorthodox baseball novel, *The Natural*, his masterpiece set in darkest Brooklyn, *The Assistant*, as well as four or five of the best American short stories I'd ever read (or ever will). The other stories weren't bad either.

In the early '50s I was reading Malamud's stories, later collected in *The Magic Barrel*, as they appeared—the very moment they appeared—in *Partisan Review* and the old *Commentary*. He seemed to me then to be doing no less for his lonely Jews and their peculiarly immigrant, Jewish forms of failure—for those

Malamudian men "who never stopped hurting"—than was Samuel Beckett, in his longer fiction, for misery-ridden Molloy and Malone. Both writers, while bound inextricably to the common life of the clan, severed their racial memories from the larger social and historical setting, and then, focusing as narrowly as they could upon the dismal, daily round of resistance borne by the most helpless of their *landsmen*, created, improbably, parables of frustration charged with the gravity of the grimmest philosophers.

Not unlike Beckett, Malamud wrote of a meager world of pain in a language all his own—in his case, an English that often appeared, even outside the idiosyncratic dialogue, to have in large part been clipped together from out of what one might have thought to be the least promising stockpile, most unmagical barrel, around: the locutions, inversions and diction of Jewish immigrant speech, a heap of broken verbal bones that looked, until he came along in those early stories to make them dance to his sad tune, to be of no use to anyone any longer other than the Borscht Belt comic and the professional nostalgia-monger. Even when he pushed this parable prose to its limits, Malamud's metaphors retained a proverbial ring. In his most consciously original moments, when he sensed in his grimly told, impassioned tales the need to sound his deepest note, he remained true to what seemed old and homely, matter-of-factly emitting the most touchingly unadorned poetry to make things even sadder than they already were—"He tried to say some sweet thing but his tongue hung in his mouth like dead fruit on a tree, and his heart was a black-painted window."

The 46-year-old man that I met in 1961 never let on that he could have written such a line, neither then nor in all the years I knew him. At first glance Bern looked to someone who'd grown up among such people like nothing so much as an insurance agent—he could have passed for a colleague of my father's, employed, as he was during the '30s and '40s, by the downtown Newark district office of the Metropolitan Life. I saw a conscientious, courteous, pinochle-playing workingman of the kind whose kibbitzing and conversation had been the background music of my childhood, a stubborn, seasoned, life insurance salesman who does not flee the snarling dog or alarm the children when he appears after dark at the top of the tenement stairwell—soberly reassuring in dark fedora and black overcoat, and carrying beneath his arm one of Metropolitan Life's large, black, oblong ledgers, the collection book which to me, as a boy, looked like a scaled-down portent of the coffin—to try to pry out of the poor breadwinner the half a buck that will prevent his policy from lapsing. He doesn't frighten anyone but he doesn't make the place light up with laughter either: he is, after all, the insurance man, whom you can only beat by dying.

That was the other surprise about Malamud. Very little laughter, no display at all of the playfulness that flickered on and off even in those barren, underheated, poorly furnished flats wherein were enacted the needs of his entombed, let alone of the eerie clowning that is the charm of *The Natural*. There were Malamud stories like "Angel Levine"—and later "The Jewbird" and "Talking Horse"—where the joke seemed only an inch away from the art, where the charm of the art was just the way it humorously hovered at the edge of the joke, and yet during all our meetings, over 25 years, I remember him telling me two jokes. Jewish dialect jokes, recounted very expertly indeed—but that was it: for 25 years two jokes were enough.

There was no need to overdo anything other than the responsibility to his art. Bern didn't exhibit himself and he didn't consider it necessary to exhibit his themes, certainly not casually to a stranger, if even among the friends he liked to assemble in the civilized setting of his own living room. He couldn't have exhibited himself even if he'd been foolish enough to try, and foolish enough to try he couldn't have been either—never being foolish was a small part of his larger burden. S. Levin, the Chaplinesque professor of *A New Life*, teaching his first college class with a wide-open fly, is hilariously foolish time and again, but not Bern. No more could Kafka have become a cockroach than Malamud could have metamorphosed into a Levin, comically outfoxed by an erotic mishap on the dark back roads of mountainous Oregon, and sneaking homewards, half-naked, at 3 A.M., the Sancho Panza beside him a sexually disgruntled, barroom waitress dressed in only one shoe and a bra. Seymour Levin the ex-drunkard and Gregor Samsa the bug ingeniously embody acts of colossal self-travesty, affording both authors a weirdly exhilarating sort of masochistic relief from the weight of sobriety and dignified inhibition that was plainly the cornerstone of their staid comportment. With Malamud as with many writers, exuberant showmanship, like searing self-mockery, was to be revealed only through what Heine called *Maskenfreiheit*, the freedom conferred by masks.

The sorrowing chronicler of human need clashing with human need, of need mercilessly resisted—and abated glancingly if at all—of blockaded lives racked with need for the light, the lift, of a little hope—"A child throwing a ball straight up saw a bit of pale sky"—preferred to present himself as someone whose needs were nobody's business but his own. Yet his was in fact a need so harsh that it makes one ache even now to consider the sheer size of it. It was the need to consider long and seriously every last demand of an overtaxed, overtaxing conscience torturously exacerbated by the pathos of human need unabated. That was a theme of his that he couldn't hide entirely from anyone who thought at all about where the man who could have passed himself off as your insurance agent was joined to the ferocious moralist of the claustrophobic stories about "things you can't get past." In *The Assistant*, the petty criminal and drifter Frank Alpine, while doing penance behind the counter of a failing grocery store that

Robert Penn Warren, the only person to win Pulitzer Prizes for both fiction and poetry, is named the first poet laureate of the United States.

he'd once helped to rob, has a "terrifying insight" about himself: "that all the while he was acting like he wasn't, he was a man of stern morality." I wonder if early in adult life Bern didn't have an insight no less terrifying about himself, maybe more terrifying—that he was a man of stern morality who could act *only* like what he was.

Essay

Ben Yagoda on the Present Tense
August 10, 1986

NO ATTENTIVE READER could fail to be aware that the present tense is in ascendancy. Jay McInerney's *Bright Lights, Big City*, Italo Calvino's *Mr. Palomar*, Margaret Atwood's *Handmaid's Tale*, Bret Easton Ellis's *Less Than Zero*, Carolyn Chute's *Beans of Egypt, Maine* and Richard Ford's *Sportswriter*—these are just some of the dozens of recent novels composed in the present. And it has become the norm for one sort of contemporary short story.

The present tense was pretty much a novelty item until a half-dozen or so years ago, primarily because the fiction writer's most precious tool is the illusion that what he is describing actually happened. The past tense helps sweep us away in the story; the present tense subtly reminds us that it is artifice after all. Fairy tales, to name a prototypical kind of narrative, start "Once upon a time," and proceed in the past tense because their listeners insist on surrendering disbelief.

Where writers did haul out the present, it was for quite specific ends. Most frequently, they have used what has been called the "historical present" to create a sense of immediacy. This is found in portentous March of Time documentaries ("Capone stays in hiding for three years") and in *Hamlet*, when the Player, quoting from an imaginary drama, describes Priam's slaughter: "Pyrrhus at Priam drives, in rage strikes wide, / But with the whiff and wind of his fell sword / Th' unnerved father falls."

The present can also serve to heighten the rhetorical quality of a work, to emphasize the artifice. Faulkner occasionally uses it this way, and so does Dickens. In the chapters of *Bleak House* narrated in the third person, he devised a taunting, compelling present-tense voice whose very tone flaunted a chilly contempt for society (and was so strong that the rest of the novel, narrated in the past tense by Esther Summerson, sometimes appears conventional almost to the point of tedium).

For Whitman, writing at about the same time, the present was one element of a very nearly biblical diction; it suggested that the events he described in *Song of Myself* did not merely take place, but were in a mysterious and transcendental way taking place: "The machinist rolls up his sleeves, the policeman travels his beat, the gate-keeper marks who pass, / The young fellow drives the express-wagon, (I love him, though I do not know him)." Ring Lardner's narrators, like the ballplayer in "Alibi Ike," talk to us in the present, as does John Updike's supermarket checker in "A & P" ("In walks these three girls in bathing suits"), because that's the way uneducated people often tell a story.

Mr. Updike wrote *Rabbit, Run* and its sequels, *Rabbit Redux* and *Rabbit Is Rich*, in the present as well. The tense suits the unmeditated life of his protagonist, Harry Angstrom; things happen to Harry, so fast that he's left bewildered. In Walker Percy's novel *The Moviegoer* and Joseph Heller's *Something Happened* we sense that the alienated narrators, Binx Bolling and Bob Slocum, speak in the present for similar reasons—to describe what has happened to them in the past tense would somehow imply that they've understood or accepted it.

Literary innovators, like Thomas Pynchon in *Gravity's Rainbow* and Calvino in *Mr. Palomar*, have periodically been drawn to the present, for much the same reason that we describe dreams in that tense—to invoke a context distinct from everyday life. A writer who helped make the present tense fashionable is Ann Beattie. Ms. Beattie recently told me that she used it in the short stories she began publishing a dozen or so years ago, and continues to call upon it frequently, for no reason other than that she imagines her scenes so vividly; she merely puts down on paper what she's "literally seeing in front of my eyes."

But that is not the whole story. If it were, so many other writers would not have picked up on her style. It is a whole school now, sometimes called "superrealists," short-story writers and occasional novelists whose work tends to appear in *The New Yorker:* Frederick Barthelme, Elizabeth Tallent, Mary Robison, Bobbie Ann Mason and others. Once in a while these authors write in the past tense, but only, one senses, to make sure that it still works.

You need only read a film treatment (a literary form always composed in the present) to realize that a key influence on this school has been the movies. The present tense lends itself to dialogue, to scenes, to the impartial observation of detail, and not to Henry James–style exegesis—circumstances not lost on a generation of authors that has spent more time looking at screens than pages.

Somewhat less obvious is the influence of journalism—specifically the New Journalism, that collection of stylistic and thematic concerns that has had so substantial an impact on nonfiction writing. The key man here is Tom Wolfe, who, beginning in the early 1960s, was drawn to scenes, and usually present-tense ones. From a 1964 Wolfe profile of Baby Jane Holzer: "Inez, the maid, brings in lunch on a tray, one rare hamburger, one cheeseburger and a glass of tomato juice. Jane tastes the tomato juice. 'Oh, —!' she says. 'It's diet.' "

Why did Mr. Wolfe's innovation prove to be so influential among both novelists and journalists? In *Simple & Direct: A Rhetoric for Writers*, Jacques Barzun writes that "motion" is "the prime virtue of prose. Knowing the value of movement, some writers fall into the present tense to narrate events in the past." In the TV age of shortened attention spans, perhaps the main challenge of writing is keeping a reader's interest. These writers try to meet it by approximating movies and television in their very readable prose.

But the real power of this way of writing springs from what's implied and not explicitly stated. Mr. Wolfe made the remarkable discovery that journalism perpetrated in scenes, and especially present-tense ones, suggests through a peculiar equation that what's being described is significant. In his essay "The New Journalism," Mr. Wolfe said one of the genre's main techniques is the recording of what he called "status details": "everyday gestures, habits, manners, customs, styles of furniture, clothing, decoration, styles of traveling, eating, keeping house, modes of behaving toward children, servants, superiors, inferiors, peers, plus the various looks, glances, poses, styles of walking and other symbolic details that might exist within a scene."

Mr. Wolfe claimed that New Journalists borrowed this posture from nineteenth-century novelists. Now, twentieth-century short-story writers are borrowing it from New Journalism. There is the same reliance on scenes, the same attention to status details (how many Kmarts have we read about in Frederick Barthelme's and Bobbie Ann Mason's stories?).

Putting this style in the hands of many of the journalists who use it is like giving an atomic bomb to Kuwait: you immediately want to close your eyes and jump under the dining-room table. But even when used by a master such as Tom Wolfe, it is something of a shell game. To describe an event in the past tense means taking a kind of responsibility for it; the I-Am-a-Camera present tense gives the unearned illusion of pure objectivity. It also obscures a highly questionable assumption: that, merely because something occurred and a reporter happened to see it, it is significant. The writer implies that he knows more than he is saying, and that the reader is smart enough to understand it, implications that are more often than not unjustified.

In fiction, too, the recording without comment of status details allows the author to wink at the reader in their shared knowledgeability. But there are other effects as well. We know that the writer has chosen these details over everything else he could have invented; by presenting them, and not telling us What It All Means, he distills a kind of polymorphous irony. On the one hand, he implies that the events represent a pattern that the characters are endlessly repeating. At the same time, we are frequently given to understand that beneath the surface is something that cannot be said—a trauma, perhaps, like an incipient divorce, or a more general sense of desperation—and is all the more palpable for being unstated.

The use of the present goes beyond technique to philosophy. Indeed, it can be seen as the logical last step in the progression of the kind of stories Chekhov and Joyce invented: stories that proceed on the assumption that expounding on meaning is no longer appropriate in fiction, rather that mundane circumstances can reveal a life in epiphany. The past tense assumes a belief in the possibility of interpretation, in the orderliness of the world, beliefs that are apparently ever harder to sustain in an age of randomness. All that these authors feel comfortable with is the cinematic presentation of data. They usually don't even give their characters last names—somehow, they wouldn't ring true, would sound too "fictional." By writing in the past, an author makes a tacit statement about his writing (it resembles the world); by writing in the present, he makes a tacit statement about the world (it resembles a movie, or a dream).

Such logic is certainly legitimate, and in the hands of the writers mentioned has produced outstanding work. Unfortunately, others use the technique without comprehending the underpinnings. They give us randomly and unimaginatively chosen details and events, signifying nothing.

Whitman tells us, "I am the man, I suffer'd, I was there," and we respect his moral and literary authority. Writers who gravitate toward the present tense don't seem to want that burden. They don't want to tell us what happened, no matter how urgently we want to be told. We want plots; they give us plot summaries, much like those we might find in the pages of *TV Guide*. This is not an illegitimate position to take. But sometimes it seems that they could try a little harder to pass beyond it.

Holocaust Funnies

Maus by Art Spiegelman
December 7, 1986

BY WILLIAM HAMILTON

ART SPIEGELMAN HAS CHOSEN to explore his painful relationship with his father, and his father's horrific experiences as a survivor of the Nazi extermination of Jews, as a comic book mouse. He isn't the only mouse in this comic book. His father is a mouse too. All Jews are mice. Nazis are cats, Poles are pigs, and non-Jewish Americans are dogs. At a

Czechoslovak sanitarium where the mother of Art Spiegelman/Artie the mouse goes to get over postpartum depression, frogs, rabbits, deer, goats, horses and elephants appear in the background.

Making a Holocaust comic book with Jews as mice and Germans as cats would probably strike most people as flippant, if not appalling. *Maus: A Survivor's Tale* is the opposite of flippant and appalling. To express yourself as an artist, you must find a form that leaves you in control but doesn't leave you by yourself. That's how *Maus* looks to me—a way Mr. Spiegelman found of making art.

Using all the quack-quack wacko comic strip conventions with the thoroughness and enthusiasm of a connoisseur, Mr. Spiegelman, a coeditor of *Raw* magazine and a teacher at New York's School of Visual Arts, draws a double tale of father and son. He does it with the wild perspective zooms the comic strips taught the movies, with pain stars and worry drips and switches from lit figures to silhouettes (a device I always suspected cartoonists originally employed to save drawing time). He uses diagrams and the same detail boxes with which Chester Gould reminded us Dick Tracy's wristwatch was a two-way radio. Bubbles rise over the heads of figures not feeling well. Dropped pills fall clear out of the frame around the mouse who knocked over the bottle. Revelation rays, crosshatched blushing, bigger, blacker lettering to signal volume or importance: the whole comic book repertory I remember adoring as a boy is lovingly employed to present this complicated, adult and unsentimental tale.

Mr. Spiegelman's protagonist, Artie, is 10 or 11 when the story begins, an anthropomorphic mouse who has a roller-skating fall. Sniffling because the friends with whom he was skating have run off, he is called over by his father and given a piece of foreboding advice: "Friends? Your friends? If you lock them together in a room with no food for a week . . . then you could see what it is, friends!"

Right from this prologue, we know the story that's coming, that Artie will draw (in two senses) out of his father. The dreadful, familiar story of the Nazi extermination of the Jews begins again, with a new set of particulars, those of the Polish life of Artie's father, Vladek Spiegelman. By setting his father's tale against his own miserable relationship with the man, Artie simultaneously presents us with this horrible persecution and its consequences 40 years after.

What is amazing is how relentlessly funny he makes it all. "I went out to see my father in Rego Park. I hadn't seen him in a long time—we weren't that close," he begins. Then, right away, a good, thematic joke—the father, who is driven crazy by everything his current wife does, snatches away the son's coat, which she is hospitably hanging up: "A wire hanger you give him! I haven't seen Artie in almost two years—we have plenty wooden hangers."

Besides imagining his father's tale in pictures, Artie shows us his own past too, in both the roller-skating fall of the prologue and a play-within-a-play

comic-within-a-comic called "Prisoner on the Hell Planet," a strip Mr. Spiegelman drew in 1972, four years after his mother committed suicide. This example
of the artist's earlier work suggests how he came to draw the victims of Hitler's
Final Solution as mice.

The characters in "Prisoner on the Hell Planet" are people. The guilt, loss,
paranoia and regret caused by a mother's suicide are expressed through human
caricatures in dense scratchboard blacks. Art Spiegelman's technique and execution here recall Posada's woodblock skeletons, Munch's *Scream* and such fabulous E.C. horror comics as "Tales of the Crypt" and "The Vault of Horror." And
like the larger story in which it is imbedded, "Prisoner" is not without humor.
Artie recollects that, while his father chanted the Kaddish (shown in Hebrew lettering) beside his wife's coffin, he himself was "pretty *spaced out* . . . I recited to
my mother from the *Tibetan Book of the Dead*!"

Growing up in America, we find our first uncommanded reading in comics.
They represent privacy and fantasy. They can become treasure. "Prisoner on the
Hell Planet" indicates they did for Art Spiegelman. He has made of them a
shrine to which he can bring his woe over his mother's suicide and the Holocaust and come away with humor, a sense of the ridiculous and some satisfying
style. The comic is as much a depiction of the artist's survival as it is the story of
his father's.

The effect of such an effort is strangely touching. Finishing *Maus* so far
(there's more to come), I felt the shiver I remember feeling during one of Duke
Ellington's jazz masses in San Francisco's Grace Cathedral when a dignified old
tap dancer began his part in the service on the solemn flagstones. The jazz mass
was so unlikely to begin with—and when it came to include a tap dancer, anything seemed possible. It showed all present how any way anyone can find to express spiritual tragedy and triumph sincerely seems sacred.

Essay

John Barth on Minimalism
December 28, 1986

"L ESS IS MORE," said Walter Gropius, or Alberto Giacometti, or Las-
zlo Moholy-Nagy, or Henri Gaudier-Brzeska, or Constantin Brancusi,
or Le Corbusier or Ludwig Mies van der Rohe; the remark (first made
in fact by Robert Browning) has been severally attributed to all of those more or
less celebrated more or less minimalists. Like the Bauhaus motto, "Form follows
function," it is itself a memorable specimen of the minimalist esthetic, of which

a cardinal principle is that artistic effect may be enhanced by a radical economy of artistic means, even where such parsimony compromises other values: completeness, for example, or richness or precision of statement.

The power of that esthetic principle is easy to demonstrate: contrast my eminently forgettable formulation of it above—"artistic effect may be enhanced," etc.—with the unforgettable assertion "Less is more." Or consider the following proposition, first with, and then without, its parenthetical elements:

Minimalism (of one sort or another) is the principle (one of the principles, anyhow) underlying (what I and many another interested observer consider to be perhaps) the most impressive phenomenon on the current (North American, especially the United States) literary scene (the gringo equivalent to *el boom* in the Latin American novel): I mean the new flowering of the (North) American short story (in particular the kind of terse, oblique, realistic or hyperrealistic, slightly plotted, extrospective, cool-surfaced fiction associated in the last 5 or 10 years with such excellent writers as Frederick Barthelme, Ann Beattie, Raymond Carver, Bobbie Ann Mason, James Robison, Mary Robison and Tobias Wolff, and both praised and damned under such labels as "K-Mart realism," "hick chic," "Diet-Pepsi minimalism" and "post-Vietnam, post-literary, postmodernist blue-collar neo-early-Hemingwayism").

Like any clutch of artists collectively labeled, the writers just mentioned are at least as different from one another as they are similar. Minimalism, moreover, is not the only and may not be the most important attribute that their fiction more or less shares; those labels themselves suggest some other aspects and concerns of the New American Short Story and its proportionate counterpart, the three-eighth-inch novel. But it is their minimalism I shall speak of (briefly) here, and its antecedence: the idea that, in art at least, less is more.

It is an idea surely as old, as enduringly attractive and as ubiquitous as its opposite. In the beginning was the Word: only later came the Bible, not to mention the three-decker Victorian novel. The oracle at Delphi did not say, "Exhaustive analysis and comprehension of one's own psyche may be prerequisite to an understanding of one's behavior and of the world at large"; it said, "Know thyself." Such inherently minimalist genres as oracles (from the Delphic shrine of Apollo to the modern fortune cookie), proverbs, maxims, aphorisms, epigrams, pensées, mottoes, slogans and quips are popular in every human century and culture—especially in oral cultures and subcultures, where mnemonic staying power has high priority—and many specimens of them are self-reflexive or self-demonstrative: minimalism about minimalism. "Brevity is the soul of wit." "Silence is golden." "*Vita brevis est, ars longa*," Seneca warns aspiring poets in his third Epistle; "Eschew surplusage," recommends Mark Twain.

Against the large-scale classical prose pleasures of Herodotus, Thucydides and Petronius, there are the miniature delights of Aesop's fables and Theophrastus' *Characters*. Against such verse epics as the *Iliad*, the *Odyssey* and the *Aeneid*—and the much longer Sanskrit *Ramayana*, *Mahabharata* and *Ocean of Story*—are such venerable supercompressive poetic forms as the palindrome (there are long examples, but the ones we remember are "Madam, I'm Adam" and "Sex at noon taxes"), or the single couplet (a modern instance is Ogden Nash's "Candy is dandy / But liquor is quicker"), or the feudal Japanese haiku and its Western echoes in the early-twentieth-century imagists up to the contemporary "skinny poems" of, say, Robert Creeley.

The genre of the short story, as Poe distinguished it from the traditional tale in his 1842 review of Hawthorne's first collection of stories, is an early manifesto of modern narrative minimalism: "In the whole composition there should be no word written, of which the tendency . . . is not to the pre-established design. . . . Undue length is . . . to be avoided." Poe's codification informs such later nineteenth-century masters of terseness, selectivity and implicitness (as opposed to leisurely once-upon-a-timelessness, luxuriant abundance, explicit and extended analysis) as Guy de Maupassant and Anton Chekhov. Show, don't tell, said Henry James in effect and at length in his prefaces to the 1908 New York edition of his novels. And don't tell a word more than you absolutely need to, added young Ernest Hemingway, who thus described his "new theory" in the early 1920s: "You could omit anything if you knew that you omitted, and the omitted part would strengthen the story and make people feel something more than they understood."

The Bauhaus Functionalists were by then already busy unornamenting and abstracting modern architecture, painting and design; and while functionalism and minimalism are not the same thing, to say nothing of abstractionism and minimalism (there is nothing abstract about those early Hemingway stories), they spring from the same impulse: to strip away the superfluous in order to reveal the necessary, the essential. Never mind that Voltaire had pointed out, a century and a half before, how indispensable the superfluous can be (*"Le superflu, chose si nécessaire"*); just as, in modern painting, the process of stripping away leads from Post-Impressionism through Cubism to the radical minimalism of Kasimir Malevich's *White on White* of 1918, and Ad Reinhardt's all but imageless "black paintings" of the 1950s, so in twentieth-century literature the minimalist succession leads through Hemingway's "new theory" to the shorter *ficciones* of Jorge Luis Borges and the ever-terser texts of Samuel Beckett, perhaps culminating in his play *Breath* (1969): The curtain opens on a dimly lit stage, empty but for scattered rubbish; there is heard a single recorded human cry, then a single amplified inspiration and expiration of breath accompanied by a brightening and redimming of the lights, then again the cry. Thirty-five seconds after it opened, the curtain closes.

But it closes only on the play, not on the modern tradition of literary minimalism, which honorably continues in such next-generation writers as, in America, Donald Barthelme ("The fragment is the only form I trust," says a character in his slender novel *Snow White*) and, in the literary generation overlapping and following his, the plentiful authors of the New American Short Story.

Old or new, fiction can be minimalist in any or all of several ways. There are minimalisms of unit, form and scale: short words, short sentences and paragraphs, super-short stories, those three-eighth-inch thin novels aforementioned, and even minimal bibliographies (Borges's fiction adds up to a few modest, though powerfully influential, short-story collections). There are minimalisms of style: a stripped-down vocabulary; a stripped-down syntax that avoids periodic sentences, serial predications and complex subordinating constructions; a stripped-down rhetoric that may eschew figurative language altogether; a stripped-down, nonemotive tone. And there are minimalisms of material: minimal characters, minimal exposition ("all that David Copperfield kind of crap," says J. D. Salinger's catcher in the rye), minimal mise-en-scènes, minimal action, minimal plot.

Found together in their purest forms, these several minimalisms add up to an art that—in the words of its arch-priest, Samuel Beckett, speaking of the painter Bram Van Velde—expresses "that there is nothing to express, nothing with which to express, nothing from which to express, no power to express, no desire to express—together with the obligation to express." But they are not always found together. There are very short works of great rhetorical, emotional and thematic richness, such as Borges's essential page, "Borges and I"; and there are instances of what may fairly be called long-winded minimalism, such as Samuel Beckett's stark-monumental trilogy from the early '50s: *Molloy, Malone Dies* and *The Unnameable*. Parallels abound in the other arts: the miniature, in painting, is characteristically brimful (miniaturism is not minimalism); Joseph Cornell's little boxes contain universes. The large paintings of Mark Rothko, Franz Kline and Barnett Newman, on the other hand, are as undetailed as the Washington Monument.

The medieval Roman Catholic Church recognized two opposite roads to grace: the *via negativa* of the monk's cell and the hermit's cave, and the *via affirmativa* of immersion in human affairs, of being *in* the world whether or not one is *of* it. Critics have aptly borrowed those terms to characterize the difference between Mr. Beckett, for example, and his erstwhile master James Joyce, himself a maximalist except in his early works. Other than bone-deep disposition, which is no doubt the great determinant, what inclines a writer—sometimes almost a cultural generation of writers—to the Negational Path?

For individuals, it may be by their own acknowledgment largely a matter of past or present personal circumstances. Raymond Carver writes of a literary apprenticeship in which his short poems and stories were carved in precious quarter-hours stolen from a harrowing domestic and economic situation; though he now has professional time aplenty, the notion besets him that should he presume to attempt even a short novel, he'll wake to find himself back in those wretched circumstances. An opposite case was Borges's: his near-total blindness in his latter decades obliged him to use the short forms that he had elected for other, nonphysical reasons when he was sighted.

To account for a trend, literary sociologists and culture watchers point to more general historical and philosophical factors—not excluding the factor of powerful models like Borges and Beckett. The influence of early Hemingway on Raymond Carver, say, is as apparent as the influence of Mr. Carver in turn on a host of other New American Short-Story writers, and on a much more numerous host of apprentices in American college fiction-writing programs. But why this model rather than that, other than its mere and sheer artistic prowess, on which after all it has no monopoly? Doubtless because this one is felt, by the writers thus more or less influenced, to speak more strongly to their condition and that of their readers.

And what is that condition, in the case of the cool-surface realist-minimalist storytellers of the American 1970s and '80s? In my conversation with them, my reading of their critics both positive and negative and my dealings with recent and current apprentice writers, I have heard cited, among other factors, these half-dozen, ranked here in no particular order:

- Our national hangover from the Vietnam War, felt by many to be a trauma literally and figuratively unspeakable. "I don't want to talk about it" is the characteristic attitude of "Nam" veterans in the fiction of Ann Beattie, Jayne Anne Phillips and Bobbie Ann Mason—as it is among many of their real-life counterparts (and as it was among their numberless twentieth-century forerunners, especially after the First World War). This is, of course, one of the two classic attitudes to trauma, the other being its opposite, and it can certainly conduce to hedged, nonintrospective, even minimalist discourse: one remembers Hemingway's early story "Soldier's Home."
- The more or less coincident energy crisis of 1973–76, and the associated reaction against American excess and wastefulness in general. The popularity

of the subcompact car parallels that (in literary circles, at least) of the sub-compact novel and the minifiction—though not, one observes, of the miniskirt, which had nothing to do with conserving material.

- The national decline in reading and writing skills, not only among the young (including even young apprentice writers, as a group), but among their teachers, many of whom are themselves the product of an ever-less-demanding educational system and a society whose narrative-dramatic entertainment and tastes come far more from movies and television than from literature. This is not to disparage the literacy and general education of those writers mentioned above, or to suggest that the great writers of the past were uniformly flawless spellers and grammarians, of wide personal literary culture. Some were, some weren't; some of today's are, some aren't. But at least among those of our aspiring writers promising enough to be admitted into good graduate writing programs—and surely they are not the *inferior* specimens of their breed—the general decline in basic language skills over the last two decades is inarguable enough to make me worry in some instances about their teaching undergraduates. Rarely in their own writing, whatever its considerable other merits, will one find a sentence of any syntactical complexity, for example, and inasmuch as a language's repertoire of other-than-basic syntactical devices permits its users to articulate other-than-basic thoughts and feelings, Dick-and-Jane prose tends to be emotionally and intellectually poorer than Henry James prose. Among the great minimalist writers, this impoverishment is elected and strategic: simplification in the interest of strength, or of some other value. Among the less great it may be *faute de mieux*. Among today's "common readers" it is pandemic.

- Along with this decline, an ever-dwindling readerly attention span. The long popular novel still has its devotees, especially aboard large airplanes and on beaches; but it can scarcely be doubted that many of the hours we bourgeois now spend with our televisions and video cassette recorders, and in our cars and at the movies, we used to spend reading novels and novellas and not-so-short stories, partly because those glitzy other distractions weren't there and partly because we were more generally conditioned for sustained concentration, in our pleasures as well as in our work. The Austrian novelist Robert Musil was complaining by 1930 (in his maxi-novel *The Man Without Qualities*) that we live in "the age of the magazine," too impatient already in the twitchy '20s to read books. Half a century later, in America at least, even the large-circulation magazine market for fiction had dwindled to a handful of outlets; the readers weren't there. It is a touching paradox of the New American Short Story—so admirably straightforward and democratic of access, so steeped in brand names and the popular culture—that it perforce appears mainly in very small-circulation literary quarterlies instead of in the likes of *Collier's, Liberty* and *The Saturday Evening Post*. But *The New Yorker* and *Esquire* can't publish everybody.

- Together with all the above, a reaction on these authors' part against the ironic, black-humoristic "fabulism" and/or the (sometimes academic) intellectuality and/or the density, here byzantine, there baroque, of some of their immediate American literary antecedents: the likes of Donald Barthelme, Robert Coover, Stanley Elkin, William Gaddis and William Gass, John Hawkes, Joseph Heller, Thomas Pynchon, Kurt Vonnegut (and, I shall presume, myself as well). This reaction, where it exists, would seem to pertain as much to our successors' relentless realism as to their minimalism: among the distinguished brothers Barthelme, Donald's productions are no less lean than Frederick's; but their characteristic material, angle of attack and resultant flavor are different indeed. So it goes: The dialogue between fantast and realist, fabulator and quotidianist, like the dialogue between maximalist and minimalist, is as old as storytelling, and by no means always adversary. There are innumerable combinations, coalitions, line-crossings and workings of both sides of the street.

- The reaction against the all but inescapable hyperbole of American advertising, both commercial and political, with its high-tech manipulativeness and glamorous lies, as ubiquitous as and more polluted than the air we breathe. How understandable that such an ambiance, together with whatever other items in this catalogue, might inspire a fiction dedicated to homely, understated, programmatically unglamorous, even minimalistic Telling It Like It Is.

That has ever been the ground inspiration, moral-philosophical in character, of minimalism and its kissing cousin realism in their many avatars over the centuries, in the fine arts and elsewhere: the feeling that the language (or whatever) has for whatever reasons become excessive, cluttered, corrupted, fancy, false. It is the Puritans' reaction against baroque Catholicism; it is Thoreau's putting behind him even the meager comforts of the village of Concord.

To the Lost Generation of World War I survivors, says one of their famous spokesmen (Frederic Henry in Hemingway's *Farewell to Arms*), "Abstract words such as glory, honor, courage, or hallow were obscene." Wassily Kandinsky said he sought "not the shell, but the nut." The functionalism of the Bauhaus was inspired in part by admiration for machine technology, in part by revulsion against the fancy clutter of the Gilded Age, in language as well as elsewhere. The sinking of the elegant *Titanic* has come to symbolize the end of that age, as the sight of some workmen crushed by a falling Victorian cornice symbolized for young Frank Lloyd Wright the dead weight of functionless architectural decoration.

Flaubert raged against the *blague* of bourgeois speech, bureaucratic speech in particular; his passion for the mot juste involved far more subtraction than addition. The baroque inspires its opposite: after the excesses of scholasticism comes Descartes's radical reductionism—let us doubt and discard everything not self-evident and see whether anything indubitable remains upon which to rebuild. And among the scholastics themselves, three centuries before Descartes, William of Ockham honed his celebrated razor: *Entia non sunt multiplicanda* ("Entities are not to be multiplied").

In short, less is more.

But if there is much to admire in artistic austerity, its opposite is not without merits and joys as well. There are the minimalist pleasures of Emily Dickinson—"Zero at the Bone"—and the maximalist ones of Walt Whitman; the low-fat rewards of Samuel Beckett's *Texts for Nothing* and the high-calorie delights of Gabriel García Márquez's *One Hundred Years of Solitude*. There truly are more ways than one to heaven. As between minimalism and its opposite, I pity the reader—or the writer, or the age—too addicted to either to savor the other.

Sherman's March to Disaster

The Bonfire of the Vanities by Tom Wolfe
November 1, 1987

BY FRANK CONROY

NOW COMES TOM WOLFE, aging enfant terrible, with his first novel, (his first novel!), six hundred and fifty-nine pages of raw energy about New York City and various of its inhabitants—a big, bitter, funny, craftily plotted book that grabs you by the lapels and won't let go. As in much of his other work, such as *The Right Stuff*, Mr. Wolfe's strategy is to somehow batter the reader into submission, using an incantatory repetition of certain emblematic phrases, (HIS FIRST NOVEL!), detailed description of people's clothing, hyperbole, interior monologue whenever he feels like it, and various other New Journalism devices he is apparently too fond of to give up. What is amazing is that he gets away with it. I read *The Bonfire of the Vanities* straight through, in two sessions on two consecutive days, and enjoyed it enormously. It swept me right up. When he writes about process he knows what he is writing about, whether it's the Wall Street bond market, the Bronx District Attorney's Office, print and television journalism, or the working habits of sleazy lawyers—the man knows how to prepare and he knows how to research. As well, he knows how to tell a story, and how to make us laugh, qualities not always present in the work of some of the more polished, more literary or ultimately more ambitious novelists of his generation.

The novel relates the fall of Sherman McCoy, an investment banker making a million a year who seems blind to everything except appearances, sex and money. He lives in the middle of New York City without knowing New York City. He seems barely to know his decorative wife, his decorative daughter or his libidinous mistress, to say nothing of himself. He's all surface is Sherman, and when he blunders off the expressway into the welfare jungle of the South Bronx in his $48,000 Mercedes, into the biggest trouble of his heretofore charmed life, he is without reserves of experience, imagination or moral awareness with which to guide himself. All he's got is adrenaline and fear, fear and adrenaline. He's a sort of carefully bred white rat in Dr. Wolfe's urban laboratory of horrors, destined to run mazes and endure shocks for our edification and amusement. (His first novel!)

The action jumps back and forth from upper-class Sherman, or to borrow some lingo from the recording industry, from Sherman's track, to the Criminal-Justice-System-in-the-Bronx track—involving Assistant D.A. Kramer (a working slob), Judge Kovitsky (burnt out), various cops and other marginally middle-class types—to the corrupt media track, involving the degenerate newspaper reporter Peter Fallow (writing for a thinly disguised *New York Post*), to the venal lower-class black track and the hypocritical and aptly named Reverend Bacon. There are dozens of minor characters on each track, and Mr. Wolfe does a fine job of keeping them all under control and in clear focus, while the major characters spiral in on each other toward the final explosive courtroom scene.

The plot is simple. Sherman screws up and the dark forces of the city close in on his rich white butt—but the presentation, or the attenuated revelation of the plot, is admirably complex, and allows for the weaving in of much interesting ancillary material. Mr. Wolfe never cheats the reader. He works hard to get every last bit of juice from every scene, every situation.

And yet, when the author has let go of your lapels and the book is over, there is an odd aftertaste, not entirely pleasant. Maybe he doesn't entirely get away with it.

Homophonic attempts to re-create regional or class accents are only irritating. " 'N thin mibby nuthun" seems clumsy rather than Southern. "Muh uhms uh shakin" seems strained. Nor is the urban black speech, Long Island WASP or New Yorkese any better. Mr. Wolfe misses, it seems to me, because of a tendency to embrace the grotesque. It is the fact of an accent, rather than the quality or nature of it, that interests him. Elmore Leonard, for instance, goes after the sound and rhythm of certain accents, and does it very well without any tortured spelling. (So does James Baldwin, for that matter.) Mr. Wolfe writes with another agenda, with a kind of malicious glee, and exaggerates in order to make fun of his characters, with whom, truth be told, he has not much sympathy.

The relentless writing about clothing becomes tiresome. As new characters enter the narrative we are immediately told, at length and in elaborate detail, what they are wearing, as if the key to an understanding of their souls might emerge from that information. Again, malice is involved. Sherman, in his $1,800 imported suit and British hand-lasted shoes, is, ipso facto, an arriviste and a poseur. A detective wearing "a sport jacket and the sort of brown pants a wife might choose to go with it" has obviously delegated too much authority. Professors wear "rotting tweeds," blacks wear running shoes. Everyone is slightly absurd. Mr. Wolfe seems unable to imagine a character who gets dressed simply to avoid being naked. The clothes are always understood to be a choice, a statement, expressing some folly or character flaw or some lie. There is so much about clothes, about appearances, that the author runs the risk of being understood to say that's all there is.

Novelists often try to show us how people have changed by describing what they do or say. Mr. Wolfe makes gestures in that direction, but he always falls back on appearances, on descriptions of surfaces. As it turns out, it doesn't matter if we believe Sherman has changed (which is lucky, because we don't). It is enough that we believe he went through the fire.

The odd aftertaste may be in part because there aren't any people in the book who seem to exist independent of the author's will, no one with enough depth to surpass his or her accent, clothing, class or situation, no one for whom believable change is possible. They are all victims of fashion or other surface forces. The fun of the book, and much of its energy, comes from watching Mr.

Wolfe eviscerate one pathetic character after another. And he is good at it, really
brilliant sometimes—whether it be a society matron or a Jewish business tycoon
making money running charter jets to Mecca for Arabs—but after a while, when
it turns out that *everyone* is pathetic (except for me and thee, of course), the fun
can turn sour. Malice is a powerful spice. Too much can ruin the stew, and Mr.
Wolfe comes close.

The Plague

And the Band Played On by **Randy Shilts**
November 8, 1987

BY H. JACK GEIGER

IN *AND THE BAND PLAYED ON*, Randy Shilts, a reporter for *The San
Francisco Chronicle* who has covered AIDS full time since 1983, takes us almost day by day through the first five years of the unfolding epidemic and
the responses—confusion and fear, denial and indifference, courage and determination.

In the beginning, Mr. Shilts writes, physicians and scientists (with the exception of a heroic and dedicated handful) did not devote appropriate attention to
the epidemic "because they perceived little prestige to be gained in studying a
homosexual affliction." Desperately underfinanced and shorthanded, epidemi-
ologists were delayed for months and years in linking all the cases of a little-
known skin cancer and bizarre infections with obscure microbes, tracking down
the chains of transmission from person to person, understanding that the root
cause was a new sexually transmitted virus spread via semen and blood.

And even when that understanding was dawning and the massive epidemic
threat was clear, as Mr. Shilts documents exhaustively, the Reagan administration ignored pleas from many scientists and physicians, cut funding mercilessly
and sent its agency heads to mislead Congressional committees by saying that
the researchers had everything they needed.

Meanwhile, he notes, gay community leaders (like everyone else!) "played
politics with the disease, putting political dogma ahead of the preservation of
human life." The mass media yawned in indifference and shunned the story
until the movie star Rock Hudson died of AIDS in the summer of 1985.

There are some troubles with this thesis, both in substance and in presentation. In his appropriate rage over indifference and lives lost, Mr. Shilts overstates
the effect earlier intervention would have had. There would have been a major

epidemic in any case because AIDS patients—unknowingly infected and capable of transmitting the virus for years before symptoms appeared—were steadily infecting others.

But this is only one of the five major stories Mr. Shilts is covering. There is the epidemiological story—the medical stumbling over clues, the exhausting tracking down and charting of cases. There is the human story: the anguish, terror, rage, denial, painful suffering and miserable deaths of specific human beings. There is the pain of their friends and lovers, the growth of fear in whole communities.

There is also the clinical story of physicians struggling to both treat and care for AIDS patients—desperately comparing notes, searching the medical journals, fighting for hospital beds and resources. There is the story of the scientific research that led at last to a basic understanding of the disease, the identification of the virus, the test for antibodies. And, finally, there is the larger political and cultural story, the response of the society, and its profound impact on all the other aspects of the AIDS epidemic.

Mr. Shilts tells them all—but he tells them all at once, in five simultaneous but disjointed chronologies, making them all less coherent.

The reader drowns in detail. The book jacket says that Mr. Shilts—in addition to his years of daily coverage of the epidemic—conducted more than 900 interviews in 12 nations and dug out thousands of pages of Government documents. He seems to have used every one of them. Reading *And the Band Played On* sometimes feels like studying a gigantic mosaic, one square at a time.

Finally, and most disturbingly, there are people missing from the book: the intravenous drug users and their sexual partners—a population that is mostly poor and black or Hispanic—who now constitute the great second wave of the AIDS epidemic, and a great share of its future. Mr. Shilts gives them a few paragraphs, no case reports, no personal or human accounts.

Not long ago, Dr. Stephen Joseph—New York City Health Commissioner, and one of the most skilled and humane of public health officials—sketched the future of the AIDS epidemic. A majority of the anticipated tens of thousands of 1991 New York City AIDS patients will be black and Hispanic intravenous drug users, their sexual partners and their babies.

How, someone asked, will two more oppressed minorities move the nation, the rest of us, to provide the needed resources? There was a long pause. "Well," Dr. Joseph at last said softly, "we'll find out what kind of people we are, and what kind of people we want to be." *And the Band Played On* is about the kind of people we have been for the past seven years. That is its terror, and its strength.

1987

Toni Morrison's *Beloved* does not win the National Book Award, prompting 48 black writers to issue a protest statement, which is published in the *Book Review* on January 24, 1988.

Essay

William Styron on James Baldwin
December 20, 1987

JAMES BALDWIN WAS THE GRANDSON of a slave. I was the grandson of a slave owner. We were virtually the same age and both bemused by our close link to slavery, since most Americans of our vintage—if connected at all to the Old South—have had to trace that connection back several generations. But Jimmy had vivid images of slave times, passed down from his grandfather to his father, a Harlem preacher of fanatical bent who left a terrifying imprint on his son's life. Jimmy once told me that he often thought the degradation of his grandfather's life was the animating force behind his father's apocalyptic, often incoherent rage.

By contrast my impression of slavery was quaint and rather benign; in the late 1930s, at the bedside of my grandmother who was then close to 90, I heard tales of the two little slave girls she had owned. Not much older than the girls themselves at the outset of the Civil War, she knitted stockings for them, tried to take care of them through the privations of the conflict and, at the war's end, was as wrenched with sorrow as they were by the enforced leave-taking. When I told this classic story to Jimmy he didn't flinch. We both were writing about the tangled relations of blacks and whites in America and because he was wise Jimmy understood the necessity of dealing with the preposterous paradoxes that had dwelled at the heart of the racial tragedy—the unrequited loves as well as the murderous furies. The dichotomy amounted to an obsession in much of his work; it was certainly a part of my own, and I think our common preoccupation helped make us good friends.

Jimmy moved into my studio in Connecticut in the late fall of 1960 and stayed there more or less continuously until the beginning of the following summer. A mutual friend had asked my wife and me to give Jimmy a place to stay and since he was having financial problems it seemed a splendid idea. Baldwin was not very well known then—except perhaps in literary circles where his first novel, *Go Tell It on the Mountain,* was greatly admired—but his fame was gradually gaining momentum and he divided his time between writing in the cottage and trips out to the nearby lecture circuit, where he made some money for himself and where, with his ferocious oratory, he began to scare his predominantly well-to-do, well-meaning audiences out of their pants.

Without being in the slightest comforted as a Southerner, or let off the hook, I understood through him that black people regarded all Americans as irredeemably racist, the most sinful of them being not the Georgia redneck (who was in part the victim of his heritage) but any citizen whatever whose de jure equality was a facade for de facto enmity and injustice.

Jimmy was writing his novel *Another Country* and making notes for the essay *The Fire Next Time*. I was consolidating material, gathered over more than a decade, for a novel I was planning to write on the slave revolutionary Nat Turner. It was a frightfully cold winter, a good time for the Southern writer, who had never known a black man on intimate terms, and the Harlem-born writer, who had known few Southerners (black or white), to learn something about each other. I was by far the greater beneficiary. Struggling still to loosen myself from the prejudices and suspicions that a Southern upbringing engenders, I still possessed a residual skepticism: could a Negro really own a mind as subtle, as richly informed, as broadly inquiring and embracing as that of a white man?

My God, what appalling arrogance and vanity! Night after night Jimmy and I talked, drinking whisky through the hours until the chill dawn, and I understood that I was in the company of as marvelous an intelligence as I was ever likely to encounter. His voice, lilting and silky, became husky as he chain-smoked Marlboros. He was spellbinding, and he told me more about the frustrations and anguish of being a black man in America than I had known until then, or perhaps wanted to know. He told me exactly what it was like to be denied service, to be spat at, to be called "nigger" and "boy."

What he explained gained immediacy because it was all so new to me. This chronicle of an urban life, his own life, un-self-pityingly but with quiet rage spun out to me like a secret divulged, as if he were disgorging in private all the pent-up fury and gorgeous passion that a few years later, in *The Fire Next Time*, would shake the conscience of the nation as few literary documents have ever done. We may have had occasional disputes, but they were usually culinary rather than literary; a common conviction dominated our attitude toward the writing of fiction, and this was that in the creation of novels and stories the writer should be free to demolish the barrier of color, to cross the forbidden line and write from the point of view of someone with a different skin. Jimmy had made this leap already and he had done it with considerable success. I was reluctant to try to enter the mind of a slave in my book on Nat Turner but I felt the necessity and I told Jimmy this. I am certain that it was his encouragement—so strong that it was as if he were daring me not to—that caused me finally to impersonate a black man.

Sometimes friends would join us. The conversation would turn more abstract and political. I am surprised when I recall how certain of these people—well-intentioned, tolerant, "liberal," all the postures Jimmy so intuitively mistrusted—would listen patiently while Jimmy spoke, visibly fretting then growing indignant at some pronouncement of his, some scathing aperçu they considered too ludicrous for words, too extreme, and launch a polite counter-attack. "You can't mean anything like that!" I can hear the words now. "You mean *burn* . . ." And in the troubled silence, Jimmy's face would become a mask of imperturbable certitude. "Baby," he would say softly and glare back with vast glowering eyes, "yes baby, I mean *burn*. We will *burn your cities down.*"

Lest I give the impression that that winter was all grim, let me say that this was not so. Jimmy was a social animal of nearly manic gusto and there were some loud and festive times. When summer came and he departed for good, heading for his apotheosis—the flamboyant celebrity that the 1960s brought him—he left a silence that to this day somehow resonates through the house.

In 1967, when *The Confessions of Nat Turner* was published, I began to learn with great discomfort the consequences of my audacity in acquiring the persona of a black man. With a few distinguished exceptions (the historian John Hope Franklin for one), black intellectuals and writers expressed their outrage at both the historical imposture I had created and my presumption. But Jimmy Baldwin remained steadfast to those convictions we had expressed to each other during our nighttime sessions six years before. In the turmoil of such a controversy I am sure that it was impossible for him not to have experienced conflicting loyalties, but when one day I read a public statement he made about the book—"He has begun the common history—*ours*"—I felt great personal support but, more importantly, the reaffirmation of some essential integrity. After those days in Connecticut I never saw him as often as I would have liked but our paths crossed many times and we always fell on each other with an uncomplicated sense of joyous reunion.

Much has been written about Baldwin's effect on the consciousness of the world. Let me speak for myself. Even if I had not valued much of this work—which was flawed, like all writing, but which at its best had a burnished eloquence and devastating impact—I would have deemed his friendship inestimable. At his peak he had the beautiful fervor of Camus or Kafka. Like them he revealed to me the core of his soul's savage distress and thus helped me shape and define my own work and its moral contours. This would be the most appropriate gift imaginable to the grandson of a slave owner from a slave's grandson.

Primo Levi is found dead at the foot of a stairwell in his home, an apparent suicide.

Bearing Witness

The Drowned and the Saved by Primo Levi
January 10, 1988

BY IRVING HOWE

T<small>O THE VAST LITERATURE</small> on the Holocaust, this modest little book forms no more than a footnote. But it's a precious footnote—a series of ripe meditations about the experience of Auschwitz, where the Italian-Jewish writer Primo Levi worked as a slave laborer during the Second World War.

Shortly before his suicide last April, Primo Levi remarked that in writing about "the tragic world" of the camps he hoped to avoid the frayed rhetoric of pathos or revenge; he chose instead to "assume the calm, sober language of the witness." His new and final book, in Raymond Rosenthal's lucid translation, employs exactly that language: humane, disciplined and, in its final impact, utterly sad.

After his liberation Levi wrote two books, now acknowledged classics, about his imprisonment in the camps: *Survival in Auschwitz* (1947) and *The Reawakening* (1963). *The Drowned and the Saved*, while a smaller work, represents Levi's concluding effort to understand an experience that, as he had himself often indicated, must finally seem beyond the reach of human understanding.

One of Levi's most striking chapters, entitled "Useless Violence," details the cruelty of the camp overlords, which seemingly had no purpose other than, perhaps, the pleasure that can come to some human beings from tormenting others. With his gift for the exact detail, Levi describes this "useless violence" from the terrors of the train transports to the humiliations of strippings, beatings, endless roll calls, tattoos and torture. It turns out, however, that from the Nazi point of view this "useless violence" was not quite useless.

Nazi logic was clear. Systematically to dehumanize both guards and prisoners meant to create a realm of subjugation no longer responsive to the common norms of civilized society; and from this very process they had set in motion, the Nazis could then "conclude" that indeed Jews were not human.

Step by step Levi shows how the humiliating stratification within the camps depended on a series of small "privileges"—small, but often making the difference between life and death. There were the little "jobs" which gave a minority of prisoners a bit of extra nourishment. There were the "better" jobs occupied by "low-ranking functionaries, a picturesque fauna: sweepers, kettle washers, night watchmen, bed smoothers (who exploited to their minuscule advantage the German fixation about bunks made up flat and square), checkers of lice and scabies, messengers, interpreters, assistants' assistants."

Moral judgment becomes more "delicate" with regard to those who occupied seemingly more advantageous positions: the barracks chiefs; the clerks, sometimes complicit in dreadful things, sometimes manipulating SS officers to soften a blow or spare a life.

Levi hesitates to judge, dealing compassionately with the "gray cases," those wretched prisoners who worked for and, if they could, against the Nazis. Even with regard to the Sonderkommandos (the details assigned to dispose of corpses in the gas chambers), Levi tries to maintain a balance of response that may be beyond human capacity.

Primo Levi's little book offers more of value, especially a discussion of the shame and guilt felt by survivors of the camps. Let me, however, turn to Levi's concluding essay, in which he recounts the correspondence he conducted with a number of Germans who read his early books about the camps and then troubled to write him. These were by no means the worst of the Germans; quite the contrary. Yet one grows a little sick at reading their pleas of extenuation, sometimes their whining evasions. Of course these correspondents don't defend the Nazis, but rarely do they confront the crucial question: How was it possible that so many Germans could vote for and then yield themselves to the Nazis?

With unruffled dignity Levi answers his correspondents, pointing out, for example, that the claim of "not having known" is often impossible to believe; that anti-Semitism, far from being a Nazi invention, was deeply imbedded in German culture; and that there are clear cases of complicity—"no one forced the Topf Company (flourishing today in Wiesbaden) to build the enormous multiple crematoria."

Whoever has come under the sway of Primo Levi's luminous mind and lovely prose will feel pained at the realization that we shall not be hearing from him again. At a time when the Holocaust, like almost everything else in our culture, has been subjected to the vulgarity of public relations, Primo Levi wrote about this most terrible event with a purity of spirit for which we can only feel grateful. This was a man.

Family Matters

Breathing Lessons by Anne Tyler
September 11, 1988

BY EDWARD HOAGLAND

ANNE TYLER, who is blessedly prolific and graced with an effortless-seeming talent at describing whole rafts of intricately individualized people, might be described as a domestic novelist, one of that great line descending from Jane Austen. She is interested not in divorce or infidelity, but in marriage—not very much in isolation, estrangement, alienation and other fashionable concerns, but in courtship, child raising and filial responsibility. It's a hectic, clamorous focus for a writer to choose during the 1980s, and a mark of her competence that in this fractionated era she can write so well about blood links and family funerals, old friendships or the dogged pull of thwarted love, of blunted love affairs or marital mismatches that neither mend nor end. Her eye is kindly, wise and versatile (an eye that you would want on your jury if you ever had to stand trial), and after going at each new set of characters with authorial eagerness and an exuberant tumble of details, she tends to arrive at a set of conclusions about them that is a sort of golden mean.

Her interest is in families—drifters do not intrigue her—and yet it is the crimps and bends in people that appeal to her sympathy. She is touched by their lesions, by the quandaries, dissipated dreams and foundered ambitions that have rendered them pot-bound, because it isn't really the drifters (staples of American fiction since Melville's Ishmael and *Huckleberry Finn*) who break up a family so often as the homebodies who sink into inaction with a broken axle, seldom *saying* that they've lost hope, but dragging through the weekly round.

Thus Ms. Tyler loves meddlers, like Elizabeth in *The Clock Winder* (1972), Muriel in *The Accidental Tourist* (1985) and Maggie Moran in *Breathing Lessons*, her latest novel. If meddlers aren't enough to make things happen, she will throw in a pregnancy or abrupt bad luck or a death in the family, so that the clan must gather and confront one another. She pushes events on people who don't want anything to happen to them, afraid that if the phone rings they may have to pick up a son at the police station, people accustomed to the idea that if anybody needs to move it usually means that he has lost his job. They don't get promotions; they hug what they have. Though once upon a time they did look up the ladder, now they're mainly trying to keep from sliding into a catastrophe such as bankruptcy, a grown child taking to drink, a bust-up between brothers and sisters who have been smothering or battering each other. Clinging to a low rung of the middle class, they are householders because they have inherited a decaying home, not because they're richer than renters, and they remain bemused or bewildered by the fortuitous quality of most major "decisions" in their own or others' lives, particularly by how people come to marry whom they do: a month or two of headlong, blind activity leading to years and years of stasis. And whatever Ms. Tyler puts them through is going to be uprooting and abrasive before it is redemptive. "Real life at last! you could say," as Maggie tells herself in *Breathing Lessons*. (The title refers to the various instructive promptings that accompany contemporary pregnancy.)

Maggie, surprised by life, which did not live up to her honeymoon, has become an incorrigible prompter. She doesn't hesitate to reach across from the passenger seat and honk while her husband, Ira, is driving. And she has horned in to bring about the birth of her first grandchild by stopping a seventeen-year-old girl named Fiona at the door of an abortion clinic and steering her into marrying Maggie's son, Jesse, who is the father and, like Fiona, a dropout from high school. Maggie's motives are always mixed. She wants to get that new baby into her now stiflingly lifeless house, and does succeed in installing the young couple in the next room, with the baby and crib being placed in hers. Jesse, in black jeans, aspires to be a rock star to escape the drudging anonymity he sees as his father's fate, in a picture frame store. "I refuse to believe that I will die unknown," he tells Ira (but eight years later is a salesman at Chick's Cycle Shop). Fiona, after the inevitable blowup, soon moves away to the house of *her* mother—the dreadful Mrs. Stuckey—where Maggie follows to spy on the baby.

Maggie is daring, enterprising and indulges her habit of pouring her heart out to every listening stranger, which naturally infuriates Ira, who, uncommunicative to start with, has reached the point where Maggie can divine his moods only from the pop songs of the 1950s that he whistles. Besides whistling, his pleasure is playing solitaire. He had dreamed of working on the frontiers of medicine, but after he graduated from high school his father, complaining of a heart problem, dumped the little family business on him, as well as the duty of supporting two unmarriageable, unemployable sisters.

Maggie, by contrast, is working quite happily as an aide at a nursing home, a job she started when high school ended. Her wishful notion that her son would make a good husband and father is based on her memory of him feeding her soup with a spoon once when she was sick. But Ira takes a far more "realistic," severely disappointed view of Jesse, and silently watches Daisy, their daughter— who at 13 months had undertaken her own toilet training and by first grade was setting her alarm an hour early in order to iron and color-coordinate her outfit for school—grow away from them and head off for college. Not long ago Daisy

1988

Ian Hamilton publishes *In Search of J. D. Salinger,* a biography that was heavily revised after Salinger successfully sued to prevent Hamilton from using his unpublished correspondence.

had stared at Maggie for the longest time with this "fascinated expression on her face, and then she said, 'Mom? Was there a certain conscious point in your life when you decided to settle for being ordinary?' "

Ms. Tyler, who was born in 1941, has 10 previous books under her belt, which, as one reads through them, get better and better. Deceptively modest in theme, they have a frequent complement of middle-aged solitaire players, anxious grandparents, blocked bachelors, dysfunctional sisters or brothers, urgent snappish teen-agers wanting fame the week after tomorrow, unfortunate small children being raised by parents not quite fit for the project, or parents suffering the ultimate tragedy of the death of a child, and they have progressed from her early sentiment in *Celestial Navigation* (1974) that "sad people are the only real ones. They can tell you the truth about things." Maggie, although exasperating, isn't sad, and like the more passively benevolent Ezra Tull in *Dinner at the Homesick Restaurant* (1982), she is trying to make a difference, to connect or unite people, beat the drum for forgiveness and compromise. As Ira explains: "It's Maggie's weakness: She believes it's all right to alter people's lives. She thinks the people she loves are better than they really are, and so then she starts changing things around to suit her view of them."

In every book the reader is immersed in the frustrating alarums of a family—the Pikes, the Pecks, the Tulls, the Learys—and though Ms. Tyler's spare, stripped writing style resembles that of the so-called minimalists (most of whom are her contemporaries), she is unlike them because of the depth of her affections and the utter absence from her work of a fashionable contempt for life.

She *loves* love stories, though she often inventories the woe and entropy of lovelessness. She likes a wedding and all the ways that weddings can differ, loves to enumerate the idiosyncrasies of children's sensibilities and of house furnishings. Temperate though she is, she celebrates intemperance, zest and an appetite for whatever, just as long as families do stay together. She wants her characters plausibly married and caring for each other. We're not introduced to the heroic theses typical of many authors in the pantheon of American letters. Her male heroes tend to have trick backs and deliberately give up, settle for decidedly less from life than they had anticipated.

The literature of resignation—of wisely settling for less than life had seemed to offer—is exemplified by Henry James among American writers. It is a theme more European than New World by tradition, but with the graying of America into middle age since World War II, it has gradually taken strong root here and become dominant among Ms. Tyler's generation.

Because Ms. Tyler is at the top of her powers, it's fair to wonder whether she has developed the kind of radiant, doubling dimension to her books that may enable them to outlast the seasons of their publication. Is she unblinking, for example? No, she is not unblinking. Her books contain scarcely a hint of the abscesses of racial friction that eat at the very neighborhoods she is devoting her working life to picturing. Her people are eerily virtuous, Quakerishly tolerant of all strangers, all races. And she touches upon sex so lightly, compared with her graphic realism on other matters, that her total portrait of motivation is tilted out of balance.

Deservedly successful, she has marked her progress by changing her imprimatur on the copyright pages of her novels from "Anne Modarressi" to "Anne Tyler Modarressi" to "Anne Tyler Modarressi, et al." to "ATM, Inc." That would be fine, except that it strikes me that she has taken to prettifying the final pages of her novels too. And in *Breathing Lessons*, the comedies of Fiona's baby's delivery in the hospital and of Maggie's horrendously inept driving have been caricatured to unfunny slapstick, as if in an effort to corral extra readers. I don't believe Ms. Tyler should think she needs to tinker with her popularity. It is based upon the fact that she is very good at writing about old people, very good on young children, very good on teen-agers, very good on breadwinners and also stay-at-homes: that she is superb at picturing men and portraying women.

Looking History in the Eye

The Satanic Verses by Salman Rushdie
January 29, 1989

BY A. G. MOJTABAI

SALMAN RUSHDIE, author most famously of *Midnight's Children*, opens his fourth and latest novel, *The Satanic Verses*, with a scene of human figures tumbling from the debris of a hijacked jumbo jetliner. The sole survivors are a strange twosome: Gibreel Farishta and Saladin Chamcha. Gibreel is a celebrated face and figure of the Indian cinema. Chamcha is a star of the dubbing trade on British radio and television.

The book moves with Gibreel and Chamcha from their past lives in Bombay to London, and back to Bombay again. For Gibreel, there is many an imaginary journey on the way—most notably to a city of sand called Jahilia (for ignorance), where a very decent, embattled businessman-turned-prophet by the name of Mahound is rising to prominence.

The Satanic Verses has sparked bitter controversy among Muslims in South Africa, where the author was prevented from appearing at a book fair by arson and death threats against all concerned with the event. Last fall the importation of the British edition of the book was banned in India as a precautionary measure against religious leaders using it to incite their followers to sectarian violence.

Some of the noisiest objections have been raised by people who have never read the book and have no intention of ever reading it. This opposition does little to educate a woefully ignorant and prejudiced Western public about the Islamic faith. And there are, I think, real problems in the text that need to be addressed.

Let us consider two issues by way of example: One of the furor-provoking episodes crops up in Gibreel's story "Return to Jahilia," where the women of a brothel called the Curtain decide to improve their trade by impersonating the wives of the Prophet. What the objectors have overlooked here is that the entire episode is one of Gibreel's dreams, a cinematic fantasy. The script may strike the reader as tasteless, but this poor taste is an accurate satiric reflection of the state of much contemporary cinema.

Deeper ground for puzzlement, if not complaint, lies elsewhere—particularly in the choice of the name "Mahound" for Mohammed. In the medieval Christian mystery plays, Mahound is always a satanic figure. How are we to understand the adoption—by a writer born a Muslim—of so defamatory a name for the prophet of Islam?

Again, it must be remembered that this is fiction. More precisely, this is a dream within a fiction—twice removed from the actual. Gibreel is, we are told, in the grip of "paranoid schizophrenia." Yet, clearly, something more programmatic is afoot here. In a direct aside to the reader, the author offers this by way of explanation:

"Here he [the prophet in Gibreel's dream] is neither Mahomet nor Moe-Hammered; has adopted, instead, the demon-tag the farangis [Europeans or foreigners] hung around his neck."

A sort of self-immunization, then? But it doesn't work like this, and who knows it better than Salman Rushdie? For much of the power of the novel lies in its ability to make clear the efficacy of our impersonations, of our monstrous descriptions of one another, to create monsters *in fact*.

It is Mr. Rushdie's wide-ranging power of assimilation and imaginative boldness that make his work so different from that of other well-known Indian novelists, such as R. K. Narayan, and the exuberance of his comic gift that distinguishes his writing from that of V. S. Naipaul. In Salman Rushdie's work, both India and England are repeopled and take on new shapes. For the Indian subcontinent there is a more commensurate bigness and teemingness, a registration of the pandemonium and sleaze of contemporary life. London neighborhoods suddenly leap to light as rich collages of transplanted Asian and African cultures. His fiction also takes on fashionable literary gestures—Joycean wordplay, magic realism and the hyperactivity, the "jouncing and bouncing" of the Coca-Cola ads that typify American culture to much of the world.

For the Western reader unfamiliar with Mr. Rushdie's work, to what can this latest novel be compared? In its entirety, it resembles only itself, but there are, in its parts, strands and shades of resemblance: to Sterne, for one, in the joys of digression; to Swift in scathingness of political satire; to the fairy and folktales of the Brothers Grimm, to Ovid's *Metamorphoses*, *The Arabian Nights*, Thomas Mann's *Transposed Heads* and the work of Gabriel García Márquez, Günter Grass, Thomas Pynchon, John Barth, Italo Calvino, *Saturday Night Live* and Douglas Adams's *Hitchhiker's Guide to the Galaxy*.

Although Mr. Rushdie explicitly evokes *Othello*—Chamcha playing a sort of Iago to Gibreel's Othello, it is not this play but the comic uproar of *A Midsummer Night's Dream* that kept coming to mind. But the lightheartedness of that midsummer frolic is not to be found here. Mr. Rushdie's work, at its strongest, is burdened with history and political freight.

Talent? Not in question. Big talent. Ambition? Boundless ambition. Salman Rushdie is a storyteller of prodigious powers, able to conjure up whole geographies, causalities, climates, creatures, customs, out of thin air. Yet, in the end, what have we? As a display of narrative energy and wealth of invention, *The Satanic Verses* is impressive. As a sustained exploration of the human condition, it flies apart into delirium.

For, often, the result of all this high-wire virtuosity is a dulling of affect, much like the blurring created by rapid hopping between channels on television: nothing seems quite real. Mr. Rushdie himself, an astute observer of the effects of fast-forwarding and remote-control devices on the way we perceive the world, takes careful note of the channel-hopping phenomenon, observing that "all the set's emissions, commercials, murders, game-shows, the thousand and one varying joys and terrors of the real and the imagined" begin to acquire "an equal weight."

But, of course, they aren't of equal weight, and after closing *The Satanic Verses* the real strengths of the book assert themselves. What finally lingers, what lives most vibrantly, for this reader, are the scenes that are grounded—the places

Vaclav Havel is elected President of Czechoslovakia, becoming the country's first non-Communist president since 1948.

where magic doesn't overwhelm the realism—the moments when Mr. Rushdie looks "history in the eye."

But I suspect that Mr. Rushdie already knows this. His book is large enough to contain, implicitly, its own self-criticism and its own advice to the author. The words of advice come near the end of the novel. They are addressed to Chamcha. Zeeny Vakil, the first Indian woman Chamcha has ever loved, is letting him have it:

> If you're serious about shaking off your foreignness, Salad baba, then don't fall into some kind of rootless limbo instead. Okay? We're all here. We're right in front of you. You should really try and make an adult acquaintance with this place, this time. Try and embrace this city, as it is, not some childhood memory that makes you both nostalgic and sick. Draw it close. The actually existing place.

Essay

Henry Louis Gates Jr. on the Literary Canon
February 26, 1989

WILLIAM BENNETT AND ALLAN BLOOM, the dynamic duo of the new cultural right, have become the easy targets of the cultural left, which I am defining here loosely and generously as that uneasy, shifting set of alliances formed by feminist critics, critics of so-called minority culture and Marxist and post-structuralist critics generally—in short, the rainbow coalition of contemporary critical theory. These two men (one a former United States Secretary of Education and now President Bush's "drug czar," the other a professor at the University of Chicago and author of *The Closing of the American Mind*) symbolize the nostalgic return to what I think of as the "antebellum esthetic position," when men were men and men were white, when scholar-critics were white men and when women and people of color were voiceless, faceless servants and laborers, pouring tea and filling brandy snifters in the boardrooms of old boys' clubs. Inevitably, these two men have come to play the roles that George Wallace and Orville Faubus played for the civil rights movement, or that Richard Nixon and Henry Kissinger played during Vietnam—the "feel good" targets who, despite internal differences and contradictions, the cultural left loves to hate.

And yet there's a real danger of localizing our grievances; of the easy personification, assigning celebrated faces to the forces of reaction and so giving too much credit to a few men who are really symptomatic of a larger political current. (In a similar vein, our rhetoric sometimes depicts the high canonical as the reading matter of the power elite. You have to imagine James Baker curling up with the *Pisan Cantos*, Dan Quayle leafing through *The Princess Casamassima*.) Maybe our eagerness to do so reflects a certain vanity that academic cultural critics are prone to. We make dire predictions, and when they come true, we think we've changed the world.

It's a tendency that puts me in mind of my father's favorite story about Father Divine, that historic con man of the cloth. In the 1930s, he was put on trial and convicted for using the mails to defraud. At sentencing, Father Divine stood up and told the judge: I'm warning you, you send me to jail, something terrible is going to happen to you. Father Divine, of course, was sent to prison, and a week later, by sheer coincidence, the judge had a heart attack and died. When the warden and the guards found out about it in the middle of the night, they raced to Father Divine's cell and woke him up. Father Divine, they said, your judge just dropped dead of a heart attack. Without missing a beat, Father Divine lifted his head and told them: "I *hated* to do it."

As writers, teachers or intellectuals, most of us would like to claim greater efficacy for our labors than we're entitled to. These days, literary criticism likes to think of itself as "war by other means." But it should start to wonder: have its victories come too easily? The recent turn toward politics and history in literary studies has turned the analysis of texts into a marionette theater of the political, to which we bring all the passions of our real-world commitments. And that's why it is sometimes necessary to remind ourselves of the distance from the classroom to the streets. Academic critics write essays, "readings" of literature, where the bad guys (you know, racism or patriarchy) lose, where the forces of oppression are subverted by the boundless powers of irony and allegory that no prison can contain, and we glow with hard-won triumph. Yet it sometimes seems that blacks are doing better in the college curriculum than they are in the streets or even on the campuses.

I suppose the literary canon is, in no very grand sense, the commonplace book of our shared culture, the archive of those texts and titles we wish to remember. And how else did those of us who teach literature fall in love with our subject than through our very own commonplace books, in which we inscribed secretly, as we might in a private diary, those passages of books that named for us what we had deeply felt, but could not say?

I kept mine from the age of 12, turning to it to repeat those marvelous words that named me in some private way. From H. H. Munro to Dickens and Austen, to Hugo and de Maupassant, each resonant sentence would find its way into my book. (There's no point in avoiding the narcissism here: we are always transfixed

On February 14, Ayatollah Ruhollah Khomeini says Salman Rushdie must die for *The Satanic Verses*.

by those passages that seem to read us.) Finding James Baldwin and writing him down at an Episcopal church camp in 1965—I was 15, and the Watts riots were raging—probably determined the direction of my intellectual life more than anything else I could name. I wrote and rewrote verbatim his elegantly framed paragraphs, full of sentences that were somehow both Henry Jamesian and King Jamesian, garbed as they were in the figures and cadences of the spirituals. Of course, we forget the private pleasures that brought us to the subject in the first place once we adopt the alienating strategies of formal analysis; our professional vanity is to insist that the study of literature be both beauty and truth, style and politics and everything in between.

In the swaddling clothes of our academic complacencies, then, few of us are prepared when we bump against something hard, and sooner or later, we do. One of the first talks I ever gave was to a packed audience at a college honors seminar, and it was one of those mistakes you don't make twice. Fresh out of graduate school, immersed in the arcane technicalities of contemporary literary theory, I was going to deliver a crunchy structuralist analysis of a slave narrative by Frederick Douglass, tracing the intricate play of its "binary oppositions." Everything was neatly schematized, formalized, analyzed; this was my Sunday-best structuralism: crisp white shirt and shiny black shoes. And it wasn't playing. If you've seen an audience glaze over, this was double glazing. Bravely, I finished my talk and, of course, asked for questions. "Yeah, brother," said a young man in the very back of the room, breaking the silence that ensued, "all we want to know is, was Booker T. Washington an Uncle Tom or not?"

The funny thing is, this happens to be an interesting question, a lot more interesting than my talk was. It raised all the big issues about the politics of style: about what it means to speak for another, about how you were to distinguish between canny subversion and simple co-optation—who was manipulating whom? And while I didn't exactly appreciate it at the time, the exchange did draw my attention, a little rudely perhaps, to the yawning chasm between our critical discourse and the traditions they discourse upon.

Obviously, some of what I'm saying is by way of mea culpa, because I'm speaking here as a participant in a moment of canon formation in a so-called marginal tradition. As it happens, W. W. Norton, the "canonical" anthology publisher, will be publishing *The Norton Anthology of Afro-American Literature*. The editing of this anthology has been a great dream of mine for a long time, and it represents, in the most concrete way, the project of black canon formation. But my pursuit of this project has required me to negotiate a position between those on the cultural right who claim that black literature can have no canon, no masterpieces, and those on the cultural left who wonder why anyone wants to establish the existence of a canon, any canon, in the first place.

We face the outraged reactions of those custodians of Western culture who protest that the canon, that transparent decanter of Western values, may become—breathe the word—politicized. That people can maintain a straight face while they protest the irruption of politics into something that has always been political—well, it says something about how remarkably successful official literary histories have been in presenting themselves as natural objects, untainted by worldly interests.

I agree with those conservatives who have raised the alarm about our students' ignorance of history. But part of the history we need to teach has to be the history of the very idea of the "canon," which involves the history both of literary pedagogy and of the very institution of the school. One function of literary history is then to conceal all connections between institutionalized interests and the literature we remember. Pay no attention to the men behind the curtain, booms the Great Oz of literary history.

But history and its institutions are not just something we study, they're also something we live, and live through. And how effective and how durable our interventions in contemporary cultural politics will be depends upon our ability to mobilize the institutions that buttress and reproduce that culture. We could seclude ourselves from the real world and keep our hands clean, free from the taint of history. But that is to pay obeisance to the status quo, to the entrenched arsenal of sexual and racial authority, to say that things shouldn't change, become something other and, let's hope, better.

Indeed, this is one case where we've got to borrow a leaf from the right, which is exemplarily aware of the role of education in the reproduction of values. We must engage in this sort of canon reformation precisely because Mr. Bennett is correct: the teaching of literature is the teaching of values, not inherently, no, but contingently, yes; it is—it has become—the teaching of an esthetic and political order, in which no person of color, no woman, was ever able to discover the reflection or representation of his or her cultural image or voice. The return of "the" canon, the high canon of Western masterpieces, represents the return of an order in which my people were the subjugated, the voiceless, the invisible, the unpresented and the unrepresentable.

Let me be specific. Those of us working in my own tradition confront the hegemony of the Western tradition, generally, and of the larger American tradition, more locally, as we theorize about our tradition and engage in canon formation. Long after white American literature has been anthologized and canonized, and recanonized, our efforts to define a black American canon are often decried as racist, separatist, nationalist or "essentialist." Attempts to derive theories about our literary tradition from the black tradition—a tradition, I might add, that must include black vernacular forms as well as written literary forms—are often greeted by our colleagues in traditional literature departments as a misguided desire to secede from a union that only recently, and with considerable kicking and screaming, has been forged. What is wrong with you people? our friends ask us in genuine passion and concern; after all, aren't we all just citizens of literature here?

Well, yes and no. Every black American text must confess to a complex ancestry, one high and low (that is, literary and vernacular) but also one white and black. There can be no doubt that white texts inform and influence black texts (and vice versa), so that a thoroughly integrated canon of American literature is not only politically sound, it is intellectually sound as well. But the attempts of black scholars to define a black American canon, and to derive indigenous theories of interpretation from within this canon, are not meant to refute the soundness of these gestures of integration. Rather, it is a question of perspective, a question of emphasis. Just as we can and must cite a black text within the larger American tradition, we can and must cite it within its own tradition, a tradition not defined by a pseudoscience of racial biology, or a mystically shared essence called blackness, but by the repetition and revision of shared themes, topoi and tropes, the call and response of voices, their music and cacophony.

And this is our special legacy: what in 1849 Frederick Douglass called the "live, calm, grave, clear, pointed, warm, sweet, melodious and powerful human voice." The presence of the past in the African-American tradition comes to us most powerfully as *voice*, a voice that is never quite our own—or *only* our own—however much we want it to be. One of my earliest childhood memories tells this story clearly.

I remember my first public performance, which I gave at the age of 4 in the all-black Methodist church that my mother attended, and that her mother had attended for 50 years. It was a religious program, at which each of the children of the Sunday school was to deliver a "piece"—as the people in our church referred to a religious recitation. Mine was the couplet "Jesus was a boy like me, / And like Him I want to be." Not much of a recitation, but then I *was* only 4. So, after weeks of practice in elocution, hair pressed and greased down, shirt starched and pants pressed, I was ready to give my piece. I remember skipping along to the church with all of the other kids, driving everyone crazy, repeating that couplet over and over: "Jesus was a boy like me, / And like Him I want to be."

Finally we made it to the church, and it was packed—bulging and glistening with black people, eager to hear pieces, despite the fact that they had heard all of the pieces already, year after year, like bits and fragments of a repeated master text. Because I was the youngest child on the program, I was the first to go. Miss Sarah Russell (whom we called Sister Holy Ghost—behind her back, of course) started the program with a prayer, then asked if little Skippy Gates would step forward. I did so.

And then the worst happened: I completely forgot the words of my piece. Standing there, pressed and starched, just as clean as I could be, in front of just about everybody in our part of town, I could not for the life of me remember one word of that piece.

After standing there I don't know how long, struck dumb and captivated by all of those staring eyes, I heard a voice from near the back of the church proclaim, "Jesus was a boy like me, / And like Him I want to be."

And my mother, having arisen to find my voice, smoothed her dress and sat down again. The congregation's applause lasted as long as its laughter as I crawled back to my seat.

What this moment crystallizes for me is how much of my scholarly and critical work has been an attempt to learn how to speak in the strong, compelling cadences of my mother's voice. As the black feminist scholar Hortense Spillers has recently insisted, in moving words that first occasioned this very recollection, it is "the heritage of the *mother* that the African-American male must regain as an aspect of his own personhood—the power of 'yes' to the 'female' within."

To reform core curriculums, to account for the comparable eloquence of the African, the Asian and the Middle Eastern traditions, is to begin to prepare our students for their roles as citizens of a world culture, educated through a truly human notion of "the humanities," rather than—as Mr. Bennett and Mr. Bloom would have it—as guardians at the last frontier outpost of white male Western culture, the keepers of the master's pieces. And for us as scholar-critics, learning to speak in the voice of the black mother is perhaps the ultimate challenge of producing a discourse of the Other.

Essay

Jay McInerney on Raymond Carver
August 6, 1989

A YEAR AFTER HIS DEATH, the recurring image I associate with Raymond Carver is one of people leaning toward him, working very hard at the act of listening. He mumbled. T. S. Eliot once described Ezra Pound, qua mentor, as "a man trying to convey to a very deaf person the fact that the house is on fire." Raymond Carver had precisely the opposite manner. The smoke could be filling the room, flames streaking across the carpet, before Carver would ask, "Is it, uh, getting a little hot in here, maybe?" And you would be sitting in your chair, bent achingly forward at the waist, saying, "Beg pardon, Ray?" Never insisting, rarely asserting, he was an unlikely teacher.

He mumbled, and if it once seemed merely a physical tic, akin to cracking knuckles or the drumming of a foot, I now think it was a function of a deep humility and a respect for the language bordering on awe, a reflection of his sense that words should be handled very, very gingerly. As if it might be almost impossible to say what you wanted to say. As if it might be dangerous, even. Listening to him talking about writing in the classroom or in the living room of the big Victorian house he shared with Tess Gallagher in Syracuse, you sensed a writer who loved the words of the masters who had handed the language down to him, and who was concerned that he might not be worthy to pick up the instrument. You feel this respect for the language—humility bordering on dread—in every sentence of his work.

Encountering Carver's fiction early in the 1970s was a transforming experience for many writers of my generation, an experience perhaps comparable to discovering Hemingway's sentences in the '20s. In fact, Carver's language was unmistakably like Hemingway's—the simplicity and clarity, the repetitions, the nearly conversational rhythms, the precision of physical description. But Carver completely dispensed with the romantic egoism that made the Hemingway idiom such an awkward model for other writers in the late twentieth century. The cafés and pensions and battlefields of Europe were replaced by trailer parks and apartment complexes, the glamorous occupations by dead-end jobs. The trout in Carver's streams were apt to be pollution-deformed mutants. The good *vin du pays* was replaced by cheap gin, the romance of drinking by the dull grind of full-time alcoholism. Some commentators found his work depressing for these reasons. For many young writers, it was terribly liberating.

One aspect of what Carver seemed to say to us—even to someone who had never been inside a lumber mill or a trailer park—was that literature could be fashioned out of strict observation of real life, wherever and however it was lived, even if it was lived with a bottle of Heinz ketchup on the table and the television set droning. This was news at a time when academic metafiction was the regnant mode. His example reinvigorated realism as well as the short-story form.

Having fallen under Carver's spell on reading his first collection, *Will You Please Be Quiet, Please?*, a book I would have bought on the basis of the title alone, I was lucky enough to meet him a few years later and eventually to become his student at Syracuse University in the early '80s. Despite the existence of several thousand creative writing programs around the country, there is probably no good answer to the question of whether writing can be taught. Saying that Faulkner and Fitzgerald never got MFAs is beside the point. Novelists and short-story writers like to eat as much as anyone else, and tend to sniff out subsidies while they pursue their creative work. For writers in the '20s, the exchange rate was favorable in Paris, and in the '30s there was the WPA, and a gold rush of sorts in Hollywood. The universities have become the creative writers' WPA in recent years.

Carver was himself a product of the new system, having studied writing at the University of Iowa Writers' Workshop and at Stanford, and later earned a living teaching. It was something he did out of necessity, a role he was uncomfortable with. He did it to make a living, because it was easier than the other jobs he'd had—working at a sawmill and a hospital, working as a service station attendant, a janitor, a delivery boy, a textbook editor. Though grateful for genteel employment, he didn't really see why people who had a gift for writing should necessarily be able to teach. And he was very shy. The idea of facing a class made him nervous every time. On the days he had to teach he would get agitated, as if he himself were a student on the day of the final exam.

Like many writers in residence at universities, Ray was required to teach English courses in addition to creative writing courses. One was called Form and Theory of the Short Story, a title Ray inherited from the graduate English catalogue. His method in these classes was to assign a book of stories he liked each week, including contemporary and nineteenth-century authors as well as works in translation. We would read the books and discuss them for two hours. Flannery O'Connor, Chekhov, Anne Beattie, Maupassant, Frank O'Connor, John Cheever, Mary Robison, Turgenev and more Chekhov. (He loved all the nineteenth-century Russians.) Class would begin with Ray saying something like, "Well, guys, how'd you like Eudora Welty?" He preferred listening to lecturing, but he would read his favorite passages, talk about what he loved in the book he had chosen. He dealt in specifics, stayed close to the text, and eventually there would come a moment when the nervousness would lift off of him as he spoke about writing that moved him.

One semester, a very earnest Ph.D. candidate found his way into this class, composed mainly of writers. At that time, the English department, like many around the country, had become a battleground between theorists and humanists, and post-structuralism lay heavy upon the campus. After a few weeks of Carver's free-ranging and impressionistic approach to literature, the young theorist registered a strong protest: "This class is called Form and Theory of the Short Story but all we do is sit around and talk about the books. Where's the form and the theory?"

Ray looked distressed. He nodded and pulled extra hard on his cigarette.

"Well, that's a good question," he said. After a long pause, he said, "I guess I'd say that the point here is that we read good books and discuss them. . . . And then you *form* your own *theory*." Then he smiled.

As a teacher of creative writing, too, Carver had a light touch. He did not consider it his job to discourage anyone. He said that there was enough discouragement out there for anyone trying against all odds to be a writer, and he clearly spoke from experience. His harshest critical formula was: "I think it's good you got that story behind you." Meaning, I guess, that one has to drive through some ugly country on the way to Parnassus. If Carver had had his way, classes and workshops would have been conducted entirely by students but his approval was too highly valued for him to remain mute.

Though Ray was always encouraging, he could be rigorous if he knew criticism was welcome. Fortunate students had their stories subjected to the same process he employed on his own numerous drafts. Manuscripts came back thoroughly ventilated with Carver deletions, substitutions, question marks and chicken-scratch queries. I took one story back to him seven times; he must have spent 15 or 20 hours on it. He was a meticulous, obsessive line editor. One on one, in his office, he almost became a tough guy, his voice gradually swelling with conviction.

Once we spent some 10 or 15 minutes debating my use of the word "earth." Carver felt it had to be "ground," and he felt it was worth the trouble of talking it through. That one exchange was invaluable; I think of it constantly when I'm working. Carver himself used the same example later in an essay he wrote that year, in discussing the influence of his mentor, John Gardner. "Ground is ground, he'd say, it means *ground*, dirt, that kind of stuff. But if you say 'earth,' that's something else, that word has other ramifications."

John Gardner, the novelist, was Ray's first writing teacher. They met at Chico State College in California in the 1960s. Ray said that all of his writing life he had felt Gardner looking over his shoulder when he wrote, approving or disapproving of certain words, phrases and strategies. Calling fouls. He said a good writing teacher is something like a literary conscience, a friendly critical voice in your ear. I know what he meant. (I have one; it mumbles.)

After almost 20 years Carver had a reunion with his old teacher, who was living and teaching less than a hundred miles from Syracuse, in Binghamton, N.Y., and Gardner's approval of his work had meant a great deal to him. In the spring of 1982, I happened to stop by Ray's house a few minutes after he heard that Gardner had died in a motorcycle crash. Distraught, he couldn't sit still. We walked around the house and the backyard as he talked about Gardner.

"Back then I didn't even know what a writer looked like," Ray said. "John looked like a writer. He had that hair, and he used to wear this thing that was like a cape. I tried to copy the way he walked. He used to let me work in his office because I didn't have a quiet place to work. I'd go through his files and steal the titles of his stories, use them on my stories."

So he must have understood when we all shamelessly cribbed from him, we students at Syracuse, and Iowa and Stanford and all the other writing workshops in the country where almost everyone seemed to be writing and publishing stories with Raymond Carver titles like "Do You Mind If I Smoke?" or "How About This, Honey?" He certainly didn't want clones. But he knew that imitation was part of finding your own voice.

I encountered Carver near the beginning of what he liked to call his "second life," after he had quit drinking. I heard stories about the bad old Ray, stories he liked to tell on himself. When I met him I thought of writers as luminous madmen who drank too much and drove too fast and scattered brilliant pages along their doomed trajectories. Maybe at one time he did, too. In his essay "Fires," he says, "I understood writers to be people who didn't spend their Saturdays at the laundromat." Would Hemingway be caught dead doing laundry? No, but William Carlos Williams would. Ditto Carver's beloved Chekhov. In the classroom and on the page, Carver somehow delivered the tonic news that there was laundry in the kingdom of letters.

Not that, by this time, Ray was spending much time at the laundromat, life having been good to him toward the end in a way for which he seemed constantly to be grateful. But hearing the typewriter of one of the masters of American prose clacking just up the street, while a neighbor raked leaves and some kids threw a Frisbee as the dogs went on with their doggy life—this was a lesson in itself for me. Whatever dark mysteries lurk at the heart of the writing process, he insisted on a single trade secret: that you had to survive, find some quiet, and work hard every day. And seeing him for coffee, or watching a ball game or a dumb movie with him, put into perspective certain dangerous myths about the writing life that he preferred not to lecture on—although he sometimes would, if he thought it might help. When we first became acquainted, in New York, he felt obliged to advise me, in a series of wonderful letters, and a year later I moved upstate to become his student.

Reading the dialogues of Plato, one eventually realizes that Socrates' self-deprecation is something of a ploy. Ray's humility, however, was profound and unselfconscious and one of the most astonishing things about him. When he asked a student, "What do you think?" he clearly wanted to know. This seemed a rare and inspiring didactic stance. His own opinions were expressed with such caution that you knew how carefully they had been measured.

For someone who claimed he didn't love to teach, he made a great deal of difference to a great many students. He certainly changed my life irrevocably and I have heard others say the same thing.

I'm still leaning forward with my head cocked to one side, straining to hear his voice.

First Impressions

Liar's Poker by Michael Lewis
October 29, 1989

BY RICHARD L. STERN

IN 1984, through an improbable set of circumstances, Michael Lewis, a 24-year-old Princeton University graduate studying at the London School of Economics, turned up in a rented tuxedo at a dinner given by the Queen Mother. He found himself seated next to the wife of a managing partner of Salomon Brothers. Mr. Lewis soon landed a job with the company—one of the most sought-after opportunities for the money-minded college generation of the 1980s.

Liar's Poker is the very funny account of his three-year, dog-eat-dog climb there. Starting as an overpaid $48,000-a-year trainee, Mr. Lewis, by 1987, was on his way to triumph as an institutional bond salesman in Salomon's London office, earning $225,000.

In London, a naïve Mr. Lewis was talked into selling some bonds from Salomon's inventory by a trader who had to get rid of them or face a loss. It didn't matter that the bonds quickly collapsed, that the company lost a new client or that the money manager who bought the bonds lost his job. Mr. Lewis performed nobly for Salomon Brothers.

But Mr. Lewis soon learned a valuable lesson. The only way to keep his clients—and perhaps assuage his growing feelings of guilt—was to protect them. So with an anxious junk bond trader standing over him and pressuring him to sell a new issue of bonds that everyone knew would go bad, Mr. Lewis cryptically told a grateful client not to touch them with a 10-foot pole.

Mr. Lewis says that he left Salomon Brothers not out of disillusionment but "more because I didn't need to stay any longer." Whatever the case, he's obviously as good a writer as he was a bond salesman. Perhaps that's because both jobs involve being able to tell a good story.

Letter

Ray Bradbury
December 17, 1989

HOW SAD THAT W. H. AUDEN CHOSE to alter his own work, changing "We must love one another or die" to "We must love one another and die." Which shifts the whole meaning in the direction of the very Doomsters most of us would like to escape. Must I interpret Mr. Auden to himself? I chose to interpret Auden's original phrase as meaning if we do not love we die. In the midst of life, surrounded by death, if we do not love someone and are not loved in return, we are a shell. In the loving give-and-take there is vital life, there is purpose, there is joy. Without love we might as well be dead. To be in love doesn't mean we ignore the darkness that surrounds us. But being in love, we are a light to one another. Damn it to hell, Mr. Auden, put your words back the way that you wrote them in the first place!

William Manchester

Anatole Broyard • Barbara Bush

John Updike • Joyce Carol Oates • Derek

Walcott • Robert Bly • Naomi Wolf • Norman

Rush • Susan Faludi • Aleksandr Solzhenitsyn

Daniel Patrick Moynihan • Francis Fukuyama

Elizabeth Marshall Thomas • Lewis Lapham

John Berendt • Cynthia Ozick • Don

DeLillo • Martin Amis

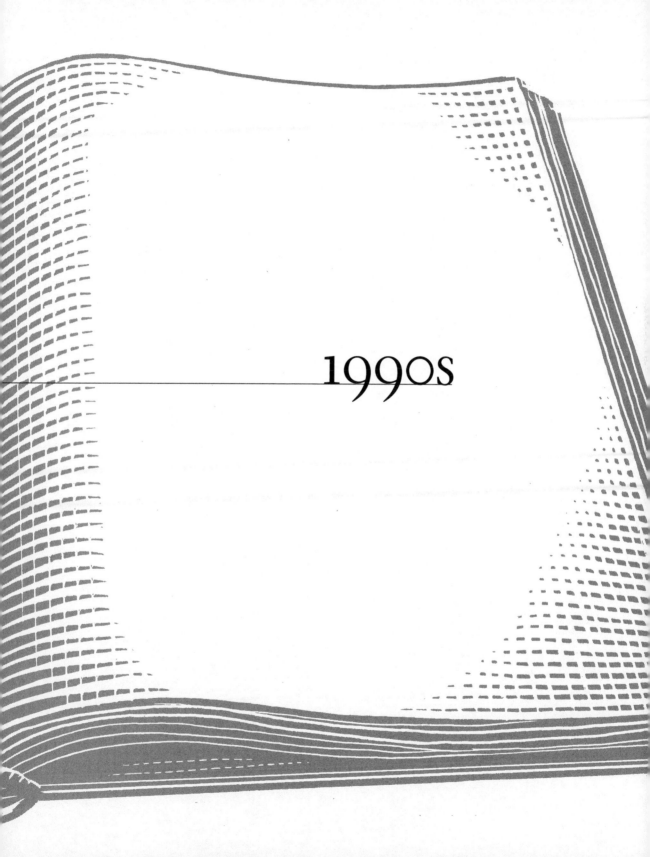

1990S

Letter

William Manchester
February 4, 1990

HENRY MENCKEN BROUGHT ME to *The Baltimore Evening Sun* in 1947, and for the next eight years—except when I was representing *The Sun* abroad—we met regularly, in his home at 1524 Hollins Street, at the paper, in the Enoch Pratt Free Library, where he gave me access to his private papers, and for lunch at the Maryland Club or his favorite restaurants, Miller's and Schellhase's, both long gone.

Long afternoons were spent walking the streets of Baltimore while he reminisced about his 50-year career there, his views of literature and society and how he had introduced America to Bernard Shaw, Friedrich Nietzsche, Joseph Conrad, Theodore Dreiser and Mike Gold's *Jews Without Money.*

Then he fell ill. Twice, his younger brother August and I brought him home in a wheelchair from the Johns Hopkins Hospital. During the last year of his life I left the Sun papers to be with him. Each morning after a hospital orderly had given him his morning rubdown we retired to his backyard. There, beneath an awning August had erected, I read him the morning newspapers, the complete works of Conrad and Twain—*Huckleberry Finn* twice—and the prefaces of Shaw.

When he felt fit, we talked, or gardened, or roamed nearby alleys for firewood, which, when we returned, August and I would saw into suitable lengths on a bench by their old pony shed. Once Mencken told me, with considerable relish, of his vasectomy and three fertile New York women who had volunteered to test its efficacy. They left him, he said, childless.

Two or three times a week I would return for an evening with him. Sometimes we passionately disagreed. He had detested Franklin Roosevelt, whom I admired extravagantly. But we were always civil, and before I would leave we always turned to music. Alfred Knopf had sent him a record player. Among the albums I brought him were three of Gilbert and Sullivan—"geniuses," he sighed.

In all our thousands of hours together I never heard Mencken insult Jews or blacks. Not once did he suggest that they be harmed, embarrassed or victimized by discrimination. Jews, he believed, were brighter, more sensitive and more talented than gentiles. But his affection for them was scarcely surprising, considering the large number of Jews who had been close to him throughout his life, both professionally and socially. "I am," he once said, "quite free of anti-Semitism."

Nor was the word "nigger" in his vocabulary. A black family lived next door;

1990

The novelist Mario Vargas Llosa loses a runoff election and fails in his bid to become president of Peru. Afterward, he declares, "Nevermore for any reason will I get involved, nevermore will I quit writing."

he was on the best of terms with them, and frequently produced surprise gifts for the two small sons. It is true that his attitude toward them was paternalistic. It is equally true that it would have been extremely difficult to find more than a few Baltimoreans at that time—including black Baltimoreans—who would have found that paternalism objectionable.

Now the diary of his later years is being published—he had expressly prohibited publication, but the lawyers found a way to thwart his instruction—and in it one finds several slurs that are taboo, even shocking, *today*. But they were not written today. They were set down, in private, at a time when racial epithets and jokes were commonly heard in polite society.

The passing of ex post facto judgments seems to be increasingly popular. A recent headline in a Connecticut newspaper read: "Old West Was Sexist"— though neither the word nor the concept of sexism existed on the frontier. Soon, perhaps, it will be disclosed that "Alamo Defenders Were Homophobes." It is sobering to reflect on the consequences were the tables turned. How would past generations judge American sexual behavior in 1990 and the abandonment of the traditional family?

If we are going to adopt generational chauvinism as dogma, many past heroes will be diminished, including liberal heroes. The kind of anti-Semitism that appears in Mencken's private diary may be found elsewhere: for example, in the early letters of Eleanor Roosevelt and Adlai Stevenson. And after FDR's crutches collapsed during a 1936 political rally in Philadelphia, he said, "I was the maddest white man you ever saw"—a remark that, in 1990, could lose an election.

Perhaps the most outrageous twisting of the Mencken diary is the charge that he was pro-Nazi. Henry Mencken was a third-generation German-American, and his view of his grandfather's homeland was hopelessly sentimental. It was a dream of pre-Wilhelmine Germany, of whimsical pipe-smoking eccentrics like Jo's beloved in *Little Women*, of Hegel and Kant, of Beethoven, Bach and, yes, Mendelssohn.

Little would have come of it had not Mencken, then the country's most controversial literary critic, been singled out for persecution during this country's anti-German hysteria in World War I. As a consequence, Mencken's attitude toward the Second World War was wholly unrealistic. He dismissed it as "Roosevelt's War," took little interest in it and was clearly unenthusiastic at the prospect of another German defeat.

But Mencken a *Nazi?* He despised the Third Reich from the outset. Any defense of Germany was impossible, he concluded, "so long as the chief officer of the German state continues to make speeches worthy of an Imperial Wizard of the Ku Klux Klan, and his followers imitate, plainly with his connivance, the monkey-shines of the American Legion at its worst."

1990

Harold Bloom proposes, in *The Book of J*, that the biblical author known to Hebrew scholars as J or "the Yahwist" was a woman. (See Samuel Butler, 1897)

442

Mencken has been silent for 34 years now. His work stands, and it towers. He was a master polemicist; he always gave better than he got, and he really needs no defense. But as one who cherishes accuracy in literary history, I am appalled by the distortions of his considerable role in it. And I am deeply offended by the smearing of my old friend by ignorant liberal bigots.

Essay

Anatole Broyard on Illness
April 1, 1990

I WAS READING SHIRLEY HAZZARD'S NOVEL *The Transit of Venus*. Though I had admired her other books, I'd always resisted this one. It struck me as too pure somehow, too heroic, larger or finer than life and therefore unreal. But now I read it with an almost indescribable pleasure. There were sentences that brought tears of gratification to my eyes and raised the hairs on the nape of my neck.

I was in a Boston hospital, propped up in bed with an intravenous feeding tube in my arm and a catheter in my urethral canal after undergoing surgery for prostate cancer. It was a double room and my roommate, a kind of thug who growled when he spoke because he had both a broken jaw and a drug habit, was spraying the air for the fourth or fifth time that day with a cloying deodorizer. He had a television set and a radio going at the same time.

The catheter hurt and the diagnosis of my case was ambiguous. When I asked the oncologist the usual question—How much time have I got?—he hesitated before answering. "I would say," he said, "that you have in the neighborhood of years."

I burrowed into the book. I was not escaping into it but identifying with it, as fervently as I have ever identified with any novel. The life Shirley Hazzard described was the kind I wanted for my neighborhood of years. Her book was the prescription that I needed and that no doctor would give me. I needed a dose of the sublime. From where I sat in my cranked-up bed, the sublime seemed to be all there was left.

I paused in my reading because I was out of shape and the beauty of the book had winded me. In my mind I composed a letter to Shirley Hazzard. After a brief description of my circumstances, I said, "You offered me an alternative. Art is our ace in the hole. I'm eating your book for lunch and it's making me hungry."

I was afraid of finishing *The Transit of Venus*. It had become my neighborhood. I put it down and went for a walk around the ward, dragging the metal rack with the IV tube and the catheter bag. From the window of an empty room I looked down at the city, which was dotted with trees. How extraordinary the real world was! Shirley Hazzard was right.

When I got out of the hospital my first impulse was to write about my illness. While sick people need books like *The Transit of Venus* to remind them of the life beyond their illness, they also need a literature of their own. Misery loves company—if it's good company. And, surprisingly enough, there isn't much good company in this rapidly proliferating field. A critical illness is one of our momentous experiences, yet I haven't seen a single nonfiction book that does it justice. Even in fiction there are only a handful of great books on the subject: Tolstoy's *Death of Ivan Ilyich*, Thomas Mann's *Magic Mountain*, most of Kafka, and Malcolm Lowry's *Under the Volcano*.

While Tolstoy is the grandfather, my favorites among these are Mann and Lowry. Kafka's illnesses are more existential than physical; they are like Kierkegaard's "sickness unto death." In *The Magic Mountain*, Mann wrote the grand, definitive romance of illness, a portrait that I would say, speaking as a connoisseur now, will never be equaled.

Mann's hero, Hans Castorp, who has only a little "moist spot" on one lung, has been sublimating his passion for Clavdia Chauchat, who is seriously ill, by reading biology books. When, encouraged by champagne, Castorp woos her, he vacillates between the language of physiology, of the doctor, and the language of the lover or poet. "Let me touch devotedly with my lips," he says, "the femoral artery that throbs in the front of your thigh and divides lower down into the two arteries of the tibia!" "The body, love, death," he says, speaking to her in French, the only language they have in common, "these three are only one. For the body is sickness and voluptuousness, and it is this that causes death, yes, they are carnal both of them, love and death, and that is their terror and their great magic!" After their first and only night together, Clavdia gives Hans an X-ray of her tubercular lungs as a souvenir.

Like Mann, Malcolm Lowry uses the delirium of illness in *Under the Volcano*, where alcoholism is the consul's disease, one that will kill him indirectly. While I have little patience with drunks, I love the consul because he makes drunkenness too seem like Mann's "fever of matter," like a slip or glitch in our composition, a hopeless reaching for happiness.

When I turned to nonfiction, to books by people who were or had been ill, I expected to find some echo of Castorp or the consul, but for the most part I was disappointed. Susan Sontag's *Illness as Metaphor and AIDS and Its Metaphors* is an elegant analysis of how we think about illness and the stigma we attach to it—the "spoiled identity" of the sick, as Erving Goffman puts it. She chooses to address herself more to the conceptualization of illness than to the daily experience of it. Approaching him panoramically rather than individually, she aims a bit high for the sick man lying flat in his hospital bed. It is not his quiddity but his place in the medical polity that occupies her. She is to illness what William Empson's *Seven Types of Ambiguity* is to literature.

In my opinion, Ms. Sontag is too hard on metaphor when she says that "the most truthful way of regarding illness—and the healthiest way of being ill—is one most purified of, most resistant to, metaphoric thinking." She seems to throw the baby out with the bath water. While she is concerned only with negative metaphors, there are positive metaphors of illness too, a kind of literary aspirin. In fact, metaphors may be as necessary to illness as they are to literature, as comforting to the patient as his own bathrobe and slippers. If laughter has healing power, so too may metaphor. Perhaps only metaphor can express the bafflement, the panic combined with beatitude, of the threatened person. Surely Ms. Sontag wouldn't wish to condemn the sick to Hemingway sentences.

What kind of book would I like to write? I'm not a doctor, and even as a patient I'm a mere beginner. Yet I *am* a critic and, being critically ill, I thought I might accept the pun and turn it on my condition. If I were to demystify or deconstruct my cancer, I might find that there is no absolute diagnosis, no single, agreed-upon text, but only the interpretation each doctor and each patient makes.

My initial experience of illness was as a series of disconnected shocks, and my first instinct was to try to bring it under control by turning it into a narrative. Always in emergencies we invent stories. We describe what is happening, as if to confine the catastrophe. The patient's narrative keeps him from falling out of his life into his illness. Like a novelist, he gives his anxiety a shape.

In the beginning I invented mini-narratives. Metaphor was one of my symptoms. I saw my illness as a visit to a disturbed country. I imagined it as a love affair with a woman who demanded things I had never done before. I thought of it as a lecture I was about to give to an immense audience, on a subject that had not been specified. Having cancer was like moving from a cozy old Dickensian house crammed with antiques, deep sofas, snug corners and fireplaces to a brand-new one that was all windows, skylights and tubular furniture.

Like anyone who has had an extraordinary experience, I wanted to describe it. This seems to be a normal reflex, especially for a writer. I felt a bit like Eliot's Prufrock, who says, "I am Lazarus, come from the dead, / Come back to tell you all, I shall tell you all." Like a convert who's had a vision, I wanted to preach it, to tell people what a serious illness is like, the unprecedented ideas and fantasies it puts into your head, the unexpected qualms and quirks it introduces into your body. For a seriously sick person, opening up your consciousness to others is like the bleeding doctors used to recommend to reduce the pressure.

What goes through your mind when you're lying, shot through with nuclear dye, under a huge machine that scans all your bones for evidence of treason? There's a horror movie appeal to this machine: beneath it you become the Frankenstein monster exposed to the electric storm. How do you appear to yourself when you sit with bare shins and no underwear beneath a scanty cotton gown in a hospital waiting room? Nobody, not even a lover, waits as intensely as a critically ill patient. On a more complicated level, it would be like explicating a difficult poem to try to capture the uncanny, painless yet excruciating sensation that comes with having a 10-inch needle thrust straight into your abdomen, a needle that seems to be writing on your entrails, scratching some message you can't make out.

What a critically ill person needs above all is to be understood. Dying is a misunderstanding you have to get straightened out before you go. And you can't be understood, your situation can't be appreciated, until your family and friends, staring at you with an embarrassed love, come to know, with an intimate, absolute knowledge, what your illness is like. The therapist Erving Polster defined embarrassment as a radiance that doesn't know what to do with itself. We need a book that will teach the sick man's family and friends, the people who love him, what to do with that radiance. If they knew how to use it, their radiance might do him more good than radiation.

I'm tempted to write a romantic book, a love offering, like Clavdia Chauchat's X-ray picture. The space between life and death is the parade ground of romanticism. The threat of illness itself seems to sound a romantic note—I've been feeling exalted since I heard the diagnosis. A critical illness is like a great permission, an authorization or absolving. It's all right for a threatened man to be romantic, even crazy, if he feels like it. All your life you think you have to hold back your craziness, but when you're sick you can let it out in all its garish colors.

As a preparation for writing, as a first step toward evolving a strategy for my illness, I've begun to take tap-dancing lessons, something I've always wanted to do. One of my favorite examples of a patient's strategy comes from a man I know who also has prostate cancer: instead of imagining his good cells attacking his bad cells, he goes to Europe from time to time and imposes Continental images on his bad cells. He reminds me that in an earlier, more holistic age, doctors used to advise sick people to go abroad for their health.

The illness genre ought to have a literary critic—in addition to or in reply to Susan Sontag—to talk about the therapeutic value of style, for it seems to me that every seriously ill person needs to develop a style for his illness. I think that only by insisting on your style can you keep from falling out of love with yourself as the illness attempts to diminish or disfigure you. Sometimes your vanity is the only thing that's keeping you alive, and your style is the instrument of your vanity. It may not be dying we fear so much, but the diminished self. A writer friend of mine who died of lung cancer used a Jamesian style in referring to his illness as a way of preventing anything ugly, rude or abrupt from arising. Another writer friend who had lung cancer was robbed of his style by a stroke that left him speechless. He died not of cancer finally, but pneumonia, as if his lungs had filled with trapped speech and he had drowned in it.

Somebody other than a doctor ought to write about the relation between prostate cancer and sexuality. As I understand it, the prostate gland is like a raging bull in the body, snorting and spreading the disease. All of the various treatments are designed to tame the prostate. When I chose hormonal manipulation over orchiectomy, I was warned that this method too would effectively cancel my libido. Yet I found this hard to believe. My libido is lodged not only in my prostate but in my consciousness, my imagination, my memory, my appreciation of women, my conception of myself—my esthetics, if you will.

There's room for hermeneutics here. Is desire itself carcinogenic? Couldn't there be another level of sexuality? Can the imagination, for example, have orgasms? Is it possible to discover an alternative mode—as the signing of the deaf is an alternative to speech—a form we haven't thought of yet, an avant-garde, nonobjective, post-modern sexuality? What would Oliver Sacks say? I never understood, in *The Sun Also Rises*, why Lady Brett and the castrated Jake Barnes couldn't think of anything to do, why all that wanting had to go begging. In my own case, after a brush with death, I feel that just to be alive is a permanent orgasm.

There's too much talk about anger among the sick and in the books about them, and I think writers should be cautioned against this. The feeling of being unjustly singled out is a dead-end kind of thinking and you can't get rid of it in Elisabeth Kübler-Ross's screaming room. I'm past middle age, and I've never been really sick before—what have I got to be angry about? Anger is too monolithic for such a delicate situation. It's like a catheter inserted in your soul, draining your spirit.

Just before he died, Tolstoy said, "I don't understand what I'm supposed to do." Very sick people feel this kind of confusion, but I'd like to point out that there's a lot they *can* do. I feel very busy now, very usefully occupied, and I'd like to write about some of the ways a sick person can divert and defend, maybe even transcend himself.

The British psychoanalyst D. W. Winnicott began an autobiography that he never finished. The first paragraph simply says, "I died." In the fifth paragraph,

1990

Millie's Book, attributed to an English springer spaniel who lives in the Bush White House, makes No. 1 on the nonfiction best-seller list.

he writes, "Let me see. What was happening when I died? My prayer had been answered. I was alive when I died. That was all I had asked and I had got it." Though he never finished his book, he gave the best reason in the world for writing one, and that's why I want to write mine—to make sure I'll be alive when I die.

First Impressions

Millie's Book as dictated to Barbara Bush by Garfield (as dictated to Jim Davis) September 16, 1990

AS TRANSCRIBED BY BARBARA BUSH, *Millie's Book* is not *Call of the Wild* or *White Fang* but, rather, a kinder, gentler book about a kinder, gentler dog. Given that it was written by a dog, one must conclude that *Millie's Book* is a miracle, or at the very least, pretty darned impressive. Most of the dogs I know would rather chew on a book than write one. Oh, sure, Millie had help from the First Lady, but Millie's wit, style and incisiveness are clearly stamped throughout.

Even though Millie's rubbed elbows—er, uh, legs—with some of Washington's more powerful politicos and no doubt been privy to some state secrets, she limits herself to sprightly accounts of digging up tulip beds, chasing squirrels and sitting on antique furniture. Not once does Millie confess that she thought about shredding some Middle Eastern diplomat's pants leg. At the very least, she could have drooled on someone's shoes.

Over all, I'll have to admit, I liked this book. I even found myself liking Millie, although I would not want that widely publicized. On my 10-point lasagna scale, I'd have to give *Millie's Book* 8 lasagnas. I think dogs in particular would enjoy reading Millie's story—then again, women, children, men and cats might enjoy it, too.

A Beautiful Brainless Guy

Rabbit at Rest by John Updike
September 30, 1990

BY JOYCE CAROL OATES

WITH THIS ELEGIAC VOLUME, John Updike's much-acclaimed and, in retrospect, hugely ambitious Rabbit quartet—*Rabbit, Run* (1960), *Rabbit Redux* (1971), *Rabbit Is Rich* (1981) and now *Rabbit at Rest*—comes to an end. The final word of so many thousands is Rabbit's, and it is, singularly, "Enough." This is, in its context, in an intensive cardiac care unit in a Florida hospital, a judgment both blunt and touchingly modest, valedictory and yet enigmatic. As Rabbit's doctor has informed his wife, "Sometimes it's time." But in the nightmare efficiency of late-twentieth-century medical technology, in which mere vegetative existence may be defined as life, we are no longer granted such certainty.

Rabbit at Rest is certainly the most brooding, the most demanding, the most concentrated of John Updike's longer novels. Its courageous theme—the blossoming and fruition of the seed of death we all carry inside us—is struck in the first sentence, as Harry Angstrom, Rabbit, now 55 years old, more than 40 pounds overweight, waits for the plane that is bringing his son, Nelson, and Nelson's family to visit him and his wife in their semiretirement in Florida: he senses that it is his own death arriving, "shaped vaguely like an airplane." We are in the final year of Ronald Reagan's anesthetized rule—"Everything falling apart, airplanes, bridges, eight years . . . of nobody minding the store, making money out of nothing, running up debt, trusting in God."

This early note, so emphatically struck, reverberates through the length of the novel and invests its domestic-crisis story with an unusual pathos. For where in previous novels, most famously in *Couples* (1968), John Updike explored the human body as Eros, he now explores the body, in yet more detail, as Thanatos. One begins virtually to share, with the doomed Harry Angstrom, a panicky sense of the body's terrible finitude, and of its place in a world of other, competing bodies: "You fill a slot for a time and then move out; that's the decent thing to do: make room."

Schopenhauer's definition of walking as "arrested falling" comes to mind as one navigates Rabbit's downward plunge. There is an angioplasty episode, recounted in John Updike's typically meticulous prose, that is likely to be quite a challenge for the hypochondriacs and physical cowards among us. (I'm not sure I met the challenge—I shut my eyes a few times.) There are candid and un-self-pitying anecdotes of open-heart surgery. We come to know how it probably feels to suffer not one heart attack but two, how it feels to strain one's "frail heart" by unconsciously (that is, deliberately) abusing one's flabby body.

A good deal is made, in the Florida scenes, of the American retired elderly. Rabbit thinks, with typical Rabbit crudeness, "You wonder if we haven't gone overboard in catering to cripples." A former mistress of Rabbit's named Thelma (see *Rabbit Is Rich*) reappears in these pages as a lupus sufferer, soon to die, not very gallantly described, when they kiss, as smelling faintly of urine. There is an AIDS patient who exploits his disease as a way of eluding professional responsibility, and there is a cocaine addict—Rabbit's own son, Nelson—whose dependence on the drug is pushing him toward mental breakdown.

The engine that drives the plot in John Updike's work is nearly always domestic. Men and women who might be called ordinary Americans of their time and place are granted an almost incandescent allure by the mysteries they present to one another: Janice Angstrom to Harry, in *Rabbit Redux*, as an unrepentant adulteress; a young woman to Harry, as possibly his illegitimate daughter, in *Rabbit Is Rich*; and now Nelson to Harry, as his so strangely behaving son, whose involvement with drugs brings the family to the edge of financial and personal ruin. Thus, though characters like Janice, Nelson and, from time to time, Rabbit himself are not very sympathetic—and, indeed, are intended by their resolutely unsentimental creator not to be—one is always curious to know their immediate fates.

John Updike's choice of Rabbit Angstrom, in *Rabbit, Run*, was inspired, one of those happy, instinctive accidents that so often shape a literary career. For Rabbit, though a contemporary of the young writer—born, like him, in the early 1930s, and a product, so to speak, of the same world (the area around Reading, Pa.)—was a "beautiful brainless guy" whose career (as a high school basketball star in a provincial setting) peaked at age 18; in his own wife's view, he was, before their early, hasty marriage, "already drifting downhill." Needless to say, poor Rabbit is the very antithesis of the enormously promising president of the class of 1950 at Shillington High School, the young man who went to Harvard on a scholarship, moved away from his hometown forever and became a world-renowned writer. This combination of cousinly propinquity and temperamental diamagnetism has allowed John Updike a magisterial distance in both dramatizing Rabbit's life and dissecting him in the process. One thinks of Flaubert and his doomed fantasist Emma Bovary, for John Updike with his precisian's prose and his intimately attentive yet cold eye is a master, like Flaubert, of mesmerizing us with his narrative voice even as he might repel us with the vanities of human desire his scalpel exposes.

Harry Angstrom, who tries to sate his sense of life's emptiness by devouring junk food—"the tang of poison that he likes"—the very archetype of the American macho male (whose fantasies dwell not, like Emma Bovary's, on romance, but on sports), appears as Uncle Sam in a Fourth of July parade in *Rabbit at Rest*, and the impersonation is a locally popular one. Rabbit, who knows little of any culture but his own, and that a culture severely circumscribed by television, is passionately convinced that "all in all this is the happiest . . . country the world has ever seen." As in *Rabbit Redux* he was solidly in favor of the Vietnam War, so, as his life becomes increasingly marginal to the United States of his time, in ironic balance to his wife's increasing involvement, he is as unthinkingly patriotic as ever—"a typical good-hearted imperialist racist," as his wife's lover put it in the earlier book.

Rabbit is not often good-hearted, however, living as he does so much inside his own skin. Surprised by his lover's concern for him, he thinks, funnily, of "that strange way women have, of really caring about somebody beyond themselves." From *Rabbit, Run* to *Rabbit at Rest*, Rabbit's wife, Janice, is repeatedly referred to as "that mutt" and "that poor dumb mutt," though she seems to us easily Rabbit's intellectual equal.

In *Rabbit at Rest*, an extreme of sorts, even for Rabbit, is achieved when, at Thelma's very funeral, he tells the dead woman's grieving husband that "she was a fantastic lay." Near the end of the novel, it is suggested that Rabbit's misogyny was caused by his mother! (Of course. Perhaps women should refrain from childbirth in order to prevent adversely influencing their sons?) It is a measure of John Updike's prescience in creating Rabbit Angstrom 30 years ago that, in the concluding pages of *Rabbit, Run*, Rabbit's ill-treated lover Ruth should speak of him in disgust as "Mr. Death." If Mr. Death is also, and enthusiastically, Uncle Sam, then the Rabbit quartet constitutes a powerful critique of America.

"Forget the Gods and Read the Rest"

Omeros by Derek Walcott
October 7, 1990

BY MARY LEFKOWITZ

TOWARD THE END of his epic poem *Omeros*, Derek Walcott suddenly interrupts his rushing narrative and asks himself whether he has not "read and rewritten till literature / was guilty as History." "When would the sails drop / from my eyes, when would I not hear the Trojan War / in two fishermen cursing?" he asks. "When would it stop, / the echo in the throat, insisting, 'Omeros'; / when would I enter that light beyond metaphor?" This apostrophe is a moving and appropriate challenge not only to the poet, but to the reader. Why are we in the present always haunted by the past, not just our past but the past of other people and peoples? Like Homer's Odysseus, we learn the answer by joining the poet on an exciting and disturbing journey "to see the cities of many men and to know their minds."

But it is the figure of the poet Homer, rather than the heroes of his poems, who serves as Derek Walcott's principal inspiration. According to ancient legend, Homer came from a humble background and had a hard and lonely life. Born the bastard son of a Greek girl living in Smyrna (modern Izmir), when he was young he traveled around the Mediterranean. But then he became blind and had to make a living as a beggar, by reciting his verse. Occasionally he was treated kindly, but more often he was driven away from the towns he visited; because he was an outsider and a hanger-on he acquired the name *Homeros*, "hostage." After much wandering, Homer finally died on the Aegean island of Ios, friendless and alone, unable to answer a simple riddle put to him by young fisher-boys.

It is this everyman's Homer, and not the comfortable court poet some people imagine Homer to have been, who inspires Derek Walcott's epic poem, and who records the past events that determine the lives of the people he describes—including that of Mr. Walcott himself and, ultimately, of all of us. This Homer is a Protean figure, infinitely knowledgeable but elusive, constantly changing shape. He is Omeros (his name in modern Greek) and also the old blind man "Seven Seas." Later he turns up as a sightless, homeless bargeman clutching a brown manuscript, only to be driven off the steps of St. Martin's-in-the-Fields church in London by a prim clergyman. He is the voice of the sea, (Winslow) Homer, and the Roman poet Virgil who guides the narrator (as he once guided Dante through hell in Dante's own epic, the *Commedia*).

In the *Iliad* and the *Odyssey* Homer needed to recall only what happened before Odysseus' return from Troy, but now the poet must reflect on an older and larger world, with new wars and new continents. If his principal characters are Antillean people with Homeric names, one also meets here Roman emperors, Spanish conquistadors, Herman Melville and James Joyce. His mind ranges from the Antilles now to the Mediterranean in antiquity to the British Empire at its height to frontier America in the Indian wars to Boston and London last week or last year to an Africa buried so deep in the memories of its exiled children that only terrible trauma can bring them to think about it. This is, as Mr. Walcott says, "a reversible world." "Art is History's nostalgia."

But his new epic does not so much tell a story as explain the feelings and reflections of some inhabitants—past, present or, like Mr. Walcott himself, intermittent—of St. Lucia in the Windward Islands. Several characters have Homeric names, but their connection with their counterparts in the *Iliad* and the *Odyssey* is deliberately tenuous and evanescent.

Helen is as beautiful as her ancient namesake, but her face does not launch a thousand ships or bring on the destruction of her city. Achille, the "main man," son of an African slave, is strong and brave like Homer's Achilles. But instead of Patroclus Mr. Walcott gives him as companion the crippled Philoctete, who suffers, like his counterpart in the ancient story, from a wound that does not heal, and whose cure marks the end of the war. But, unlike his Greek namesake, Philoctete lives among men, enduring his pain. Achille also does not inflict his resentment on his friends, nor does he kill Hector, even over Helen. Hector dies as the result of his own recklessness, but the poem ends not with his funeral, but with the continuing existence of the survivors who learn to live with their memories.

When, toward the end of the poem, the narrator encounters Omeros, he complains he can no longer use the gods who dominate the action of the *Iliad* and the *Odyssey*. "Forget the gods," Omeros advises, "and read the rest." In their place Mr. Walcott puts forces even more pitiless and unpredictable than the gods of Olympus: nature, the sea, violent changes of weather, lizards and iguanas and the jungle foliage that casts debris and disorder onto the landscape.

When Homer's Achilles goes down to the sea, he finds his goddess mother Thetis ready to come to his aid, but Achilles must trust himself to a beautiful but unfeeling Sea-Mother (*mer-mère*) who can support or destroy him.

The gods brought order to Homer's world, but in Mr. Walcott's epic, Odysseus (and all of us who like him are exiles) must return to a home whose character has changed over time, even to the point where we can no longer recognize it. Yet these references to the ancient past, brief and insubstantial as they may seem, form the foundation of Mr. Walcott's poem. They endow his new characters and situations with heroism; they suggest that their experiences, particular as they are to specific places and present times, are also timeless and universal.

The narrative of *Omeros* is exciting and memorable, despite the absence of the chases, duels and descriptions of violent deaths in the Greek epics. At the end, Helen returns to Hector; a war-wounded Englishman in exile finds he can talk to his dead wife with the aid of one Ma Kilman, the wise old woman who runs an establishment called the No Pain Café and who also somehow recalls the ancient African remedy that cures old Philoctete's incurable wound. In place of action there is an increasing awareness of other people's suffering. Like Odysseus and the legendary Homer himself, everyone (including the narrator and reader) learns from his or her wandering and exile, even if it is only how better to understand what has happened.

Perhaps most surprisingly of all, we discover that it is the remote past, antiquity and military history, that matters, rather than modern concerns about money or self-promotion. Mr. Walcott's epic is a significant and timely reminder that the past is not the property of those who first created it; it always matters to all of us, no matter who we are or where we were born.

Accentuate the Masculine

Iron John by Robert Bly
December 9, 1990

BY MIHALY CSIKSZENTMIHALYI

I T IS REFRESHING these days to read a book that does not lay the blame for America's collective ills on social injustice, the savings and loan scandal, Iraq or the National Endowment for the Arts, but—get this—on defective mythology. The reason so many young people are ruined by drugs or senseless violence, according to Robert Bly (who is well known for his verse as well as for his recent forays into the reconstruction of the male psyche), is that to grow up as a wholesome adult one needs not only material comforts but the wise guidance of one's elders; and that is becoming increasingly scarce.

Anthropological literature is filled with accounts of how the Hopi Indians or the Arapesh of New Guinea nudge their youth into adulthood with the help of myths, symbols and initiation rituals. It is generally understood that such cultures would not endure unless elders spent a great deal of energy passing on their knowledge and values to the younger generation. But one could read a towering stack of enthnographies without encountering the suggestion that perhaps the same necessity holds also for us. Primitive people may need myths and rituals, because, well, they are primitive, aren't they? We, being rational, need none of that. Just give us the facts and the truth shall set us free.

It is with this dry Cartesian notion of human development that Mr. Bly takes issue. He starts with the assumption that boys don't become men or girls women by simply getting older and better informed. They also need a spiritual infusion from myths and mentors, in the form of a caring relationship that gradually discloses to the young what adulthood is all about. According to Mr. Bly, women in the last few decades have begun to rediscover what femininity means, while for men—separated from their fathers and from other male models—the concept of masculinity gets progressively blurred. To grow up healthy, young males need a positive ideal of manhood, and Iron John intends to provide it for them.

The model explored in this book is an archetypal character who recurs in myths and literature from the Gilgamesh to the brothers Grimm. Iron John is a hairy wild man who inhabits the forests and helps aimless young princes in their quest for fame and fortune. Mr. Bly's reading turns this Iron John into a perfect combination of untamed impulses and thoughtful self-discipline. This, and not the macho idols of the 1950s or the androgynous flower children of the 60s, should be our guiding ideal of mature masculinity. Although Iron John is an unregenerate male, man and woman can be whole only through each other. Mr. Bly does not believe that blurring the distinctions between the genders makes sense. As in biological development, integration requires prior differentiation; a fulfilling relationship requires a masculine man and a feminine woman.

It is possible that people who think of themselves as liberated will find Mr. Bly's theses somewhat reactionary. After all, why assume that the two genders need different myths, or that women can't initiate boys into manhood? Why not assume a generic human psyche, and unisex role models? To these questions Mr. Bly gives reasonably convincing answers. Four million years in which men and women prospered by maximizing complementary characteristics, eons that etched different patterns on the neural networks of the two genders, cannot—

with all the good will in the world—be erased in a few decades. Nor can the subtle tendrils of culture, which entangle us in traditional gender roles, be cut without running the risk of bleeding the sap out of a growing man, or woman.

In terms of what it tries to accomplish, Mr. Bly's book is important and timely. We need powerful jogs such as this to help us remember that, moon shots and genetic engineering notwithstanding, we are still befuddled creatures needing all the help we can get from the distilled experience of the ancients of the tribe.

However, the overall style of the book is a bit disappointing. Donald Hall once commented, "Bly moves like a huge hummingbird from Jung flower to Zen Flower, from the Buddha to the Great Mother," and this modus operandi is very much in evidence in the present volume—except that the field of flowers has expanded to include a few up-to-date anthropologists, psychologists and the headlines of the daily papers.

Mr. Bly, like other rehabilitators of ancient myths (such as Joseph Campbell, Robert Graves, Carlos Castaneda), tries to reflect the complexity of existence by making every symbol, image or event both good and bad, helpful and dangerous. Soon all the landscape is filled with ambivalent characters flashing red and green, stop and go, do this but watch out for the consequences. The great King is the ideal father not to be confused with the real father, and he is to be looked up to but escaped from, admired but abandoned, and so forth. This approach shows a sophisticated understanding of the dialectical nature of psychic reality, but it is also rather confusing. It suggests that a young man better forget about growing up unless he has the sensitivity of a Jung, the brains of an Einstein and the determination of a General Patton, plus a good dose of luck.

Mirror, Mirror

The Beauty Myth by Naomi Wolf
May 19, 1991

BY MARGO JEFFERSON

I AM GAZING AT A GLOSSY, full-color, seven-page advertisement for a new line of cosmetics produced by Ultima II. They are called the Nakeds II. The Nakeds offer "HUNDREDS OF SHADES IN EVERY NUANCE OF NEUTRAL . . . FOR WHENEVER A WOMAN WANTS THE LOOK OF LESS FOR SATURDAY" (she's likely to be around trees, bushes and other naturalistic props), "THE LOOK OF MORE FOR WORK" (more money, more competence, hence more facial armature), "OR FOR EVENING, THE LOOK OF WOW!"

It's utterly ridiculous—still, I can't help liking the packaging, those cream-colored makeup containers with black piping that so resemble ladies' hatboxes in the photograph on the three-page foldout. But that's my weakness, and it's there to be played on. How could it be otherwise, Naomi Wolf asks in *The Beauty Myth*, a sweeping, messy, vigorous, callow but stouthearted book dedicated to the proposition that the icon of the educated, middle-class woman as wife, mother and tasteful sexual appliance has been replaced by the icon of the educated, middle-class, wage-earning woman as a flaw-free specimen of physical perfection.

Ms. Wolf, a graduate of Yale who is now a Rhodes scholar at New College, Oxford, believes that from the Cult of Domesticity to the Feminine Mystique to the Beauty Myth and its backlash—that is, over the past 35 years—

> inexhaustible but ephemeral beauty work took over from inexhaustible but ephemeral housework. As the economy, law, religion, sexual mores, education, and culture were forcibly opened up to include women more fairly, a private reality colonized female consciousness. By using ideas about "beauty," it reconstructed an alternative female world with its own laws, economy, religion, sexuality, education, and culture, each element as repressive as any that had gone before.

Ms. Wolf maps out this "alternative female world" by recording just about every form of obsession and exploitation a $20 billion-a-year cosmetics industry, a $33 billion diet industry, a $300 million cosmetic-surgery industry and a $7 billion pornography industry can nurture and supply.

Is this new information? No (as Ms. Wolf's plentiful footnotes verify), but it is information we keep refusing to process, and we must be reminded of it until we begin to do so. As a feminist muckraker and media critic, Naomi Wolf does her work well. But as a feminist cultural historian, she has two big problems. The first is the intellectual equivalent of beauty follies. She overdoes glittery, special-effect metaphors—beauty as the cult millenarianism; beauty as the Iron Maiden, a body-shaped casket painted with the limbs and face of a young woman that served as a medieval instrument of torture. She is also addicted to cosmetic touch-ups of her thesis in the form of brief quotations and one-liners from critics, scholars and poets through the ages.

I'll put the second problem in question form: Why does every generation frame its recognition of lies and injustice in the claim that no previous generation has ever suffered them so acutely? I believe Ms. Wolf when she writes that "today's children and young men and women have sexual identities that spiral around paper and celluloid phantoms: from *Playboy* to music videos to the blank female torsos in women's magazines, features obscured and eyes extinguished, they are being imprinted with a sexuality that is mass-produced, deliberately dehumanizing and inhuman."

But I don't believe this is taking place "for the first time in history": it's taking place at this moment in history through the particular methods that media and technology provide. After all, the conventions, excesses and grotesqueries of the beauty industry were securely in place by the 1920s.

As for beauty standards—from body shape to feature size—they were a lot more restrictive and bigoted just 25 years ago than they are now, and while Ms. Wolf is right to say that the muscled and worked body in fashion today has its alien and bionic side, the 1950s exaggeration of "natural" female flesh and curves was just as artificial and (if you lacked them) debilitating. One body canonized pseudowomanliness; the other appropriates pseudomanliness. Beauty is such a strange thing—it's a fantasy, a pastime and a profession (like sports), and we bring a daunting range of emotions and associations to it. I like the fact that Ms. Wolf ends her book by saying we need more, not less of it.

The Beauty Myth shows us yet again how much we need new ways of seeing. I regret that it also shows how much we need new ways of writing—polemics and manifestoes that will make room amidst their facts and theories for the contradictory particulars of each reader's life.

The Candidate

Mating by Norman Rush
September 22, 1991

BY JIM SHEPARD

THE NARRATOR of Norman Rush's *Mating*—who through almost 500 pages remains persistently unnamed—opens her sprawling comedy of manners by announcing, "In Africa, you want more, I think." And she does want more: there she is, 32 years old, a would-be Ph.D. in anthropology with an exploded thesis on her hands, tired of her own company with no one left behind or on the horizon, "feeling sexually alert" and circulating in Gaborone, the capital of Botswana. She doesn't want "to be a candidate any more, not for a doctorate or anything else." She's certain she's "on the verge of a confused but major experience," an experience she can't initiate alone. She needs a companion. When it comes to intellect, she tells us, "My preference is always for hanging out with the finalists."

And along comes the ultimate finalist: Nelson Denoon, at the pinnacle of the academic vineyard wherein she labors with the peasantry. He's beautiful, heretical, feminist and interdisciplinary, someone who not only studies why the world has to be so unpleasant but who is also actively trying to do something about it: as a pragmatic and apparently successful utopian, he has set up a miraculous and self-sustaining Eden in the Kalahari Desert, run by and for dispossessed and abused African women. To prove her commitment, resourcefulness and grit—to prove her qualifications as a suitable companion—she resolves to cross the hundred miles of desert alone to find him and his Eden.

All of this is presented in an allusively freewheeling first-person narrative that provides exhilarating evidence of an impressive intelligence at work and play. Readers receive a palpable sense of having their education sternly tested—and expanded—by Mr. Rush's novel. Geography, history, political science, economics, literature, biology, popular culture and utter trivia—the narrator and her beloved Denoon hash everything out, and in doing so are encyclopedic in the extreme, segueing from bats to Boers to Borges to Botswana.

The narrative itself represents the heroine's reconsideration of her relationship with Denoon, her emotions recollected in the shakiest of tranquillities, a strategy that allows for endless asides, digressions, minilectures, documents entered in evidence and, most of all, hindsight. But all of her attempts to, as she puts it, get "inside the moat," to be embraced by the perfect man and perfect community, only point out to her how problematic the paradox of her position as a feminist is becoming: for all her gifts, she's relying for happiness and a sense of purpose on a male.

Not everything that Mr. Rush attempts in this extraordinarily ambitious novel comes off. It's striking that someone as self-conscious as the narrator would fail to make more of the Harlequin Romance elements of her tale. Some of the wordplay is more wearing than charming. The irony of this narrator never being named is too clearly Meaningful. A certain amount of rambling does take place.

If these seem like relatively small complaints, they are. Mr. Rush has created one of the wiser and wittier fictive meditations on the subject of mating. His novel illuminates why we yield when we don't have to. It seeks to illuminate the nature of true intimacy—how to define it, how to know when one has achieved it.

"For me love is like this," the narrator tells us. "You're in one room or apartment which you think is fine, then you walk through a door and close it behind you and find yourself in the next apartment, which is even better, larger, more floorspace, a better view. You're happy there and then you go into the next apartment and close the door and this one is even better. And the sequence continues, but with the odd feature that although this has happened to you a number of times, you forget: each time your new quarters are manifestly better and each time it's breathtaking, a surprise, something you've done nothing to deserve or

Nadine Gordimer becomes the first South African to be awarded the Nobel Prize in Literature.

make happen. You never intend to go from one room onward to the next — it just happens. You notice a door, you go through, and you're delighted again."

It's a measure of the success of this first novel that the above also describes the reader's experience of Mr. Rush's vigorous and luminous prose.

The War on Women

Backlash by Susan Faludi
October 27, 1991

BY ELLEN GOODMAN

JUST AS ANITA HILL'S ACCUSATIONS of sexual harassment provoked spontaneous outrage, this book will have a spine-stiffening effect on any woman who thinks she is paranoid. Yes, says Ms. Faludi, they are after you.

Ms. Faludi is at her best in debunking the studies, experts and trend stories that made their way into our collection of "common wisdom" in the last decade. She skewers the data, the data collectors and the data purveyors.

Ms. Faludi's eye ranges from Washington in the Reagan years to Hollywood in the *Fatal Attraction* years, from the fate of advertising's new Breck Girl to the final chapter of the best seller *Women Who Love Too Much*. She is particularly keen in sighting the contradictions between what the new right advocated and how it lived.

But *Backlash* is not just a critique of revisionism — although it would make wonderful reading for a mass-media class. Nor does Ms. Faludi turn up a conspiracy.

Nevertheless, with wit and a breezy, sharp style, she traces the cumulative damaging effect of the backlash. Attention turned away from the notion that women had too little equality and toward the idea that they had an overdose of the evil stuff. In the process, the '80s became the decade of the biological clock, the mommy track and post-feminism instead of family leave, the equal rights amendment and feminism.

Backlash is, however, sometimes guilty of the sort of trend reporting that it criticizes. Ms. Faludi marshals her evidence, but leaves out pieces that don't fit her puzzle. Yes, NBC put a jiggle show on television about student nurses called *Nightingales*, but it was killed by the outrage from nurses. Yes, Hope was the homebound madonna of *thirtysomething*, but in the last episode she was breaking out while her husband, Michael, was having a midlife crisis.

And while the leaders of the counterassault tried to twist and stall the women's movement, they weren't quite as successful as *Backlash* suggests.

There have been voices countering the counterassault. It hasn't been all push back and no shove forward. *Thelma and Louise* came from somewhere. So did Anita Hill.

What is also missing is recognition of the difference among hostility, hypocrisy and plain old ambivalence. The backlash told women they couldn't have it all and shouldn't even try. But no one invented the ambivalence that many working mothers feel. Ms. Faludi's dark portrait of the new men's movement could also be many shades grayer.

But this is an invigorating and thorough report from the battleground of "the undeclared war against American women." It may do more than give us a quick trip through the '80s. It portends the next set of trend stories. The women's movement that refused to die despite its many obits is just about due for a media resurrection.

Sparing the Udmurt

Rebuilding Russia by Aleksandr Solzhenitsyn
November 24, 1991

BY DANIEL PATRICK MOYNIHAN

IN 1979 *Newsweek* published a forum on the coming decade. In a brief entry, I proposed that the 1980s would see the breakup of the Soviet Union. If any American read a word of this, I have no record of the event. But one Russian did. Aleksandr Solzhenitsyn and his wife invited me and my wife to spend a day with them in their home near Cavendish, Vt.

Taking our leave after a vast, old-fashioned 4 o'clock dinner, I asked Mr. Solzhenitsyn if he believed he would ever be able to return home. "I had thought," he replied, "I would be back by now."

Well, the Soviet Union has broken up. No one anticipated it more than Aleksandr Solzhenitsyn. And now he has written a succinct, at times breathless, essay, which was originally published in the Soviet Union in September 1990 as a supplement in the newspaper *Komsomolskaya Pravda*. *Rebuilding Russia*, wonderfully well translated by Alexis Klimoff, is instructive because it offers Mr. Solzhenitsyn's own proposals, but it is fascinating in what it says about how the breakup came about.

Ethnicity: it is the great hidden force of the age (a fact still lost on what is called our "intelligence community"). Mr. Solzhenitsyn begins here.

"In the course of three-quarters of a century," he says, "to the sound of incessant proclamations trumpeting 'the socialist friendship of peoples,' the communist regime has managed to neglect, entangle, and sully the relationship among . . . peoples to such a degree that one can no longer see the way back to the peaceful coexistence of nationalities, that almost drowsy non-perception of distinctions that had virtually been achieved—with some lamentable exceptions—in the final decades of pre-revolutionary Russia."

The American reader may be tempted to discount that talk of "peaceful coexistence" and the "almost drowsy non-perception of distinctions" in some pastoral past. But the evidence is with Mr. Solzhenitsyn, who is, after all, scarcely a man given to avoiding unpleasant facts. For example, one may consult David Fromkin's *Peace to End All Peace* on the *douceur de vivre* of Ottoman Iraq. The world has known worse things than those empires.

But they could not last, or in any event, did not. At the beginning of the twentieth century, nationalism, the ethnic demand for separate states, was rising all across Europe, notably in the Hapsburg and Romanov empires (and Ireland and Norway and Quebec, but let's not get started).

There is a sense in which the Marxists just lucked into this. The ethnic masses were stirring; the Marxists labeled them toiling masses. Workers of the World united to undo the Emperor, the Czar, the Sultan, the whomsoever. The pre-revolutionary writings of Lenin and Stalin are filled with discussions of the Nationality Question.

American scholars are firm in the view that the phrase "self-determination" originated with Woodrow Wilson in 1917. Not so. The Bolsheviks put it into their platform in 1903 (and the Ukrainians into the United Nations Charter in 1945). In 1913, Stalin, who was to become the first Commissar of National Minorities, was asking, "What is to be done with the Mingrelians, the Abkhasians, the Adjarians, the Svanetians, the Lesghians?"

Mr. Solzhenitsyn's view is that they must leave the new Russian state.

Substantial groups like the Tatar, Bashkir, Udmurt, Komi, Chuvash, Mordva, Mari, and Yakut. . . . The smallest national groups: the Nenets, Permyak, Evenki, Mansi, Khakas, Chukchi, Koryak, and other peoples I cannot enumerate here. They all lived well in the Tsarist "prison of peoples" and it is we, the communist Soviet Union, who have dragged them toward extinction. We must lose no time in offering our help in restoring them to life and vigor. It is not yet too late.

Every people, even the very smallest, represents a unique facet of God's design. As Vladimir Solovyov has written, paraphrasing the Christian commandment: "You must love all other people as you love your own."

But when it comes to living arrangements, you live with your own.

Mr. Solzhenitsyn's dream is the return of an entity that might be called "Rus," consisting of the Little Russians (Ukrainians), Great Russians and Byelorussians, and located in the Russian heartland ("we all sprang from precious Kiev"). The remaining 12 republics and assorted jurisdictions, with their numerous ethnic groups, must go.

The real issue is to get on with rebuilding society. He is mostly for democracy. Two Cheers, as E. M. Forster would say. For Mr. Solzhenitsyn, democracy works well in small units, where the voters know the candidates personally and exercise "self-restraint." He cites Switzerland as his ideal, along with "citizens' assemblies" in the United States (clearly thinking of the New England town meeting).

In his 1978 Harvard commencement address, Mr. Solzhenitsyn seemed at times contemptuous of American democracy with its pusillanimous peaceniks and consumer orgiasts. But that was then. He was but two years over here and further from Russia than ever. In *Rebuilding Russia* he comes across as a thoroughly practical man, even something of an eighteenth-century man. As, you might say, Jefferson. Or Madison, who wrote of the "fugitive and turbulent existence" of ancient republics, and might find the Russian tough-mindedness of this essay refreshing.

It appears to me, at all events, that Mr. Solzhenitsyn has understood the major twentieth-century thinkers very well, among them the philosopher Karl Popper, who wrote that "one chooses democracy, not because it abounds in virtues, but only in order to avoid tyranny"; and the economist Joseph Schumpeter, who said, in cautioning against ignoring the context of time and place, that democracy was "the surrogate faith of intellectuals deprived of religion." Mr. Solzhenitsyn would build a democracy from the ground up, beginning with small regions—towns, groups of villages, "areas up to the size of a county"—and on the whole he would build slowly. He has no enthusiasm for the secret ballot, which was in fact an unthinkable notion when the United States got started. He would have a lot of indirect representation. Well, so did the Framers of the American Constitution.

Mr. Solzhenitsyn has not a great deal to say about the judicial branch. But what in this indomitable man's life would have given him any firsthand experience of an independent judiciary?

And so, great joy to him and to his people—to all those peoples. There is one other thing. I touched on it in that 1979 article. Who gets the warheads? That is not resolved in this book, and possibly could not be. Which could ruin everything Aleksandr Solzhenitsyn all but sacrificed his life to achieve.

It's All Over Now

The End of History and the Last Man by Francis Fukuyama
January 26, 1992

BY WILLIAM H. MCNEILL

BACK TO HEGEL" is not a rallying cry many Americans are likely to find plausible, yet this is what Francis Fukuyama advocates in this quixotic and tightly argued work of political philosophy. Actually, Mr. Fukuyama—a consultant at RAND and the former State Department official who caused a stir three years ago with his essay "The End of History"—does not really recommend Hegel, but an interpretation of Hegel by a French intellectual named Alexandre Kojeve (to me, entirely unknown), who explained in 1947 that History with a capital "H" had reached its logical end with the emergence of liberal democracy. In *The End of History and the Last Man*, Mr. Fukuyama adds a dash of Nietzsche to this strange cocktail, which is where the Last Man in his title comes from.

Mr. Fukuyama's invocation of German political philosophy aims to correct what he sees as a serious defect of Anglo-American political thought. Hobbes, Locke and Madison, he says, based their political theory on a lopsided view of human nature. By appealing only to reason and desire, their liberalism left out a third element of human nature, which, according to Mr. Fukuyama, is of special importance for politics. This he calls *thymos*, a term borrowed from Plato that he translates as "spiritedness" or "desire for recognition." When properly satisfied, *thymos* arouses pride; when frustrated it results in anger. A failure to assert it brings a sense of shame.

Thymos, Mr. Fukuyama argues, is the principal motor of politics, impelling some men, throughout history, to assert personal mastery over others. But the genius of liberal democracy, dating from the American and French Revolutions, is that *thymos* could now begin to find universal satisfaction in shared citizenship. Freedom, in short, was perceived as a goal for all, and the struggle for mastery that had dominated the past now reached its logical and necessary conclusion. History (capitalized to signify a "meaningful order to the broad sweep of human events") came to an end.

To be sure, not all the countries of the world have yet achieved liberal democracy. But Mr. Fukuyama argues that they are all bound to get there, sooner or later, since human nature requires it. Until that time, history continues in the old way in the illiberal parts of the globe, and the End of History affects only Europeans, Americans and the inhabitants of a few other nations, such as Japan.

Mr. Fukuyama is not entirely blind to these dimensions of social life, but he only considers nationalism, which, he holds, can "fade away as a political force" by becoming "tolerant like religion before it." Oddly, he says nothing about race feeling, which appears to be on the rise in Europe as well as in the United States. He likewise skips over religiously defined identities and rivalries, so prominent in the Middle East, which he presumably thinks will eventually sink toward the sort of political marginality that Protestantism and Catholicism have attained in this country and in most of Western Europe. Similarly, he says nothing about class conflict, perhaps because he thinks that Marxism has now been so discredited that refutation of one of its primary doctrines is unnecessary.

Finally, it seems worth pointing out that Mr. Fukuyama's philosophical approach entirely omits the biological and ecological setting within which human society and politics inevitably exist. Even if his End of History were to arrive, the enduring equilibrium he attributes to liberal democracy, because it "gives fullest scope to all three parts" of the human soul, would confront serious outside disturbances arising from the instabilities in the natural environment created by our technology and ever-increasing numbers. Under such circumstances, tumults like those of the past would surely continue, even if, from Mr. Fukuyama's point of view, History had somehow lost its right to a capital letter.

As a professional historian, I am bound to point out that Mr. Fukuyama is so eager to address the grand sweep of History that he does not bother much with the details of history (without a capital letter). Thus, for instance, he asserts that Hobbes profited from the ideas of Newton, who was all of 11 years old when *Leviathan* was published. He also tells us that the English civil wars of the seventeenth century were fought between Catholics and Protestants, thereby administering a posthumous conversion to some of the antagonists in those all-Protestant conflicts.

Yet such errors, however egregious, are really beside the point. As a thinker and theorist of politics, Mr. Fukuyama deserves to have his argument taken seriously. Trying to do so, I find myself quite in sympathy with his effort to base politics on something more than the calculus of material self-interest. Ever since economists achieved the status of national soothsayers through their success in generating new concepts and statistics for maximizing war production during World War II, economics has pervaded public discourse in the United States far more than it deserves to. Americans, like other human beings, clearly do respond to noneconomic motives; and what Mr. Fukuyama refers to as *thymos* does, in fact, frequently outweigh material self-interest, impelling individuals to engage in acts of collective self-assertion or to display behavior that sometimes puts their lives at risk.

Nonetheless, the lesson Mr. Fukuyama derives from his reading of History seems to me fundamentally false. His argument that all the human past was no

Oops!

The Bridges of
Madison County

*BY ROBERT JAMES
WALLER*

Published: April 1, 1992.
Reviewed: March 28, 1993.

465

more than a fumbling progress aimed at the perfection of liberal, capitalist democracy, as exemplified here and in a few other countries, simply reformulates a longstanding vision of the United States as embodying an earthly perfection toward which all other peoples have been expected to aspire. The exotic Germanic garb in which Mr. Fukuyama expresses this self-flattering image may give fresh life to this myopia. But when Asian models of social and economic efficiency seem to be gaining ground every day, and when millions of Moslems are at pains to sustain the differences, great and small, that distinguish them from Americans, it is hard to believe that all the world is destined to imitate us.

My basic difference with Mr. Fukuyama is this: I do not believe that human nature is uniform and unchanging. Rather, whatever penchants and capabilities we inherit with our genes are so malleable that their expression takes infinitely diverse forms. Personal identification with a group of fellows is the basic guide for most behavior; and groups define themselves by marking the ways they differ from outsiders. This, I believe (in contrast to Mr. Fukuyama), assures permanent institutional diversity and cultural pluralism among humankind.

1993

On June 6, the *Book Review* publishes color for the first time. It's the Summer Reading issue, and features a picture of a big spotted snake.

First Impressions

The Hidden Life of Dogs by Elizabeth Marshall Thomas
August 1, 1993

BY JEFFREY MOUSSAIEFF MASSON

OUR KNOWLEDGE OF ANIMALS seems shrouded in clichés: What do dogs dream about? Chasing cats, we think. But the truth is we have no idea what dogs dream about. It is not impossible that they dream about their own unhappy childhoods. Michael, a gorilla brought from Africa and taught American Sign Language, apparently once signed that he was sad. Asked why, he related the story of seeing his mother killed by hunters in the jungle during his capture when he was small.

Elizabeth Marshall Thomas is an anthropologist and a novelist, and she is gifted in both fields. She observes closely and sympathetically and writes with clarity, depth and engagement. Her latest book, *The Hidden Life of Dogs*, is informative, delightful, innovative and full of an intimate knowledge of canine life.

We humans, at last, are becoming aware that our supposedly unique capacities (speech, esthetic sense) are not the yardstick by which all other animals are to be measured. The fact that a dog cannot speak does not mean that it does not have complicated thoughts, complex emotions or the capacity to suffer. Why, after all, should dogs not feel compassion, wonder, gratitude, love, disappointment and other subtle emotions? They clearly do, and deciphering these emotions is only a question of being able to read the signs.

This is what Ms. Thomas is so good at doing. She had the wonderfully original idea (at least, I have not heard of anybody else doing it) of following her dogs on their daily rounds. She simply let them loose, then watched them and, as much as physically possible, joined them in their escapades. The result is a fascinating glimpse into the canine world, possibly deeper and more accurate than any we have had until now. Even Konrad Lorenz's famous book *Man Meets Dog* is flawed by presuppositions that are absent here.

While field biologists have learned in recent years to be as unobtrusive as possible in observing and following animals (Cynthia Moss's book *Elephant Memories* is an outstanding example), this technique has rarely been attempted with domesticated animals. In the literature about dogs, we learn little about the intimate relation of dog to dog. Dog stories, even the better ones, may tell you a great deal about human emotions and human psychology and how humans feel about dogs, but they tell you relatively little about dogs themselves. No book I have read has taught me more about the inner lives of dogs than this one.

Freud is said to have asked, "What does a woman want?" and he never found the answer. Ms. Thomas asks what dogs want, and gives this answer: "They want each other. Human beings are merely a cynomorphic substitute, as we all know."

Rather than despising anthropomorphism, Ms. Thomas uses it sparingly, but with great empathy and without apology. After all, she observes, just as we need to see dogs in human terms, dogs need to see us in dog terms.

Some readers might feel that the author has turned her dogs into impossibly wise Zen masters. But canine wisdom, whether hers or theirs, is more benign and persuasive and certainly less pretentious and manipulative than the wisdom claimed by most members of our species.

Letter

Lewis Lapham
October 24, 1993

EVERY PUBLISHING SEASON sponsors at least one cause célèbre, and in New York this fall the merchants of high-end literary opinion assigned the show window to a book that dwells, not surprisingly, on themselves. *New York Days* is a sentimental memoir in which the author, Willie

1994

Catching up, the *Book Review* reviews its first CD-ROM, "Microsoft Art Gallery," on March 6.

Morris, describes his tenure as the editor of *Harper's Magazine* in the years 1967–71 as a lost golden age of American letters, when journalism was poetry and all the writers at all the tables at Elaine's were the natural children of William Faulkner or Henry James.

My own memory of the time and place so flatly contradicts his portrait in nostalgic pastel (in the specific instances as well as the general propositions) that on reading his book and its attendant publicity, I assumed that one of us was looking at the reverse images seen in a mirror. What Mr. Morris presents as a golden age I remember as an age of tinsel; his cast of fearless prophets I remember as a crowd of self-important pharisees; the books that he names as the last page proofs of authentic journalism (among them *In Cold Blood*, by Truman Capote; *Miami and the Siege of Chicago*, by Norman Mailer; and *The Best and the Brightest*, by David Halberstam) I would name as the first spawn of the synthetic melodrama that leads, more or less directly, to *Oprah* and *Geraldo* and Joe McGinniss pretending to be Teddy Kennedy; what to Mr. Morris's mind appears as disinterested reporting appears to my mind as relentless self-promotion, and well before I had reached the end of *New York Days* I thought that it captured, all too perfectly, the spirit of an age that debased the currency of its idealism with the coinage of celebrity.

Given the prevailing rates of inflation cheapening the measures of value elsewhere in the society, the loss of definition and purpose in what used to be called the fourth estate was probably inevitable. Before 1960 most of the writers and editors working on newspapers in New York understood that they had more in common with carpenters or stonemasons than they did with diplomats or poets. Many of them were self-educated, and they hired themselves out as journeymen, not as immortal artists. Having come of age in the 1930s and '40s, they were schooled in the lessons of poverty, and they tended to identify with the crowd in the bleachers rather than with the swells in the box seats. If asked to state their occupation, they would have said "reporter" or "newspaperman" (the term "journalist" pertained only to Englishmen and fops), and they sought to write a simple and translucent prose, the idea being to make more clearly visible the subject of the story.

1994

In September, Aleksandr Solzhenitsyn, who has returned to Russia, becomes the host of his own television talk show. Before long, he cancels the guests and does all the talking himself. A year later, the program is dropped for low ratings.

I was attracted to the trade in the late 1950s because it seemed to offer a means of questioning the delusions of grandeur that were beginning to afflict the American oligarchy. As an apprentice member of that oligarchy, educated at a New England prep school and Yale University, I understood that in return for admission to the box seats the guests were expected to admire the benign wisdom of the corporations buying the golf balls or the salmon on toast. Not wanting to pay the price of a ticket, and admiring instead the skepticism of Ambrose

Bierce, H. L. Mencken and I. F. Stone, I assumed that the newspaperman who did his job correctly couldn't expect to be welcomed with grateful applause at the nation's better country clubs.

So bleak a prospect didn't sit well with the temper of the times. The '60s were about having it both ways—a reputation for principled objection and first-class hotel suites at the political conventions, a publisher's advance extended to six figures and a blue work shirt signifying the author's contempt for money. The voices of conscience decorated the dinner tables of power, and within a year of President John F. Kennedy's glamorous arrival in the White House, the suddenly respectable "profession of journalism" was attracting volunteers from Harvard and Princeton. The new recruits arrived with bound volumes of the absolute truth, comfortable in the assumption that the aura of academic entitlement conferred the badges of moral as well as intellectual superiority. The rates of pay kept pace with the expanding wealth of the communications industries, and by the end of the decade the higher-priced operatives found it easy to regard themselves as the peers of the political and theatrical figures about whom they composed their best-selling romances. The ambiguity of the Vietnam War compounded the confusion, and just as the moralists among them came to imagine that they were better qualified to govern the country than the candidates elected to public office, so also they dressed themselves in the mantles of self-righteousness.

If before 1960 most people recognized irreducible differences among journalism, literature, politics and the movies, the distinctions dissolved under the technical and epistemological pressures of the next 10 years. The lines between fact and fiction became as irrelevant as they were difficult to distinguish, and the several forms of expression once known as the lively arts fused into the common alloy of the mass media. News was entertainment and entertainment was news, and everybody was staging his or her shows and special effects in the same theater of celebrity.

Under the rubric of what was beginning to be called the new journalism, magazine writers claimed the exemptions of novelists *manqué*. The presumption allowed them to arrange the materials at hand (descriptions of scene, tones of voice, fragments of conversation, impressions of character, etc.) into whatever designs attracted the most applause and the highest fees. By substituting the veneer of a precocious style for the weight of fact, and making little or no distinction between subject and object (the interviewer being as important as, often more important than, the interviewee), they presented their own advertisements for reality as literal renderings of the world of historical event.

The technique worked reasonably well on the margins of society—among

1995

People everywhere are reading Jane Austen's books. They've discovered (or rediscovered) them via the movies.

Hell's Angels and hopeful movie actresses, on tour with politicians, Jackie Onassis and other journalists. The technique didn't work so well among people who didn't need the publicity. Unless the journalist first translated himself into a sycophant, he had trouble gaining access to the higher tiers of authority. Who would talk to the fellow except in lies and half-truths? Certainly not newspaper publishers or network executives; nobody in the investment banks, the Pentagon, the influential law firms, the White House or the corporations. The high-priced journalists of the day resolved the dilemma by taking to heart the lessons of the Age of Aquarius and *Jesus Christ Superstar,* and they began to write books—ostensibly about war, or politics, or the Presidency—that could have been uniformly entitled "All About Me."

Very little of the supposedly tough-minded journalism that appeared in *Harper's Magazine* during the late 1960s risked giving offense to the wisdom in office. The putative champions of liberty took up the cry of dissent only after it had become profitable and safe. The magazine published its denunciations of the Vietnam War when the crowds of angry students were already in the streets; the sentiments in favor of the civil rights movement appeared at a time when they had become the stuff of corporate advertising.

An air of conscience-stricken protest was in keeping with the spirit of the age, and most of the people who showed up in Elaine's in the years 1967–71 understood the joke. The humor and good feeling of the place was grounded in the tone of irony, but Mr. Morris was one of the people who believed their own press notices.

First Impressions

Midnight in the Garden of Good and Evil by John Berendt
March 20, 1994

BY GLENNA WHITLEY

T HE VOODOO PRIESTESS looked across the table at her wealthy client, a man on trial for murder: "Now, you know how dead time works. Dead time lasts for one hour—from half an hour before midnight to half an hour after midnight. The half-hour before midnight is for doin' good. The half-hour after midnight is for doin' evil. . . . Seems like we need a little of both tonight."

When he began living part of the year in Savannah, Ga., John Berendt, a columnist for *Esquire* and a former editor of *New York* magazine, was looking for—what? Respite from the big city? A charming little Southern town dripping with humidity and history to observe as fodder for a novel? What he found was a cultured but isolated backwater, a town where who your great-grandparents were still matters, where anti-Yankee resentments are never far from the surface and where writers from New York are invited to midnight voodoo ceremonies in graveyards.

Mr. Berendt's writing is elegant and wickedly funny, and his eye for telling details is superb. He frequently veers off and includes overheard conversations, funny vignettes and bits of historical and architectural data—a method that a lesser observer might have botched but that works wonderfully here. *Midnight in the Garden of Good and Evil* might be the first true-crime book that makes the reader want to call a travel agent and book a bed and breakfast for an extended weekend at the scene of the crime.

1995

Martin Amis upsets the London literary world when he sinks his teeth into an advance of almost $800,000 for his novel *The Information*.

The Names Have Been Changed

Primary Colors by Anonymous
January 28, 1996

BY MICHAEL LEWIS

THIS BOOK WAS WRITTEN by an artful thief, someone who knew just how much he could steal and get away with it. Although it is advertised as a novel, it tells the story of the 1992 Democratic primaries pretty much exactly as they must have appeared through the eyes of George Stephanopoulos. Almost every character, incident and setting has been drawn directly from life, and the author does everything in his power to make sure that we do not miss the connections. Bill Clinton is recast as Governor (of a small Southern state) Jack Stanton, complete with bimbo eruptions, a draft problem and a strident wife (here named Susan). The pious Governor of New York, Mario Cuomo, has become the pious Governor of New York, Orlando Ozio; Gennifer Flowers has become Cashmere McLeod (with tapes); Hope, Ark., has become Grace Junction (the state is unnamed). Even the journalists are impossible to miss: the oenophile R. W. Apple Jr. of *The New York Times* makes a cameo appearance as the oenophile A. P. Caulley of *The New York Times*. It is a strange reversal of the usual conventions of fiction. Only the identity of the author remains unknown to the reader.

The author, whoever he or she is, makes about as much effort to cover his tracks through literature as he does through life. He has lifted his emotional

1996

A Manhattan court rules that Random House, which has sued to get back a $1.2 million advance paid to the actress and steamy-book writer Joan Collins, must instead pay her an additional $1 million.

infrastructure—or at any rate the book's central relationships—from *All the King's Men*, Robert Penn Warren's fictionalized account of the rise of Huey Long. Again, he seems to want us to know that he has done it. The narrator Jack Burden has become the narrator Henry Burton. The central object of unfeeling politicosexual attention, Sadie, here has become Daisy, or Daise, as she is affectionately and anagrammatically known.

But the most startling piece of petty larceny is the book's central relationship: Henry and Stanton. (That is, Stephanopoulos and Clinton.) Henry watches his governor with the same blend of love, awe, resignation and revulsion as Jack Burden did The Boss. Even the cascading, demotic rhythms of his voice are modeled on Warren.

Of course, you cannot borrow wholesale from a novel of the early 1940s and remain credible in the mid-1990s. The author has had to make a number of minor alterations, some very clever, to tailor Robert Penn Warren's package to the Clinton campaign. As a scion of the Louisiana overclass, Jack Burden was unable to serve his rising populist governor without betraying class and family. You can't get away with that sort of aristocratic conceit any longer; the upper class has long abandoned its posture of moral superiority toward practical political climbers. The upper class now underwrites practical political climbers. The author solves this problem—and gives us a protagonist a bit more sympathetic than the average Yuppie in the bargain—by having Henry be the scion of black civil rights leaders. In working for Stanton, Henry is made to feel by nearly every black person he encounters that he is selling out both his class and his family.

The only trouble is that Henry seems occasionally to forget that he is black. Or rather he is black when it serves the author's purpose but not when it doesn't. He finds himself in bed with white women across the Deep South, for instance, without a passing mention of the color of his skin. And can anyone imagine Hillary Clinton reaching across and "tousling" the hair of an Afro-American? I can't. (Though I can easily imagine her reaching across and tousling the hair of George Stephanopoulos.) If nothing else, the author's tangle with fiction reinforces the impression that the more plausible and vivid passages, which seem to be pure invention, in fact come straight from inside the Clinton campaign.

Primary Colors is an odd book. But maybe the oddest thing about it is how good it is. In spite of its sins it is far and away the best thing I have read about the 1992 campaign; it breaks all the rules and lives to tell about it. The author's portrait of Mr. Clinton is astonishingly powerful. I doubt that anyone who reads the book will ever again think of the President in quite the same way. I'm not quite sure why this should be, except there is a wonderful honesty about it, a refusal to give in to the conventional interpretation of people and events that cripples so

1996

Anonymous enjoys a surprise best seller with *Primary Colors* while Joe Klein gets rich.

much that is written about politics. There is a whole set of emotions lurking just below the surface in politics that for whatever reason almost never get described in print.

The person who wrote this book has the not entirely respectable gift of the realist: he makes art out of what he has seen. So who did it? From what he steals and how he steals it the author offers you a literary equivalent of one of those computer-generated crime sketches. White, male, young, extremely observant, gifted with the language, a bit tortured and conflicted but not so much that he is unable to pursue his ambition. Above all, he was very close to the campaign (though it could be argued that anyone who watched C-Span was). Possibly a journalist, but if so one with unusual access to insiders. More likely an insider himself. If George Stephanopoulos was planning to write a novel to make sense of his experience, he's been beaten to the punch by some reporter or underling. Then again, maybe he wasn't. You never know.

Heaven Is Hell

The Puttermesser Papers by Cynthia Ozick
June 15, 1997

BY JACK MILES

CYNTHIA OZICK has an amphibious talent. She is interested in ideas to the extent that they yield stories and stories to the extent that they yield ideas. Literary intellectuals ("Wait'll you meet him!" one Ozick character crows. "He's got this *mind*") may groan when the novelist in Ms. Ozick intrudes on the critic. Lovers of pure story may sigh when the critic breaks the novelist's spell. But others read Ms. Ozick for the fun of just this double-crossing. Her latest book, *The Puttermesser Papers*, is a crazy delight. Its author doesn't fall between two stools, she floats there.

The word "papers" in the title properly suggests that these five previously published episodes from the imagined life of Ruth Puttermesser have been collected rather than constructed. The first paper, "Puttermesser: Her Work History, Her Ancestry, Her Afterlife," introduces the protagonist, age 34, as a New York Jew who has quit the "blue-blood Wall Street" law firm where she was going nowhere fast. She is now working in the Department of Receipts and Disbursements of the City of New York, where she is going nowhere even faster. Twice a week, Puttermesser visits her Uncle Zindel for a Hebrew lesson, and the plot, we think, is about to thicken. But suddenly a voice breaks in:

"Stop. Stop, stop! Puttermesser's biographer, stop! Disengage, please. . . . Puttermesser is not to be examined as an artifact but as an essence. Who made her? No one cares. Puttermesser is henceforth to be presented as given."

So much for the pointillistic tedium of characterization. Fill in the dots yourself, reader. "Hey! Puttermesser's biographer!" this overture section ends. "What will you do with her now?"

What Ms. Ozick does with her is contained in the second Puttermesser paper, "Puttermesser and Xanthippe," in which we are reminded that Puttermesser, now 46, is a feminist. ("She always said 'humankind' instead of 'mankind.' She always wrote 'he or she' instead of just 'he.' ") What many busy feminists secretly crave, of course, is a wife. Dumped by her lover, demoted and then fired by her boss, Puttermesser gets something even better. She creates—in her sleep, from the soil of the many potted plants in her apartment—a girl golem who calls herself a daughter but conducts herself like a superspouse and indeed insists on the name Xanthippe, for Socrates' ball and chain.

Now we are on the terrain Ms. Ozick loves best: a fantasy landscape rich in allegorical possibilities and low in conventionally novelistic requirements. The original golem, created in the sixteenth century (as Ms. Ozick explains) by the Great Rabbi Judah Loew, cleansed Prague. Puttermesser's golem has a bigger project ahead. She will cleanse New York:

> Ah, how this idea glowed for Puttermesser! . . . Mobs transmuted into troops of the blessed, citizens bursting into angelness, sidewalks of alabaster, buses filled with thrones. Old delicate Prague, swept and swept of sin, giving birth to the purified daylight, the lucent genius, of New York!

Shades of S. J. Perelman! Ms. Ozick loves the comic flounce of overstatement and cleverly contrives situations in which she can get away with it. Xanthippe, a sendup of the great woman behind every great man, gets Puttermesser elected mayor of New York. But as Leah, the name Puttermesser has always fancied for her child, Xanthippe also mimes the perfect Jewish daughter. ("Why were you created?" Puttermesser asks. To which she responds, "So that my mother should become what she was intended to become.") "The Golem Cooks, Cleans and Shops," one chapter heading reads. Does she ever! But growing skyward, as all golems do until they are destroyed, she also becomes a sexually insatiable giantess, bedding (to exhaustion) Mayor Puttermesser's entire administration. Finally, Puttermesser has to uncreate her.

In the next installment, "Puttermesser Paired," Ms. Ozick's heroine, now in her 50's, takes up with a painter named Rupert Rabeeno, a younger man who copies—or, as he puts it, "reenacts"—master paintings. Puttermesser, by now a lonely retiree rather than a practicing lawyer, introduces him to the novels of her beloved George Eliot, casting herself as Eliot and Rupert as Eliot's paramour, George Henry Lewes.

In time, Rupert shakes free of his tutor and develops an arresting thesis about the late Eliot, a set of biographical observations and speculations that in another format Ms. Ozick could have written up as a psychohistorical essay. Here, though, she turns them into a love story with an O. Henry ending. (Ms. Ozick, one recalls, has won the O. Henry Prize four times.)

The best of Ms. Ozick's stories are a kind of commentary. "Puttermesser and the Muscovite Cousin," the fourth section of the book, strikes me as a commentary on the way that for decades the phrase "Russian Jews"—meaning American Jews of Russian descent—has summoned up images of art, intellect and the ardor of the radical. Puttermesser's cousin Lidia—all vulgarity, materialism and hustle—represents a goodbye to all that, Russian Jew confounding "Russian Jew."

The comrades this new arrival encounters on the Upper West Side are best characterized by the "social visionary" Schuyler Hartstein, founder of *Shekhina*, a Jewish magazine intended to serve as the socialist alternative to a rival capitalist journal called *Motherwit*. As Ms. Ozick describes it, a Shekhina fundraiser attracts, among others, "Bert Waldroon, the playwright and activist, and Kirkwood Plethora, grown surprisingly elderly by now, her trademark single earring masking a hearing aid. . . . And there were, of course, the politically consecrated—atheists mainly, apparently unoffended by what they called Sky Hartstein's 'religious orientation.' "

Lidia, invited by Hartstein to share her wisdom as "one born into the Experiment, no matter how late," comes bluntly to her point: "Foolish American peoples! In Soviet stupid peoples more smart!" When Lidia takes her black-market earnings and flies off to join her old boyfriend in Sakhalin, Puttermesser misses her, and we know why.

Puttermesser dies in her late 60's, raped and murdered by a burglar in a ski mask. The book's final section, "Puttermesser in Paradise," stages this grisly crime as a kind of ballet viewed through a scrim. Then, in heaven, Puttermesser's dreams begin to come true. She marries Emil Hauchvogel, the man who got away some 50 years earlier. And she has the son she never had on earth: "They circumcised him and planted the tiny gold foreskin under an olive tree, and every olive on every branch began to take on the color of gold." But husband and son soon evaporate, for where past and future are one, to have is also to have not: "The secret meaning of Paradise is that it too is hell." The book ends with a wistful poem, whose last stanza is:

> *Better never to have loved than loved at all.*
> *Better never to have risen than had a fall.*
> Oh bitter, bitter, bitter
> butter
> knife.

Last words of a lady who couldn't quite cut it. Puttermesser, the narrator says, means "butter knife." Ms. Ozick makes comedy of her own necessity as a literary centaur, half artist and half scholar. She makes a deeper comedy of Puttermesser's ancient ache as a childless celibate alone with her books and the memory of her transcendent hopes for love, for literature and for the lovers of literature. "O may I join the choir invisible," as George Eliot once cried. You may, Ruth, you will, but you know what Lidia would say about *that*.

Surviving the Cold War

Underworld by Don DeLillo
October 5, 1997

BY MARTIN AMIS

EXPECT A LOT FROM THE NEXT SENTENCE. Among its other virtues, the title of Don DeLillo's heavily brilliant new book gives a convenient answer to the Big Question about the American novel: Where has the mainstream been hiding? The grand old men, the universal voices of the late-middle century (predominantly the great Jews, and John Updike), are getting older and grander, but the land they preside over looked to be shrinking. Furthermore, it seemed that their numbers were not being replenished by writers of comparable centrality. Was this an epochal change, a major extinction? No. It was a strategic lull.

Something atomized the mainstream. The next wave of genius was there, but not visibly, not publicly. Inasmuch as the mainstream was an institution, these writers could not work within it. They went underground, they sought an underworld of codes and shadows: incognito, incommunicado, and quietly dissident, their literary reputations largely cult-borne. But now the condition that caused the great discontinuity in American letters has come to an end. The novelists are climbing out of the bunker. Don DeLillo's exact contemporaries, Robert Stone and Thomas Pynchon, seem poised for a fuller expansion. DeLillo himself, however, suddenly fills the sky. *Underworld* may or may not be a great novel, but there is no doubt that it renders DeLillo a great novelist.

The new novel is Don DeLillo's wake for the cold war. According to its argument, the discontinuity in American cultural life had a primary cause: nuclear weapons. The hiatus was inaugurated on the day that Truman loosed the force from which the sun draws its power against those who brought war to the Far East, and was institutionalized four years later when the Soviet Union started to attain rough parity. Cosmic might was now being wielded by mortal hands, and by the State, which made the appropriate adjustments. The State was your enemy's enemy; but nuclear logic decreed that the State was no longer your friend. In one of the novel's childhood scenes, the schoolteacher (a nun) issues her class dog tags:

> The tags were designed to help rescue workers identify children who were lost, missing, injured, maimed, mutilated, unconscious or dead in the hours following the onset of atomic war. . . . Now that they had the tags, their names inscribed on wispy tin, the drill was not a remote exercise but was all about them, and so was atomic war.

Nuclear war never happened, but this was the nuclear experience, unknowable to anyone born too soon or too late. In order to know what it was, you have to have been a schoolchild, crouched under your desk, hoping it would protect you from the end of the world. How people rearranged their lives around this moral void, with its exorbitant terror and absurdity is DeLillo's subject. Perhaps it always has been. The new novel, at any rate, is an 827-page damage-check.

Underworld surges with magisterial confidence through time (the last half century) and through space (Harlem, Phoenix, Vietnam, Kazakstan, Texas, the Bronx), mingling fictional characters with various heroes of cultural history (Sinatra, Hoover, Lenny Bruce). But its true loci are "the white spaces on the map," the test sites, and its main actors are psychological "downwinders," victims of the fallout from all the blasts—blasts actual and imagined. DeLillo, the poet of paranoia and the "world hum," pursues his theme unstridently; he is tenacious without being tendentious. Yet even his portraits of bland, hopeful, pre-postmodern American life—his Americana—glow with the sick light of betrayal, of innocence traduced or abused. The "great thrown shadow" has now receded and terror has returned to the merely local. MAD (Mutual Assured Destruction) was exploded; and the bombs did not detonate. Still, the press-ganged children who wore the dog tags must live with a discontinuity in their minds and hearts. DeLillo's prologue is called "The Triumph of Death," after the Breughel painting. In the end, death didn't triumph. It just ruled, for 50 years. I take DeLillo to be saying that all our better feelings took a beating during those decades. An ambient mortal fear constrained us. Love, even parental love, got harder to do.

The protagonist, Nick Shay, works for a company called Waste Containment. And *Underworld* is among other things a witty and dramatic meditation on excreta, voidance, leavings, garbage, junk, slag, dreck. A drunken spectator at the 1951 Dodgers-Giants playoff leans forward and disgorges a length of "flannel matter. He seems to be vomiting someone's taupe pajamas." A newlywed on his honeymoon finds that "his BMs" (daily "hygiene" is another euphemism) "are turning against him": "that night Marvin had to make an emergency visit to the hotel toilet, where he unleashed a fire wall of chemical waste." This is human waste, forgivable waste. But then there is nuclear waste: the stuff that never goes away and makes heaven stop its nose.

In DeLillo's beautifully tender anxiety-dream, *White Noise* (1985), the famous "airborne toxic event" was the result of a military-industrial accident. But it was also DeLillo's metaphor for television—for the virulent ubiquity of the media spore. Explaining a recent inanity of his daughter, Shay's coworker "made a TV screen with his hands, thumbs horizontal, index fingers upright, and he looked out at me from inside the frame, eyes crossed, tongue lolling in his head." DeLillo's way with dialogue is not only inimitably comic; it also mounts an attack on the distortions, the jumbled sound bites, of our square-eyed age. "I'll quote you that you said that." "She's got a great body for how many kids?" "They put son of a bitches like you behind bars is where you belong." "I'm a person if you ask me questions. You want to know who I am? I'm a person if you're too inquisitive I tune you out completely." "Which is the whole juxt of my argument."

It should be said in conclusion that those who stay with this book will experience an entirely unexpected reward. *Underworld* is sprawling rather than monumental, and it is diffuse in a way that a long novel needn't necessarily be. There is an interval, approaching halfway, when the performance goes awful quiet. But then it rebuilds, regathering all its mass. As I noticed the surprising number of approximations DeLillo settles for ("a kind of sadness," "sort of semidebonaire," "a certain funky something"), my feelings about the author began to change. Reading his corpus, sensing the rigor of his language, the near-inhuman discipline of his perceptions and the peeled eyeball of his gaze, you often feared for the man's equilibrium. Yet who was the man? DeLillo is normally quite absent from his fiction—a spectral intelligence. *Underworld* is his most demanding novel but it is also his most transparent. It has an undertow of personal pain, having to do with fateful irreversibilities in a young life—a register that DeLillo has never touched before. This isn't Meet the Author. It is the earned but privileged intimacy that comes when you see a writer whole. The critic F. R. Leavis called it the "sense of pregnant arrest."

"But the bombs were not released. . . . The missiles remained in the rotary launchers. The men came back and the cities were not destroyed." Just so. Now that the cold war is gone, the planet becomes less "interesting" in the Chinese sense (ancient animadversion: May you live in interesting times). But it isn't every day, or even every decade, that one sees the ascension of a great writer. This means that from now on we will all be living in *more* interesting times. Which is my whole juxt.

Editors' Choice
1972–1997

Editors' Choice

The Children of Pride: A True Story of Georgia and the Civil War

BY ROBERT MANSON MYERS

FROM 6,000 LETTERS written among several branches of a Southern family between 1854 and 1865, Robert Manson Myers has woven 1,200 into a massive and touching portrait of a bygone society. Beginning on a summer afternoon with a mother's description of her peaceful pursuits, followed by a reply from her son, a student in Boston, describing abolitionist riots, we are caught up in the slowly unfolding tragedy of the Civil War. Never before have we been made quite so aware of the public and private life of town and plantation, of the religious and political beliefs, the joys, sorrows, loves, recreations, education, illnesses and deaths of people in that time and place. One cannot forget a mother's description of her encounter with a Yankee soldier bent on stealing her valuables, or the thoughts of a woman at war's end, when she must leave the home she came to as a bride and face an unknown future. Mr. Myers has added hundreds of pages of biographical and historical information that make the volume a matchless record of the rise and fall of nineteenth-century Southern civilization. If ever an editor can be said to have written a book, *The Children of Pride* is that book.

Henry James: The Master, 1901–1916

BY LEON EDEL

WITH THE PUBLICATION OF the fifth and final volume of his biography, Leon Edel brings to a close a literary labor of 20 years. The only works that invite comparison with Edel's achievement—the only ones which trace the lives of major modern writers with a complete scholarly fidelity and yet emerge as works of literary distinction in their own right—are George D. Painter's *Proust* and Richard Ellmann's *James Joyce*. James came of age in the era of Emerson and Ruskin; he died in 1916, at the age of 72, having quarreled with H. G. Wells and received the homage of the young Ezra Pound. As a boy, James lived in the Paris of the Second Empire; in his old age he dined with Herbert Asquith and Winston Churchill. He knew Flaubert and Turgenev as well as Boston Brahmins, Conrad, Crane and Kipling, as well as members of the Bloomsbury group and the young Hugh Walpole and Somerset Maugham. He belonged, moreover, to a brilliant literary family, and he supported himself through decades of unremitting labor in the literary marketplace, which was not overly sensitive to his value or his distinction. He moved in the large world, and he created a large world of his own: he was a great novelist and great critic. Mr. Edel's achievement is to have written, with literary, historical and psychological perspicacity, a life worthy of one of the few American writers who can be called a master.

Fire in the Lake: The Vietnamese and the Americans in Vietnam

BY FRANCES FITZGERALD

THIS IS THE RICHEST kind of contemporary history; it places political and military events in cultural perspective—something rarely done in the hundreds of books written about Vietnam during the last dozen years. In analyzing the stabilities and instabilities of Vietnamese society, FitzGerald shows how the country is undergoing, not a civil war, but a revolution, a term she carefully defines in its Vietnamese context. She tells how the Vietnamese have adapted communism both to their Confucian heritage and the imperatives of modernization and how they have been able to organize so effectively against all military odds. She describes the serial frustrations of the French and Americans in Vietnam and explains the irrelevance of "pacification." She is superb at clarifying the differences between Vietnamese and American cultures. Her choice of significant anecdotal detail to enrich her generalizations is masterly. She combines wise reading with vivid and compassionate reportage. This is the best book on Vietnam so far; it is sadly overdue by at least five years.

The Coming of Age
BY SIMONE DE BEAUVOIR

FROM HER PRODIGIOUS reading in world literature and her personal observation Simone de Beauvoir has single-handedly established a history of and a rhetoric for the process of aging. In confronting a subject of private anguish and universal public silence she draws skillfully and easily on both scientific and artistic evidence, on ethnology, psychology and physiology, on medicine and sociology, on painting, poetry and fiction. The book is a *catalogue raisonnée* of the causes and effects of aging; but as well as being encyclopedic it has a passionate theme: the steady degradation of old age at a time when there are more and more elderly people. De Beauvoir reports movingly on the predicament of the aged in the modern world, whether as the result of poverty, illness or enforced idleness, within the family, at work, in institutions and in society at large. Her analyses and reportage are complemented to great effect by her vignettes of famous historical figures in old age—the sexual tenacity of Victor Hugo in his seventies, the pathetic jealousy of Tolstoy's wife until his death at 81, Goya's late rejuvenation, Gide's complaints of the extinction of desire, Michelangelo's obsession with death. Although *The Coming of Age* is a synthesis of available knowledge, de Beauvoir has shaped the material into a pioneering work.

A Theory of Justice
BY JOHN RAWLES

MORE THAN 20 YEARS in the making, this book is a magisterial exercise in "moral geometry," as demanding as it is rewarding. Although it was published in 1971, it was not widely reviewed until 1972, because critics needed time to get a grip on its complexities. In fact, it may not be properly understood until it has been studied for years—as it certainly will be, in political science and philosophy courses. Rawls's achievement has been to restate, revise and breathe new life into the idea of the social contract as a basis for political structures. The social contract gave way in the nineteenth century to the utilitarian concept of "the greatest good for the greatest number." But Rawls demonstrates that utilitarianism is incompatible with our intuitions about justice and fairness (as embodied, for instance, in the U.S. Constitution). At home with contemporary philosophical techniques and concerns, such as decision and game theory, Rawls turns the problem of justice into a problem in rational choice. His notion of "justice as fairness" consists not only of the right of each person to the most extensive liberty compatible with a like liberty for others; it also insists that social and economic inequalities are tolerable only when they are to *everyone's* advantage, not just to the advantage of a majority. The talented or socially advantaged person hasn't *earned* anything: "Those who have been favored by nature, whoever they are," he writes, "may gain from their good fortune only on terms that improve the situation of those who have lost out." Rawls's arguments for this proposition are persuasive; its political implications may change our lives.

Editors' Choice

Gravity's Rainbow

BY THOMAS PYNCHON

THOMAS PYNCHON'S novel is one of the longest, darkest, most difficult and most ambitious books in years. Its technical and verbal resources bring to mind Melville, Faulkner and Nabokov and establish Pynchon's imaginative continuity with the great modernist movement of the early years of this century. *Gravity's Rainbow* is bone-crushingly dense, compulsively elaborate, silly, obscene, funny, tragic, poetic, dull, inspired, horrific, cold and blasted.

Set in England, France and Occupied Germany in 1944 and 1945, it is thick with references and flashbacks to World War I and Weimar, to England and America in the twenties and thirties, even to German South West Africa at the turn of the century. The central plot concerns the search for a V-2 rocket, a symbol of the "sexual love of death" which Pynchon suggests is the driving paranoid force behind modern history. The novel bristles with allusions to literature, music, art, to military and industrial history, to pop culture, physics and Pavlovian psychology.

Pynchon is capable of the most intricate literary structures — plots and counterplots and symbols and facts that twist in time and space. In his universe the characters become mechanical men whose trajectory toward death is touched by a manic and comic impulse or a vague free-floating anguish. For all its power and intelligence Pynchon's novel is a magnificent ruined necropolis, but its teetering structure towers above the surrounding literary shacks and hovels.

The Summer Before the Dark

BY DORIS LESSING

O F ALL THE POSTWAR English novelists, Doris Lessing is the foremost creative descendant of that "great tradition" which includes George Eliot and D. H. Lawrence. Her new novel *The Summer Before the Dark* is her most artful exploration of her major themes: the relation of self and society, intelligence and feeling, madness and health, and, above all, the role of modern woman.

The Summer Before the Dark is about a profound change in the life of a 45-year-old London housewife whose time of caring for her husband and children is over. Her family gone for the summer, she takes a job with an international service organization and discovers that mothering is marketable. She travels abroad and enters into an affair with a young man, only to find that he is deathly ill. She returns to London, ill herself, slowly pulls herself together, and at last goes home restored to health, wiser, more critical, and more at ease with the idea of growing old and eventually dying.

There is little about the outward trappings of the book that is new, nor is Doris Lessing interested in "writing well." Yet, her moral intelligence and strong, unfettered feeling have produced a work on the border between traditional narrative and stream-of-consciousness. It is rare in contemporary fiction to find a work at once unironically sincere and still intelligent: in its subject and scale, *The Summer Before the Dark* confirms the sense that Doris Lessing is a plain-speaking, somewhat awkward, but immensely attractive master of modern fiction.

Macaulay: The Making of a Historian

BY JOHN CLIVE

A GIFTED BIOGRAPHER has rescued a great man from Victorian pieties and patronizing historiography and restored him to heroic and human stature. *Macaulay: The Making of a Historian* takes him from his birth in 1800, into a severe and repressive Evangelical milieu, to 1839, when he had just formulated the modern educational and legal systems of India. The portrait embraces half a dozen themes. There is the physically unattractive and personally abrasive Macaulay attaining extraordinary social success by dint of his rhetoric; Macaulay the competitor, forging a spectacular public career by his brilliant polemical writing and debates on the issues of the day; polymath Macaulay, voraciously appropriating the classics, history, literature and poetry of his tradition, and assuming an easy familiarity with its creators; Macaulay the prism of progressive nineteenth-century political thought whose "principal endeavor," Clive shows, "was to accommodate the new forces released by the French and Industrial revolutions"; and Macaulay the private man, his conscience dominated by a gloomy father, and his emotional life ruled by his dependence on the domestic attentions of his two sisters.

Thomas Babington Macaulay is an overwhelming figure. An author less skillful than Clive would have tried to charm the reader by relying on Macaulay's rhetorical excesses or impress him by condescending to Macaulay's historical judgments. Instead, Clive has written a surprisingly intimate life, psychologically sophisticated without being presumptuous. It is also a pleasure to read.

1974

Editors' Choice

Watership Down

BY RICHARD ADAMS

HERE IS THE *Odyssey* and *Iliad* of rabbits, for people of all ages—a splendidly written adventure story, a rather broad allegory, a meditation on bravery, a text on ecology, a lecture against totalitarianism and a passionate act of imaginative projection. Fiver, Hazel and Bigwig, in the English fantasy tradition of Tolkien's *Lord of the Rings* and C. S. Lewis's *Chronicles of Narnia*, are original and quite moving creations.

Roll, Jordan, Roll: The World the Slaves Made

BY EUGENE GENOVESE

IN THE WORDS of our reviewer, David Brion Davis, this history is "the most profound, learned and detailed analysis of Negro slavery to appear since World War II." "Genovese, an American Marxist historian, has produced an enormously rich account of both the socio-economic system of slavery and the slaves' and masters' inner experience of it. His book significantly reevaluates such stereotypes as the black Mammy and the black slave-driver and provides a brilliant analysis of the role of Christianity in slave culture.

Darwin on Man

BY HOWARD E. GRUBER AND PAUL H. BARRETT

HOWARD E. GRUBER AND PAUL H. BARRETT print for the first time Darwin's notebooks from 1837 to 1839, crucial years when he sifted and winnowed the ideas that decades later led to *The Origin of Species* and one of the dominant theories of modern times. Darwin's thoughts and observations on man and nature, accompanied by Gruber's essay on scientific creativity in general and Darwin's intellectual processes in particular, make a startling and important record of the young scientist.

Something Happened

BY JOSEPH HELLER

THE AUTHOR OF *CATCH-22* has turned his back on expansive comedy and tried his hand at claustrophobic tragedy, composing an anguished novel of suburban manners and morals. What he adds to the genre is a relentless and deliberately exhausting psychoanalytic monologue. A serious, painful and important book that offers a portrait of a representative postwar American man whose existence is seen as a kind of narcissistic death-in-life.

All God's Dangers: The Life of Nate Shaw

BY THEODORE ROSENGARTEN

THE WORDS OF AN ALABAMA sharecropper provide an encompassing portrait of the rural South during much of the twentieth century. This old, powerful black man's recollections of his political experiences with the Sharecropper's Union, his time in jail, his struggles with exploitative whites, have great clarity and force; Shaw's rich language and high storytelling style make this an eloquent book.

The Gulag Archipelago

BY ALEKSANDR I. SOLZHENITSYN

WHILE NOT IN A class as literature with his *The First Circle* and *One Day in the Life of Ivan Denisovich*, this is a terrifying human document—the history of the imprisonment, brutalization and often the murder of tens of millions of innocent Soviet citizens by their own Government during Stalin's rule, from 1929 to 1953.

Dog Soldiers

BY ROBERT STONE

ROBERT STONE'S novel is a dark descendant of Conrad's and Hemingway's adventure stories, a tale of Vietnam and California, a narrative meditation on the 1960s. The author of A *Hall of Mirrors* here makes intelligent, imaginative and horrifying connections between the Vietnam war, the counterculture and heroin. It is melodramatic, cruel, witty and grim. Stone is a highly accomplished writer.

1975

Editors' Choice

The Dead Father

BY DONALD BARTHELME

THIS BOOK IS the author's most sustained, ambitious and successful work. The several volumes of short stories, a collection of parodies, and the one previous novel (*Snow White*, a short, sardonic deformation of the fairy tale) established Donald Barthelme as the supplest of ironists; but the very playfulness that was his virtue and his subject matter (for the most part the same that the media dealt with straight) indicated a cautiousness and want of seriousness. *The Dead Father*, an Oedipal fugue, is deadly serious. The title character is an overwhelming figure, now dead, now moribund, now ominously alive. It (the father is more object than person) instructs, threatens, punishes, rewards, means well yet is anguishingly inept, pities himself, brags, advances, retreats—while his children try to ignore him, attend him, escape him, are captured. Most other "experimental" ventures seem mild compared to *The Dead Father*. In the Freudian sense, it is a brave book.

Humboldt's Gift

BY SAUL BELLOW

THE NOVELIST at 60 adopts the guise of Charles Citrine, narrator and protagonist of *Humboldt's Gift*, a frenzied, raffish, sorrowing novel. It is a story of literary success and failure: set against Citrine's swelling international reputation is the slow death and madness of Von Humboldt Fleisher (in real life

Delmore Schwartz), who lived out the bourgeois script for the romantic poet (the agony and the ecstasy, and now you pay for it, you dog!). This tale of two cities—Bellow-Citrine's Chicago and Humboldt-Schwartz's New York—is full of episodes, memories, arias, essays, jokes, lyric flights, and meditations on death and the way of the artist in America. These tumble from Citrine's baroque mind in a dense and crowded book. The scenario is confused and unsatisfying, but Bellow's smart, urban voice has never been wittier.

Against Our Will: Men, Women and Rape
BY SUSAN BROWNMILLER

THIS FEMINIST TRACT that seems destined to take its place beside de Beauvoir's *The Second Sex*, Friedan's *The Feminist Mystique* and Kate Millet's *Sexual Politics*. Drawing evidence from many sources—literature, legal and military history, contemporary media—she examines rape in war, riots, pogroms; in plantations, prisons and dark alleys; the rape of whites and blacks, of children and slaves. She examines social attitudes toward rape, the psychology (male and female) of rape, the rapist as hero, the victim as masochist, and comes to the conclusion that the threat and act of rape are part of a fundamental and fearful power relationship between men and women. Her conclusions will strike some as extreme, but her manner is steady and reasoning throughout.

The Problem of Slavery in the Age of Revolution: 1770–1823
BY DAVID BRION DAVIS

THIS MOST RECENT VOLUME in the author's study of slavery in the West, begun nine years ago, opens against a background of intense social reform in Europe and America. In England and the Continent abolitionists debated; in America the Founding Fathers, faced with the problems of casting a constitution and creating a United States, effected disastrous compromises between the interests of New England idealists and Southern planters. The origins and uses of slavery is a subject that has generated many studies in recent years; this book, by submitting the material to one overall view and adding its own insights, makes a special claim on our attention.

The War Against the Jews
BY LUCY S. DAWIDOWICZ

Lucy S. Dawidowicz asked herself three questions: "How was it possible for a modern state to carry out the systematic murder of a whole people for no other reason than that they were Jews? How was it possible for a whole people to allow itself to be destroyed? How was it possible for the world to stand by without halting this destruction?" By examining the long tradition of anti-Semitism in Germany and Eastern Europe, by showing the translation of idea into action under the Nazi regime, by a dry accumulation of facts and close attention to the mechanics of slaughter, by a careful investigation of the varied Jewish response, Dawidowicz has immeasurably increased our understanding. One caution: the style is graceless.

Ragtime
BY E. L. DOCTOROW

With a crazy mix of historical personages (Ford, Houdini, J. P. Morgan, Emma Goldman) and pop-cartoon characters (a Latvian socialist who becomes a movie mogul, a black pianist who leads a guerrilla action against the establishment), *Ragtime* re-creates pre–World War I America. Doctorow has not so much rewritten history as invited us to dream about it: to see it again through the psyche of the seventies. His antique Sunday-supplement images, weirdly deformed, move us along from absurdity to absurdity with openmouthed fascination. Its combination of camp nostalgia, unabashed sentimentality and literary innovation made *Ragtime* one of the big best sellers of 1975.

A Sorrow Beyond Dreams
BY PETER HANDKE

A novelist and playwright of exquisite subtlety brings his great gifts of edge and clear-sightedness to this memorial for a lost soul. *A Sorrow Beyond Dreams* is a meditation on the life and death of his mother, a housewife who committed suicide at 51. Born into the meanest circumstances, raised in the Germany of National Socialism, without education and finally without hope, this everywoman speaks (although she did not have the words to speak) for all the under-beings of the world who pass through life without living a life.

Edith Wharton

BY R. W. B. LEWIS

THIS CAPACIOUS, scholarly biography is the story of an enormously productive, troubled yet satisfying life. From 1913 until the Depression she was generally considered the most accomplished American novelist (a view that even this eloquent revivification of her work is unlikely to reestablish). Using hitherto unknown Wharton material, Lewis smoothly narrates the facts of her life—the struggle to become an independent woman; the unhappy marriage; a long love affair; friendships with Henry James, Bernard Berenson, the young Kenneth Clark, Percy Lubbock; the fortune she made from her books and stories; her generosity; the travels in Europe; the poetry; and, most surprisingly, the secret sexual garden (Edie was a lady but apparently a woman too). The best literary biography of the year.

Far Tortuga

BY PETER MATTHIESSEN

PETER MATTHIESSEN'S tale is a visionary novel of the sea, told in Caribbean dialect and poetic log-book descriptions of the water, wind, clouds, birds and sea life. It follows the voyage of a decrepit schooner hunting green turtles off the Central American coast, and of its nine-man crew, caught in an outmoded way of life. The book's ambition is to plot the boundaries of nature and culture, to locate its mongrel crew at the juncture of history and ecology. It risks a lot and demands considerable patience: the dialogue is eccentric, and the descriptions can seem precious, self-indulgent, mere exotic picture-painting; the narrative is melodramatic and has pretentions to myth; but the originality of its form, the sustained beauty and rhythms of its language, and its precise and serious love of its subject reward our attention and engage our affections.

I Would Have Saved Them If I Could

BY LEONARD MICHAELS

THERE IS A FEROCIOUS vitality and intelligence at work here; Michaels seems to have tapped some electric current of moral rage, lust, wit, sorrow, narrative violence. The effect is a kind of super-realism, as if Flannery O'Connor had been urbanized and speeded up. Michaels writes of childhood on the Lower East Side, of graduate school in the fifties, of marriage, sex, politics, apocalyptic paranoia in the sixties. Funny, desperate, manic, overwrought, he scatters allusions like buckshot (Byron, Trotsky, Borges, Kafka). But these are always stories, filled with characters, not silhouettes—they suffer and bruise.

Guerrillas
BY V. S. NAIPAUL

SET IN AN INDEPENDENT Caribbean island, this is a novel about the politics of the Third World. A white South African liberal with a dead heart; his English mistress, the personification of radical chic; a Chinese-black revolutionary, bisexual, with a taste and a hatred for white women; assorted political opportunists; native aristocracy and low-life—copulate, plot and betray, as a sudden spontaneous uprising threatens life and position. In the background U.S. helicopters hover, ready to restore order and maintain interests. This nasty, spare, intelligent novel seems as much written against the white, middle-class reader as for him—a story of Graham Greene's or Joseph Conrad's told from the other side. Probably the best novel of 1975.

The Gulag Archipelago: 1918–1956, Volume II
BY ALEKSANDR I. SOLZHENITSYN

READING THE GULAG books is harrowing, but exalting too: one senses the primitive impulse of man to record; this happened, and it must not be forgotten. That he could, inside the country, collect the material, interview over 200 camp survivors, and save the manuscript for publication is a heroic achievement. The outside world has known for decades of the suffering of Russians at the hands of their leaders; now it knows more. But it will probably be these volumes, either through samizdat circulation or eventual open publication, that will eventually inform the Russians themselves of their suffering.

The Great Railway Bazaar
BY PAUL THEROUX

THEROUX WENT BY TRAIN from London across Europe, through the Orient, back via Japan and the Trans-Siberian Railroad. He tells you what he saw and how he felt, delights and disappointments, landscapes, rooms, streets, meals. He is a delicious novelist (begin with *Saint Jack* if you haven't read him); here every new meeting is the start of a new novel. His style is effortless, ironic, various, enjoying itself as it pleases you. It is travel writing in the grand tradition—curious places, politics, strange people, every day a new adventure.

Editors' Choice

Speedboat

BY RENATA ADLER

SPEEDBOAT is a quintessentially New York book with its radical-chic parties, conversations with analysts, late-hour excursions to Elaine's, its encounters with rats, cab drivers, early morning stealers of the neighbor's Sunday *Times*. It is elegantly written, often funny, vivid in its presentation of the absurdities, the small and great horrors, the booby traps with which our daily existence is strewn. It is a brilliant collage, an assemblage of tiny anecdotes, vignettes, overheard conversations, aphorisms and reflections. These bits and pieces—many of them the verbal equivalent of found objects—are shaped for us by the sensibility of the narrator, a highly intelligent, vulnerable woman in her mid-thirties. In the presentation and analysis of her specimens, Renata Adler is an exquisite craftsman. Her style is luminously exact, subtle in its rhythms, capable of both concrete immediacy and arresting generalizations.

To Jerusalem and Back: A Personal Account

BY SAUL BELLOW

VISITING ISRAEL for several months in 1975, Bellow kept an account of his experiences and impressions. It grew into an impassioned and thoughtful book. Bellow delights in the liveliness, the gallantry of Israeli life: people on the edge of history, an inch from disaster, yet brimming with words and arguments. We get talk from intransigent right-wingers intent upon a "greater Israel," from anxious "doves" who want to stretch out a hand of peace in behalf of survival, from writers who feel the country's obsession with politics is stifling them, and from a masseur at the King David Hotel, a body-culture nut, who seems to have stepped right out of a Bellow story. Bellow delights not with sappy tourist delusions but with a tough critical spirit: his Israel is pocked with scars and creases, and all the more attractive.

The Uses of Enchantment: The Meaning and Importance of Fairy Tales
BY BRUNO BETTELHEIM

EACH FAIRY TALE is a magic mirror which reflects some aspects of our inner world, and of the steps required by our evolution from immaturity to maturity"—by the light of this axiom Bruno Bettelheim, the psychoanalyst, has written a charming book about enchantment, a profound book about fairy tales. *The Uses of Enchantment* cannot enforce the use of fairy stories without a matrix of family security and social consensus; but at the least it shows us how cunningly, how lovingly, the anonymous generations of "a happier age" prepared their children for the challenges of life and guided them toward sexual, ethical health, once upon a time.

Women of the Shadows
BY ANN CORNELISEN

ANN CORNELISEN worked for years for a British group called Save the Children Fund, which was involved in establishing day nurseries for Italian children, and she settled down in the village of Torregreca. In this book she expresses outrage, awe and disillusionment with what she calls the "fatal symmetry" of southern Italian life. The men are the guardians of their illusions, with their elaborate jealousies, their obsession with betrayal, the rituals of restriction with which they isolate and try their wives. The wives know better, that no one else could possibly covet anything of theirs. Ann Cornelisen knows these women so well, and her regard for them is so loving, complicated and despairing that her book is worth a shelf of dissertations on Italian village life.

The Damnable Question: A Study of
Anglo-Irish Relations
BY GEORGE DANGERFIELD

GEORGE DANGERFIELD'S masterly new book brings together a massive number of "facts" (familiar and unfamiliar) and "truths" (palatable and unpalatable) about Anglo-Irish relations between 1800 and 1922 (with the rising of April 1916 the keystone) and weaves them together in a narrative that is a model of history as a literary art. It is an agreeable, a Dangerfieldian irony perhaps, and perhaps a portent, that the book itself should be the work of an Englishman deeply sympathetic to Ireland, blessed with a humane and civilized understanding of the two nations.

October Light
BY JOHN GARDNER

JOHN GARDNER is the dazzling virtuoso among recent novelists: a plausible impersonator, ventriloquist, puppet-master and one-man band. *October Light* is a lavishly talented, often impressive work, clearly his best book since *Grendel*. It concerns the struggle of two archetypal granitic Vermont Yankees (an aged brother and sister) and in dramatizing their conflict reaches into the depths of what might be called, loosely, the Protestant soul.

Roots: The Saga of an American Family
BY ALEX HALEY

ALEX HALEY'S book begins in Gambia West Africa in 1750 with the birth of one of his ancestors, Kunta Kinte, born of Omoro and Binta Kinte, of the Mandinka tribe, and of the Muslim faith. We are in his skin and in his darkness and presently we are shackled with him in his terror, rage and pain, his stink, and the stink of others on the slave ship that brings him here. *Roots* is a study of continuities, of consequences, of how a people perpetuate themselves, how each generation helps to doom, or helps to liberate, the coming one.

World of Our Fathers
BY IRVING HOWE

IRVING HOWE has written a great book about two generations of "bedraggled and inspired" Jewish immigrants on the Lower East Side, and beyond, in virtually all of their social and cultural bearings and in most of their political and economic ones. A work of history and art, it is also a complex story of fulfillment and incompleteness.

Heat and Dust
BY RUTH PRAWER JHABVALA

IN *HEAT AND DUST,* Ruth Jhabvala intertwines two very different narratives—one going on in the present, the other exhumed from the past—across the obliterating gulf of half a century. They both concern English women devoured by India. Like Forster, with witty precision she renders the barriers of incomprehension and futility that persist between the English and Indians.

The Woman Warrior: Memoirs of a Girlhood Among Ghosts
BY MAXINE HONG KINGSTON

MAXINE TING TING HONG KINGSTON is a young Chinese-American writer, and *The Woman Warrior* is her first book. It is a brilliant memoir. It shocks us back to the mystery of a stubbornly, utterly foreign sensibility; no other book since André Malraux's melancholy artifice, *La Tentation de l'Occident,* even starts to do this. *The Woman Warrior* is about being Chinese, in the way *Portrait of the Artist* is about being Irish. It is an investigation of soul, not landscape. Its sources are dream and memory, myth and desire. Its crises are the crises of a heart in exile from roots that bind and terrorize it.

Born on the Fourth of July
BY RON KOVIC

ON THURSDAY NIGHT, July 15th of last year, in front of millions of Americans, Ron Kovic, a young Vietnam veteran in a wheelchair, seconded the nomination of a Vietnam draft resister as the Democratic Party's candidate for Vice President of the United States. Ron Kovic turned 30 on America's 200th birthday. For the past nine years he has been paralyzed from the waist down as a result of wounds suffered in Vietnam. Kovic's book records his growth from neighborhood kid-next-door, high school wrestling champion, worshiper of the Mickey Mantle–era Yankees and Audie Murphy–era war hero, and the first in his class to rush forward to meet the Marine recruiters visiting his school, into what he has become today: a man who has written the most personal and honest testament published thus far by anyone who fought in the Vietnam War.

André Malraux

BY JEAN LACOUTURE

IN THIS BIOGRAPHY Lacouture is not out to dynamite André Malraux but to circumscribe him, using much the method Malraux himself employs in his monologues on art. Lacouture prowls round and round, hoping a change of lighting, a new perspective, will answer the plainest of questions: Real identity (?) Real provenance (?) Real dates (?) And he is as fair and as objective as possible as he sorts out the red herrings, the myths, the outright falsehoods from so-called facts, documentary evidence, and other people's memories, which may be no more reliable than Malraux's own.

The Autumn of the Patriarch

BY GABRIEL GARCÍA MÁRQUEZ

AS IS TO BE EXPECTED from García Márquez, this novel about a Latin American dictator is mystical and surrealistic in its excesses, its distortions and its exotic language. It is a supreme polemic against any society that encourages or even permits the growth of such a dictator. García Márquez objectifies the monster—with the whistle of his hernia, or the seed of his unknown father, or his discovery that a lie is more comfortable than doubt. And these facts, under the hand of this master novelist, accumulate to embody a most complex and terrible vision of Latin America's ubiquitous, unkillable demon.

Details of a Sunset: And Other Stories

BY VLADIMIR NABOKOV

VLADIMIR NABOKOV'S new collection of his old stories, *Details of a Sunset* (1924–1935), is much concerned with different kinds of loss—exile, failure of romantic love and family love, the death of a wife, the death of a son, the death of one's self—and yet the effects of these stories are mainly exhilarating, even affirmative. Even if we don't consider the subjects or the events in Nabokov's stories, it must seem that his imagination—simply in what it sees and in the way it speaks—has demonic powers. Therein lies much of its pleasure for readers, a literary experience reminiscent of *Alice in Wonderland*, another playfully verbal world where the perversities of plot, wittily qualified by lots of pain and apprehensions of death, full of exotic and subterranean perceptions, leave one thrilled and pleased.

Hearing Secret Harmonies

BY ANTHONY POWELL

THE PUBLICATION of *Hearing Secret Harmonies*, the last of the 12 volumes of Anthony Powell's *A Dance to the Music of Time*, is unmistakably a literary event. He has created and sustained a raffish and eccentric world that is recognizably his own. Set between 1921 and the '60s, the series is populated with a sometimes rich and sometimes seedy assortment of upper-class and Bohemian types, old Etonians, society hostesses, dissolute stockbrokers, shady but charming gentleman-jockeys who run nightclubs and marry four or five times, the eccentric offspring or widows of peers, adulterous countesses who were once mannequins. There is now such a thing as "a typical Anthony Powell character" or "a situation right out of Anthony Powell"—no small achievement for a novelist. Certainly he ranks with the radically different Doris Lessing as the best of the novelists now writing British fiction.

A Voice from the Chorus

BY ABRAM TERTZ (ANDREI SINYAVSKY)

A VOICE FROM THE CHORUS, based on letters sent by Sinyavsky from Soviet prison to his wife, is a long and loose series of philosophical and literary meditations. The author moves easily from the myth of Oceania to Celtic legends, from the vertical structure of icons to the architecture of old Orthodox churches, from Rembrandt's *Return of the Prodigal Son* to ancient Japanese painting and the poetry of Anna Akhmatova and Osip Mandelstam. For Sinyavsky, the "craving to write gospels instead of novels" is at the core of Russian literature. He also remarks: "A Russian does nothing but tempt God with various rational proposals about the best way to run the world. Russians give a lot of trouble to God." Sinyavsky's work, like that of Solzhenitsyn, should trouble everyone.

The Easter Parade

BY RICHARD YATES

THE EASTER PARADE explores the lives of a woman and her two daughters in New York; it is a sad tale of marriage and divorce, and a still sadder one of sexual liberation. Taking upon himself a seemingly thankless task, Yates writes powerfully of exasperating people, of people who refuse to shape up, of experience that never ripens into wisdom, of reality persistently stunned, but never evaded for long.

Editors' Choice

Delmore Schwartz: The Life of an American Poet

BY JAMES ATLAS

DELMORE SCHWARTZ (1913–66), poet, short-story writer, novelist, playwright, critic, professor, editor, legendary conversationalist, wretched husband, lover, aging fornicator, wino, brawler, pillhead and frightened psychotic, was a salient figure in a generation of extremely gifted writers, among whom he established intimate and often excruciating connections. James Atlas's biography of Schwartz offers more information than any single friend could possibly possess. In a style clear, precise and graceful this book reads with the pleasure of a good novel.

Samuel Johnson

BY W. JACKSON BATE

THIS JUDICIOUS and faithful narrative of Johnson's life shows our kinship with the man as no other biography, not even Boswell's, has done. Bate is unfailingly perceptive and moving and with great skill interweaves the life and the work. Of this magisterial book it might justly be said, as Johnson said of *Paradise Lost*, that it is not the best only because it is not the first.

Falconer

BY JOHN CHEEVER

O N I T S S U R F A C E *Falconer* seems to be a conventional novel of crime, punishment and redemption—a story about a man who kills his brother, goes to prison for it and escapes. Actually, it is a kind of contemplation in short-hand, a meditation on the abstraction Cheever has always called "home" but has never before located specifically in the life of the spirit.

Afterimages

BY ARLENE CROCE

A R L E N E C R O C E ' S capacity for large, tellingly documented judgments about dance, its audiences, its cultural implications in the film as well as in the theater, is equal to her capacity for the most beautifully detailed and exciting descriptions of particular dance movements. In these pieces, ranging back to 1966 and originally published in *The New Yorker* and other magazines, Arlene Croce shows herself to be a dance critic of the highest distinction.

Gates of Eden: American Culture in the Sixties

BY MORRIS DICKSTEIN

M O R R I S D I C K S T E I N has written the first comprehensive appraisal of the '60s in America. With excellent literary judgment and judicious sympathy he covers politics and culture, the rise of a new sensibility, the "new journalism," fiction, rock music, black writing and black nationalism, and concludes with an autobiographical sketch that nicely reveals the relationship of the observer to the things observed.

A Book of Common Prayer

BY JOAN DIDION

T H I S I S Joan Didion's third and most ambitious novel: it investigates the breakdown of social relationships in the last two decades, particularly as it affects parents and children. Didion's language is spare, sardonic, elliptical, understated. She, like the narrator of this book, has been an articulate witness to the most stubborn and intractable truths of our time, a memorable voice, partly eulogistic, partly despairing, always in control.

Every Child's Birthright: In Defense of Mothering
BY SELMA FRAIBERG

SELMA FRAIBERG, known to a generation of parents as the author of a luminous account of childhood, *The Magic Years*, continues in this eloquent and touching book her investigation of the first years of life and the crucial importance to a child of a mother's attention. She persuasively argues that Government policy in the dispersal of welfare and requirements for day care has been chosen not for the good of children but for the convenience of politicians.

Dispatches
BY MICHAEL HERR

NOTHING ELSE has come so close to conveying how different the Vietnam War was from any other we have fought, how different were the methods used and the men who fought it. Michael Herr's style derives from the era of acid rock, the Beatles films, and a druggy Hunter Thompson once-removed-from-reality appreciation of the Great Joke. The best book to have been written about Vietnam.

Chinese Shadows
BY SIMON LEYS

THIS BOOK by a noted Sinologist is a report of six months in 1972 spent in Peking and surrounding provinces: it describes the government's systematic destruction of Chinese culture and warns Western intellectuals not to be taken in by the carefully staged tours, which may forge "friendship between peoples" but prevents friendship between persons.

Day by Day
BY ROBERT LOWELL

THIS, Lowell's last book of poetry, published shortly before his death last fall, continued his verse autobiography and his struggle to dismember and reconstitute the English lyric. In it he wrote of a wife, children, the seasons, ill health, acquaintances, friends living and dead, a walk, a photograph, a poetry reading, a dinner out, shaving, making love, insomnia, fishing—life led day by day. By the end of his life every word in the language had its distinct musical value, so that he could within a feather's weight say what happened.

Song of Solomon

BY TONI MORRISON

USING BLACK FOLKLORE, fantasy, fable, song and allegory, Toni Morrison has written a brilliant prose tale that surveys nearly a century of American history as it impinges on a single family.

The Path Between the Seas: The Creation of the Panama Canal, 1870–1914

BY DAVID MCCULLOUGH

THIS BOOK TELLS the long and complicated tale of the Panama Canal, the largest, most extensive undertaking (except for war) the world has ever seen. There have been scores of previous volumes on the subject, but none is so thorough, readable, fair or graceful in the handling of the myriad materials, particularly the neglected story of the initial participation of the French.

Coming into the Country

BY JOHN MCPHEE

JOHN MCPHEE has written a big book about Alaska, our last frontier. Besides describing the wild grandeur of our 49th state he devotes much of his most artful prose to the peculiarly American types who went north to begin life over. With this book McPhee proves to be the most versatile journalist in America.

India: A Wounded Civilization

BY V. S. NAIPAUL

OVER A PERIOD of 14 years novelist V. S. Naipaul made four extended visits to India. He developed a painful, even oppressive, but evidently inescapable relationship with the country and found it not only, as his subtitle indicates, wounded but mortally so. Indian society, he asserts, has actually "broken down." This is an indispensable book for anyone who wants seriously to come to grips with the experience of that tortured land.

Robert Frost: The Work of Knowing
BY RICHARD POIRIER

BRUSHING PAST the stale views of Robert Frost as our last native sage or an accomplice of nature's charm, Richard Poirier starts from a recognition of how fiercely contrary, how wittily tough-minded Frost's best poems can be. Poirier is at his best when charting the strategies of mind by which Frost dramatizes the interplay between human desire and external reality.

The Gentle Barbarian: The Life and Work of Turgenev
BY V. S. PRITCHETT

THIS IS A WORK of cameo refinement, yielding pleasure from start to finish. Ivan Turgenev emerges in complex shading, a figure slightly absurd, mostly lovable, rich in foible, but still a master of fiction, the kind of writer who transforms personal weakness into imaginative strength.

The Professor of Desire
BY PHILIP ROTH

THIS, Roth's 10th book, is a thoughtful, stylistically elegant novel about the paradox of male desire—that lacerating sexual passion which may lead to happiness but cannot survive it. This book is more a high-level discourse adorned with wit, with rhetorical devices new and ancient, than it is fiction.

Staying On
BY PAUL SCOTT

THE STORY of a British army colonel and his wife who stayed on in India at the end of the British rule in the '40s, this finely detailed, sad and comic novel concludes Paul Scott's account of the end of Empire and the partition of India.

On Photography
BY SUSAN SONTAG

EVERY PAGE of *On Photography* raises important and exciting questions about its subject, and raises them in the best way—in a context of clarity, skepticism and passionate concern, with an energy that never weakens but never blusters, and with an admirable pungency of thought and directness of expression. These six elegant and carefully connected essays are not really about individual photographers, nor solely about the art, but rather about the act of photography at large, the plethora of the product, the puzzles of its nature.

Letters on Literature and Politics: 1912–1972
BY EDMUND WILSON

IN THESE LETTERS one sees that the whole sweep of world literature lay in Wilson's grasp, to be sifted, judged, protected. One sees his eagerness to share every pleasure of literary discovery. His determination to live out the idea of the man of letters and his stubborn insistence upon speaking his own mind were heroic. For anyone interested in literature or the literary life in America over the past 60 years, these letters are a treasure, a feast.

Editors' Choice

In Patagonia
BY BRUCE CHATWIN

THIS IS A TRAVEL BOOK to stand on the small shelf with Graham Greene's *Journey Without Maps*, Somerset Maugham's *The Gentleman in the Parlour* and Paul Theroux's *The Great Railway Bazaar*. Riding and walking through Patagonia, which comprises southern Argentina and parts of Chile and Tierra del Fuego, Bruce Chatwin detoured, meandered and circled back, interviewing sheep ranchers, observing the flora and fauna, collecting old tales, such as the true story of Butch Cassidy and the Sundance Kid, who went to Patagonia in 1901 on the run from the Pinkertons.

The Stories of John Cheever

THESE 61 STORIES of New York and suburban life are a gift at once sweet and sad, nourishing and voluptuous. They are filled with nostalgia, which the dictionary abruptly calls "homesickness as a disease." In Cheever's case, the disease has brought forth works of art, particularly such stories as "The Enormous Radio," "The Housebreaker of Shady Hill," "The Bus to St. James's," "The Country Husband," "The Swimmer" and "The World of Apples."

Discipline and Punish: The Birth of the Prison
BY MICHEL FOUCAULT

IN THIS AMBITIOUS WORK of cultural history, Foucault argues that the origins of modern social control can be found in the "enlightened" creation of the modern prison. The prison reformers of the eighteenth century invented our modern treatment of criminals and other social deviants as individual "cases" that require "cure" and "adjustment." They also created thereby the all-pervasive rule of disciplinary surveillance: the compilation of minute, controlling data about citizens—the tools of bureaucracy and totalitarianism.

E. M. Forster: A Life
BY P. N. FURBANK

THIS BIOGRAPHY is not likely to be superseded for years to come. Besides a plenitude of fascinating stories that make it so enjoyable, the book provides the means by which one can come to terms with the somewhat uneasy but intense admiration that Forster still inspires in the sympathetic reader. Mr. Furbank has made admirable use of the prodigious amount of material—letters, journals, commonplace books, etc.—that were placed at his disposal. One leaves this biography grateful to both author and subject.

Final Payments
BY MARY GORDON

THE GRAVESIDE is an appropriately grim and melodramatic locale for the opening scene of Mary Gordon's remarkable first novel. For 11 years Miss Gordon's heroine Isabel Moore had nursed her dour Catholic father through his strokes; at his death she is given her freedom but loses her identity. We are made to care about Isabel's arrested emotional development, her agony of guilt—that is the genuine achievement of *Final Payments*.

The Flounder
BY GÜNTER GRASS

A GARGANTUAN TALE that spans the period from the Stone Age to the 1970s, *The Flounder* is Günter Grass's first major novel in 15 years and one of the most exuberantly inventive works in recent European fiction. Within the framework of a modern fable, Grass tells and retells an assortment of historical anecdotes and ribald tales—all variations on the battle of the sexes through the ages (each also keyed to a particular food staple). Grass recovers the point of view of the anonymous masses usually left out of official history.

A Savage War of Peace: Algeria 1954–1962
BY ALISTAIR HORNE

ONLY 16 YEARS have passed since the end of the war in Algeria, but history is moving so fast that the details of the story have been largely forgotten. Alistair Horne has interviewed many witnesses with many different viewpoints and has read and digested the innumerable books about the Algerian question. The result is a book that provides as full and objective a history of the Algerian war as we are likely to see for some years.

Facts of Life
BY MAUREEN HOWARD

MAUREEN HOWARD'S memoir of her past is divided into sections entitled Culture, Money and Sex. Of these the most interesting is the section on culture—a tribute to the excellence of Maureen Howard's writing, given that either of the other subjects, as we all know, is of far greater potential interest. What moves us most is the depiction of an Irish Catholic family in Bridgeport, Conn., in the 1940s and her portrait of the artist as a young woman.

Leon Trotsky
BY IRVING HOWE

OF THE THREE giant figures of the Russian Revolution, Trotsky is the dominant and most dramatic. His immense vitality was matched by his versatility. Irving Howe, within the limits of the Modern Masters series, has written an excellent short account that he calls a "political essay." It is particularly valuable for its discussion of democratic socialism and the emergence of the totalitarian state.

The World According to Garp
BY JOHN IRVING

JOHN IRVING'S fourth novel is pleasing, convoluted and self-reflecting. Through its formal sinuosities it is also a study of family life in the age of the women's movement and a treatise on how reality is processed by fiction. Mr. Irving's talent for storytelling is so bright and strong that he fully re-creates our time with its lurid and unending public melodrama.

Lying Low
BY DIANE JOHNSON

A BEAUTIFULLY CONSTRUCTED, elegantly written novel, powerful in its impact. The action occupies four days, which begin with the killing of a hen by a neighborhood dog and end with a catastrophe that is at once surprising and plausible. It is one of Diane Johnson's triumphs that she can capture and make interesting the sheer "dailiness" of existence within a framework that could easily have lent itself to melodrama.

Stories
BY DORIS LESSING

D ORIS LESSING is the great realist writer of our time, in the tradition of the major novelists of the nineteenth century—a tradition of large moral concerns, an earnest and affirmative view of human nature, a dead-eye for social types. This new collection of all her short fiction (except the African stories) should repair any misunderstanding about the breadth of her sympathy and the range of her interests and, above all, the pleasures of reading her.

Wrinkles
BY CHARLES SIMMONS

A STRIKING EXPERIMENT in fictional form, *Wrinkles* consists of 44 brief essays or meditations, each on the past, present and future of an unnamed middle-aged writer. The method feels like a kind of spiritual exercise. If this is a book of sadness, it is not really a sad book: Mr. Simmons has a marvelous recall of the touching comedy of growing up. The author is a member of the Book Review staff.

The Coup
BY JOHN UPDIKE

J OHN UPDIKE has betaken himself—imaginatively at least—to Africa. The trip has done him good, for he has returned with one of his strongest novels, a book that stands with the two *Rabbit* novels and *The Centaur* as an example of what this extraordinarily prolific novelist can do when his imagination, as well as his language, is strenuously engaged. Updike has had the fictional audacity to project a black among blacks, a militant and culturally, though not sexually, puritanical Marxist-Muslim, the redoubtable Col. Félix Ellelloû, president and dictator of a sub-Saharan nation with the biblical name of Kush. This comedy of absurd cultural juxtaposition (which, like Waugh's, can sometimes bare a wonderfully menacing set of teeth) is sustained beautifully throughout.

The Eye of the Story: Selected Essays and Reviews
BY EUDORA WELTY

IN THIS INVIGORATING selection of her nonfiction (some of which appeared in these pages), Eudora Welty constantly touches the place where literary critic and creative writer meet. She uses the words "pleasure" and "sweetness" without embarrassment or sentimentality, always leading us back to the books themselves. Writing of Ford Madox Ford, she says that what was due him was not only honor and study but "the response of love," and the response of love is what Miss Welty brings to the writers who matter to her.

Inventing America: Jefferson's Declaration of Independence
BY GARRY WILLS

THERE IS NO better account, at least in such brief compass, of the fears, divisions, loyalties and priorities of the men who dominated the Continental Congress and who altered and established the Declaration of Independence. While Garry Wills has obviously done meticulous research, his greatest assets are a sharp eye for revealing detail, a flair for detecting hidden strings of power and influence and a shrewd sense of how the delegates perceived and used one another. This book is also one of the best studies of Jefferson yet to appear.

1979

Editors' Choice

The White Album

BY JOAN DIDION

THE TITLE ESSAY of Joan Didion's new collection is probably the best short piece on the late 1960s, even better than *Slouching Towards Bethlehem*, that remarkable account of the Haight-Ashbury flower children from which her previous collection took its name. Other articles here include a description of an elaborate recording session of The Doors in which everything is there except the essential Door, Jim Morrison; a press conference with a slogan-spouting Huey Newton in the Alameda County Jail; an interview with Eldridge Cleaver in which there is much talk about the publisher's advance for *Soul on Ice* ($5,000). Most of the pieces deal with California subjects, and all of them manifest not only Joan Didion's intelligence, but her instinct for details that continue to emit pulsations in the reader's memory.

King of the Jews

BY LESLIE EPSTEIN

MAKING NOVELS out of the holocaust has often proved a hopeless enterprise. Readers have been numbed by the magnitude of the horror involved or else revolted by a kind of pornography of violence. Leslie Epstein, in contrast, has focused on the morally ambiguous politics of survival in the person of Isaiah Chaim Trumpelman, chief elder of the Jewish Council (Judenrat) in a Polish ghetto. Drawn into a position of absolute power and absolute impotence in which no human being could function with any moral coherence, Trumpelman is clearly modeled on the historical figure Mordechai Chaim Rumkowski. This novel is a lesson in what artistic restraint can do to help us imagine the dark places of history.

Sleepless Nights
BY ELIZABETH HARDWICK

THE SUBJECT of Elizabeth Hardwick's subtle and beautiful novel is memory, and the "I" whose memories are in question is entirely and deliberately the author. We recognize the events and addresses of Elizabeth Hardwick's life not only from her earlier writings but from the poems of her husband, the late Robert Lowell; we recognize the rainy afternoons and dyed satin shoes and high-school drunkenness of adolescence, the graduate years at Columbia, the households in Maine and Europe and Boston and on West 67th Street in New York. Her meticulously transcribed histories yield a terrible point: In the culture under study, life ends badly. The freedom to live untied to others, however desired that freedom may be, is hard on men and hard on children and hardest of all on women.

Gödel, Escher, Bach: An Eternal Golden Braid
BY DOUGLAS R. HOFSTADTER

THIS SENTENCE IS FALSE." The unsettling effect of such statements was for a long time attributed to the ambiguity of common language. However, even the most carefully contrived logical systems give rise to such paradoxes when they refer to themselves, as the mathematician Kurt Gödel showed in 1931. Douglas R. Hofstadter, a professor of computer science, has written an enormous and ingenious essay on Gödel's theorem; the drawings of the Dutch artist Maurits Cornelis Escher, which depict in exquisite detail illogical physical structures and occurrences; and Johann Sebastian Bach, whose fugues comment on themselves so richly.

Eighth Day of Creation: Makers of the Revolution in Biology
BY HORACE FREELAND JUDSON

IN THE LAST 25 years our understanding of the biochemistry of life has profoundly deepened. The remarkable human and scientific story of this change has never been better told. Mr. Judson spent 10 years in research, and he lets the events, such as the discovery of DNA, unfold as they happened. Along the way we learn each participant's view of the key moments preceding the final illumination. One finishes the book with a great sense of elation and of admiration for what man, at his best, can accomplish.

The Nabokov–Wilson Letters: Correspondence Between Vladimir Nabokov and Edmund Wilson, 1940–1971
EDITED BY SIMON KARLINSKY

THESE TWO eminent figures from widely separated backgrounds had much in common. Both put literature before any other cause, both were linguists, both admired each other's work, both had reason for gratitude to each other, and before their famous public quarrel over Nabokov's annotated translation of *Eugene Onegin* both enjoyed each other's pugnacity. All this is told in a brilliant and entertaining epistolary record of the most fertilizing of literary friendships.

White House Years
BY HENRY KISSINGER

HENRY KISSINGER'S TASK, as he saw it on taking office in the administration of Richard M. Nixon in January 1969, was to end the Vietnam War, manage a "global rivalry" and nuclear-arms race with the Soviet Union, reinvigorate alliance with European democracies and integrate recently formed nations into a "new world equilibrium." How did he do? This 1,500-page book, which is more record than assessment, perhaps because the former Secretary of State has written so soon about his management of the complex and turbulent events of 1969 to 1973, is nonetheless bound to become an important historical document.

The Culture of Narcissism: American Life in an Age of Diminishing Expectations

BY CHRISTOPHER LASCH

RANGING WITH much virtuosity over the whole of American life, Christopher Lasch finds evidence only of change and decay. This is a civilized hellfire sermon, with little promise of salvation. Having lost our sense of communion with the past, we feel no responsibility for the future. Our schools, our attitudes toward sex, the family and old age, our acquiescence in the rule of bureaucracy, our muddled liberal attitudes toward punishment, even our acceptance of the corruption of sport into showbiz are all signs of this decline. This is a black and forceful survey of the way we live now.

The Executioner's Song

BY NORMAN MAILER

WHAT WAS EXPECTED to be Norman Mailer's "Gary Gilmore book" (as an earlier effort had been his "Marilyn Monroe book"), that is, an account of and contemplation on the life and death of a convicted murderer, turned instead into an astonishing thousand-page novel about the American West. Mailer, a great and obsessed stylist, used a meticulously limited vocabulary and a voice as flat as the horizon to produce a book ambitious to the point of vertigo.

The Rise of Theodore Roosevelt

BY EDMUND MORRIS

OF ALL OUR PRESIDENTS, Theodore Roosevelt had the most unlikely blend of brilliance, learning, outrageousness and inscrutability. He was to attain frenzied popularity but was later to wreck his own party and meet with indignation and criticism that has become more penetrating ever since. A biographer could not ask for a more stirring subject, and Edmund Morris has done a magnificent job in this first volume, which carries Roosevelt up to but not into the White House. It is a sweeping narrative of the outward man and a shrewd examination of his character.

A Bend in the River

BY V. S. NAIPAUL

FOR SHEER abundance of talent there can hardly be a writer alive who surpasses V. S. Naipaul. Whatever we may want in a novelist is to be found in his books: an almost Conradian gift for tensing a story, a serious involvement with human issues, a supple English prose, a hard-edged wit and a personal vision. Best of all, he is unafraid to use his brains. *A Bend in the River,* set in an unnamed East African country a bit like Uganda, concerns the tragic aftermath of independence, when power falls into the hands of the army and "The Big Man." Perhaps Naipaul's prime achievement is his ability to hold fast to the bitterness before his eyes.

The Habit of Being

BY FLANNERY O'CONNOR
EDITED BY SALLY FITZGERALD

SINCE HER DEATH in 1964, Flannery O'Connor's reputation has grown to a point where it isn't eccentric to regard her as at least the equal of any American writer of short stories. The letters that make up this volume begin when she is 23 and working at Yaddo and end 16 years later, six days before her death; they tell us a great deal about her attitudes toward her own work and literature in general. They are sober, folksy, intimate or playful, a little guarded perhaps in emotional matters but, because of that, without sentimentality. They seem to come from a moral age we scarcely remember.

The Boer War

BY THOMAS PAKENHAM

FOR BRITAIN, the Boer War (1899–1902) was the most costly and humiliating adventure in the hundred years between Waterloo and 1914. It set a stamp of British decline on the new century and ended "Pax Britannica." Thomas Pakenham has brought an original view to the war, its underlying motives and leading personalities with an authority that commands respect, even if not every historian will agree with it. The war began with the Boers' refusal to permit white "Uitlanders" equality of rights, along with British cupidity for gold and empire. It ended with the loss of 22,000 British, 25,000 Boer and 12,000 African lives.

The Man Who Kept the Secrets: Richard Helms and the CIA

BY THOMAS POWERS

RICHARD HELMS gave the best part of his life to the spy business. He joined the Office of Strategic Services in 1943, attended the Central Intelligence Agency's birth in 1947, became chief of its clandestine arm in 1952, and finally head of the whole operation in 1966. As Thomas Powers says, nobody's career offers such "an ideal pathway through the secret history of the last 30 years." Is Helms a hero, a victim, a monster of the secret state, or just a nice American guy doing a decent job for his country? Mr. Powers doesn't take sides and in consequence has produced one of the best spy stories in a long time, all the better for being nonfiction.

The Ghost Writer

BY PHILIP ROTH

THE VOICE THAT Roth developed for his first-person narrations—notably *Portnoy's Complaint*, *My Life as a Man* and recently *The Professor of Desire*—is surely one of the most distinctive and supple in American fiction. In this very short novel it is the voice of the narrator, Nathan Zuckerman, a young writer who pays a visit of homage to the eminent Jewish writer E. I. Lonoff. There ensues an extraordinary story in which Anne Frank, miraculously saved from the Holocaust, appears as Lonoff's mistress—or so Zuckerman imagines. *The Ghost Writer*, Roth says, is about the surprises that the vocation of writing brings.

Sideshow: Kissinger, Nixon and the Destruction of Cambodia

BY WILLIAM SHAWCROSS

WILLIAM SHAWCROSS, the British journalist who has worked as a reporter in Indochina and Washington, claims to have interviewed over 300 people, corresponded with many others and examined several thousand pages of unpublished Government documents obtained under the Freedom of Information Act (some classified Top Secret) before coming up with this indictment of Henry A. Kissinger and Richard M. Nixon in their treatment of Cambodia. Mr. Shawcross raises such issues as the legality of the secret bombing, the way the bombing and subsequent invasion spread the fighting, the deliberate prolongation of the war in Cambodia and the avoidance of a negotiated settlement.

Too Far to Go: The Maples Stories
BY JOHN UPDIKE

So many of John Updike's characters seem to inhabit the suburbs of Splitsville and to toy with infidelity as soon as the shower presents are unwrapped that one thinks of them as naturally polygamous. This reputation has come in part from the stories Mr. Updike has written about Richard and Joan Maple. Seventeen are collected here—the most civilized stories imaginable, and because of this, the most tender.

1980

Editors' Choice

Falling in Place
BY ANN BEATTIE

IN THE SIX YEARS since her work first began to appear *The New Yorker*, Ann Beattie has become for many readers the representative young American novelist and short-story writer. Yet nothing she has written did quite prepare us for this novel. Not that her stories or settings have changed, but there is a new fancy to her characters' feelings and a much greater range and number of characters and points of view: from a 40-year-old ad agency man and his disillusioned wife to his alcoholic mother, his tricky boss, terrified but cool best friend, down through his 25-year-old mistress, his surly 15-year-old daughter to his 10-year-old son, who is too fat. *Falling in Place* is a deliberately understated, wry comedy of manners, an ever so slightly bittersweet version of, say, Flaubert's parodies of provincial life. Miss Beattie is a prodigiously gifted and developing writer who has started to come of age.

Christianity, Social Tolerance, and Homosexuality
BY JOHN BOSWELL

JOHN BOSWELL argues that after hundreds of years of indifference, the Church became hostile to homosexuality during the thirteenth century. This paralleled the rise in intolerance toward other minorities, notably heretics, Jews and Muslims. The cause of the new feeling was associated with the general systemization of politics and culture during the high Middle Ages, which made all forms of distinctiveness—whether sexual, doctrinal or ethnic—seem undesirable. St. Thomas Aquinas, who elaborated the theory that homosexuality was "unnatural," is Mr. Boswell's principal villain. Although the book's findings are startling enough, they are not half so startling as the book itself, which displays the sweep and control that one finds only in the work of a major historian.

Italian Folktales
BY ITALO CALVINO

ITALO CALVINO'S *Fiabe Italiane* was published in Italian 24 years ago, and has now been translated into an English that is colloquial but never corny, plainspoken, economical, wry and flexible and sometimes stunningly lyrical. Calvino for two years read and sorted numerous collections, old and new, bad and good, of Italian tales, searching out the best, and retelling them with his exquisite storyteller's skill. He is possibly Italy's most brilliant living writer; this collection stands with the finest folktale collections anywhere.

Loon Lake
BY E. L. DOCTOROW

IN *LOON LAKE* E. L. Doctorow has fashioned a world of mirrors, a fascinating, tantalizing novel in which nearly every image or episode has its counterpart somewhere else in the book. Like Mr. Doctorow's earlier *Ragtime*, *Loon Lake* evokes a period in our history: in this case the 1930s, with backward glances to the '20s and earlier. If *Ragtime* is a work of brilliant surfaces, then *Loon Lake* is a work of brilliant parts. The experience of reading it—even its pages of bad poetry—is exhilarating.

Man in the Holocene
BY MAX FRISCH

THE SWISS WRITER Max Frisch is a leading contender for the Nobel Prize. Certainly his published work, written over a 45-year period, has the variety and originality of style, the weight and humanity of substance that we expect, and occasionally get, from Nobel laureates. *Man in the Holocene* has about it the aspect of a classic, not because it imitates an ancient author, but because of its lucidity and elegance of form, its severe impersonality, its restraint, its universality. Reading about the slow, inexorable decline of the 74-year-old retired engineer and widower, Herr Geiser, one doesn't say, "This might have happened"; one says, "This happens, inevitably, wherever there are humans." This luminous parable of indeterminable purport is a masterpiece.

Walt Whitman

BY JUSTIN KAPLAN

THIS BIOGRAPHY of Whitman forgoes detailed comment on the poems and uses them chiefly to illustrate the life. Justin Kaplan's taste is very near impeccable, and by his emphases and omissions a critical view of Whitman's best work is silently conveyed; and Mr. Kaplan's human insight makes psychological connections that illuminate, often by delicate juxtapositions of texts, a whole tract of poetry. Whitman sometimes seems like nineteenth-century America itself, condensed into one allegorical embodiment exhibiting all its embryonic interests and potential identities.

China Men

BY MAXINE HONG KINGSTON

MAXINE HONG KINGSTON'S first book, *The Woman Warrior*, was a brilliantly realized attempt to understand herself in relation to Chinese women. *China Men*, using the same techniques—the blend of myth, legend and history, the fevered voice, relentless as a truth-seeking child's—is impelled to understand the men with whom she is connected: her father, grandfather, brother—all mythic figures. Mrs. Kingston has achieved this understanding, from the side of the woman, the daughter, the victim. Hers, then, is the victory, not only of comprehension, but also of forgiveness.

The Cost of Good Intentions

BY CHARLES R. MORRIS

THIS BOOK DESCRIBES the turbulent period in New York City's history from 1960 to 1975, when at last the strained financial structure collapsed under pressures that had been building for 15 years. If this book did only that, the author would deserve honor and credit for setting the historical record straight on one of the most complex, critical domestic occurrences of our time. But by tracing what city officials *thought* was happening, as well as what was really happening, Charles R. Morris has produced something more—a meticulous case study of "good intentions" gone awry and of mistakes made because policy makers were unaware of the terrain shifting beneath them.

Nature and Culture

BY BARBARA NOVAK

DRAWING ON DIARIES, letters and contemporary texts on esthetics, science and philosophy, Barbara Novak creates a thoroughly convincing case for her thesis that the content of nineteenth-century American landscape painting is religious. Time and again she illustrates how ingrained in American thought is the belief that nature, especially wild nature, is more than merely a sight to see, that it is the earthly manifestation of the divine. Once popularized, such an idea, which has its roots in the Transcendental pantheism of Emerson and Thoreau, explains why camping out can be experienced as a religious pilgrimage by Americans, who revere Yosemite more than Lourdes. Professor Novak's account of what nineteenth-century American artists thought and wrote about what they painted, as well as what they surmised from what they read, gives one a concrete sense of the landscape painter as a religious sightseer, painting the shrines of the natural world with the piety that the artists of other cultures used to depict local deities.

Conrad in the Nineteenth Century

BY IAN WATT

BECAUSE HE IS SO ODD a writer, Joseph Conrad has needed a critic who would, in both senses of the word, let him live. Live, first of all, in his time and with his gifts, in his environment, among ideas, other artists, the men and women he knew; and, second, live despite taking frank account of his glaringly evident faults: his inability to handle sex, his fragmentary style of composition, his often grandiloquent prose. Ian Watt has done these things with more success than any writer since Conrad's death in 1924.

The Collected Stories of Eudora Welty

THE RICHNESS of Eudora Welty's talents resists a summing up. We can place her with her models, Chekhov and Katherine Anne Porter: She is always honest, always just. And she is vastly entertaining. The stories are magnificent. Her youthful need to watch became a life devoted to observation. There is a superb vigilance in Eudora Welty, a present tense. Each work is responsive to its time: History, especially in the South, must not reflect romantic distortions. It is only by the rigorous observation which we find in her *Collected Stories* that the present is verified and the past kept useful and alive.

1981

Editors' Choice

The Chaneysville Incident

BY DAVID BRADLEY

LIKE THE AUTHOR, the narrator of David Bradley's second novel is young, black and a college professor. His quest and the quest of the book is to unravel the mystery of "the Chaneysville incident," which occurred at the time of the Underground Railroad, when 13 runaway slaves, about to be recaptured, were shot instead—at, so the tale goes, their own urgent request. Along the way, Mr. Bradley synchronizes five different kinds of rhetoric, controls a complicated plot, conveys much information, handles an intricate time scheme, pulls off a couple of final tricks that dramatize provocative ideas and generally keeps things going at a remarkable pace.

Bad Blood

BY JAMES H. JONES

THE TUSKEGEE Study of Untreated Syphilis in the Negro Male, the subject of this book, was a 40-year deathwatch over the lives of more than 400 black sharecroppers in Macon County, Ala. There, from 1932 to 1972, the United States Public Health Service conducted a "study" in which treatment was deliberately withheld from syphilitic men in an effort to determine the natural course of the disease. The intention was to prove that syphilis was "different" in blacks. As an authentic, exquisitely detailed case study of the consequences of racism in American life, this book should be read by everyone who worries about the racial meanings of Government policy and social practice in the United States.

Haydn: Chronicle and Works
BY H. C. ROBBINS LANDON

THIS LEVIATHAN of a biography, a document-crammed, five-volume, 3,248-page study that costs $325, will take its place beside such indispensable musical biographies as Thayer's Beethoven and Spitta's Bach. Every scrap of Haydn scholarship has been drawn together in the 17-pound package; but Mr. Landon's broader contribution has been to place each piece of music in a social, political and intellectual framework for the musical layman. No one can read these volumes, or even dip into them, without being enthralled by an entire culture and its creators.

Philosophical Explanations
BY ROBERT NOZICK

A STRIKINGLY ORIGINAL and imaginative attempt by a first-rate philosopher to deal with the classic problems of philosophy in a new way and by so doing to make philosophy once again more relevant to the concerns of laymen. To simplify Mr. Nozick's approach, he seeks to free philosophical investigation from the tyranny of proof and substitute the more flexible process of explanation. Such questions as "How is free will possible, if all actions are causally determined?" or "How is it possible for the subjective experiences of thinking, feeling and perceiving to find a place in the objective world?" become, through Mr. Nozick's methods, once again available to useful inquiry.

Old Glory
BY JONATHAN RABAN

AT AGE 7, in Norfolk, England, Jonathan Raban read *Huckleberry Finn* for the first time and began to dream of the Mississippi. Finally, in 1979, age 37, he met the living river. He flew to St. Paul, bought a very small boat and started the 1,400-mile trip down to New Orleans. *Old Glory* is the account of that trip and a stunning success. Mr. Raban seems to have stopped in every town and talked to every person along the whole 1,400 miles. He had expected to find a country of conformists, but was delighted to learn that Americans are true eccentrics and individuals, a high compliment from an Englishman.

Housekeeping

BY MARILYNNE ROBINSON

ONE SHOULD READ this first novel as slowly as poetry, and for the same reason: The language is so precise, so distilled and so beautiful one does not want to miss any pleasure it might yield up to patience. The protagonist and narrator of *Housekeeping* is a quiet, dreamy girl named Ruth who has lost her father in an accident and her mother to suicide. When her grandmother dies, she passes through the hands of two aunts to a third, the eccentric Sylvie, and begins to lose touch with reality. Since Ruth tells her own story, the tightly controlled lyricism of the language loses its definition at the book's close; but, still, *Housekeeping* is an extraordinary performance.

Midnight's Children

BY SALMAN RUSHDIE

THIS BRASH, knowing, massive, aggressive novel is to modern India what Günter Grass's *The Tin Drum* is to modern Germany. It concerns the narrator's growing up in Bombay between 1947 and 1977, and also India's growing up from independence on August 15, 1947, to Indira Gandhi's Emergency Rule of 1977. The "midnight children" of the title are the 1,001 children born during the first hour of independence. Each of them is miraculously gifted. The narrator Saleem, for instance, is telepathic; others can travel through time; one can change sex at will. They are seen to be the hope of the nation. But the half that survive till 1977 are sterilized and finally *sperectomized*, or drained of hope—as, Mr. Rushdie seems to say, India itself has been.

The Gate of Heavenly Peace

BY JONATHAN SPENCE

CHINA'S MODERN REVOLUTION did not start with Mao Zedong's Long March in 1935, but four decades earlier with the seizure of power in 1898 by the constitutional monarchists. Jonathan Spence tells the story of this long revolution in unique fashion, through the lives and written testimony of its intelligentsia, chiefly men and women of letters. These witnesses range from the scholar and philosopher Kang Youwei (1858–1927), who led the reforms of 1898, to Ding Ling, still living, who spent three years under Kuomintang house arrest and later was either exiled or imprisoned by the Communists for a total of 18 years. There is in this chronicle of politics and thought much "felt life," that quality Henry James so valued in fiction.

A Flag for Sunrise

BY ROBERT STONE

SQUALID, spectacular, agitated, littered with ancient ruins and riddled with more spies than you can shake a cloak at, Central America seems almost too much of a good thing for a novelist: the treasure of Sierra Madre tarted up for the apocalypse. Robert Stone, setting his new, now novel in an imaginary but circumstantial version of this place, is taking a serious risk; but the risk is worth it, the wager is won. Stone converts clichés into people, and people into questions. This novel, Stone's third, has the pace and suspense of a first-class thriller and brilliantly catches the shifting currents of contemporary Latin American politics.

The White Hotel

BY D. M. THOMAS

REMARKABLE IN CONCEPTION and unusual in structure, *The White Hotel*, a novel by the English poet D. M. Thomas, is composed of fictional letters to, from and about Sigmund Freud; two compositions by a woman patient, one in verse, the other in prose, which describe with much erotic detail a fantasized affair with Freud's son Martin; a long analysis by Freud of "this unfortunate woman's case"; and finally a narrative of her unhappy life, during which she suffers the European agonies of World War II. What *The White Hotel* sets out to perform is nothing less than a diagnosis of our epoch through the experience of an individual; it comes close to achieving that remarkable goal.

Prisoner Without a Name, Cell Without a Number

BY JACOBO TIMERMAN

AT 2 IN THE MORNING of April 15, 1977, 20 armed men in civilian clothes arrested Jacobo Timerman, editor and publisher of a leading Buenos Aires newspaper. Thus began 30 months of imprisonment, torture and anti-Semitic abuse. Timerman's crime, apparently, was his fervid Zionism (although there was no law against Zionism) and his insistence on maintaining a free newspaper. Charges against him were never defined by his oppressors, the military men from the wing of the armed forces that came into control of the Government in 1977; and, unlike 15,000 other Argentines, "the disappeared," Timerman was eventually released into exile. His testimony constitutes one of the most gripping and important books to be published this year: gripping in its human stories, not only of brutality but of courage and love; important because it reminds us how, in our world, the most terrible fantasies may become fact.

Rabbit Is Rich

BY JOHN UPDIKE

RABBIT ANGSTROM keeps coming back. John Updike published *Rabbit, Run* in 1960, *Rabbit Redux* in 1971, and now *Rabbit Is Rich*. One reason Rabbit has this power may be that he is not Updike, but the one who didn't leave Pennsylvania, didn't go to Harvard, didn't become a dazzling novelist. Updike might see him in a real or imagined trip home, at a reunion or a wedding: My God, he's still there. What's he *doing*. He must weigh 225 at least. Runs the Toyota Agency, the one his father-in-law let him into 10 years ago. He and Janice have been married for 23 years now. . . . In *Rabbit Is Rich* Updike fulfilled the fabulous promise he offered with *Rabbit, Run* and *The Centaur* 20 years ago.

Editors' Choice

The Burning House
BY ANN BEATTIE

THIS IS ANN BEATTIE'S third collection of stories in eight years, and a new Beattie is almost like a fresh bulletin from the front: We snatch it up, eager to know what's happening out there on the edge of that shifting and dubious no-man's-land known as interpersonal relations. Her characters are on maintenance doses, getting from one day to the next, one lover to the next. By now she has absolute control over this material. Compared to the earlier stories, these are less strange, more narrowly and intensely focused, more accomplished. The mood is not bloody-minded; rather it is sorrowful. No one is better than Ann Beattie at evoking the floating, unreal ambiance of grief.

Waiting for the Barbarians
BY J. M. COETZEE

IMAGINE what it must be like to live as a serious writer in South Africa: an endless clamor of news about racial injustice, the feeling that one's life is mortgaged to a society gone rotten with hatred, an indignation that exhausts itself into depression, the fear that one's anger may overwhelm and destroy one's fiction. About all these matters J. M. Coetzee, a South African writer in his early 40's, has evidently thought deeply, and in his new novel he has found a narrative strategy for controlling the tension between subject and author. He tells the story of an imaginary Empire, set in an unspecified place and time, yet recognizable as a "universalized" version of South Africa. At the Empire's edge live barbarian tribes, which the so-called Third Bureau claims are preparing to mutiny. Troops are sent; first there are reports of victory; but finally they return, dazed and bedraggled. The Empire fades; the barbarians remain. A power of historical immediacy gives this novel its thrust, its larger and, if you wish, universal value.

Tumultuous Years

BY ROBERT J. DONOVAN

THIS SECOND VOLUME of Robert J. Donovan's history of Harry S. Truman's Presidency deals with his elected term in office, 1949 to 1953. The author, a journalist turned historian, has spent a decade absorbing the materials of a period that now seems to have contained the seeds of all the most pressing troubles and issues of our times. The lucid, orderly narrative deals vividly with the Korean War and the clashing personalities of Truman and Gen. Douglas MacArthur, as well as with such crucial postwar events and issues as the establishment of NATO, the "loss of China," the entrenchment of the cold war, the decision to develop the hydrogen bomb, the impact of Senator Joseph McCarthy. In addition to sketches of the senior figures involved—Truman himself, Secretary of State Dean Acheson, James Forrestal, MacArthur—there are revealing glimpses of rising young men, including Richard Nixon and Lyndon Johnson.

Schindler's List

BY THOMAS KENEALLY

AMONG THE CARPETBAGGERS who followed the German Army into Poland in 1939 was a young Sudeten German named Oskar Schindler, who had a reputation for womanizing and giving lavish parties for his influential friends. He was rewarded with one of Cracow's plums: He was appointed *treuhandler*—read plunderer—of a prosperous Jewish-owned enamelware factory. Against every probability Schindler became a possessed man, ready to risk everything in a daring scheme to rescue 1,300 Jewish workers from certain death. Using fictional techniques, the versatile Australian novelist, Thomas Keneally, tells the true story of a man who saved lives that the sinews of civilization were bent on destroying.

Years of Upheaval

BY HENRY A. KISSINGER

IN THE SECOND VOLUME of his interminable yet endlessly fascinating memoirs, Henry A. Kissinger mourns the burden of carrying a crippled President, but still cannot help celebrating his own incomparable feats of survival. As Richard Nixon's Presidency expired, Mr. Kissinger's already great influence soared. This volume recounts that incredible year between the summers of 1973 and 1974, in which the refugee from Nazi Germany became the most glamorous and probably the most powerful man in America. The book begins with his baptism as Secretary of State by a grudging President floating in a swimming pool in San Clemente and ends with the President on his knees at the door of the Lincoln Bedroom in the White House. In between are many brilliant personal portraits of American and world leaders and some vivid lessons in diplomatic strategy.

The Fate of the Earth

BY JONATHAN SCHELL

THIS IS A WORK of enormous force. There are moments when it seems to hurtle, almost out of control, across an extraordinary range of fact and thought. But in the end, it accomplishes what no other work has managed to do in the 37 years of the nuclear age—make us confront head-on the nuclear peril in which we all find ourselves. "If, in a nuclear holocaust," says Jonathan Schell, "anyone hid himself deep enough under the earth and stayed there long enough to survive, he would emerge into a dying natural environment." The surfaces of the earth would cool, the vegetation would wither away, the waters would become contaminated and the ozone layer, which protects all living things on earth, would disappear. In a word, this would become a dead planet. With arduous and painstaking argument, Mr. Schell asks that we recognize this and do something about it.

Bronx Primitive

BY KATE SIMON

TODAY WE THINK of Kate Simon as so privileged, sophisticated and cosmopolitan that we gladly consign to her great cities of the world, designating them Kate Simon's Paris, Kate Simon's London, New York, Rome, Mexico City—glamorous places she has made deliciously intimate to readers of her travel books. But she grew up Jewish in the Tremont Avenue section of the

Bronx, having been brought there by her young immigrant parents direct from the Warsaw ghetto, with only a brief stopover on the Lower East Side. And now she turns her powers of observation upon herself as a child and upon the sidewalks, the stoops, the public schools and the railroad flats of the Bronx she grew up in. The result is a superb record of one particular immigrant experience.

Aké

BY WOLE SOYINKA

AKÉ provides Wole Soyinka's readers with the best possible way of understanding his work. Playwright, poet, novelist, polemical essayist and now autobiographer, Mr. Soyinka is unquestionably Africa's most versatile writer and arguably her finest. In *Aké* he has produced an account of his childhood in western Nigeria that is destined to become a classic of African autobiography. For all its seriousness, this is not a solemn book. It is written in supple English, full of good humor and lyric grace, mingling the sounds and smells of village life, his Christian upbringing and the presence of his African ancestors.

Isak Dinesen

BY JUDITH THURMAN

THIS BIOGRAPHY of Karen Blixen is an extremely satisfying work. Well researched, sympathetic, fair and imaginative, it tells the story of "Isak Dinesen," the author of *Seven Gothic Tales* and *Out of Africa*, who as Baroness Blixen led a highly interesting and varied life, spanning two continents and more than two cultures. She died in 1962; here, 20 years later, she emerges from myth and anecdote as witch, sibyl, lion hunter, coffee planter, aristocrat and despot, a desperately sick but indestructible woman. She steps from Judith Thurman's pages with all the force of legend and all the human detail of a real person made by real circumstance.

Dinner at the Homesick Restaurant

BY ANNE TYLER

THIS IS ANNE TYLER'S ninth novel. It is funny, heart-warming, wise, edging deep into truth that is psychological, moral and formal—deeper than Miss Tyler has gone before. The setting is Baltimore. The focus is Pearl Tull, 85 and dying, whose ruminations center partly on a moment 35 years before, when her husband, a traveling salesman, announced that he was clearing out for good; partly on the years of ferocious labor that followed; partly on the mystery of the character of her three children. We're speaking about an extremely beautiful book.

Bech Is Back
BY JOHN UPDIKE

SINCE 1970 Henry Bech has been one of John Updike's several alter egos. In *Bech: A Book*, Bech was the author of three novels and was beginning to find that leading the literary life was easier than writing. Now, in *Bech Is Back*, his dry period has stretched to 13 years. At last he relinquishes his timidities, marries his mistress, finishes a long-awaited best-selling book and exchanges his shyness for disillusion, thereby becoming a formidable literary figure. *Bech Is Back* is not really a novel but an entertaining group of linked stories. One, "Bech Wed," is a small and witty masterpiece of domestic relations and the literary life.

Aunt Julia and the Scriptwriter
BY MARIO VARGAS LLOSA

THIS COMIC NOVEL, the work of the Peruvian writer Mario Vargas Llosa, is an homage to two real people who gave shape to his artistic and personal life: an ascetic Bolivian who all day, every day, wrote scripts for radio soap operas and the author's Aunt Julia. In both the novel and real life, Vargas Llosa married his Aunt Julia; and, as a young radio newsman in Lima in 1953 he worked with the Bolivian. The brightest achievement of Vargas Llosa's wild fantasy is his portrait of the artist as an obsessive fountain of make-believe worlds, which blend not only with one another but with his fictional reality.

Editors' Choice

Cathedral

BY RAYMOND CARVER

THERE ARE ARTISTS who reach the strange by staying with the ordinary. Raymond Carver, an American writer now in his mid-40s, has been writing stories for some years that create this effect. His settings are American towns, semi-industrial and often depressed. His characters, plebeian loners struggling for speech, now and then find work as factory hands and waitresses. The action skids across the troubles of daily life and then, through some eerie turn of chance, collapses into failed marriages and broken lives. Familiar enough on the surface, these stories leave one with tremors that resemble the start of a mental breakdown. *Cathedral*, Mr. Carver's third collection, after *Will You Be Quiet, Please?* and *What We Talk About When We Talk About Love*, shows a gifted writer struggling for a larger scope of reference, a finer touch of nuance.

During the Reign of the Queen of Persia

BY JOAN CHASE

THE QUEEN of this novel's title is Gram, an intractable old tyrant who has cursed and battled through a difficult life in rural Ohio and won her way to the promised land of bingo games and movie matinees and who rules her household of women—daughters and granddaughters—with a hard and knobby hand

and a tongue like a rasp. *During the Reign of the Queen of Persia* is a Norman Rockwell painting gone bad, the underside of the idyllic hometown, main-street, down-on-the-farm dream of Middle America. This first novel takes its place with other important contemporary fictions that depict the condition of the American woman.

The Name of the Rose
BY UMBERTO ECO

IMAGINE A MEDIEVAL CASTLE run by the Benedictines, with cellarers, herbalists, gardeners, librarians, young novices. Imagine that, one after the other, half a dozen monks are found murdered in the most bizarre ways. Imagine that a learned Franciscan is sent to solve the mystery and at the end of the narrative it turns out that all these horrible crimes were committed for highly ethical and cultural reasons. These are the bare bones of a first novel by a famous Italian practitioner of semiotics (the philosophy of signs and symbols). *The Name of the Rose* has been a best seller in Europe and, shortly after the publication of this excellent translation by William Weaver, went to the top of the best-seller list here. Imagine!

Attlee
BY KENNETH HARRIS

THIS EXCELLENT new biography does justice to the remarkable politi-cian who was England's Prime Minister from 1945 to 1951. With skill and grace, Kenneth Harris's book traces the transformation of the young man about London into the social reformer who became the leader of the Labor Party. (In-cidentally, it also succeeds in that notoriously difficult literary task, the depiction of a happy marriage—Attlee's lasted 42 years.) Attlee has been easy to underesti-mate; but Churchill, who knew him well from his participation in Churchill's wartime coalition Cabinet, called him "an honorable and gallant gentleman, and a faithful colleague who served his country well at the time of her greatest need."

The Price of Power

BY SEYMOUR M. HERSH

THIS COLOSSAL EFFORT by an award-winning, former reporter for *The New York Times* attempts to show that the image of mastery and public service conveyed by Henry Kissinger in his memoirs is just one more skillful deception. Seymour Hersh, who spent years stalking his prey and conducting, reportedly, more than 1,000 interviews, examines the personal politics and motivations of the Nixon administration, the conduct of Kissinger-Nixon foreign policy and its results, fundamental issues of constitutional government and political ethics. He comes up with a portrait of an operation that lies somewhere between that of the Borgias and the Mafia. Mr. Hersh's sources—neither Mr. Kissinger nor Mr. Nixon would talk with him—were necessarily largely the disappointed and disgruntled. Nonetheless, no student of the Nixon "White House years" and the "years of upheaval"—to use words from the titles of Mr. Kissinger's volumes—will be able to ignore this book.

Modern Times

BY PAUL JOHNSON

THIS HISTORY of the world from the 1920s to the 1980s takes in all continents and major countries. Paul Johnson, the English journalist and historian, sees the history of modern times as in great part the history of how the vacuum formed by the decline of religion has been filled. "Nietzsche rightly perceived," Mr. Johnson writes, "that the most likely candidate would be what he called the 'Will to Power' "; and it is precisely the Will to Power that, since the end of World War I, has made this such an unsettled and bloody century. There is a great deal of intellectual pleasure to be had from this distinguished and provocative work of history.

Ironweed

BY WILLIAM KENNEDY

THE THIRD in a series of three Albany-set novels, following *Legs*, about the gangster Legs Diamond, and *Billy Phelan's Greatest Crime*, *Ironweed* concerns Billy Phelan's father, a former mechanic, major-league third baseman, lush and murderer, who is now back in Albany after 22 years on the lam. The time is the Depression, and the supporting cast includes crooks, bums, cons, gamblers and working stiffs. William Kennedy practices a tough-minded and defiant humanism that will leave many readers chastened but feeling good.

Chronicle of a Death Foretold

BY GABRIEL GARCÍA MÁRQUEZ

THE COLOMBIAN NOVELIST is best known for his *One Hundred Years of Solitude* and his 1982 Nobel Prize. His new novel, *Chronicle of a Death Foretold*, is a short, strange and ingeniously conceived metaphysical detective story in which the detective, García Márquez, reconstructs the events associated with a murder that occurred in a Caribbean town 27 years before. Thus, as a character in his own novel, the author interviews people who remember the murder, studies documents assembled by the court, accumulates many kinds of data—dreams, weather reports, gossip, philosophical speculation—and creates a chronicle of what happened. This murder will stand among the many in modern literature as one of the most powerfully rendered.

The Moons of Jupiter

BY ALICE MUNRO

THIS FOURTH COLLECTION of stories by the Canadian writer Alice Munro is her strongest yet. Witty, subtle, passionate, its protagonists are women nearing or in their 40's who are negotiating difficult domestic or sexual changes in their lives. Mrs. Munro's literary performance has little to do with situation and everything to do with character. Shrewd, amused, self-aware, her women are risk-takers, plucky, independent, sexually vibrant. Their intelligence beckons to the reader, who likes them not only for the dangers they pass through but for their alertness to the pleasure of the passage.

The Rosenberg File

BY RONALD RADOSH AND JOYCE MILTON

WERE JULIUS AND ETHEL ROSENBERG guilty of transmitting American atomic secrets to the Soviet Union in the 1940s, or were they cold-war scapegoats whose execution was a grave miscarriage of justice? From this definitive study of extensive government files opened under the Freedom of Information Act and from hundreds of interviews, the authors have developed the argument that both contentions are true—that Julius Rosenberg played a central role in a Soviet espionage ring and transmitted material he believed contained important atomic secrets, but that Klaus Fuchs, the English physicist, had already given those secrets to the Russians; that Ethel Rosenberg was not deeply involved in her husband's activities but knew about them; that the FBI was aware of her limited role; that some of the evidence against the Rosenbergs was questionable and probably false; that nearly all those involved—from the KGB to the FBI to some of the Rosenbergs' "defenders"—were willing to see them die for their own partisan interests.

The Anatomy Lesson
BY PHILIP ROTH

THIS IS THE THIRD PART of Philip Roth's fictional trilogy of Nathan Zuckerman, American Jewish novelist. In the first, *The Ghost Writer*, Zuckerman the beginner tastes critical approval without popularity; in the second, *Zuckerman Unbound*, he attains fame and wealth with *Carnovsky*, a novel like Roth's own *Portnoy's Complaint*; now, in *The Anatomy Lesson*, he suffers from internal demons and constant physical pain that may or may not have an organic base. In a succession of brilliant monologues, the hero portrays himself as a bankrupt writer, bereft of ideas, subject matter and self-confidence, but still bound to his profession as he is to his aching body. Despite the funny high and low comedy, this Zuckerman finale has had a mixed critical reception.

The Social Transformation of American Medicine
BY PAUL STARR

A MEDICAL-INDUSTRIAL COMPLEX of profit-making companies is already firmly established in American medicine and growing at a spectacular rate. Profit-making conglomerates own chains of hospitals, nursing homes, kidney dialysis centers, diagnostic laboratories, pharmacies, medical office buildings, ambulatory surgical centers, and shopping mall emergency centers. In this monumental study, Paul Starr describes what the change will eventually mean to physicians, who will lose control of the practice of medicine, and to patients, who will become mere customers for their services. Mr. Starr traces the roots of our contemporary health-care system to a changing culture and a shifting economy and makes its growth and development clear and comprehensible. This important book is written with wit, irony and great style.

Hugging the Shore

BY JOHN UPDIKE

THIS LARGE SELECTION of the essays and reviews John Updike has published alongside his novels, stories and poems over the past eight years stands beside his earlier collections, *Assorted Prose* (1965) and *Picked-Up Pieces* (1975), and documents his achievements as a man of letters. As before, Mr. Updike is concerned with the general conditions of cultural life as far as they can be deduced from the humanities. In the new collection he reviews anthropologists like Claude Lévi-Strauss, travelers like Jonathan Raban, historians like Isaiah Berlin, theologians like Karl Barth, actresses like Louise Brooks and Doris Day, literary critics, a philosopher, five poets and nearly every novelist on the scene except Norman Mailer.

1984

Editors' Choice

The Bourgeois Experience: Victoria to Freud.
Volume One: Education of the Senses
BY PETER GAY

IN THE FIRST of what Peter Gay promises will be at least five volumes of "history informed by psychoanalysis," facades are ripped away from the proper homes of the Victorian middle class to reveal fascinating sexual lives upstairs and down. People who were skeptical about Victorian virtue right along might have suspected all this, but Mr. Gay has ransacked diaries, letters, court files, medical logs, and books and read between the lines to find evidence for this entertaining and illuminating history. He sometimes expresses wonder at how little our forebears knew about sex as they started out in life, but he makes a powerful case that they learned quickly how to get in on the action.

Brothers and Keepers
BY JOHN EDGAR WIDEMAN

JOHN EDGAR WIDEMAN is a former Rhodes Scholar, a teacher of literature and the author of six novels. His brother, Robert, 10 years younger, is in a Pennsylvania prison serving a life sentence for murder. In this harrowing and eloquent book, the older brother sets out to explore the poor black environment of their youth to find how they turned out so different. His search leads him to the discovery of what an extraordinarily perceptive man his younger brother has become; the speech and presence of Robert Wideman in this book are unforgettable. But it also leads the author to rediscover the depths of racial prejudice and the ways society has of degrading and finally forgetting those it finds troublesome. Robert Wideman emerges as a man who knows who he is, but his older brother is not sure of himself now, and his doubts give rise to brooding, brilliant monologues about his own motives and feelings.

Dawn to the West: Japanese Literature in the Modern Era

BY DONALD KEENE

DONALD KEENE, the Columbia University expert on Japanese literature, is no stranger in Japan. These two massive volumes, essays on every aspect of Japanese writing since 1868, were translated into Japanese and published in Tokyo for scholars and students at the same time they appeared here. There is no comparable one-man treatment of Japanese literature in any language. Mr. Keene has mastered Japanese literary culture from inside and delivered it up in concrete, detailed accounts of a huge array of novels, stories, poetry, drama and criticism, all done in an easy style and his own independent voice. Eventually he will cover all of Japanese literature.

Deadly Gambits: The Reagan Administration and the Stalemate in Nuclear Arms Control

BY STROBE TALBOTT

THE GOAL of arms-control negotiators in the Reagan administration may not be reduction in nuclear weapons or even American nuclear superiority over the Soviet Union. From the account of the inside maneuvering over arms control given by Strobe Talbott, the biggest prize in the exhausting infighting among government agencies, principally the State and Defense Departments, seems to be simply Presidential preference for one side or the other. Behind his vivid presentation of the backbiting, backstabbing world of Washington politics, there is a somber lesson about what happens to nuclear arms control and foreign policy when the interest of the President is concentrated not on the substance of the matter but on what sounds good to Americans.

Him with His Foot in His Mouth and Other Stories
BY SAUL BELLOW

THEY ARE NOT precisely confessional, but the five recent stories in this collection are filled with more real people than anything else the Nobel Prize winner has written. There is rich laughter here and many sympathetic characters. Saul Bellow's own voice is clearly heard in most of them; he has leveled the maze and laid out all the clues to his lifetime enterprise, and a very intellectual project it is. But if it is tempting to read the stories as the closest we are likely to get to an autobiography from Bellow—an assortment of friends and relatives of the author from more than 60 years are transformed into fictional characters—that temptation should be given into carefully. For the ideas in the stories really add up to a reprise of Western intellectual civilization.

In Her Own Right: The Life of Elizabeth Cady Stanton
BY ELISABETH GRIFFITH

THIS YEAR'S presidential campaign, with Representative Geraldine Ferraro on a national ticket, would have warmed Elizabeth Cady Stanton's heart. Up to a point. Stanton undoubtedly would have felt the woman should have been at the top of the ticket, not second on it. In popular history and belief, Susan B. Anthony has long been seen as the principal nineteenth-century women's leader. But Elisabeth Griffith's well-rounded biography of Stanton makes a compelling case that she was at least the equal of Anthony and in most respects a good deal more radical. Her vigor, warmth and cantankerous humor come out strongly in this biography, and the battles she fought are fought again in a new and sympathetic light.

Life & Times of Michael K
BY J. M. COETZEE

IT IS SOUTH AFRICA, certainly. Michael K, who knows only what is emotional and obvious and has no capacity for abstractions or philosophy, is a victim of a cruel society, certainly. The official country is at war with a large part of its own people, certainly. Yet these certainties, added up, make up but a small part of the great story that emerges from J. M. Coetzee's short tale, in which small moral disclosures pile up from page to page until the book becomes an overwhelming indictment of the self-deceptions of human stupidity. Michael K is a man whose only sustenance, "the bread of freedom," in the end cannot be found. As in his earlier *Waiting for the Barbarians,* Mr. Coetzee proves himself an absolute master of moral fiction.

Lives of the Poets: Six Stories and a Novella
BY E. L. DOCTOROW

IN E. L. DOCTOROW'S sixth and subtlest work of fiction, half a dozen short stories are drawn together by a final novella that reveals the life and soul of the (fictional) writer of the stories and a great deal about the predicaments of modern man. In the light of the novella, passion and idealism surprisingly appear in the writer, whose own experiences among the culturati of New York echo those of the characters he has created in the stories. The many ironies created by Mr. Doctorow's reflexive method cut through laughter, grief, outrage and cynicism and lay open the heart of a man hungering for seriousness in a world that feeds mostly on cruelty and frivolity.

Machine Dreams
BY JAYNE ANNE PHILLIPS

THE MACHINE DREAMS are nightmares that pass from father to son and then, after both are dead, to daughter in this complex first novel in which family legends rise to the level of myths. The machines belong mainly to wars, the one the father survived and the one the son did not, but they are also the kinds of vehicles a deus ex machina rides. In this case, the reference is ironic, since the god never rescues the actors from fate. Their concerns are familiar, and the novel's thrilling shocks arise from ordinary moments that suddenly burst with deep meaning we had not anticipated.

The Memory Palace of Matteo Ricci
BY JONATHAN SPENCE

HOW DOES Jonathan Spence do it? A few years ago in *The Gate of Heavenly Peace,* he appeared to write about a handful of Chinese writers and delivered a whole revolution into his readers' imaginations. This time he builds on a little treatise on mnemonic arts written by a sixteenth-century Jesuit missionary and conjures up Ming-dynasty China and Europe during the Counter-Reformation. Here are Matteo Ricci, who went to China on his mission just 400 years ago, and the Emperor Wanli, along with flights of Oriental bureaucrats, scholars and artists and cohorts of cardinals, Vatican bureaucrats and European thinkers—all come robustly to life. They have never looked better. Mr. Spence is also a fine teacher; one leaves this crowd with more than a suspicion that in 400 years of intellectual and technological progress, we may have traded a richness of mind and memory for cold, spare rationalism.

The Quality of Mercy: Cambodia, Holocaust and Modern Conscience
BY WILLIAM SHAWCROSS

FROM 1978 TO 1980 Cambodia was the center stage of human horror, as the Khmer Rouge warred against their former allies, the Communists of Vietnam. Press reports told of the appalling starvation of the Cambodians. The British journalist William Shawcross looks closely at how people and international agencies responded to the crisis. Almost everyone but the International Committee of the Red Cross comes out as self-aggrandizing, misguided or incompetent in this telling, moving account. But what brought such a large world response to the crisis in the first place? In chapters that are bound to remain controversial for many years, Mr. Shawcross argues that, in just the right circumstances at just the right time, the world was suddenly reminded of the Holocaust of the Jews in Europe under the Nazis, and people responded as much to their memories as to what they knew of Cambodia.

The Unbearable Lightness of Being
BY MILAN KUNDERA

WITH CUNNING, wit and elegiac sadness, Milan Kundera, the celebrated Czechoslovak émigré writer, expresses the trap the world has become in this relentless novel about four people who are born of images in Mr. Kundera's mind—a doctor and his dedicated wife and a frivolous, seductive woman painter and her good, patient lover. The stories of this quartet, all of whom die or fade from the book, are engrossing enough. But this writer's real business is to find images for the disastrous history of his country in his lifetime. He uses the four pitilessly, setting each pair against the other as opposites in every way, to describe a world in which choice is exhausted and people simply cannot find a way to express their humanity.

Walt Whitman: The Making of the Poet

BY PAUL ZWEIG

PAUL ZWEIG, who died earlier this year, has made the first successful attempt to show the origins of *Leaves of Grass* and the poet who suddenly appeared in that 1855 volume and immediately became the ancestor of countless American voices. Using every scrap Whitman left, the testimony of hundreds of contemporaries, and newspapers and other publications of the age, Zweig is able to trace the growth of Whitman's conviction that he had a calling to become the orator of the American people. He re-creates a whole culture and then convincingly presents the absorption of that culture into one fascinating, powerful poet.

The War of the End of the World

BY MARIO VARGAS LLOSA

REVOLUTION IS NOT all it is cracked up to be. Mario Vargas Llosa's novel, based on a real millenarian uprising in northern Brazil in the nineteenth century, is such a powerful tale of adventure, peopled by such resplendent and horrifying characters, that it needs no moral—but it is hard to avoid that one. The revolutionary sect he creates seems to spring naturally from the basic tenets of Christianity and humanity's shared longing for freedom, but it becomes the enemy of order and the church, and it consumes itself. The passionate eloquence of the Peruvian novelist drives his story through history and across the world, but his own faith in reason is as clear as his vision of the rarity of individual freedom in a world threatened by the sleep of moral imagination.

With a Daughter's Eye: A Memoir of Margaret Mead and Gregory Bateson

BY MARY CATHERINE BATESON

THERE IS NO BIOGRAPHY quite like this one of Margaret Mead by her daughter. First, Mead, who had hundreds of close personal friends and did not want any of them to share that friendship with one another, is difficult to nail down. Also, Miss Bateson spends a good deal of her vivid narrative on her father, Gregory Bateson, like Mead and Miss Bateson herself a noted anthropologist, so her book is really about her relationships with two people. The result is not only a biography of Mead and Bateson but a warm story of growing up with two brilliant eccentrics and coming out of the experience a wise and strong person. The book is unique in that the author is as memorable in it as its twin subjects.

1985

Editors' Choice

The Abandonment of the Jews: America and the Holocaust, 1941–1945

BY DAVID S. WYMAN

WOULD THE REACTION be different today?" is David S. Wyman's question as he opens his inquiry into the response of Americans in the early 1940s to evidence that Hitler was exterminating the Jews of Europe. With exemplary clarity and thoroughness, the historian produces devastating evidence to show that the White House, the State Department, Congress and the military all resisted suggestions that they act to stop the mass murders or rescue the Jews. The Americans, along with the British, even expressed fear that the Nazis might change their policy and begin to expel Jews; representatives of both Governments feared a large influx of Jewish refugees into their nations. American Christian churches fell into nearly total silence, and even the American Jewish community, torn by bitter feuding, was ambivalent and timorous in lobbying for a rescue of the European Jews. Very few individuals, from President Roosevelt down, emerge with any credit from this searching and exhaustive study of official United States documents.

All Fall Down: America's Tragic Encounter with Iran
BY GARY SICK

GARY SICK, the staff member on Iran in the National Security Council during the Carter administration, gives a balanced, fair and convincing account of the Iranian crises of 1978–80. He analyzes carefully the shifts in American policy in the early '70s that left Washington a hostage to Teheran, and with shrewd and impartial insight into the characters of the top American officials involved, he reveals the internal struggles within the administration—first as the Shah's regime collapsed and then as the American Embassy and its personnel were captured shortly after the Ayatollah Khomeini began consolidating power. Mr. Sick's cool, sharp and restrained analysis suggests serious questions about how foreign policy is made, how far the United States can pursue global strategies and whether this country can do anything effective once the regime of an allied country becomes destabilized.

Common Ground: A Turbulent Decade in the Lives of Three American Families
BY J. ANTHONY LUKAS

COVERING A GREAT DEAL more than its subtitle suggests, this is a huge study of Boston in the 1970s, when it was under the pressure of court-ordered busing to achieve school desegregation. The three families J. Anthony Lukas focuses on include only a handful of the hundreds of people in a multi-layered account of the moral fabric of a city and the vastly different social universes of its neighborhoods. Eventually the turmoil surrounding the desegregation efforts is seen in the context of history, not just national history or that of Boston but the history of the little villages cities are made up of and in many cases even the histories of individuals.

Flaubert's Parrot
BY JULIAN BARNES

DRAWING GUSTAVE FLAUBERT out of hiding from behind his doctrine of impersonality in art, Julian Barnes has written a high literary entertainment. He calls it a novel, but it is a hybrid that combines biography, fiction and literary criticism, and the whole performance is done with great brio. As Mr. Barnes's hero, an English doctor, searches for trivia about Flaubert across France, a Flaubert who is anything but trivial is conjured up, and the world he so painstakingly constructed in his own fiction is amusingly stood on its head.

Mr. Barnes's novel richly parodies Flaubert and, parrotlike, uses his words and many free associations based on them to write a subversive biography of the great novelist. It is witty, prodigally inventive, warm and humane, and it would have infuriated Flaubert. Reading it, one can feel, perhaps share, the triumph Mr. Barnes must have felt in writing it.

Footsteps: Adventures of a Romantic Biographer
BY RICHARD HOLMES

THE FOOTSTEPS of the title are those of Richard Holmes following four, or perhaps a dozen, nineteenth-century literary heroes across Europe in four pocket biographies, of Robert Louis Stevenson, Mary Wollstonecraft (plus some Wordsworth), Shelley (along with an entourage) and the poet Gérard de Nerval (with another entourage, which includes Baudelaire). His own journeys also give us something like an autobiography—a wry picture of a gypsy scholar tracking down the identities of other people. There is something more here that is hard to define, but Mr. Holmes provides the key when he mentions at the outset that 10 years before, he had been writing a novel about a group of friends "caught up in May '68" in Paris. By the end of *Footsteps*, he has become a self revealed by its interaction with others, not only the dead quartet of writers but the many living people he encountered in his quest. His is the biography of a biographer defined by his own times.

House
BY TRACY KIDDER

MARKED BY CLARITY, intelligence and grace, this book about building a house is much more than that—it is the story of the clients and the architect and most of all the four craftsmen who actually built the structure outside Amherst, Mass. Most of these people, including the craftsmen, share backgrounds as upper-middle-class children of the '60s. This commonality and the choices that have molded their lives are like spiritual blueprints from which the house rises. The intellectual, moral and emotional issues that emerge from Tracy Kidder's narrative open the windows and doors of the house of a generation and let us look inside. The book reads like a fine old-fashioned novel that proceeds calmly to a conclusion that gives the reader deep pleasure.

Love Medicine
BY LOUISE ERDRICH

THERE ARE seven narrators and twice that many unforgettable characters in this lyrical first novel about an American Indian family in the Middle West. Miss Erdrich is a poet, and she uses the different voices to compose a cumulatively wondrous prose song filled with sorrow and laughter. In her hands the tawdry world of her heroes and villains becomes a shining place of baroque decay. Her writing is meticulous—every word and sentence is perfectly placed to achieve the effect she wants. The voices in this rich tale belong to characters who will not leave the imagination once a reader has let them in. *Love Medicine* is a brilliant debut.

Mr. Palomar
BY ITALO CALVINO, TRANSLATED BY WILLIAM WEAVER

IN THESE ADROIT and witty meditative fictions, if Mr. Palomar is a lens to let Italo Calvino look at the phenomena of the world, the lens often turns into a mirror that reflects the reflecting intellect back on itself. And if Mr. Palomar is discovering his place in the world through a series of disquisitions on visual experiences, cultural developments and the cosmos, those discoveries dissolve under his intellectual scrutiny. Calvino is on the high wires, on lines of thought strung out above the big international circus. What is impressive about *Mr. Palomar* is a sense of the safety net being withdrawn at the end, of beautiful, nimble, solitary feats of imagination being carried off not so much to dazzle an audience as to outface what Philip Larkin calls "the solving emptiness / That lies just under all we do."

Move Your Shadow: South Africa, Black and White
BY JOSEPH LELYVELD

JOSEPH LELYVELD first reported from South Africa for *The New York Times* in the 1960s, and he returned in the '80s. In an extraordinary feat of journalism, he reveals the advance of apartheid in appalling detail and uses a range of personal experiences with both blacks and whites that no white South African could duplicate to illustrate the petrifaction of South African society in the last 20 years. The force of the book comes from his determined adherence to the principle of reporting only the circumstances of his own life and his own experiences in the troubled nation. While his understanding of and sympathy with black South Africans are unsurpassed by any other white reporter's, he reveals a deep appreciation as well of the thinking and the fear of whites at many levels of the society.

The Old Forest and Other Stories
BY PETER TAYLOR

PETER TAYLOR'S best stories are like miniature novels—dense with observation and analysis. In this collection there are a number of the best, and the title story is as good as anything he has written. For many readers that means it is a great deal better than most writing being done now. His measured and civilized voice belongs to the age of John Cheever and John O'Hara and sounds wonderfully refreshing amid the current uproar. And while he is very much a Southern writer whose principal concerns are family relationships, there could hardly be a writer less Gothic or rhetorical. He is the artist of the normal. Set in large cities of the middle South, the 14 stories in this collection include several new ones and some early work like "Porte Cochere" and "The Scoutmaster."

The Periodic Table
BY PRIMO LEVI

PRIMO LEVI—best known for his two books about his imprisonment at Auschwitz during World War II, his liberation by the Soviet Army and his difficult return to his home in Italy—is a chemist, and his new book, translated by Raymond Rosenthal, reveals that for a chemist the periodic table of elements, the terror of so many students, is pure poetry. He titles the 21 pieces here "Argon," "Chromium," "Zinc" and so on. The essays are at once what he calls "confrontations with Mother-Matter," portraits of people, analytical "tales of militant chemistry" and imaginative reflections on social and political life. Such components are successfully integrated in this beautifully crafted book because in Mr. Levi's vision no aspect of nature is impermeable to human intelligence. As he considers the elements and human beings, he also fills in some gaps left in the two books about his Holocaust experiences, but there is much more here—a wealth of wisdom about human relationships and values and the beauty of the world.

1986

Editors' Choice

Arab and Jew: Wounded Spirits in a Promised Land
BY DAVID K. SHIPLER

ISRAEL HAS EXISTED with the West Bank, the Golan Heights and the Gaza Strip as part of its internal life longer than it existed without them. Since the Six Day War in June 1967 an entire generation has grown up to serve in the Israeli Army without ever having known the nation Israel originally was, in which questions of conscience were mostly ethnocentric. David K. Shipler, chief of the Jerusalem bureau of *The New York Times* from 1979 to 1984, examines the changes in the nation in the last 19 years. With freshness and originality he presents war and friendship, terrorism and intermarriage, social and sexual attraction and repulsion and many more contrasting topics in a wealth of narratives, anecdotes and conversations that are never hackneyed. Together, they form a subtle and revealing picture.

Arctic Dreams: Imagination and Desire in a Northern Landscape
BY BARRY LOPEZ

BARRY LOPEZ cannot wait to get up in the morning. What is so prodigious about him is not so much his impressive travels in the Arctic, but his happiness in them. No one else can go on and on so well with indefatigable pleasure about landscape, the sky and sea and especially about the riot of bird and

sand and sea life. He shoots for epiphanies, but he is good at summarizing scientific information too, and he gives fascinating glimpses of past travelers like
the fantastic sixth-century Irish monk St. Brendan, who explored the North Atlantic for seven years. Part rhapsody and part history, the book displays a mag-
nificently nonchalant assurance at times, and Mr. Lopez has dappled it with
footnotes that swing among his memories and afterthoughts and that are as interesting to read as his lyrical text.

Crossing the Line: A Year in the Land of Apartheid
BY WILLIAM FINNEGAN

A N EASY, conversational style and a talent for succinct characterization
and evocation of place make William Finnegan's account of a year spent
teaching in a Cape Town high school a vivid tale of South Africa's agony. Mr.
Finnegan, who is an American, recounts his experiences in a "colored" (mixed-
race) school in 1980, a year when mixed-race and black students all over the
Cape staged boycotts demanding better education. After the boycott was broken,
the author began to discover the ruthless efficiency of the government's
apartheid program, and in stories about his students and colleagues, officials and
ordinary citizens, he richly details the appalling power of the system.

FDR: The New York Years: 1928–1933
FDR: The New Deal Years: 1933–1937
BY KENNETH S. DAVIS

T HE SECOND and third volumes in Kenneth S. Davis's biography of
Franklin Delano Roosevelt promise that when he has finished, his work
will at least rival the histories of the New Deal written by Arthur M. Schlesinger
Jr., Frank Freidel and James MacGregor Burns. The volume on the years when
Roosevelt was Governor of New York has much greater sweep than its subtitle
suggests; it tells more effectively than anyone has yet done how the New Deal
was born in the battles among the remarkable people he assembled in his
"brains trust," and it shows what was happening to the whole nation in those critical times. Similarly, the highly dramatic volume on his first term as President,
rich in historical substance, political thought and character portraiture, is unmatched in the meticulous density of its material. Most impressive is the unfolding portrait of Roosevelt; chapter by chapter he becomes more complex,
even mysterious.

The Handmaid's Tale

BY MARGARET ATWOOD

IN THE REPUBLIC of Gilead the female population is divided into classes based on functions—the Marthas (houseworkers), Econowives (workers), Handmaids (childbearers), Aunts (thought controllers) and Wives. Men (the Commanders) run the nation. Margaret Atwood's cautionary tale of postfeminist future shock pictures a nation formed by a backlash against feminism, but also by nuclear accidents, chemical pollution, radiation poisoning, a host of our present problems run amok. Ms. Atwood draws as well on New England Puritan history for her repressive twenty-second-century society. Her deft sardonic humor makes much of the action and dialogue in the novel funny and ominous at the same time.

John Maynard Keynes: Volume One: Hopes Betrayed 1883–1920

BY ROBERT SKIDELSKY

THIS IS THE first biography of the economist to bring together the two sides of his early life—the formidable public person he was by the age of 30 and the circus rider of the social and homosexual whirl of Bloomsbury. The private Keynes in Robert Skidelsky's judicious account is by turns charming and insupportable, cutting and kind, snobbish and unpresuming, while the public one is serious, hardworking and crushingly intelligent. Mr. Skidelsky shows how the intellectual world of Cambridge University at the turn of the century, and the philosophy dominant there, formed the personality of the man who began life as a member of the elites among the elite, but who eventually challenged the established order and supplied the intellectual ammunition to bring it down.

The Life of Langston Hughes: Volume One: 1902–1941, I, Too, Sing America

BY ARNOLD RAMPERSAD

ARNOLD RAMPERSAD'S biography of Langston Hughes reads like a novel, quickly and steadily sweeping the reader—with appropriate itch, anger, fear, exhilaration, triumph or pain—through the poet's life up to the beginning of World War II. Here was a man who as a child was seldom with his mother and scarcely knew his estranged father. Raised by a grandmother, he was virtually on his own from the age of 13. Yet by the time he was 25, he had traveled and worked in Africa and Europe and mastered several languages and he was one of the best-known black poets in the United States. The book provocatively introduces the leading figures of the Harlem Renaissance, along with a galaxy of others in politics, literature and the arts. Its dramatic, sometimes painful, last chapter leaves one eager to see the next volume.

A Machine That Would Go of Itself:
The Constitution in American Culture
BY MICHAEL KAMMEN

MICHAEL KAMMEN'S anecdotal history is committed to a survey of sentiments at the grass roots about our most fundamental political document. It is hardly comforting reading, although it is often amusing. The bizarre ignorance of the Constitution among Americans for two centuries possibly explains the passionate fury with which political groups of every stripe have debated it. An illuminating exploration of literature comparing our written Constitution with the unwritten one of Britain leads Mr. Kammen to conclude that Americans have taken much pride, and little interest, in their form of government. Part of the problem is that people have thought of the Constitution as a perpetual motion machine that, once started, needs no further attention. Mr. Kammen's engaging book ought to shake that faith.

The Man Who Mistook His Wife for a Hat:
And Other Clinical Tales
BY OLIVER SACKS

WITH THE LUCIDITY and power of a gifted short-story writer, Oliver Sacks, an eminent neurologist, writes about two dozen patients who manifest striking peculiarities of perception, emotion, language, thought, memory or action. His decidedly original approach to neurological disorders—he writes like a philosopher-poet—is insightful, compassionate, moving and on occasion, especially when he plays naïve about neurological literature, infuriating. His eminently humane approach, and his willingness to take seriously the ordinary locutions people use to talk about their conditions, are entirely to his credit. There is no one else who writes about what used to be called simply "mental problems" with such understanding and such delightful literary and narrative skill.

Out of India: Selected Stories

BY RUTH PRAWER JHABVALA

THE 15 SHORT STORIES in this collection were chosen by Ruth Prawer Jhabvala from four volumes written over the years. In a long introduction she eloquently explains how the vast reality of India has come into the imagination of this woman who was born in Germany of Polish Jewish parents and who has lived most of her life in the subcontinent. Her milieu is middle-class and Hindu, and her stories are mostly domestic, but she has a fine satiric eye for the modern Westernized young people who scandalize their elders and for the ashrams where young and old go on spiritual quests. There is not a shoddy line or unnecessary word here; the book has the hallmark of balance, subtlety, humor and beauty.

A Perfect Spy

BY JOHN LE CARRÉ

A TENSE BALANCE between the narrative drive of the plot and the artfulness of the style makes this espionage novel perhaps the best in John le Carré's oeuvre. Many readers have come to expect Byzantine plotting in his fiction, but here the structure is straightforward, although in its vivid characterization and spiraling story line the novel is modeled on Dickens. But its greatest force derives from its autobiographical aspects. The protagonist, a spy named Magnus Pym, reveals a haunting picture of his father, Rick Pym, a tantalizing presence but not much of a father. It is his need to fill the void in himself created by his harrowing relationship with the vacant Rick that drives Magnus to the high-pressure world of spying. Mr. le Carré mines this vein deeply, creating parallelisms, symbols, psychological motivations and complex metaphors that echo and expand in this epitome of the literature of paranoia that is so exactly suited to our times.

The Progress of Love

BY ALICE MUNRO

MANY OF THE 11 short stories in this collection, by the Canadian writer Alice Munro, have the moral and historical density of other people's novels. They are remote from the techniques and ambitions of current experimental fiction and give us worlds so like our own that reading them is, at times, emotionally risky. The stories are unflinchingly and audaciously honest, uncompromising in their dissection of the ways in which we deceive ourselves in the name of love. The bleakness of the book's vision is enriched by Ms. Munro's exquisite eye, and ear, for detail. If life is heartbreak, it is also uncharted moments of kindness and reconciliation.

Roger's Version
BY JOHN UPDIKE

ITS TITLE SUGGESTS there might be very different versions of this story from the one told by its narrator, a professor of divinity, and clues planted in the text seem to warn the reader not to trust him, especially when he imagines in great detail the affair his wife is having with a graduate student in science (even as he is pursuing the young daughter of his own half sister). The unresolved enigma at the heart of John Updike's challenging novel makes the arguments the professor and the scientist, who is a fundamentalist Christian, have about faith and reality deep and disturbing. It also gives Mr. Updike's characteristic preoccupations with eroticism, theology, domestic realism and vivid physical description an illusory quality—as though the author is daring the reader to question the reality of his own perception of everyday life at least as acutely as he might doubt the existence of God or the reality of the unseeable, possibly unimaginable, world of physics that scientists so confidently manipulate.

Saints and Strangers
BY ANGELA CARTER

ANGELA CARTER'S VOICE is literary but not precious, deep but not difficult, funny without being superficial, and indifferent to formulas. The humor in the 8 stories (better to call them concoctions) in this volume is a blend of English distance and American wackiness. Like the poet in the story called "The Cabinet of Edgar Allan Poe," all the protagonists are historically grounded characters who have to live by "disordered wits" where "there is no reason for anything to be real." Lizzie Borden and Charles Baudelaire's mistress, Jeanne Duval, are among them. So are an Edwardian cook of magic soufflé and even Shakespeare's Puck, who, in a tale that slyly exposes and mocks our taste for the erotic, achieves one of the wickedest self-transformations in modern fiction.

The Vanished Imam: Musa al-Sadr and the
Shia of Lebanon

BY FOUAD AJAMI

M USA AL-SADR seems to display within a single life the full range of the Middle Eastern enigma. He was born in Iran, became the inspired leader of Lebanon's Shiite community and disappeared—he is presumed dead—on a visit to Col. Muammar el-Qaddafi's Libya in 1978 when he was 50 years old. In this impassioned, luminous book, Fouad Ajami, himself a Lebanese Shiite, who is a professor at the Johns Hopkins University, tells Sadr's story in a way that throws light on the pervasive ambiguity that is the political, religious and social condition of the Middle East. Perhaps only someone as subtle and sophisticated as Musa al-Sadr, who has been compared to Gandhi and Jesus but also to Rasputin, can be effective in seeking peace in such a situation. Mr. Ajami's story of his life and his people may give Americans a deeper understanding of Lebanon and the Middle East than any other book.

Velázquez: Painter and Courtier

BY JONATHAN BROWN

T HE LIFE of the great Spanish painter Diego de Velázquez was extraordinary, and Jonathan Brown has made it enthralling. The painter's astonishing ability to paint directly from life manifested itself when he was still a youth, and he quickly became not only the court painter to King Philip IV but the master of the King's collections, for which he acquired some of Europe's greatest art. His own most magnificent work was done at a time when his duties, and his strange, utterly fascinating quest to become ennobled, filled his days with anxiety, intrigue and terrible labor. Read in context, the pictures, often interpreted by critics and artists but never so well as by Mr. Brown, mean far more than ever before. In the plates of this book, by far the best ever devoted to Velázquez, they invite one into the brilliant depths of the painter's imagination and the triumphant struggle of his life.

Whites

BY NORMAN RUSH

O NE OF THE WHITES in black Africa depicted in the short stories included in this collection by a former codirector of the Peace Corps in Botswana says that absence of real commitment is what makes doing good overseas so attractive to Americans now, because—no matter what happens—the visiting whites know they have done their best. The failure of American idealism and technology is the underlying subject of all the stories. Most of Norman Rush's whites cannot shoulder "the white man's burden" anymore because they can't even lift up their own spirits; their loss of conviction is complete. But in two stories an American woman and a male dentist accept the full bounty of Africa's generosity, intelligence and vitality in very surprising ways.

Editors' Choice

An Arrow in the Wall: Selected Poetry and Prose
BY ANDREI VOZNESENSKY, EDITED BY WILLIAM JAY SMITH AND F. D. REEVE

RUSSIAN TRADITION is rich with poets who, like Pushkin, act as secret truth-tellers countering the official line. Andrei Voznesensky is deep in the Pushkin tradition when he writes about Caesar but means Stalin and about cruel Turkish janizaries who are really Russian soldiers. Nonetheless, what one feels powerfully in these poems and prose pieces from three decades is the poet's passionate love of his country and of Russian traditions. This is by far the best attempt to bring a Russian poet into a Western context; it is not possible to produce in English the extraordinary music of Mr. Voznesensky's language, but these translations, by a number of hands, reveal that the core of his meaning comes across very well, even without his linguistic virtuosity in Russian.

Beloved
BY TONI MORRISON

BY TURNS RICH, graceful, rough, colloquial, eccentric and lyrical, this novel about bondage and freedom lets us know American black slavery as those who experienced it did—in a parentless, childless and spouseless world where the sudden disappearance of people was quite legal. A survivor, Sethe, is trying to build a new life when the ghost of her little daughter, Beloved, appears. Ghosts are treated with the same magnificent practicality that transforms everything in this book, and it is the return of Beloved that allows other characters to reveal the pain of the past and Sethe to achieve a self-accepting peace. Toni Morrison's verbal authority compels belief; she blends a knowledge of folklore with a highly original treatment that keeps the reader guessing and discovering, right up to the last page.

The Bonfire of the Vanities
BY TOM WOLFE

TOM WOLFE'S first novel positively hums with energy. Mr. Wolfe thoroughly understands what he writes about in this big, bitter, funny book about New York City and its denizens: Wall Streeters, politicians, policemen, jailbirds, sleazy lawyers and con men in television and journalism. And he knows how to tell a story; the novel's pace is so fast it is like falling downstairs at times. His characters may lack depth and his attempts to make the reader hear their accents can be downright annoying, but this novel has scores of fine scenes, set pieces, a strong story line and some psychologically penetrating writing. Dozens of minor characters speeding along different tracks of an admirably complex plot are kept in perfect control while the major ones spiral in on one another toward the last explosive moment.

Chaos: Making a New Science
BY JAMES GLEICK

CHAOS, an unlikely name for a field of science, has emerged in the past 20 years from a collection of unsolved problems that originally attracted the attention of only a few scientists. In a mostly successful essay in popularization, James Gleick, a science reporter for *The New York Times*, has written a taut, exciting history of this now fashionable enterprise. His artful use of examples demonstrates the near ubiquity of chaos, from weather (and weather predicting) to the orbits of stars to the sporadic recurrence of plagues. He also draws deeper connections, most startlingly one between the science of chaos and the new mathematical field of fractal geometry. Clearly the masters of chaos have fun, and in this book the reader shares it.

The Counterlife

BY PHILIP ROTH

THE COUNTERLIFE turns on itself halfway through and reads itself front and rear, before and after, like a swing. The daring structure of Philip Roth's novel, in fact, is likely to make it continually surprising even on rereading. Returning here, and writing his own (posthumous) story, is Nathan Zuckerman, who was supposed to have been all wrapped up in the trilogy-plus-novella *Zuckerman Bound.* Zuckerman, himself a creator of Rothian characters, is really the creation of Peter Tarnopol, the novelist in *My Life as a Man,* we are assured. Are we to believe it? There are twists and turns in *The Counterlife* that disabuse us of easy belief; down its byways we hear all of Mr. Roth's fictions whispering to one another. His old themes and concerns are here, but now we understand them differently. But do we? Mr. Roth's sport with the nature of reality becomes an exhilarating contest for his reader.

The Embarrassment of Riches: An Interpretation of Dutch Culture in the Golden Age

BY SIMON SCHAMA

THE PANORAMA of seventeenth-century life in this history is as skillfully composed as the canvases of the great Dutch painters, reproductions of which march through the book by the hundreds, dazzling readers of Simon Schama's re-creation of an era when stupendous wealth flooded the Netherlands. But this is not a mere tale of riches. Mr. Schama explores the household and moral economy of the nation together; his quasi-anthropological description of historical behavior as social process is a vast emporium of the mental bric-a-brac making up the collective conscience of a people. This conscience was troubled by the ruptures wealth made in the restraints of Calvinist inhibition. The moral ambiguity of the culture plays over Mr. Schama's revelations of the lives of the burghers like light and shadow in a Rembrandt, turning these ceremonious and self-congratulatory figures into vivid dramatic actors in a magnificent pageant.

Evelyn Waugh: The Early Years 1903–1939

BY MARTIN STANNARD

THIS, the first of two volumes in a definitive biography, is a step toward the canonization of Evelyn Waugh as a master. It is a biography for the serious student, filled with relentless detail. But the detail reveals how Waugh cut his brightest jewels from the raw rubble of experience. Martin Stannard's analysis of early Waugh works, from reviews and travel pieces to novels and stories, uncovers brilliant forgotten passages. Mr. Stannard's thesis is that, from the outset, Waugh was a driving force, and the picture he draws is of the writer as self-promoter and tireless workman; Waugh had to earn every penny he spent, and he was no mean spender. He was an aristocrat manqué and an insufferable snob who liked to lampoon the unfortunate and mock innocence. Yet he was one of the most bewitching writers in the language, and it is precisely as writer that he comes to life here.

The Fatal Shore
BY ROBERT HUGHES

RICH WITH BIZARRE, winning characters, this history of Australia as a British penal colony in the eighteenth and nineteenth centuries has all the elegance one expects of Robert Hughes. In recent years many Australian historians have written about the penal system (it was once a neglected subject, if not taboo), but this is the most full-blooded, monumental book yet about the formation of a nation partly by people who had been deported from England to penal colonies in the southern island continent so harsh that some prisoners sought death sentences to escape them. These colonists' children, however, became rugged patriots, and through them something of the penal experience passed into the national character. Mr. Hughes tells a story that has epic range and the fascination of a great adventure.

The Ice: A Journey to Antarctica
BY STEPHEN J. PYNE

THE MAGNITUDE and variety of ice are staggering, as a reader of Stephen J. Pyne's meditative and exciting exploration of the earth's cold, white underside will soon discover. Mr. Pyne, a historian, brings to the book an encyclopedic acquaintance with the development of Western thought, an audacious scientific curiosity that led him to master disciplines most of us have never imagined and a commanding style; his writing dizzies the mind but conveys a view that interweaves physical science with humanistic perception. This is not a travel book or romantic excursion. Antarctica appears here as a force that changes the movement of the planet, and its ice mirrors the evolving intellectual life of mankind during the last few centuries. The implications of *The Ice* are vast.

Life and Death in Shanghai
BY NIEN CHENG

A N ABSORBING STORY of resourcefulness and courage, this personal account of the Chinese Cultural Revolution of the 1960s has magnificent moments of resistance to tyranny and stupidity, as well as bludgeoning recollections
of brutality and torture. Nien Cheng, who was imprisoned for more than six
years by Red Guards on trumped-up charges, and whose daughter was murdered, spares us none of the details. But her memoir is told in a voice of calm
defiance that leaves one all the more astonished at the ecstatic irrationality of
her persecutors, the mindlessness of the entire movement and the triumphant
spirit that made Mrs. Cheng an adversary hordes could not defeat. To read her
book is to experience humiliation, terror, despair, anger and hope and, at last, to
gain a deep understanding of the value of the sovereign individual in a mobbish
world.

The Making of the Atomic Bomb
BY RICHARD RHODES

T HIS MAJOR HISTORICAL synthesis brings to life the men who created
the nuclear era. Richard Rhodes, a novelist as well as the author of several
nonfiction books, has used the vast literature on the subject, along with his own
interviews of survivors, to create a work in which the makers of the new world
speak in their own voices. He resists writing a novelistic history, but instead
plumbs the natural depth and drama of this great story. He points no accusatory
fingers and avoids the apocalyptic sermons that mar many books on the atomic
bomb. The result is a book resonant with human wisdom, and folly, that makes
us look at ourselves, our century and our future directly, soberly and, surprisingly, with a glimmer of hope.

More Die of Heartbreak
BY SAUL BELLOW

T HE CALAMITOUS WIT of *The Adventures of Augie March* and *Herzog*
is back in this refreshingly youthful novel about people rearranging one another's lives as they attempt to rescue their own. Here the relationship between
a 35-year-old citizen of the world and his uncle, a world-famous scientist who has
married a woman 20 years his junior, is the vehicle for exposing widening circles
of betrayal, deceit and conspiracy over sex and money—the stakes in a kind of

cosmic con game. Amid the laughter there is Saul Bellow's customarily serious purpose, the mind of this writer always stands outside itself, mercilessly examining its own working and tracking the great issues of the age. The comedy runs deep here because the characters, even the most brutally venal, have a tragic capacity.

Staring at the Sun
BY JULIAN BARNES

THE MAGIC of this brilliant novel is masked by the almost reportorial language Julian Barnes uses to trace the life of a woman who, at the age of 100, comes to a breathtaking literary epiphany in the next millennium. The book flashes between extremes of enchantment and disenchantment as Mr. Barnes breaks the barriers of conventional time and genre and creates characters from ideas and language. Italo Calvino once said the reader, knowing the future, is wiser than the writer. Mr. Barnes has taken the risk of leaping into the future and pre-empting the reader's advantage. A disenchanted God and an enchanted technology (a computer called The Absolute Truth) enter his heroine's life, but it is she who is the true sorceress, one who escapes her "second-rate life" and shows us a spectacular vision that turns out to be not mere trickery, but reality.

The Truly Disadvantaged: The Inner City, the Underclass, and Public Policy
BY WILLIAM JULIUS WILSON

IN THEIR ANALYSES of the relentless growth of a black inner-city underclass in spite of War on Poverty and Great Society programs, both liberals and conservatives have misread the basic structural changes in the American economy during the past 20 years, according to William Julius Wilson, a University of Chicago sociologist. His new book, by far the best exploration of the problem, demonstrates that it is the loss of traditional jobs in cities that has created the present crisis. No government program to date has addressed the jobs question meaningfully. His own broad policy agenda stresses a tight labor market and general economic growth along with European-style family allowances and increased investment in child care. Some may disagree with that program, but Mr. Wilson's study of this cancerous poverty is totally convincing—and chilling.

Veil: The Secret Wars of the CIA 1981–1987

BY BOB WOODWARD

T HE UPROAR over this book's account of a deathbed interview of William Casey by Bob Woodward tended to make it seem a sensational piece of work when it was published in October. In fact, its few sensational revelations are not what is most compelling about it. *Veil* is a penetrating, profane, illuminating portrait of the American intelligence community. This is not historical archeology, but real-time intelligence, the best look we are likely to have for a long while inside this strange business, and into the lives and motivations of its practitioners. Obviously one can question whether Casey was really letting Mr. Woodward in on the truth in many cases or merely using him; but in most of the situations he writes about Mr. Woodward exposes the reality of the intelligence world, and his book is as engrossing as any spy thriller.

World's End

BY T. CORAGHESSAN BOYLE

A LIVELY CAREER that had produced mostly superior literary horseplay in language-intoxicated works since the late 1970s is transformed by *World's End*, a novel that indicates T. Coraghessan Boyle has no foreseeable limits as a writer. In this story that pulls together two worlds 300 years apart, there are dozens of characters—Indians, merchants, hippies, many others—who come fully to life not as clowns or victims, but as agents in Mr. Boyle's visionary treatment of power, manipulation and treachery. There is a ceaseless reaching for broader contexts. The themes Mr. Boyle develops as his story shuttles between epochs make us grasp in new terms their connection with the American social and political experiment. His mastery of history is the secret of the accomplishment here. Mr. Boyle has lost none of the qualities that marked him a witty writer before, but now he has challenged his own disengagement; passion, need and belief breathe with striking force and freedom through this smashing good novel.

Editors' Choice

Arabesques

BY ANTON SHAMMAS, TRANSLATED BY VIVIAN EDEN

DESPITE its autobiographical qualities, this book, by a Christian Arab who writes lyrical Hebrew and considered himself an Israeli, is called a novel by its author perhaps because its real aim is the discovery, or creation, of a self, not merely the story of a self already made. In an arabesque of movement between two voices called the Teller and the Tale, Anton Shammas conducts a hunt for a heritage that rivals anything in Dickens. He creates a world in which the present searches into the past even as the past peers into the future. His tale is set in a time of vengeful troubles when state security, religion and economics dictate death; suspicion, bravery and betrayal are everywhere; and violence is as common as climate. But Mr. Shammas is a true artist who keeps his heart clean and his eye clear, so that these conditions rise around us naturally as we read.

Battle Cry of Freedom: The Civil War Era

BY JAMES M. MCPHERSON

JAMES M. MCPHERSON'S BOOK—eloquent but unrhetorical, scholarly but not pedantic, succinct and comprehensive at the same time—may be the best volume ever published about the Civil War. Everything Mr. McPherson touches drives his narrative forward, and yet there is not a hint of ostentation from the first sentence to the last. He makes the war steal up on the reader the way it did on the nation, teaching the most important and dreadful truth of all—that no more than ordinarily sinful men and women, and able and patriotic politicians, and a nation enjoying unrivaled prosperity, can make irretrievable and deadly blunders. It is the timeliest possible lesson for us now, and we get it here from a great teacher.

Bernard Shaw: Volume One, 1856–1898: The Search for Love
BY MICHAEL HOLROYD

THERE SHOULD BE no need of another biography of George Bernard Shaw for perhaps a century, when the passing of time may require one. In this first of three projected volumes, Michael Holroyd gives us the child Shaw in Dublin, Shaw the struggling novelist and ghostwriter, the indefatigable letter writer, the virgin philanderer, Shaw the champion of Ibsen and the perfect Wagnerite—and all this before he hits his stride as a playwright. And, what is most important, Mr. Holroyd has got Shaw's intrusive fingers, which have been everywhere in previous accounts, out of his own life story, and he has written his book in his own admirably clear and concise style, free of Shavian echoes.

A Brief History of Time: From the Big Bang to Black Holes
BY STEPHEN W. HAWKING, ILLUSTRATED BY RON MILLER

PHYSICS in the twentieth century is a tale of two revolutions. Einstein taught us that gravity, the weakest of nature's forces, is best described as a warp in space-time. And at the level of nuclear particles, quantum mechanics turned nature into a game of probability. Stephen W. Hawking of Cambridge University, who has survived Lou Gehrig's disease for more than two decades, has been a world leader in the effort to bring these two provinces together. In a jaunty and absolutely clear little book, he shares ideas about the universe, its origins and its fate, with everyone who can read, along with some provocative revelations of his own motivations, hopes, mistakes and prejudices. His book is a rare sharing of confidence by a scientist with uncommon courage, a dazzling vision and an impish sense of humor.

A Bright Shining Lie: John Paul Vann and America in Vietnam

BY NEIL SHEEHAN

IF ONE BOOK captures the Vietnam War on the Homeric scale, this is it. Neil Sheehan tells the story of the war through the focus of John Paul Vann, an army officer who faced down South Vietnamese politicians and American generals to expose the corruption that undermined our efforts and later was President Nixon's civilian adviser in Vietnam until he was killed in a helicopter crash in 1972. It is a dramatic device that lets Mr. Sheehan bring the very palpable feel of the war to us with passionate power—especially after, halfway through this long book, he surprises us with the revelation that Vann was not only brave, resourceful and incorruptible, but also selfish and duplicitous. The war story and Vann's story do not fully overlap, so the book is a montage, and what a montage it is.

Coming of Age in the Milky Way

BY TIMOTHY FERRIS

WITH A LYRICAL FLAIR Timothy Ferris recounts humanity's growing knowledge of the universe from the earliest cosmologies to the burst of discoveries of the twentieth century, presenting the story as the consummate human adventure. He also reveals enough of the arrogance and foolishness of scientists along the way, and of the ignorance, panic and prejudice of rulers, religious leaders and ordinary people, to make us understand that genius is sometimes fed by jealousy, and scientific progress sometimes measured by failure. Even though it is feverish and breathless toward the end, where it deals with a bewildering array of new sciences and discoveries, this book is a glorious adventure for the reader.

Dictionary of the Khazars: A Lexicon Novel in 100,000 Words

BY MILORAD PAVIC, TRANSLATED BY CHRISTINA PRIBICEVIC-ZORIC

THIS EBULLIENT and generous celebration of the reading experience should be read just about any way except cover to cover. Milorad Pavic assembles not one but three dictionaries (Christian, Islamic and Hebrew), in which each entry is a story about a lost people who lived in the Balkans 1,000 years ago. With its chronologically disturbed entries and cross-referencing, it looks complex but surrenders easily to any reconstructed reading you choose. From this feast of folkloric anecdotes and legends, you make your own story, or hundreds of them. And what stories they are, about such things as a hen that lays "time eggs," seasons that contain two years going in opposite directions, dream hunters who plunge into other people's dreams and purloin bits of them and a man who turned his soul inside out and slipped it on like an inverted glove. The novel gives a tantalizing life-after-death illusion of an inexhaustible unending text.

Libra

BY DON DELILLO

THE RICHEST NOVEL so far by Don DeLillo pitches into the history of the assassination of President Kennedy from angles that at first disorient us and finally leave us feeling we have understood something—about ourselves and history and the nature of perception—that can only be grasped from history on the margins, what people don't want to know. Mr. DeLillo has a merciless ear for language and a mastery of people's elliptical speech that allow him to turn commonplace moments into the work of genius. It is the accumulation of those moments that makes his portraits of Lee Harvey Oswald and many others moving and frightening, and the Kennedy murder as tragic and dramatic as are the catastrophes of the great classical tragedies, but with an entirely American twist.

Love in the Time of Cholera

BY GABRIEL GARCÍA MÁRQUEZ, TRANSLATED BY EDITH GROSSMAN

THIS SHINING and heartbreaking novel may be one of the greatest love stories ever told. Inspired by the long pursuit of Gabriel García Márquez's mother by his father, it is the tale of a vow of love that takes 51 years to fulfill. Writing with impassioned control and out of a maniacal serenity, the author creates language at once classical and familiar, opalescent and pure, that is able to praise and curse, laugh and cry, fabulate and sing and soar. Mr. García Márquez redeems the silences of history about a Caribbean haunted by centuries of war and disease that have brought so appallingly many people down. This may be the only way to write about love; without the darkness there might be romance, erotica, social comedy, soap opera—all also present in this book—but not the

Big L. There is nothing like the final chapter, symphonic, sure in dynamics and tempo, moving us unerringly among hazards of skepticism and mercy to an end that makes us realize this novel can return our worn souls to us.

The Magic Lantern: An Autobiography
BY INGMAR BERGMAN, TRANSLATED BY JOAN TATE

IT IS NOT AUTOBIOGRAPHY in the usual sense. For instance, there is much less about films than you might expect, even though Ingmar Bergman is the most thoroughly artistic filmmaker ever. And there is not much about his wives or other lovers, nor about his children. But there are gripping revelations, especially about his childhood, told in an unrelentingly honest manner. It is a random, anecdotal, unchronological book that gives you a picture of a highly emotional and not very adaptable soul. It holds you as many of his films do, and his story deals in totally unpredictable ways with a life filled with maladies and rages as well as with an intense love of theater. As in many of his films, by the end he has revealed things you may find it discomforting to know and a central character whom you may not like but who is stamped into your imagination.

Original Intent and the Framers' Constitution
BY LEONARD W. LEVY

THOSE WHO have been hearing a great deal about the original intention of the Framers of the Constitution in the past decade, and certainly those conservatives who have insisted on limiting interpretation to "original intent," will be surprised by this lively book by a leading constitutional historian. With rigorous scholarship and vigorous wit, Leonard W. Levy demonstrates that the Framers themselves did not regard their debates as the final word on the meaning of the Constitution; they expected the Republic to develop naturally as it grew. Mr. Levy uses his fine analytical powers, his crackling humor and the gifts of a superb teacher to help us understand, and take comfort in, the fact that judges must go right on interpreting the spacious words of the Constitution as they have always done.

Parting the Waters: America in the King Years 1954–63
BY TAYLOR BRANCH

TAYLOR BRANCH has reached into the crevices of history where much of the change in the nation occurred unnoticed to produce a sweeping history of the beginnings of the civil rights movement. To be sure, there are moments of high drama that will be familiar to most readers, remembered by many—the bus boycott in Montgomery, Ala., the Selma march, the byzantine negotiations between Attorney General Robert Kennedy and J. Edgar Hoover over wiretapping the Rev. Martin Luther King Jr. But what accounts for the power of Mr. Branch's book is the knowing, careful buildup of little human dramas, the heroism, determination, pettiness and bewilderment behind the great campaigns. People who were involved in the movement will come upon scenes they witnessed, battles they were part of, to find them brilliantly illuminated. Mr. Branch's book deepens, expands and fulfills the memories of many of us and the history of a time of great change in the nation.

The Rise and Fall of the Great Powers: Economic Change and Military Conflict from 1500 to 2000
BY PAUL KENNEDY

PROFESSIONAL HISTORIANS now tend to abjure the notion that we can learn from history, but Paul Kennedy has produced a work of almost Toynbeean sweep that not only is relevant to our times but is clearly meant to be read by policy makers. As he surveys the rise and eclipse of Spain, France and England through 400 years and the rise of America, Mr. Kennedy avoids determinism and argues that it is always political skill that accounts for the maintenance of hegemony; the failure of shrewd political intelligence is the principal reason for the decline of great nations. His scholarship is great, his eloquence powerful and his argument convincing. He by no means endorses notions of the inevitable decline of the West; he poses a challenge to American leaders that they can meet, although he seems not entirely confident they will.

Stories in an Almost Classical Mode
BY HAROLD BRODKEY

HAROLD BRODKEY'S considerable reputation rests mainly on his stories that have appeared over the past 25 years in *The New Yorker*, and they make up the bulk of this book. Mr. Brodkey's gifts are remarkable even though they often cause pain to the reader. For he is a great protractor; his sentences often seem interminable, and the reader comes away from them exhausted. But his efforts to feel deeply are often palpable and tremendous. The dominant theme of almost all the stories is the child's vision of the world and its people, and when the vision is realized it is often infused with a horrified pity. Mr. Brodkey does not recollect in tranquillity, but in a kind of poetic fury. Yet the last story is a kind of gentle apocalypse, and it seems right to end a book that tries to make sense of a frantic world with a Hawthorne-like tale of the end of that frantic world.

The Tenants of Time
BY THOMAS FLANAGAN

THIS MASTERLY historical novel is centered on an Irish village for half a century up to 1908, but it is a novel of the world and time and there are scenes in London, Paris, Dublin, Venice, Chicago, and literary references that reach back to myth and forward infinitely. It teems with hundreds of characters and stories within stories and is told in a vast choir of voices, each distinct and eloquent. All these appealing and annoying and strange and familiar characters are seeking to recover their own past. By the end we tend to agree with them that history cannot be captured and yet we have to acknowledge that Thomas Flanagan has in fact just written it, in a magnificent piece of fiction. There is scarcely a single assumption any reader will come to this book with—whether about historical fiction or the history of England and Ireland or the proper conduct of great Victorian women—that will not be shaken to the core.

Where I'm Calling From: New and Selected Stories
BY RAYMOND CARVER

SINCE 30 of these 37 stories have appeared in other collections, presumably the intention was to invite re-evaluation. The point is well taken. It turns out that Raymond Carver, who died this year, was not the minimalist he is said to be, but stands squarely in the line of American realism. His stories create meaning through form, and the best of them are works of great conceptual beauty. Through the often bleak lives of his characters, he evokes a bafflement that does not render an absence of meaning but an awkwardness in the face of meaning. His is an attempt to create a hush, not to achieve silence, but to hear better. What happens most powerfully and often in the stories is the imagining by one character of another character's life, as if the replication of one's own life in another could rescue one from the terrors of randomness or help one find the germ of myth in unstructured experience. That expresses the rationale of this writer's artistic practice, and his fiction transforms our perception. We finally see in it the point made by Henry James, that beauty is the form of address made by the world to the human soul.

Editors' Choice

Billy Bathgate

BY E. L. DOCTOROW

A STORY of a 15-year-old boy's journey to adulthood with plenty of cliffhang-ing adventure, *Billy Bathgate* is E. L. Doctorow's shapeliest novel. In the Bronx of the 1930s Billy links up with the legendary mobster Dutch Schultz. Schultz, who becomes something of a capricious parent to the boy, is one of many characters who walk right off the page. Mr. Doctorow has the ability to en-compass events in their entirety; the novel is packed with complex and oddly beautiful street scenes, filled with grime and color. Billy, the narrator, may be unnaturally eloquent, but the reader who grants Billy his gift of language is re-warded with passages of writing so intense and vivid that the story is wholly trust-worthy and compelling.

Citizens: A Chronicle of the French Revolution

BY SIMON SCHAMA

SIMON SCHAMA challenges enduring prejudices with prejudices of his own in this provocative and stylish account of the first few years of the French Revolution. But above all he tells a story—with baroque eloquence and rococo sparkle. In his thesis, the ancien régime was progressive, not reactionary, and the Revolution became a holy war in which personal scores became politi-cal causes and the joy of living gave way to the joy of watching other people die. Mr. Schama is at his most powerful when denouncing the Revolution's dependence on killing for political ends. The Reign of Terror of 1793, he argues, was merely the heady stirring of freedom of 1789 with a higher body count. Although this grand argument is exaggerated and readers who want to see the Revolution's positive side must read a different work, *Citizens* is a most intelligent book.

Federico García Lorca: A Life
BY IAN GIBSON

IT TOOK IAN GIBSON almost 20 years of research to produce his classic biography of the Spanish Civil War's most gifted victim. He goes to the heart of Federico García Lorca's explosive genius in theater, poetry and music and captures the chiaroscuro of his life as no one else has done. Moreover, Mr. Gibson sees Spanish culture from the inside and gives the reader a sense of Spanish life that is utterly real. He traces three intertwining threads of Lorca's life—religious belief, sexuality and social concerns—and demonstrates that his searing criticisms of society were inseparable from his religious and sexual iconoclasm. Mr. Gibson is disarmingly candid about the impossibility of always discovering the truth, but his account of the poet's life, and of the political murder that ended it, rings true.

Foucault's Pendulum
BY UMBERTO ECO

BRILLIANTLY TRANSLATED by William Weaver from Umberto Eco's Italian, this novel is an intellectual triumph. Its pages are crammed with information—appropriately, since Mr. Eco is a semiotician, a professor of signs, codes and hidden meanings. No one should know as much as he does, but he shares it all—mountains of learning sculptured into grand landscapes on which the ultimate conspiracy, one to synthesize all conspiracies, is played out by bands of modern-day Knights Templar, Rosicrucians, Masons, Jesuits, Nazis and diabolicals of many stripes who are trying to seize not power over the earth but the power of the planet itself. Mr. Eco fakes nothing. The novel teases, amuses, baffles and enchants one, but every detail is authentic. *Foucault's Pendulum* is an encyclopedic detective story playfully constructed by a master, manipulating his own invention—a long, erudite joke.

From Beirut to Jerusalem

BY THOMAS L. FRIEDMAN

THOMAS L. FRIEDMAN, who has won two Pulitzer Prizes, reported on Lebanon and Israel from 1979 to 1988, first for United Press International and then for *The New York Times*. This book, the most intelligent account of those years in the Middle East one is likely to find, is a story of how the past cripples the present. In Beirut Mr. Friedman, Pandemonium's resilient correspondent, reveals a surreal world filled with bizarre episodes always involving death. But he never loses his sharpness or humor. In Israel he becomes introspective, mulling over his role as an American Jew who dislikes some Israeli policies, but that does not impede him from giving the most persuasive, concise analysis of Israel's political paralysis. Mr. Friedman is obsessive, but not irritating—his stories are too astonishing, and he is too engaging for that.

Harold Macmillan: Volume One: 1894–1956, Volume Two: 1957–1986

BY ALISTAIR HORNE

THIS MOST READABLE and enjoyable biography of a man who in his long parliamentary career underwent an almost complete change of public character is particularly good on the subtleties of Harold Macmillan's introverted, elusive nature. Alistair Horne's account of the lifelong affair Macmillan's wife began early in their marriage, with one of his Tory Party associates, is especially moving. It explains a great deal about Macmillan's loneliness and the persona he carefully created. Mr. Horne also reveals the sources of Macmillan's liberal social ideas and deftly traces his remarkable diplomatic career during World War II. The story of his tenure as Prime Minister, when he presided over Britain's retreat from world power, is a mirror of a nation. Macmillan lived 92 years, most of them near the heart of power, and Mr. Horne's biography has the sweep of a century that transformed the world.

A History of the World in 10½ Chapters

BY JULIAN BARNES

POST-MODERNIST but accessibly straightforward, Julian Barnes's fifth book may seem less a novel than an assembling of fictions and essays. This comedy of ideas has much to do with transforming journeys—from the story of Noah through one about a young woman who sets to sea on a raft to escape nuclear Armageddon and another about a film star re-creating a missionary's disastrous trip down a Venezuelan river to an account of an astronaut who finds God in space and returns to earth to find what he thinks are Noah's remains. The centerpiece is a luminous meditation on Géricault's painting *The Raft of the Medusa* in which the picture of the doomed craft emerges as a transcendent allegory. The many stories here are given their dominant tone, and humor, by an undercurrent of gentle, self-reflective irony. The book demystifies its subjects and mocks its own ambition; it is a playful, witty gathering of conjectures by a humanist who loves ideas.

How War Came: The Immediate Origins of the Second World War, 1938–1939
BY DONALD CAMERON WATT

AFTER FOUR DECADES of research Donald Cameron Watt has written a diplomatic history in the grand style, a masterly study of European diplomacy during the year preceding Hitler's invasion of Poland in 1939. There is much to be learned about folly in this tale of how British hesitation, French ambiguity, blind Soviet suspicions, Italian vanity, American fecklessness and the slippery particularism of Eastern European states thwarted containment and let a malevolent Hitler hurl the world into war. Mr. Watt affirms that individuals count in history and gives sharp portraits of every politician and diplomat of any significance from all countries in what is a veritable biographical dictionary of prejudice, delusion, selfishness, venality and moral corruption. This book leads to serious reflection on the deep obligation of society to choose its leaders wisely.

If the River Was Whiskey
BY T. CORAGHESSAN BOYLE

T. CORAGHESSAN BOYLE'S third collection of short stories has all the linguistic acrobatics and hip, erudite audacity one expects from this author. He lampoons our most terrible fears and ridicules our cupidity, racism and insensitivity. His imaginative leaps and somersaults are often breathtaking. He is fluent in a vast number of slick American dialects and, being a four-star general of hyperbole, he creates a parade of outsize characters who are fun, often hilarious. But two of these stories give something more. One is an eloquent love story about the redemptive powers of water, and of love. And the title story, about a boy and his alcoholic father, is the most powerful and poignant Mr. Boyle has ever written. He evokes the shared pain of these two people with a sure hand, and we come away with a deep respect for the author.

A Peace to End All Peace: Creating the Modern Middle East 1914–1922

BY DAVID FROMKIN

THERE HAS BEEN a great deal of historical research into the present-day Middle Eastern situation, but now David Fromkin has pulled it all together in a single book that sums up everything cogently but not simplistically. Although it is based solely on English-language sources, it is about the breakup of the Ottoman Empire at the close of World War I and its consequences for the Western powers, the Soviet Union and the Middle East. He demonstrates how Britain's obsession with maintaining its routes to India and keeping Russia out of the Middle East led to the creation of a political map of that region that is remarkably close to the one we know today. He mistakenly gives Winston Churchill far too central a role in all this, and he wrongly reads pessimism into the political thinking of the British at the time. But this outstanding book puts most pieces of the Middle East puzzle into place in a way that no one volume has done before.

The Remains of the Day

BY KAZUO ISHIGURO

THIS STRIKINGLY ORIGINAL novel by a young Japanese-British writer is a beguiling comedy of manners that imperceptibly becomes a heart-rending study of personality, class and culture. A straitlaced butler makes an obliging narrator as he reveals in wry and funny ways aspects of his character he would try to hide if he could even recognize them. Kazuo Ishiguro's command of the butler's corseted idiom is perfect in the progressive revelation of unintended ironic meaning. Underneath what the butler says are a moving series of chilling revelations about his own buried life and, by implication, a critique of the social machine of Britain at a time (1956) when the nation has just lost its world power. With affection, humor, irony, compassion and understanding, Mr. Ishiguro presents the butler—and Britain, its politics and culture—from every point on the compass.

The Satanic Verses

BY SALMAN RUSHDIE

SALMAN RUSHDIE is a storyteller of prodigious powers; in this novel he draws on resources ranging from Homer to Joyce to *Saturday Night Live*. His central characters—Gibreel, the angel Gabriel turned satanic, and Chamcha, a hapless victim with horns and a tail—fall from an unlikely heaven to an unlikelier hell in Bombay and London. But their real world is in nightmares, the dreams of Gibreel that make up the spinoff narratives that keep the novel whirling. And the tale of Chamcha and his father forms a novel within the novel. In the imaginative avalanche of stories that fill the book Mr. Rushdie probes our ability to conjure up monstrous descriptions of one another, to create monsters in fact. At its strongest, it is burdened with history and politics; the most vibrant scenes are those in which the author looks history in the eye, scenes of expatriation and political exile in which the magical veil Mr. Rushdie throws over the whole book does not conceal the hard realism underneath.

The Shawl

BY CYNTHIA OZICK

IN THE TWO STORIES in this brief volume Cynthia Ozick looks deeply into the soul of perhaps the most disturbing character she has ever created and pulls off the rare trick of making art out of what repels us. In one story, which brings the Holocaust as close as possible to the claustrophobia and absorption of a fairy tale, a woman watches Nazi concentration camp guards kill her infant daughter. In the next, Ms. Ozick explores the connections among idolatry, maternity and philosophy as the woman—now old and demented in Miami—makes a relic of her dead baby's shawl. The story of this brilliantly realized character is excruciating but not depressing; Ms. Ozick's art mediates chaos and lights the night of the soul with flashes of insight about culture and memory, and with humor. If she imagines here the worst that can happen, she also reminds us that history often proves to have the darkest imagination of all and that there are lives that put paranoia to shame.

Editors' Choice

Biting at the Grave: The Irish Hunger Strikes and the Politics of Despair

BY PADRAIG O'MALLEY

TEN IRISH REPUBLICAN Army members in a Northern Ireland prison—including Bobby Sands, who was elected to the British Parliament in the midst of his ordeal—died in hunger strikes in 1980–81. Their macabre enthusiasm for the ancient art of dying for Ireland produced incalculable results that continue to ripple through British and Irish politics and life. In an eloquent and haunting book, Padraig O'Malley, who was born in Dublin and now teaches in Boston, makes the fanaticism of these men and their supporters, the obdurate and morally discredited tactics of the British government and the hopeless combat of the Protestant and Roman Catholic factions in the Northern Ireland struggle explicable, and exposes the politics behind it.

The Complete Poems of Anna Akhmatova

EDITED BY ROBERTA REEDER

ANNA AKHMATOVA —the high priestess of Russian poetry—saw her husband shot, her son imprisoned twice by Stalin, her work banned in the 1930s and late '40s, and she knew few peaceful moments before her death in 1966 at the age of 76. To her the role of the poet was to remember and bear witness. Conscience, repentance, suffering have an effortless place in her great poetry and testify to the purgation she underwent in her work. Sonorous, calm, deliberate in movement, her Russian has no English equivalent, but in this admirably restrained and accurate translation, by Judith Hemschemeyer, sense and message strike with all the weight of the original. To render the entire corpus of such a poet into proportioned, forceful English is a remarkable achievement, and so are these two beautifully made volumes.

Friend of My Youth
BY ALICE MUNRO

THE STORIES of Alice Munro—a hugely gifted chronicler of the lives of people of habitual spiritual frugality in Ontario—have made her one of the world's great totemic writers. In this, her sixth collection of stories, the country has darkened and the principal characters are older than those in previous books; they are now baffled and bitter survivors of seismic cultural upheavals. But these troubled men and women are compulsively curious and the lucky have moments of near epiphany that sparkle through life's malevolence. Each story is a marvel of construction, with parallel narratives of inquiry and introspection. Ms. Munro, who has deepened the channels of realism, is a writer of extraordinarily rich texture; her imagery stuns or wounds and her sentences stick to the rough surfaces of our world.

Lawrence of Arabia: The Authorized Biography of T. E. Lawrence
BY JEREMY WILSON

A CUBE of reading matter may be inhibiting, but this vast biography of one of the most enigmatic figures in modern times will endure beside T. E. Lawrence's own book *The Seven Pillars of Wisdom* as Lawrence's monument, and future books about the great soldier and adventurer will be merely commentaries on it. Jeremy Wilson does not spoil a splendid story by academic dryness, but he has acquired some of Lawrence's austerity. He is a skilled analyst of human nature and he uses the enormous Lawrence archive made available to him to sweep away many of the Lawrence myths, leaving the man himself perhaps even more mysterious than he seemed before. It is a wholly convincing performance and only a sour critic would find fault with its police-court clarity.

London Fields

BY MARTIN AMIS

MARTIN AMIS has taken the apocalyptic genre into sinister byways in this bitter tragicomedy of life in a world going noisily to hell. His dark vision of life has always been relentless, but this novel, a virtuoso depiction of a wild and lustful society in a dying world, is a large book of comic and satirical invention. It offends every imaginable sensibility. Mr. Amis's mordant satire turns his characters into caricatures, but those caricatures have a vitality and erotic intensity seldom found in modern fiction. *London Fields* is not a safe book; it is moved not by plot but by the density of its language and its language is demonically alive.

My Son's Story

BY NADINE GORDIMER

IN THIS UNNERVING tour de force, a "coloured" boy in South Africa stumbles into the secret life of his father, a leader of the movement to end apartheid. He is stunned by the casualness of the infidelity and by the expectation that he will become a conspirator of silence. His perplexity gives way to a sardonic voice that keeps reminding us that this novel is meant to look with nuanced force at moral complexity, ambiguity and hypocrisy. But Nadine Gordimer, who has a keen eye for the exceedingly precarious moral situation of everyone in her violently unjust country, has an uncanny ability to portray each of her characters with sympathy and subtlety. She can expose the evil of the world without damning the people caught in it, people we come to value as we know them.

Omeros

BY DEREK WALCOTT

THE TITLE of Derek Walcott's 325-page poem is the Greek name of the epic poet Homer, but it is the blind, homeless old poet himself rather than Homeric heroes who inspires this enthralling story in verse. Mr. Walcott's vividly realized characters are the ordinary people of the Caribbean islands. Their story is as rich as that of any epic and, as it unfolds, it encompasses the whole world and all our histories; their experiences become timeless, universal. No poet rivals Mr. Walcott in humor, emotional depth, lavish inventiveness in language or in the ability to express the thoughts of his characters and compel the reader to follow the swift mutations of ideas and images in their minds. This wonderful story moves in a spiral, replicating human thought, and in the end, surprisingly, it makes us realize that history, all of it, belongs to us.

Possession: A Romance
BY A. S. BYATT

A PLENITUDE of Dickensian surprises awaits the reader at the end of this novel about competing academics who come into comically mortal combat when one of them discovers that two Victorian poets, a man and a woman, whom they all guard jealously as their idols and the sources of their incomes, had more than a passing interest in each other. A. S. Byatt is a gifted observer of details and she uses them brilliantly in this very Victorian "romance" of a detective story that satirizes academia but also becomes a concoction in the manner of Jorge Luis Borges. She creates characters who might have stepped out of Dickens or P. G. Wodehouse directly into a post-modernist novel and, along the way, writes fine Victorian verse and prose, and opens every narrative device of fiction to inspection without ever ceasing to delight.

Rabbit at Rest
BY JOHN UPDIKE

WITH THIS, the most brooding, most demanding and most concentrated of all of John Updike's longer novels, the Rabbit quartet, and Rabbit, come to an end. Its final word, spoken by Rabbit himself, is "Enough." Navigating the stumble toward death of this antihero, one can only think of Schopenhauer's definition of walking as "arrested falling." Inevitably, this novel will make one reflect also on the previous three and what becomes most clear is that the being which most illuminates all four books is not Rabbit or any other character but the world through which he moves on his long decline, meticulously recorded by one of the most gifted American realists. The Rabbit novels, for all their grittiness, make up Mr. Updike's surpassingly eloquent valentine to his country.

The Search for Modern China
BY JONATHAN D. SPENCE

THE CENTRAL THEME in this volume—a comprehensive explanation of four centuries from the decline of the Ming dynasty to the death of the democracy movement in June 1989—is China's troubled search for identity in the modern world. The significance of that struggle is not limited to China.

Jonathan D. Spence uses fiction and poetry to breathe life into historical processes, folk songs to galvanize entire peasant movements and diplomatic correspondence to reveal the complexity of official thinking about China's destiny. He reveals the inner lives of historical characters and shows, rather than merely tells, the continuity of Chinese history, the links between the Manchu emperors and Mao Zedong and between the protesters of Tiananmen Square and intellectual rebels of the long past. This superb history will challenge and enrich Western thinking about contemporary China.

Simone de Beauvoir: A Biography
BY DEIRDRE BAIR

DURING THE LAST six years of Simone de Beauvoir's life, Deirdre Bair spent a great deal of time with her, armed with tape recorder and notepad. Her demystifying biography of the serious, frumpy mother of feminism, the Mother Courage of existentialism and left-wing politics in France, the epitome of bourgeois rebelliousness, leaves de Beauvoir better understood than her own works do. And it is reassuring to find out at last the extent to which de Beauvoir lived a life independent of Jean-Paul Sartre and how she achieved for herself the intellectual and erotic freedom she claimed all women ought to have. Ms. Bair addresses her subject from a strongly American point of view and while her references to French intellectual history are not always insightful, her tone of wonderment comes at the right points in the narrative.

The Things They Carried
BY TIM O'BRIEN

THIS COLLECTION of interrelated and coherent stories about Vietnam belongs high on the list of best fiction about any war. The narration passes through the stories from character to character, including one named Tim O'Brien. They contradict one another about incidents, undermine one another's versions. Thus Mr. O'Brien gets beyond literal descriptions of what these men went through. He makes sense of war's unreality—and of why he has further distorted that unreality in his fiction—by exploring the workings of imagination, by probing his memory of the terror and fearlessly confronting the way he has dealt with it as a soldier and a writer. He not only crystallizes the Vietnam experience for everyone; he exposes the nature of all war stories.

Tropical Gangsters

BY ROBERT KLITGAARD

ROBERT KLITGAARD, an administrator for two and a half years of a World Bank project to reform the economy of tiny, impoverished Equatorial Guinea, understands that transferring skills is more important than transmitting cash, and that neither givers nor recipients of aid programs know how to do it. His style is more that of a novelist or travel writer than of an economist, and his tale of lethargy and corruption among the Equatorial Guineans and indifference and frustration among foreign experts has the twists and surprises of fiction. But it is not made up. A reader learns much from it about why our approaches to the Third World are often mischievous failures. In the end it even leads one to question the wisdom of the whole process of what we call development.

Vladimir Nabokov: The Russian Years

BY BRIAN BOYD

NABOKOV'S LIFE reads like a work by a very imaginative creator. In this first volume of his biography, Brian Boyd gives us a definitive life of the writer and a superbly documented chronicle of his time—from the brilliant last years of the czars through the 1917 Revolution and the decades of exile in Europe before Nabokov sailed for America in 1940. Mr. Boyd's great gift for drawing life and literature together makes his book especially rewarding for people who do not read Russian, for during his first 20 years of exile Nabokov wrote 8 novels, 50 stories, 4 plays, 100 poems and much more that is still untranslated. And he is especially good on the central theme of so much of Nabokov's work, his relationship with his father, the dedicated liberal political leader. The assassination of his father in Berlin in 1922 produced a trauma that reverberates through most of Nabokov's writing; Mr. Boyd allows us to feel its full resonance.

1991

Editors' Choice

Complete Collected Stories
BY V. S. PRITCHETT

V. S. PRITCHETT at the age of 90 has gathered 82 stories, written over 65 years, that he wants to preserve. They differ vastly in length and style, but all illustrate the strangeness of the ordinary, reflecting a child's clarity of vision but with a slightly corrupt knowingness. In addition to their intrinsic beauty, these tales provide rich allusions to life in England through this century: changing cultural surfaces, alterations in manners, sinking values. But through the changes human passion obstinately prevails, and Pritchett celebrates it. His characters are mostly commonplace people who may seem comic or tedious until one realizes that great passions move them. His work is an exaltation of life.

Consciousness Explained
BY DANIEL C. DENNETT

THE AUDACIOUS TITLE of this book, which attempts a scientific explanation of the feeling we have of being aware and self-deliberating, is emblematic of the style of Daniel C. Dennett, a provocative philosopher who is fully conversant in psychology, neuroscience and computer science. His book can be tough reading, but his writing is incisive, bright and often humorous. He arrives at a theory of his own to explain how our neural machinery has evolved to give us an uncanny reflective capacity that has led people for millenniums to suppose the body is inhabited by a spirit. But even those who reject his theory will value his illuminating attacks on previous scientific explanations and his extraordinarily clear syntheses of other theories of mind, brain and consciousness. Mr. Dennett's book is the best example in many years of science aimed with wonderful accuracy both at scientists and at general readers.

Holocaust Testimonies: The Ruins of Memory
BY LAWRENCE L. LANGER

ANALYZING HUNDREDS of taped interviews with Holocaust survivors kept in a video archive at Yale University, Lawrence L. Langer demonstrates that they often speak from "common memory," recalling events in an ordered and detached way. But often they speak from "deep memory," reliving chaotic, brutal and degraded reality with a sense of irrecoverable loss. He argues persuasively that habitual references to the survivors as embodiments of the "invincible" or even "noble" human spirit are wrong. During the Holocaust, he says, the self functioned on the edge of extinction, and the personal histories of its victims are utterly beyond our evaluation. Despite being frequently quite abstract and full of psychological theory, this book has great power, never more so than in the extensively quoted recollections of these fugitives from the worst of hells.

The Journals of John Cheever
BY JOHN CHEEVER

THIS GENEROUS SELECTION from a journal John Cheever kept for more than 35 years shares with his fiction four main subjects: nature, God, home and sex. It lets us see the beast crouching in the bushes of the well-kept houses that fill his stories. Loneliness, at the center of all his work, accounts for his obsessive idealization of home and hearth, and the journal reflects his anguish at the conflicts that idealization created. Wanting to be a good husband and father, he was an alcoholic and a bisexual who hated his double life. Some readers may wish less dirt were exposed, but all can luxuriate in this rich prose, especially when Cheever writes about writing. That he struggled against terrible odds is evident here; but he left behind work of great beauty in all his books, including this one.

A Life of Picasso: Volume One, 1881–1906
BY JOHN RICHARDSON, WITH THE COLLABORATION OF MARILYN MCCULLY

THIS, the first of four long-awaited volumes of the biography of Pablo Picasso, has the steady, unhurrying pace of Victorian biographies. John Richardson was long a neighbor of Picasso's in the south of France and had the trust of the artist and his widow, as well as of countless friends of theirs. His affectionate tale, filled with a tumult of reminiscence, is also hardheaded, putting to an end many legends the painter himself helped create. Not only Picasso but hundreds of others spring to life, and Mr. Richardson makes vivid the intrigues, jealousies, enmities, passions and loves of the extraordinary people who became involved with Picasso. The volume ends, tantalizingly, with a thrilling description of Picasso's preparations in 1906 to begin *Les Demoiselles d'Avignon*, a painting that would change the direction of all art.

Mating
BY NORMAN RUSH

NORMAN RUSH'S first novel, about a woman anthropologist seeking perfect love and the perfect lover, another anthropologist who has created a utopia in Africa, is one of the wisest and wittiest fictional meditations ever written on the subject of mating. It illuminates the nature of true intimacy. At their happiest, the lovers arrive at a state that is exalting in its seeming inexhaustibility. All this is presented in an allusive, freewheeling first-person narrative of impressive intelligence. The reader's education is tested and expanded by the fast and self-conscious company of the narrator and her beloved, people whose mordant wordplay is sly and pleasantly unobtrusive. If such brilliant writing is not enough, this woman's quest is a grand adventure across a land that assaults and seduces all the senses.

Maus: A Survivor's Tale II: And Here My Troubles Began
BY ART SPIEGELMAN

IT MAY LOOK like a comic book, but *Maus II* is serious, subtle and eloquent pictorial literature. In his first *Maus* (1986) Art Spiegelman created a character, Artie Spiegelman, who was struggling to understand his parents, Vladek and Anja, survivors of Auschwitz; but he never directly told the story of the Holocaust. Here, without sentimentality or melodrama, he confronts it in tales of incidents that may be incommunicable. One might expect a strip portraying Jews as mice, Germans as cats and other people as different kinds of animals to be distracting. But the animals allow one to follow the fable without drowning in horror. The struggle to transform history into art is a central part of the drama here. The reader, sucked into the heart of the maelstrom, develops insights that are beyond the capacity of the characters; that is a mark of Mr. Spiegelman's mastery of narrative.

The Truth About Chernobyl
BY GRIGORY MEDVEDEV

THE REVELATIONS in this classic in the history of nuclear power are shocking, and its drama is gripping. Grigory Medvedev, chief engineer at Chernobyl when it was built in 1970 and a Soviet government energy official at the time it exploded in 1986, investigated the explosion on site and interviewed many of its victims before they died of radiation burns. His book, which is translated by Evelyn Rossiter, begins slowly and somewhat technically, but soon becomes a taut drama; it gives the locations of all the people in the reactor building, along with their fears and doubts second by second, as the monster they tried to control began to rock in a wild dance before it ripped apart, spewing more radiation than any explosion or bomb, ever. If this is a tale of official incompetence, it is also one of the heroism of many men and women who rushed into the facility to rescue the injured and contain damage at the cost of their lives. The implications of this book for the future of nuclear power are chilling.

Two Lives
"Reading Turgenev" and "My House in Umbria"
BY WILLIAM TREVOR

THE BEAUTIFULLY COMPOSED surfaces of William Trevor's storytelling in these two novellas are nicely deceptive, for the reader is gently jolted into seeing beneath them the rippling complexities inherent in being human. In one tale a woman is confined to a mental institution after the failure of a doomed marriage from which she had taken refuge in a passionate attachment to her cousin, whose early death not only did not end her fervor but endowed her with a strange freedom. In the other a woman novelist injured in the bombing of a train takes other survivors into her home as she recovers; but as she heals she finds the great injury of her life is her past. In both novellas Mr. Trevor shuffles scenes from the past and the present—some of them darkly comic—subtly underlining ways in which these two different lives illuminate each other. In a wry but compassionate way he shows how fragments in the "peepshow of memory" can make up a life.

Wartime Lies

BY LOUIS BEGLEY

IN THIS MASTERLY first novel, Louis Begley, a Manhattan lawyer who as a boy managed to escape the Nazis in his native Poland, tells the tale of Maciek, a Jewish boy who also survives, but at enormous cost. The boy is too young to judge the cruelties he suffers, and his voice has a fine, unguarded authority, especially since the story is framed in the perspective of the cultivated and wary middle-aged man he later becomes. Maciek, whose mother died at his birth, spends the war years in the care of an aunt fiercely determined to survive. From her he learns the terrible discipline of deception at an age when deceit costs him his soul but failure to deceive would cost his life. At the end the man in midlife, faithful to the dark irony of little Maciek's fate, confines his childhood to the empty realm of lies and thus, without saying so, underlines the saving value of fiction, in which lies can be reconciled with truth.

Editors' Choice

The Ant and the Peacock: Altruism and Sexual Selection from Darwin to Today
BY HELENA CRONIN

HELENA CRONIN, who studied philosophy before she became a researcher in zoology at the University of Oxford, is a lucid explainer of science for readers with no scientific training; she brings to her engaging book the spirited style of a naturally gifted writer. The ant of her title stands for the conundrum of altruism—why certain creatures sacrifice themselves for others; and the peacock stands for the puzzle of sex differences—why some male animals are dangerously ornamented. Charles Darwin and Alfred Russel Wallace independently discovered evolution and published their theories together in 1858. But they disagreed deeply on how to explain altruism and sex differences in the light of natural selection; their disagreements continue among evolutionists today. Ms. Cronin's pursuit of the conflicting ideas is a surprising adventure, a revelation of how scientists think. Her book is a fascinating history of the development of scientific theory and the growth of a global scientific community.

The English Patient

BY MICHAEL ONDAATJE

FOUR PEOPLE left behind in a Tuscan villa as World War II sweeps north out of Italy grapple for a truth no human being can ever find: an Englishman slowly dying of burns from an airplane crash, a Canadian nurse stubbornly caring for him, a friend of her family who is a professional thief turned military spy and a Sikh soldier in the British army charged with defusing hidden German bombs and mines. These people are so brilliantly drawn and singular they seem like icons in a mosaic, representing innocence, passion, loss and endurance. The kinesthetic quality of the descriptions of air warfare and bomb disposal in the novel gives an eerie beauty to scenes that make chills run through a reader, but the author's probing of his characters' inner passions fills one with even more apprehension. In the end this intensely theatrical tour de force reveals, if not a great peace at the heart of the human mystery, a vision of how heroic the struggle is.

Jazz

BY TONI MORRISON

WITH HER CUSTOMARY virtuosity Toni Morrison brings us into the heart of Harlem early in this century, a Harlem permeated with the thrum of the music evoked by her title, a Harlem to which black people fleeing from fear in other places came to find their riskier selves. Her episodic novel, played out in intense prose rhythms, is about three people who came together simply because they were put down together—powerless innocents enchanted and deceived by the music of the world, who believed life would be good to them. A cosmetics salesman, the son of a wild cave woman, purveys illusion until he himself is caught in a romantic illusion spun by a foxy teenager whom he kills. His wife, luxuriating in the thralldom of jealousy and obsessed by longing for the baby she never had, seeks to possess the image, memory and soul of the dead girl. Ms. Morrison always conjures up worlds with complete authority; this time it is a world without soft lights or shadows, drawn in the bold strokes of a poster.

Kissinger: A Biography

BY WALTER ISAACSON

HENRY KISSINGER has not wielded power in Washington for 16 years, but curiosity about him remains so intense that he continues to be one of the most famous people in the world. When Walter Isaacson began work on this book, the former Secretary of State became so intrigued he opened up access to friends and records and gave the *Time* magazine editor many hours of interviews. That may have been one of his gravest miscalculations ever. Based on enormous documentation and years of interviews, this biography, in range and research, is the book to end all books on Mr. Kissinger. It is compulsive, and compulsory, reading. As the evidence accumulates, it becomes a devastating portrait of a refugee from Nazi Germany who became one of the most admired men in America. But he profoundly distrusted the politics of popular democracy, here and in other countries, and he joined with President Richard M. Nixon to run the government as if it were a two-man conspiracy.

Lincoln at Gettysburg: The Words That Remade America

BY GARRY WILLS

IN THIS BRIEF, bracing and provocative book, Garry Wills, the historian and columnist, argues that in the Gettysburg Address Abraham Lincoln, with consummate skill, changed the Constitution from within, making the hope it embodies triumph over its words by insinuating the ringing affirmation of equality from the Declaration of Independence into people's minds as the foundation of the American government. Single-handedly he made Jefferson and the signers of the Declaration the true founding fathers of the nation and created the notion of a national citizenship. Mr. Wills demonstrates word by word that, in a century when orators were steeped in the classical traditions of formal speech, Lincoln was the greatest master of all; he created a revolution in style so effective that all modern political prose is indebted to the Gettysburg Address.

The Lost Upland

BY W. S. MERWIN

WITH THE AGILE eloquence of the impassioned poet he is, W. S. Merwin, in three stories that form a pastoral epic, draws readers into the lives of people in the Dordogne region of southwest France where he has had a house for several decades. He creates a texture of soil and water, vine and garden, castle and hovel, mist, sunshine and moonlit shadows so sensuous that one feels one has known this upland for a lifetime. Mr. Merwin is adept at treating human behavior as part of nature and at fashioning a sense of place from people's conduct. These people view the unwelcome present through the prism of the past, thus the title of the book and the sweet longing it leaves behind. The truffle-rich foie gras of one village permeates a tale of gossip, decadence and genteel rascality in the first story; the taste and smell of a vintner's private *cru* seep into the last, about the waning of an old culture. And in the middle story Dordogne shepherds are transformed into heroes of the struggle we all wage against time, with greater zest the more we realize no one ever wins it.

Outerbridge Reach
BY ROBERT STONE

AN UNSETTLING MORAL PROPOSITION can be glimpsed behind this novel: that seeing through everything and believing in nothing may be the most stupid way to cheat oneself of life. An advertising copywriter for a boat company—he is a middle-aged Vietnam veteran and a parody of a Hemingway hero—volunteers to sail solo around the world in a race after the company's owner, who was to make the race, disappears. The adman's wife suppresses her fears about the adventure and decides it may revitalize her husband and their marriage. But a filmmaker producing a documentary about the boat has an affair with her while her husband battles the sea alone. Even richer in literary allusions than Mr. Stone's other books, and told in a gritty idiom, this shapely novel has great power. Like a thriller it makes us care intensely about what will happen next and who will be hurt. And it is impossible to read the last dazzling hundred pages without feeling something terrible has happened and no one is to blame.

Regeneration
BY PAT BARKER

PAT BARKER has been the model of a working-class realistic novelist, but here she leaps the lines of gender, class, geography and history at once. And she takes another daring chance: her novel is about real people who published their own memoirs. *Regeneration* is the story of the British poet Siegfried Sassoon, a World War I combat hero who in 1917 writes a highly publicized letter protesting the war and is sent by a baffled government to a hospital where the distinguished neurologist and psychologist W. H. R. Rivers is pioneering treatments for shell shock. As an intense father-son relationship develops between the men, Ms. Barker's themes—war and madness, war and manhood—make the madness of war more than metaphor. But, in the tradition of literary realism, she confronts reality without polemics, anger or artifice. Her story becomes a magnificent antiwar novel and a wonderful justification of her belief that plain writing, energized by the named things of the world, will change readers profoundly by bringing them deep into imagined lives.

Young Men & Fire
BY NORMAN MACLEAN

THIS GREAT BOOK about young firefighters who parachuted into a 1949 Montana forest fire shortly before it blew up into a firestorm that killed 13 of them is a magnificent drama of writing, a tragedy that pays tribute to the dead and offers rescue to the living. Norman Maclean was 74 years old in 1976 when he began a quest to discover what really happened in the fire, and ill health in his last few years prevented him from completing his book before he died at 88. But, if it lacks the finish he wanted to give it, *Young Men & Fire* has searing power. Maclean's search for the truth, which becomes an exploration of his own mortality, is more compelling even than his journey into the heart of the fire. His description of the conflagration terrifies, but it is his battle with words, his effort to turn the story of the 13 men into tragedy, that makes the book a classic. He does not try to win a brawl with truth but to pay his respects to it. He struggles openly and dramatically with the literary forms of tragedy, allowing into his notion of the tragic uncertainty, mystery, even absurdity—in a word, the modern condition. In the end he has let us see how all true artists work.

1993

Editors' Choice

Across the Bridge: Stories
BY MAVIS GALLANT

THE WORLD Mavis Gallant creates in these 11 stories is urban (mostly Paris or Montreal), deeply conservative and, for all its urbanity, old-fashioned. In the title story, timeless as a fairy tale, everything is stock—except the writing. The material is a staple of popular romantic fiction, which Mrs. Gallant subverts with intelligence and wit. Not every story here is that successful. This writer is a scalpel-sharp anatomist of stupidity, and while this skill can make her work very funny, occasionally her humor works at the expense of her characters. But she has few equals. One story here, "Forain," is as close to perfection as possible, a marvel of wit, feeling and tact in which each detail is exact and telling. That and the title story alone would make this book one of the best collections of fiction in years.

Balkan Ghosts: A Journey Through History
BY ROBERT D. KAPLAN

THE SUSPICIOUS, angry people of Bulgaria, Greece, Albania, Romania and what was once Yugoslavia—especially uprooted peasants with fantasy-enriched histories—think they are fatefully alien to one another, but Robert D. Kaplan, a journalist who has reported on this region for several magazines, demonstrates with gusto that they do indeed form an unhappy whole. The Balkans, boiling into fury once again, have a special fascination, for Communism not only failed to resolve any of the region's historical controversies (layers of them built up for more than a thousand years); it suppressed and thus magnified them, so now it seems the mixture of memory and folklore that is popular history has suddenly sprung out of a forgotten grave into appalling life. Mr. Kaplan occasionally falls prey to gullibility, but the fantastic stories he gathers bring one closer to understanding the real history of the Balkans.

Before Night Falls
BY REINALDO ARENAS

IN THIS MEMOIR, Reinaldo Arenas—a gifted, untaught novelist who was denied recognition in Castro's Cuba, and imprisoned and tortured as a homosexual before he escaped from the island in the 1980 Mariel boatlift—links his personal history with a political meditation on his country, told from the point of view of an abandoned son. The role is right: Arenas, who had AIDS, committed suicide in New York in 1990, leaving a note that accused Fidel Castro not only of Cuba's tragedy but of his own. His book reveals Cuban officialdom as unprincipled and corrupt in its liteary politics, and in its macho sexual pretensions. Arenas was one of the world's great loners, and was almost as alienated in America as in Cuba, finding the very Americans he wanted to be closest to—intellectuals and gay men—morally flabby. What makes his memoir so poignant and haunting is what he never acknowledges explicitly: that his standard of liberation was absolute, his innocence made him vulnerable to unending hurt, and the freedom he sought exists nowhere.

The Collected Stories
BY WILLIAM TREVOR

IN MORE THAN 80 stories filling a thousand pages and written over 30 years, one might expect to find some sameness. But William Trevor's pure intensity of attention finds an endless new set of subjects and tones in a world worn smooth by handling. His is work of impeccable strength and a profundity rare in the history of short fiction. Because his prose is as plain and natural as daylight, his tremendous achievement seems effortless. Though he shares much of the richness of his countrymen Yeats and Joyce, he avoids their sourness of spirit, and though his vision of the human tragedy can be as dark as that of the Greeks, it is also deeply, though never entirely, comic. There is always the rising hint of faint laughter here. His perfect sympathy with human beings lays out the tragic implications or the mere foolishness of the simple Irish people he writes about, but a native tenderness spares them his malice.

The Fate of the Elephant

BY DOUGLAS H. CHADWICK

NATIONAL GEOGRAPHIC sent Douglas H. Chadwick, a wildlife biologist, out to make a survey of elephants everywhere, and his book is a kind of elephantocentric view of the world. What emerges is the conviction that preserving elephants is closely related to protecting human beings; both species use up habitat voraciously, and both adapt cunningly to the devastation they leave behind. Mr. Chadwick glides right over some critical issues, but he has good moral taste and an expansive, shrewd knowledge of the world lights his tour of elephant lands: Kenya, Tanzania, Central Africa, India, Thailand, Malaysia, Zimbabwe, even Hong Kong and Japan, where the ivory markets grow despite the world's efforts to restrain them.

The Island: Three Tales

BY GUSTAW HERLING

THE THREE TALES in this volume rightfully belong to the canon of great works of literature. Gustaw Herling, who lives in Italy but writes in his native Polish, has taken a long time to come to the attention of the world. Until the fall of Communism, his fiction was banned entirely in Poland, and in the West it has been translated only very slowly. Yet any reader approaching these stories will find a timeless world like no other. A Herling story is multilayered, complex and told in a detached voice that bespeaks a wonderful air of courtesy toward the reader; this writer is a supremely civilized man. In each story—two of them connect morally and physically the actions of people deeply separated by time and distance—he probes with thrilling delicacy the infinite and eternal consequences of human decisions and intentions. Mr. Herling's vision is humanistic, compassionate, illuminating; it can leave one speechless with gratitude.

Jesus' Son: Stories

BY DENIS JOHNSON

IN THIS tour de force of compression and moral entropy, Denis Johnson uncovers a universe under the spell of addiction, malevolence, faith and uncertainty. His 11 stories demand to be read like a novel structured along a kind of Cubist chronology. The narrator is a kin of some of Samuel Beckett's great spokesmen, unable to construct a well-made story, unable even to get the facts of his own life straight as he staggers from habit to addiction, participating along the way in abortions, car crashes, drug deals and murder. Mr. Johnson is always compassionate and skeptical. The damaged psyches of his characters keep his readers off balance, and often laughing, but even the sense of humor here seems deranged, menacing; it is all part of the admirable, startling art of this fearless detective of the tortured paths of Americans' moral lives.

Judge on Trial
BY IVAN KLIMA

IVAN KLIMA'S BOOK, first circulated as an underground text in the 1970s in Czechoslovakia, is likely to survive as the key version of the late-twentieth-century Eastern European political novel, rivaled only by the work of Milan Kundera. Conceived with great intellectual and moral ambition, this many-layered story about a man on the inside of the old regime who acts prudently in his emptiness places the moment of Communist repression in a vastly larger history and thus raises hope for the political orders of the future. This is work in the tradition of Elias Canetti and Arthur Koestler, an honest examination of the agonized pain of Middle European history that suggests that it still has something to disclose to the moral future.

The Last Panda
BY GEORGE B. SCHALLER

ALTHOUGH GEORGE B. SCHALLER says this sinewy book was "reluctantly written," no one who cares about life on earth should miss it. In 1980 Mr. Schaller became the first scientist the Chinese Government had ever allowed to study the panda in the wild, and the experience proved far more difficult than his celebrated studies of lions and gorillas. No scientist is better at bringing the reader into his world. He has the gifts of clarity, eloquence and passion, and they make some of what he reveals unnerving. Human efforts to save the panda have been not only late and halfhearted, but so often fundamentally loony that one is embarrassed for our species. "The panda has not evolved to amuse humankind," he warns. And why has humankind evolved? That question the reader cannot avoid.

Lenin's Tomb: The Last Days of the Soviet Empire

BY DAVID REMNICK

A CONFLUENCE OF OBSERVATION, digging, knowledge and reflection that is classy journalism, this book is a record of almost four years beginning in 1988 when David Remnick, a *Washington Post* reporter, was assigned to Moscow. In it the Russian democrats, now a beleaguered cadre, come to the fore; these were their best years. A gallery of figures emerges, not all of them remembered much now in the West, sketched with a force close to Balzac's. And while the author is sometimes too sentimental, he gives sweeping panoramas of collective farm workers, laborers and miners. He argues convincingly that what did in the old Soviet leadership, right down through Mikhail Gorbachev, was its unending assault not only on people but on memory. By making a secret of history, it made its people increasingly distracted, and desperate, until they overthrew it.

Mazurka for Two Dead Men

BY CAMILO JOSE CELA

C AMILO JOSE CELA, the 1989 winner of the Nobel Prize in Literature, constructs here perhaps his most mesmerizing fiction, about life during the first four decades of this century in his native Galicia, a life so brutal that the Spanish Civil War, when it occurs, seems a mere continuation of the ordinary. This is a seamless world, with no distinction between human life and nature, and the narrative voices, uniformly vulgar but never obscene, have a monotony that gives them a kind of liturgical cadence, endowing them with an aura of truth. These are the voices of classical tragedy and the argumentative voices of the law; thus they give an active role to death in the development of a fiendishly haunting story based on the simple premise that if you kill someone, sooner or later you will pay because the universe must be justified.

A Moment of War: A Memoir of the Spanish Civil War

BY LAURIE LEE

L AURIE LEE is 79, but in his youth this English poet joined the Republicans in the Spanish Civil War, and now, before his sight fails entirely, he sets down what happened. More than most, this was a war fueled by illusion; Mr. Lee had his share of that. He was also an unlicked country lad, and his ignorance made him adaptable, protected him. He is not ignorant now. His enormously sophisticated book, a testament to the morality and weakness of humanity, has the plainness of Orwell but the metaphorical soaring of a poem. There is an echo of the 1930s in the prose, but you can hear the maturity of the man and writer as he traces the steps of a youthful combatant whose thoughts are mostly silent to the reader. This has the effect of making *A Moment of War* the reader's own story, and the terrible judgment about life that came to Mr. Lee when he finally killed a man a judgment of the reader.

Shylock: A Legend and Its Legacy
BY JOHN GROSS

VILLAINY IS GOOD DRAMA, so Shylock has become a touchstone of acting through the centuries. But Shylock is larger than *The Merchant of Venice*, larger than theater; and since Hitler showed the world the natural end of anti-Semitism, actors, directors and audiences have all cringed from gazing directly at the Shylock whom Shakespeare created. John Gross, in a book that whisks away a whole world of sophistry, looks at 400 years of Shylocks; it is not only a study of a literary masterpiece, but of history, psychology and changing mores; of imagination, intelligence and evil; of Henry VIII, Elizabeth I and Freud; Edwin Booth, Henry Irving and Olivier. By returning the play, and its performances, to the realities from which they rose, Mr. Gross returns it, and Shylock, to us. This is a singular gift of restoration and a rare example of the gentle power of impassioned reason presented in measured language.

Travels with Lizbeth
BY LARS EIGHNER

THIS MODERN AUTOBIOGRAPHY of a supertramp re-creates in lavish detail the grammar, outlook and economy of the unhoused life as its author, a fortyish hitchhiker, zigzags between Austin, Tex., and Los Angeles. Lars Eighner has a weird prose style, which he uses with deadpan irony; his voice is by turns grandiloquent and simple, and his vision of the world involves abrupt distortions of scale, as people who are all-important at one moment shrink to ciphers in the next. Objects stir him more than human beings; he can rhapsodize over found scraps, like the personal computer, fished out of a Dumpster, on which he wrote this book. Lizbeth is his dog. She shares his wild life, and, while his language about her is often strangely distant, it allows her to become a compelling character in his odyssey—as strange as any he encounters.

Editors' Choice

Balzac: A Life

BY GRAHAM ROBB

"I AM NOT DEEP," said Honoré de Balzac, "but very wide." Graham Robb, as chatty and urbane as his subject, confidently negotiates the vast expanses of Balzac's life in an unusually witty biography that reads somewhat like a detective story as Mr. Robb tracks down the connections between the life and the work of the greatest novelist of the nineteenth century. Balzac regarded dissipation as an investment in friends and patrons, but also in the tumult of personal experience he poured into his novels (*The Human Comedy* alone has more than 2,000 acutely realized characters). Few literary lives are as exciting; Balzac amazes and exhausts one as he tosses in financial rapids, skirts suicide, gambles, smokes opium, seduces women, fathers bastards and creates in prodigious outbursts of writing a world almost as turbulent as he was himself.

Conquest: Montezuma, Cortés, and the Fall of Old Mexico

BY HUGH THOMAS

AMAZINGLY, Hugh Thomas has located archival treasures in Spain that were missed by scholars for centuries, and he has written an encyclopedic history that supplants William H. Prescott's legendary *History of the Conquest of Mexico*, published 141 years ago. Lord Thomas eloquently conjures up the grandeur, fury, mystery and tragedy of this epic story; and his sensitivity to the personalities of the principal figures, and to their voices, which he evokes from his documents, makes it all new. *Conquest* does not offer the comforts of heroes and villains, but it greatly deepens our understanding of the terrible—and probably unfathomable—moment when two peoples, each believing itself the chosen, met in blood and fire to give birth to a new world.

A Frolic of His Own
BY WILLIAM GADDIS

EVEN IF THE READER has to pay close attention to the continuous, minimally punctuated speech of dozens of characters which makes up the entire narrative of this exceptionally rich novel, the payoff is worth it. In this misanthropic and often hilarious comedy, William Gaddis holds up the legal profession, its minions and dupes, to mockery, and then extends the ridicule to a wide spectrum of contemporary American culture—presented with Swiftian glee as an unholy stew of greed, ignorance, illiteracy, corruption and childish folly. His powers of mimicry allow him to flesh out the distinct, often appalling, personalities of his characters through nothing more than their spates of words, and readers who laugh their way right through to the end may find it impossible to get the rhythms and sounds of those voices out of their imaginations.

In the Lake of the Woods
BY TIM O'BRIEN

ON THE SURFACE this novel is a mystery story about a woman who disappears after her husband's political career collapses when his great secret—as a soldier he had been at the My Lai massacre in Vietnam—is exposed. But, like Tim O'Brien's other novels, it traces the line between a literal but unknowable truth and a truth whose only evidence is the story containing it. Here he turns his concerns about truth, time and responsibility inward, letting them weigh on one character, the husband, whose inner architecture is more emblematic than personal. There are sections of conventional narrative; others that collect evidence on the case from interviews and excerpts from books or public records; and others obsessively puzzling over what really might have happened. At bottom, this is a tale about the moral effects of suppressing a true story, about the abuse of history, about what happens to you when you pretend there is no history.

The Language Instinct
BY STEVEN PINKER

STEVEN PINKER gathers data from many fields—including cognitive neuroscience, developmental psychology and speech therapy—to demonstrate that the roots of language are in our genes. He firmly places the wiring of the brain for language in the framework of Darwinian natural selection in a well-written, witty book that makes even the most difficult material accessible to average readers. His argument may raise hackles—as it already has done among some psychologists and anthropologists—because it seems to doom the liberal notion that human behavior can be made better by improvements in culture and environment. But Mr. Pinker argues, with a fascinating array of evidence, that in fact the diversity of the world's cultures is superficial and that the most human trait, language, is produced by evolution; we are born with it, in all its complex grammatical elaboration.

The Moral Animal: Evolutionary Psychology and Everyday Life
BY ROBERT WRIGHT

IF THE ARGUMENT that language is genetic is tough to swallow, look at Robert Wright's thesis: the source of human morality is genetic. Genes account for the battle of the sexes, friendship, hypocrisy, generosity, selfishness, the whole kit and kaboodle. As Mr. Wright reports on how the science of evolutionary psychology has developed, he wants to upend received wisdom about our sense of right and wrong in general, arguing with consistent and good-humored irreverence that in the wake of Darwin we have to reconstruct morality from the ground up. The thinking of this excellent journalist is provocative, challenging and illuminating; as he develops his own arguments he precisely outlines the world of sociobiology and lets us see where the contending forces shaping it fit in. Many arguments in his book are debatable, but none are facile; this fiercely intelligent book is a feast of clear thinking.

Naturalist
BY EDWARD O. WILSON

IN A WISE personal memoir, Edward O. Wilson—a giant in contemporary biology, a pioneer in evolutionary biology, a world authority on ants and one of the founders of sociobiology—recalls a life which, from the outset, was captivated by a compulsion for close observation of living things and a passion to synthesize what we know about them. Its readers will learn much about the risks, the long labor, and the moral and intellectual intensity of a life devoted to science, and about the harrowing ordeal this gentle scientist went through when many academics in other disciplines created a political furor over his seminal 1975 book *Sociobiology*, which they contended would be an instrument of cultural determinism and racism. A mixture of loneliness, amusement, curiosity and intellectual rigor makes the voice of this thoughtful man unforgettable.

Open Secrets: Stories
BY ALICE MUNRO

ALL THE STORIES in this collection are lessons. And it is no mere coincidence that the time frame of almost all of them is an entire life; but they draw on the complexity of a mature and vigilant sensibility. Alice Munro's daring adventure is to try to apprehend the mystery of existence in time, the unique quality of a person's fate. Since delving into mystery starts with language, people in her stories are constantly telling stories or struggling to understand them — in confessions, rumors, letters, conversations, newspapers. But often they do not know the meaning of their own stories. In any case, there are always puzzles of love, time, death, spirit that cannot be apprehended through language; they are the open secrets that cannot be talked into clarity, but which Ms. Munro patiently prods and turns and pokes until, in story after story, they yield lessons — partial, ambiguous and momentous.

Stalin and the Bomb: The Soviet Union and Atomic Energy, 1939–1956
BY DAVID HOLLOWAY

USING ONCE-SECRET Russian archives, David Holloway examines nuclear weapons in the Soviet Union with an eye to the part their development played in starting the cold war. His hardheaded study gives little comfort to liberals and none to revisionist historians. The first Russian atomic bomb was indeed developed with the help of espionage, but even without it the Russians would have built a bomb a few years later, and their hydrogen bomb was entirely their invention. Could the cold war have been short-circuited if American leaders had told Stalin about work on our atomic bomb early on? No. Stalin saw immediately that if anyone else had the weapon and he did not the Soviet Union was lost. What makes this book so readable is Mr. Holloway's capacity to evoke the character of so many Russian scientists and political leaders, and to make them understandable without ever being naïve about them. As a result we get a more complete story of Russian nuclear weapons than we have had yet about our own.

A Way in the World
BY V. S. NAIPAUL

PURSUING his lifelong obsessions—what it means to become a writer and what happens in postcolonial societies when foreign power recedes, leaving behind chaos and cruelty—V. S. Naipaul fashions this book out of nine linked narratives: some personal, some historical, some novelistic. The American publisher calls it a novel, the author does not. Whatever it is, it is a disturbing meditation on the relationships among personal, national and world histories and on inheritance and immortality. That it is an archeology of the colonial impulse becomes clear in tales of Christopher Columbus (1451–1506), Sir Walter Raleigh (1554–1618) and the failed Venezuelan revolutionary Francisco Miranda (1750–1816), each adrift in the Gulf of Desolation, between Trinidad and Venezuela, as his life nears its close. Driving them all is a simple urge to create themselves anew. It is the human urge, to make ourselves up as we go along— sometimes with dramatic consequences for the world.

W. E. B. Du Bois: Biography of a Race, 1868–1919
BY DAVID LEVERING LEWIS

THE SUBTITLE of this first volume of David Levering Lewis's life of Du Bois is the key to it: during the first half of his life, Du Bois—as he developed into a pioneering historian, the leading crusader for black rights, and finally the father of Pan-Africanism and a founder of the National Association for the Advancement of Colored People—became totally identified with the struggle of the black race, and gave it a magnificent voice. Mr. Lewis gives us an enormous amount of information as he explores Du Bois's academic achievements, his political growth and, above all, the growth of Du Bois's powerful sense of self. That made him the leader he was and, as Mr. Lewis makes clear, it made him often unbearable to others. Mr. Lewis tells a well-known story in such rich detail and with so many fresh insights that one ends this volume eager to see the next.

Editors' Choice

The Haunted Land: Facing Europe's Ghosts After Communism
BY TINA ROSENBERG

TINA ROSENBERG thinks efforts by Eastern Europeans to establish a new order may be doomed unless they face up to what they all did under the collapsed Communist regimes. She writes about East Germany, Poland, Slovakia and the Czech Republic in personal terms, focusing each account on an individual to point up the moral uncertainties nagging people at all social levels: How much of the past should be revealed? Who should be punished? Who can judge? Should everyone who thrived in the old order be shorn of all gains? Who should see the files? What constituted collaboration? The portraits drawn by this compassionate reporter make one feel the fear weighing on people as they try to rebuild, along with the treacherous sense of comfort that entices many to evade personal responsibility for letting tyranny succeed as long as it did.

In Confidence
BY ANATOLY DOBRYNIN

NO OTHER AMBASSADOR in modern times has played such a long and crucial role in international affairs as Anatoly Dobrynin, the Soviet envoy in Washington from 1962 to 1986, and none has written about his experience with fewer inhibitions. His is the most revealing account of the cold war to have come out of Russia so far; it opens up a great seam in hitherto impenetrable Soviet history. His revelations of how some great crises were resolved through secret channels of negotiation are fascinating. But what truly astonishes one is his frank exposure of 40 years of blunders by the leaders in Moscow and the energy with which he condemns some of them—especially Mikhail Gorbachev, whom Mr. Dobrynin blames for the collapse of the Soviet empire. At first, readers may wonder whether he tells the truth; by the end of the book they will have no doubt.

Independence Day
BY RICHARD FORD

FRANK BASCOMBE, the antihero of *The Sportswriter* (1986), is back—no longer a writer but a real estate salesman, 44, divorced ("I wanted somebody with a true heart," his ex-wife says; "that wasn't you"). Personal relationships, especially with women, puzzle him more than ever; it is not, he says, as if he doesn't exist, just that he doesn't "exist as much" as other people. So his attempts to turn his current affair into something deeper fizzle out, and his efforts to help his troubled teenage son during a Fourth of July weekend trip veer toward tragedy. If the novel's story line is thin, the character sketches are brilliant work by a master of the craft. With wisdom and wry wit, Richard Ford makes Bascombe a man who takes his place alongside Willy Loman and Rabbit Angstrom in our literature.

The Information
BY MARTIN AMIS

MIDLIFE CRISIS is something else in Martin Amis's dazzling novel about literary envy in London. Richard, a failed novelist, can't stand the huge success of his best friend, Gwyn, whose stinking-bad novels make him a fortune. Richard, indignant and resentful, tries to redress the cosmic imbalance with the help of some of Mr. Amis's usual menagerie of dangerous netherworlders, who turn Richard's dicey game against him. All the characters become pawns in an accelerating chess match they have no control over. Mr. Amis, the prince of hip, is in top form; his humor is more daring than ever, and his mastery of phrase and metaphor makes his gorgeous, dark invention crackle. He is also smart about being smart: at just the right moments he sinks the blade of his satire into himself.

The Island of the Day Before
BY UMBERTO ECO

THIS GRAND and deliriously writerly novel is a book of many books that
regenerates literary traditions as it unfolds a tale of warfare, romance and
shipwreck during the most exciting period of our intellectual history, the mid-
seventeenth century. Umberto Eco's narrative surface is sensually alluring, cool
and glittery, but for all its lucidity and charm, there is always something else
going on: if the plot turns on blood, ambition, intrigue, spying, love, death and
damnation, there is a profound agenda here that urgently if playfully makes us
aware of the steady continuity of human thought—the conspiracy of the world
to be known. This novel, translated by William Weaver, is really a book about
telling, reminding us that the only clarity we are capable of reaching is the story
we tell to compel time and the universe to take on meaning.

The Life of Graham Greene: Volume Two: 1939–1955
BY NORMAN SHERRY

NORMAN SHERRY, the biographer as bloodhound, tracks Graham
Greene—who found peace only in drink, drugs, sex and war—through
tangled love affairs, international conflicts and spy capers on four continents.
This volume covers the years of his greatest novels and film scripts, and exposes
all the intricate connections between the life and the fiction. Mr. Sherry spells
out what was a grotesquely complicated life in a compulsively readable, astutely
humane story that, in other hands, might have been just salacious. Perhaps most
startling is his account of Greene's career in Britain's intelligence services during and after World War II. His boss was the traitor Kim Philby. Greene kept in
close touch with Philby all his life; Mr. Sherry produces evidence at least suggesting that Greene in his later years may have turned Philby, once a double
agent for Moscow, into a double agent for the West.

Lincoln
BY DAVID HERBERT DONALD

THERE MAY BE 7,000 books about Abraham Lincoln around, but
David Herbert Donald's biography is so lucid, richly researched, scrupulous and gritty that one cannot imagine a more satisfying one. In it Lincoln's life
is a series of abrupt triumphs and setbacks that constantly threaten to sink him
into oblivion. He is no simple hero: he has principles aplenty, but he is wily in

pursuit of them, driven by blazing ambition. He knows all there is to know about how to get things done, often by dissimulation; that he learned in the squalid political infighting of Illinois courthouses. And he loves political battles—never more than when he leads the country in its direst crisis. Mr. Donald's voice is confident, earthy and restrained, and therein lies his book's cumulative power; it comes alive in the mind, and the last page is unforgettable.

Overcoming Law
BY RICHARD A. POSNER

THE CHIEF JUDGE of the United States Court of Appeals in Chicago— a Reagan appointee, no less—has written the sharpest and most thoughtful book on the plight of law in years, one that lashes conservatives and liberals alike. The judge is deliciously sarcastic about most lawyers, judges and law professors, whom he finds a lazy pack dedicated to legal precedents and ignorant of the real world. He insists that law will be reformed only when all of them direct attention to the real-world effects of their arguments and decisions—and that means they have a lot to learn about their fellow citizens and about other disciplines that might sharpen their thinking: economics, sociology, history and more. Law is "a public good of immense value," he argues, but ordinary people increasingly don't see it that way, and unless they do it will disappear.

Sabbath's Theater
BY PHILIP ROTH

OUT OF THE WAY, all you afternoon trash-talk television show hosts, and Madonna too—kids, mere kids. In the great game of sex and outrage, Philip Roth remains unchallenged. To feel tumultuously alive, touch the nasty side of existence, says the protagonist of *Sabbath's Theater*, Mr. Roth's richest novel. There is plenty of the nasty in this virtuoso performance by our best literary stand-up comic. But the menacing sense of last things in the story of an aging man leaving his wife, going to a funeral and arranging for his own death gives a depth and resonance to the jokes and rascally fun found in none of his other books. The verbal play is almost tactile, like slaps, as the narrative moves from third-person comic to first-person perverse confession, but there is a polemical energy that lifts it beyond verbal playfulness; at times the message is painful.

The Stories of Vladimir Nabokov

EDITED BY DMITRI NABOKOV

THE DENSITY and richness of these 65 stories—including 13 never published before—make them overwhelming if one tries to read them right through. They have to be explored one by one in many moods. Nabokov wrote nine in English, one in French; 55 were written in Russian between 1920 and 1940, during his European exile. Most deal with a remembered, enchanted Russia or the raffish world of the impoverished diaspora. Nabokov's youthful passions for butterfly collecting, chess and poetry fused to endow his prose with a peculiar intensity and trickiness. In language that strains at the limits of the expressible, he used infinitely precise sensory minutiae to encode the mingled miracles of being and our perception of it. He was the great poet of consciousness, and his stories continue to change a reader's response to the world, no matter how many times one comes back to them.

Zola: A Life

BY FREDERICK BROWN

HOW DID ÉMILE ZOLA—who always proclaimed that the writer must stand above politics—become the moral conscience of France during the Dreyfus affair, taking on the establishment so effectively that he may have been murdered for what he did? Frederick Brown, in the best biography of Zola ever, shows how his childhood and early journalism made him hate duplicity; he was determined to force readers to look only at "the facts" in his novels, without romantic or patriotic illusions. In a richly detailed examination of the books and the realities they reflected, Mr. Brown makes clear that it was that resolve that moved Zola to shame the entire political class of France in his last years. For the first time the man, the artist and the firebrand who forced a nation to look its own hypocrisy in the eye can be seen as the same person—perhaps not an engaging man, but a great one.

Editors' Choice

After Rain

BY WILLIAM TREVOR

EACH STORY by William Trevor in this new collection turns on lying, concealment or unbridled truth-telling; and these dislodging faults in the texture of reality are linked with cruelties ranging from mere spite to fraud, sectarian violence and murder. But the great casualties here are marriages; in the 12 stories there are seven divorces, six adulteries, pervasive sexual jealousy, several loveless marriages and four children from broken homes. The stories lack the ironic wit that lightens Mr. Trevor's novels, but by avoiding closure he gives them a kind of optimism: hope may be underground but there is a tangible sense of fairness about what happens to people. It springs from Mr. Trevor's silent introduction of other perspectives behind each point of view. A reader's insight is not limited to what a victim sees; other interpretations are always implied. It is as though the author's knowledge is not absolute, but contingent on the thoughts and expressions of his creations; his only access to their reality is what they say or think. This narrative discipline frees the characters from the wheel of determinism. Mr. Trevor's role in creating them fades to invisibility, leaving his readers in the presence of something very like life.

Angela's Ashes: A Memoir

BY FRANK MCCOURT

FRANK MCCOURT, a teacher, grandfather and occasional actor, was born in New York City, but grew up in the Irish town of Limerick during the grim 1930s and '40s before he came back here as a teenager. His recollections of childhood are mournful and humorous, angry and forgiving. His father was an idler, a drunken sentimentalist who sang patriotic songs, lost the few jobs he could find, drank the welfare money and finally wandered off to England, leaving his family behind to survive on handouts, donations from Roman Catholic charities and occasional petty larceny. If his mother, Angela, was woebegone, she had reason to be. At first there are seven McCourt children in this always present-tense tale, but by the end, as Mr. McCourt returns to New York, there are only four, the others having died of childhood diseases. The most moving chapters in this engaging book are those recounting his education at the hands of passionate classicists and one about his own childhood illnesses and a long stay in a hospital where his great friend is a dying girl. Mr. McCourt's voice is that of a fine Irish-American raconteur, aware of his charm but diffident about it, and he casts a spell with a memorable story induced by powerful circumstances.

Bad Land: An American Romance

BY JONATHAN RABAN

EARLY IN THIS CENTURY open land in the West still seemed to cry out for cultivation, calling to what Jonathan Raban identifies as "the intense, adhesive attraction of self to soil." What really cried out was an advertising campaign by railroads, luring immigrants to fill the spaces the rails crossed. In one of the most illuminating books written about rural America in many years, Mr. Raban, a literary Englishman who migrated to the United States six years ago, shows us how the towns and farms of eastern Montana were settled—and later unsettled when reality shattered the dreams. There is a mix of optimism, enterprise and salesmanship in this tale that would make it almost unnoticeable to most Americans. Mr. Raban is keenly aware of how the whole notion of landscape is constructed; his imaginative reach recaptures the momentum of the settlers' migration, and their idealism, not only from official records, newspapers and memoirs, but even from schoolbooks of the age. He gives this material not the ironic glance his previous books might make us expect, but respectful attention. In *Bad Land* we find an affectionate reasonableness about this bewildering nation that reminds us how much it is always nourished by the hopes of immigrants.

The Collected Stories of Mavis Gallant

THIS 887-PAGE VOLUME of 52 stories written over half a century reveals clearly what an ambitious and accomplished anomaly Mavis Gallant is. An expatriate in spirit long before she left her native Montreal for Paris in 1950, she is fascinated by the modern displaced citizen of an ever more mobile world. Her characters do not flee from home; they start out homeless, spending their lives conniving at accommodation with a century that started in horror and is ending in hollowness. As they discover that history does not mean continuity, they draw readers irresistibly into their own myopic quests for a reliable perspective on life. Mrs. Gallant primes us to expect them to be good or bad, but never hints which are which; and in her stories tragedy can turn to comedy in a sentence. Except for a satiric streak that has grown more explicit recently, her style, amazingly versatile from the start, has changed little. But she has radically reshaped the short story decade after decade; some of the newer stories are accordions, interlinked tales that suggest a new novelistic mutant. In a real sense her style and attitude are her message. Her disregard of tight plot and momentum makes up her theme: our destiny is to wander, misinterpreting as we go along—just as she has dared to drift in a disorienting century, trusting to her own imaginative compass. It has been a great trip.

The Life of Nelson A. Rockefeller: Worlds to Conquer, 1908–1958

BY CARY REICH

THE FIRST VOLUME of this oversize but vivid account of Nelson Rockefeller's life is the story of one long and spectacularly successful lunge for power. There are times when readers may wish Cary Reich had not given the whole case history of every minor character bobbing along in Rockefeller's wake or that he had been able to describe Rockefeller's few years at the State Department in something less than 300 pages. But this portrait of a maddeningly elusive character is probably as nuanced as any we will ever get. Beginning as the son of one of America's richest men, Rockefeller dominated his brothers by the power of his personality and the world around him by gregarious charm. He was the driving force behind the far-flung Rockefeller business and philanthropic empire and he was a key player in foreign policy initiatives under Presidents Franklin Roosevelt, Harry Truman and Dwight Eisenhower before he ran for governor of New York as the decade of the 1950s ended. The parade of the powerful, the rich and the celebrated through it keeps this huge volume endlessly fascinating. And then there is the parade of beautiful women Rockefeller had such a good eye for. Except in style, this book might be a robust eighteenth-century novel.

The Moor's Last Sigh
BY SALMAN RUSHDIE

No RETORT to tyranny could be more eloquent than Salman Rushdie's new novel, his first since he went into hiding after *The Satanic Verses* inspired Iranian religious leaders to call for his execution in 1989. Ostensibly this is the picaresque saga of the rise, decline and extinction of an ancient Portuguese family in India, told by its last member. The family is marked by lunacy, betrayal, wild sexual confusion and crude lusts for power. The watershed events of Indian history intrude. The denouement is pyrotechnical. But hidden in this carnivalesque wrapping is a bitter cautionary tale. The cataclysm occurs when the family, its once strong religious beliefs now terminally weak, encounters the new absolutist religious spirit arising in India. It is obvious Mr. Rushdie is dealing, subtly and by analogy, with the situation that created his own predicament. What else is here? A biting parody of the family saga novel; a celebration of Bombay in its cosmopolitan years; a masterly rendition of jokey, punning Indian English; a dark assessment of Indian religious nationalism; and a mordant reflection on the future of serious art. If the language of the novel is heavily ornamented, the brio and wit make all the dazzle seem quite natural.

Selected Stories
BY ALICE MUNRO

IN ONE OF HER earlier short stories, Alice Munro has a writer say she looks at her work as "a sort of wooing of distant parts of myself," and, even as Ms. Munro's stories have grown richer, almost Elizabethan, in their evocations of nature, texture and fabric, that wooing of distant parts has made the world—usually some part of her native Canada—an ever more haunted, mind-saturated place. Ms. Munro's complex, involved plots are profoundly meditated; she achieves intense clarity in phrase and image; she has exceptional psychological insight and honesty; her reach is bold and she is gritty. Most of her heroines start young and grow up to discover the world's romantic possibilities, marital fury and the heavy strange dullness of adult life in which love guarantees no happiness, and nature, no matter how hard it is, never lies. Her later stories—which probe the tectonics of human earthquakes and explore violence not only in subject but in technique—have often triumphantly reconstructed the world of her ancestors in such scope and depth that one has to go back to Tolstoy and Chekhov to find anything comparable. Through the decades her brilliantly polished stories have made her a large literary figure, and the short story a more important genre than before.

The Song of the Dodo: Island Biogeography in an Age of Extinctions
BY DAVID QUAMMEN

ISLAND BIOGEOGRAPHY is a new science concerned not only with islands but with the whole natural fabric of life. Because they are isolated and relatively small, islands can reduce animals and plants to rarity, and then chance factors—a dry spell, brief infertility—can end the species. Mankind has now carved up the entire earth into islands, David Quammen says, so we are looking at the possibility of the last extinction. That is his subject. But the performance is something else. Very seldom is science written like this. Mr. Quammen is not a professional environmentalist or a scientist. He is an accomplished essayist and a novelist and his book is a richly elaborated work of literary craftsmanship full of roaring adventures, madcap flights of imagination and people wilder than the animals they stalk with him. He is intelligent, playful and free of cant, so his bad news unaccountably uplifts us, making us rejoice in the ornery strangeness and amazing vitality of nature. Islands, even while they put species in danger, are, to use his words, the flywheels of evolution, and as he makes us see the giddy fecundity of nature he induces a smile again and again over our very fragility.

Editors' Choice

American Pastoral

BY PHILIP ROTH

THIS NOVEL is a lament for the death of the dream of assimilation that was precious to the children of Jewish immigrants of Philip Roth's genera- tion. Nathan Zuckerman returns to New Jersey for a high school reunion and meets again his boyhood hero, Swede Levov, the admirable athlete who duti- fully took over the family business, married a beauty queen and grew rich. But after Swede dies, Zuckerman undertakes an imaginative investigation into this success story and finds disaster. Swede's only daughter at 16 had joined the Weathermen, planted bombs in public buildings, lived destitute in hiding for years, became a radical devotee of an Oriental religion and finally returned to New Jersey, where Swede has a shocking meeting with her shortly before his death. What this beautifully elaborated tale dwells on is the deaths she caused, the damage she spread through her family, and on an insistent question: how is it possible that these good parents could raise this dislocated person? A hint of an answer is heard in an apparently innocent little contest, when the girl was very young, between Swede's father and his wife's Roman Catholic mother for the soul of their granddaughter. The themes the old people sound reverberate in vir- tually every conversation among other characters here, exchanges that have nothing to do with religion but ask just as pointedly how much we can share without losing our souls. Thus the tone of this allegory—a remarkable mixture of rage and elegy.

American Scripture: Making the Declaration of Independence

BY PAULINE MAIER

MOST HISTORIANS have treated the Declaration of Independence as a central document of the Age of Enlightenment, a product of the natural rights philosophy of John Locke and other British theorists. And most people see Thomas Jefferson as its author, a claim Jefferson made the year he died. Now, with good-humored feistiness and some mockery of official pieties, Pauline Maier presents the Declaration as the embodiment of the American mind and colonial experience rather than as the work of Jefferson or the progeny of any philosophy. The big deal in 1776, she argues persuasively, was the popular decision to get out of the British Empire; independence was a necessity, not a philosophical choice. With striking originality, she sets the famous document in the context of 90 local declarations of independence issued beforehand by colonies, cities, towns and grand juries; the people had declared independence before the Continental Congress did. She shows Jefferson cobbling together his draft from his own preamble to the Virginia Constitution and George Mason's early version of Virginia's Declaration of Rights (which said all men are created equal). And she reproduces the editing done in two days by the Congress, so we can watch the delegates shortening and improving Jefferson's draft. The July 4 document, virtually ignored for a generation after it appeared, became the great American scripture only after it was enlisted as a weapon in partisan political battles of the early nineteenth century.

The Blue Flower

BY PENELOPE FITZGERALD

PENELOPE FITZGERALD'S early novels were comedies of contemporary British eccentricities so sharp that she got a reputation as an almost disreputably enjoyable author. As she moved on to stories about other countries and other eras, her habitual insight and authority carried over naturally into these more historically complicated settings. Her new novel makes the greatest leap of all; it is her most recondite and challenging book, and as authentic a piece of imagination as one can find about a writer—in this case the great German Romantic Novalis (1772–1801). Here he is a philosophy student in the 1790s, his mind exploding with ideas and his heart falling captive to a spirited teenage girl. There is no better introduction than this novel to the intellectual exaltation of the Romantic era, its political ferment, its uncertain morals, its in-

nocence and refusal of limits. It is also a wholly convincing evocation of that notoriously difficult matter, genius; its presence in Novalis and his siblings fairly
crackles in these quiet pages. The book also reaches far beyond its story, becoming an interrogation of life, experience, human horizons and love (its re-
minders of what it feels like to be in love the first time are luminous). As always,
Fitzgerald's economy is next to miraculous, and the language is an enchantment: without a hint of mimicry, she uses virtually undetectable shifts in emphasis and phrasing to conjure up the tone of the German of eighteenth-century
Saxony; it rings true.

Huxley: From Devil's Disciple to Evolution's High Priest

BY ADRIAN DESMOND

THIS RACY BIOGRAPHY of Thomas Henry Huxley (1825–95) is a portrait of the modern age being born. Huxley was a superb scientist and
Adrian Desmond writes about science as lucidly as anyone can, but Huxley was
also the great apostle of Darwinism, and Desmond vividly sketches his ferocious
assaults on the structures of Victorian society—religion, class, education—as he
molded Darwin's scientific revolution into a social engine to overthrow the old
order. The man and the historical transformation are one in this intensely dramatic, amusing account. It does not try to make either the man or his age too coherent; Huxley was a bizarre, intricate character, and there was a sense of
chaos—the reader can feel it—as the established regime crumbled and Huxley's
version of evolution became the ideology of the new industrial order. He was the
most contentious man alive; he was also prodigiously energetic and cunning. To
see the rise of science, and the middle class, amid such political tumult is to gain
a new insight into history. He created the idea of "the scientist" as the idol of the
new age. He coined the word *agnostic* and proudly applied it to himself. Gifted
publicist and social engineer that he was, he sold the world on the ideals of skepticism, experimental openness, objectivity and undogmatic clarity. The idea of
being lofty, above politics and wholly objective may have been absurd in Huxley's case, but it was seductive enough to change the entire outlook of later generations.

Into Thin Air: A Personal Account of the Mount Everest Disaster

BY JON KRAKAUER

UNTIL MAY 1996, 630 people had climbed Mount Everest and 144 had died on it. That spring at least 30 expeditions of tourists made the climb. On May 10 a rogue storm blew up, and eight people in three separate expeditions approaching or leaving the summit died. Jon Krakauer, a 42-year-old writer, was with one team, assigned by *Outside* magazine to report on the commercialization of Everest. Although 12 people died altogether in 1996, he says, a record, 84 made it to the top, so it was a safer-than-average year. Krakauer explains the economic incentives for experienced climbers to lead groups of amateurs up the mountain, the even greater incentive for Nepal to license the trips and the total lack of incentive to limit the numbers risking their lives. When things go wrong in the death zone, the last 2,000 feet, and eventually they do, even the world's best guides cannot save the tourists, or themselves. But his book does more than report on lethal tourism. He wrote it to "purge Everest from my life." It didn't. It may put Everest ineradicably into your mind. This deftly constructed tale lets you sense the excruciating torture of climbing five miles high, the exhilarating and terrifying disorientation of oxygen starvation, the capricious moods of wind and snow, the strange seductiveness of death at odd moments. His re-creation of the storm that killed his companions swirls around the reader like the gale itself and gives this appalling struggle with death a horrifying intimacy.

Mason & Dixon

BY THOMAS PYNCHON

THOMAS PYNCHON'S finest novel is a book of heart, fire and genius. Its structure is classic comedy: the astronomer Charles Mason, as straight man, and the surveyor Jeremiah Dixon, to whom the madcap is just a reflex, bumble along in the mid-eighteenth century drawing the line that separated Pennsylvania from Maryland and West Virginia, the North from the South. The narrator says history needs tending by fabulists, counterfeiters and cranks, and Pynchon gleefully joins the company. The story of this map-making becomes an investigation into the order of the universe, aiming to convince us that reason is inadequate to penetrate the world's mysteries. The book's abundant humor balances on the thin edge of anachronism; history, myth, anecdote and hyperbole are perfect equals. The style is bumptiously Fielding-esque, but subversively pumped up with allusions not only to yesterday and today but to Pynchon's other novels and many twentieth-century masters of fiction; the allusiveness and self-awareness are a good part of the fun. The robust characters—merchants, prostitutes, barmen, Indians, caffeine addicts, a talking dog, cabalists, sailors, poets, clerics, along with historical icons like Washington, Franklin, the Penns and Baltimores—wrestle with a reader's understanding. As for Mason and Dixon: they are Pynchon's deepest creations; we know them from youth to death and, for all their confusion, surliness, resentment and loneliness, they inspire sympathy, perhaps even affection.

The Puttermesser Papers
BY CYNTHIA OZICK

FICTION, SCHMICTION—Cynthia Ozick is a literary centaur, half-scholar, half-artist, who loves a fantasy landscape with infinite allegorical possibilities, and she cheerfully leaves it to the reader to fill in the blanks when she feels like popping out of her story into commentary. What holds these five pieces together is simply Ruth Puttermesser (the word means butter knife, and the book ends with a funny, poignant poem about love and butter knives), a New York Jew whose mental life is richer than all the financial markets and political offices she floats through and who has to wait for heaven to realize her best dreams and worst apprehensions. Along the way she creates a female golem who makes Puttermesser mayor of New York but who also grows gigantic and has to be unmade when her sexual appetites exhaust the Mayor's entire administration. Next Puttermesser and a new lover take on the roles of George Eliot and her lover, George Henry Lewes—a caper that allows Puttermesser to deliver some brilliant literary insights, including a few into the work of Ozick. After an interlude with Puttermesser's Russian cousin—a breathtaking sendup of Upper West Side intellectuals and their critics—Puttermesser is in Paradise, married, with a son, and grown woefully wise about heaven. These papers can hardly be said to have a beginning or end, but when they stop, one is surprised to feel so deeply possessed by the painfully comic spirit of Puttermesser.

Toward the End of Time
BY JOHN UPDIKE

FROM WORD 1 John Updike undermines readers'—and critics'—logical assumptions in this novel, for the text is the journal of a 66-year-old man, Ben Turnbull, who at the end of his own time seems freed of time. His journal reveals not only the world but the wanderings of his wits. So what if a woman turns into a deer his wife had wanted him to kill? So what if he jumps from a

United States in the next century, disintegrating after a war with China, to ancient Egypt, or to virtual reality? So what if characters appear and disappear like phantoms in a dream? Our sense of logic rises from time, and here time is drizzling into a black hole. Turnbull's journal is like *Walden* gone haywire; Ben is brilliantly observant of nature, but if Thoreau's gaze is innocent, Ben's is a gritty-eyed squint. And unlike Thoreau, Ben has women: a wife (the unvoiced struggle as each watches for the other to croak first is an entrancing game); a middle-class slut, or a deer, who inspires lust, guilt and longing for lost youth as they rollick through contortions of very Updikean sex; and a barely nubile gang moll who brings back to Ben his prepubertal self. No matter; soon enough time melts Ben's potency to ooze, and he is as ruthless in describing decay as he was in depicting his sexual romps and obsessions. Indeed, if Ben's ruthlessness is evenhanded, so is his alarming intelligence; it falls on every scene, person, object and thought in the book, giving it an eerie ambiance.

Underworld

BY DON DELILLO

DON DELILLO has always been a harshly original writer, rich in dangerous alienation, with great gifts of eye, ear, nose, palate and fingertip. But his reputation was cult-borne. With *Underworld* he fills the sky. In this novel he diagnoses the debilitation of the cold war, by probing into how people rearranged their lives around the moral void of an absurdity, mutually assured destruction. From its opening, at one of baseball's greatest games, to its inspired epilogue in a Central Asian institution filled with radiation-misshapen humans, it surges with magisterial confidence through half a century. But its true locations—test sites—are not on maps, and its characters live, psychologically, downwind from them. Here bland, hopeful American life glows with the sick light of betrayal, innocence abused; everyone's better feelings take a beating, and ambient moral fear pinches everyone—not only his invented characters but a host of cultural heroes who appear, from J. Edgar Hoover to Lenny Bruce. The protagonist is an entrepreneur of waste; the novel bursts with witty and dramatic conjurings of garbage, voidance, slag. The dialogue is a rockingly comic attack on our mental excreta: the distortions and sound bites of the television age. DeLillo was absent from his fiction before, an unbodied intelligence, but here is an undertow of personal pain he has never touched. This is his most demanding novel and yet his most transparent, giving the reader the privileged intimacy that comes from seeing a writer whole.

Virginia Woolf

BY HERMIONE LEE

VIRGINIA WOOLF said a biographer had to be like the miner's canary, "testing the atmosphere, detecting falsity, unreality and the presence of obsolete conventions." She might have been writing about Hermione Lee. This exceptionally well-researched, beautifully written and graceful life rescues Woolf from her iconic standing and restores her to human dimensions. Among the obsolete conventions Lee avoids are the politicized agendas of the academy and jargon-ridden psychoanalytic speculations. Without special pleading—Woolf's faults are in full view—she maintains a real modesty in the face of the irreducible nature of the writer, but she is capable of shrewd psychological conjecture about Woolf's intellectual and imaginative growth. She vividly re-creates the world Woolf was born into in 1882, a maze of formalities and reticences, and then leads us through changes that, slow in coming but shocking in effect, made all that seem light-years away by the time Woolf was 50. She convinces us that Woolf, contrary to previous assumptions, reveled in a deep intimacy with her husband, Leonard. Finally, she makes a persuasive case for the underlying sanity of this woman as she battled her own madness and shows the brilliant literary uses she made of her instability; as Woolf said, her madness kept her sane. In the end, without being told so by Lee, the reader is pretty sure to conclude that Woolf was personally heroic in life and that, against all odds, she had become a great writer.

The Whole Shebang: A State-of-the-Universe(s) Report

BY TIMOTHY FERRIS

THE WHIMSICAL TITLE refers to what cosmologists do. They are trying to account not for the physics or chemistry or any one aspect of the universe, but for the composition, history, appearance and operation of the whole thing. As Timothy Ferris—an admirably knowledgeable journalist and a great guide for ordinary readers—says, this is a big order. So is his book. The sweep is vast: in eight chapters he canvasses the theory of the Big Bang, the dynamism of the universe, the shape of space, the origins of the chemical elements, the debate over the dark matter that makes up most of the universe, the mystery of the clumping together of stars and galaxies, the search for a Darwinian explanation of the history of the universe and the hope of finding one unified theory to explain everything. Then he gets to the really big stuff: the inflation of the universe and what that implies, where it all came from, how quantum mechanics works and why it suggests there may be many universes, and how humanity, the source of all these theories, fits into a scientific explanation of the whole shebang. Ferris's theorists are not just thinking machines; some are as strange and unyielding as the universe they study. He has a gift for making readers understand not only what the scientists know but how they know it. Finally, as in no previous book of his, Ferris sticks his neck out here, showcasing at least one theory that cannot be tested for years.

Index

Page references in **bold face** indicate locations of major discussions